BRIAN GOODALL

THE PENGUIN DICTIONARY OF
HUMAN GEOGRAPHY

PENGUIN BOOKS

PENGUIN BOOKS

Published by the Penguin Group
Penguin Books Ltd, 27 Wrights Lane, London W8 5TZ, England
Penguin Books USA Inc., 375 Hudson Street, New York, New York 10014, USA
Penguin Books Australia Ltd, Ringwood, Victoria, Australia
Penguin Books Canada Ltd, 10 Alcorn Avenue, Toronto, Ontario, Canada M4V 3B2
Penguin Books (NZ) Ltd, 182–190 Wairau Road, Auckland 10, New Zealand

Penguin Books Ltd, Registered Offices: Harmondsworth, Middlesex, England

First published 1987
5 7 9 10 8 6 4

Copyright © Brian Goodall, 1987
Diagrams by Kathleen King
All rights reserved

Printed in England by Clays Ltd, St Ives plc
Filmset in Monophoto Times

To Rita

PREFACE

This work is a companion volume to *The Penguin Dictionary of Physical Geography* (J. B. Whittow, 1984). The decision to write two dictionaries, one of human geography, the other of physical geography, was made primarily because of the explosion of geographical terms in current usage witnessed over the last three decades. It was not made in the light of any possible division of human geography from physical geography, since the authors of both dictionaries subscribe to the importance of an integrated approach – one which emphasizes the people–environment theme – within the discipline of geography. This view of geography can be supported while recognizing that human geography is, in many ways, a hybrid discipline which has recently experienced fundamental changes in its ways of thinking – in its philosophy, its methodologies and its focal interests. These changes began with the adoption of the positive philosophy of the natural sciences in the 1950s. Alongside this 'new geography' a variety of humanistic and radical approaches have subsequently developed. The result is a significant expansion of the discipline's language: new terms and concepts have appeared, and further terms and concepts have been borrowed from other disciplines, especially the social sciences. Human geographers have frequently infused the latter with meanings of their own, as has also happened with certain everyday words which are used in a special way.

The range of terms selected for inclusion in the two dictionaries is intended to extend their use beyond A-level and similar studies to students involved in tertiary-level education. It is hoped that the non-geographer requiring some familiarity with geographical terms will also find the dictionaries useful for reference. In compiling *The Penguin Dictionary of Human Geography* an attempt has been made to include all terms currently used by human geographers working with the range of studies referred to above. The objective is to provide the student with a single reference volume which covers not only the purely human geographic terms, but also those common to the social sciences and to people–environment relationships, as well as planning and basic quantitative techniques. Several terms regarded as obsolete by some academic geographers have been included because they may be encountered in older textbooks frequently still in use; there are also a number of 'popular' terms which are met in books purporting to explain human geography to the layman. The terms selected are primarily English language ones and an attempt has been made to explain differences between British and American usage wherever these occur. Foreign-language terms have been included when they are in common international use. Although words with only a local connotation have been kept to a minimum there is a bias towards country-specific terms, especially in respect of the British system.

*

The companion dictionaries of human geography and physical geography are planned along similar lines. They therefore share broadly comparable formats, each using the Penguin method of cross-referencing (namely ◊ = *see*, ◊◊ = *see also*).

Metric units have been adopted throughout, although in many instances, especially in historical terms, imperial measurements are used and the metric equivalent quoted.

The dictionary is dedicated to my wife – her patience and forbearance have been remarkable over the several years this project has been underway. Without her support and encouragement it would not have been completed.

Burghfield Common, July 1985   B.G.

ACKNOWLEDGEMENTS

I would like to thank friends and colleagues in the geography fraternity with whom I have, from time to time, discussed a variety of topics which greatly helped in clarifying my ideas. In particular I am grateful to John Whittow, author of the companion dictionary, for advice, and to Ian Fenwick, Peter Hall, Geoff Lucas and Bob Parry, who have been of assistance in various ways. I must also thank Jane Brookling and Rosa Husain, who shared the typing of the manuscript, and Kathleen King, who drew the diagrams.

For kind permission to reproduce certain diagrams I gratefully acknowledge the following: Fig. 2, Countryside Commission, *Protected Areas in the United Kingdom*, 1984; Fig. 22, W. Bunge, 'Detroit humanly viewed: the American urban present', from *Human Geography in a Shrinking World*, by R. Abler, D. Janelle, A. Philbrick, and J. Sommer © 1975 by Wadsworth Publishing Company, reprinted by permission of the publisher; Fig. 23, E. Bylund, 'Theoretical considerations regarding the distribution of settlement in inner North Sweden', *Geografiska Annaler Series B*, 42, 1960; Fig. 31, E. M. Horwood and R. R. Boyce, *Studies of the Central Business District and Urban Freeway Development*, University of Washington Press, 1959; Fig. 80, R. Rothwell, 'The role of technology in industrial change: implications for regional policy', *Regional Studies*, 16, Cambridge University Press, 1982; Fig. 103, J. E. Vance, Jr, *The Merchant's World: The Geography of Wholesaling*, Prentice Hall, 1970; Fig. 123, P. J. Rimmer, 'The search for spatial regularities in the development of Australian seaports, 1861–1961/62', *Geografiska Annaler Series B*, 49, 1967; Fig. 154, J. Friedmann, *Regional Development Policy: A Case Study of Venezuela*, M I T Press.

A

a posteriori statement A statement or prediction made on the basis of existing experience. ◊ *a priori statement*.

a priori statement A statement that can be proved true or false by reasoning (and not by experience). ◊ *a posteriori statement*.

aborigines A term used generally to describe the original inhabitants found living in an area when it was first discovered by Europeans but particularly to the wandering tribesmen who migrated into Australia from Southern Asia some 40,000 years ago. The latter are the only surviving members of the ◊ *Australoid* race.

abortion The termination of a pregnancy in its early stages by the expulsion of a human embryo or foetus from the womb before it is able to survive. It may be spontaneous or purposely caused, i.e. induced. The latter is a method of ◊ *birth control*.

absenteeism Absence from work. It may be involuntary, due to illness or other causes, or voluntary.

absolute distance ◊ *geodesic distance*.

absolute location ◊ *location*.

absolute rent ◊ *Marxist theory of rent*.

absorbing barrier ◊ *diffusion barrier*.

accelerator A process by which changes in the ◊ *demand* for ◊ *consumer goods* bring about even larger fluctuations in the demand for ◊ *capital goods* used to make them. It is a factor which tends to accentuate booms or slumps in the economy (◊ *business cycle*). Demand for capital goods comprises two distinct elements: (i) demand arising from the need to replace worn-out or obsolete capital goods and (ii) demand for the provision of additional productive capacity where there is an increasing demand for consumer goods. ◊ *multipliers*.

acceptable dose limit A primary standard for a ◊ *pollutant*, being the dose which has either no or acceptable short/long-term effects on human health or on plant and animal species which the pollutant comes in contact with. ◊ *emission standard*, *environmental capacity*.

accessibility A variable quality of a ◊ *location*. The concept expresses the ease with which a location may be reached from other locations and therefore summarizes the relative opportunities for contact and interaction. Accessibility has normally been measured in frictional or geometric terms which emphasize (i) a connection component (that of being able to reach a location) and (ii) a movement component (that of being able to get there quickly/cheaply). Accessibility has been accorded a central role in much classical and modern ◊ *location theory*, where it reflects the relationship of a location to the ◊ *transport system*. Particular *accessibility* is calculated from one point in a transport system, while *general accessibility* is calculated from a large number of points in the system. The influence of accessibility on location decisions can be illustrated in the case of retailing, where traditional city-centre shopping activities locate in accordance with *general accessibility* to the distribution of consumers: functions such as garages and cafés take advantage of the *arterial accessibility* associated with major traffic routes entering the city centre; and specialized functions, such as produce markets and entertainment, reflect the *special accessibility* attached to locations with particular environmental conditions or historical circumstances.

Accessibility is now recognized as involving, besides geometry, equally important social and economic dimensions because of its consequences for the resources/opportunities available to people at different locations. ⬦ *centrality*, *connectivity*, *friction of distance*, *proximity*.

accessibility index A simple measure of ⬦ *accessibility* in a ⬦ *network* which, for any selected ⬦ *node*/place, represents the sum of the distances from it to all other nodes/places. Distance can be measured in ⬦ *cost-distance*, ⬦ *time-distance* or any other relevant terms. Thus the accessibility index overcomes the major deficiency of other network indices (⬦ *alpha index*, ⬦ *beta index*, ⬦ *cyclomatic number*, ⬦ *gamma index*), which disregard the actual distances and the quality of movement. The sum of the accessibility indices for all nodes/places gives the ⬦ *dispersal index*.

accommodation (1) A general term used to describe living and working premises. ⬦ *accommodation unit*.

(2) The relationship between ⬦ *immigrants* and the receiving society when, during the early period of contact, there is the least degree of adaptation and acceptance consistent with the peaceful coexistence of the two groups. The newcomers are therefore able to retain or rebuild their own social and cultural patterns. It is a compromise characterized by toleration. ⬦ *acculturation*, *assimilation*.

accommodation land Small enclosed fields on the edge of town where animals can be kept after being purchased for slaughter.

accommodation unit A planner's term for a unit of housing occupied by one ⬦ *household*. The unit can be a separate house, maisonette, flat, etc.

accounting price ⬦ *shadow price*.

accretion A process of peripheral addition to the ⬦ *built-up area* of a town, normally comprising a non-traditional plan-unit and forming a component of either a residential area or a ⬦ *fringe belt*.

acculturation A process of cultural change initiated by either the conjunction of two or more cultural systems or, more likely, the transference of individuals from their original societies and cultural settings to new socio-cultural environments. In the former case the borrowing of items from one ⬦ *culture* by another means that the cultures coming into contact with one another are both affected. In the latter case the term describes the process and degree of acquisition and learning by the immigrant of the ways of behaviour (including roles, habits, attitudes, values, knowledge) of the receiving society, e.g. an ⬦ *ethnic group* loses its individual culture as it is absorbed into a wider society. ⬦ *accommodation* (2), *assimilation*, *melting-pot concept*, *socialization*.

accumulated demand Total ⬦ *demand* for a good by one ⬦ *consumer*, either individual or institutional, over a relatively long period of time. It implies that the demand is relatively constant in expression but susceptible to periodic satisfaction.

Ackerman formula An attempt, by E. A. Ackerman, to explain the size of a country's ⬦ *population* in terms of the area's resource endowment, economic characteristics and economic history. Expressed as a formula:

$$P = \frac{RQ(TAS_t) + E_x + T_r \pm F - W}{S}$$

where P = size of population
R = amount of resources

Q = factor measuring natural quality of resources
T = physical technology factor
A = administrative techniques factor
S_t = resource stability factor
E_s = scale economies element
T_r = resources added through trade
F = institutional element and 'friction' loss element consequent upon institutional characteristics of society
W = frugality element (wastage or intensity of use)
S = standard of living

⟡ *optimum population*, *overpopulation*, *underpopulation*.

acquisition behaviour The buying of one ⟡ *firm* by another (⟡ *takeover*) or the joining together of two firms (⟡ *merger*) resulting in changes in ownership or control. Such behaviour may be classified into:
(i) *Diversification acquisitions*, which extend the range of product lines produced by a firm.
(ii) *Horizontal acquisitions*, whose purpose is to reduce the competition faced by a firm.
(iii) *Vertical acquisitions*, which are designed to assure material supplies or product markets.

acre A unit of Imperial measure of area. The *statute acre*, a legal measure of land in Britain, was based on the amount of land which a plough team (a man with two oxen) could plough in a day. Edward I attempted to standardize the area in 1305. The *statute acre* today = 4,840 yd^2.

$$640 \text{ acres} = 1 \text{ mile}^2$$
$$1 \text{ acre} = 0.4047 \text{ hectar}$$
$$2.47106 \text{ acres} = 1 \text{ hectare}$$

Local or *customary acres* of varying extent were in use in different parts of Britain as late as the early 19th century, e.g. the Cheshire acre was 10,240 yd^2, the Hereford acre only 3,240 yd^2.

action area An area, indicated in a ⟡ *structure plan*, where major change is expected by ⟡ *development*, ⟡ *redevelopment* or improvement. Action is therefore required on a comprehensive basis at an early date (i.e. within the following ten years). A ⟡ *local plan* is prepared to guide such action.

action space A subset of all ⟡ *locations* within a given area, comprising those locations which an 'actor' (e.g. shopper, intended migrant) knows about and with which he or she could potentially interact. The individual has sufficient information about these locations to assign them ⟡ *place utilities* which reflect the individual's preferences. Action space is therefore the area within which the individual makes decisions about where to live, work, shop, etc. ⟡ *activity space*, *awareness space*, *behavioural environment*, *information field*, *operational space*, *space*.

active filtering ⟡ *filtering*.

active locators Manufacturing ⟡ *firms* which are not dependent upon the locational experiences of others and are willing to pioneer new locations. Such adaptive behaviour is almost certainly related to the size of firm, although in the case of multi-plant firms past precedent within the company may be heeded. ⟡ *location leader*, *passive locators*.

active migrants ⟡ *Migrants* who seek out suitable destinations which, in their eyes, guarantee future prosperity. ⟡ *migration*.

active population Or *labour force*. There are three slightly different interpretations:
(i) the population of working age within a country (broadly speaking the adult population).
(ii) the ⟡ *working population*, which includes both men and women who are normally employed and those who may be tempor-

arily unemployed. This is the most common interpretation.

(iii) the employed population, being those men and women actually engaged in productive employment at a given time. ⬦⬦ *activity rate*, *dependency ratio*, *secondary labour force*.

activity allocation models Planning ⬦ *models* which are used to predict where activities will be located in an area. Prediction usually follows a three-stage procedure. The first involves temporal extrapolation or some other method (e.g. ⬦ *economic base*) to forecast future population levels, housing needs and employment structure. The second stage determines where, within the area, the activities locate, i.e. the activity allocation using, for example, a ⬦ *Lowry model*. The third stage models movement patterns, e.g. journeys to shop, to work, in the area. The earliest activity allocation models constructed separate sub-models for manufacturing, retail and residential location based on ⬦ *gravity model* approaches.

activity rate That proportion of a nation's or area's total population of employable age which is gainfully employed. Male and female rates may be calculated separately. ⬦⬦ *active population*, *manpower forecasting*, *working population*.

activity space A limited component of the ⬦ *behavioural environment*, also known as (direct) *contact space*, which is the ⬦ *space* in which the majority of an individual's activities are carried out, i.e. those places visited regularly by an individual. Activity space usually consists of discrete ⬦ *locations* and can be mapped either as a point pattern or by a ⬦ *time–space prism*. A series of hierarchically nested activity spaces can be recognized, reflecting an individual's varied activities – *familial space*, *neighbourhood space*, *economic space*, and *urban sector social space*. ⬦⬦ *action space*, *contact field*, *daily-life environment*, *indirect contact space*, *social space*.

actual range ⬦ *breaking-point*. ⬦⬦ *range*.

actuarial data Demographic data relating to ⬦ *births* and ⬦ *deaths* and forming part of ⬦ *vital statistics*.

adaptation level theory An attempt to explain why ⬦ *perceptions* of objects differ from reality. Where significant characteristics vary between objects of a given type, a particular object is not perceived as it really is, but its characteristics are compared to a subjective average of all similar characteristics experienced in the past. This subjective average or frame of reference is the *adaptation level*. For example, once a location acquires some quality of centrality, it is likely to be perceived as more central than it actually is by people who habitually live in less central locations.

adaption ⬦ *adoption and adaption*.

adaptive re-use A North American term used to describe the conversion of ⬦ *inner city* buildings from one use to another, e.g. from blue-collar workplaces to offices, from warehouses to residences for white-collar workers, etc.

additional worker hypothesis A labour economist's view which suggests a positive relationship between increases in the ⬦ *unemployment rate* and increases in the ⬦ *active population*. Increasing unemployment rates can result in new entrants into the labour force, especially into the ⬦ *secondary labour force*, in cases where the head of a household becomes unemployed and other members of that household seek jobs in order to maintain household income. ⬦⬦ *discouraged worker hypothesis*.

adit, adit-mine, adit-mining An adit is a horizontal opening by which a ⬦ *mine* is entered or drained. It is found in hill areas where seams of minerals outcrop at the surface and can be mined directly from the hillside. It has fallen into disuse in Britain, as the easily accessible deposits have been exhausted. ⬧ *bell pit*, *drift mining*.

administrative principle ⬧ *central place theory*.

adobe An unburnt brick dried in the sun. The term is also applied to a house or structure made of such bricks.

adolescent Becoming adult. Adolescence is the period in an individual's life between childhood and maturity. ⬧ *general age group*.

adolescent towns ⬧ *age of towns scheme*.

adoption and adaption An idea applied particularly to locational decisions involving choice of non-optimal locations, a distinction being made between adoptive and adaptive behaviour. Certain activities or locations are said to be adopted by chance because the ⬧ *decision-makers* in question act with imperfect information, or with no information, or without perceiving the information available. Such locations may be non-optimal. In contrast the adaptive viewpoint focuses on rational decision-making in which the activity or firm adapts itself to the system or environment after careful and full consideration of all relevant information, so leading to the choice of the ⬧ *optimum location*.

The adoptive stance acknowledges that, while the locational choices of individual firms may appear quite random if viewed case by case, this random behaviour takes place within a competitive economic environment. Hence firms choosing non-economic locations will be eliminated in time, while the other randomly located firms are adopted by the system.

adoption intensity The degree of ⬧ *market penetration* of an ⬧ *innovation* per unit area.

adult death rate A term usually taken to mean the ratio of deaths of persons over 1 year of age to the size of the population at the mid-year, expressed as a rate per 1,000

population. ⬧ *death rates*, ⬧⬧ *child mortality rate*.

advance mining A method of underground mining in which extraction proceeds from the base of the shaft outwards to the boundary of the deposit. ⬧ *bord and pillar*, *longwall mining*, *mine*.

advanced gas-cooled reactor ⬧ *AGR*.

adventitious population That ⬧ *population* resident in a rural area but dependent upon an urban area for making a living. Today the terms ⬧ *commuter* and ⬧ *exurban* are more likely to be used to describe such people.

advocacy planning A type of ⬧ *planning* in which the planner represents the interests of a particular social group in the planning process and his allegiance and responsibility is solely to the needs of this group. ⬧⬧ *allocative planning*, *innovative planning*.

aesthetics The branch of philosophy concerned with the principles of beauty, and the standards of taste and ⬧ *value*.

affinity A term used to describe the spatial attraction of one type of activity to another. Clustered patterns of activity locations often occur as a result of affinity. ⬧⬧ *complementarity*.

affinity environment A spatially bounded ⬧ *social environment* based on voluntary residential choice and characterized by a shared preference among residents for salient attributes such as ethnicity (⬧ *ethnic group*), ⬧ *life style*, income, occupation, age, family status and religion. Such an environment minimizes the psychological stress of urban living at the same time as maximizing access to specific social facilities desired by the residents, such as specialized food markets, places of worship, etc.

afforestation The usual meaning today is the planting of trees on land previously in another use to form a ⬧ *forest* (⬧ *reforestation*). In an earlier legal sense the term applied to the placing of an area under forest law, e.g. by Norman kings as royal hunting ground. ⬦ *forestry*.

age of towns scheme A descriptive classification proposed by Griffith Taylor which formalizes the contrasts between different sizes of ⬦ *town* in terms of land use patterns. Five categories are recognized: (a) *infantile towns*, with a haphazard distribution of houses and shops, and no factories; (b) *juvenile towns*, in which a differentiation of zones begins with a concentration of shops; (c) *adolescent towns*, in which scattered factories make a first appearance; (d) *early mature towns*, showing a clear separation of high-class housing from other residential areas; and (e) *mature towns*, with separate commercial and industrial areas and four zones of housing, from mansions to shacks.

age/sex pyramid, age/sex structure The composition of the ⬦ *population* of a country or area according to its *age and sex structure*, summarized in terms of age groups and expressed in a ⬦ *frequency distribution* or ⬦ *histogram*. The histogram usually takes the form of a *pyramid* in which the population is built up in one-, five- or ten-year age groups, with males on one side, females on the other, and with the base representing the youngest age group and the apex the oldest (⬦ Fig 1). The horizontal bars are drawn proportional in length to the actual numbers in each age group or to the percentage of the population in each group.

age-specific birth rates ⬦ *birth rates*.

age-specific death rates, mortality rates ⬦ *death rates*.

age-specific fertility rates ⬦ *fertility rates*.

agglomeration A term used in a broad sense to describe the spatial grouping together of activities and people for mutual benefit. In a more particular context it is applied to the association of productive activities in close proximity to one another which improves their efficiency through the collective use of infrastructure (⬦ *agglomeration economies*). The tendency for activities to concentrate generates large market areas and aids the circulation of capital, commodities, labour and information. ⬦ *centralization, concentration, polarization*.

agglomeration economies A term used to describe all the ⬦ *external economies* experienced by a productive unit and derived from its particular locational association with a large-scale spatial cluster of economic activities (⬦ *agglomeration*). Agglomeration economies can be subdivided into ⬦ *localization economies* and ⬦ *urbanization economies*. ⬦ *economies of environment*.

aggregate travel model A procedure for estimating the total distances involved in serving a market from alternative locations. The point of minimum total distance for each location is given by:

$$A_i = \sum_{j=1}^{n} Q_j \, T_{ij}$$

where A_i = aggregate distance travelled to serve the market from plant location i
Q_j = expected sales at market j
T_{ij} = distance (or transport cost) between i and j

In a general form the model can be applied to any situation where the trips made by individuals associated with a given activity need to be aggregated. ⬦ *market potential*.

agistment The pasturing, on payment of a due, of one person's animals on another's land. In the case of ⬦ *common land* it signifies the letting of a commoner's right to pasture stock to another person.

AGR (advanced gas-cooled reactor) A type of nuclear reactor in which heat extraction is by carbon dioxide gas under pressure. Heat from the gas is transferred to water in a heat exchanger and converted into steam for a turbo-generator to produce

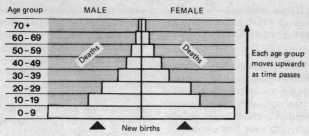

(a) High death rate

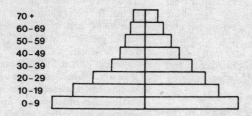

(b) Effect of reduction in death rate

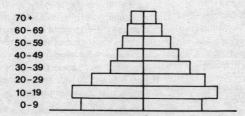

(c) Effect of reduction in birth rate (after 10 years)

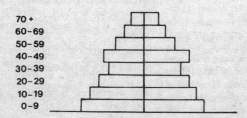

(d) Effect of reduction in birth rate (after 40 years)

Fig. 1 Age/sex pyramids

electricity. It is the successor to the ◊ *Magnox* reactors in the UK nuclear power programmes. The fuel is uranium dioxide in stainless-steel cladding. ◊ *nuclear energy*.

agrarian Modern terminology makes a distinction between agricultural (◊ *agriculture*) and agrarian in respect to landed property and cultivated land. Agrarian relates to matters of ◊ *land tenure* and considerations arising from land ownership.

agrarian reform A large-scale, government-sponsored change in the institutional setting of rural society and agriculture involving not only ◊ *land reform* but also the rationalization of rural settlement patterns, schemes for improved educational and other social ◊ *infrastructure*, and increased capital funding for agriculture.

agricultural area An area of land utilized for ◊ *agriculture*, including ◊ *arable*, ◊ *grassland* and other ◊ *pasture*.

agricultural belt ◊ *country belt*.

agricultural consolidation ◊ *land consolidation*.

agricultural co-operative ◊ *co-operative*.

agricultural density Agricultural population per unit of cultivated land or crop area (which allows for multiple cropping). ◊ *comparative density, density, man–land ratio, physiological density*.

agricultural geography As a branch of ◊ *economic geography*, agricultural geography today studies the spatial variation in patterns of agricultural activity, seeking to describe and explain crop and stock distributions, agricultural practices and organization, and agricultural marketing. Previously it has concentrated on delimiting and classifying agricultural areas, describing where crops, etc. were produced, with an emphasis on relationships with the physical resource base. The explanation of agricultural land use now emphasizes economic factors, input

costs and market opportunities, including the way in which these are influenced by ◊ *location*, farm size, ◊ *land tenure* systems, labour supply, etc. Location has been singled out in developing theory to explain agricultural land use (◊ *agricultural location theory*), but the limitations of ◊ *normative* economic approaches have led to increasing interest in the behavioural approaches to farmers' decision-making. (◊ *behavioural geography*.)

Within agricultural geography there is still a concern with defining and classifying land use, for example in terms of ◊ *crop combinations*, and in recognizing land's potential productivity (◊ *land capability*). Other developments parallel interests elsewhere in geography, such as the study of spatial ◊ *diffusion*, applied in agriculture at a farm-by-farm level to the spread of animal diseases and to product and process innovations, and to the study of the spatial impact of government policy influencing the agricultural sector via the control of agricultural markets. Agriculture's role in economic ◊ *development* is also singled out, especially in respect of economic advancement in less developed countries, where maximum food production is viewed as a necessity to support rapidly growing populations, as well as providing a basis for industrial development. ◊ *economic rent, Green Revolution*.

agricultural holding As defined by the United Nations Food and Agriculture Organization, an agricultural holding is simply a basic unit for agricultural production. It is defined more precisely in the UK Farm Survey as any area of 5 acres (2·02 hectares) or above used for the growing of crops, including grass, which is farmed separately as a self-contained unit

agricultural land classification ◊ *land classification*.

agricultural location theory A framework for identifying the important variables which determine the spatial ◊ *equilibrium* pattern of agricultural production. The focus is on the form of agricultural production that would best be carried out at a given location, i.e. the location is known, as is the level of market demand, and the problem is to determine the optimum crop/stock and cropping/stocking system. The approach adopted is a ◇ *normative*, economic one which stresses the importance of distance/transport costs in relation to prices received for products and rent paid for land. Since the internal spatial extent of the typical agricultural enterprise is relatively large, differences in land prices/rents associated with different spatial positions and resource endowments are of major locational significance and it is critical to investigate the substitution relationship between rent and transport outlays. Applied to the study of a single crop, the approach helps explain land use intensity, and to several crops, the understanding of land use competition. The classical formulation is the ◇ *von Thünen model*. ◇◇ *economic margin of cultivation*, *economic rent*.

agricultural residual A term used to describe parcels of land which remain in agricultural use after being more or less engulfed by the outward expansion of the urban built-up area. ◇◇ *urban sprawl*.

Agricultural Revolution The term is most commonly applied to the changes which transformed Britain's countryside in the 18th and 19th centuries. During that period ◇ *agrarian* change took place at a rapid rate and on a large scale, leading to a fast rise in agricultural output and productivity, as the agricultural industry strove to satisfy an expanding market. The changes comprised many interacting elements: in agricultural techniques, such as ◇ *crop rotations*, selective breeding, improved implements and liming, etc.; in structural elements, such as the dissolution of ◇ *open fields*, ◇ *enclosure* of wastes, farm consolidation and the extension of arable

land; and in institutional arrangements, ranging from the 'spirit of improvement' to the modification of the law to facilitate change in agriculture.

There is some controversy, however, in dating the Agricultural Revolution in Britain. The traditional view places it between 1760 and 1843, while there is also support for a second view which dates it from 1560 to 1767. A third school of thought suggests a *Second Agricultural Revolution* from 1818 to 1880, relating to development in animal feed, fertilizers and field drainage, etc. A *Mechanical Revolution*, dating from 1914, associated with mechanization based on the internal combustion engine, is also recognized. There is an alternative view, that of the *Gradualist School*, which argues that the development of modern agriculture is spread over such a long period of time that the idea of a revolution is hardly tenable.

agricultural system In order to produce a crop or rear livestock, ◇ *factors of production* need to be brought together in varying proportions, combined in different ways and adjusted to physical conditions. The resulting arrangement constitutes an agricultural system, of which there are numerous examples. ◇ *collective farming*, *commercial grain farming*, *convertible husbandry*, *dairying*, *dry farming*, *dryfield farming*, *European peasant farming*, *extensive agriculture*, *factory farming*, *high farming*, *hill farming*, *horticulture*, *hydroponics*, *market gardening*, *Mediterranean agriculture*, *mixed farming*, *monoculture*, *monsoon agriculture*, *paddy farming*, *part-time farming*, *pastoral farming*, *peasant farming*, *plantation agriculture*, *ranching*, *sedentary agriculture*, *sericulture*, *shifting cultivation*, *subsistence agriculture*, *terrace cultivation*, *tropical peasant farming*, *truck farming*, *vegeculture*, *viticulture*, *wet-rice cultivation*. ◇◇ *system*.

agriculture In a strict sense (and in the original use of the term) agriculture means the practice of cultivating the soil. The present-day interpretation is much wider and includes not only the growing of crops but all forms of livestock raising, including the use of natural vegetation for feeding the animals and the gathering-in of crops, whether for subsistence or exchange. Hence the science and practice of *farming*. ◊ *alternate agriculture*, *cultivation*.

agroforestal A term which covers both agricultural and forest uses of land. It is used in two situations: (a) when there is no clear distinction between agricultural and forest land, e.g. where woodland is used for grazing; and (b) when the combined agricultural and forest productive area is differentiated from built-over and unproductive areas.

agronomy A science which deals with the theory and practice of soil management and crop production.

agro-town A compact and densely populated form of rural settlement, common in parts of Mediterranean Europe, in which the majority of the ◊ *active population* are engaged in agriculture. With populations of 20,000 or more such towns support a range of retail and service functions although they do not form part of an integrated ◊ *urban system*. Workers have to travel daily to work the land, often as labourers on large estates, which surround the agro-town. The inefficiency of this is reflected in the decreasing intensity of cultivation with increasing distance from the town.

aid A term used to describe the transfer of resources from developed to underdeveloped countries. It takes various forms – capital funds, technology, expertise, export credits, educational scholarships and other training schemes, etc. Practices range from bilateral agreements providing aid from one country to another to the work of multilateral agencies (e.g. the UN

Food and Agriculture Organization, UNESCO, the International Monetary Fund, the World Bank, and Inter-American, African and Asian Development Banks) which collect resources and redistribute them on a variety of criteria. Independent charitable organizations, e.g. Oxfam, may also be involved.

The provision of aid is seen as a means of stimulating ◊ *development* in the underdeveloped countries, but in practice the flow of resources may be a two-way process with interest payments on loans, etc. being made to the developed countries. Where this happens the underdeveloped country's ◊ *dependence* upon a developed country may be intensified.

The pattern of aid shows a concentration of flows to ◊ *Third World* countries.

air corridor ◊ *corridor*.

air transport and regional development Air transport can play different roles in the various stages of economic development of a new region today. K. S. Sealy suggests a three-stage model:

(i) *The pioneer phase*. Aircraft are used for aerial resource surveys, to establish the first camps and to aid in the construction of surface links where potential resources justify exploitation.

(ii) *The exploitation phase*. Once primary land routes have been established, aircraft specialize in passengers and freight.

(iii) *The final phase*. Where growth of industry and settlement occur, surface modes of transport will come to dominate and air transport assumes a more 'normal' role, concentrating on passengers, mail and specialized freight.

airport An airfield designed for use by civil aircraft and equipped to facilitate the movement of passengers and cargo, by providing terminal facilities which expedite the transshipment of traffic from surface to air transport.

Airports may be classified according to

the facilities available, reflecting the type of traffic and runway length:

(i) *Major international*, capable of handling the largest commercial aircraft on an all-the-year-round basis and having full customs, immigration and catering services. It has a minimum of two runways: one not less than 3,750 m for take-off, the other not less than 2,500 m for landing.

(ii) *International*, similar to (i) except that it has one runway not less than 3,050 m.

(iii) *Medium and short-haul* international and domestic services on a year-round basis. Similar to (ii) but with a runway not less than 2,550 m.

(iv) *Seasonal international charter* and domestic scheduled services, with a runway not less than 2,550 m.

(v) *Occasional charter services*, business and training operations, with a runway not less than 2,000 m.

(vi) *Short charter and domestic services* and all aspects of general aviation. A runway of 1,600 m.

(vii) *General aviation* and short take-off and landing (STOL) aircraft, with a runway minimum of 1,220 m. ⬦ *public safety zone*.

algorithm A step-by-step procedure or set of rules for performing a calculation. It is usually supported by a formal mathematical proof. ⬦ *simplex algorithm*.

alienation The state in which a person is indifferent to or estranged from the material environment, either from nature or from the means of production via labour market processes.

alliance A temporary political association between ⬦ *states* for their mutual benefit. It is restricted in its sphere of operation. Examples include the Council of Europe and the ⬦ *North Atlantic Treaty Organization*.

allocative planning One of two types of ⬦ *planning*, recognized by J. Friedmann, concerned to achieve the optimal allo-

cation of resources between all of the competing needs or uses within a society. Also known as *regulatory planning*. ⬦ *advocacy planning*, *innovative planning*.

allometric growth. A term used to describe the systematic, differential growth of parts within a complex growth structure, e.g. the relationship of population growth to increasing distance from the city centre.

allotment (1) Originally a legal term for the allocations of land set aside for landless villagers when former ⬦ *open fields* and pastures were parcelled out at the time of the ⬦ *enclosure* awards.

(2) The modern use, derived from (1), is as in *allotment garden*. Small pieces of land, privately or publicly owned, which are let annually and cultivated by the allotment-holder for the production of vegetables and fruit for consumption by himself or his family. Under the 1947 Agriculture Act allotments should not exceed 40 poles (0·25 acre, 0·1 hectare) in extent.

Alonso model A model developed by W. Alonso to explain the pattern of ⬦ *land use* and ⬦ *land values* in urban areas. The model emphasizes economic factors, particularly ⬦ *accessibility* and the trade-off between transport costs and land prices/rents. It may therefore be regarded as a development of the ⬦ *von Thünen model* of agricultural land use and rents.

The model starts with a rigorous assumptive base: of a perfect land market, all jobs concentrated in the city centre, given household preferences and incomes, etc. Each household must decide how near the city centre it wishes to live, faced with the knowledge that the further away from the centre it lives the greater its transport costs and the less, therefore, it has available to spend on land and other goods. Given household income and spending on other goods, a ⬦ *bid-rent curve* can be determined which represents the set of prices the household could pay for land with increasing distance from the city centre. Different households have different bid-rent curves, because of differences in income, spending on other goods, etc., from which a residential bid-rent curve can be deduced. Each household can choose where to live on this curve and this will depend upon the household's relative preference for space versus accessibility. Alonso assumes that households have a positive preference for land/space. The extent to which preferences can be indulged is a function of income and, since land is more plentiful and cheaper at the urban fringe, it is the highest-income groups who choose to live there at low densities while lower-income groups are found at higher densities nearer the city centre.

The analysis can be extended to retail, manufacturing and other land uses. Bid-rent curves can be established for these and, as they value accessibility more highly than do households, residential uses are excluded from the central area. The basic pattern of urban land use/land values produced is one of segregated land uses in concentric rings around the city centre. Certain of the assumptions can be relaxed without undermining the validity of the model's general principles.

alp A high mountain pasture, above the tree-line, combined with periodic settlement. ⇭ *saeter*, *shieling*.

alpha index A measure used to calculate the complexity of a ⟡ *network*. It is calculated as the ratio of the observed number of ⟡ *fundamental circuits* (⟡ *cyclomatic number*) to the maximum number of fundamental circuits that may exist in a network:

$$\text{Alpha index } (\alpha) = \frac{e - v + p}{2v - 5}$$

where $(e - v + p)$ = cyclomatic number
e = number of ⟡ *routes*
v = number of ⟡ *nodes*
p = number of graphs or sub-graphs

$2v - 5$ = maximum number of circuits

The alpha index varies on a scale from 0 to 1, i.e. from no circuits to the maximum number. Thus the higher the index the more integrated the network. It is used by geographers in the analysis of transport networks in particular. ⟡ *beta index*, *cutpoint index*, *cyclomatic number*, *detour index*, *gamma index*, *König number*, *Shimbel index*.

alternate agriculture A system of farming, also known as the *Norfolk System*, implying the practice of arable farming for fodder crops introduced into England in the early 18th century. It involves the sowing of temporary grass and clover ⟡ *leys*.

alternative energy sources Sources of heat and power that do not rely on ⟡ *fossil fuels* or ⟡ *nuclear energy*. They include ⟡ *solar power*, ⟡ *hydroelectric power*, ⟡ *wind energy*, ⟡*wave energy*, tidal energy, biological energy sources, ⟡ *geothermal energy* and ocean thermal energy conversion.

ambient energy sources Or *benign energy sources*. Sources of power that arise from harnessing natural forces and, in particular, those sources whose utilization leads to no net input of heat into the earth, e.g. ⟡ *hydroelectric power*, ⟡ *wind energy*.

ambient standard Or *environmental quality standard*. A standard which sets the permissible level of ⟡ *pollution* in the environment. Such standards are usually determined in relation to damage to health, public services and ⟡ *amenity*. Individual discharge levels can then be determined for sources of pollution so as to comply with the ambient standard. ⟡ *emission standard*.

amenity, amenities An abstract concept describing those natural and people-made qualities of the ⟡ *environment* from which people derive pleasure, enrichment and satisfaction. Conditions or facilities that make a place more pleasant and attractive. ⟡ *amenity conservation*.

amenity conservation The maintenance of the natural environment for the protection of wildlife and ⟡ *landscape*, and the provision of areas for informal ⟡ *recreation*.

Amerind A term made up from the first syllables of 'American Indian' to designate a member of the race of people inhabiting the New World before its occupancy by Europeans.

analogue model ⟡ *model*.

analogue theory A formal theory of model-building in which a simplified but structural representation of a particular system or activity is created by the selective abstraction of elements from a real-life situation.

analysis of variance The standard ⟡ *parametric test* of difference between three or more ⟡ *samples*, applicable to data measured on an ⟡ *interval scale*. The object of the test is to decide whether the samples come from a common, normally distributed population. The rationale is to find out whether there is more variation between the samples than within them by testing whether the ⟡ *arithmetic means* of the samples differ significantly from each other. If the samples are all drawn from the same population and drawn at ⟡ *random* the ⟡ *variance* measured, either within or between samples, should not differ very much and the lower the value of F (the ratio of the between samples variance and the within samples variance). Where between-sample variance is very much greater than within-sample variance, the greater the value of F, and the less likely that the samples are drawn from the same population. Also known as the *F-ratio test* and *ANOVA*.

analytical regionalization An approach to regional classification which starts from a large area, e.g. the world or a continent, and divides it into sub-classes on the basis of a number of principles. Hence a process of logical division to produce a regional system. ⟡ *regionalization*.

anarchism A political philosophy which sees government and laws as undesirable and advocates the abolition of the ⟡ *state*. In its place would be the voluntary co-operation of largely self-sufficient groups. The philosophy has been a foundation for critiques put forward in ⟡ *radical geography*.

anchor tenant In a planned shopping centre, anchor tenants are the major ⟡ *shopping goods* outlets, such as department stores, with a large trade-generation potential which serves to attract smaller shops. Anchor tenants are spaced strategically throughout a centre in order to create an even flow of shopping traffic. They are often offered special rental terms.

anchorage ⟡ *harbour*.

ancient monument An ancient building, structure, earthwork or cave which is scheduled by the Department of the Environment to be in their guardianship. It may be owned by a local authority, central government, or a private person, and is protected against alteration or demolition without the Secretary of State's consent. ⟡ *scheduled monument consent*.

ancillary linkages Connections or ⟡ *linkages* between unlike functions such that both benefit. They lead to a mixing of unlike functions in an area, e.g. office buildings and restaurants.

Angerdorf A ⟡ *green village* type found primarily in eastern Germany and dating back to the period of eastern colonization of the Germans. It is characterized by an oblong-shaped central green and generally associated with ⟡ *open fields*. This type of settlement was common in eastern England, Germany east of the Elbe, in Poland, Denmark and Skåne before ⟡ *enclosure*.

◊ *Gewanndorf, Haufendorf, Runddorf, Strassendorf, Waldhufendorf*.

animal–land ratios ◊ *stocking rates*.

animal unit months The amount of forage necessary to carry one cow or five sheep for one month, used as a basis for expressing ◊ *carrying capacity* on American rangelands. ◊ *range (2)*.

anomie A situation where two or more conflicting sets of ideas exist within the same society such that the possibility of realizing the aims or objectives of one set is hindered or prevented by the presence of the others.

ANOVA ◊ *analysis of variance*.

antecedent boundary ◊ *boundary*.

anthropics A discipline covering all knowledge about people.

anthropocosmos The world of people as distinguished from the great world or cosmos beyond people's reach.

anthropogeography A somewhat misleading term which has been broadly interpreted as the geography of people on an anthropological basis. More specifically it represents a German conception of human geography developed by F. Ratzel (in his *Anthropogeographie*, 1882 and 1891) which demonstrates the possibility of studying scientifically the relations between human communities and their ◊ *geographical environment*, including their distribution over the earth.

anthropology The study of human beings. The term was previously restricted to physical characteristics and measurement of people, such as skull shapes and sizes (◊ *cephalic index*), and the evolution of the human species from anthropoid (ape-man) ancestors. It now also embraces ◊ *ethnology* and ◊ *ethnography* and so includes the development of technical skills to make implements, etc., social organization, religion and culture, linguistics and spatial distributions. ◊ *social anthropology*.

antipodes Places on the earth's surface directly opposite to each other. The term is used loosely in Britain to refer to Australia and New Zealand.

anti-utopia A modern term created to describe the anti-ideal place. Not to be confused with ◊ *dystopia*. ◊ *cacotopia*.

anyport A generalization of the process of ◊ *port* growth suggested by J. A. Bird on the basis of observed (largely British) experience of the seaward expansion of large multi-functional ports keeping pace with growth in trade and increases in vessel dimensions. Bird identified six eras in the development of a port's installations:
(i) The *primitive port*, located on the estuary shore where a ◊ *harbour* can be found and where there is dry ground to establish a town.
(ii) *Marginal quay extension*, as the port begins to extend along the town waterfront and the quays begin to outstrip the areal growth of the town.
(iii) *Marginal quay elaboration*, which provides additional quayage, without increasing the port area, by the building of short jetties and the cutting of small docks into the banks.
(iv) *Dock elaboration*. Increasing traffic and size of vessels leads to the building of wet-docks, downstream from the original port area, with road and rail connections.
(v) *Simple lineal quayage*. At some stage it becomes difficult to expand docks for larger vessels and the outlines of dock quays must be simplified and extended.
(vi) *Specialized quayage* to cater for the growth of, first, bulk cargoes and, later, container and ◊ *RO-RO* traffic.

Each era is ended by the start of the next in the succession, but, although eras supersede one another, the installations from earlier eras remain and are usually modified and/or down-graded in function. Hence various eras of port development co-exist and capital investment normally ensures the continued use of older installations, rather than their immediate abandonment. Accordingly anyport can be said to represent a process of port expansion seawards, spreading down-river in a fairly contiguous fashion and leaving relatively little space between older and newer quays.

A longer-term view suggests that even major ports are subject to a process of *seaward migration* of port activities, involving the closure of older wharfs and docks unable to cope with traffic congestion and increasing size of ships. ⬦▷ *port-outport model*.

AONB ⬦ *Area of Outstanding Natural Beauty*.

apartheid A policy of racial ⬦ *segregation* involving separate development for the peoples of different ⬦ *ethnic groups*, instituted in South Africa by the Nationalist government which came into power in 1948. Its objective is to preserve the privileged position of the white minority of European descent. Non-whites must live in officially segregated areas which have inferior social services and are denied basic political rights. Regulations prohibiting mixed marriages and requiring non-whites to carry identification papers have been relaxed. In an extension of the policy, *Bantustan homelands* have been created for the Republic's indigenous black Africans since 1959, e.g. Bophuthatswana, Transkei. These occupy the poorest and least accessible parts of the country.

apparency ⬦ *imageability*.

apparent time The time of day at any given place, reckoned by the diurnal movement of the sun, as registered, for instance, by a sundial. Synonymous with ⬦ *local time*. ⬦▷ *equation of time*, *standard time*.

applied geography The application of geographical knowledge and skills to the solution of society's problems, both economic and social, at world and local scales. Because applied geography has tended to tackle particular problems as they came to prominence it has not developed a coherent theoretical base. Such problems have occurred notably in underdeveloped areas, where L. D. Stamp's pioneering efforts singled out ⬦ *population pressure*, economic ⬦ *development* and ⬦ *quality of life*. Contributions were also prominent in the field of town and country or ⬦ *physical planning*, where applied geography's role was enhanced by the ⬦ *quantitative revolution* and extended into other public sectors, such as health care. Outside the public sector applied geography has been related to locational consultancy work, especially in retailing.

appraisal well A well drilled close to another, proven well to gain information about a reservoir's or field's characteristics in order to help determine its commercial potential. Also known as an *outstep* or *delineation well*. ⬦▷ *development well, wildcat well*.

appraisive perception The ⬦ *value judgement* people make about places, e.g. such-and-such is a pleasant place to live in. It implies some evaluation of the place(s) concerned. ⬦▷ *designative perception, perception*.

aquaculture The management of aquatic environments to increase production of organic materials for harvest. Plant products may be grown in people-modified aquatic environments but most effort focuses on the possibilities of increasing the production of animal protein from rivers, lakes and oceans. ⬦▷ *fish farming*.

aqueduct An artificial channel or structure (usually raised like a bridge over low ground) for carrying water cross-country over long distances.

aquifer recharge In water management (i.e. aquifer management and river regulation) excess river flows may be diverted down boreholes to recharge aquifers (underground water-bearing layers of porous rock through which water can flow after it has infiltrated the upper layers of soil) that have been overpumped.

arable land Land suitable for ploughing. The term is commonly used, however, to describe land actually ploughed and cropped, but including ⬦ *fallow*, short ⬦ *ley* grassland and ⬦ *market gardens*. ⬦⬦ *grassland, pasture, tillage*.

Arbeiterbauern ⬦ *worker-peasant*.

arboretum A collection of living trees which are maintained for the study and display of their variety of form and colour.

arboriculture The cultivation of trees. ⬦⬦ *silviculture*.

archaeology The scientific study of civilizations through the physical remains of their past activities. The word is commonly applied to the study of prehistoric civilizations' remains but does cover the systematic study of all antiquities. ⬦⬦ *environmental archaeology, industrial archaeology, spatial archaeology*.

archipelagic waters A ⬦ *maritime zone* created by the establishment of archipelagic ⬦ *baselines*. International agreement allows archipelagic states to draw straight baselines joining the outermost points of their outermost islands subject to four conditions:
(a) The system of straight baselines must not depart to any appreciable degree from the configuration of the archipelago.
(b) The ratio of water to land within the baselines must not exceed 9:1.
(c) No segment of the straight baseline should exceed 125 nautical miles.
(d) No more than 3% of the segments may measure between 100 and 125 nautical miles.
Archipelagic waters bear a stronger similarity to ⬦ *territorial waters* than to ⬦ *internal waters* and the archipelagic state must

allow the traditional fishing rights of other states within waters enclosed by the baselines and must also allow states which have laid submarine cables through the area when it consisted of ⬦ *high seas* to repair those cables. The right of innocent passage still applies through archipelagic waters, but the archipelagic state may designate shipping lanes through them to be followed by alien vessels.

area (1) A general term used by geographers to refer to some clearly defined ⬦ *space*; often used interchangeably with ⬦ *region*.
(2) A precise term for the extent or measurement of a surface, measured in square units, e.g.

British units: $9 \text{ ft}^2 = 1 \text{ yd}^2$
$4,840 \text{ yd}^2 = 1$ ⬦ *acre*
$640 \text{ acres} = 1 \text{ ml}^2$

The relationships between British and SI units are:

$$1 \text{ ft}^2 = 0.0929 \text{ m}^2$$
$$1 \text{ acre} = 0.4047 \text{ hectares}$$
$$(= 4,050 \text{ m}^2)$$
$$2.47106 \text{ acres} = 1 \text{ hectare}$$
$$1 \text{ ml}^2 = 2.5899 \text{ km}^2$$
$$0.386103 \text{ ml}^2 = 1 \text{ km}^2 (= 100 \text{ hectares})$$

area-based policies Those public policies with a deliberate bias to favour or penalize certain geographical areas relative to others. Such policies are applied at various spatial scales from the intra-urban, e.g. housing policy introducing ⬦ *general improvement areas*, to the national, e.g. interregional ⬦ *industrial location policy*. Such ⬦ *positive discrimination* is administratively more convenient than discrimination in favour of households or individuals. ⬦⬦ *development areas*.

Area of Outstanding Natural Beauty (AONB) An area in England or Wales of high ⬦ *landscape* quality and unspoilt character, not being in a ⬦ *National Park*, designated by the Countryside Commis-

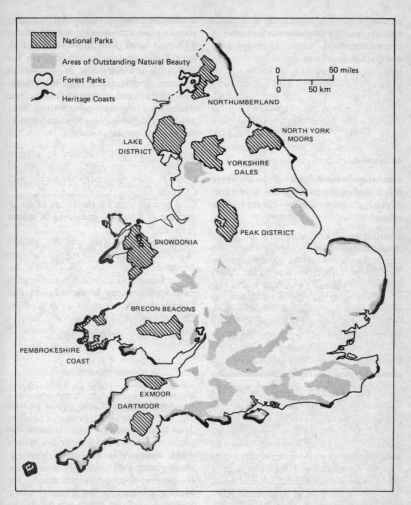

Fig. 2 Areas of Outstanding Natural Beauty, Heritage Coasts and National Parks in England and Wales

sion under the 1949 National Parks and Access to the Countryside Act. The purpose of the designation is to encourage the planning and management of such areas in order to conserve and enhance their natural beauty, which includes protecting flora, fauna, and geological as well as landscape features, and so maintain their role in contributing to the wider enjoyment of the countryside. AONBs are the responsibility of local planning authorities. Their distribution is shown in ◊ Fig. 2.

areal association The comparative variation/similarity between two or more spatial or ◊ *areal distributions* from place

27

to place within the same study area. Since spatial distributions are collections of geographic facts, areal or *geographical association* may also be defined as the similarity between two or more sets of geographic facts collected for the same unit area. Where two distributions reach high values in the same places and low values in similar, other, places they are said to show close areal or *geographical association*. ⬦ *association, coefficient of geographical association*.

areal classification A term used to denote a ⬦ *classification* or subdivision of areas which is established without regard to the spatial contiguity of members of the classes.

areal differentiation The process by which geographers construct ⬦ *regions* to describe and interpret the differences in the different areas of the earth's surface. It was first conceived in a descriptive ⬦ *idiographic* vein (⬦ *regional geography*), but recently analyses of ⬦ *regional differentiation* have been reinstated as a central focus of modern human geography as part of the attempt to interpret and understand how regional disparities occur. ⬦ *chorography*.

areal distribution A distinction can be drawn between, on the one hand, a pattern or arrangement of events/facts on the surface of the earth and, on the other hand, a distribution of their frequency in a set of areas plotted as a two-dimensional ⬦ *histogram*. An areal distribution represents a set of magnitudes assigned to areal units, with the values plotted against the additional dimensions of contiguous geographical space. The result is a surface summarizing the distribution in the dimensions of magnitude and geographical space. ⬦ *spatial distribution*.

areal organization The recognition of specific spatial patterns of organization, e.g. of local government within a country, of the functions of a multinational firm.

arithmetic–geometric ratio (A/G ratio) A principle used to estimate the abundance of certain types of ore deposits. It is based on the idea that as the grade of the ore decreases arithmetically its abundance increases geometrically until the average abundance in the earth's crust is reached. Therefore as demand increases and high-grade ore deposits are exhausted mining will move to poorer and poorer ores, which are assumed to be progressively more and more abundant. This is too simplistic a view, since the A/G ratio is applicable only to a very limited number of ores, and the economic and energy costs of working ores of lower and lower grade need to be considered.

arithmetic mean The measure usually implied by the term ⬦ *average*. It can only be applied to ⬦ *interval data* and is that value of the variable series which is numerically most representative of the whole series. The arithmetic mean is calculated by adding together all the values in a series or data set and dividing by the number of values:

$$\text{Arithmetic mean} = \bar{x} = \frac{\Sigma x}{n}$$

where Σx = summation of all values of x
$\quad\quad\; n$ = number of values of x

Thus every value in a series is taken into account and an exact answer is obtained which is suitable for further mathematical development. Extreme values, high or low, do have a disproportionate effect. The arithmetic mean is the quantity about which squared deviations are minimized, hence the sum of deviations from the mean of a series equals zero and the average deviation from the mean is also zero. This latter relationship has a proper statistical name: the *first moment* about the mean. ⬦ *average, geometric mean, harmonic mean, median, mode*.

arithmetic mean centre ⬦ *mean centre*.

arterial ribbon ⟡ *ribbon development.*

Article IV Direction Order An order, issued by the Secretary of State for the Environment, in areas of special character (e.g. ⟡ *national parks*, ⟡ *conservation areas*), which has the effect of suspending the ⟡ *General Development Order*. This means that those classes of ⟡ *development* normally exempted are brought under planning control, e.g. small extensions to houses, fences, etc.

aspiration level A psychological notion representing an expected or desired level of reward or return to an ⟡ *entrepreneur* or individual. The level depends on the amount of information available to a decision-maker. ⟡ *satisficer concept.*

aspiration region A perceived area or space within which an individual, household or firm would expect to obtain a certain level of satisfaction or return from undertaking some action. Its boundaries will be defined by upper and lower limits set by criteria specified by the individual, etc. on the basis of information available at a given time. The aspiration region for a household seeking a new residence would therefore relate to the areas in which they would like, and could afford, to live. ⟡ *search space.*

assart The process of clearing ⟡ *forest* or waste land for cultivation, associated particularly with the 12th and 13th centuries. To assart land without licence was a grave offence for, whereas the waste of the forest consisted of cutting down trees that might grow again, assart was uprooting them so that the forest was destroyed. Where land was assarted by licence from the Crown, *assart rents* were payable. New assart land was sometimes divided between all ⟡ *freeholders* according to their share in the older arable land.

assembly costs A manufacturer's ⟡ *transport costs* incurred in assembling the necessary raw material inputs at his place of production. Also known as *procurement costs.* ⟡ *distribution costs, locational costs.*

assimilado policy A colonial policy, as used by Portugal, under which a colonial subject may become 'civilized' or assimilated, i.e. acquire education and adopt a European way of life. ⟡ *assimilation.*

assimilation The process by which persons of diverse ethnic and racial backgrounds come to interact and intermix, free of constraints, in the life of the larger community or nation. It may be distinguished from ⟡ *accommodation*, but ⟡ *acculturation* and *integration* are similar processes. The rate of assimilation depends on factors such as race, religion, economic status, attitudes, education, intermarriage, etc. The extent of assimilation is frequently reflected in the level of ⟡ *residential segregation.*

Two forms of assimilation are recognized: (i) *Behavioural assimilation*, involving a process whereby members of a group are integrated into a common cultural life with other groups as a result of sharing the experience and history and acquiring the memories, sentiments and attitudes of these other groups. (ii) *Structural assimilation*, which refers to the distribution of migrant ethnics amongst the groups and social systems of a society. In particular it considers their distribution through the system of occupational stratification. Structural assimilation is most likely to occur after behavioural assimilation. ⟡ *melting-pot concept.*

assisted areas Parts of a country where special measures are considered to be necessary to encourage the growth and proper distribution of industry. ⟡ *area-based policies, development area, development district, industrial location policy, intermediate area, special area.*

associated number ⟡ *König number.*

association A statistical term implying a systematic or regular change in one

◊ *variable* as another variable changes. Alternative terms are ◊ *correlation* and covariation. ◊◊ *areal association, geographical association.*

at-grade intersection The point at which two or more ◊ *roads* meet at the same level. ◊◊ *grade-separation.*

atavism, atavistic A term denoting resemblance to grandparents, or even more remote ancestors, rather than to parents.

attitude A relatively enduring and consistent set of opinions or way of thinking about particular persons, objects or events. It often implies that a ◊ *value judgement* has been made. ◊◊ *natural attitude.*

attribute A quality or characteristic of a person or thing. In statistics, the term is retained for a feature/characteristic that is confined to a ◊ *nominal scale* of measurement, e.g. a population characteristic such as race, religion. ◊◊ *variable.*

Australoid One of the primary ◊ *races* of people, represented today by the ◊ *Aborigines* of Australia, possibly the oldest of all the surviving races of humans. Australoid peoples are characterized by dark skin, wavy hair and large teeth. ◊◊ *Caucasoid, Khoisanoid, Mongoloid, Negroid.*

autarchy Absolute sovereignty or despotism involving absolute or autocratic rule by a government or individual. ◊◊ *anarchism.*

autarky National or regional economic self-sufficiency and independence.

authority constraints Limits on human behaviour/activities which determine precisely when and where people and organizations can meet for activities requiring contact between persons and exactly who can participate in such joint activities; e.g. legal opening hours of shops determine working hours for shop assistants and opportunities to shop for customers. ◊◊ *capability constraints, coupling constraints.*

Autobahn In West Germany, a ◊ *road* of ◊ *motorway* standard.

autocorrelation ◊ *space–time autocorrelation, spatial autocorrelation, temporal autocorrelation.*

automation That part of the process of technological development in which a sequence of industrial processes is controlled automatically and self-regulated. It involves the replacement of human labour by increasingly sophisticated machines. It differs from mechanization in degree rather than kind in that, in the case of automation, it is human mental, rather than physical, processes which are being replaced for a great many industrial operations.

autonomous activities ◊ *basic activities.*

autonomous invention ◊ *invention.*

autonomous investment ◊ *investment.*

autonomy The right of self-government.

autoroute In France, a ◊ *road* of ◊ *motorway* standard.

autostrada In Italy, a ◊ *road* of ◊ *motorway* standard.

avenue A tree-lined path/road leading to a 17th-century country house. The name is derived from the French '*avenir*' meaning 'to come to'. The avenue was commonplace in Britain in the 19th century. The term is also used to describe any wide street or road in an urban area, especially in North America.

average A term used loosely to indicate any central tendency but usually synonymous with ◊ *arithmetic mean.*

average age of childbearing For a woman who at the end of her childbearing span had had only one child, the average age of childbearing would be her age on the date of birth of her child. If she had had two children it would be her age midway between the dates of birth of her two children, etc. For a ◊ *cohort* of women it would be their average age at the time when half of their children were born. Average age of childbearing has been calculated in an attempt to understand changes in ◊ *fertility rates*. Thus a period of decline in the average age of childbearing concentrates the amount of childbearing taking place in each year of observation and keeps the crude ◊ *birth rate* high even if ◊ *cohort fertility* is moving downwards; whereas a period of increase in the average age of childbearing spreads births more thinly over a span of years and depresses the yearly birth rates.

aviation A spatial activity concerned with supplying an air ◊ *transport* service. ◊ *commercial aviation, general aviation.*

awareness space A ◊ *space*, e.g. an urban area, containing those places or locations about which the individual, e.g. an intended migrant, has knowledge before a search begins. ◊ *Preference space* is contained within awareness space. ◊ *action space, activity space, contact field, search space, virtual space.*

axiom A truth which is self-evident or a universally accepted principle or rule. Axioms are basic building blocks in ◊ *laws* and ◊ *theories.*

B

baby boom population cycle Or *future ◊ population cycle*. The baby boom is a feature of countries which have brought their general level of ◊ *fertility* to a low level. If socio-economic conditions are conducive to a lowering of the age of marriage or a reduction in the spacing of births, the ◊ *birth rate* rises rapidly while the ◊ *death rate* remains at a relatively low level (◊ Fig. 3). Eventually the birth rate declines and relative stability is re-established, but in the meantime there has been a boost in the size of the overall population.

BACAT ◊ *LASH*.

backcountry In recreation management, any area where dispersed ◊ *off-road recreation activities* are stressed, i.e. a recreation area (for hiking, cross-country skiing, canoeing, etc.), in contrast to ◊ *wilderness*.

background concentration (of pollutants) The background concentration of ◊ *pollution* in a particular area is that level of pollution which would exist in the absence of any local sources of pollution.

backhaul The return trip of a vehicle transporting goods or freight. If the vehicle has to return empty or in ballast (heavy material to improve stability) the transport or freight charge for the outward journey will have to be high enough to pay for the costs of the return. The possibility of a ◊ *return cargo* is important if vehicles would otherwise return unladen, and lower rates (*ballast rates*), deriving from backhaul economies if a cargo can be obtained, may be offered in the direction of the lighter flow to stimulate return cargoes.

backward linkage ◊ *linkages*.

backwash effects One of the sets of interdependencies (◊ *spread effects*) recognized by G. Myrdal as characterizing the dynamic aspects of ◊ *core–periphery* structures in developing his ◊ *cumulative*

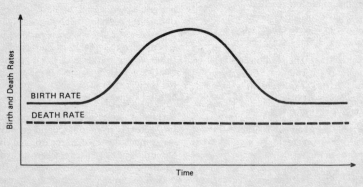

Fig. 3 Baby boom population cycle

causation theory of economic growth. Backwash effects represent the negative effects of economic growth in the core region on its periphery; they therefore increase the disparity between core and periphery. The effects take the form of the spontaneous development of spatial flows of labour, capital and commodities from the periphery to the core and so support the further ◊ *concentration* of activity in the expanding core. Called *polarization effects* by A. O. Hirschman. ◊◊ *centralization*, *polarization*.

backwoods A term first used in the USA to denote the sparsely settled, uncleared forest land to the west of the early settlements; at best an area of pioneer settlement. It is now commonly applied to any region of wild, uncleared forest land, sparsely settled and far removed from centres of urban population.

balance of payments A systematic record of the relation between the payment of all kinds made from one country to the rest of the world and its receipts from all other countries. The *current account* is that part of the balance of payments account which shows all payments made or received in respect of goods and services, including payments of interest on past lendings and borrowings. The *capital account* shows all payments made or received by way of settling old debts or creating new debts. ◊◊ *balance of trade*, *exports*, *imports*, *terms of trade*.

balance of trade The relationship between payments for a country's ◊ *imports* and receipts for its ◊ *exports*. This 'visible balance' is only part of the ◊ *balance of payments*. ◊◊ *terms of trade*.

balanced neighbourhood Processes of ◊ *segregation* generate ◊ *natural areas* within the urban residential mosaic whereby each group within an urban society occupies its own separate residential area. In contrast the balanced neighbourhood is a planning concept which envisages each ◊ *neighbourhood* as a balanced cross-section of the whole urban society, such that all groups are equally represented in the neighbourhood.

balk, baulk An unploughed piece of land in an ◊ *open field* serving as a *foot-balk* to give access to the ploughed portions; or as a *boundary-balk* between two ploughed portions; or as an *untilled balk* used for grazing; or as a *headland* for turning the plough team.

ballast rates ◊ *backhaul*.

ballast voyage A journey made by an oil tanker or other vessel with sea water carried in the oil tanks as ballast to provide essential stability for the vessel on the empty leg of its journey. The ballast is usually discharged at sea along with any residual oil from the tanks; consequently the practice is a major contributor to oil ◊ *pollution*.

balneology The science of bathing, particularly the therapeutic use of natural mineral waters.

Bamboo Curtain An ideological ◊ *frontier* which, by analogy with the ◊ *Iron Curtain*, represents the limit of Chinese communist influence.

bar-graph A diagram comprising a series of bars, if placed horizontally, or columns, if placed vertically, which are proportional in length to the quantities they represent. In *simple* bar-graphs, each bar represents a total value; in *compound* bar-graphs, each bar is divided to show constituents as well as total value. ◊ Fig. 4.

barrage A large, usually concrete, structure across a river to impound a body of water much deeper than the original river. Some distinguish barrage (where no hydroelectric power station is present) from ◊ *dam* (where a power station is present) but this is not universally accepted.

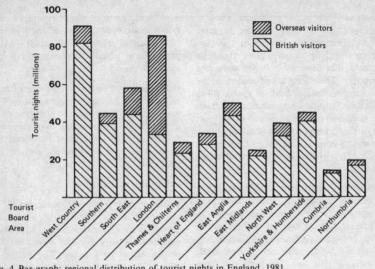

Fig. 4 Bar-graph: regional distribution of tourist nights in England, 1981

Barrages· are usually concerned with annual water storage, a dam with perennial storage.

barrier ◊ *diffusion barriers.*

barrier effect (of boundaries) ◊ *boundary effect.*

barrow A communal burial mound for chiefs, family and other prominent people first raised over graves in the ◊ *Stone Age.* The practice continued into Saxon times. Barrows are chiefly found in areas of chalk and other limestone uplands throughout Western Europe. The largest rarely contained more than a dozen graves. The earliest, Stone Age, ones were referred to as *long barrows*, some being up to 200–300 ft (61–91·5 m) long and 50 ft (15·25 m) wide. These contrast with the *round barrow* or *tumulus* of the ◊ *Bronze Age.* Round barrows can be subdivided according to shape: (i) *bowl*, resembling an upturned bowl; (ii) *bell*, a slightly flattened bell surrounded by ditch and mound; and (iii) *disc*, resembling a shield with small mound forming the boss of the shield.

base load The minimum steady level of demand, and therefore load, on an electricity supply system over a given time period, usually expressed in watts or multiples thereof. ◊ Fig. 5. ◊ *base load plant.* ◊ *electricity generation, load duration curve, load factor, load following, peak load.*

base load plant An electricity generating plant which is kept running continuously to meet the ◊ *base load* demand of an electricity supply system. As demand rises above this base load, additional generating capacity must be brought into use; the order in which this is done is carefully controlled for the system as a whole on the basis of a hierarchy of generating costs (called a *merit order* in the UK). Power stations having the lowest marginal generating costs are highest in the merit order and supply the base load. Conversely power stations having the highest marginal generating costs supply the ◊ *peak load.* For generating systems having nuclear as well as fossil-fuel power stations, the nuclear ones are higher in the merit order since

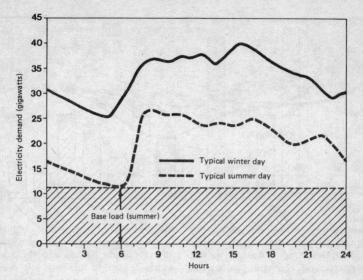

Fig. 5 Base load

they have low fuel costs and very low marginal running costs.

base price ◊ *basing-point pricing*.

baseline The current rules for drawing baselines from which the ◊ *territorial waters,* ◊ *contiguous zones* and ◊ *exclusive economic zones* are measured and which mark the outer limits of ◊ *internal waters* were established in 1958 at the first United Nations Conference on the Law of the Sea. Normally the low-water line would mark the baseline around the coasts of any country, including the coasts of any islands which the country owns. The low-water line varies throughout the year along most coasts but the rules do not specify which low-water mark should be used. It is up to the government of the country to select one and mark it on a large-scale chart so that other governments can be aware of the locations. Deviations from the selected low-water baseline are permitted in two special circumstances:

(i) along short sections of coast to link up longer sections where the low-water line is used, e.g. straight lines across mouths of rivers and entrances to harbours; also across bays where the mouth of the bay does not exceed 24 nautical miles. States may also include bays wider than 24 nautical miles on historical grounds, although ◊ *historic bays* are not defined in the rules, but merely mentioned as bays to which the normal rules do not apply.
(ii) along comparatively lengthy sections of coast which are deeply indented or cut into or where there is a fringe of islands along the coast, straight baselines may be constructed. ◊ Fig. 6.

basic activities ◊ *Economic base theory* divides the economic activities in a region into two groups – basic activities and ◊ *non-basic activities*. Basic activities are those economic activities which contribute directly to the economic base of a region by bringing in money from outside the

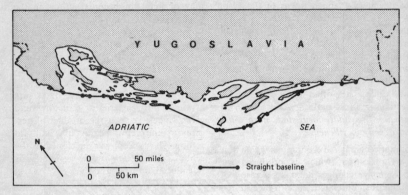

Fig. 6 Baseline

region, e.g. by exporting products; i.e. they constitute that proportion of activities in a region dependent upon markets outside the region. Also known as *autonomous activities*, *carrier industries*, *city-forming activities*, *exogenous activities*.

basic costs The minimum ◊ *costs* in manufacturing industry which must be paid irrespective of location, such as the costs of ◊ *raw materials* at the points where they are mined and the costs of ◊ *labour* at its cheapest point. ◊ *locational costs*.

basic industry ◊ *heavy industry*.

basic/non-basic ratio The relationship, for any city or region, between the proportion of workers employed in ◊ *basic activities* and the proportion employed in ◊ *non-basic activities*. The distinction between the two sectors is clearer in theory than in practice and the categorization may have to be made on the basis of a pragmatic set of rules. The ratio indicates the magnitude of the response in non-basic activities for a given change in basic activities. The proportion of non-basic employment increases as city or region size increases and also varies for any city or region over time. ◊ *economic base theory*.

basic unemployment ◊ *unemployment*.

basin cultivation A method of cultivation found on the margins of the tropics, especially in Nigeria, Ghana and the Sudan, which is used to minimize soil erosion resulting from torrential rainfall. Each field is divided into numerous small basins surrounded by low earth ridges so as to trap the water and allow it to sink in, rather than run off rapidly.

basin irrigation ◊ *irrigation*.

basing-point pricing A discriminatory ◊ *pricing policy* whereby a rigid pattern of ◊ *delivered prices* is imposed and systematically followed by all firms in an industry. The system operates by fixing a *base price* at a single location. The price quoted to any consumer is this base price plus the ◊ *freight charge/rate* from the base point to the consumer's location, whether or not the consumer buys the good from the base point or some other location. All producers, irrespective of location, quote an identical delivered price to any one consumer. A variation on the system involves *multiple basing* points, in which case the price to any consumer is the base price plus the freight charge from the nearest base point to the consumer. ◊ *Pittsburgh plus system*. ◊◊ *blanket rate pricing, postage stamp pricing, uniform pricing*.

bastide town Planned towns of the 12th, 13th and 14th centuries, mostly in France, that displayed a return from medieval irregularity to the formal layout of the Roman era. They were generally small, with some variation in form to suit local conditions, and enclosed by a protective wall/ditch. They often had a castle and a rectilinear street pattern. Also known as *newton, Neustadt, nieuwstad, nova villa, novus burgus, villeneuve.*

bazaar economy An economy in which that part of output which is produced for ◊ *exchange* changes hands as a result of numerous, unrelated, face-to-face transactions between buyer and seller (often also the producer). Transactions are normally centred upon an actual market place, and price is often determined by haggling. Such an exchange system reflects a very limited development of a retail and wholesaling system. ◊ *market economy.*

beating the bounds ◊ *perambulation.*

bedroom town ◊ *dormitory town.*

behaviour contagion An important element of much ◊ *decision-making* involving the imitation of those whom the decision-maker regards as reliable or prestigious.

behavioural assimilation ◊ *assimilation*

behavioural environment Human behaviour is not a simple and straightforward reaction to the objective or ◊ *phenomenal environment* but a reaction to a partial and distorted psychological representation of that ◊ *environment*. The behavioural environment nests within the ◊ *perceptual environment* and is that part of the latter which draws a behavioural response from an individual or towards which a person's behaviour is directed. The behavioural environment is a subjective milieu which governs a person's reactions or actions and, although it only partly reflects 'objective reality', it is the environment in which rational human behaviour begins and decisions are taken. Those decisions may or may not become actions in the phenomenal environment.

Since the same objective environment may have quite different meanings for people whose past experience, cultural setting, etc. differ, the behavioural environment represents a psycho-physical field in which phenomenal facts are arranged into patterns or structures and given values, i.e. it is the product of perception interpreting reality in a cultural setting. The concept was developed by the school of ◊ *Gestalt psychology* and was introduced into geography by W. Kirk. Also known as the *decision environment* and the *task environment.* ◊ *action space.*

behavioural geography An approach to ◊ *human geography* which adopts the methods and concepts of ◊ *behaviourism*, a general movement which has spread into the social sciences in recent years from the behavioural sciences, to explain spatial patterns of behaviour in terms of cognitive processes. The behavioural approach views people as 'thinking' persons and is interested in the way in which people come to terms with their physical and social environments, i.e. the cognitive processes through which individuals codify, respond to and react upon their environments. The real world is viewed from the perspective of those individuals whose decisions affect locational or distributional patterns in order to derive generalizations about individual and group spatial behaviour.

It has been suggested that behavioural geography was both a logical outgrowth of and a critique of the ◊ *quantitative revolution.* The latter stressed ◊ *economic man* and the optimality of spatial behaviour, but interest focused increasingly on how decisions were made in practice. The approach was developed and formalized, particularly in the 1960s, in studies of innovation ◊ *diffusion*, ◊ *decision-making*, ◊ *cognitive mapping*, etc. The emphasis, however, has been on the individual's 'mechanical' responses to spatial and social structures rather than on an understanding of the motivations underlying the behaviour (◊ *humanist geography*). ◊ *behavioural environment, bounded rationality, cognition, operational environment, perception, perceptual environment, phenomenal environment.* ◌ *authority constraints, capability constraints, coupling constraints, cognitive map.*

behavioural matrix A framework, devised by A. Pred, within which locational ◊ *decision-making* can be analysed. Decision-making is represented in a matrix (◊ Fig. 7) as a function of two vectors: the quantity and quality of perceived information available in an ◊ *operational environment* to a decision-maker and the ability of the decision-maker to use that information. With the passage of time decision-makers should obtain more/better information and should become more skilled in its use. In terms of the matrix this means a decision-maker should move diagonally down to the right towards cell B_{nn}, which represents perfect decision-making. ◌ *decision environment, economic behaviour.*

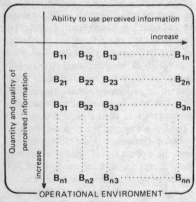

Fig. 7 Behavioural matrix

behaviourism A perspective on behaviour which views everyday actions in terms of a ◊ *stimulus–response model*, i.e. a particular stimulus in the external environment (e.g. ringing of a telephone) causes an action in response by a person (hearer gets up to answer it). Classical behaviourism is concerned only with such superficially observable behaviour and its determinants which are found outside the person concerned. The perspective is applied in ◊ *behavioural geography* to facilitate an understanding of patterns of spatial behaviour. ◌ *cognitive behaviourism, neobehaviourism.*

bell pit A term describing an early type of ◊ *mining* in which a seam or vein of minerals was removed from around the base of a shallow shaft. The pit was abandoned when the roof became unsafe and surface depressions today mark where the pit has since caved in. Chalk in Buckinghamshire and coal and other minerals in the Black Country and the Peak District, were mined from bell pits.

beneficiation A preliminary treatment process (such as concentration, pelletization or sintering) in which low-grade ores are enriched at their site of occurrence. The beneficiation process therefore reduces the amount of waste material in the ore and increases the ◊ *transferability* of the ore.

benefit–cost analysis ◊ *cost–benefit analysis*

benign energy sources ◊ *ambient energy sources.*

berewick A subsidiary or outlying portion of an estate.

best practicable means A pragmatic approach to the control of emissions from scheduled industrial processes. The term was introduced by the 1906 Alkali Act and referred to by the UK Alkali Inspectorate in controlling emissions from oil refineries, cement works, petrochemical plants, etc.

The idea has been much criticized, since it is seen as a loophole which may allow an industry to emit noxious or harmful substances in greater amounts than would have been allowed had absolute standards been set. It implies, however, that while better ◊ *emission standards* are obtainable, industry must not be unduly penalized in its operations as the costs of pollution are offset by the socio-economic benefits of a thriving industrial sector.

beta index The simplest measure of overall ◊ *connectivity* in a (transport) ◊ *network*. The beta index measures how easy it is to move from one ◊ *node* to another as the ratio between the number of ◊ *edges* and the number of nodes in a network.

$$\text{Beta index }(\beta) = \frac{\Sigma e}{\Sigma n}$$

where Σe = number of edges
Σn = number of nodes

The beta index has a range from zero to a maximum of 3·0 for planar graphs and infinity for non-planar graphs. Broadly, beta values below 1·0 describe ◊ *branching* and disconnected networks; exactly 1·0 a network with only one ◊ *circuit*; and values above 1·0 circuit networks of varying complexity. ◊◊ *alpha index, cutpoint index, cyclomatic number, detour index, gamma index, König number, Shimbel index.*

beta weights Standardized ◊ *regression coefficients.*

betterment The increase in the value of land (including the buildings thereon) which arises as a result of central or local government action, whether positive, e.g. by the execution of public works or improvements, or negative, e.g. by the imposition of restrictions on the use of certain privately owned land. Since it can be argued that community action generates such increases in land value, and because the increases in value enjoyed by particular landowners are fortuitous and unearned, it follows that the increase (or part of it) should properly pass to the community. Various attempts have been made to

collect betterment in Britain, such as ◊ *development charges* from 1947 to 1953, betterment levy from 1967 to 1971, development land tax from 1976. In practice betterment has proved difficult to assess, since it is widely diffused and difficult to distinguish from the effects of population growth, inflation, etc.

betterment migration ◊ *migration.*

Betti number ◊ *cyclomatic number.*

bias Systematic ◊ *error* or distortion in a data set. Bias may derive from a variety of sources, e.g. ◊ *sampling* procedures which include or give rise to unrepresentative proportions of different parts of a population; and in the case of surveys from nonresponse, question wording, respondent and interviewer attitudes.

bid-rent (bid-price) curve A bid-rent curve indicates how much a person (farmer, householder, retailer, etc.) is prepared to pay for a unit of land at varying distances from the market/city centre. It describes the ◊ *trade-off* of cheaper land rents with increased transport costs due to increased distance from the market/city centre and represents a series of rents to which the person is indifferent, i.e. equally satisfied at any point on the bid-rent curve. The height of the curve (i.e. the value of the

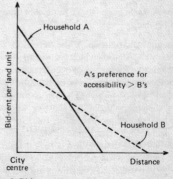

Fig. 8 Bid-rent curve

bid-rent at the market/city centre) depends, for a producer, on the difference between a product's market price and its production costs, and, for a householder, on income and preferences. Its shape (i.e. the rate at which the bid-rent declines with distance) depends on the transportation characteristics of the product in the case of producers and preference for ◇ *accessibility* in the case of householders (◇ Fig. 8). Such a bid-rent curve assumes that household incomes, product prices, transport cost structures, etc. are constant. Any change in one of these factors would generate a new bid-rent curve for each person. ◇◇ *Alonso model, location rent.*

bilateral trade ◇ *Trade* between two countries. A strict interpretation would require the value of goods and services exported by country *A* to country *B* to be exactly matched by the value of the exports from country *B* to country *A*. The development of bilateral trade dates primarily from the Great Depression of the 1930s. ◇◇ *countertrade.*

bill of lading A legal document of title and stamped receipt for goods which specifies the contract of carriage between the shipper and the shipping company.

binary system A positional method of counting using only two digits, zero and 1.

bing A waste heap from a mine in Scotland. ◇◇ *tip heap.*

binomial distribution A theoretical ◇ *frequency distribution* which is concerned with the relative frequency of occurrence of two numbers or, rather, sets of conditions or repetitions of events. The two conditions are discrete, mutually exclusive and together represent the sum total of the ◇ *probability.* The prime characteristic of the binomial distribution is that it reflects the frequency (or probability) with which these two different conditions are likely to occur for any given number of occurrences

being considered. Its use in geographical research has been limited, largely because the probability associated with any locational event in a spatial pattern is very small, but it has been used to test whether the characteristics of a sample are those that would have occurred with a random selection. ◇ *binomial test.*

binomial test A ◇ *non-parametric* test, based on the ◇ *binomial distribution* as a sampling distribution, used to compare two sets of dichotomized data, e.g. the two sets of data might represent the number of small and large fields on north- and south-facing slopes, and be regarded as samples of a single population of fields. The proportion of small fields in each 'sample' can be considered an estimate of the proportion of small fields in the total population and any difference attributed to chance rather than aspect. The binomial test will calculate the probability of obtaining such a difference as great as that between the two samples.

bioculture A general term used occasionally for the husbandry of animals. The most common form is ◇ *ranching.*

biological depopulation ◇ *depopulation, rural depopulation.*

biological energy sources Major supplies of fuel energy represented principally by petroleum and coal, derived many millions of years ago from plant and animal remains. ◇ *energy.*

biological time A type of time closely associated with attitudes and perceptions and with behaviour constrained by the ◇ *built environment.* It refers to a person's system of internal clocks which control and indeed determine wide areas of behaviour. These rhythms are called *circadian* because they tend to conform to a 24-hour cycle, e.g. the sleep–wake cycle. These nest into seasonal or circannual rhythms which, in turn, nest in lifetime rhythms. ◇ *psychological time, socio-ecological time.* ◇◇ *time geography.*

biorights The right of endangered species or unique landscapes to remain unmolested.

biotic potential of population The theoretical rate of growth of a human population which is allowed to develop in an optimal environment of unlimited extent. Such population growth follows an exponential form.

birth control The conscious attempt to control population growth by the deliberate use of ◊ *contraception* and other 'unnatural' methods, including ◊ *sterilization* and induced ◊ *abortion*. Birth control is seen as essential in helping achieve a levelling-off of current rates of population growth to a sustainable steady state. But birth control is slow to take effect because (a) a large proportion of the world's population is young and even if the next generation's mothers (who are already alive) have only two children the population will continue to rise for thirty to forty years, and (b) programmes have had only limited success, since some Third World governments are suspicious that they are a trick to prevent them becoming more affluent, while there is a large body of religious opinion opposed on moral grounds to any form of artificial birth control.

A. Sauvy suggests that the use of the term is bad for two reasons: it suggests a command or mastery which is not present, and most advocates exclude abortion, which is a method of preventing birth.

Family planning is an alternative term.

birth rates Birth rates are usually expressed as the number of babies born per thousand population per year. This is the *crude* or *live birth rate* and is the most common index of ◊ *fertility*.

$$\text{Crude birth rate} = \frac{\text{No. of live births} \times 1000}{\text{Total (mid-year) population}}$$

It is termed crude birth rate because the denominator contains persons who have either no chance of giving birth at all (e.g. men, girl babies, old women) or who have different probabilities of giving birth (married and unmarried women), but also because it makes no allowances for differences between populations in their age distribution.

To overcome the latter disadvantage *age-specific birth rates* are calculated for specified age classes, normally five-year age groups. Similarly, when comparing birth rates between parts of a country *standardized birth rates* can be calculated to overcome the effect of regional or urban–rural variations in age composition. Birth rates are standardized by calculating the rate which would have occurred if the age composition of an area had been that of the country as a whole. Birth rates are a function of (a) demographic variables such as the number of women of childbearing age, the prevailing age of marriage, the number of married women, the number of childless women, family-size norms, the average interval between successive births, etc., and (b) other variables such as the proportion of young women at school, the level of education of mothers, the income of fathers, prevailing economic conditions, the availability of housing, etc. ◊◊ *natural change component*.

bivariate correlation ◊ *correlation*.

black box approach The term black box is used by psychologists and others to refer to a group of functions of the brain which are known in outline but which are not known component by component. Thus a particular response (feeling, emotion) may occur to a given stimulus, but how the brain functions in translating that stimulus to a particular response is not fully known, i.e. the mediating process performed by the human mind/brain is not understood. The brain is sometimes called a black box. The

41

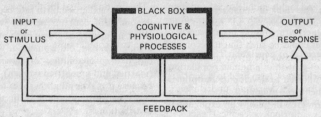

Fig. 9 Black box

above idea is used as a ◊ *model* of a ◊ *system* whose internal characteristics (structure and functioning) are not understood but whose ◊ *stimulus–response* characteristics can be studied in detail, i.e. attention is directed to the character of the outputs which result from identified inputs (◊ Fig. 9).

With respect to spatial systems use of the black box between symbolic stimulus and overt decision has moved human geography some way towards an understanding of the behavioural process, but there remains a lack of full knowledge of its workings.

black economy ◊ *informal economy*.

black house An early, rudimentary dwelling, with centre hearth, which housed both family and beasts. Built in areas of wood scarcity, gale-force winds and high rainfall, it therefore had to have very thick walls which were packed outside with turves. Black houses are found in the Outer Hebrides and south to Tiree, and can be compared to the ◊ *long house* of the Highland Zone in Britain.

blanket rate pricing A type of ◊ *transport rate* structure for goods, similar to a *postage stamp pricing* (◊ *uniform pricing*), in which a different uniform rate is adopted in different zones. The blanket rate charged for shipments to a zone customarily rises with the distance of the zone from the origin of the shipment. It has been used in transcontinental rail movement since the 19th century. Its advantage to the operating

company is that it greatly simplifies rate quotations and publication of rate schedules. For a manufacturer such a pricing system has no effect on the choice of location within a zone.

blight The effect of social or functional change, taken together with the ageing of buildings, on the value or standard of buildings. It involves a degree of subjectivity regarding the non-acceptance of obsolescent buildings and neighbourhoods as well as the more factual aspects of the progressive depreciation of real property. Various types of *blight* have been recognized:

(i) *Economic*, in which changes in the demand for goods result in a lowering of the socio-economic level of use of buildings.

(ii) *Functional*, in which there is a decline in a building's capacity to render a service consequent upon changing technology and mobility of population.

(iii) *Frictional* or *environmental*, which is brought about by the deleterious effect of certain activities upon their surroundings.

(iv) *Social*, which is equated with a loss of prestige.

(v) *Physical*, which is the deterioration of buildings due to age and lack of maintenance.

In all cases blight involves a loss of productivity, and property-owners react by disinvesting. Blight is a response to change in a growing urban system due to the conflict between fixed building resources and highly mobile social and economic demands. As such it is a diseconomy of urban growth, and the misallocation of resources could be such that it becomes a major policy issue for urban government.

block enclosure A term used to describe an area of formal ◊ *enclosure* undertaken *en bloc* at a given point in time. It contrasts with the informal, piecemeal enclosure which may have taken place over a longer time span.

blockbusting An overt tactic used by realtors (estate agents) to direct and control the growth of black residential areas in the North American city. It involves the use of scare tactics to increase the rate of white turnover. ◊ *lily-whiting.*

blood-group indices There are four main blood groups: A, B, AB and O. These groups differ in the presence or absence of two factors (A and B) in the red blood cells and in the presence or absence of two factors (anti-A and anti-B) in serum. The same four groups are found among all people: random tests indicate that in the world's population generally the groups are present in the proportions A 38%, O 37%, B 18% and AB 7%, but the frequency of each group within a given population varies with ◊ *race* and geographical distribution.

The racial affinities between one population and another can be expressed in the form of an index derived from comparing their respective *blood-group ratios* and summing the differences irrespective of sign, as in the table below.

The limiting values for the index are 0 and 200 and the lower the value of the index the more comparable the racial affinity of the two populations.

bocage A type of rural landscape with small fields enclosed by low, hedged banks and/or a line of pollarded trees. The term was originally used to describe landscape in north-west France, i.e. Brittany and Normandy.

body ballet A term used by D. Seamon in developing a particular phenomenological perspective to the understanding of everyday experiences. Body ballet is one of two types of behaviour (◊ *time–space routine*) which are housed within the ◊ *body-subject*: it represents a set of integrated gestures and movements which sustain a particular taste or aim. Body ballets are frequently an integral part of manual skill or artistic talent, i.e. the simple hand, leg and body movements needed in performing any work, leisure activity, etc. ◊ *place ballet.*

body-subject Part of D. Seamon's phenomenological schema for understanding everyday experiences, using a term borrowed from M. Merleau-Ponty to describe an intentional body force. Body-subject is the inherent capacity of the body to direct behaviours of the person intelligently, and thus function as a special kind of subject which expresses itself in a preconscious way usually described by such words as 'automatic', 'habitual', 'involuntary' and 'mechanical'. Thus body-subject underlies and guides our everyday

	Population X	Population Y	Difference
A	37	40	3
O	38	44	6
B	17	10	7
AB	8	6	2
			—
		Index of racial affinity =	18

movements, which take the form of ◊ *body ballets* and ◊ *time–space routines*.

body territory ◊ *personal space*.

boiling water reactor (BWR) A type of ◊ *light water reactor*.

bonded A term used to describe a warehouse when it has been approved by Customs as being secure and suitable for the storage of goods that are liable for duty which has not yet been paid.

bondland Old cultivated land, as distinguished from ◊ *assart* land.

bookland Land granted by a Saxon king to a subject and the title confirmed by charter.

boot-strap strategy An approach to ◊ *urban renewal* which involves the conservation and upgrading of existing properties without displacing the occupants. It is based on the belief that everything is improvable and worth improvement. ◊◊ *rehabilitation*.

booth A temporary shelter, cowhouse or herdsman's hut probably associated with the practice of ◊ *transhumance*.

bord and pillar An underground coal-mining technique, commonly used in the United States for deep mining operations. It involves 'blocking-out' areas of coal by a roadway network of squares, rectangular blocks or pillars and extracting coal by means of conventional or continuous processes. Coal-pillars are efficient roof supports, but a significant proportion of coal is left behind unless the pillars are replaced by steel or timber supports. ◊◊ *advance mining*, *longwall mining*, *pillar and stall*.

border, border zone (1) A district or zone lying along each side of the ◊ *boundary* which separates one country from another. ◊◊ *frontier*, *march*.
(2) The actual ◊ *boundary* between two countries.

borough Originally, in England and Wales, a settlement given privileges in trade, landholding and self-government by means of a charter granted by the king or a lord. Such settlements, often fortified places, already possessed urban functions or quickly acquired them as a result of its charter. *Royal boroughs* were granted charters by the king, *seigneurial boroughs* by a lay or ecclesiastical lord. The former's privileges were more secure and generous.

The term *parliamentary borough* was used of a town constituency in England which returned one or more members to Parliament. Within the local government system which evolved in England and Wales in the late 19th century (1888 Local Government Act) *county boroughs* were created: this status was reserved for large towns which had the status of an administrative ◊ *county*. County boroughs were abolished as part of the reorganization of local government which took place in 1974 (under the terms of the 1972 Local Government Act). ◊◊ *burgh*.

borrowing innovations The concept that an economy or an ◊ *entrepreneur* may be innovative by adapting and using original ideas or devices developed by others. Imagination and skill in application may in some cases serve as substitutes for more basic inventiveness. ◊ *innovation*.

boss nexus A term utilized by P. S. Florence to describe a particular psychological motive of an ◊ *entrepreneur*, namely, that of love of power. Such a motive could lead to the rejection of a ◊ *merger* if the entrepreneur were to be submerged in another organization. ◊◊ *free man nexus*, *hobby nexus*.

boulevard A landscaped ◊ *avenue* or thoroughfare in towns, especially one lined with trees and laid out with lawns, etc.

boundary A boundary is often interpreted as a line demarcating recognized limits of established political units, such as ◊ *states*

and administrative areas. The preferred definition, however, is as a vertical interface between state sovereignties where they intersect the surface of the earth: the extension down to the centre of the earth is according to international agreement which allocates rights to all subterranean resources, but similar agreement has not yet been reached over the upward extension into air space because of difficulties in agreeing an upper limit. Boundaries therefore have no horizontal extent and all are artificial in the sense of being determined by people. The boundary concept has evolved as states have been forced to compete for space and fixed limits needed to be specified. Four stages in the development of international boundaries may be recognized:
(i) *Allocation*: the general political decisions on the division of territory.
(ii) *Delimitation*: the selection of a specific boundary within a broad allocation zone.
(iii) *Demarcation*: the marking of the boundary location by posts, buoys, etc.
(iv) *Administration*: continuing arrangements for the maintenance and operation of the boundary.

There are two principal classification systems applied to boundaries:
(i) *Generic boundaries*, based on origin, are of four types:
(a) *Physical boundaries*, which follow some physical feature.
(b) *Ethnic boundaries*, which separate peoples of differing cultural characteristics.
(c) *Historical boundaries*, which follow old political lines.
(d) *Geometric boundaries*, which are straight lines following a meridian of longitude or a parallel of latitude.
(ii) *Functional boundaries*, based on cultural relationships, are of two main types:
(a) *Antecedent boundaries*, which precede the close settlement and full development of associated cultural landscapes, etc. In the course of this de-

velopment the presence of the boundary is taken into account as groups subsequently occupying the area adjust to it. Totally antecedent or *pioneer boundaries* are drawn before any settlement takes place and exist in virginal form until the arrival and settlement of colonists.
(b) *Subsequent boundaries*, which are delimited after the close settlement and development of an area. Where they coincide with established cultural, ethnic or economic patterns they are described as *consequent boundaries*, but where they ignore such patterns they are referred to as *superimposed* or *discordant boundaries*.
◊ *frontier*, *boundary mark*, *relict boundary*.

boundary dispute There are four types of disagreement between countries which may arise in respect to ◊ *boundaries*:
(i) *Territorial boundary disputes*, which result from some quality of the neighbouring borderland which makes it attractive to the country initiating the dispute.
(ii) *Positional boundary disputes*, which concern the actual location of the boundary.
(iii) *Functional boundary disputes*, which arise over state functions applied at the boundary.
(iv) *Trans-boundary resource development disputes*, which concern the use of transboundary resources, such as a river or a coalfield, and have as their aim the creation of some organization which will govern the use of the particular resource.
A solution to type (i) and (ii) disputes can be found only by altering the boundary in favour of the claimant, but type (iii) and (iv) disputes can be solved without a boundary change.

boundary effect ◊ *Boundaries* act as a barrier or filter to all types of spatial interaction between countries and regions. Such effects are most significant in an economic sense through association with ◊ *tariff* and ◊ *quota* restrictions, but they also serve to reinforce cultural differ-

45

ences. They emphasize the difference between ◊ *geodesic distance* and ◊ *functional distance.* ◊◊ *halo effect.*

boundary estimation ◊ *breaking point.*

boundary mark Marks, natural or made by people, used to denote the limits of land ownership, and civil or ecclesiastical jurisdictions. From early times natural features, such as streams, boulders and trees, were used, to be supplemented later by hedges, banks, ditches and roads. The most common surviving boundary marks, e.g. carved stones, were put up during the 19th century, when ◊ *parish* boundaries were re-drawn.

boundary waters Those water features (e.g. seas, lakes, rivers) within which a ◊ *boundary* is drawn. ◊◊ *internal waters, territorial waters.*

boundary zones Areas in the vicinity of ◊ *boundaries* which share distinctive characteristics as a result. ◊◊ *border zone.*

bounded rationality The notion that represents a person's limited capacity to formulate and solve complex problems. The view of the ◊ *decision-maker* as globally rational ◊ *economic man* is not tenable because information is not free but must be obtained within time and money constraints and because decision-makers have limited ability to process and use the information they acquire. Optimal decisions are therefore unattainable and a decision-maker is conceived of as constructing a simplified model of the real situation which he or she can deal with, and as behaving rationally with respect to this model, i.e. with respect to a number of pre-selected alternatives out of a much larger set of alternatives. Also known as *cognitive rationality.* ◊ *behavioural matrix.* ◊◊ *satisficer concept.*

bounded spaces Bounded spaces are simply subdivisions of the earth's surface with a ◊ *boundary* surrounding them. There are two types according to the nature of the boundary:
(i) *Legal or legally bounded spaces* are those in which a person's rights and obligations are defined by law. Such rights and obligations change when the boundary is crossed: the latter is usually identified by a tangible barrier.
(ii) *Conceptual or conceptually bounded spaces* have no legal basis but are subscribed to by a large number of people because of common characteristics and/or conditions of access. The boundary surrounding such ◊ *spaces* is usually much more vague and ill-defined. ◊◊ *spatial fields.*

bovate A measure of the amount of land in early times required to support a farming unit, in this case as much land as one ox could plough in a year. The bovate was essentially a measure of ancient tillage or ◊ *open field* arable, and was the normal unit of tenure in the ◊ *Danelaw.* Generally synonymous with ◊ *oxgang.* Once determined, such land denominations took on further connotations, as they were used as a basis for taxation, rents, services, etc., and bovates remained in use for such purposes until the early 15th century.

brachycephalic Broad-headed: defined by anthropologists as a skull with a ◊ *cephalic index* of $\geqslant 83 \cdot 1$.

brain drain The persistent loss of the most capable people of a country or region, especially their young people, by ◊ *emigration* due to the lure of opportunities and benefits elsewhere.

branch plant A second or subsequent manufacturing plant established by a ◊ *firm.* The motivation may be to meet an expanding demand, or to respond to changing geographical patterns of markets or to changing structures of costs. Such plants may manufacture a complete product or only one element/component in a product. ◊◊ *industrial movement, truncated firm.*

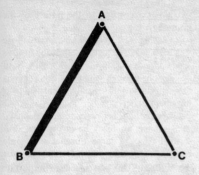

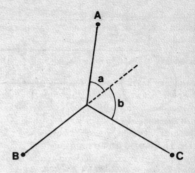

(a) Relative volumes of traffic between A, B and C

(b) Branching angles : a(B to A), b(B to C)

Fig. 10 Branching angle

branching angle The angle of branching of routes in a ⟡ *network*. Generally the magnitude of the angle between a branch route and the main stem will be smaller the greater the proportion of total movement along that branch. This suggests that the less important the branch relative to the main route it is linking up with, the greater the angle of branching, as ⟡ Fig. 10 shows.

branching network Or ⟡ *tree*. A ⟡ *network* in which there is only one possible path between a pair of places, i.e. a set of connected lines without any complete loops, as illustrated in ⟡ Fig. 11. ⟡⟡ *circuit network*.

breaking point The interaction breaking point between two towns is defined as a point up to which one town exercises the dominating retail trade influence and beyond which the other town dominates. The point can be calculated as follows:

$$d_{jk} = \frac{d_{ij}}{1 + \sqrt{\dfrac{S_i}{S_j}}}$$

where d_{jk} = distance of breaking point from town j

d_{ij} = distance between towns i and j

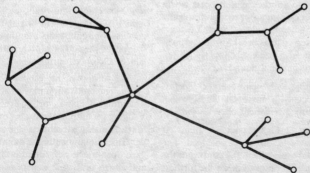

Fig. 11 Branching network

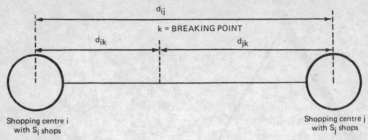

Fig. 12 Breaking point

S_i = number of ◊ *shopping goods* outlets in town *i*

S_j = number of shopping goods outlets in town *j*

◊ Fig. 12 demonstrates the relationships between these parameters. The relative importance of the towns can be measured in a variety of ways, e.g. their populations could be substituted for shopping goods outlets. Applying this concept to a series of neighbouring towns allows boundaries of ◊ *market areas* to be estimated. ◊◊ *Reilly's law, retail gravitation.*

breaking bulk, break-of-bulk The function of a wholesaler, importer, etc. in dividing up a single commodity load into quantities or sizes to meet the particular requirements of individual retailers, manufacturers, etc. This frequently takes place where the commodity is transferred from one transport mode to another, e.g. at ports where the transfer is from water to land transport for imported commodities. Such locations may be referred to as break-of-bulk points. An artificial break-of-bulk is often assumed at national boundaries.

brecks Supposedly temporary ◊ *enclosures*, especially from forest lands, which often became permanent ones. ◊◊ *intake.*

bridge-point, bridging point A point at which a river is, or can be, bridged. The term is used especially in the context of the lowest bridging point to mean the furthest point downstream at which a river could

be bridged. This was often an important factor in the original location of a town.

bridgehead A fortified area established in enemy territory, especially on the far side of a river protecting the end of a bridge nearest the enemy. The idea has been extended to the territorial control by one ◊ *state* across a river which primarily forms the ◊ *boundary* between the two states, e.g. the Dutch bridgehead across the River Meuse at Maastricht.

bridle path, bridle way A path or way fit for the passage of horses but not of vehicles. The legal implication is that right of way is restricted to pedestrians and horse-riders.

bright-lights district That specialized part of the ◊ *central business district* where entertainment facilities are concentrated.

British Summer Time (BST). A ◊ *standard time*, sometimes known as *daylight saving time*, first introduced in Britain in 1916. It is in use for about seven months each year, from near the end of March until near the end of October, during which clocks are set one hour in advance of ◊ *Greenwich Mean Time. Double BST*, whereby clocks were advanced two hours, was instituted between 1941 and 1947.

broch A massive circular stone tower with very thick hollow walls and a central courtyard open to the sky, found on the islands and north and west coasts of Scotland. Brochs date originally from the 4th to 2nd centuries B C and represent fortified homesteads.

Bronze Age One of the major phases of prehistoric culture (⟡ *Iron Age*, *Stone Age*) based on the technological skills employed in making implements and weapons. The Bronze Age is the period when these were made of bronze (an alloy of copper and tin). No exact dates can be given, nor does it necessarily denote a fixed chronological period in history, but it marks a stage in the development of human culture through which many peoples of the world have passed in their progress from the Stone Age to the Iron Age. For the British Isles it is generally accepted that the Bronze Age covered the 18th to 5th centuries B C.

BST ⟡ *British Summer Time*.

budget line ⟡ *iso-outlay line*.

buffer state A ⟡ *state*, usually independent, situated between two or more powerful and usually rival neighbouring states. It serves the purpose of helping to allay direct conflict between them and so contains their expansionist policies.

building density The ratio of the total floor area of a building to the net site area (within the property boundaries). ⟡ *plot ratio*.

building line A standard regulating the layout of development prescribing a line at a given distance from the middle of a road which indicates the nearest limits of future buildings in relation to that road.

Building Preservation Notice To secure the preservation of any building of architectural or historic interest which is not a ⟡ *listed building*, a local authority may serve a Building Preservation Notice which prevents the demolition, alteration or extension of the building. This notice has the effect of protecting the building for six months, thus giving time for considering whether or not it should be listed.

built environment That part of the physical surroundings which are people-made or people-organized, such as buildings and other major structures, roads, bridges and the like, down to lesser objects such as traffic lights, telephone and pillar boxes. ⟡ *environment*.

built-up area A term, commonly used in planning, for the area of a town or city which is covered by buildings and which has no internal space for further similar development. ⟡ *urban fence*, *urban tract*.

bulk carriers Ships which are specifically designed to carry bulk cargo, i.e. cargo not packed in any form of container. Such ships may be designed for a particular bulk commodity, such as supertankers for oil, or designed for several commodities, such as ⟡ *'obo' vessels*. With supertankers a distinction may be made between a V L C C (very large crude carrier) of 200,000–450,000 tons, and a U L C C (ultra-large crude carrier) of over 450,000 tons.

burg A type of settlement built by the Danes in the Midlands during the 8th century. It was copied by the Anglo-Saxons in Wessex, and had spread to Mercia by the 10th century. It comprised a refuge, military headquarters and a market, and also often a mint. The later ⟡ *shires* of the area were centred upon burgs.

burgage (1) A form of tenure found in ⟡ *boroughs*, and common by the 12th century, in which all forms of service, except perhaps military service, were commuted to a fixed money rent.
(2) The plot of urban land held by a ⟡ *burgess*, which consisted of the house, a yard and a ⟡ *garth*. The size of plot varied enormously, but generally it had a narrow frontage onto the street with a long narrow strip of land behind. The burgage would have a fixed rent as a contribution to the borough. The burgage arrangement, whereby valuable frontage space was shared out,

is accommodated most effectively in a rectangular ⟡ grid system.

burgess An inhabitant of a ⟡ borough, usually a ⟡ freeman, who had special privileges and duties, such as holding by ⟡ burgage (tenure) and doing watch and ward.

burgess rights Privileges accruing to ⟡ burgess tenements, which included free marriage of daughters, confirmation of widows' dowers, and freedom from tolls on all merchandise bought and sold by burgesses, as well as the usual tenants' rights.

burgh Originally the term had the same meaning as ⟡ borough, but it is now restricted to towns in Scotland possessing a charter. Three classes of burgh can be recognized depending on the origin of the charter: a royal burgh obtained its charter from the crown, a burgh of barony from a baron, and a burgh of regality from a lord who exercised certain rights of justice.

bush fallowing ⟡ land rotation.

business cycle The well-defined and repetitive oscillations in the economic business level of an area, nation or larger segment of the world. Also known as the trade cycle, it implies alternating periods of trade boom and slump and was especially characteristic of 19th-century business activity. The average duration, from one boom to the next, was eight years. Employment, production, wages, prices and profits rise together during the boom, only to decline in the ensuing slump. While all industries are affected, the fluctuations are most marked in the capital goods industries (⟡ accelerator). Although various theories have been put forward to explain the cycle, fluctuation in demand is considered most important. ⟡ Kondratiev cycle, regional cycle.

buy-back agreement ⟡ countertrade.

by-law housing Housing built in Great Britain from 1870, after legislation had been passed which laid down certain standards, particularly of ⟡ density, which had to be followed by builders in urban areas.

by-product A useful, but secondary, product which is made during the making of something else (the latter being the main purpose of the manufacturing process). ⟡ complementary product, joint product, supplementary product.

C

cacotopia A Greek word meaning 'a bad place' and used to refer to mountain paths, passes, etc. P. Geddes and L. Mumford used it to mean 'hell', but it is more commonly used to replace ◊ *anti-utopia*.

cadastral survey A survey made to demarcate landed properties. The area, boundaries, value, location and ownership of each holding is recorded in a ◊ *cadastre*.

cadastre A public record or register of land/property ownership, land values and land use. ◊ *cartulary*.

cairn A pile of rough stones, of varying height, often found on a peak or summit ridge and raised as a monument or mark of some kind. Some may date back to the ◊ *Bronze* and *Iron Ages* and mark ancient burial sites. Medieval documents record the use of others as parish ◊ *boundary marks*. More recent *waymarker cairns*, usually much smaller than the ancient ones, have been erected as ◊ *landmarks* to indicate paths, especially over moorland routes lacking natural landmarks.

calendar year The system by which time is divided into fixed periods or ◊ *years*, which are subdivided into months and days. The year, the month and the ◊ *solar day* are natural periods of time used in the preparation of a calendar. The year corresponds to the period of the earth's revolution around the sun (365 days 5 hrs 48'46"); the month to the period of the moon's revolution around the earth; and the day to the period of rotation of the earth on its axis.

A problem arises because the year is not an exact multiple of the period of the moon's revolution around the earth or of the solar day. To arrive at a solar year of 365·25 days, three consecutive years of 365 days are followed by a ◊ *leap year*, of 366 days. Since a leap year is 14'11" longer than the true year, the *Gregorian calendar* (New Style) now in use corrects for this by making centurial years leap years only when they are exactly divisible by 400. Thus 1700, 1800 and 1900 were ordinary years but 2000 will be a leap year. As a result the 'error' is reduced to less than 1 day in 3,000 years.

calibration Most ◊ *models* contain ◊ *parameters* within their mathematical structure which will differ when a model is applied to different parts of the world, or different regions or urban areas within a country. The calibration process involves fitting the theoretical model to a particular data set, i.e. a complete set of data is assembled for a base year at some past point in time for all the input and output variables of the model, and the calibration process finds the 'best' values of the parameters that reproduce in the model as closely as possible the known results for the base year. Once a model has been successfully calibrated it can be used to predict unknown values of the dependent variable(s).

call-in power The Secretary of State for the Environment has the power to call in for his own decision any application for ◊ *planning permission* submitted to a local planning authority. His decision is then final, there being no grounds for appeal on planning terms. Call-in is most likely in cases of applications that involve a substantial departure from the provisions of a ◊ *development plan*, mineral workings, or a matter of more than local importance.

calorie As defined by physicists, the heat required to raise the temperature of 1 gramme of water by 1°C. This is a minute quantity of heat in practical terms. When used in respect of human nutritional requirements, it means ◊ *kilocalorie*.

calorie intake and requirements ◊ *nutritional requirements*.

Canada Land Inventory A comprehensive national scheme for ◊ *land evaluation* in Canada, using computerized data storage and retrieval. It originated from recommendations for a ◊ *land capability* map at the Resources for Tomorrow conference in 1961 and has its formal roots in the 1961 Agricultural Rehabilitation and Development Act. Preliminary studies commenced in 1963 and a geographic data bank storing information about the whole of settled Canada was in routine use by the end of the 1960s. It contains data collected both by census agencies and by field scientists, some of the latter especially for the Inventory. Locational referencing is by geodetic latitude and longitude, with data automatically digitized on entry. The inventory's purpose was to measure and describe the potential of every part of Canada (excluding incorporated areas) for recreation, for supporting wildlife, for growing timber and for agriculture.

canal A people-made waterway constructed primarily to join rivers, lakes and seas for the purpose of inland navigation, but also used in the case of distribution channels for irrigation water and even water supply. The earliest canals were built in Mesopotamia around 4000 BC. At first they could run only on the level and were therefore restricted to flat country, but with the introduction of the lock, enabling sections of a waterway to be artificially raised or lowered, canals could cross different levels of terrain. Long-distance canals therefore became possible from the 16th century. In Britain the main canal-building period was from the 1760s to the 1820s, when waterways were cut to facilitate the cheap transport of bulky goods. ◊ *ship canal*.

canonical correlation An analytical procedure which assesses the relationship between a large number of independent ◊ *variables* and a large number of dependent variables. These two sets of variables, each of which can be given a theoretical meaning as a set, represent the basic input for canonical correlation analysis, which determines linear combinations of the variables within each set. Each linear combination from one set maximally correlates with a corresponding linear combination from the other set. These linear combinations are the *canonical variates* and come in associated pairs. Thus the canonical variates are composed of coefficients that reflect the importance of the original variables in the set. The first pair of canonical variates selected have the highest possible intercorrelation, the second pair accounts for the maximum amount of the relationship between the two sets of variables left unaccounted for by the first pair, and so forth. The amount of ◊ *correlation* between each corresponding pair of canonical variates is the canonical correlation between them, and its square represents the amount of ◊ *variance* in one canonical variate that is accounted for by the other canonical variate. It is therefore a technique with considerable capabilities for data reduction.

capability constraints Limits on human behaviour/activities arising from the biological construction of human beings and/or the tools they can command. Such limits are essentially temporal in effect, e.g. the need of a person to rest for a period of time and to eat at regular intervals. The regularity and duration of such physiological constraints determine when, and for how long, other activities can be engaged in. ◊ *time–space prism*. ◊◊ *authority constraints, coupling constraints*.

capacitated network A ◊ *network* with known maximum capacities for handling flow along ◊ *links* or through ◊ *nodes*.

capital (1) The town within a country, province or state where political authority is concentrated, i.e. the seat of government. Various political–geographical classifications of capitals have been attempted. The distinction between *natural capitals*, which have evolved to reach capital status, and *artificial capitals*, which are custom-built to serve the capital function, is now generally regarded as futile. H. De Blij suggested a morphological approach based on a capital's position in relation to state territory and ◊ *core areas* which recognized:

(i) *Permanent capitals*, e.g. London, Paris, which have retained their pre-eminence through successive stages in the politico-territorial evolution of their state.

(ii) *Introduced capitals*, e.g. Brasilia, Madrid, which were established to replace former foci in order to perform new and different functions.

(iii) *Divided capitals*, which cover the rare cases where the capital function is divided between two towns, e.g. in South Africa the legislature is in Cape Town and the government in Pretoria.

(2) One of the ◊ *factors of production*. It includes all things/wealth deliberately made by society for use in the production of further wealth. It is described as *real capital* when it consists of buildings, machines, material stocks, etc. Real capital may be subdivided into:

(i) *Fixed capital:* factories and other buildings, transport systems, physical plant, machinery and equipment. Such capital is relatively immobile because it is

costly and difficult to move from a fixed location.

(ii) *Floating* or *circulating capital:* raw material and fuel stocks, goods in the process of manufacture, etc.

(iii) *Specific capital:* equipment that cannot normally be used for any other purpose than that for which it was originally designed and constructed.

(iv) *Non-specific capital:* equipment that is flexible and can be used in a variety of processes. ◊◊ *capital goods*.

Capital can also be regarded as money to obtain the inputs necessary to commence production, in which case it is known as *financial capital, investment capital* or *money capital*.

The term *working capital* combines aspects of real and money capital since it includes inventories of materials and completed goods, easily realizable assets (including certain investments and short-term debts owed to the firm) and actual cash or bank balances. ◊◊ *economic overhead capital, social overhead capital*.

capital, social ◊ *social overhead capital*.

capital account ◊ *balance of payments*.

capital deepening The growth of the stock of ◊ *capital goods* more than proportional to the growth of the labour force. ◊◊ *capital widening*.

capital goods Manufacturing output may be subdivided into two types of goods – capital goods and ◊ *consumer goods*. Capital goods are those outputs which are themselves used to produce further goods. Also known as *production capital*. ◊ *capital* (2).

capital intensive A form of production in which a high proportion of ◊ *capital* (2) is used in relation to the amount of ◊ *labour* employed. Oil refineries and petrochemical plants, which require much capital investment into equipment and automatic machinery but employ a relatively small labour force, are examples of capital intensive industry. ⟡ *labour intensive*.

capital-shortage unemployment ⟡ *unemployment*.

capital widening The growth of the stock of ⟡ *capital goods* proportional to the growth of the labour force. ⟡ *capital deepening*.

capitalism An ⟡ *economic system* for the general production of goods and services based on private enterprise, in which most of the resources/means of production and the power to exploit them are in the hands of relatively few private individuals and are subject to largely uncontrolled economic ⟡ *competition*. Thus the 'actual producer', i.e. the worker, is separated both from the means of production and from the good he/she produces. This separation is effected through the wage-labour market which transforms worker's labour into goods according to price signals. Therefore the ⟡ *values* connotation of this term usually implies the ⟡ *profit motive* and the exploitation of the worker. ⟡ *market economy, neocapitalism, state capitalism*.

carn A Gaelic term for ⟡ *cairn*.

carrier industries ⟡ *basic activities*.

carrying capacity The maximum intensity of use, at a given level of management, which a natural or people-made ⟡ *resource* can sustain without an unacceptable degree of deterioration of the character and quality of the resource or the product of the use of that resource. The concept was originally applied to animal : land ratios expressed either in terms of the number of a particular domestic animal or of livestock units or the equivalent per area (⟡ *souming, stocking rate*). These ratios related to the level of use pasture will tolerate without permanent destruction. The term is extended to apply to the area of land under cultivation needed to support one person (⟡ *population carrying capacity*), and hence to the maximum number of users who can be sustained by a given set of land resources for a particular purpose, such as recreation (⟡ *rated capacity, recreational carrying capacity*).

The concept is also applied to the carrying capacity of a road or railway, measured in terms of the maximum number of passengers per hour it is capable of carrying under optimum conditions.

cartel A central selling organization formed by producers to control production and marketing and so avoid competing with one another. Each member is assigned a specific share in the total output of a commodity and all members are bound by a code of rules: if the specified output is exceeded some penalty, e.g. a fine, is imposed on the erring member. ⟡ *oligopoly*.

cartesian space Two-dimensional ⟡ *space* involving a regular, rectangular grid based on two co-ordinate axes, perpendicular to each other, with an arbitrary origin or zero point. Co-ordinates measure on an ⟡ *interval scale* and provide a method of grid referencing to establish location in space.

cartogram A term with some variation in meaning, although all agree that a cartogram is a map on which statistical information is presented in diagrammatic form. The broadest use of the term would regard any statistical map as a cartogram, including those using symbols to display quantitative data on a map. The accepted specific use is for a highly abstracted and simplified map in which the base is not the true scale, i.e. a particular map projection transforming topographical space according to statistical factors so that the largest units mapped relate to the greatest statistical values. Geographical features are roughly preserved in so far as each unit is bound by its true neighbours. ⟡ Fig. 13 depicts a cartogram of UK counties by size of voting population in 1966.

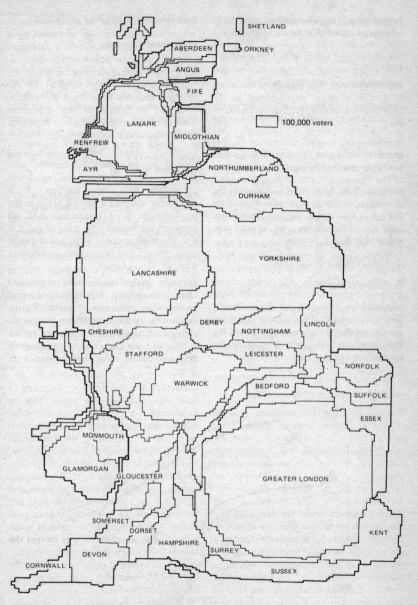

SHETLAND
ORKNEY
ABERDEEN
ANGUS
FIFE
LANARK
MIDLOTHIAN
RENFREW
AYR
NORTHUMBERLAND
DURHAM
YORKSHIRE
LANCASHIRE
CHESHIRE
DERBY
NOTTINGHAM
LINCOLN
STAFFORD
LEICESTER
NORFOLK
WARWICK
BEDFORD
SUFFOLK
MONMOUTH
ESSEX
GLAMORGAN
GLOUCESTER
GREATER LONDON
SOMERSET
DORSET
KENT
HAMPSHIRE
SURREY
DEVON
CORNWALL
SUSSEX

☐ 100,000 voters

Fig. 13 Cartogram: UK counties by 1966 voting population

cartography The art, science and technology of making charts and maps, together with their study as scientific documents and works of art. It provides a formal system for the presentation and communication of spatial data.

cartometry Techniques for making measurements from maps and their subsequent analysis.

cartulary A record (or list) of lands and privileges granted by charter. ⟡ *cadastre*.

carucate The term which replaced the ⟡ *hide* (⟡ *yardland*) in areas of Danish influence in England in the late 9th century and the 10th century. Carucates were subdivided into ⟡ *bovates*.

cascade diffusion ⟡ *diffusion*.

cascading system ⟡ *systems analysis*.

cash crop A ⟡ *crop* grown with the object of producing a surplus for sale or barter (as contrasted with a crop grown primarily for the sustenance or use of the grower and his family). ⟡ *catch-crop*.

cash economy ⟡ *informal economy*.

cash tenancy ⟡ *tenancy*.

caste An exclusive social division based solely on birth, to which a person belongs throughout their life and which totally restricts choice of occupation and marriage partner. Members of the higher castes enjoy many privileges, but those in the lowest castes (formerly known as 'untouchables') are condemned to the most menial labour.

catastrophe theory A mathematical approach for dealing with qualitative discontinuities, e.g. a change from one stable state/equilibrium to another, in a dynamic ⟡ *system*. Changes in the state are represented by a trajectory on a surface (⟡ Fig. 14) in a 'state space', defined by the system's control parameters which can alter continuously. The trajectories may conform to elementary kinds of discontinuous catastrophe where the system changes abruptly from one state to another. The methodology is in its early stages of development, but the approach

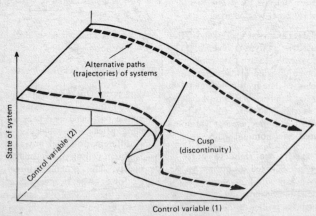

Fig. 14 Catastrophe theory

has been used in simple modelling in historical geography and urban and regional science.

catastrophism A school of thought which considers that the basic elements of the ◊ *landscape* were formed by sudden catastrophic occurrences.

catch-crop A term used primarily to describe a quick-growing ◊ *crop* grown between two main crops in a ◊ *rotation*, e.g. after harvesting an early cereal crop, ryegrass may be sown to provide autumn fodder for cattle or sheep, then, towards the end of winter, the remainder of the catch-crop can be ploughed in to provide a quick-decaying green manure and the land prepared for sowing a new crop of cereals in the spring.

The term is also used for a quick-growing crop planted between the rows of a main crop or in place of a failed crop. Use is thus made of land that would otherwise be temporarily unproductive. ◊ *interculture*, *multiple-cropping*.

catchment area In planning and marketing geography, that area or sphere of influence from which the vast majority of retail sales for a particular shopping centre or development are derived. ◊ *complementary region*, *market area*, *service area*.

categorical data analysis A set of statistical methods used to analyse ◊ *nominal scale data*. Categorical data are data which can be fitted or subdivided into unique categories or classes. The methods of analysis are similar to ◊ *regression* except that they can handle situations where either or both the dependent and independent variables are measured on a nominal scale.

cattlegate (gait) The right to graze a number of beasts, fixed according to the holder's gate (*cowgate* = pasture for one cow on the common grazing), on a piece of land which the holder of the right either owns in common with the possessors of other gates or has acquired by grant from the owner of the land. ◊ *common rights*. ◊ *stint*.

Caucasoid One of the primary ◊ *races* of people, found in Europe, North Africa and from the Middle East to northern India. It is the most variable in physical appearance of all the major races: skin colours range from clear white through pink or ruddy to light brown or olive; hair, of fine to medium texture, ranges in colour from platinum blond to red and dark brown; and eye colour varies from pale grey-blue or green to various shades of brown. Caucasoid peoples have high and narrow noses and thin lips, and blood group A is much more common than group B. ◊ *Australoid*, *Khoisanoid*, *Mongoloid*, *Negroid*.

causal analysis, cause and effect analysis An approach to scientific explanation in geography based on the assumption that prior causes can explain observed phenomena. Thus the relationship between two objects or events or sets of objects or events is such that one object is explained in terms of the other. Causality laws are ◊ *deterministic*, i.e. if the cause is present, the effect must follow. In recent years calculations of ◊ *probability* have been included in causal analyses.

causeway A raised track crossing marshes, fens and flood plains of rivers.

CBD ◊ *central business district*.

ceiling price The maximum price which a potential buyer is prepared to pay to obtain a particular real property interest. Ceiling prices are subjective valuations, and different potential buyers will arrive at different ceiling prices for the same real property. The potential buyer's ceiling price for a given property therefore represents the maximum sum he/she is prepared to pay in the last resort to obtain that property. ◊ *floor price*.

Celtic field An imprecise term referring to all fields of regular shape which were laid out in this country before the Saxons established themselves. Origins may be as early as the 6th century B C, while some probably remained in use after the withdrawal of Roman rule early in the 5th century. The fields were small in size (1–1·5 acres; 0·4047–0·6061 hectares), approximately rectangular and surrounded by earth banks, stone walls or hedges. They were commonly found on the higher slopes or tops of hills associated with settlements dating from the ◊ *Bronze Age* to the end of the Roman period. ◊◊ *lynchet.*

census An official enumeration or count of the population or other things, e.g. production, traffic, with the statistics relating to them. Most common is the *Census of Population*, which is a complete enumeration of all persons in a defined area at a specified time on the census day. The universality of coverage is stressed and details are recorded for all people who are either within a given area at the particular time (◊ *de facto population*) or who normally reside within the area (◊ *de jure population*). The modern census is more than a count of people, since it aims to present as comprehensive a picture as possible of the demographic, social and economic characteristics of the people in a country. The census therefore provides a primary source of information about the population of a country.

To be of value a census should be taken regularly. In the United Kingdom the first official census was taken in 1801 and every decade thereafter with the exception of 1941.

The types of data collected by censuses vary enormously between countries. In order to promote comparability between countries the United Nations recommends that every census should include: the total population; age–sex structure and marital status; place of birth and citizenship or nationality; mother tongue, literacy and educational qualifications; economic status; urban or rural place of residence; household or family structure; and ◊ *fertility.* ◊◊ *floating population.*

Census Metropolitan Area (CMA) The basic area used in Canada for measuring the extent of ◊ *urbanization.* The population of the urbanized core of the area is > 100,000. ◊ *metropolitan area.*

Central American Common Market (CACM) A trade agreement establishing a ◊ *common market*, among the Central American countries of Costa Rica, El Salvador, Guatemala, Honduras and Nicaragua in order to stimulate mutual trade via the reduction and elimination of ◊ *tariffs.*

central business district (CBD) Originally an American term indicating the heart of the city (◊◊ *downtown*) but now commonly used throughout human geography to describe the nucleus of the urban area which acts as a focus of commercial, social and civic life. Generally the CBD is the older, historical retail and office hub of the city and has developed around the focus of the city's mass intra-urban transportation facilities. Being the position of greatest ◊ *accessibility* to the whole urban area it contains the major concentration of high-order commercial land uses. It therefore has the densest land use within the city, the tallest buildings, the highest land values and fully built-on sites. The CBD is of restricted spatial extent and often shows considerable specialization of land use into separate sub-districts, i.e. a 'district of centralized districts' (◊ Fig. 15), which reflect a search for ◊ *external economies.* Also, but less commonly, referred to as the *central commercial district, central traffic district, downtown business district.* ◊◊ *central city, concentration grade, kernel, seven lives of downtown, zone of assimilation, zone of discard.*

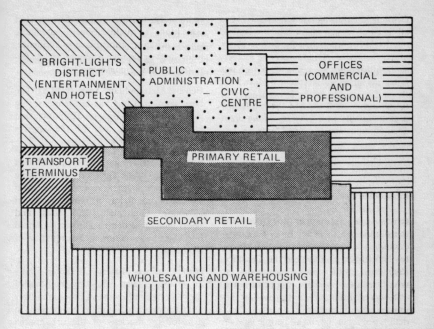

Fig. 15 Central business district

central business height index (CBHI) An intensity-of-use index calculated for a block or a site in the ◊ *central business district*. It is measured as the ratio of the square footage of floor space in buildings devoted to typical CBD activities to the ground-floor area of the building in square feet, i.e.

$$CBHI = \frac{\text{Total central business uses floor space}}{\text{Total ground-floor space}}$$

It measures what the height of each block or site would be in terms of floors if all the central business uses were spread uniformly over the whole block or site, and values greater than 1 are considered indicative of the CBD.

Also known as *total height index, use/height index*.

central business index (CBI) A composite index used by R. E. Murphy and J. E. Vance to define the spatial extent of the ◊ *central business district*. For each block both the ◊ *central business height index* and the ◊ *central business intensity index* are calculated and all blocks meeting the requirement:

CBI = CBHI of ⩾ 1·0 plus CBII of ⩾ 50%

are regarded as part of the central business district.

central business intensity index (CBII) An intensity-of-use index calculated for a block or a site in the ◊ *central business district*. It relates the square footage of floor space devoted to typical CBD activities to the square footage of all floor space in the block or site, i.e.

$$\text{CBII} = \frac{\dfrac{\text{Total central business}}{\text{user floor space}}}{\text{Total floor space}} \times \frac{100}{1}$$

The critical value is taken as 50%. ◊ *concentration grade*.

central city A term used in the USA for the municipality in a ◊ *metropolitan area* which contains the ◊ *central business district*.

central commercial district ◊ *central business district*.

central limit theorem A theorem, based on ◊ *probability* theory, which lies at the heart of ◊ *sampling* theory. It states that, no matter what the form of the ◊ *frequency distribution* of the population of measurements for some variable x, the sampling distribution of the sample means that $\bar{x}$ taken from that population approaches a ◊ *normal distribution* as the size of the samples taken increases.

central place An urban centre or settlement node whose primary function is to provide the population of the surrounding area with goods and services. Central place ◊ *functions* are therefore essentially distributional and are dispensed from a given location – the central place – to customers who are spatially scattered. ◊ *central place theory*. ◊◊ *complementary region*.

central place theory A theory explaining the number, location, size, spacing and functions of settlement within an ◊ *urban system*. The theory proceeds by ◊ *deduction* to produce a ◊ *normative model* of the spatially efficient settlement pattern under specified conditions, assuming that decisions are made by entrepreneurs (shopkeepers) to maximize profits and by consumers to maximize utility. Central place theory originated with the pioneering work of W. Christaller, a German economic geographer, who asserted that settlements acted solely as ◊ *central places* retailing goods and services to surrounding areas. Using the concepts of ◊ *range* (maximum distance a consumer will travel to purchase a good) and ◊ *threshold* (minimum level of business for an ◊ *establish-*

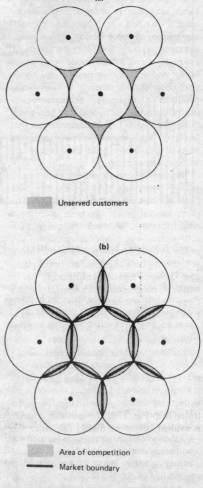

(a)

Unserved customers

(b)

Area of competition

Market boundary

Fig. 16 Central place theory – delimitation of market areas

ment to be economically viable) Christaller demonstrated that, while these differed between retailing activities, groups of establishment or orders of ◊ *functions* with similar characteristics could be recognized.

Each order of functions is associated with a central place and the problem is to locate that place in order to minimize distance travelled by consumers while maximizing the profitability of each establishment. This ◊ *centrality* requirement, assuming a uniform distribution of population and purchasing power, and transport costs varying linearly with distance, produces a triangular arrangement of central places, each with a hexagonal ◊ *market area*. ◊ Fig. 16 demonstrates that hexagons are the most efficient shape of market area to serve an area completely without any overlap.

The underlying logic of the overall spatial pattern is that settlements with large populations will be able to support more central place functions and more establishments of each function than settlements with small populations. A ◊ *hierarchy* of central places evolves from settlements with the smallest populations and lowest-order establishments (with smallest ranges and thresholds), which form the densest network, to those in the next order forming a less dense network, and so on, Christaller recognizing seven levels in all. At each level every central place contains all the functions of the lower level(s) so that it has a nested group of market areas of lower-order places which it serves. The pattern which would result with three orders of settlement is illustrated in ◊ Fig. 17a. The spatial hierarchy is evident, since the higher the order the smaller the number of settlements and the greater the distance between nearest neighbours. There is only one centre of the highest order and the number of centres below it (after the second order) increases in a ratio (◊ *k-value (1)*) of 3: the sequence is

1, 2, 6, 18, 54, 162, 486, i.e. lower-order centres and their complementary market areas ◊ *nest* within those of larger centres according to a rule of threes. Thus the market area of the higher-order place includes a third of the market area of each of the six neighbouring lower-order places, as ◊ Fig. 17a shows. This arrangement, which minimizes the aggregate distance travelled by consumers, is referred to as the *marketing* or *supply principle*. Although aggregate distance is minimized, the transport network is not the most efficient because the important transport links between the larger places do not pass through intermediate places (◊ Fig. 17b). If the population of central places is proportional to their number of establishments and volume of business the result is a stepped hierarchical form of ◊ *city-size distribution*.

Christaller suggested two variants of the above pattern:

(i) *The traffic* or *transport principle*, which involves a *k*-value of 4 (nesting according to fours, whereby the market area of a higher-order place includes a half of the market area of each of the six neighbouring lower-order places, as ◊ Fig.18a shows) to generate that hierarchy of places which results in the most efficient transport network, for as many places as possible are located on the main transport routes connecting the higher-order centres: ◊ Fig. 18b.

(ii) *The administrative* or *political-social principle* involves a *k*-value of 7 (a nesting arrangement whereby the market area of the higher-order place includes the whole of the market areas of each of the six neighbouring lower-order places: ◊ Fig. 19a). Efficient administration is the control principle and, since market areas cannot be split administratively, they must be allocated exclusively to a single higher-order place. The associated transport network is shown in ◊ Fig. 19b.

Christaller's approach was refined by

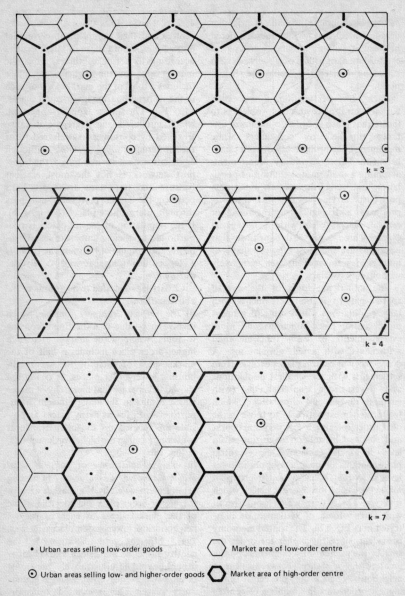

* Urban areas selling low-order goods ⬡ Market area of low-order centre

⊙ Urban areas selling low- and higher-order goods ⬢ Market area of high-order centre

Figs. 17a, 18a, 19a Central place theory – market areas = ($k = 3$) (market principle), $k = 4$ (transport principle) and $k = 7$ (administrative principle) hierarchies.

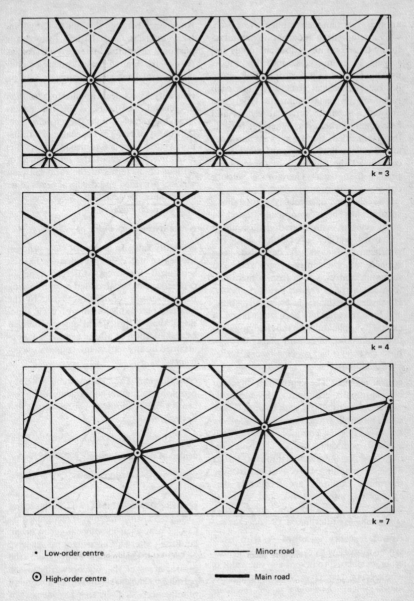

k = 3

k = 4

k = 7

• Low-order centre   —————— Minor road

⊙ High-order centre   ━━━━━━ Main road

Figs. 17b, 18b, 19b Central place theory – corresponding transport networks for $k = 3$, $k = 4$ and $k = 7$ hierarchies.

another German geographer, A. Lösch, who attempted to incorporate manufacturing (based on ubiquitous materials and serving local markets) into his model urban system. Lösch proposed a more flexible hierarchical structure, since each function or establishment type was allowed a separate range, threshold and hexagonal market area. Wherever feasible these coincided, but Lösch's system does not stipulate that every settlement must contain all the functions of those places smaller than itself. Therefore a smooth city-size distribution results.

The theory, particularly Christaller's version, has been empirically tested in many regions, with deviations accounted for by a variety of cultural and environmental factors. It has also been applied at the intra-urban scale to shopping centres, which form a hierarchy focused on the ◊ *central business district*. However, the theory is essentially static, and little research has been undertaken to extend its applicability to the changing relative importance of central places through time. ◊ *entry zone, packing theory, settlement hierarchy.*

central planning The centralized direction of national economic development, associated particularly with ◊ *state socialism*. The public ownership of the ◊ *factors of production* is commonplace in such socialist economies, since it is a requirement for the effective implementation of central planning. Directives which cover the entire economy are frequently disaggregated into sectoral and regional targets; thus spatial and non-spatial ◊ *planning* are interlinked. ◊ *collectivism.*

central tendency measures A term used synonymously with ◊ *averages* of various types, calculated to describe in one value a whole set of data. ◊ *arithmetic mean, geometric mean, harmonic mean, median, mode.*

Central Treaty Organization (CENTO) An alliance between the United Kingdom, Iran, Pakistan and Turkey formed for purposes of mutual defence and seen as part of the United States' policy of containment of Russian influence.

centrality As a concept applied to ◊ *location* in general, centrality is interpreted as 'enjoying a state of high ◊ *accessibility*', i.e. the quality of being at the centre of a transport system. Applied to urban centres it is a relative measure of the importance of settlements in terms of the ratio between services provided and the local needs of its inhabitants. ◊ *centrality value, index of centrality.* ◊ *nodality.*

centrality index ◊ *index of centrality.*

centrality value In ◊ *central place* studies, the degree of ◊ *centrality* imparted to each settlement for every different type of ◊ *function* can be calculated by multiplying the relevant ◊ *location coefficient* by the number of establishments of each functional type. A functional index is derived by the addition of all the centrality values attained by any settlement. ◊ *index of centrality.*

centralization The spatial trend whereby people and activities concentrate into a few centres or locations. ◊ *concentration and centralization.*

centre firms ◊ *dual economy.*

centre of minimum travel ◊ *median centre.*

centre–periphery hypothesis ◊ *core–periphery model.*

centrifugal forces One of two counteracting forces (◊ *centripetal forces*) recognized by C. C. Colby as producing change in urban land use patterns. Centrifugal forces drive people and businesses away from the central areas of the city outwards to the periphery. They are made up of a merging of influences – a desire to leave one part of the city and the urge to go to another. Five forces are recognized:

(i) The *spatial force*, where congestion in the centre uproots and the empty spaces of the periphery attract.

(ii) The *site force*, involving the need for a special site which cannot be met in the intensively used central area.

(iii) The *situational force*, resulting from the nuisance and other disturbances in the central area and the promise of more amenable conditions at the periphery.

(iv) The *force of social evolution*, which contrasts the land values, taxes, etc. between centre and periphery.

(v) The *status and organization of occupance*, in which the obsolescence and inertia of the central area stands in opposition to the dynamism and freedom of the periphery.

centrifugal migration ♢ *migration*.

centripetal forces The second of C. C. Colby's counteracting forces (♢ *centrifugal forces*) influencing change in urban land use patterns. Centripetal forces attract, and hold, people and businesses to the centre of the city. They derive from the attractive qualities of that part of the city, namely:

(i) The *site attraction*, often the quality of the natural landscape that invited the original occupance.

(ii) The *functional convenience* associated with the maximum ♢ *accessibility* of the central area to the entire surrounding region.

(iii) The *functional magnetism* which results in the mutual attraction of like and unlike activities.

(iv) The *functional prestige*, stemming from an established reputation.

centripetal migration ♢ *migration*.

centrography The study of descriptive statistics for the measurement of central tendency and dispersion in two-dimensional distributions, such as spatial patterns. Centrography flourished in the 1920s and 1930s in the USSR and was commonplace in the USA, where the Geography Branch of the US Bureau of the Census still reports on the centre of gravity of population after each census. It enjoyed some revival in North America from the 1960s. It is sometimes referred to as *geostatistics*. ♢ *macrogeography*.

centro-symmetric ordering The process by which the functions of the ♢ *urban core* separate out into a geographical pattern of clusters or sets.

centuria A Roman land allotment made up of blocks, based on the *jugerum*, or the amount of land a two-ox team could plough in one day. In practice, therefore, the individual blocks or fields varied in size and there is disagreement about how many jugera there are in a centuria.

centuriation The system of dividing land into square plots in the Roman period. It was used especially to apportion land to retired soldiers after the civil wars of the first century BC. It is unlikely to be found in Britain.

cephalic index A measure of skull shape used to describe head-form amongst population characteristics in studies in physical ♢ *anthropology*. The index is the proportional ratio of breadth to length measured between certain agreed points on the living head, i.e.

$$\text{Cephalic index (CI)} = \frac{\text{Maximum breadth of head}}{\text{Maximum length of head}} \times \frac{100}{1}$$

Individuals may then be classified as:

(i) ♢ *Dolichocephalic*, having a CI $\leqslant 75.9$.

(ii) ♢ *Mesocephalic*, having a CI of 76–83.

(iii) ♢ *Brachycephalic*, having a CI $\geqslant 83.1$.

certainty In decision-making, a situation or strategy in which the decision-maker has complete knowledge of all the outcomes of proposed actions, i.e. each outcome has a ♢ *probability* = 1.0. The only problem for the decision-maker is one of choice between outcomes. ⟡ *risk*, *uncertainty*.

ceteris paribus The scientific method of keeping other factors constant in order to isolate one or certain factors for analysis. The Latin meaning is 'other things being equal'.

chain migration ⟡ *Migration* flows over long distances within a country have historically involved a considerable amount of chain migration. Most migrants move relatively short distances, but the moves are predominantly in one direction to form a flow. As people migrate from B to A, they are replaced in B by other migrants from C, who in turn are replaced by others from D. Most of the massive redistribution of population in England during the Industrial Revolution was carried out in such fashion by short-distance moves cumulating towards the new industrial towns. ⟡ *migration chain*.

channelization The regulation of conflicting road traffic movements into separate paths of travel to facilitate the safe and orderly movement of both vehicular and pedestrian traffic. This is achieved by means of road markings, raised islands, controlled intersections, etc.

character of goods theory In a departure from the division of goods into ⟡ *convenience*, ⟡ *shopping* and ⟡ *speciality goods*, L. V. Aspinwall arranged goods along a continuous scale based on their marketing characteristics. These characteristics relate to the proportion of sales passing through various trade channels of distribution (e.g. supermarkets, department stores). The important characteristics are the replacement rate at which goods are bought, the gross margin available to meet channel costs, the services required by consumers, the time involved in consumption, and searching time on the part of purchasers. The lower the total of measurements on

these five characteristics the longer the channel of distribution.

charter group A term used to describe the host population when discussing the initial relationship of an in-migrant group with its new area. The first ⟡ *ethnic group* to settle previously unoccupied territory becomes, according to J. Porter, the charter group of the society because, as the original and effective possessor of that territory, it enjoys a position of control. That group is able to retain many privileges and prerogatives, among which are decisions concerning which other groups are to be let in and what they will be permitted to do. The charter group provides the dominant matrix into which new ethnic groups have to fit. Porter's definition which imputes dominance to the first ethnic group to enter an area may be too restrictive, since there are cases of later ethnic groups establishing themselves as dominant.

chase An unenclosed tract of country used for hunting, normally on marginal land of poor soils. Such areas were common in Norman and Plantagenet times but the term is now obsolete, although its occurrence in place names, e.g. Cannock Chase, Chevy Chase, Waltham Chase, is an indication of the former use of the land.

chi square test (χ^2) A ⟡ *non-parametric* statistical ⟡ *significance* test used to compare two ⟡ *frequency distributions* using ⟡ *nominal scale* data. It is one of the most flexible and commonly used statistical tests designed to work on absolute frequencies. The test may be used in one of two ways: (i) The one-sample chi square test is used to compare a single sample with an 'expected' distribution, i.e. to determine whether the sample has been drawn from a population having specified characteristics. The test compares observed frequencies (O) with a set of expected frequencies (E) to establish the ◊ *probability* of the difference being the result of chance or ◊ *sampling error*, e.g. between the locations of a certain activity in an area (O) and the spatial distribution of some influential factor (E).

(ii) The chi square test for two or more independent samples is used to determine the probability that the samples were drawn from different populations, e.g. whether the number of workers in each ward of a city in n occupational categories are likely to be random samples from the same parent population.

child mortality rate The age-specific ◊ *death rate* for children aged one year or more but less than five. The numerator is the number of deaths of children aged 1·0 to 4·9 years in a given period and the denominator the total number of children of that age in the area during the period.

chorography The study of the ◊ *areal differentiation* of the earth's surface in which the emphasis is on the delineation and description of particular ◊ *regions*. The term, attributed to B. Varen (Varenius), was widely used in the 17th and 18th centuries, when it implied a special or ◊ *regional geography* as distinguished from geography, dealing with the earth in general, and topography, dealing with small areas. The present usage of the term is limited, although some American geographers use 'chorographic' to describe an area of sub-continental scale and *'chorographic map'* as one with a scale between 1 : 500,000 and 1 : 5,000,000. ◊◊ *chorology*.

chorology A rarely used term which is largely synonymous with ◊ *chorography*, although it includes an explanation, as well as a delineation and description, of the causal relations of phenomena within a particular region. It is identified with the 'science of regions' as used by F. Marthe

and F. von Richthofen in the late 19th century. The term was subsequently used in a wider context by A. Hettner in recognizing three groups of sciences – the systematic or material, the chronological or historical, and the chorological or spatial (which had two branches: astronomy, the arrangement of things in the universe, and geography, the arrangement of things on the earth's surface).

choropleth map A ◊ *thematic map* utilizing areally based data and employing distinctive colour or shading proportional to density by statistical or administrative area. ◊ Fig. 20.

chronogeography ◊ *time geography*.

c.i.f. pricing Cost, insurance and freight. The term used of goods shipped where the price quoted to the customer includes freight and insurance charges. Thus c.i.f. pricing is a pricing policy under which a producer offers his goods at a uniform ◊ *delivered price* to customers irrespective of their distance from the origin. The producer ships the goods, meeting all charges up to 'on board' and paying the freight, insurance, etc., and spreads these costs over all customers irrespective of location. It allows the producer to pass on part of the real cost of supplying distant customers to those who are closer to the factory. ◊ *freight absorption, uniform pricing.* ◊◊ *f.o.b. pricing.*

Cinque Port A ◊ *port* which was a member of the medieval federation of ports (originally five, whence the name) situated on the south-east coast of England and having jurisdiction especially for defence purposes along the coast from Seaford to Birchington from the 12th to 14th centuries. The ports in order of precedence were Hastings, Sandwich, Dover, Romney and Hythe, to which were added Rye and Winchelsea.

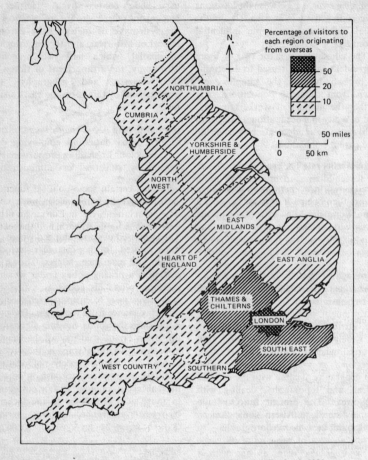

Fig. 20 Choropleth map: regional importance of overseas visitors to England, 1981

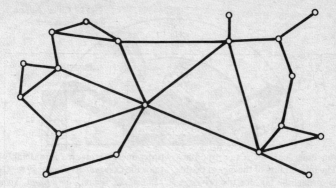

Fig. 21 Circuit network

circuit network A ◊ *network* in which there is more than one path or route between at least two places, i.e. sets of connected places with one or more loops, as illustrated in ◊ Fig. 21. ◊ *fundamental circuit, Hamiltonian circuit.* ◊◊ *branching network.*

circuity, index of ◊ *detour index.*

circular and cumulative causation ◊ *cumulative causation.*

circularity ratio A measure of the shape or form of a geographic area:

$$\text{Circularity ratio} = 4A \times P^2$$

where A = area
P = perimeter

The lower the value of the ratio the more compact the shape. Alternative indices are listed under ◊ *shape measures.*

circulating capital ◊ *capital* (2).

circulation The movement of goods, services, activities and individuals through an economic–geographic ◊ *system.*

city A term used generically today to denote any urban form but applied particularly to large urban settlements. There are, however, no agreed definitions to separate a city from the large ◊ *metropolis* or the smaller ◊ *town.* Originally the term

indicated certain socio-political functions and implied predominance in trade–commercial relations, e.g. in Europe an urban settlement with a cathedral and the seat of a bishopric, in the United Kingdom and the Commonwealth a title conferred on a settlement by royal charter or letters patent.

Within ◊ *central place theory* an attempt has been made to distinguish city from town on the basis of a larger number and greater diversity of retail and service functions. Indeed, small cities – with a population of 20,000–200,000, serving a market area of up to 1,000,000 people – acting as regional centres at the bottom of the wholesale ladder are distinguished from large cities – with a population of 200,000–500,000, serving a market area with between 1,000,000 and 3,000,000 people. ◊◊ *dispersed city, functional classification of cities, garden city, gateway city, linear city, millionaire city, optimum size of city, overbounded city, plug-in city, pre-industrial city, primate city, underbounded city, urban area.*

city-filling activities ◊ *non-basic activities.*

city-forming sector ◊ *basic activities.*

city of death In W. Bunge's 'total city', based on a study of Detroit, the de-

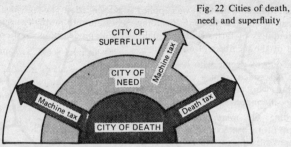

Fig. 22 Cities of death, need, and superfluity

teriorating inner core of a metropolitan centre. The inhabitants of the city of death pay both a machine tax, for the privilege of using the machinery necessary to life itself, and a death tax, collected by overcharging for food, housing, loans, etc. ◊ Fig. 22 shows the relationship between the city of death, the ◊ *city of need* and the ◊ *city of superfluity*. ◊◊ *inner city*.

city of need W. Bunge's term for much of the contiguous built-up area of metropolitan centres whose inhabitants keep pace with the demand for 'machine-minders', i.e. its children are trained as 'factory fodder' to the levels needed to operate machines. Its inhabitants, like those in the ◊ *city of death*, also lose by paying a machine tax for the privilege of using the machinery necessary for life itself. ◊ Fig. 22. ◊◊ *city of superfluity*.

city of superfluity W. Bunge's term for the 'outer city' containing relatively few inhabitants but an abundance of wealth and power, compared to the ◊ *city of death* and the ◊ *city of need*. Its inhabitants are the owners of the machines and businesses which extract the machine tax and death tax and they live in a commuter culture marked by an extreme separation of work from home. ◊ Fig. 22. ◊◊ *suburbia*.

city region An area that surrounds an urban settlement which functions as the regional centre. This area is tied to the regional centre for higher-order functions although oriented to local towns for lower-order ones. It is an area considerably larger than the ◊ *urban settlement area*. ◊◊ *complementary region, hinterland, sphere of influence, Umland*.

city-serving activities ◊ *non-basic activities*.

city-size distribution A ◊ *frequency distribution* of urban settlements for any area or country in different size categories (usually population). Observed distributions can be compared with a theoretical or empirical model (e.g. ◊ *central place theory*, ◊ *primate city distribution*, ◊ *rank-size rule*).

civic centre That part of a ◊ *town* or ◊ *city* in which the principal public buildings (e.g. town hall, municipal offices, public library and other civic buildings) are located.

civil day ◊ *solar day*.

civitas A Roman term for the native tribal divisions of e.g. Britain and Gaul, incorporated for administrative purposes into the Romans' own system.

clachan A term, equivalent to ◊ *hamlet* or even ◊ *village*, used in the Highlands of Scotland and Ireland to describe a traditional form of rural settlement, i.e. a cluster of farmhouses and associated outbuildings usually grouped without any formal plan. Clachans consisted of up to twenty farmsteads, and a communal arable system was sometimes practised. In the Scottish case the presence of a church was regarded as essential, and the clachans were the equivalent of ◊ *kirktouns* (◊◊ *ferm-*

touns), but in Ireland the term was applied to any small rural settlement including those groupings of farmsteads originally occupied by the members of one family.

clan A group of people who believe that they are descended from a common ancestor, but who cannot trace their full genealogical connections.

clapboarding Or *weatherboarding*. The practice of fitting protective timbers on the outside of buildings, formerly commonplace in south-east England. Boards are fixed horizontally to the framework of a building, overlapping from top to bottom in order to keep rain out.

class A rank or order of society composed of individuals of equal standing. It is a multi-dimensional concept in which the three main dimensions are position in the economic system, status in society and power. A class is therefore a social group comprising a large number of individuals of similar ◊ *social status*, income and culture. Its members display similar ◊ *life styles* and have similar material and economic bases.

There is a primarily hierarchical classification based largely upon economic phenomena, since members of a class share the same position in society's ◊ *division of labour*. The Marxist interpretation emphasizes this common economic relationship to society and its origins in the development of ◊ *capitalism*, a relationship governed by the ownership of the means of production.

It is possible for an individual to move from one class to another, e.g. upwards by personal merit, good fortune or marriage. Class differs in this context from ◊ *caste*, in which an individual remains permanently in the group into which he/she was born. ◊◊ *dual society*, *social mobility*, *social polarization*, *social rank*, *socio-economic groups*.

class rates ◊ *Freight rates* which apply to all items that are moved in small quantities. ◊◊ *commodity rates*.

classification The statistical generalization of data into mutually exclusive categories using predetermined criteria.

classificatory scale ◊ *nominal scale*.

classified roads ◊ *Roads* which form part of an international, national or regional network or which are important as local through roads. In many countries technical standards for design are specified for each class of road.

Clawson method An approach to ◊ *recreation* demand measurement and prediction derived from economics and developed by M. Clawson, an American land economist. The approach centres around the estimation of a ◊ *demand* schedule for a recreation facility. That schedule reflects the price people would be prepared to pay for their enjoyment, and the notional price can be taken as a measure of the benefit they derive from their recreational experience. Demand schedules depend on the population distribution around the recreation facility and on the transport costs people incur in using that facility.

clear felling The practice, in forest management, of removing all trees and vegetation from an area as part of the timber extraction operation. Clear felling is highly controversial because of its negative environmental, aesthetic, recreational and wildlife impacts. ◊◊ *deforestation*, *selective logging*, *shelter belt system*.

clearance areas A clearance area procedure is used by a local authority for areas of unfit housing where it intends to demolish the buildings, clear the site and rebuild. An area can be so designated not only if the houses are unfit for human habitation, but also where the arrangement of the houses or streets is dangerous or injurious to the health of the inhabitants, providing the local authority is satisfied that the best method of dealing with the conditions in the area is the demolition of all buildings in the area.

cleared-site value The present value of the net income that can be earned by investing in the new building necessary to put the site to its optimum use. Cleared-site value is thus an economic valuation of location or rent-paying ability and represents the sum of money available to purchase the existing interests in a site/property after allowing for the costs of clearing the site. ◊ *economic life of a building.*

clee rent A payment made by all commoners for their rights to pasture cattle and sheep on the ◊ *common.* ◊ *common rights.*

clone colonization A second-stage settlement process in the colonization of a previously unoccupied area whereby short-distance migration out from the initial settlements by the sons of the first settlers and then their sons, etc. describes the settlement diffusion pattern. There are several possible ways in which the pattern may evolve through time (◊ Fig. 23).

closed economy The economy of a society or group in which the exchanges that take place are mainly confined within that group, and exchanges with other societies or outsiders are extremely limited. ◊ *open economy.*

closed forest A forest in which trees are the dominant life form and the canopy is fully enclosed. ◊ *open forest.*

closed population A ◊ *population* in which there is no ◊ *migration* inwards or outwards and whose growth depends entirely on the difference between ◊ *births* and ◊ *deaths.*

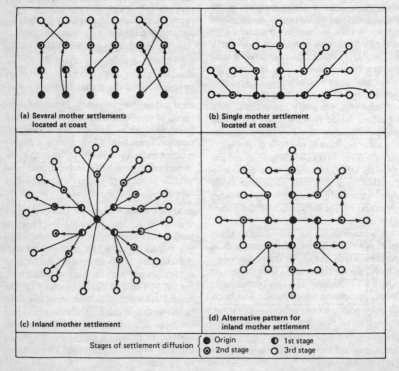

(a) Several mother settlements located at coast

(b) Single mother settlement located at coast

(c) Inland mother settlement

(d) Alternative pattern for inland mother settlement

Stages of settlement diffusion {
● Origin
◉ 2nd stage
◑ 1st stage
○ 3rd stage
}

Fig. 23 Clone colonization

closed system A ◇ *system* with clearly defined boundaries across which no movement or exchange of material or energy occurs. Such closed systems tend towards maximum ◇ *entropy*, as the fixed amount of energy available is used up through work performed and change only occurs through innate or given differences within the system itself. ◇ *open system*.

Club of Rome A body founded in 1968 by an international group of philosophers, economists, managers, scientists, technologists and others. The Club's object is to understand the workings of the world as a finite ◇ *system* by studying the interactions of economic, scientific, biological and social components of the present human state, in the hope of being able to predict the results of present actions and policies and to formulate alternative policies where deemed necessary on environmental and survival grounds.

cluster A term used loosely to describe the close proximity or grouping of settlements or other activities in any spatial distribution.

cluster analysis A statistical technique of ◇ *classification* designed to take a given set of data and to reduce them step by step into a smaller number of classes. The procedure is based on collapsing the most similar pair of observations into one class, then joining the next most similar, and so on, down to the desired number of classes. The criterion for collapsing the first, and subsequent, pairs is greatest similarity, represented by the shortest distance on a linear scale between the relevant observations. The procedure may be represented diagrammatically as a ◇ *linkage tree* in ◇ Fig. 24. Hence it is also known as *linkage analysis*.

Fig. 24 Cluster analysis

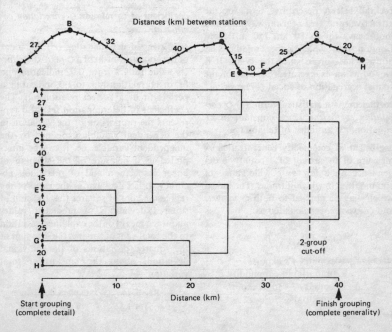

CMA ◊ *Census Metropolitan Area.*

coast protection A form of environmental management, now recognized as an appropriate sphere for collective action, designed to allay the progressive degradation of the land by coastal erosion processes. In the United Kingdom each maritime local authority is a coast protection authority for its own area and able to carry out such protection work as might appear necessary to it for the protection of the land within its jurisdiction. Sea defence works can be undertaken to protect the land from erosion and encroachment by the sea and against flooding. These involve engineering solutions such as groynes, sea walls, bulkheads, revetments and breakwaters.

coastal shipping A term describing the domestic traffic in goods and commodities undertaken in small cargo ships and contrasting with ◊ *ocean shipping*, which involves international trade.

cocktail belt A descriptive term for the attractive rural area near railway lines and motorways up to 80 km (50 ml) from London into which upper middle-class housing has spread since the 1940s. It is viewed as an exaggerated example of the spatial segregation of social ◊ *classes*.

coefficient As a statistical term: (1) ◊ *correlation coefficient*; (2) a constant in an equation; (3) an index of reliability.

coefficient of commodity concentration A measure of the extent of a country's dependence on a few or a wide range of commodities in which it trades. The index, which may be applied to both ◊ *imports* and ◊ *exports*, is calculated as:

$$C_{jx} = 100 \sqrt{\left(\frac{X_{ij}}{X_j} \right)^2}$$

where X_{ij} = country j's exports (imports) in commodity i

X_j = country j's total exports (imports)

C_{jx} = index of concentration of exports (imports)

The index may range between a value of 100 and $100/\sqrt{n}$ (where n = number of commodities). The closer the index is to 100 the more concentrated the country's export (import) trade into certain categories. ◊ *commodity concentration, coefficient of geographical concentration, export concentration, import concentration.*

coefficient of compactness A measure, similar to the ◊ *radial shape index*, of the shape or form of a geographic area, calculated as:

Coefficient of compactness = $A/\sqrt{2\pi \int d^2{}_i\, dxdy}$

where A = area

d = distance of an indefinitely small rectangle of length dx and width dy from the centroid of the area

coefficient of concentration ◊ *Gini coefficient.*

coefficient of correlation ◊ *correlation coefficient.*

coefficient of determination (r^2) An index of the goodness-of-fit of a ◊ *regression* line. Its value ranges from 0·0, indicating 'no fit' or no relationship, to 1·0, indicating a perfect fit or a perfect relationship. The coefficient of determination (r^2) also represents the proportion of the variation in the dependent variable explained by the independent variable, i.e. it can be interpreted as a measure of the strength of linear association and of prediction accuracy. It is calculated as the ratio of the regression sum of squares (i.e. the sum of squared deviations of predicted values about the mean) or the explained variation to the total sum of squares (i.e. the sum of the squared deviations of the individual deviations about their mean) or total variation:

$$r^2 = \frac{\text{Regression } SS}{\text{Total } SS} = \frac{\text{Explained variation}}{\text{Total variation}}$$

coefficient of geographical association A measure of the similarity in the spatial distributions of two phenomena, being a version of the general ⬦ *Gini coefficient*. It does not measure ⬦ *association* in the true sense, since it measures what proportion of one variable would have to be re-allocated between areas in order to make it correspond with the distribution of the other variable:

$$\text{Coefficient of geographical}\atop\text{association} = \frac{\Sigma_i |F_i|}{100}$$

where F_i = the difference between two activities in area i, summed for all areas either positive or negative deviations. Its value can range from 0.0, indicating exact correspondence in the two spatial distributions, to 1.0, indicating total dissimilarity. The results are dependent upon the number and size of areas used: a few large areas give characteristically low values of the coefficient. Also called *coefficient of linkage* and *coefficient of similarity*. ⬦ *areal association*. ⬦ *coefficient of localization*.

coefficient of geographical concentration A measure of a country's dependence on ⬦ *trade* with a limited or large number of other countries. The index may be applied to both ⬦ *imports* and ⬦ *exports*, and is calculated as:

$$G_{jx} = 100 \sqrt{\Sigma\left(\frac{X_{sj}}{X_j}\right)^2}$$

where X_{sj} = country j's exports to (imports from) country s
X_j = country j's total exports (imports)
G_{jx} = index of concentration of export trade (import trade) with certain partners

The index may range between a value of 100 and $100/\sqrt{n}$ (where n = number of trading partners): the closer the index is to 100 the more concentrated a country's exports (imports) with one other country. ⬦ *coefficient of commodity concentration*.

coefficient of linear correlation ⬦ *product–moment correlation coefficient*.

coefficient of linkage ⬦ *coefficient of geographical association*.

coefficient of localization A measure, based on the ⬦ *Gini coefficient*, which indicates the extent to which employment in a particular industry is localized in one or a few regions or dispersed over all regions. It represents a single measure of the extent to which that employment is concentrated areally by comparison with some other spatial distribution, such as total employment or population. The comparison is in percentage terms and the actual computation involves: (1) subtracting for each region its percentage share of national employment in a particular manufacturing industry from its percentage share of all manufacturing employment in the nation; (2) adding all the positive differences (or all the negative); and (3) dividing that sum by 100. The limits to the coefficient are 0.0 and 1.0: 0.0 if the given industry is distributed in exactly the same way as the base magnitude and 1.0 if the entire industry is concentrated in a single region.

The basic idea has been extended to various other comparisons, e.g. ⬦ *coefficient of geographical association*. ⬦ *coefficient of redistribution, localization curve*.

coefficient of multiple correlation (R) A descriptive statistic that represents the strength of the relationship between three or more variables in a ⬦ *multiple regression* analysis.

coefficient of redistribution A variant of the ⬦ *coefficient of localization*, being essentially a measure of the deviation between two spatial distributions of the same phenomenon taken at different key points in time, e.g. a comparison for two successive census years of the percentage distribution of population by region. The earlier percentage distribution is taken as the base and the deviations of the later percentage distribution from it computed (as in calculating the coefficient of localization). The limits are 0·0, indicating no redistribution has taken place between the two time periods, and 1·0, implying a complete redistribution.

coefficient of risk ◊ *significance level.*

coefficient of similarity ◊ *coefficient of geographical association.*

coefficient of specialization A measure of the degree to which the ◊ *industrial mix* of a region's economy differs from that of the nation as a whole. The calculation, similar to that for any index based on the ◊ *Gini coefficient*, involves (1) subtracting for each industry its percentage share of total regional employment from its percentage share in national employment; (2) adding all the positive differences (or the negative); and (3) dividing that sum by 100. The limits are 0·0 to 1·0: if the region has an industrial mix identical to that of the nation the value will be 0·0 and if all the employment in a region is in a single industry the coefficient approaches 1·0. The coefficient can also be used to compare a region's industrial mix at different points in time.

It is also known as the *index of regional specialization*, and even as an *index of diversification*. ◊ *Gibbs–Martin index of diversification.*

coefficient of variation The degree of variability or ◊ *dispersion* of observations about a mean value is measured by the coefficient of variation. It is calculated by expressing the ◊ *standard deviation* of a data set as a percentage of its ◊ *arithmetic mean*, i.e.

$$CV = \frac{\sigma}{\bar{x}} \times 100$$

where σ = standard deviation
$\bar{x}$ = arithmetic mean

The coefficient of variation therefore gives a relative rather than an absolute measure of variability. Hence, it is occasionally referred to as an *index of variability.*

cogeneration The production of two useful forms of ◊ *energy* from a single process, e.g. in a factory the steam needed for industrial processes or space heating is first run through turbines to generate electricity.

cognition A psychological term relating to the processes by which human beings obtain, store, use and operate upon information. It includes knowing, sensing, perceiving, remembering, imagining, reasoning, judging, deciding, etc. A cognition process denotes the complex way in which ◊ *perceptions* and stimuli are translated by the human brain into some recognizable structure. The use of a cognitive approach in ◊ *humanist geography*, especially ◊ *phenomenology*, seeks a contextual or true understanding of objects and spatial behaviour. ◊ *cognitive behaviourism, cognitive dissonance.*

cognitive behaviourism Cognitive or *environmental behaviourism* describes the situation where people react to their ◊ *environment* as it is perceived rather than as it really is. People interpret the environment through their previous experience and knowledge, giving a subjective or ego-centred interpretation of environment.

cognitive description The lowest order of scientific explanation used in geography as recognized by D. Harvey. Cognitive description involves the straightforward description of what is known, based on an ordering or ◊ *classification* of the data collected. The classification follows predetermined ideas about its structure and no theory is therefore explicitly involved. Advocates of ◊ *hermeneutic approaches* stress the importance of cognitive description on the grounds that the quality of the explanation depends more on the depth of ◊ *cognition* than on methodological procedures. ◊ *morphometric analysis.*

cognitive dissonance The non-fitting relationships among ◊ *cognitions* and between cognitions and reality. Beliefs about places do not match geographical reality and the individual is therefore motivated towards behaviour that does not accord with what would be expected from consideration of the available information about the objective environment.

cognitive mapping A process, comprising a series of psychological transformations, by which an individual acquires, codes, stores, recalls and decodes information about the relative locations and attributes of phenomena in his/her everyday spatial environment. The picture, which is the product of this process in the individual's mind, can be considered as a *cognitive* or ◊ *mental map.*

cognitive rationality ◊ *bounded rationality.*

cohort A group of persons who experience a certain ◊ *vital event* (e.g. birth, marriage) during the same specific period of time and who are subsequently analysed as a unit throughout their lifetimes. Thus, all babies born in a given year form a *birth cohort.*

cohort fertility The total number of live births to a particular birth or marriage ◊ *cohort.* When the childbearing years of all women in the cohort are completed, the *cohort total* ◊ *fertility rate* would be the average number of children born per woman. ◊ *fertility.*

cohort-survival method A method of ◊ *population projection* which takes account of differences in ◊ *birth* and ◊ *death rates* for various age groups. The initial population is disaggregated into ◊ *cohorts,* customarily five-year age groups, according to sex and racial origin. As a cohort progresses it

becomes subject to different mortality, fertility and marriage risks at different periods of time. These risks are applied to each cohort so that, at the end of the period, the cohort which survives will be substantially different from the cohort which sets out at the beginning of the period.

The number of survivors of each cohort is calculated from age-specific ◊ *life tables,* for time intervals of usually one to five years. For each time interval the natural increase of population is projected by (1) obtaining the expected number of births by multiplying age-specific fertility rates by the average number of women in each of the cohorts of childbearing age, and (2) calculating the number of survivors of those births via ◊ *infant mortality* rates. The number of survivors of this new, lowest age group are then added to the number of survivors in the time interval up to the forecast date.

It is sometimes referred to as *longitudinal analysis.* ◊ *growth composition analysis.*

Colby hypothesis A dynamic explanation of urban development based on ◊ *centrifugal* and ◊ *centripetal forces.*

collective consumption The ◊ *consumption* of ◊ *public goods* which, because their characteristics inhibit their sale on markets, have to be consumed by groups of people, e.g. defence.

collective farming A type of farm organization started in the USSR and now also practised in other east European countries, communist China, North Vietnam and North Korea. The land, which is state-owned, is compulsorily amalgamated into large *collective farms* which are either leased permanently to a large group of shareholder farm workers who run the holding as a single unit (◊ *kolkhoz,* ◊ *kung-she*) or are run by a manager and worked by labourers as directed (◊ *sovkhoz*). A proportion of the produce is delivered to the government, and the workers receive shares of the proceeds from the sale of the remainder according to work done. ⟡ *ejido*, *kibbutz*, *moshav*.

collective goods ⟡ *public goods*.

collectivism A general term applied to all political and economic systems based on ⟡ *central planning* by the state. ⟡ *state socialism*.

colonia In the Roman settlement of Britain, a colonia (pl. *coloniae*) was a settlement of retired soldiers.

colonialism The policy of a ⟡ *state* seeking to establish and maintain its rule or authority over another state or alien people, implicitly less developed than itself. It was practised by a succession of European states, especially before the First World War, as national development was accompanied and extended by colonial expansion. Thus colonialism is related to uneven economic development and facilitated the expansion of ⟡ *capitalism*. While most colonial territories have gained formal independence, it can be suggested that colonialism has been replaced by ⟡ *neo-colonialism*. ⟡ *economic imperialism*, *imperialism*, *internal colonialism*.

colonization A term used not only in the sense of establishing a ⟡ *colony* or colonies as a result of pursuing a policy of ⟡ *colonialism* but also to describe the organized settlement of a new area on a large scale. This area may be internal or external to a country.

colony (1) A settlement in a new country formed by a body of people, often in an undeveloped and sparsely inhabited area. It also refers to the community so formed. (2) In a more formal political context, the territory occupied or conquered by a distant state and controlled by it. ⟡ *colonialism*, *dependency*. (3) On the intra-urban scale, a number of people of one nationality or particular

occupation living in one quarter or district of the city, e.g. an artists' *colony*. ⟡ *ethnic area*.

combination The amalgamation or ⟡ *merger* of ⟡ *firms* in order to achieve greater economic strength and profitability. There are two types:
(i) *Horizontal combinations*, where the member firms are all engaged in the same stage of production.
(ii) *Vertical combinations*, where the member firms are engaged in different stages of production of the same commodity or commodities. ⟡ *horizontal expansion*, *integration*, *vertical expansion*.

combination index ⟡ *crop combinations*.

COMECON ⟡ *Council for Mutual Economic Assistance*.

command economy ⟡ *redistributive economy*.

commensal linkage ⟡ *linkages*.

commercial action space ⟡ *action space*.

commercial aviation Scheduled and charter services by air transport. ⟡ *aviation*, *general aviation*.

commercial compensation ⟡ *countertrade*.

commercial geography An early term for ⟡ *economic geography*. It dealt with the study of what was produced where.

commercial grain farming An ⟡ *agricultural system* in which large areas of mid-latitude grasslands are given over to the cultivation of a single grain crop, most commonly wheat. The system is highly mechanized but does not make intensive use of land or labour. Wherever rainfall is adequate there is a tendency for this system to give way to rotational farming.

commercial grazing ⟡ *ranching*.

commercial linkage ⟡ *linkages*.

commercial reserves ⟡ *reserves*.

commercial ribbon A North American term

in origin, meaning the service and retail use of frontages along major radial roads into an urban area. These natural strip developments, which include petrol and service stations, restaurants and motels, etc., are usually only a block wide and serve demands originating from the passing traffic. The uses are not functionally related, since each 'shopping' visit is a single-purpose stop. Also known as *commercial strips*.

commercial strip ◊ *commercial ribbon*.

commodity (1) In economics, a good or service which satisfies a particular and distinct want felt by consumers.
(2) In economic geography, an item shipped from the ◊ *primary* to the ◊ *secondary sector*. As such commodities are distinguished from ◊ *products*, which are items moving from secondary to ◊ *tertiary sectors*, and from ◊ *goods*, which move from the tertiary sector to ◊ *consumers*.

commodity concentration A term, applicable to both a country's ◊ *imports* and its ◊ *exports*, which describes a situation where one or a few imports (exports) dominate a country's total import (export) trade. ◊ *coefficient of commodity concentration*. ◊ *export concentration*, *import concentration*.

commodity rates ◊ *Freight rates* applicable to a few items, e.g. grain, iron ore, that are moved in large quantities. They are usually lower than the ◊ *class rate* for the corresponding distance.

common ◊ *common land*.

common field A term often used synonymously with ◊ *open field*, but which J. Thirsk suggests should be restricted to those open fields which had common rules for cultivation and grazing, e.g. arable land cultivated in common using ploughs and animals owned by several people and over which community grazing rights were exercised after harvest and during ◊ *fallow* periods.

common field system Fields, comprising strips, over which common rules of cultivation and grazing operated. The classical ◊ *open field* system was therefore a common field system as practised throughout the well-populated parts of medieval England for the intensive cultivation of corn. ◊ *field system*, *strip field*.

common grazing Land owned by a single proprietor but leased to several tenants for the pasturage of animals in common. In the Highlands of Scotland such common grazing was located beyond the ◊ *head-dyke*.

common land An area of private property over which a number of people have legal rights which they exercise in common. All common land is therefore in the possession of what the law terms a 'legal person'. Originally this was the lord of the manor but now is usually the local authority in towns and a private individual or commercial company in rural areas. Such common land was not only the waste land of the manor over which ◊ *commoners* were given rights to certain products but also cultivated land subject to certain rights of common (whether these rights were exercisable at all times or only during specified periods). ◊ *common rights*.

Much common land was enclosed for cultivation during the 18th century and the rights of usage were transferred to the lords of the manor, but parliamentary Acts in the 1860s and 1870s restricted further ◊ *enclosure* of the commons. Today such land has to be registered as common land under the Commons Registration Act of 1965, and a legal register is kept of who holds what rights.

Thus the general public does not have legal right of access to all common land – only in towns for air and exercise. Many commons in rural areas are now being treated more like those in towns, i.e. as places for recreation. ◊ *commonable land*.

common market Basically a single ◊ *market* covering the combined territories of the participating ◊ *states*. Within that market area the states seek to lower or abolish all governmental restrictions on the movement of goods, persons, services and capital between member countries. They also agree to establish a uniform trade policy towards non-member countries, which involves harmonizing the external ◊ *tariffs* and export incentive schemes of member countries. Hence, a form of international economic integration. ◊◊ *free trade area*.

common of estover ◊ *common rights*.

common of pannage ◊ *common rights*.

common of pasture ◊ *common rights*.

common of piscary ◊ *common rights*.

common of turbary ◊ *common rights*.

common-property resource A ◊ *resource* for which no individual/private ownership rights exist and for which no rent/price is payable for its use, e.g. fish in the ocean, fresh air. Such resources, not owned by anyone, are considered to be 'owned in common'. ◊ *commons, the*.

common rights Under a communal agricultural system (◊ *open field*, for example) the agriculturalist, in return for certain payments and services, obtained access to certain land uses which were regarded as rights. These rights were often exercised in common and represented the right of one or more persons to take or use part of the produce of another's soil. Usually the owner of the soil or land was the lord of the manor. There were six basic rights:
(i) *Common of estover*: the right to take sufficient wood from the ◊ *demesne*, the lord's waste or woods for fuel, the making of implements, the building and the repair of houses and fences.
(ii) *Common of pannage*: the right to turn pigs into the woods, waste or ◊ *demesne*. (◊◊ *pannage*.)

(iii) *Common of pasture*: the most important of the rights of common, the right to graze animals on the waste land of the manor. (◊◊ *pasture*.)
(iv) *Common of piscary*: the right to take fish from streams or lakes.
(v) *Common of turbary*: the right to take peat or turf for fuel. (◊◊ *turbary*.)
(vi) *Common in the soil*: the right to take stones.

Such common rights may still exist today, although there has been an increasing limitation of rights to more sharply defined classes of user and also a severe restriction of land subject to such rights, since they were extinguished as a consequence of ◊ *enclosure* in many areas.

common use A type of ◊ *multiple use* of land in which the same tract is put to two or more primary uses, e.g. forestry and recreation. The physical possibilities and limitations of such common use depend on the ◊ *compatibility* of the uses. ◊◊ *parallel use*.

commonable land Land used communally for only part of the year, e.g. arable land which, after harvest, was pastured by the commonable animals until seed-time.

commoner A commoner holds ◊ *common rights* and has a say in the management of ◊ *common land*. Originally entitlement to these privileges stemmed from the occupation, either through ownership or rental, of a holding in the ◊ *open field* or a ◊ *toft*.

commons, the The concept of the commons is one of the common ownership of ◊ *resources* of value to society. The term derives from ◊ *common land* used for pasture but has been extended to cover all common environmental resources – land, air, water, etc. (◊◊ *common-property resource*). It was popularized by the American conservationist Garrett Hardin, who argued that the more an individual (or corporation) exploited the commons, the greater the long-term harm to the quality of life enjoyed by society as a whole.

communal tenure A form of ◊ *land tenure* in which ownership of land is vested in the community.

communality In a ◊ *factor analysis*, the common ◊ *variance* of any individual variable accounted for by a given set of factors. The total variance of individual variables can be divided into three types:
(i) *Common*: that proportion of the total variance that correlates with other variables.
(ii) *Specific*: that proportion of the total variance that does not correlate with any other variable.
(iii) *Error*: chance variance due to errors of sampling, measurement, etc.

communication The transfer or movement of information from person to person and place to place. It is either 'interpersonal', through the face-to-face contact of persons or groups, or 'mass', via the technological devices of the mass media.

communications A term used interchangeably in Britain with ◊ *transportation* to describe all means or networks of communicating between places, e.g. road, rail, radio, telegraph. North American usage is restricted to the means of moving information.

community A group of interacting persons, occupying and sharing a limited territorial space for residence and for work, which functions to meet common needs generated in sharing this space and establishes characteristic forms of social interaction underpinned by shared values. Viewed both as a spatial–temporal and as a social system, community represents the smallest spatial system which encompasses the major features of everyday life in society. ◊ *neighbourhood*, *non-place community*, *place community*, *rural community*, *social network*.

community centre The second order recognized among urban shopping centres, with a greater depth of retailing than ◊ *neigh-*

bourhood centres. Community centres are based on a large variety store or junior department store and contain some specialist clothing shops, supermarkets, banks, etc. Typically, they comprise 9,290–27,500 m² (100,000–300,000 ft²) of selling space and cater for 50,000–150,000 people. ◊ *regional centre*.

Community Development Project (CDP) One of two main strands in the urban programme directed at ◊ *deprivation* (◊ *urban aid*) developed in the United Kingdom by the Home Office in the early 1970s. The CDP approach focused on twelve deprived ◊ *neighbourhoods* and represented an attempt at action research into a better understanding and more comprehensive tackling of social needs, especially in older urban areas, through the closer co-ordination of central and local effort, both official and unofficial, informed and stimulated by citizen initiative and involvement. Each CDP was to run for a five-year period and the project has now been phased out. There was a mixture of approaches in the twelve projects, but most turned to the structural or class-conflict analysis as the most satisfactory explanation of the problems faced in their areas.

community efficiency index An example of a measure used to highlight the differences in social conditions which occur at a local scale. The index is derived by summing the ranks of individual administrative units for variables grouped under four headings – dwelling condition, health, social control, welfare. These units are then re-ranked within each of these four headings and the new sets of ranks summed for administrative units across the four headings to give a combinatorial index of community efficiency for each administrative unit.

commuter, commuting Commuting is the term used to describe journeys to and from work. Various commuting flows are recognized:

(i) The traditional centripetal movement of suburban residents to jobs in the central city. Known as *in-commuting*.

(ii) *Reverse commuting* or *incommutation*, related to the suburbanization of jobs employing people who are residents of the inner areas of cities. Also known as *out-commuting*.

(iii) *Lateral commuting*, which has developed along with the evolution of outlying clusters of employment opportunities, such as greenfield industrial estates, and suburban and dormitory housing estates.

A commuter is therefore a person who travels regularly between home and workplace. A *daily commuter* makes the return journey between place of residence and workplace each working day, whereas a *weekly commuter* is a person who lives away from home during the working week. Originally the term was applied to season ticket holders using suburban railways who paid a commuted sum in lieu of daily tickets. ◊ *commuter belt*, *commuting distance*, *commuting ratio*. ◊◊ *daily urban system*.

commuter belt The zone from which a city daily draws workers or ◊ *commuters* from residences outside the city to work in the city. ◊◊ *daily urban system*, *labourshed*.

commuting distance The distance from a person's place of residence to their place of work.

commuting ratio The proportion of a workforce in a given area whose journey to work in terms of ◊ *commuting distance* (normally to a workplace outside the area) qualifies them to be regarded as ◊ *commuters*.

compaction index An attempt to quantify the 'shape' of areal units which uses a circle, the most compact two-dimensional shape, as a basis for comparison. The compaction index is measured as the ratio of the area of the spatial unit being studied to the area of the smallest inscribing circle (◊ Fig. 25).

$$\text{Compaction index} = \frac{\text{Area of spatial unit}}{\text{Area of smallest inscribing circle}}$$

Maximum compaction, i.e. where the shape of the spatial unit is a circle, gives an index value of 1·0, and the less compact the shape the lower the value of the index. ◊◊ *shape measures*.

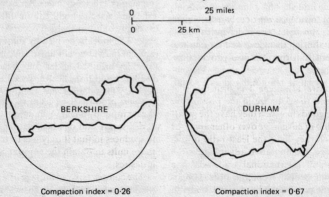

Fig. 25 Compaction index

compactness ratio Compactness is a spatial property that can be considered as the spatial distribution of an areal unit about some central point. A circle therefore represents the two-dimensional shape with maximum compactness. The compactness ratio is a commonly used measure of the shape or form of areal units and the term has been used for two alternate measures:

(i) Compactness ratio $= \dfrac{2\sqrt{\pi A}}{P}$

(ii) Compactness ratio $= \dfrac{1 \cdot 273^A}{L^2}$

where A = area of the spatial unit
P = perimeter of the spatial unit
L = longest (major) axis of the spatial unit

In both cases circular areas give index values of 1·0 and the less compact the shape the lower the value of the compactness ratio. Also known as the *shape index*. ⟡ *shape measures*.

compage A 'total' ⟡ *region*, distinguished by a community of feeling among its inhabitants as well as by all the features of the physical and biotic environment functionally associated with human occupance of the earth. The term was introduced into geography by Derwent Whittlesey in refining certain aspects of ⟡ *regional geography*.

company town A ⟡ *town* or urban settlement whose ⟡ *economic base* is dependent upon the activities of a single ⟡ *firm* or plant to the extent that the firm also provides the houses, etc.

comparative advantage The principle that areas tend to specialize in the production of those goods in which they have the greatest ⟡ *ratio of advantage* over other areas, or for which they have the least ratio of disadvantage. Comparative advantage is the basis of all international trade and the maximum benefit from the operation of this principle would be derived under a system of ⟡ *free trade*. It is therefore basic to the understanding of national (regional) ⟡ *specialization* whereby all countries (regions) benefit from the ⟡ *exchange* of products even if all countries (regions) have the ability to satisfy their needs from domestic production.

The principle applies as long as areas have different ratios of advantage for two or more goods. Consider the case where one area has an absolute advantage in the production of all goods, e.g. country A can produce wheat at two-thirds the cost of its production in country B and cotton at half the cost of cotton production in country B. Country A will then specialize in cotton production (in which it has the greater ratio of advantage) and country B will produce wheat (in which it has the lesser ratio of disadvantage). Assume the above cost differentials are reflected in the following net output/unit output figures:

	Country A	Country B
Cotton	90	45
Wheat	60	40 ·

For 9 units of cotton A will trade 6 units of wheat (these being equivalent to the cotton production in terms of factor inputs): similarly, for 9 cotton units B will trade 8 units of wheat. There is then a basis for trading 9 cotton units for from 6 to 8 units of wheat. Determination of the actual trading ratio will depend upon the ⟡ *terms of trade*. Suppose the trading equilibrium is set at 9 cotton units to 7 wheat units. Country A, producing cotton, will gain 1 unit of wheat over and above what it could produce itself from an equivalent factor input by engaging in trade. Country B will save 1 unit of wheat in every 8 units it produces in that it only has to trade 7 of those units to obtain the amount of cotton it desires.

The comparative advantage of a country (region) can stem from its natural resource endowment, its economic endowment of labour and capital, and the characteristics of space in terms of access to markets. ◊ *Heckscher–Ohlin theorem, initial advantage.*

comparative cost analysis A basic, general procedure whose objective is to determine, for any given industry, the ◊ *comparative advantage* of alternative locations with respect to total costs of production on the basis of an established or anticipated pattern of markets and a given geographic distribution of raw materials and other productive factors used in the industry. It is derived from ◊ *industrial location theory* and can be used not only from an industry's point of view to aid the selection of new locations and assess the efficiency of existing locations but also from a region's point of view to determine its industrial growth prospects.

The analysis proceeds by calculating the total production costs which the industry would incur at each of the locations to be compared. The location with the lowest production costs (including transport costs) would be the most desirable location. The important magnitude is the difference in total costs from location to location, and therefore the analysis need consider only those costs which vary between locations (components of production and transport costs that do not vary between locations may be ignored). While this may lead to considerable savings in research time, comparative cost analysis really offers a practical means of making a rational choice among alternative locations only in those industries where relatively few locations and few inputs are involved.

comparative density A type of ◊ *physiological density* in which the total population is related to land area weighted according to its ◊ *productivity* (e.g. 1 km² of cultivated land = 3 km² of grassland). ◊◊ *man–land ratio.*

comparative mortality figure ◊ *death rates.*

compatibility An important concept, relating to the ◊ *multiple use* of land, which describes the ability of two or more activities/uses to share/coexist on a given site or area of land. Three possibilities may be recognized:
(i) *Complete compatibility*, where two or more activities can take place at the same time on the same site.
(ii) *Partial compatibility*, where two or more activities can use the same site but have to do so at different times in order to avoid conflict, i.e. they require ◊ *time zoning.*
(iii) ◊ *Incompatibility*, where two or more activities cannot use the same site even at different times, i.e. they require ◊ *space zoning.*

Compatibility depends on the nature of the activities themselves, on the way in which they are practised (including intensity of land use) and on site characteristics. The concept has been most widely used in the study of recreational activity.

compensation test ◊ *Kaldor–Hicks compensation test.*

compensation trade ◊ *countertrade.*

compensation variation A measure of 'willingness to pay' based on the maximum amount a person(s) would be willing to pay to maintain or retain a commodity. That amount is normally lower than the ◊ *equivalent variation.*

competition A ◊ *market* condition in which buyers and sellers of relatively similar standing seek to improve their economic well-being by securing favourable terms for ◊ *exchange.* ◊◊ *imperfect competition, monopolistic competition, oligopoly, perfect competition, pure competition.*

competitive hinterland ◊ *hinterland.*

competitive linkage ◊ *linkage.*

complementarity (1) The relationships of two places (regions) when one place (region) has a surplus of a commodity

while the other has a deficit of the same commodity. It is therefore a prerequisite of ◊ *trade* and of spatial interaction, being one factor in E. L. ◊ *Ullman's bases for interaction*. In the wider context complementarity of places is dependent upon the concept of *comparative advantage*.
(2) The relationships between activities at a given location in the sense that (a) certain activities need to use the products and services of and be in close contact with other specialized activities in order to function efficiently (◊ *linkage*), and (b) certain activities, together with other specialized activities, provide a more complete range of goods and services.

complementary labour Different categories of ◊ *labour* may be regarded as being jointly supplied, i.e. the supply of one kind of labour in an area depends on how much of another kind is there. A local population or potential labour force almost always consists of an assortment of people of different ages, sexes and physical and mental capabilities. Hence if most jobs available in an area are in coal-mining and therefore employ men, there is likely to be a surplus of female labour. This represents a complementary labour situation and the excess female labour might provide a bargain labour supply for certain firms, i.e. an advantageous labour location for an activity using female labour. ◊ *dual labour market*, *indirect integration*.

complementary linkage ◊ *linkage*.

complementary products In any process which produces two or more products, those products may be complementary products in the sense that the production of one commodity benefits the production of another commodity, e.g. a leguminous crop preceding a cereal one in a crop rotation. ◊ *joint products*, *supplementary products*.

complementary region The ◊ *region* or area served by a ◊ *central place*. It includes re-

lationships in both directions – town to country and country to town. Complementary regions may be recognized at all orders in the central place hierarchy. ◊ *city region*, *service area*.

completed family size An alternative to ◊ *fertility rates* as a measure of population replacement. Because of the marked variation which may take place in the timing of childbearing within marriage, specific fertility rates and ◊ *reproduction rates* may fluctuate considerably from year to year, even when the completed family size remains fairly constant. The completed family size approach involves following for a group of women, married in a particular year (a marriage ◊ *cohort*) or born in a particular year (a generation), the growth of their families throughout their lifetimes. The results can then be used to predict future population levels.

Completion Notice For ◊ *planning permissions* granted since the 1968 Town and Country Planning Act became law, a Completion Notice may be served on developers who have started work on a ◊ *development* for which permission has been granted but who have then suspended work for some reason. The uncertainty about when the development will be completed creates difficulties for the local planning authority in assessing new allocations of land for further development. A Completion Notice may therefore be served which states that the planning permission lapses after the expiration of a specified period (of not less than one year).

components of change An accounting framework for studying changes in the level of economic activity, especially manufacturing, in a region or area that focuses attention at the plant/factory/establishment level. The analysis may be made in terms of the number of plants and/or the numbers in employment. The changes in any one area over a given time

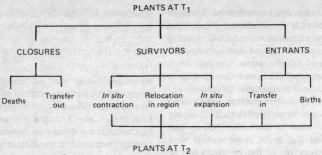

Fig. 26 Components of change

period are divided into the following components:

(i) *In situ* changes, resulting from the expansion, contraction and relocation within the area of plants existing at the start of the period and still operating at the end of the period.

(ii) Closures, resulting from the 'death' of some plants and the movement out of the area of other plants.

(iii) Entrants, resulting from the 'birth' of completely new plants and the movement into the area of other plants.

The net change in the number of plants in an area between time T_1 and time T_2 is summarized in ◊ Fig. 26. For employment the net change = (employment in new entrants) + (net change in employment in survivors) − (employment in closures).

composite household A ◊ *household* which includes one or more ◊ *hidden households*. ◊◊ *household fission*.

comprehensive development The complete ◊ *development* or ◊ *redevelopment* of a sizable area, especially within a town, as a phased operation in accordance with a comprehensive plan for the whole area. ◊◊ *piecemeal development*.

compulsory purchase A power granted to government bodies to obtain land they require compulsorily rather than through the operation of the market. Thus a *compulsory purchase order* is an official

order, served on a private landowner by a government body, for the compulsory acquisition of private property which is required for public use or in the public interest. ◊ *eminent domain*.

conacre A system of ◊ *land tenure* in Ireland in which small portions of land, even individual fields, were available for leasing. The duration of the letting was eleven months according to E. E. Evans and a year and a day according to I. H. Adams. Since fields let in conacre were worked as part of a farm, the system frequently led to fragmented farms.

concealed household ◊ *hidden household*.

concealed unemployment ◊ *unemployment*.

concentrated decentralization A term describing the strategy evolved to deal with the problems of population growth and overcrowding in pressurized metropolitan regions. At first growth was accommodated at the periphery of the ◊ *metropolis*, so increasing concentration at the centre of the region. The strategy of concentrated decentralization emerged as a deliberate attempt to create a better balance between the central urban areas and the surrounding ◊ *hinterlands* by dispersal of the growth into small/medium-sized towns not too distant from the metropolis and including overspill ◊ *new towns*. ◊◊ *decentralization, expanded town*.

concentration and centralization The tendency towards the clustering or ◊ *localization* of economic activity, and therefore people, in and around a relatively small number of urban centres. Also referred to as ◊ *agglomeration* and ◊ *polarization*. Spatial concentration and centralization is fostered by market factors, information sources and decision-making/control centres, as well as by inter-activity ◊ *linkages* and other ◊ *external economies*. It arises largely from the fact that economic activity is becoming more and more organized in units of increasing size and within a hierarchical organization structure.

concentration grade A method, applied on a street-by-street basis in ◊ *central business district* retail studies, designed to identify those streets where the shops specialize in retailing ◊ *durable goods*. For any street the concentration grade may be calculated as:

$$\text{Concentration grade} = \frac{\text{\% floor space selling durable goods in the street of the total of such floor space in the CBD}}{\text{\% floor space selling convenience goods in the street of the total of such floor space in the CBD}}$$

◊ *central business intensity index*.

concentric diversification ◊ *diversification*.

concentric zone theory One of three major theories (◊ *multiple nuclei theory*, *sector theory*) of ◊ *urban morphology*. Developed by E. W. Burgess on the basis of studies in Chicago, the theory argues that urban land uses can be represented as a series of consistent, concentric zones. Five zones are recognized: (1) the ◊ *central business district*, (2) the ◊ *zone in transition*, (3) a zone of independent working men's homes (second-generation immigrant settlement), (4) a zone of better residences (basically middle-class) and (5) the commuters' zone (high-class residences). The concentric pattern (◊ Fig. 27) arises from the hypothesis that urban rents and transport costs are substitutable and through a system of competitive bidding land uses are sorted according to their ability to benefit from and therefore pay for proximity to the central position of greatest ◊ *accessibility*. Since the many activities of the city are not all equally susceptible to changes in accessibility their ◊ *bid-rent* curves vary in shape, but similar activities are likely to be found at similar distances from the CBD.

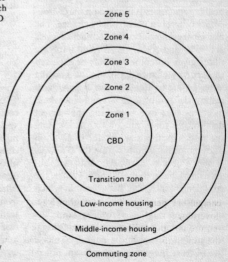

Fig. 27 Concentric zone theory

The theory also describes the growth of the city. Growth depends on new residents (immigrants) moving into the second zone and this initiates a process of ◊ *invasion and succession* whereby the residents of the other zones are displaced outwards towards the urban periphery. Hence the theory is sometimes known as the *concentric zone growth theory* or the *concentric growth theory*.

concept of natural subsidy ◊ *natural subsidy*.

conceptual spaces ◊ *bounded spaces*.

condominium A ◊ *territory* governed by two (or more) other ◊ *states* jointly.

conference lines A term used to describe shipping companies that have banded together in a *'conference'* to protect their common interests. This allows control to be exercised over ◊ *freight rates*, charges and other dues and also over sailing schedules to ensure no overlap.

confidence interval, confidence level, confidence limits The term confidence level indicates the degree of certainty with which a statement may be made about a statistical ◊ *population*. It is based on the ◊ *probability* of a result occurring by chance. The two most commonly used confidence levels are 95% and 99%, the former implying that a given outcome will only be expected to occur by chance 1 time in 20, and the latter 1 time in 100. Thus in ◊ *hypothesis* testing the use of a 95% confidence level indicates that one is making the correct decision 95 times out of 100 in rejecting the null hypothesis when an observation or outcome lies wholly within the ◊ *critical region*. For any particular statistical analysis maximum and minimum values, the confidence limits, can be set within which an observation will lie with a specified level of confidence. The range between the confidence limits is the confidence interval. Generally the higher the confidence level the wider is the confidence interval.

confirmatory statistics Statistical methods used to test ◊ *hypotheses*. ◊ *exploratory data analysis*. ◊◊ *descriptive statistics*, *inferential statistics*.

conflict theory A ◊ *paradigm* which views conflict within institutions or other spatial, social and economic areas as more important in inducing change than functional or consensus relationships. *Conflict models* emphasize the internal and structural nature of conflict and its roots in basic social relationships. Conflict occurs over the distribution of such socially valued items as economic resources, power and status, and is characterized by the constraints some members of society exercise over other members. *Conflict resolution* considers the processes for reaching decisions when parties to the decisions oppose each other. ◊◊ *consensus model*.

confluence town A town whose urban functions derive in large measure from a convergence of waterways. ◊◊ *gap town*.

congested region A ◊ *region* in which the level of ◊ *economic development* has reached a scale at which ◊ *diseconomies* can be detected. Diseconomies arise from continuing increases in the intensity of use of resources, in particular the transportation system, and eventually this leads to a reduction in industrial efficiency. Major ◊ *metropolitan areas* in advanced industrial nations are representative of such congested regions.

congestion Congestion results from using some existing facility, especially a transport link, beyond its holding or ◊ *carrying capacity*. On any transport route the level of congestion (or degree of retarded flow) depends on traffic volume, ◊ *modal split*, ◊ *transport network* characteristics, and the availability and acceptability of public transport. Effects include increased costs and time delays associated with travel, a proportion of road accidents, and environmental pollution. In so far as the full ⟡ *social costs* of congestion are not borne by transport users it represents an ⟡ *externality* to the urban or national economy. ⟡ *crowding*.

conglomerate diversification ⟡ *diversification*.

congruent environment An ⟡ *environment* that facilitates, or at least does not impede, people in following a ⟡ *life style* they desire. ⟡ *incongruent environment*.

conindustrialization G. Renner's term for the massive regional concentration of manufacturing that ultimately emerges from the development of symbiotic relationships in industry. ⟡ *agglomeration*, *industrial complex*.

conjugal family ⟡ *nuclear family*.

connectivity In ⟡ *graph theory*, the degree to which the ⟡ *nodes* of a ⟡ *network* are directly connected to each other. More generally it indicates the degree of internal connection in a transport network. The higher the ratio between ⟡ *links* and nodes in a network the greater is the connectivity. Connectivity can be measured via the ⟡ *beta index* and the ⟡ *gamma index*.

connectivity index ⟡ *gamma index*.

connectivity matrix ⟡ *graph theory*.

conscripted immigrants 'True' ⟡ *second-generation immigrants*, i.e. children born to immigrant parents in the country of emigration. The decision to migrate was not theirs, but their parents'. ⟡ *immigration*.

consensus models of society Sociological models which emphasize the structural and ⟡ *normative* integration of social systems, and which regard social conflict as an aberrant or transitory phenomenon. Societies are seen as having an optimum/equilibrium condition, in terms of which functional integration is assessed, or as characterized by a consensus on values and norms. Sociological consensus models, such as structural functionalism, developed through biological analogies, stress the functional unity of the social organism. In organismic models, the analysis of social phenomena and institutions proceeds in terms of the relationship of the part to the effective survival of the whole, and integrated functioning or consensual social activity is defined as a necessity for the survival of the social system. ⟡ *conflict theory*.

consequent boundary ⟡ *boundary*.

conservation Conservation embraces a wide range of concepts. Strictly speaking it means 'preservation', to retain intact or unchanged. This implies a 'saving' from change, e.g. a unique natural habitat threatened by urban development. In a wider sense conservation implies the planning and management of ⟡ *resources* so as to secure their wise use and continuity of supply, while maintaining and enhancing their quality, value and diversity. Conservation, in either sense, can be applied to a great variety of phenomena: not only natural resources – plants, animals, landscape, etc. – but also people-made objects, including historic buildings, ancient monuments, paintings, sculptures, etc.

In relation to natural resources, conservation can involve the protection of species from exploitation at one end of the spectrum, to sustaining food production while maintaining or even improving the quality of the environment at the other end. Four types of conservation have been recognized in this context:

(i) *Species conservation*, involving the protection of plant and animal species which are under threat from any form of exploitation.

(ii) *Habitat conservation*, which seeks to maintain representative habitat types over the full, natural ecological range.

(iii) *Land use conservation*, which seeks to balance the competing forms of land use with natural ecosystems.

(iv) *Creative conservation*, which aims to

make use of landscapes produced by society – from motorway verges to derelict mineral workings and spoil heaps.

Similarly, conservation of the ⟡ *built environment* may protect individual buildings of architectural or historic merit from destruction; may maintain representative areas of our economic and social history; and may also encourage the purposeful use of old buildings as part of a plan to enhance the quality of the environment. ⟡ *amenity conservation, resource management*.

conservation area An area, designated by a local planning authority, of special architectural or historic interest, the character or appearance of which it is desirable to preserve or enhance. Such statutory protection was first introduced under the 1967 Civic Amenities Act and represented a logical growth of the established code of officially recognizing and safeguarding buildings of special architectural and historic interest. ⟡ *listed building*.

conservative migration ⟡ *migration*.

consolidation ⟡ *land consolidation*.

conspicuous consumption T. Veblen's term to describe the wasteful and ostentatious use of goods, demonstrating the wealth and social position of an individual. ⟡ *consumption*.

constant returns, law of A condition in which, when all the ⟡ *factors* of production are increased in a given proportion, the amount of the product is increased in the same proportion. ⟡ *diminishing returns, economies of scale*.

consultative space ⟡ *social space*.

consumer A person who uses a ⟡ *good* or ⟡ *service*. Certain generalizations are made in economic analysis about *consumer behaviour* in distributing limited income among an infinite variety of goods and services available. It is assumed that (i) the consumer will arrange his expenditure so that the relative marginal ⟡ *utility* of all the goods he consumes will be in the same proportion to their relative prices; (ii) a fall in the ⟡ *price* of a good, other things being equal, will increase his consumption of it (a rise in price having the opposite effect); and (iii) a rise in his real income will normally result in an increased consumption of goods (a fall in real income having the opposite effect). While exceptions to these generalizations do occur they are of sufficient validity to be regarded as reasonable assumptions in the analysis of consumer behaviour. ⟡ *opportunity set, predisposition*.

consumer goods Products or articles in the actual form in which they are used by the domestic ⟡ *consumers* who buy them. They therefore directly satisfy human wants or desires.

consumer's surplus The excess of the price which a person would be willing to pay rather than go without a good, over that price which he actually does pay.

consumption The process of using ⟡ *goods* and ⟡ *services* to satisfy wants. It can thus refer, legitimately, to the purchase by an individual or family of goods and services supplied by firms. The *consumption function* is a behavioural equation expressing the relationship between consumption and income. ⟡ *collective consumption*.

consumption-possibility line ⟡ *iso-outlay line*.

contact field A term used to describe the spatial distribution of all the acquaintances of an individual, group or organization. It is equivalent to ⟡ *activity space* and therefore more restricted than ⟡ *action space*, ⟡ *awareness space* or ⟡ *behavioural environment*. ⟡ *daily-life environment*.

contact number A measure of shape of an area, defined as the number of neighbours touching that area. Empirical studies suggest a spatial regularity in that mean values of contact numbers for different areas

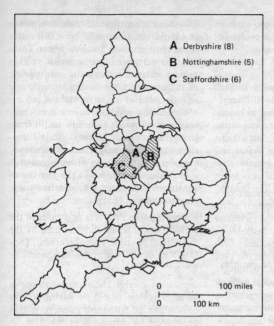

A Derbyshire (8)
B Nottinghamshire (5)
C Staffordshire (6)

0   100 miles
0   100 km

Fig. 28 Contact numbers of three English counties

converge towards 6. From ⬦ Fig. 28 it can be seen that the contact number for Nottinghamshire is 5, for Staffordshire 6, and for Derbyshire 8. ⬦ *shape measures.*

contact possibilities ⬦ *index of contact possibilities.*

contact space ⬦ *activity space.*

contagious diffusion ⬦ *diffusion.*

containerization The method of handling all manner of cargo in large containers which was developed world-wide in the 1960s to encompass road, rail and ship transport. The cargo container is a steel or aluminium box of standardized size, 8 × 8 ft (2·6 × 2·6 m) and in 10 ft (3·3 m) lengths from 10 ft (3·3 m) to 40 ft (13·1 m) in which the cargo, some 25–30 tonnes, uniform or mixed, is packed by the dispatcher. The use of uniform containers greatly reduces handling costs, allowing efficient loading

and unloading by means of standardized fixtures and machinery, as well as easy direct transfer from one transport mode to another. Container-handling depots have been established at road and rail terminals, and at major ports. ⬦ *fishy-back principle, piggy-back principle.*

contextual effect A term used in ⬦ *electoral geography* to describe a situation in which voting behaviour is influenced by a particular local issue or context as well as by more general forces. Where the local and general contexts reinforce each other the result will not be affected, but where the local issue runs counter to the general force the result will be different from that expected. Voters may therefore find themselves in a conflict situation where their usual loyalties are countered by a local influence. The effects on election results occur when the latter prevail and votes are cast differently than would be the case in the absence of such conflict. ⟡ *friends and neighbours effect, neighbourhood effect.*

contextual space ⟡ *space.*

contiguity test A simple test of ⟡ *spatial autocorrelation* designed by M. F. Dacey. Using a ⟡ *nominal scale* the test is based on an analysis of 'joins' for areas with common boundaries: a 'join' may represent two areas with the same characteristic or two areas of contrasting characteristics. The number of 'joins' of each type can be tested for randomness. The contiguity test has been used in geography to test for (i) a tendency for an activity or phenomenon to agglomerate in space; (ii) contiguity in the residuals from regression; and (iii) functional linkage, in particular the influence of proximity on diffusion patterns.

contiguous zone A ⟡ *maritime zone*, located beyond the ⟡ *territorial sea*, over which a coastal ⟡ *state* exercises certain exclusive rights. Although international legislation on contiguous zones is not cut and dried, according to the Informal Composite Negotiating Text agreed at the United Nations 3rd Conference on the Law of the Sea held in 1977 the contiguous zone may

not extend more than 24 nautical miles (44·4 km) from the same baseline as is used for the territorial sea. Since the above Text gives the territorial sea a width of 12 nautical miles (22·2 km) the contiguous zone is a zone 12 nautical miles wide on the outer edge of the territorial sea.

Within the contiguous zone a state may exercise the control necessary to prevent infringement of its customs, fiscal, immigration and sanitary/health regulations in respect of its ⟡ *territory* or territorial sea, or to punish infringement of any of those regulations committed within its territory or territorial sea. The relationship between the contiguous zone and the other maritime zones (⟡ *continental shelf*, ⟡ *exclusive economic zone*, ⟡ *internal waters*, ⟡ *territorial sea*) is illustrated in ⟡ Fig. 29. ⟡ *zone of diffusion.*

continental shelf The relatively flat seaward extension of the world's land-masses found off the coasts of many continents, with its outer edge marked by the continental slope, at a depth of about 200 m (610 ft), which marks a transition zone between the continental shelf and the ocean depths.

Where coastal ⟡ *states* are bordered by

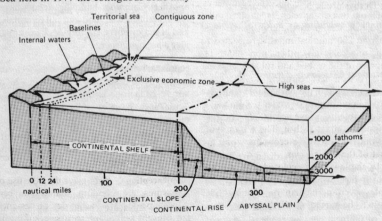

Fig. 29 Contiguous zone and other maritime zones

continental margins which are wider than 200 nautical miles (370 km) (◊ *exclusive economic zone*), they are entitled to claim the continental shelf as a fifth ◊ *maritime zone* (◊ Fig. 29). The political significance of the continental shelf is of recent origin, dating from the time when exploitation of underwater resources, other than fisheries, became a feasible prospect. In an attempt to resolve states' claims to ◊ *sovereignty* over the seabed and subsoil of the continental shelf the United Nations, through its 1958 Law of the Sea conference, produced the *Continental Shelf Convention* giving states rights to exploit mineral resources of their coastal waters to a depth of 200 m (610 ft), or beyond if exploitation was technically feasible. This convention was replaced in the 1977 Informal Composite Negotiating Text (United Nations 3rd Conference on the Law of the Sea), under which coastal states are permitted to claim the seabed and the subsoil of submarine areas which extend beyond their ◊ *territorial seas* throughout the natural prolongation of their land territory to the outer edge of the continental shelf. The 1977 Text had introduced the exclusive economic zone and rights in respect of that zone already comprehend the continental shelf out to a distance of 200 nautical miles (370 km). Claim to the continental shelf beyond 200 nautical miles is restricted to the mineral and other non-living resources of the seabed and subsoil, together with organisms belonging to sedentary species which at the harvestable stage are either immobile on or under the seabed or are unable to move except in constant physical contact with it. The waters lying beyond the exclusive economic zone are part of the ◊ *high seas*.

In shallow, semi-enclosed seas, e.g. the North Sea, where the claims of coastal states overlap, median or dividing lines have to be agreed. ◊◊ *Hedberg zone*.

contingency table A table, in the form of a

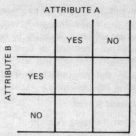

Fig. 30 Contingency table

matrix with rows and columns, which sets out data, i.e. observed frequencies, on the basis of two or more ◊ *attributes*. If there are two attributes data are arranged in a 2 × 2 contingency table (◊ Fig. 30), and observations can be classified in any one of four ways. A contingency table may be of any size and represents a first step in assessing whether two criteria of classification are independent of one another. ◊ *cross-tabulation*. ◊◊ *chi square test, gamma, Somer's D.*

continuous variable In theory a ◊ *variable* which can take on any value between plus and minus infinity, i.e. whatever two values are mentioned, it is always possible to imagine more possible values in between them. In practice many variables treated as continuous may take on only a positive value (including zero), e.g. distance in km. ◊◊ *discrete variable*.

contour mining ◊ *strip mining*.

contour ploughing A type of field cropping that follows the natural contour of the land, with the farmer ploughing along a slope rather than up and down the slope. It is therefore a conservation measure designed to reduce soil erosion and gullying. ◊◊ *strip cropping*.

contraception ◊ *Birth control* by the use of measures, e.g. condom, diaphragm, cervical cap and intra-uterine device, designed to prevent sexual intercourse resulting in conception. In recent years the contraceptive pill has become commonplace, as have ◊ *sterilization* and vasectomy techniques (although the latter, by convention, are not included as contraceptive techniques). Contraception excludes induced ◊ *abortion* (which is used after conception has occurred).

contract rent ◊ *rent*.

contractual tramping A method by which commodity shippers are encouraged to make use of vessels for periods longer than a single voyage via attractive offers of substantial freight discounts on long-term charters and contracts of affreightment extending up to fifteen years. This system has in large measure replaced the former 'open' tramp trade.

control system A ◊ *process–response system* in which the key components are controlled by some intelligence. ◊ *systems analysis*.

control variables ◊ *Variables* (or ◊ *attributes*) used for dividing a ◊ *sample* into relevant sub-groups. Such control variables may be used to guide sampling decisions as well as analysis of data.

controlled tipping Now the most common method of domestic refuse landfill disposal. Refuse is tipped in layers, compacted and covered at the end of every working day with an inert layer of suitable material to form a seal. It therefore reduces the public nuisance and health hazards compared to the earlier practice of 'open' tips.

conurbation A term coined by Patrick Geddes to describe the continuously built-up area formed by the coalescence of several, originally separate, expanding settlements. The emphasis is placed on the continuity of the physical built-up area, and the term has tended to give way recently to the terms ◊ *metropolitan area* or ◊ *metropolitan labour area*, which emphasize function interdependence.

convenience centre ◊ *neighbourhood centre*.

convenience goods ◊ *Goods*, of ◊ *low-order*, which are purchased by ◊ *consumers* at fairly regular, short intervals; which individually represent a small fraction of a consumer's weekly income; and for which selection or choice is relatively unimportant: e.g. groceries. Since purchases of convenience goods are made to meet day-to-day requirements they are likely to be purchased from the nearest shopping centre (◊ *neighbourhood centre*).

convenience store A category of retail shop selling ◊ *convenience goods*, visited frequently by any consumer to buy perishable foods and other items of daily use.

conventional name Places in many parts of the world where English is not spoken are known to us by Anglicized names which are not used at the places to which we apply them. Such a name is a conventional name or *exonym*, e.g. Cologne (Köln), Lisbon (Lisboa), Turin (Torino) – the local or ◊ *geographical name* is in brackets. Similarly other nations use conventional names for British places, e.g. Londres, Londen (for London). There is some international pressure to give priority to the geographical name, but there are problems of transliteration of names from non-Roman scripts.

convergent linkage ◊ *linkage*.

conversion The physical alteration of an existing building, usually to permit a higher density of occupation. In its most common form, single-family houses are modified to accommodate two or more self-contained household units. ◊ *economic life of building*, *gentrification*.

convertible husbandry The system of continually tilling improved land under an alternation of grain and grass crops in place of the ancient division of the cultivated area between permanent arable and permanent grass. The system was introduced as early as the 13th century but did not become widespread until the 18th and 19th centuries.

co-operative An association of farmers, organized for their mutual benefit in production and marketing or both. Co-operatives act as purchasing and distributing agents for seeds, feeding-stuffs and fertilizers, as grading and selling agents for produce, and as joint owners of farm machinery. The co-operative system allows farmers to operate their own holdings as individuals, yet offers the advantages of bulk-purchasing, grading and standardization, and of large-scale contract marketing, which reduce costs to the farmer, so improving efficiency and increasing profits.

Copper Age The period or cultural phase of people's evolution, which preceded the ◊ *Bronze Age*, about the middle of the second millennium. Stone was still the most important material for tools, but copper was used especially for ornaments.

coppice A term applied to both the woodland and the wood production system which involves the cutting-back of young broadleaved trees to a stump in order to exploit early growth. Cut-over stumps produce fresh shoots from side-buds just above ground level in the year following harvesting: a coppiced tree is therefore one without a single trunk. The shoots provide a crop of poles and when these are felled the cycle is repeated. Such woodland is cut over periodically, both casually and in strict rotation, every ten to fifteen years in the United Kingdom, depending on the species of tree. The process can continue for 100 years or more. Hazel and sweet chestnut are most commonly used for coppice. *Copse* is a shortened form of the term coppice. ◊ *coppice with standards.* ◊ *pollard.*

coppice with standards A traditional system of woodland management whereby timber trees are grown above a coppiced woodland. It is used in particular as a method of exploiting oakwoods, in which all the trees except a rather open network of tall, well-formed oaks – the *standards* at about twenty per acre (fifty per hectare) – are felled, leaving plenty of space for hazels and other underwood to grow and be ◊ *coppiced* at intervals of ten to fifteen years. The coppice layer may be two-storeyed: (i) a 'large coppice' layer of ash and maple regularly cut about 1 yd (1 m) from the ground, and (ii) a 'small coppice', the layer of canopy closest to the ground and comprising hazel and hawthorn. The large coppice layer is not always present.

copse ◊ *coppice.*

copyhold A form of ◊ *land tenure* in which title was substantiated by the tenant's ability to produce a copy of the entry in the ◊ *court roll* noting his acquisition of the property by inheritance or some other means. It developed out of villein tenures in the later Middle Ages and by the 16th century some 30% of landholding in England was held by copyhold. Thus a *copyholder* was a tenant who held by copyhold.

cordon survey Or *screenline survey.* A cordon survey is normally conducted on traffic routes at specially selected points, which together represent a cordon around the survey area (such as an urban area or a central business district) and permit the easy and comprehensive measurement of traffic flows. The cordon principle may also be used in ◊ *O-D surveys.*

core ◊ *urban core.*

core area A term used to embrace past and present areas of political dominance, areas of intense national or cultural consciousness, and areas of economic leadership (◊ *core region* in the latter case). In political geography it is used to refer to some central area in which or about which a

◊ *state* originates and which acts as the catalyst about which the state's subsequent growth takes place. This normally results from the core area being more richly endowed with natural resources and, from an early date, supporting a relatively high population density at higher cultural and economic levels than elsewhere in the state. The commercial ascendancy and the ability to support military power allow the rulers of the core area to extend political control over adjacent areas. Thus the state expands with the accretion of territory around its core.

core–frame concept A refinement of the traditional ◊ *central business district*, depicting the latter as comprising two distinct parts in a core–frame pattern (◊ Fig. 31). There is an inner core, the central part of the ◊ *downtown* area, distinguished by intensive use of high-value land, with consequent marked vertical usage in high-rise buildings, and a concentrated daytime population. It is the focus of the public transport system and a centre of specialized activities with strong functional links between shops and various offices.

The core is surrounded by a less intensively developed frame in which, since it has much lower land values, there is more likely to be horizontal than vertical expansion and the various functional sub-areas – wholesaling, off-street parking, light manufacturing etc. – are not so strongly interlinked.

core–periphery model A model of the spatial structure of an ◊ *economic system*, based on the unequal distribution of power in economy and society, consisting of two major components: a centre or ◊ *core region* and a periphery. The core region dominates the periphery in most economic, political and social respects. This ◊ *dependence*, structured through the relations of exchange between core and periphery, is essentially a form of internal ◊ *colonialism*.

Fig. 31 Core–frame concept

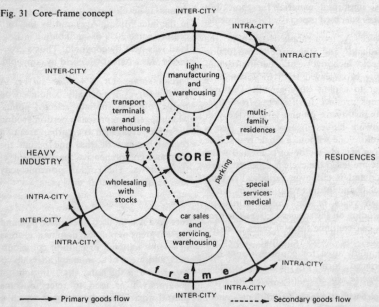

The concentration of economic power, wealth, innovation and productivity at the core serves to maintain the core's advantage in exchange and allow core region institutions to determine the development path of the peripheral regions. Such unequal relations may be reinforced by the implementation of economic policies which favour the core at the expense of the periphery and may also be maintained by migration and capital flows from periphery to core ($\diamond$ *cumulative causation*). The model has also been referred to as the *centre–periphery hypothesis*. $\diamond$ *peripherality, polarized development, spatial structure and national economic development.*

core region John Friedmann's term for the concentrated metropolitan economies, comprising one or more clustered cities and the encompassing area, with a high potential for generating and absorbing $\diamond$ *innovation* and economic growth. $\diamond$ *core area, spatial structure and national economic development.*

corn rent A $\diamond$ *rent* payment expressed in terms of the price of corn in an area. The payment therefore varies in amount with changes in the price of corn.

Cornell system A system of $\diamond$ *land evaluation* incorporating economic parameters.

corner area An area off the main flows of transportation or geographically on the edge of a region, i.e. a peripheral area.

corrected noise level An index of industrial $\diamond$ *noise* which measures the level of noise emitted from industrial premises in dB(A) ($\diamond$ *decibel A-scale*), corrected for tonal character, intermittency and duration in accordance with the appropriate British Standard.

correlation A statistical term for the strength of the $\diamond$ *association* or relationship which exists between the values of two (i.e. *bivariate correlation*) or more $\diamond$ *variables* (i.e. *multiple correlation*) in the analysis of

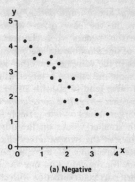
(a) Negative

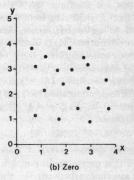
(b) Zero

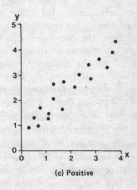
(c) Positive

Fig. 32 Correlation

◊ *interval* and ◊ *ratio data. Positive correlation*, in the case of a two-variable comparison, occurs when changes in the values of one variable are accompanied by changes in the values of the other variable in the same direction, i.e. larger values on one variable tend to go with larger values on the other. *Negative correlation* occurs when larger values on one variable tend to go with smaller values on the other, i.e. the values of the two variables change in opposite directions. If there is no clear tendency for the values on one variable to move in a particular direction with changes in the other variable then the situation approaches *zero correlation*. These three situations are illustrated on scatter diagrams in ◊ Fig. 32. The term, sometimes referred to as *covariation*, is used in a number of contexts: (1) ◊ *autocorrelation*, (2) ◊ *correlation coefficient* (r), (3) ◊ *coefficient of determination* (r^2), (4) ◊ *coefficient of multiple correlation* (R), (5) coefficient of multiple determination (R^2), (6) ◊ *multiple correlation*, (7) ◊ *partial correlation*, (8) . ◊ *product–moment correlation*, (9) ◊ *Spearman rank correlation*.

correlation coefficient (*r*) A descriptive statistic that measures the strength of the linear association between the values of variables, i.e. the extent to which variations in the values of one variable are linked to variations in the values of the other variable(s). No causal link can be deduced from the correlation coefficient alone. A correlation coefficient, usually represented by the symbol r, ranges in value from $+1.0$ to -1.0. Those two values of r represent, respectively, perfect positive and perfect negative ◊ *correlation* (◊ Fig. 32). ◊ *Kendall's tau, product–moment correlation, Spearman's rho*.

correlogram analysis A method in time series analysis used to the serial ◊ *correlation* structure among the ◊ *variable* values at lags of 1,2,3, . . . *n* time periods, i.e. the ◊ *temporal autocorrelations* between the values of x_t (variable x at time period t) and x_{t-1} (variable x at time period t minus 1), x_t and x_{t-2}, x_t and x_{t-3}, and so on. The periodicity of the fluctuations can be established, e.g. peaks in time cycles related to outbreaks of epidemic disease.

Correlogram analysis can be extended to the analysis of spatial data series by allowing for spatial lag, e.g. permitting analysis of the spatial spread/clustering of the disease as well as its time periodicity.

corridor (1) A negotiated extension of the ◊ *territory* of one ◊ *state*, interrupting the territory of another, to give it access to the sea or an international waterway. For example, the pre-1939 Polish corridor, agreed as part of the settlement at the end of the First World War, which gave Poland access to the Baltic Sea, or the Leticia corridor obtained by Colombia (under principles enunciated in the 1921 Barcelona Convention of Freedom of Transit) from Peru in 1922 to provide access to the Amazon River. ◊ *landlocked state*.
(2) The term has been extended to the case of an *air corridor*, which gives airway access to a place, e.g. to West Berlin, and more generally to any prescribed international air-route over a country.

cosmography The science which describes and maps the general features of the universe, both the heavens and the earth. A term rarely used today.

cosmopolitan A term used to describe person(s), attitudes and places whose characteristics reflect their 'belonging to all parts of the world', i.e. free from national prejudices and at home in all parts of the world.

cost The amount of expenditure incurred in obtaining the services of a ◊ *factor(s) of production*. The approach now used is in terms of the opportunities or alternatives forgone (◊ *opportunity cost*). ◊ *cost curve, cost structure, cost surface, fixed costs, marginal cost, overhead costs, prime costs*, *production costs, variable costs.* ⟡ *basic costs, locational costs, occupancy cost, on-site costs, private costs, procurement costs, ripening costs, social costs, sunk costs, terminal costs.*

cost–benefit analysis A technique for the comprehensive enumeration and evaluation of proposed public investment projects, undertaken from the viewpoint of the community. In contrast to the profit-and-loss accounting approach of normal business management to private investment proposals, cost–benefit analysis assesses the wider implications of public schemes, including the full ⟡ *social costs* and ⟡ *social benefits*, i.e. it attempts to quantify the ⟡ *externalities* involved. Cost–benefit analysis therefore appears to offer a practical way of assessing the desirability of projects and ensuring, where alternatives exist, that the most worthwhile is selected: a considerable improvement in decision-making procedures.

The technique was initially developed in the United States to appraise public sector investment in river basin and harbour schemes, but many of its early applications in the United Kingdom were in the planning field, in particular urban transport, e.g. the Victoria underground line. There are three stages in an analysis: (i) The identification of all the relevant costs and benefits of a project. (ii) The placing of monetary values on the costs and benefits, including those items which do not normally have market prices attached to them, e.g. air pollution. This also involves the use of ⟡ *discounting* to reduce costs and benefits occurring over different time periods to a common base. (iii) The use of the resulting cost–benefit ratio as an input to decision-making.

While cost–benefit analysis is conceptually simple, in practice its application raises a number of problems, and the technique has come under considerable criticism in recent years. Delimitation of

the items to be included among costs and benefits is not straightforward, especially if double counting is to be avoided. Placing market values on the intangible costs and benefits is difficult, as there is no objective method of judging ⟡ *shadow prices*. The discount rate(s) adopted is/are critical to the present value of future costs and benefits, and the comparison of aggregate costs and benefits ignores distributional considerations. ⟡ *cost–effectiveness analysis.*

cost curve A graph of the relationship between cost of production and volume of output for a given plant or firm. Three cost curves are commonly used: (i) The *total cost curve*, which plots the total cost of given volumes of output. (ii) The *average cost curve*, which typically slopes downwards to the right at low levels of output, to rise again owing to ⟡ *diminishing returns* after minimum average cost has been reached. (iii) The ⟡ *marginal cost* curve, which plots the cost of each additional unit of production. The relationship between the three curves for a given plant is shown in ⟡ Fig. 33.

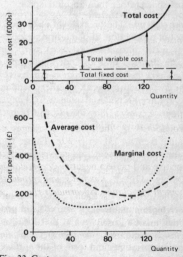

Fig. 33 Cost curves

cost-distance A measure of the ◊ *distance* between two locations in terms of the money cost of movement. ◊◊ *geodesic distance*, *time-distance*.

cost–effectiveness analysis An alternative to ◊ *cost–benefit analysis*, although the exact meaning of the term is not always agreed upon. Some of the techniques falling under this umbrella are of a financial nature, such as cost-minimization procedures, but the most widely accepted interpretation is that it is a technique for finding the best or most effective way of using a given financial budget. The former (cost-minimization) generates the cheapest method of accomplishing a defined objective, the latter the maximum benefit from a given expenditure. ◊ *Planning, programming and budgeting* is an extension of cost–effectiveness analysis.

cost of living index ◊ *Index of Retail Prices*.

cost space A form of perceived or relative ◊ *space*, based on ◊ *cost-distance* and/or ◊ *time-distance*. Decisions concerning human spatial behaviour are based on such cost space rather than absolute space.

cost structure The breakdown of the total cost of production, at plant, firm or industry scale, into its constituent parts, in particular the cost of individual inputs such as ◊ *factors of production*. Analysis of the cost structure reveals whether an industry (or firm) is material intensive, ◊ *capital intensive*, ◊ *labour intensive*, etc. with respect to expenditure on inputs.

cost surface Spatial variations in the cost of production represented as a three-dimensional surface with distance along the two horizontal axes and money cost on the vertical axis. Each point on the surface represents the aggregate costs of production for a given scale at that location. Cost isopleths (◊ *isodapanes*) detail the spatial variations and form of the surface. Such cost surfaces can also be drawn for the cost of individual factors of production, such as land, labour and materials. ◊◊ *profit surface, revenue surface*.

cottage industry A system of employment in which rural labour/craftsmen, aided by their families, work at home either on their own account or organized centrally by ◊ *entrepreneurs* who deliver raw materials and collect the finished goods. Workers are paid according to the number of articles produced. The system was common in Britain before the ◊ *Industrial Revolution* but now survives primarily in non-industrialized countries. ◊ *domestic industry*. ◊◊ *factory system*.

cottager The occupier, sometimes also the owner, of a ◊ *tenement* having common rights attached to it, often with a ◊ *croft* attached as well.

cotter A holder of a small piece of land held in return for services to the lord of the manor. The system possibly originated with bondmen in the days of serfdom, or in a later period when, owing to pressure of population, it became impossible for all to have a reasonable share of the available cultivable land.

Council for Mutual Economic Assistance (COMECON) An international economic organization formed under Russian hegemony to promote harmonization of supply and demand within the Soviet bloc and to develop patterns of regional specialization leading to the steady advancement of welfare of all the participating ◊ *states*. It was founded in 1949, with its headquarters in Moscow, by the USSR, Bulgaria, Czechoslovakia, Hungary, Poland and Romania; East Germany was admitted in 1950, Mongolia 1962, Cuba 1972. Yugoslavia became an associate member in 1964. Albania was a member from 1949 until 1962.

counted data ◊ *nominal scale*.

counterfactual explanation An approach in

historical studies, based on the comparative method, which compares a hypothetical reconstruction of what might have happened in the past against the record of what actually took place. The approach, used particularly in econometric history, emphasizes the importance of theory in postulating counterfactual situations and of quantitative methods, such as ⟡ *simulation* techniques, in implementing them. It is suggested that counterfactual explanation might be used in ⟡ *historical geography*.

counterpurchase ⟡ *countertrade.*

counterstream effect The tendency of those places which have high rates of inward ⟡ *migration* also to have high rates of outward migration. It was noted as long ago as the 1880s in E. G. Ravenstein's pioneer statement of migration principles.

countertrade, compensation trade A ⟡ *trade* arrangement under which ⟡ *export* sales to a particular country are made conditional upon accepting ⟡ *imports* from that country. A wide variety of exchange agreements exists and a basic distinction is made between *commercial compensation* and *industrial compensation*. Commercial compensation refers to the exchange of unlinked goods in a special deal between the countries under which transactions are usually completed within three years. Three types of commercial compensation are recognized: (i) *barter*, involving the direct exchange of goods without any transfer of funds under a single contract; (ii) *counterpurchase*, where separate contracts cover the sale of goods by country X to country Y and the commitment of country X to buy goods from country Y (the value of the goods exchanged under the two contracts need not be the same); and (iii) *pre-compensation* or *evidence account*, which allows exporters to maintain a balance between exports and counter-imports over a period of time (e.g. a multinational firm with a local manufacturing subsidiary in a developing country may be required to ensure counterpurchased exports of equivalent value to their subsidiary's imports of materials and components).

Industrial compensation involves country X accepting goods produced in country Y using plant or machinery imported from country X, and the agreements involve larger sums of money and longer periods of time than with commercial compensation. Industrial compensation takes the form of either a *buy-back agreement*, involving one contract for the sale of the factory and another for buying back some of its output, or *offset* (also known as *forced technology transfer*), whereby a developing country seeks to incorporate components made in that country in the factory or its finished products so obtaining indirect access to technology.

Other forms of countertrade are *framework agreements*, long-term arrangements within which individual agreements taking any of the above forms of commercial or industrial compensation are set, and *switch trading*, where imbalances in long-term bilateral agreements lead to large credit surpluses in one of the countries which are made available to a third country (i.e. if country X has a large surplus with country Y, imports to X from country Z can be funded by the export of goods from Y to Z).

Countertrade allows countries suffering from liquidity crises to continue to import goods despite their shortage of foreign exchange; it allows certain countries to gain access to protected markets in other countries; it offers a means by which countries can acquire advanced technology; it acts as an export subsidy for countries whose exports are overvalued or uncompetitive on the open market; and it enables countries to export their primary products in the face of low world demand. However, countertrade is discriminatory and therefore works against the multilateral principles of the General Agreement on Tariffs and Trade (GATT).

Until the late 1970s countertrade was primarily a trading policy used by communist countries but in the 1980s it has become more widespread, proving especially attractive to ◊ *Third World* countries and even finding some support among OECD (Organization for Economic Co-operation and Development) countries. ◊◊ *bilateral trade*, *multilateral trade*.

counterurbanization A process of population ◊ *decentralization*, first noted in the USA in the early 1970s when population statistics showed ◊ *metropolitan areas*, especially the larger ones, losing population by net migration to non-metropolitan areas. Various explanations include the increased costs of living in large cities, the improvements in personal mobility which allow certain individuals/families to realize their preference for living in small cities/rural areas, and the relocation of manufacturing industries in search of cheap labour in a period of economic crisis. ◊◊ *deconcentration*.

counterweight city ◊ *métropoles d'équilibre*.

country (1) Any political unit or ◊ *state* on a national scale, regardless of whether it is dependent or independent.
(2) Land put to agricultural and rural uses, such as fields, woods and open spaces, with few houses and other buildings.

country belt A stretch of ◊ *country* (2) around and between towns. It is used for agriculture or as parkland, some of which may be in public (urban) ownership. Also referred to as the *agricultural belt* or *rural belt*.

country park A park, or pleasure ground, established in Great Britain under the 1968 Countryside Act with help from the Countryside Commission as a means of providing, or improving, facilities for the public enjoyment of the countryside. Country parks are normally at least 25 acres (10 hectares) in extent and provide urban dwellers with opportunities to enjoy the countryside by short walks, picnics, or just sitting and admiring the view, as well as by more active outdoor recreational pursuits, such as horse-riding, sailing, etc. The parks must therefore be accessible to large numbers of people; must have the capacity to absorb them and support a wide range of facilities; and should ease pressure on the more remote and solitary places, and hence reduce the amount of damage to the countryside caused by recreation. ◊◊ *forest park*, *national park*.

county One of the traditional units of local government in England and Wales (◊◊ *borough*, *parish*). The county, as a territorial division, has its origin in feudal times, when it was the area granted by the Crown to an earl in return for the acceptance of feudal obligations. County was the Norman equivalent of the Old English ◊ *shire*. Thus, from an early period, the county was regarded as a ◊ *community*, and approached the Crown as a corporate body. In addition to administrative functions the county was also a unit for preservation of the peace and assessment of taxation by commissioners appointed by the county court. Political representation on a county basis evolved in the 13th century.

Subsequent reforms, enacted particularly in the 19th and 20th centuries, have extended and restructured the functions performed, delimited the relationships with central government more clearly, and altered areal boundaries, but the county remains the basic unit for local government.

coupling constraints Limits on human behaviour/activities which arise because of the need of people and organizations to join together to fulfil some common purpose. The act of 'joining' must be co-

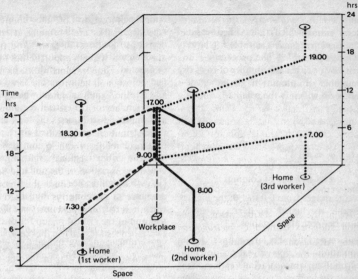

Fig. 34 Coupling constraints

ordinated in both ⬦ *space* and time. T. Hägerstrand terms the set of constraints which operate on the act of joining 'coupling constraints'.

The operation of such constraints is a major cause of some of the highly regular temporal and spatial flows characteristic of modern society – 'bundles' of activities are formed in order to fulfil our needs and wants and to perform our roles in society, e.g. the journey to and from work. It follows that such 'bundles' are possible only if they occur within the daily ⬦ *time–space prism* of all participants (⬦ Fig. 34). ⬦ *authority constraints, capability constraints.*

court roll Medieval records of a court's activities, including tenurial agreements (⬦ *copyhold*), so called because the parchment on which the record was written was filed as a roll.

covariance, analysis of Essentially a combination of ⬦ *regression* analysis and the ⬦ *analysis of variance.* Its application in

geography – to transport, urban spacing, migration and population change problems – has not been very rewarding.

covariation ⬦ *correlation.*

cover crop A quick-growing crop planted between main ⬦ *crops* to protect cleared land from the danger of soil erosion, a practice especially important in areas liable to torrential downpours, e.g. tropical forest. When the cover crop has served its purpose it is usually hoed or ploughed in, hence leguminous plants able to enrich the soil are favoured. ⬦⬦ *catch crop, interculture.*

cover set In a hierarchical structure, a set at a given level $(N + 1)$ that covers sets at a lower level (N), e.g. the set {parishes} at level N is related to the cover set {counties} at $N + 1$. Cover sets are used in ⬦ *Q-analysis.*

covert A small, planted wood or piece of scrub woodland, with low undergrowth, maintained to provide 'cover' for foxes in hunting country or game birds and deer.

Cramer's *V* A ◊ *non-parametric* measure of ◊ *association* which is a modified version of the ◊ *phi coefficient* suitable for larger ◊ *contingency tables*. The procedure is to adjust *phi* for either the number of rows or the number of columns in the table, depending on which is the smaller:

$$\text{Cramer's } V = \left(\frac{\varphi^2}{\min (r - 1), (c - 1)} \right)^{\frac{1}{2}}$$

where $\varphi = phi$
   r = number of rows
   c = number of columns

Its value ranges from 0·0 to 1·0: the higher the value the higher the degree of association between the variables.

crannog An ancient lake dwelling: a settlement built on the edge of a lake, consisting of an artificial brushwood and rubble island with an oak log surface, topped by a single, circular homestead. In Ireland crannogs date from the ◊ *Neolithic*, but in Scotland they are ◊ *Iron Age* or later.

created space ◊ *space*.

creole In the West Indies and certain parts of the American mainland, a person born and naturalized in the country but of European (frequently French or Spanish) or African Negro ◊ *race*. The term has no connotation of colour, although there is an increasing tendency to think of mixed blood being involved.

critical group In ◊ *pollution* emission monitoring, that group of individuals most at risk to a particular discharge. If the critical group is receiving doses/exposures below those recommended as acceptable it is assumed that the population at large is exposed to 'safe' levels of discharge. Success in monitoring ionizing radiation releases from nuclear reactors, and the discharge of heavy metals into estuaries, depends on the ease with which the critical group can be identified.

critical points, critical region, critical values An integral part of the null ◊ *hypothesis* decision procedure is the ◊ *significance level* at which null hypotheses are to be accepted or rejected. The level of significance is specified before a statistical test is conducted, and it is the significance level which defines the boundary of the critical region. As in all sampling distributions the total area of the distribution when plotted corresponds to a probability of 1·0. Within this total area the critical region is that region in which one is critical of the null hypothesis, i.e. with a significance level of 0·05 there is a chance of rejecting the null hypothesis when it is true only five times in 100. The location of the critical region for one- and two-tailed tests (◊ *tail*) on the ◊ *normal distribution*, using a 0·05 significance level, is illustrated in ◊ Fig. 35. In the one-tailed

(a) One-tailed test, with critical region in the upper tail

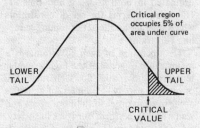

(b) Two-tailed test

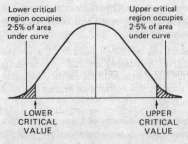

Fig. 35 Critical region

case the critical region is located in one of the tails, whichever is specified by the alternate hypothesis, i.e. the critical region occupies 5% of the total area under the curve describing the sampling distribution. In the two-tailed case the upper and lower critical regions each occupy 2·5% of the area under the curve.

The critical value or critical point is therefore the value of the statistic beyond which the result of the test is significant at a stipulated significance level. In general the calculated value of the test statistic must be greater than or equal to the critical value in order to permit the null hypothesis to be rejected. Critical values have been calculated at various significance levels for all the major statistical tests.

critical theory A school of thought, with origins in classical ◊ *Marxism*, whose central focus is the relationships between social structure and social change which exist under ◊ *capitalism* and their restructuring through a process of critique. The latter involves a rational and public scrutiny of all activities, a rational reconstruction of the conditions that made actions possible, and a reflection on the structures which constrained human action. The origins of the critical theory of society lie in the work of the Frankfurt school in the 1920s and 1930s, and later developments are associated with Jürgen Habermas.

croft, crofting A system of farming, particularly in the Highlands and Islands of Scotland, whereby the arable land of small farms, previously held in common, was divided among the joint tenants into separate crofts, while the pasture remained in common. The impetus for the development of the crofting system was given by the reallocation of ◊ *runrig* lands into individual holdings, which started after the 1745 Rebellion and was accelerated by the 19th-century clearances as landowners displaced small farmers to make way for sheep.

Crofting is largely subsistence farming, since the produce of the croft is consumed by the crofter and his family, except for wool and sometimes milk and cattle. It may be supplemented by seasonal work, e.g. in fishing. The croft is a family inheritance, though not necessarily owned by the family. Crofts are grouped into a wider co-operative organization, the ◊ *township*. The Crofter Holdings (Scotland) Act, 1886, designated a croft as a rented holding of less than 50 acres (20 hectares) in extent and/or an annual rent of less than £30 (now £50). Typical crofts have from 2 to 10 acres (0·8 to 4 hectares) of arable.

cromlech ◊ *dolmen*.

crop Food and other plants grown on a ◊ *field* rather than a ◊ *garden* scale. ◊ *cash crop*, *catch crop*, *cover crop*, *cryophilous crop*, *cultivation*, *double-cropping*.

crop combinations A method of analysis, first developed by J. C. Weaver, for delimiting agricultural regions on the basis of multi-crop patterns. The method starts from the observation that single-crop situations are uncommon and that in most areas farmers usually grow a variety of crops of different degrees of importance. Crop combination regions are delimited as a result of the statistical assessment of land use patterns.

The method compares the proportions of an observed distribution with a series of hypothetical distributions. The latter are calculated for even distribution between 1-crop (i.e. ◊ *monoculture*, 100% of land in one use), 2-crop (i.e. 50% of land in each of two crops), 3-crop, ... *n*-crop categories. For each sub-area the percentage of land occupied by each crop is determined and the crops ranked from greatest to lowest. The observed percentages of cropland are compared with the theoretical percentages to determine which hypothetical category most nearly approximates the observed distribution. The comparison is based on the sum of the squared differences between each category of the hypothetical distribution and the observed distribution. That hypothetical distribution which generates the smallest sum of the squares is the one that best approximates the actual crop combination.

crop mark Aerial photographs, especially those taken during dry periods, often reveal differences in the colour and height of crops. These crop or *vegetation marks* largely depend on the amount of moisture which the plants can draw from the soil. They are most pronounced in grasses and cereal crops, which change colour and grow shorter in the shallower soil above hard features like buried road surfaces or the foundations of ruined buildings and grow taller over covered refuse pits and former ditches. These variations are too subtle to be detected at ground level, but crop marks on aerial photographs have revealed medieval farming patterns, hedgerow positions and boundaries, as well as disused roads and sites of archeological interest. ⟡⟩ *shadow site.*

crop rotation A farming practice in which a systematic succession of different crops is grown in each ⟡ *field* of a farm. The advantages of crop rotation include the maintenance of soil nutrients (since the crops are chosen to be complementary in their nutrient requirements and their contributions to fertility); more effective control of weeds and pests and a reduction in the risk of disease; and the combatting of soil erosion. Modern rotations take from two to eight years to complete a full rotation cycle. ⟡⟩ *land rotation.*

cross-section A description, representative of a society and its landscape, at a particular point in time. It is used as a working method in ⟡ *historical geography* when reconstructing 'past geographies'. ⟡ *synchronic analysis.* ⟡⟩ *vertical theme.*

cross-tabulation The display or splitting-up of observations/cases within a category into sub-categories on the basis of what is known about them on two or more classificatory ⟡ *variables.* Such a display is the basis for ⟡ *contingency table* analysis and the relationship depicted in a cross-tabulation may be summarized in a measure of ⟡ *association* or a test of statistical ⟡ *significance.*

crowding A physical and experiential state which exists when a person feels shut in or hemmed in by other persons or things. It depends in part on ⟡ *density* as well as on the particular purpose an individual has in mind (⟡ *recreation carrying capacity*). ⟡⟩ *congestion.*

crowding index The number of persons per house, used as a measure of ⟡ *density* within a ⟡ *dwelling* unit.

crude birth rate ⟡ *birth rates.*

crude death rate ⟡ *death rates.*

cryophilous crop An arable ⟡ *crop* which needs a certain amount of cold weather in order to produce flowers later in its growing period. If such crops do not undergo this cold (below a certain low temperature, though it need not be below $0°C$) their growth remains vegetative or they form only abortive flowers which do not produce seeds. Cereal crops such as wheat, barley, oats and rye; peas and some kinds of beans; root crops like mangolds, sugarbeet and potatoes; clover and lucerne; and fruit trees (apple, pear, peach, etc.) are all cryophilous. The low-temperature requirement does not exist with *non-cryophilous crops.*

cube law A generalization of the electoral bias in a two-party contest under a single-member constituency electoral system. The law states that the ratio of the percentage of the seats won by the two contesting parties (S_1/S_2) equals the cube of the comparable ratio for the percentage of the votes cast for each party $(V_1/V_2)^3$. Where $V_1 > 50\%$, then $S_1 > V_1$, and electoral bias occurs without any electoral abuse.

cultivation The systematic preparation and use of ◊ *land* for the growing of ◊ *crops*. ◊ *basin cultivation, intensive cultivation, mixed cultivation, primitive cultivation.* ◊◊ *agriculture, farming, horticulture, market gardening, tillage.*

cultivation limit As normally interpreted, the altitude at which ◊ *cultivation* is no longer physically viable. ◊ *growing season, physical margin of cultivation.* ◊◊ *economic margins of cultivation.*

cultural configuration A term used by N. Ginsburg to denote the system of ◊ *social organization*, including values, goals and objectives.

cultural ecology The study of the interactions of societies with one another and with the natural ◊ *environment* in order to understand and explain the processes of adaptation and transformation that operate to alter social institutions, human behaviour and environment.

cultural geography A systematic branch of geography which focuses on the identity of communities and societies at local, regional and national scales, with a central emphasis on people–environment relationships. Because of the breadth of interest, cultural geography had, at one time in North America, a very general meaning equated by some with the whole field of ◊ *human geography*, but in recent years the term has come to be synonymous with the much narrower geographical tradition concerned with cultural differences. In Europe the term has always had a more specific connotation; in the United Kingdom it is associated with descriptive ◊ *regional geography*.

Cultural geography depends heavily on direct field observations and has its origins in the seminal work of Carl Sauer, who emphasized the way in which the differential impact and succession of culture groups was imprinted in the exploitation, form and personality of the landscape (◊ *cultural landscape*). Detailed attention has been given to a variety of themes, including the domestication of plants and animals, agricultural practices, people's impact on ◊ *ecology*, the origin and spread of ◊ *cultures*, settlement features (e.g. house types, building materials), language and religion.

cultural hearth The centre or area of origin of a culture group associated with a particular ◊ *cultural landscape*. ◊◊ *hearth areas*.

cultural landscape The people-made ◊ *landscape* which results from the fashioning of a natural landscape by a ◊ *culture* system. It is therefore a heritage of many eras of natural evolution and of many generations of human effort. The study of cultural landscapes is pursued through the accurate, systematic description of those visible and concrete elements associated with human occupation and utilization of the land. In the German literature it is referred to as *Kulturlandschaft*.

cultural resources ◊ *resources*.

culture Culture is now viewed in cultural anthropology from two points of view – as *cultural code* or as ◊ *social structure*. In the former case culture is regarded as a historically transmitted code of acquired beliefs which supplements instinctive behaviour in human beings, i.e. it is a pattern of meanings, endlessly copied and persistently up-dated, through which people communicate and develop their knowledge about life and their attitudes towards it. The latter case sees culture as a network or system of social relations. Concepts of culture, especially interpreted as cultural code, have been central to the work of French ◊ *regional geography* and of the Berkeley school dealing with ◊ *cultural landscape*. ◊◊ *genre de vie*.

culture contact The interaction of different culture groups or different ◊ *genres de vie* as a result of ⟡ *migration*, or territorial expansion.

cumulative causation The process whereby impulses to economic growth or economic decline within countries or regions are, via the operation of market forces, self-reinforcing. This is a consequence of ⟡ *multiplier* and scale economy effects. For example, in the growth case, the location of new industry in a region will create extra jobs and demands for other factors of production. So additional income is generated for the region's inhabitants, and their spending of that income increases the size of the regional market, creating opportunities for the expansion of existing firms and the establishment of further new firms. An upward spiral is thus set in motion: ⟡ Fig. 36 illustrates the simple nature of the cumulative process.

The internal growth momentum is further reinforced, according to G. Myrdal, by the nature of the spatial interaction between the expanding region and other areas. The process operates to increase the inequalities between regions, since the growth of the expanding region continues to take place at the expense of other regions owing to the fact that spatial flows of labour and capital focus on the expanding region, i.e. lagging regions lose skilled and enterprising workers and locally generated capital (⟡ *backwash effects*). The influx of productive factors to the expanding region further stimulates the cumulative process there, for example by adding both to the size of the market and to the supply of labour.

The concept is also referred to by the longer title *circular and cumulative causation*.

current account ⟡ *balance of payments.*

curvilinear regression ⟡ *polynomial regression.*

customary acre ⟡ *acre.*

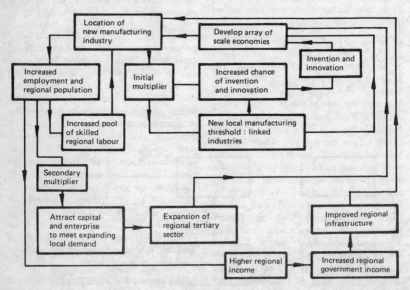

Fig. 36 Cumulative causation

customs duty ◊ *tariff.*

customs union A type of international economic integration of two or more ◊ *states* to create a common ◊ *tariff* area. This is achieved by reciprocal abolition on the part of the states concerned of tariffs and other barriers to ◊ *free trade*. There is free trade within the customs union, and a common external tariff towards states outside. ◊ *common market.*

cut-over area Formerly forested area that was once highly profitable for timber production but because of abuse in the felling/extraction process is no longer productive.

cutpoint A point or ◊ *node* in a graph or ◊ *network* the removal of which creates additional, separate components which do not feature in the original graph. Thus for the graph shown in ◊ Fig. 37 the removal of

point *Z* creates three new components.

The number of new components created as a result of removing a node is its *cutpoint index*. This index accounts for the part played by each node of a network in connecting together that network, i.e. the higher the cutpoint index the more critical the node to the overall ◊ *connectivity* of the network. ◊ *alpha index, beta index, cyclomatic number.*

cycle of human behaviour A conceptual framework, formulated by F. S. Chapin, to demonstrate how individual- or group-held values concerning the use of a particular site or area set in motion a four-phase cycle of behaviour which culminates in the site or area being put to a particular use. The four phases (◊ Fig. 38) are: experiencing needs and wants; defining goals; planning alternatives; deciding and acting.

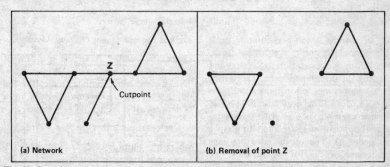

Fig. 37 Cutpoint

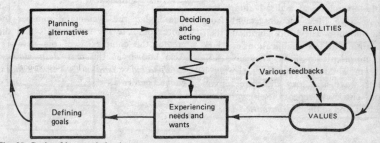

Fig. 38 Cycle of human behaviour

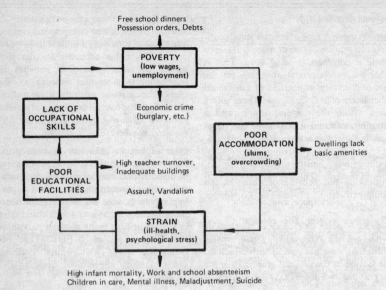

Fig. 39 Cycle of poverty

cycle of poverty A self-perpetuating cycle of social malaise and ◊ *deprivation* transmitted from one generation to the next and reflecting the interdependence of unskilled work, low incomes, poor living conditions and poor educational opportunities (◊ Fig. 39). For example, people with poor educational opportunities are likely to go into unskilled work. The low incomes they earn have consequences for where they can afford to live and the educational opportunities for their children. Their children start school at a disadvantage and may receive little encouragement from their parents. They too complete their education with few qualifications and lack a future-oriented outlook. They have difficulty in obtaining jobs and earning a decent wage and they therefore remain poor. The cycle repeats itself with their children, and so on. ◊ *transmitted deprivation*.

cyclical unemployment ◊ *unemployment*.

cyclomatic number A simple measure of ◊ *connectivity* used in network geometry. The cyclomatic number indicates the number of ◊ *fundamental circuits* in a ◊ *network*. It is measured as follows:

Cyclomatic number $(\mu) = e - v + p$

where e = number of ◊ *links* (routes)
v = number of nodes
p = number of graphs or subgraphs

The higher the cyclomatic number the more complete the connections and the greater the complexity of the network. Also known as the *first Betti number*. ◊ *alpha index, beta index, cutpoint index, gamma index*.

D

daily-life environment A person can only be in one place at a time. Therefore there are only so many opportunities open to a person within a limited time and a limited range of distance. This opportunity set is a person's daily-life environment or *life space*. ⟐ *activity space, contact field*.

daily urban system The concept of an extended urban area defined on the basis of the ebb and flow of daily ◊ *commuting* and activity patterns and representing, therefore, the ◊ *daily-life environment* of the area's residents. The daily urban system develops as the influence of the urban area reaches out, absorbs and reorganizes the surrounding territory. Countries such as the United States and the United Kingdom can be divided into daily urban systems covering most of their national ◊ *space-economy*. ⟐ *laboorshed, metropolitan labour area, urban system*.

dairying An ◊ *agricultural system* involving livestock production on specialist ◊ *farms* for the production of milk and other dairy products. Modern dairying is a product of the last century and reflects the growth of urban incomes, improvements in transport, and advances in science and technology. Specialized dairy farms represent a substantial capital investment but are relatively ◊ *labour intensive* and small in land area. Although dairy farmers enjoy a regular cash income throughout the year, supplementary activities may include pig breeding and the rearing of beef calves.

dam A barrier built across a lake or the course of a river to impound the flow and raise the level of the water, so creating a ◊ *reservoir* for perennial storage (this distinguishes it from a ◊ *barrage*). The supply of water may be used for domestic purposes, for ◊ *irrigation*, for hydroelectricity production, or for maintaining water levels in canals. The dam can also be used to regulate the flow of water as a flood control measure.

Danelaw Those districts in northern and north-east England settled by the Scandinavians in the 9th and 10th centuries and in which Danish customary law subsequently prevailed.

DATAC areas Small areas, outside ◊ *development areas*, revealed in the mild recession of 1958–9 to be suffering severe ◊ *unemployment*. These were designated DATAC areas and were eligible to receive financial assistance towards projected industrial investment under the 1958 Distribution of Industry (Industrial Finance) Act. The designation was withdrawn in 1960 with the passing of the Local Employment Act.

daughter settlement ◊ *mother settlement*.

davoch A unit of agricultural land in Scotland subject to fiscal and military assessment which did not conform with any standard of areal measurement. It was probably the nucleus of a single stretch of arable, becoming in time the equivalent of the ◊ *hide*.

day population The population of residential areas during working hours. It comprises mainly women and children, but also retired and unemployed persons. ⟐ *night population*.

daylight indicators It is generally accepted that buildings where people live and work should receive adequate daylight under average conditions. Daylight indicators are angle controls used for establishing the permissible heights of buildings in relation to surrounding streets and near-by buildings so as to ensure adequate daylighting (amount of daylight falling on the outer face of a building) to the new buildings and to prevent undue diminution of the amount of daylight received by existing buildings and streets. Thus, daylight indicators act as a control on the spacing of buildings on a site. ⟡ *sunlight indicators.*

daylight saving time ⟡ *British Summer Time.*

de facto population Or *enumerated population.* At the time of a ⟡ *census* in the United Kingdom each individual is recorded at the place where he/she is found. The de facto population represents all persons, including visitors, in an area at the time of the census, i.e. the 'present-in-area' population. ⟡ *de jure population.*

de jure population The resident population of an area. Where a ⟡ *census* has been conducted on a de facto population basis, the number of visitors has to be deducted from the population total to find the population normally resident in the area at the time of the census.

de jure space Legally ⟡ *bounded space.*

dead ground An area which is invisible to an observer at a particular point in the field because of the form of the intervening land surface (⟡ Fig. 40)

dead land A term originally suggested by F. T. Aschman to describe blighted vacant land, i.e. sites which remain vacant because of clouded ownership titles, tax delinquencies or obsolete subdivision layouts. ⟡ *blight.*

deadweight tonnage The weight in tons (2,240 lb.) of the cargo, fuel, stores (including fresh water and baggage) and crew on board a merchant ship when down to her safe ⟡ *load line.* It is a measure of the cargo carrying and earning capacity of a ship. ⟡ *displacement tonnage, gross register tonnage, net register tonnage.*

death rates Or *mortality rates.* Death rates are frequently calculated simply as the number of deaths per year as a rate per 1,000 ⟡ *population.* This is the *crude death rate,* i.e.

$$\text{Crude death rate} = \frac{\text{Number of deaths} \times 1,000}{\text{Total (mid-year) population}}$$

It is referred to as a crude rate because it does not consider the age and sex composition of the population at risk and is therefore not a reliable indicator of relative ⟡ *mortality.*

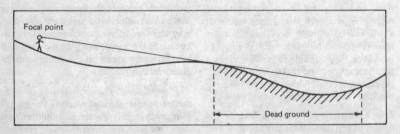

Fig. 40 Dead ground

To overcome this disadvantage *specific death rates* are calculated, either for males and females separately or for different age groups, normally five-year groups, the latter being *age-specific death rates*. The basis of their calculation is the same, i.e. to relate the number of deaths in a year of persons in a specified group to the total number of persons in that group in the mid-year population.

Standardized death rates can be calculated to overcome the effect of regional and urban–rural variations in age composition. The direct method of standardizing death rates is to use the national population as the 'standard' and calculate the death rates which would have occurred if the age composition of the region were identical to that of the nation. Any difference between the standardized death rates and the region's specific death rates would be accounted for by differences in mortality between the two populations. There are two methods – the *comparative mortality figure* (C M F) and the *standardized mortality ratio* (S M R).

$$CMF = \frac{\sum {}^s p_x \cdot {}^a m_x}{\sum {}^s p_x \cdot {}^s m_x} \times 1,000$$

where ${}^s p_x$ = number of people in the standard population of age x

${}^a m_x$ = death rate in the actual regional population at age x

${}^s m_x$ = death rate in the standard population at age x

i.e.

The sum of deaths which would have occurred per age group in the standard population if the death rates of the region had applied

_____

The sum of the total deaths per age group in the standard population

$$SMR = \frac{\sum {}^a p_x \cdot {}^a m_x}{\sum {}^a p_x \cdot {}^s m_x} \times 1,000$$

where ${}^a p_x$ = number of people in the actual regional population at age x

${}^a m_x$ and ${}^s m_x$ as defined above

i.e.

The sum of the total actual deaths per age group in the regional population

_____

The sum of the deaths which would have occurred if the death rates in the region had been those of the standard population

Death rates are influenced by an individual's age and sex, marital status, ◊ *social class*, occupation and ◊ *life style*. ◊ *adult death rate, child mortality rate, infant mortality, life table, mortality, natural change component.*

decay A process, not wholly understood, whereby property declines in appearance and structural stability, and the surrounding area suffers social degeneration. ◊ *blight, economic life of a building, obsolescence.*

decentralization The movement of people, jobs and activities from the centre or core of major ◊ *metropolitan areas* to suburban and outlying locations within their ◊ *daily urban system*, i.e. a phenomenon of intraregional relocation. This spatial relocation is generated by ◊ *centrifugal forces*: within the urban areas demands for increased space and the desire to avoid congestion, pollution, high land values, etc. generate movement to suburban and ◊ *greenfield sites*. This redistribution may be into preplanned zones: ◊ *concentrated decentralization,* ◊ *overspill*. The term is applied to particular types of land use, hence *industrial decentralization, office decentralization.* ◊ *dispersed city, urban sprawl.*

decibel (dB) A logarithmic unit for measuring the relative loudness of noise, i.e. the sound level. The reference level is taken as the quietest sound that can be heard by someone with normal hearing at a frequency of 100 hertz: this reference sound level is 10^{-12} Watts (W). Thus a jet aircraft, 100 m away at take-off, generates a noise of approximately 1W, which is 10^{12} times as powerful as the reference level. It can therefore be said to differ from the reference level by

$$\log\left(\frac{\text{aircraft noise power}}{\text{reference power}}\right) = \log 10^{12} = 12\,\text{bels}.$$

Since bels are too large for convenience decibels are used instead (by introducing a factor of 10). Therefore the jet aircraft has a take-off noise of 120 decibels. ◊ *decibel A-scale, noise indices, perceived noise decibels.*

decibel A-scale (dB(A)) A frequency weighted noise unit, commonly used in the measurement of industrial and traffic ◊ *noise.* The decibel A-scale corresponds approximately to the frequency response of the ear and therefore correlates well with loudness. ◊◊ *corrected noise level, decibel, perceived noise decibels.*

decision environment ◊ *behavioural environment.*

decision-making Goal-seeking persons and organizations are faced with a problem of choice, and decision-making is the process whereby alternative courses of action are evaluated and a decision made as to the appropriate action. A decision-making perspective was introduced into location analysis, particularly industrial location, as part of the 1960s behavioural approach (◊ *behavioural geography*). The decision-making approach stresses that real world (location) decisions are rarely optimal in the sense that profits are maximized or costs incurred minimized.

Geographical case studies have concentrated on determining stages in the decision-making process and the range of factors considered, but the understanding of the decision-making context itself remains limited, even where theoretical frameworks regarding decision-making under conditions of ◊ *risk* and ◊ *uncertainty* are introduced. ◊ *rational model of decision-making, routine decisions, strategic decisions.* ◊◊ *behavioural matrix.*

declining region A ◊ *region* characterized by absolute economic decline, involving the closure of manufacturing and other establishments, the removal of ◊ *capital* and the ◊ *emigration* of labour. ◊◊ *depressed region, downward-transition region.*

deconcentration A type of ◊ *decentralization* in which productive activities are encouraged by the negative ◊ *externalities* of large urban areas to move to smaller places. ◊ *filter-down theory of industrial location.*

dedication scheme A scheme, originally introduced under the 1947 Forestry Act but revamped in 1974, whose purpose is to encourage private landowners to plant/replant and manage their woodlands following plans agreed with the Forestry Commission. Those plans are designed to ensure sound forestry practice, effective integration with agriculture, environmental safeguards and such opportunities for public recreation as may be appropriate. Private landowners enter into a *dedication agreement* via a deed of covenant and in return get a single planting grant (higher rates are paid for broad-leaved trees) plus an annual management grant during the period of establishing the plantation. The scheme also applies to the rehabilitation of existing unproductive woodland by selective planting and natural regeneration. The scheme applies to areas of 10 hectares (25 acres) or more – smaller areas may be eligible for the ◊ *small woods scheme.*

deduction A method of reasoning from principles to facts, i.e. from the general to the particular. Deductive method begins by investigating the principal forces de-

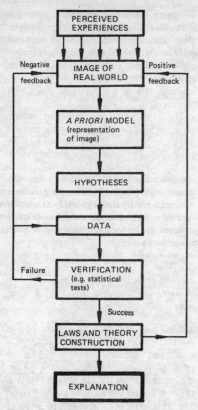

Fig. 41 Deduction

termining a given class of phenomenon and, via logical reasoning, demonstrates that from certain of the premises and propositions all other propositions must follow – it produces general ◊ *laws* and ◊ *theories* in accordance with which such phenomena operate. ◊ Fig. 41 is a simple summary of the deductive method. ◊ *scientific method*. ◊◊ *induction*.

deep seabed The seabed and subsoil beyond the limits of national jurisdiction, i.e. the ◊ *exclusive economic zone*. It is referred to in the United Nations Convention on the Law of the Sea as 'The Area', in which the

resources are designated as part of the Common Heritage of Mankind. Exploitation of those resources is governed via a permit process by the International Seabed Authority, and royalties accruing to that Authority are to be placed in a United Nations fund for economic development. ◊◊ *high seas*.

deepways Underground lines of ◊ *transportation* for private or mass-transit vehicles. It is argued by some planners that a complete system of such lines is indispensable to the solution of urban traffic problems.

deer forest An extensive tract of moorland/upland, usually devoid of trees, managed to provide deer-stalking. ◊◊ *chase*.

defensible space A living, residential ◊ *environment* which can be used by inhabitants for the enhancement of their lives and at the same time provide security for their families, neighbours and friends. ◊◊ *bounded space*.

defensive diversification ◊ *diversification*.

deficiency payment ◊ *guaranteed prices*.

deforestation Or *disafforestation*. A term which is used today to describe the complete felling and clearance of a ◊ *forest* but which in a historical–legal sense meant the freeing of a tract of land from forest law, i.e. the reduction of forest to the status of ordinary land.

deglomeration economies Forces (◊ *diseconomies*, *external diseconomies*) leading to the ◊ *deconcentration* of industrial and other activity from major ◊ *metropolitan areas*. ◊◊ *agglomeration economies*.

degrees of freedom The maximum number of observations or categories that can be freely assigned before all the rest are completely determined. Thus, in very simple terms, if there are 40 observations to be placed in three categories, once 15 observations have been assigned to the first category and 13 to the second, the number of observations in the third category has been determined – with three categories there are 2 degrees of freedom. The number of degrees of freedom represents in some way the size of the sample, or samples, involved in the statistical test: in some tests it is simply the sample size but in others it has to be specially calculated.

de-industrialization The cumulative weakening of the contribution of ♢ *manufacturing industry* to a national economy, whether measured in terms of output, exports, investment or employment. It is the absolute decline in employment in manufacturing which is usually stressed.

delineation well ♢ *appraisal well*.

delivered price The ♢ *price* of a commodity or good delivered to the consumer's location. The extent to which the delivered price quoted to any given consumer reflects the true costs of both production and transport depends on the ♢ *pricing policy* adopted by the supplier.

demand The willingness and ability of ♢ *consumers* to pay for a particular good or service. A *demand curve* is a graphical presentation of a demand function showing how much of a good will be bought per unit of time at any given price,

assuming the other influences governing demand, e.g. income, remain unchanged. With demand on the horizontal axis and price on the vertical axis, the demand curve typically slopes downwards to the right, reflecting the tendency of people to consume less of a good as its ♢ *price* increases.

The terms 'expansion' and 'contraction' of demand describe changes in demand attributable to changes in the price of the good only. The slope of the demand curve at any point reflects the ♢ *elasticity of demand*. The terms 'increase' and 'decrease' in demand are reserved for changes in demand attributable to changes in other factors, e.g. income, since they mean more or fewer goods are demanded at any given price than formerly, i.e. a point on a new demand curve. Market price of a good is determined by the intersection of the demand curve with the ♢ *supply* curve. ♢ *accumulated demand, effective demand, joint demand, option demand*.

demand cone The spatial representation of the relationship between ♢ *demand* for a good and distance from a market or production point. In principle the greater the distance from the market the higher is the ♢ *price* (by the amount of the freight) and consequently the smaller the quantity

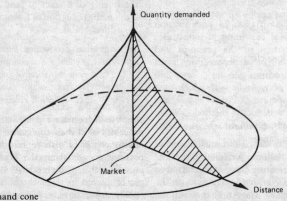

Fig. 42 Demand cone

demanded. Thus each market/supply point is surrounded by a demand cone (◊ Fig. 42). ◊◊ *price funnel.*

demand curve ◊ *demand.*

demand-deficient unemployment ◊ *unemployment.*

demesne That part of the ◊ *manor* lands which the lord had not granted out but retained for his own use. It might or might not be intermingled with his tenant's holdings in the ◊ *open field.* The demesne land was cultivated directly for profit by the lord using *villein labour.* The latter system declined from the 14th century as services were commuted to rent payments; as the corn hectarage was reduced; as the demand for land to rent, and hence, rents, increased; and as it became difficult to find good reeves and bailiffs.

demilitarized area ◊ *neutral zone.*

demographic ageing A change in the age structure of a population whereby the proportion of old people (those over sixty or sixty-five years of age) in the total population increases. ◊◊ *old-age index.*

demographic coefficient A crude index intended to give a measure of the future ◊ *population pressure* in an area by relating existing ◊ *population density* and population increase. Since there are alternative ways of measuring population increase, the demographic coefficient may be calculated in two ways:

Demographic coefficient either, $= dR$

where d = population density
R = ◊ *net reproduction rate*

or $\quad = dt$

where t = rate of ◊ *natural increase*/1,000 population

demographic index A combinatorial measure, representing ◊ *population density* and growth rates, ◊ *birth* and ◊ *death rates,* ◊ *infant mortality* rates, and population

density in cultivated areas, developed by B. J. L. Berry in his factor analysis of ◊ *development* variables. ◊◊ *technological index.*

demographic relaxation theory The theory that ◊ *overpopulation* causes war. When people lack space or ◊ *territory* they are held to feel a need to spread out and take the land and wealth of others. Even if they do not succeed, the losses incurred would reduce the population, bringing everything back to 'normal'. War, therefore, is seen as having a social function of demographic relaxation.

demographic response theory An attempt to explain modern demographic history in terms of 'multiphasic' response. The theory postulates that the increase in a population's natural growth rate (which in turn is the result of a secular decline in mortality) creates a series of responses – delayed marriage, increased celibacy, ◊ *abortion,* ◊ *contraception,* and overseas and rural–urban ◊ *migration* – designed to maintain the population's rising prosperity. Empirical support is deduced from the population histories of north-west European countries and Japan. ◊◊ *demographic transition.*

demographic revolution A term used to describe the widespread adoption, originating in 18th-century France, of the use of contraceptive methods in marriage. ◊◊ *birth control, contraception.*

demographic transition The demographic transition is a general model of changes through time in ◊ *vital rates.* It is regarded as the modern ◊ *population cycle,* being based on the experience of developed countries which have passed through the processes of ◊ *industrialization* and ◊ *urbanization.* It is also represented as the path of escape from the ◊ *Malthusian population cycle.* The model (◊ Fig. 43) suggests four phases:

(1) The *high stationary phase,* during which

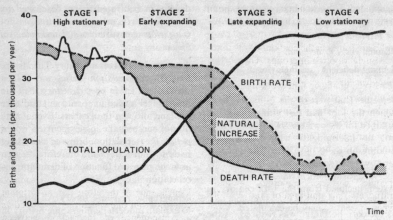

Fig. 43 Demographic transition

both ◊ *birth* and ◊ *death rates* are high and total population remains at a low, fluctuating level. The fluctuations are due to erratic changes in the death rate as a result of famine, war and disease.

(2) The *early expanding phase*, which sees a continuing high birth rate but a steady decline in the death rate, hence ◊ *life expectancy* increases and total population expands at an increasing rate. The fall in the death rate is the result of improved and more reliable nutrition, improved medicine and sanitation, and greater political stability which reduces the incidence of wars.

(3) The *late expanding phase*, which witnesses the stabilization of the death rate at a low level and a reduction in the birth rate as society becomes industrialized and urbanized. The rate of total population expansion is slowed down.

(4) The *low stationary phase*, by which time both birth and death rates have stabilized at a low level and total population is again stationary but at a high level. Some fluctuation in the birth rate may be experienced.

The demographic transition is sometimes referred to as *Thompson–Notestein theory* after W. S. Thompson, who drew attention to the differences between population structures of major world regions, and F. W. Notestein, who developed demographic transition theory more fully. ◊ *demographic response theory.*

demography The scientific and statistical study of ◊ *population*, and in particular the size of populations, their development and structure. It therefore focuses on the empirical, mathematical and statistical analysis of ◊ *births* and ◊ *fertility*, ◊ *deaths* and ◊ *mortality*, and ◊ *migration* processes and their effects on population size, structure, composition and distribution, and on the causes and consequences of changes in these variables. ◊ *demographic transition, population accounts, population equation, population policy, population theory.* ◊ *demographic relaxation theory, dependency ratio, family, marriage rate, nuptiality, net reproduction rate.*

dendogram ◊ *linkage tree.*

dene hole A narrow shaft up to 6·25 m (20 ft) deep, ending in a bell-shaped chamber or series of chambers and galleries. Dene holes are found in the chalklands of southern England, often in groups. Their origin is uncertain but most probably they are marl pits, chalk or flint workings, dating from the ◊ *Stone Age*. A more romantic explanation, but less plausible, is that they are 'Dane holes' – hiding-places for property during the Danish invasions of the 7th and 8th centuries.

density A measure of the number of items (people, workers, buildings, animals, traffic, etc.) per unit area of land. Various types of density may be calculated: ◊ *agricultural density, comparative density, employee density, employment density, network density, physiological density, population density, residential density, traffic density.* ◊◊ *carrying capacity, density gradient, density–size rule, floor space index, land absorption coefficient, man–land ratio, occupancy rate, persons per room, plot ratio, space standards.*

density gradient The rate at which intensity of land use falls off with increasing distance from some central point. A density gradient therefore describes a pattern of ◊ *distance decay.* A theoretical justification can be deduced from spatial models such as the ◊ *Alonso* and ◊ *von Thünen models,* but most attention has concentrated upon intra-urban population density gradients. Following the empirical study of urban areas throughout the world, Colin Clark proposed a negative exponential form for the rate of population density decreases at a decreasing rate with increasing distance from the city centre.

density–size rule A relationship, noted by R. H. Best on the basis of empirical evidence, between urban size (expressed in population terms) and intensity of land use: namely, as the population size or urban area increases the ◊ *land provision* (hectares/1,000 population) declines exponentially, i.e. the ◊ *density* of development in persons per hectare rises at a decreasing rate.

dependence A conditional relationship, especially between two or more ◊ *states/ societies,* which implies dependence in the sense of the dominance of one state over another, or even the control by one state of another, as in ◊ *colonialism* and ◊ *imperialism.* Hence the ability of one state/ society to function and develop derives, in large measure, from its links with another dominant, imperialist state/society. Dependence is therefore not an original condition but one which has developed as a consequence of interaction between states/societies.

dependency A territory subject to rule by another ◊ *state.* The term, or even *dependent territory,* is now commonly used in place of colony.

dependency ratio The number of children (aged under 14) and old people (aged 60 or 65 and over) in a population as a ratio of the number of adults (aged 15–59/64).

$$\text{Dependency ratio} = \frac{\text{Children } (<14) + \text{aged } (>60 \text{ or } 65)}{\text{Adults } (15\text{–}64)}$$

It is a useful comparative indicator of the proportion of the population that those employed or potentially active (◊ *active population, working population*) have to support. ◊◊ *dependent population.*

dependency ties M. M. Webber's term for the ◊ *linkages* relating individuals, groups, firms and other entities to one another when viewing the city as an operating system. These dependency ties are the invisible relations that bring various interdependent business establishments, households, voluntary groups and personal friends into working associations with each other.

dependent population The total ◊ *population* of an area less the ◊ *working population*, i.e. those of pre-school and school age, the retired, others in full-time education, etc. ◊ *dependency ratio*.

depletion In the context of resource use, a reduction in the total amount of a ◊ *resource* ultimately available for use by society. ◊ *depletion policy*.

depletion policy Government policy concerned with establishing guidelines as to how fast society should be using up its ◊ *resources*, particularly exhaustible or non-renewable ones. Attempts to formulate depletion policies imply that an optimal depletion rate – i.e. a rate of use which is better than all others, neither too fast, nor too slow – can be determined for the extraction and consumption of such resources. There are, however, problems in identifying such rates in practice, because the technically optimal rate may differ from the broader, economically optimal rate of use which, in turn, will differ from a narrowly commercial or profit-maximizing rate, and because of the difficulty of ensuring equity between generations. ◊ *resource management*.

depopulation The decline in the total ◊ *population* of an area. The term should be reserved for those areas where numbers are diminishing absolutely. It is normally applied only to rural areas (◊ *rural depopulation*).

depreciative behaviour Actions or behaviour which violate societal or institutional norms. The term covers a variety of formal and informal 'rule' violations, e.g. from dropping litter in public places to vandalism in recreational and other areas.

depressed area, depressed region A ◊ *region* that has already achieved a high level of industrial development but now is in a state of economic depression compared with other regions or with some national norm. Typically a problem region of advanced industrial nations. ◊ *declining region, downward-transition region*.

deprivation In modern society poverty cannot be judged in absolute terms. Deprivation is a relative term which reflects the view that people can be said to be deprived when they lack the resources to obtain the types of diet, to participate in the activities and have the living conditions and amenities which are customary, or are at least widely encouraged or approved, in the societies to which they belong. Thus persons may suffer a sense of deprivation when there are other people who are demonstrably better off than themselves and with whom they may be compared, even though they are not objectively deprived in the more usual sense of having to go without completely. ◊ *multiple deprivation, transmitted deprivation*.

derelict land Legally, derelict land should be interpreted as land which has been abandoned by its owner but, more commonly, it is taken to mean land which has been so damaged by extractive or other industrial processes, and/or by serious neglect, that it is unsightly in its existing state and is incapable of beneficial use without undergoing remedial treatment. The latter interpretation involves the problem of reconciling economic and aesthetic approaches, since (a) land which may appear spoiled or degraded may not be economically derelict, e.g. a waste tip at a coal mine still in use, and (b) land which may be economically derelict need not give offence to the eye, e.g. neglected scrub woodland. K. L. Wallwork subdivides derelict land into three categories:

(i) *Extant dereliction*, i.e. land now derelict, as officially defined.

(ii) *Potential dereliction*, i.e. land that will become derelict, on cessation of the present use, unless some remedial action is taken, e.g. mineral workings.

(iii) *Partial dereliction*, i.e. land in the initial stages of degradation, e.g. land damaged by mining subsidence, and land which has been derelict and, although never reclaimed, has been put to other uses, e.g. a worked-out quarry used for tipping. ◊ *derelict land clearance area.*

derelict land clearance area Rates of grant and territorial coverage of state aid in the United Kingdom to assist local authorities with the acquisition and reclamation of ◊ *derelict land* have changed several times since 1949. Derelict land clearance areas are specially designated areas, first introduced in the early 1970s, in which special aid is available from central government to help tackle the derelict land problem.

desalination The process by which the dissolved solids in sea or saline water are partially or completely removed to make the water suitable for domestic, agricultural or industrial use. The main techniques used are distillation, electrodialysis, freezing and reverse osmosis.

descriptive statistics ◊ *Statistics* that describe a situation or survey population in quantitative terms. Data are described numerically so that their magnitude and spread can be expressed meaningfully and concisely, e.g. ◊ *central tendency* and ◊ *dispersion* measures, and ◊ *index numbers.* ◊ *exploratory statistics, inferential statistics.*

descriptive theory ◊ *positive theory.*

deserted village Or *lost village.* A settlement whose name appears in early records but which is no longer inhabited. Traces of the deserted village can still be found in the modern landscape, e.g. an isolated church; masonry lumps embedded in the meadows; roughly rectangular mounds in linear hollows in a field; or, perhaps, a prolific growth of nettles. Such villages may have been overcome by disaster, e.g. bubonic plague, or suffered from ◊ *depopulation*

consequent upon ◊ *enclosure* and ◊ *engrossing.* More than 1,300 deserted villages have been identified in England, mainly in the Midlands and the eastern half of the country where ◊ *open fields*, arable cultivation and late enclosure were characteristic. There are considerable numbers elsewhere in the British Isles, but their sites are more difficult to find.

desertification The spread of desert-type conditions in arid and semi-arid regions. Although climatic change is a possible cause, it is thought that increasing human pressures are a major factor in the rapid expansion of desert conditions in the marginal areas around the true deserts. Thus, overgrazing, supplemented by wood-cutting for fuel, by vegetation clearance for cultivation and by burning, lead to the removal of organic material, to the breakdown of soil structure and hence increased loss of rainfall by direct surface evaporation, and to soil erosion, deflation and dune reactivation.

design speed A speed selected for design purposes which will determine those features of a ◊ *road* – such as curvature, super-elevation and sight distance – upon which the safe operation of vehicles depends.

design standard ◊ *specification standard.*

designative perception Those ◊ *perceptions* that people have of the ◊ *attributes* of places which are devoid of any evaluation of those attributes, e.g. town A is a long way from here, or town B is located on the coast, or town C has a cold climate. ◊ *appraisive perception.*

desire line A straight line (i.e. shortest) connection between two locations representing the origin and destination of a trip. Also termed a *dyad.* The number of desire lines connecting two locations is an indication of the intensity of demand for

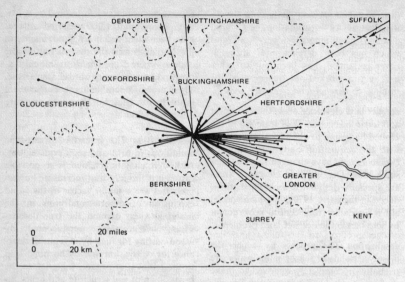

Fig. 44 Desire line: origins of visitors to Cowleaze Woods (summer Sunday afternoon, 1976)

movement between those two locations, as shown in ◊ Fig. 44. ◊◊ *flow line*.

determination, coefficient of ◊ *coefficient of determination*.

determinism The philosophical doctrine that all human action is not free but directly controlled by some ◊ *law* or force that elicits a particular reaction, i.e. there is an inevitability of occurrence of some set of events or relationships due to the influence of physical conditions (◊ *environmental determinism*) or economic forces (◊ *economic determinism*).

deterministic A term describing a viewpoint which asserts, usually under specified conditions, that the relationships between phenomena are invariant and which may therefore be expressed symbolically – if *x*, then *y* and only *y*, i.e. every time a particular event (*x*) occurs, another particular event or prescribed sequence of events (*y*) is certain to follow. ◊◊ *causal analysis*, *probabilistic*.

deterministic model ◊ *model*.

detour index A measure of how directly movement may be made on a ◊ *network*. It is calculated as the ratio of the shortest actual ◊ *route* distance between a given pair of ◊ *nodes* and the direct, straight-line or ◊ *geodesic distance* between the same two nodes, i.e.

$$\text{Detour index} = \frac{\substack{\text{Shortest distance} \\ \text{on network} \\ \text{between 2 nodes}}}{\text{Direct distance}} \times 100$$

The minimum value of the index is 100, representing a direct route with no detour: high ratios suggest a weakly connected network but may also reflect the indirectness or deviousness of the individual routes connecting nodes.

Also referred to as the *index of circuity* and as the *route factor*. ◊◊ *alpha index*, *beta index*, *cyclomatic number*, *gamma index*, *König number*, *Shimbel index*.

devaluation An official reduction in the

value of a national currency in terms of gold and other currencies.

development (1) In a ◊ *planning* context, development is defined in the United Kingdom under the Town and Country Planning Acts as the carrying-out of building, engineering, mining or other operations in, on, over or under the land or the making of any material changes in the use of any buildings or other land. ◊◊ *development control, land conversion process.*
(2) In a wider meaning development is a process of becoming larger, more mature or better organized. Ideally such a process is indigenous and without internal conflict in the sense that human beings and societies progress to the fullest possible extent under conditions of their own free choosing. The term is used, however, in an economic and social context to describe the state of nations and the historical processes of change experienced by them, e.g. from a geographical viewpoint the extent to which the natural resources of a nation have been brought into productive use. Thus a particular set of characteristics are viewed as indicators of the level of development. In the narrowest sense the characteristics are those which signify ◊ *economic growth* and describe the stages by which a nation progresses from a subsistence agricultural base to an advanced industrial society (◊◊ *development stages theory of growth, industrialization*). In addition to the usual economic measures (such as per capita levels of and rates of increase of production and consumption) the concept of development now subsumes associated social, cultural and political changes, as well as welfare measures which reflect distribution of goods, wealth and opportunities within a nation. ◊◊ *least developed countries, modernization, Rostow model.*

Development Area An area or region in the United Kingdom scheduled by the gov-

ernment to receive aid through ◊ *positive discrimination* under ◊ *regional policy*, i.e. an ◊ *area-based policy* favouring regions of below average economic performance. Essentially the first Development Areas were ◊ *depressed regions* in the 1930s and were defined in the 1945 Distribution of Industry Act on the basis of the earlier ◊ *special areas.* Significant changes have been made since 1945 in the nature and level of financial and infrastructural aid available and in the spatial extent of the areas covered (◊◊ *intermediate area, special development area*). In addition to the positive inducements to investment in Development Areas, negative controls on the location of new activity in non-development areas have been in force at various times (◊ *industrial development certificate, office development permit*).

development bottleneck Key factors, situations or conditions that obstruct ◊ *development* even though other conditions would permit it. In a region with good labour supplies and natural resource endowment a lack of local leadership or capital investment could inhibit the region's development.

development charge The 1947 Town and Country Planning Act nationalized development rights and the associated ◊ *development values* and imposed development charges on developers of land (compensation was also payable to those who lost development rights). All owners were therefore placed in the position of owning only the existing (1947) use rights and values in their land (◊ *existing use value*). Developers were to pay a development charge amounting to 100% of the increase in the value of land resulting from ◊ *development* permitted as a result of the granting of ◊ *planning permission.* Development charges were seen as an effective method of collecting ◊ *betterment*, but owing to the practical difficulties of operating the scheme and its effects on the land market they were abolished in 1953.

development continuum A term used by B. W. Hodder to stress that ◊ *development* depends on a total or balanced ◊ *economic system.* Development over time, space and sectors is a highly related process, the components of which are inextricably linked. No one sector of economic activity should be over-emphasized as a panacea for development. Thus Hodder suggests that any division between agricultural and industrial sectors is probably false and arbitrary, since a large part of the industrial sector depends on agriculture for its raw materials and is aimed at feeding back into agriculture its products and techniques. Moreover, after a certain threshold in the development of agricultural systems the feedback of technology from industry to agriculture is crucial.

development control The process by which local planning authorities exercise their statutory duty to control all ◊ *development* in accordance with the provisions of their ◊ *development plans* (◊◊ *local plan, structure plan*). The control is possible by virtue of the obligation upon all developers to seek ◊ *planning permission* for new development. ◊◊ *completion notice, enforcement notice, general development order, stop notice, use classes order.*

development corridor A special case of an ◊ *upward-transition region* that connects two ◊ *core regions.*

development districts Small areas, based on employment exchange areas, designated under the 1960 Local Employment Act by the government to receive aid through ◊ *positive discrimination* under ◊ *regional policy.* The criterion for delineation was primarily the existence of an ◊ *unemployment* rate greater than $4\frac{1}{2}\%$. Development districts replaced ◊ *development areas* only between 1960 and 1966 as the

spatial units singled out by an ◊ *area-based policy* favouring regions of below average economic performance.

development plan A development plan comprises a series of documents containing a local planning authority's main objectives for land use in its area over a period of years. Development plans were introduced under the 1947 Town and Country Planning Act: '1947 type' development plans indicated the manner in which local planning authorities proposed that land in their area should be used, whether by ◊ *development* or not, and the stages by which any such development should be carried out. It was required that the plan should define sites of proposed roads, public and other buildings and works, airfields, parks, pleasure grounds, nature reserves and other open spaces, or allocate areas of land for agricultural, industrial, residential or other purposes. The plans were subject to ministerial approval and to review every five years.

The system of development plans and ◊ *development control* set up under the 1947 Act operated for two decades without significant change, but a system appropriate for the mid-1940s tended to develop its own rigidities in the face of the increasing tempo of economic and social change. This was particularly true of development plans, which acquired a misleading appearance of certainty and stability, as well as proving difficult to keep up to date. Consequently the system was revised by the 1968 Town and Country Planning Act: the respective roles of central and local government were redefined and a framework provided for a greater degree of ◊ *public participation.* In essence the new approach (predicated on the reorganization of local government into unitary authorities) was to give a single authority responsibility for preparing a broad strategic ◊ *structure plan*, within which detailed ◊ *local plans* were elaborated and development control administered. The development plan for an area now includes the structure plan and any alterations to it with the Minister's notice of approval, together with any local plans and alterations to them with the local planning authority's resolution of adoption.

development region J. Friedmann's term for ◊ *planning region*.

development stages theory of growth Or *sector theory of growth*. A theory suggesting a sequential path of ◊ *development* through which all nations would progress, reflected in changes in the dominant occupation of the ◊ *labour force* consequent upon changes in ◊ *comparative costs* and changes in income ◊ *elasticities of demand*. Thus a rise in per capita income in different areas at different times has generally been accompanied by a resource reallocation, with a decline in the proportion of the labour force engaged in ◊ *primary activities*, and a rise first in ◊ *secondary* and then in ◊ *tertiary* and ◊ *quaternary activities*. It is argued that the rate of occurrence of such sector shifts, and the resultant internal evolution of ◊ *specialization* and ◊ *division of labour*, provide the main dynamic of ◊ *economic growth* in an area. The rate of shift in the relative importance of different sectors is explained by the income elasticities of demand for their products and by different rates of change in labour productivity. As incomes rise, the demand for products supplied by the secondary, tertiary and quaternary sectors rises faster than the demand for primary products, and these sectors therefore grow faster.

This sector explanation may be extended into a stage theory version:
(1) In the first stage a region has a self-sufficient ◊ *subsistence economy*, with little investment or trade, in which the basic agricultural population is distributed according to the localization of natural resources.
(2) With improvements in transport, the region develops trade and specialization.

A second stratum develops carrying on simple village industries to serve agriculture.
(3) With increasing inter-regional trade, the region progresses through a succession of agricultural crops from extensive grazing to cereals to dairying and horticulture.
(4) Increasing population, allied to diminishing agricultural returns, forces the region to develop secondary activity, i.e. to industrialize.
(5) The final stage witnesses the development of tertiary and quaternary activity producing for export. ◊ *economic base theory, Rostow model*.

development value The potential value of a site or land if it were to be developed to its ◊ *highest and best use*. Where a site has development or redevelopment potential the market price it will command will therefore be greater than its ◊ *existing use value*.

development well After ◊ *wildcat* and ◊ *appraisal wells* have proven crude oil or natural gas to be present in economically workable quantities in a discovery, further wells drilled into the same reservoir are termed development wells. ◊ *directional drilling*.

devolution The process by which the central government of a ◊ *state* transfers certain powers to individual political sub-units within its ◊ *territory*. It is most often considered where linguistic and cultural minorities seek a degree of political ◊ *autonomy* within a state.

dewpond A pond constructed to maintain a supply of drinking water, particularly for livestock, in an area of high permeability such as chalk or limestone country. Dewponds are scooped-out hollows, 19·5 m to 29·5 m (20 to 30 yd) across, traditionally lined with puddled clay and flints, although modern ones are lined with plastic sheeting. The oldest probably date from the 17th century. The water supply is not maintained by dew, being more dependent upon rain (and today even artificial supply).

diachronic analysis The study of the processes by which changes in one component of a ◊ *system* are transmitted throughout that system. In geography such processes of change and transformation have been studied in traditional ◊ *historical geography* by the reconstruction of a course of events as a ◊ *vertical theme*, but more formal analytical procedures deriving from ◊ *systems analysis* have recently been applied throughout geography. ◊ *synchronic analysis*.

diagonal linkage ◊ *linkage*.

dialectic The investigation of truths by systematic reasoning in which contradictions or opposites are synthesized. It proceeds from an assertion, or thesis, to a denial, or antithesis, and finally reconciles the two through a synthesis. The synthesis then forms a new thesis, i.e. each resolution produces its own contradiction, and the process is repeated until an ultimate, universal synthesis is reached.

differential rent ◊ *Marxist theory of rent*.

diffusion The spread or movement of a phenomenon over space and through time. Studies of diffusion in modern geography, stimulated by the work of T. Hägerstrand

in the 1960s, include the movement of migrants, the spread of settlements, innovations, information, crops and diseases. Diffusion processes have been distinguished (◊ Fig. 45) on the basis of either the character of the dispersal, i.e. expansion or relocation, or the structural character, i.e. contagious or hierarchical.

Expansion (or *expansive*) *diffusion* is a process of transmission through a population from one location to neighbouring locations or decision points. In this expansion the phenomenon being diffused remains, and is often intensified, in the originating location, with new members being added to the population in such a way as to alter the spatial pattern of the population as a whole. Expansion diffusion can be subdivided:

(i) *Contagious* or *epidemic diffusion* involves transmission processes that depend upon direct contact. The spread takes place in a centrifugal manner from the source location(s) outwards in a pattern which emphasizes the importance of proximity and interaction between actual adopters (acceptors, infectors, etc.) and potential adopters.

(ii) *Cascade diffusion* describes a process that transmits a phenomenon through a system of ordered centres, locations or decision points and is commonly termed *hierarchical diffusion* by geographers when

Structural character \\ Dispersal character	EXPANSION	RELOCATION
CONTAGIOUS	*e.g. spread of agricultural innovation amongst farmers in a region*	*e.g. migratory labour*
HIERARCHICAL	*e.g. spread of clothing fashions and popular music*	*e.g. filter-down relocation of manufacturing firms*

Fig. 45 Diffusion: types of processes

specifying movement upward or downward in a ◊ *hierarchy*, e.g. innovations which occur primarily in large central places diffuse horizontally between centres of the same level in the central place system and vertically down the hierarchy to smaller central places.

Relocation diffusion is in essence a similar process, but the phenomenon being diffused evacuates the old location(s) as it moves to new locations, i.e. its movement pattern comprises successive relocations that may by-pass certain potential locations. Relocation diffusion has been modelled on both an industry-specific basis (emphasizing the importance of the sectoral, technical–economic environment of the industry for the speed and extent of the transmission process, and reflecting the degree of market concentration, size structure of firms, etc.) and a firm-specific basis (emphasizing the internal characteristics of firms, such as management attitudes, information interrelationships, etc.). ◊ *diffusion barriers, epidemic models, paracmastic process.*

diffusion barriers All processes of ◊ *diffusion* may be affected by barriers which either absorb or stop diffusion processes or reflect and channel those processes. Diffusion barriers are therefore used to model the reduction in transmission or interaction. In most cases diffusion barriers are 'permeable' rather than absolute, allowing part of the energy or message of the diffusion pulse to go through. There are four types of barrier, in decreasing order of blocking effectiveness (◊ Fig. 46):

(i) *Superabsorbing barriers*, which absorb new contacts and destroy original transmitters.

(ii) *Absorbing barriers*, which absorb new contacts but leave original transmitters intact.

(iii) *Reflecting barriers*, which absorb new contacts but allow the transmitter to make another contact in the same time period.

(iv) *Direct reflecting barriers*, which do not absorb contacts but reflect them randomly.

In practice diffusion barriers do not

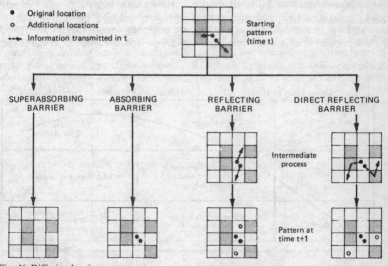

Fig. 46 Diffusion barriers

have to be real, in the form of physical features, but only perceived.

diffusion wave ◊ *innovation wave.*

diffusionism An anthropological concept, prevalent around 1900, that all ◊ *cultures* shared a common origin, with civilization being passed on along trade routes and through tribal contact, gradually spreading out from a single cultural centre. The concept was based on the assumption that human beings were naturally uninventive and, therefore, that parallel evolution was rare.

digitizing The translation of an analogue line, such as an areal boundary or a river, into discrete digital co-ordinates. The resultant co-ordinate sets are suitable for use in computer-assisted ◊ *cartography.*

diminishing returns Or *law of variable proportions* or *law of proportionality.* A physical principle, applicable to any productive system, that whenever successive inputs of a (variable) ◊ *factor of production* are added to a limited fixed factor a point is soon reached after which the additional or marginal output of the product per unit of input decreases. The

law relates to quantities per unit of time. It can be stated more precisely: If the quantity of one factor of production is increased by equal increments, from zero, the quantities of other factors of production remaining fixed, the resulting increments of output, or marginal product, will increase at first, reach a peak and then diminish. As ◊ Fig. 47 illustrates, every ◊ *production function* involves three points of diminishing returns: the total product increases at an increasing rate until the marginal product reaches its peak. From this point on the marginal product diminishes, while the total product continues to increase but at a decreasing rate. The total product reaches a maximum at the same point as the marginal product becomes zero – any addition of variable inputs beyond this point results in a negative marginal product and a decrease in total product. The average product reaches a maximum at the point at which it intersects the declining marginal product curve and remains positive so long as there is any total product.

Nature and technology often impose such constraints on productive activities by restricting the availability of ◊ *land,* ◊ *labour* and ◊ *capital.* ◊ *Entrepreneurs*

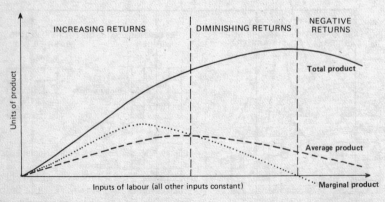

Fig. 47 Diminishing returns

should be aware that such contraints will make certain factor combinations become at first more and then increasingly less productive. ⟡ *economies of scale.*

direct contact space ⟡ *activity space.*

direct marketing A term used in ⟡ *agriculture* to cover farm-door sales, farm shops, roadside stalls, mobile shop deliveries, urban market stalls and 'pick-your-own', i.e. direct selling by farmer to consumer, cutting out any 'middle man'. ⟡ *marketing.*

direct reflecting barrier ⟡ *diffusion barrier.*

directional drilling A technique of drilling oil or gas wells from an offshore drilling platform that starts with a vertical bore diverted by as much as 60° from the vertical (⟡ Fig. 48). As many as forty wells

may be drilled from a single platform, so enabling a wide area of the oil or gas field to be exploited, lowering the cost of drilling and minimizing interference with other uses of the seas. ⟡ *development wells.*

Dirichlet polygons Polygons having the geometric property of containing within them areas that are nearer to the enclosed point (centre) around which they are constructed than to any other given point (centre). They are constructed (⟡ Fig. 49) by

(a) Lines drawn to connect adjacent points

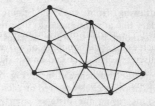

(b) Mid-points of lines

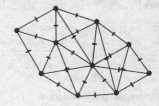

(c) Dirichlet polygons

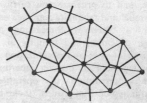

Fig. 49 Dirichlet polygons via inter-point lines

(i) drawing lines from each point to each adjacent point, (ii) bisecting each of these inter-point lines to give its mid-point, and

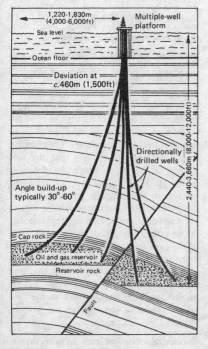

Fig. 48 Directional drilling

129

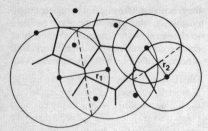

Fig. 50 Dirichlet polygons using intersecting circles

(iii) drawing from each mid-point a boundary line at right-angles to the original inter-point line to create a series of convex polygons. Such polygons give a median-line division of space. An alternative method of delineation (◊ Fig. 50) involves drawing circles centred on each of the points, using the distance apart as radius. The side of the polygon between the two points is located by drawing a line through the points of intersection of the circles.

Dirichlet polygons, also referred to as *Thiessen polygons* or *Voronoi polygons*, are used in the description of point patterns and especially to define spheres of influence, as around urban centres.

disafforestation ◊ *deforestation.*

disaster preparedness Action which is designed to minimize loss of life and damage, and to organize and carry out rescue, relief and rehabilitation in cases of disaster. It involves forecasting and warning; education and training of the population at risk; and organization for and management of disaster situations, including preparation of operational plans, training of relief groups, stockpiling of supplies and earmarking of funds. ◊ *disaster prevention.* ◊◊ *natural hazard.*

disaster prevention Measures designed to prevent natural phenomena from causing or resulting in disaster or other emergency situations. It involves the formulation of long-range policies and programmes, including legislation and regulatory measures, to prevent or eliminate the occurrence of disasters. ◊ *disaster preparedness.* ◊◊ *natural hazard.*

discontinuance order A power available to a local planning authority to serve notice on an activity/land user to discontinue the existing use of a site. An order can be made 'if it appears to a local planning authority that it is expedient in the interests of the proper planning of their area'. The order requires ministerial confirmation and involves compensation being paid to the user. Under this power action can be taken against any ◊ *development* (or use), but it would appear that an order will be confirmed only where the case is a strong one, e.g. a ◊ *non-conforming activity* creating a major nuisance. ◊◊ *revocation order.*

discordant boundary ◊ *boundary.*

discounted cash flow A common economic technique used to evaluate the relative profitability of alternative projects. There are two variants – the net yield and net present value methods. Both base their evaluation of a project on the present cash value of a sum(s) to be received at some future date(s) (◊ *discounting*). The criterion in the net yield method is that the best project is that from which the proceeds would yield the highest rate of compound interest in equating the present value of the project with future proceeds. In the net present value method an appropriate discount rate is stipulated: the present value of the cash inflow is determined using this rate, and the original cost of the project is subtracted therefrom. The resulting surplus is the net present value of the project and the best project is the one which generates the highest net present value.

discounting, discount rate In any investment the distribution of costs and benefits through time is important. In order to decide whether an investment is worthwhile the present value of forecast revenues and cost flows through time needs to be established. That present value is determined by discounting and is such an amount as will, with compound interest at a prescribed rate, equal the sum(s) to be received or the cost(s) to be incurred in the future. The prescribed rate is the discount rate and there are two major conceptual approaches to the determination of the appropriate discount rate, which may be either a social ◊ *time preference rate* (a normative measure of the relative value of present and future consumption) or a social ◊ *opportunity cost* (which allows for the displacement of alternative investment). ◊◊ *cost–benefit analysis*, *discounted cash flow*, *net present value method*.

discouraged worker hypothesis A view held by certain labour economists that high and persistent periods of ◊ *unemployment* are characterized by withdrawals from the ◊ *labour* force of workers who feel there is little prospect of their obtaining work in the near future. Such workers may only re-enter the labour force when job prospects improve markedly. ◊◊ *additional worker hypothesis*.

discovery–depletion cycle A concept applicable to the exploitation of ◊ *non-renewable resources*, especially minerals, which recognizes that the limit to the use of such a resource is a finite quantity. The discovery–depletion cycle, or *exploitation cycle* or *production depletion curve* as it is alternatively called, represents a generalized exploitation pattern (◊ Fig. 51) and is based on observed relationships over time between the variables of cumulative discoveries, cumulative production and ◊ *proven reserves*. Six stages are recognized: discovery; development; rapid expansion (as discovery rate outstrips production rate); mature or peak production (as rate of discovery of new reserves falls); decline (as reserves are depleted consumption falls); and exhaustion. The cycle is experienced for the resource as a whole, as well as for particular mining districts and individual mines. The passage of the cycle may be extremely erratic and the length of the normal cycle highly variable.

discrete variable A ◊ *variable* in which the possible values are clearly separated from one another, e.g. family size. ◊◊ *continuous variable*.

discretionary time ◊ *leisure*.

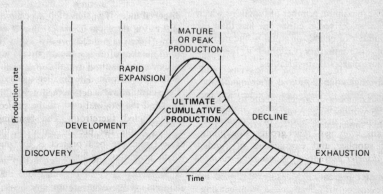

Fig. 51 Discovery–depletion cycle

discriminant (discriminatory) analysis A procedure developed in response to problems of indecision encountered in ◇ *classification* where certain cases could conceivably belong to more than one class. Some method of discriminating among the given classes and of facilitating the classification of new cases with the least likelihood of error was required. Thus discriminant analysis statistically distinguishes between two or more groups of cases in which the researcher selects a collection of discriminating (independent) ◇ *variables* that measure characteristics on which the groups are expected to differ. The mathematical objective of discriminant analysis is to weight and to combine linearly the discriminating variables so as to ensure that the groups or classes are as statistically distinct as possible. This is done by forming one or more linear combinations of the independent variables. Discriminant functions are of the form:

$$D_i = d_i1Z_1 + d_i2Z_2 + \ldots d_ipZp$$

where D_i = score on the discriminant function i

d = weighting coefficient

Z = standardized value of the p discriminating variables used in the analysis

The maximum number of functions which can be derived is either one less than the number of classes or equal to the number of discriminatory variables if there are more classes than variables.

discrimination ◇ *positive discrimination*.

diseconomies A general term to describe the diminishing returns or profitability that sometimes result from greater size, as in the case of a city, or greater output, as in the case of a plant. ◇ *external diseconomies*. ◈ *economies of scale*.

disgavelling ◇ *gavelkind*.

disguised unemployment ◇ *unemployment*.

disintegration A term used to describe a ◇ *firm*'s or ◇ *establishment*'s response to internal pressures for growth which involves splitting off parts of the production process to separate firms or establishments. Such disintegration may be *vertical* – in which case either the earlier or the later stages in a production process are split off – or *horizontal* – in which case the production process is replicated in the new firm/establishment in a location which serves a new market. ◈ *integration*.

disjointed incrementalism A term used in a planning context to describe a situation or strategy of 'muddling through'. The approach of this strategy is not the realization of some long-term goal but the solution of immediate, pressing problems. It therefore represents a process of continuous reaction to a succession of problems, i.e. an incremental process. This entails considering alternative policies which differ only marginally from current ones, so restricting the number of alternatives considered but also making the problem of choice more manageable. Any unforeseen, unpredicted consequences can be tackled later in the serial chain of decisions. ◈ *rational model of decision-making*.

disparking The conversion of ◇ *park* to farmland.

dispersal index The sum of ◇ *accessibility indices* for all places (◇ *nodes*) in a ◇ *network*. Taken as it stands, or divided by the total number of nodes, the dispersal index provides a measure of overall ◇ *accessibility* within a network. The smaller the index the more accessible places are to each other. ◈ *dispersion value*.

dispersed city (1) A cluster of physically discrete cities (i.e. ones separated by tracts of agricultural land) which function together economically as a single urban unit at a higher level of organization. Such clusters have been rationalized as a truncation in the ◇ *central place* hierarchy in such areas and its replacement by a group of lower-order cities with complementary specialist activities. It is equally likely that such clusters are due to entirely local variations in settlement evolution.

(2) A description of a built-up pattern resulting from the redistribution and growth outwards of an urban population from an existing centre into the countryside, i.e. an urban population in a rural setting. Also referred to as the *spread city*. ⟡ *commuter belt, dormitory settlement, ex-urban, urban sprawl*.

dispersed settlement A term used to describe a pattern of ⟡ *rural settlement* where most of the people live in scattered farmhouses and cottages, rather than in ⟡ *hamlets* or ⟡ *villages*. It contrasts with ⟡ *nucleated settlement*. ⟡ *Einzelhof*.

dispersion In statistics the spread of values in a set of data. Dispersion can be measured in various ways, some parametric (⟡ *coefficient of variation, mean deviation, standard deviation, variance*) and others non-parametric (⟡ *inter-quartile range, quartiles, range*).

Geographers are also concerned with the spread of observations or objects in the spatial dimension, i.e. over some area or about some central location. In this case the degree of dispersion is described in terms of a continuum ranging from clustered (at one end), through random, to uniform (at the other). ⟡ Fig. 52. ⟡ *nearest neighbour analysis, quadrat analysis*.

dispersion, index of ⟡ *index of dispersion*.

dispersion value If the distance between pairs of ⟡ *nodes* in a ⟡ *network* is expressed in terms of intervening ⟡ *links* along the shortest ⟡ *paths* connecting them, the dispersion value represents the grand total of the number of links to be traversed in connecting each node to every other node. The dispersion value provides a measure of the network's size in terms of all the paths within it. ⟡ *dispersal index*.

displacement migration ⟡ *migration*.

displacement tonnage A measure of ⟡ *tonnage* used of warships, being the weight of water displaced (in effect the weight of a vessel when fully laden). ⟡ *deadweight tonnage*.

disposal notification area Under the 1975 Community Land Act a local authority can designate areas in which anyone proposing to dispose of a substantial interest in land would first be required to inform the local authority – hence, disposal notification area. The purpose is to safeguard the local authority's position in

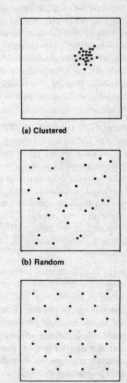

(a) Clustered

(b) Random

(c) Uniform

Fig. 52 Dispersion

respect of the public acquisition of development land. The local authority would be able to say, on notification, whether or not they proposed to acquire the relevant interest.

dissimilarity, index of ◊ *index of dissimilarity*.

distal margin ◊ *fringe belt*.

distance Distance, the spatial dimension of separation, is a fundamental geographical property influencing ◊ *location* and ◊ *movement*. Distances are conventionally shown true to their length on an absolute scale of kilometres or miles (◊ *geodesic distance*), but it may be more appropriate to measure them in relative terms, since distance is viewed primarily as a barrier to ◊ *spatial interaction* (◊ *cost-distance, functional distance, individual distance, social distance, time-distance*). ◊◊ *distance decay, expected distance, friction of distance, isodistantes, marriage distance, psychic distance, sight distance, standard distance.*

distance decay The concept of declining intensity of any pattern or process with increasing ◊ *distance* from a given point or location. Also referred to as *distance lapse rate.* Thus the degree of ◊ *spatial interaction* is inversely related to distance and this has been recognized both in classical theories of spatial structure, for example ◊ *central place theory*, and in empirical efforts to specify distance decay functions, as in ◊ *gravity modelling*.

distribution (1) That branch of ◊ *economics* which examines the determination of payments (◊ *interest, profits, rent* and *wages*) to the ◊ *factors of production* for their contribution to the work of production.
(2) That part of ◊ *service industry* responsible for the distribution of material goods to consumers, i.e. the distributive trades of ◊ *retailing* and ◊ *wholesaling*.
(3) In ◊ *statistics*, the mathematical description of the pattern of variation or scatter of observations displayed by a population. In particular the underlying probability rules that generate observations. ◊ *bionomial distribution, frequency distribution, normal distribution, Poisson distribution.*

distribution costs The costs of transporting finished goods to market. ◊◊ *assembly costs, transport costs.*

distributor hierarchy, distributor network A system of distributor ◊ *roads*, connecting one to another, through an orderly sequence of function and importance. A primary distributor network is the network required in a town to give access to and between the main areas of development. Distributor roads are designed for the efficient movement of motor vehicles and therefore generally have no direct frontage access.

distributor route ◊ *route*.

district According to K. Lynch, medium-to-large sections of a city, conceived of as having two-dimensional extent, which are immediately identifiable to the inhabitants and which usually have local names. While such districts are always identifiable from the inside as having some recognizable common character, they are also used for exterior reference. ◊ *edge, landmark, node, path.* ◊◊ *neighbourhood.*

district heating The technique of heating a whole section of a city (comprising commercial, industrial or domestic premises) by a network of pipes employing hot water or steam as energy carriers from a central boiler or heat source. In Iceland heat comes directly from ◊ *geothermal sources* but is usually produced by a central unit such as a heat-only boiler. District heating is relatively common in Scandinavia and Eastern Europe.

district plan ◊ *local plan*.

districting algorithm A computational procedure for delimiting electoral constituencies according to size constraints.

The procedure is politically neutral and therefore prevents the ◊ *gerrymandering* of boundaries. ◊◊ *electoral geography.*

diversification (1) A strategy of firm growth involving an increase in the number of industrial sectors in which a firm is active. Diversification may be:

(i) *Horizontal*, in which new products are developed or adopted for existing markets which require only minor adjustments of equipment and technological skills. It is normally undertaken during the early stages of firm development to exploit production capacity and technological competence more efficiently.

(ii) *Concentric*, which involves the widening of product use in order to supply new markets.

(iii) *Conglomerate*, which involves a simultaneous broadening of products, markets and technology. The strategy may be viewed as *defensive diversification*, a solution to short-run problems such as reducing risks, using spare capacity and escaping from the adverse effects of a decline in size, or as *offensive diversification*, where a firm is exploiting the opportunities in industries that are growing rapidly.

(2) The process of developing a wide range of industry in an urban or regional economy, indicating that there is no unusual dependence on or specialization in particular industries. ◊ *index of diversification.*

diversification curve ◊ *localization curve.*

diversion curve A technique used in traffic assignment to assess the proportion of motor vehicle drivers likely to switch to a new route if constructed. For any trip there are usually several alternative routes, each with its own 'travel resistance' depending on its characteristics of speed, distance, travel time and level of service. The travel resistance of different routes can be quantified in the form of diversion curves. Three types of diversion curve are in current use: (a) the travel time ratio curve, (b) the distance and speed ratio curve, (c) the travel time and distance saved curve (illustrated in ◊ Fig. 53).

divided capital ◊ *capital (1).*

divided circle A diagrammatic device whereby a circle is subdivided into sectors, each of which is proportional in size to the value it represents.

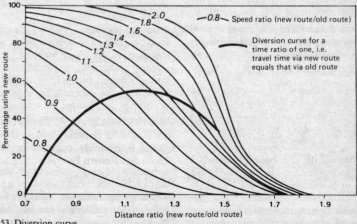

Fig. 53 Diversion curve

divided state An exception to the rule that a people and ◊ *territory* are united under a clear-cut system of sovereign government. In this case ◊ *sovereignty* is divided, disputed or vested in an international organization and a divided state exists, e.g. Germany, Korea and Vietnam.

division of labour The ◊ *specialization* of ◊ *labour* involving the division of the production process into a number of parts, each part undertaken by a separate worker or group. Such division of labour has accompanied agricultural, industrial and commercial development and its advantages stem from the fact that individuals gain greater skill and dexterity by performing one job rather than several. It also allows differences in individual aptitudes to be exploited and encourages the use of machinery, so resulting in increases in ◊ *productivity* and improvements in quality.

dolichocephalic Long-headed: defined by anthropologists as a skull with a ◊ *cephalic index* ≤ 75·9.

dolmen A prehistoric monument, consisting of a large, unhewn, flat roof-stone resting on several upright stones, which served as a ◊ *Neolithic* burial chamber. In Great Britain the term is synonymous with *cromlech* (Welsh for bent, flat stone).

domestic industry The production of goods in the home for local use. ◊◊ *cottage industry*, *factory system*.

domestic product ◊ *Gross Domestic Product*.

dominant industry An industry which dominates another industry or industries in an ◊ *input–output* framework by exercising a measure of control over the latter's output. Thus industry *i* dominates industry *j* if the flow of goods or services from *j* to *i* is a greater proportion of *j*'s output than the flow from *i* to *j* is of *i*'s output. ◊◊ *key industry*.

dominion A term, not much used today, for a self-governing ◊ *state*, formerly a ◊ *colony* of the United Kingdom but now quite independent, which recognizes the loose association of the Commonwealth of Nations of which the sovereign of the United Kingdom is the head.

dormitory settlement, dormitory town, dormitory village Rural settlements from which the resident ◊ *active population* commute to employment elsewhere. Such settlements are the result of the growth and redistribution of population of large urban/metropolitan centres. The term is most frequently applied to rural villages into which commuters have moved, displacing the original population, and which have then been expanded by developing new housing estates. ◊◊ *commuter belt*, *dispersed city*, *metropolitan village*, *urban sprawl*.

double-cropping The use of a given piece of land to produce two full ◊ *crops* each year. ◊◊ *multiple-cropping*.

downtown A term symbolizing, for Americans, the heart of the city. This central zone, perhaps the original urban core, with its well-articulated sub-districts, is more commonly referred to in geographical literature as the ◊ *central business district*. ◊◊ *seven lives of downtown*.

downward-transition region Peripheral areas containing old-established settlements which are characterized by either stagnant or declining rural economies with low agricultural productivity, or the loss of a primary resource base by the depletion of mineral production, or ageing ◊ *industrial complexes*. ◊ *region*. ◊◊ *declining region*, *depressed region*.

drift, driftway ◊ *drove road*.

drift mining Mining of minerals by driving horizontal tunnels into the side of a hill in which mineral deposits occur in nearly horizontal strata. Similar to ◊ *adit mining*. ◊◊ *mine*.

drift net Drift or *gill nets* are used principally in herring ◇ *fishing*. The net is made up of sections about 46 m (50 yd) long and 9 m (10 yd) deep, and may extend up to 5 km (3 ml). The top corners of each section hang from large floats, while the rest of the net's top, about 2m (6 ft) below the surface, is buoyed up with a line of corks. A heavy cable or warp holds the bottom of the net down. The net is towed gently along by the fishing boat drifting with the wind. During the night herring move into the surface waters to feed on the plankton there. When confronted by the drift net the fish attempt to swim through, but the net is gauged so that only small fish escape and the larger fish are trapped by their gill covers as they try to retreat out. The net is hauled in at first light. ◇◇ *seine fishing, trawl fishing*.

drove road A 'road' – a broad, grassy track – used by drovers taking cattle, sheep and other animals to ◇ *fairs* and ◇ *markets*. Before the middle of the 18th century drove roads were ill-defined tracks, but with the development of droving to get large herds of Scottish and Welsh cattle to the growing towns of England they became highways for animals. Drove roads declined in the early 19th century following the spread of railways. Also known as *drifts* or *driftways*. ◇◇ *greenways*.

drubbel A small, open, clustered ◇ *hamlet*.

dry farming A system of ◇ *extensive* agriculture allowing the production of crops without ◇ *irrigation* in areas of limited rainfall. Dry farming involves conserving soil moisture through mulching (to resist capillarity and protect the moist earth from the sun's heat), frequent fallowing (usually only a single crop is grown in two years, the crop being alternated with ◇ *fallow*), maintenance of a fine tilth by cross-ploughing, repeated working of the soil after rainfall and removal of any weeds that would take up some of the moisture. This system is used in the drier parts of areas practising ◇ *Mediterranean agriculture* and has allowed the extension of arable cultivation into the North American prairies and parts of Australia in the late 19th century and, more recently, into the Russian steppes. Dry farming, however, remains vulnerable to severe drought.

dry point settlement A ◇ *settlement*, in a region of wet soils or liable to floods, located at a site free from flooding.

dry-stone wall A feature of much hill country in Britain, dry-stone walls are built without mortar. Many were constructed in the 19th century as part of the ◇ *enclosure* of open grazing, especially in areas too exposed for hedgerows. Most such walls are wider at the base than at the crown and are usually capped with coping stones. The walls are typically constructed of two outer layers of large, flattish stones enclosing an inner fill of smaller, rounded stones, and are often reinforced with 'through' bands of even larger flat stones.

dryfield farming A form of ◇ *subsistence* agriculture involving an intensive tillage system which is used where a lack of water restricts the growth of very high-yielding cereals such as rice. The emphasis is on dry grains, even where ◇ *irrigation* is practised, i.e. maize, wheat, millet and sorghums, which are rotated with crops such as soybeans and garbanzos. It is found in south and south-east Asia, as well as North Africa and Mexico.'

dual economy An ◇ *economy* based upon two separate/distinct economic systems which co-exist in the same geographical space. Dualism is characteristic of many developing countries, in which some parts of a country resemble advanced economies while other parts resemble traditional economies, i.e. there are two circuits of production and exchange. One system reflects the intense ◇ *development* of certain economic activities, often as a result of foreign investment, to exploit an abundant natural resource for which demand is high. It is characterized by modern ◊ *capital-intensive* industry, extensive trade and commercial transactions. This system may be quite isolated from the general economic pattern of the country as a whole, where most of the people live in relative poverty, caught up in a system involving ◊ *labour-intensive* industry, local services and limited trade. The concept has generated a substantial body of development theory in which the uneven nature of development and the barriers to its progress have been emphasized.

The concept is also applicable to most developed ◊ *market economies* which show a two-part industrial–regional structure. Heartland or ◊ *core regions* are dominated by meso-economic organizations or *centre firms* (large, efficient, oligopolistic firms), strong in resources. Peripheral regions have traditional microeconomic structures or peripheral firms, which .may be subdivided according to their relationships with the core into:
(i) *Satellite firms*, which are functionally linked, backward or forward, to centre firms.
(ii) *Competitive fringe firms*, which are non-dominant firms competing with centre firms in their 'home' industry.
(iii) *Free agent firms*, a residual category of firms specializing in the production of unique articles.

dual labour market A concept which views the labour market as being subdivided into a *primary* sector/market (broadly synonymous with the internal labour markets of large organizations, which offer not only good financial rewards but also good working conditions, career prospects and often substantial fringe benefits) and a *secondary* sector/market (where the jobs available provide low wages and a few fringe benefits, poor working conditions, high labour turnover, little chance of

enhancement, and often arbitrary and capricious supervision). Mobility between the two sectors is very limited.

dual society A society in which there are primarily two ◊ *classes* – the very poor and the very rich. A dual society is characteristic of many less developed countries.

dual water supply The public supply of water to buildings using one system of supply for potable water and another for non-potable water, offering opportunities for greater efficiency and possibly greater safety.

dumping The selling of products at a price below true average cost, usually in export markets.

duopoly The provision of a good or service by only two suppliers, who between them control the price and level of production, i.e. the industry comprises just two firms. ◊ *monopoly, oligopoly.*

durable goods ◊ *High-order goods* whose use extends over a long period of time, e.g. furniture, clothing, electrical equipment. Such goods are purchased infrequently by the individual consumer, they often represent a multiple of the consumer's weekly income, and selection/choice is an important factor in their purchase. ◊ *convenience goods, shopping goods.*

duty free area ◊ *free trade area.*

duty free zone Or *free trade zone.* Terms used interchangeably with ◊ *free port*, but especially for small areas in which customs regulations of the host country are relaxed.

dwelling A building, or part thereof, forming separate self-contained premises, designed to be occupied by a single ◊ *family* for residential use. ◊ *slum dwelling.*

dyad ◊ *desire line.*

dynametropolis A ◊ *metropolis* which exhibits continuous growth like the ◊ *dy-*

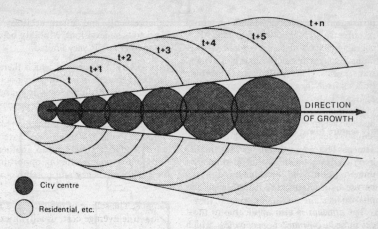

Fig. 54 Dynapolis

napolis. A dynametropolis contains all the phenomena that characterize a dynapolis, only intensified in scale and complexity.

dynapolis The dynamic city which, as expounded by C. A. Doxiadis, has a plan-form that allows for growth of all its parts, i.e. with a parabolic unidirectional growth axis which can expand in space and time, as shown in ◊ Fig. 54.

dystopia A bad or evil place; another and more precise term for ◊ *anti-utopia*.

E

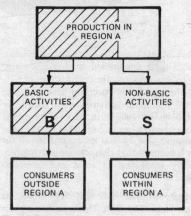

early mature towns ◊ *age of towns scheme*.

easement The name given, in law, to a person's right to restrict the freedom of another's use of land, or to guarantee his own use of it. Easements therefore place limits on certain ownership rights: they may be *affirmative easements*, giving the right to secure limited access to the land for a specific purpose such as the maintenance and use of a road or pipeline, or *negative easements*, which prevent the owner of the land from erecting a structure so as to obstruct light or air. ◊> *wayleave*.

ecological fallacy Conclusions drawn at a given level of analysis apply only at that level. Any assumption that those conclusions necessarily hold at a more disaggregate level, particularly at the level of the individual persons or other entities concerned, is called the ecological fallacy.

ecology The scientific study of the mutual relationships between organisms, both plant and animal, and their ◊ *environment*. Ecological ideas have influenced geography during the 20th century, not only in expected realms such as biogeography, but also more generally in respect of the emphasis on relationships between people and their (physical) environment within a single, bounded, geographical area. ◊ *fire ecology*. ◊> *human ecology*.

economancy The ◊ *by-product* economy resulting incidentally from ◊ *conservation*.

economic base (export base) theory A theory explaining the ◊ *economic growth*/decline of a city or region in terms of the nature and size of its ◊ *basic activi-*

Fig. 55 Economic base theory

ties. The local economy is subdivided into two mutually exclusive sectors (◊ Fig. 55):
(i) *Basic activities* (*B*), or export base, which includes all industries for which effective demand is external to that area. Such basic industries would be expected to have ◊ *location quotients* greater than 1·0, since the area must have more than its proportionate share of such industries.
(ii) *Non-basic activities* (*S*), or residentiary industries, which meet a demand internal to the area, i.e. supply the resident population.

The level of activity in the basic sector is therefore set by forces outside the area, and changes in that level will result in changes in the non-basic sector, and hence in total employment and population. Basic activities are the 'carrier' transmitting the effects of external income shifts to the home area. Increases (decreases) in demand for products of the basic sector will therefore lead to the increase (decrease) of total activity within the area, the magnitude of these changes being determined by the ⟡ *basic/non-basic ratio.*

In shorthand terms the economic base relationships, usually measured in employment terms (*E*), are:

$$E = B + S$$
$$S = kE$$
$$\therefore E = B + kE$$

indicating that the level of economic activity is determined by basic activity. The constant (coefficient) *k* expresses an assumed fixed relationship between basic and non-basic activities over time. The impacts of changes in basic activities on employment can be calculated via the base multiplier:

$$E = \frac{1}{1-k} B$$

i.e. a unit increase in *B* generates

$$\frac{1}{1-k}$$

units of additional employment. Though the growth rate of an area may be explained in the short run more by basic/export activity growth than by any other one factor, economic base theory has been criticized both for its mechanical application and its conceptualization. The use of a constant or 'normal' basic/non-basic ratio for any area is questionable, since the ratio could be expected to change with growth as non-basic activity increases in relative importance as an area grows in size as a response to increased local market opportunities. The basic/non-basic ratio is also an average which masks differences between basic activities in respect of the amount of residentiary activity generated. Then there are problems in identifying industries to be assigned to the basic sector. A major criticism is the undue importance attached to export industry in

determining the level of economic activity, since the purchase of imports by an area will have a negative multiplier effect which is ignored by this theory. However, economic base theory has provided a foundation for much regional economic analysis, its advantages being that it is quick and simple. ⟡ *development stages theory of growth, index of surplus workers, multiplier, staple theory of economic development.*

economic behaviour The individual and collective pursuit of material well-being. ⟡ *Economic man* seeks to expend a minimum of effort in bringing ⟡ *resources* under his control and to redistribute them in a manner which will give him the greatest satisfaction. Economic behaviour therefore involves the exercise of choice, that choice being made in most cases at the margins of expenditure. ⟡ *Equilibrium* is reached for the individual when there is no way in which a shift of his expenditure from one thing to another could improve his material well-being. ⟡ *Pareto optimality.*

economic blight ⟡ *blight.*

economic determinism The doctrine, developed in its most influential form by Karl Marx and Friedrich Engels, that the economic basis of society is the major factor in determining its other social institutions. ⟡ *determinism.* ⟡ *environmental determinism.*

economic efficiency The relationship between the value of output and the value of input – the higher the ratio the greater the efficiency. There is also an objective of maximizing or improving the relationship. ⟡ *spatial efficiency.*

economic geography The geography of people making a living, dealing with the spatial patterns of production, distribution and consumption of goods and services. Economic geography, formerly known as ⟡ *commercial geography,* involved, at first, the compilation of a factual record of production in different parts of the world. The emphasis upon ◊ *commodities* and the geographical conditions and methods of their production encouraged the fragmentation of economic geography, with the conventional subdivision by sector into ◊ *agricultural geography*, ◊*industrial geography* and ◊ *transport geography*.

The development of economic geography over the past three decades has witnessed the substitution of analysis for description, leading to an identification of the factors and an understanding of the processes affecting the spatial differentiation of economic activities over the earth's surface. This transformation was consequent upon the incorporation of ◊ *neoclassical economics* into economic geography, and explanations are largely based upon ◊ *economic determinism* as the guiding principle. ◊◊ *geonomics*.

economic growth The increase of the productive capacity and output of a country, usually measured in terms of ◊ *Gross National Product*. Economic growth is therefore reflected in an increase per head of population in the ◊ *production* of goods and services of all kinds available to meet final demands, e.g. goods and services for domestic ◊ *consumption*, ◊ *capital goods* for accumulation and export goods

to pay for imports. Economic growth has become the cornerstone of economic policy for most countries, although it is being increasingly questioned because of its failure to differentiate between the production of useful and trivial outputs. ◊ *development stages theory of growth, Harrod–Domar model, Rostow model*.

economic growth, stages of ◊ *Rostow model*.

economic imperialism The power exercised by one ◊ *state* over another through economic strength. Although no overt political control of the state receiving ◊ *aid* exists, the volume of investment capital provided, or of exports purchased, makes it difficult for the recipient state to follow an independent policy. ◊◊ *colonialism, imperialism, neocolonialism*.

economic indicators Particular ◊ *economic statistics* which are sensitive to changes in the state of industry, trade and commerce. In the United Kingdom these include the statistics of ◊ *unemployment* and unfilled vacancies; money supply, bank advances, gold reserves, basic material and fuel prices, and retail prices; wage rates and earnings, retail sales and hire purchase debt; ◊ *terms of trade* and industrial output. ◊◊ *social indicators*.

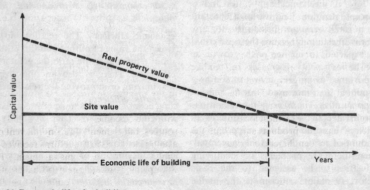

Fig. 56 Economic life of a building

economic life The period of commercial use of a ◊ *capital good* or other durable product. The length of the period depends on the rate of ◊ *obsolescence*, physical life and changing economic circumstances. ◊◊ *economic life of a building*.

economic life of a building The period over which the capital value of an existing building exceeds the capital value of the cleared site (◊ Fig. 56). ◊◊ *cleared-site value, conversion, site value*.

economic man A model of human behaviour in which a person is completely rational in satisfying his/her wants and pays no regard to the interests of others. The model assumes the maximization of certain utility functions, such as profit maximization. Given complete information and a perfect ability to utilize that information in a rational way, economic man maximizes returns and minimizes costs. As an abstraction or first approximation the concept has been particularly useful in classical economic analysis, allowing the prediction of optimal strategies from the options available. Its introduction into economic geography produced a series of deterministic normative models. ◊ *economic behaviour*. ◊◊ *behavioural matrix, optimizer*.

economic margin ◊ *marginal analysis*.

economic margins of cultivation The limits for a given crop or husbandry activity where production becomes unprofitable. Such margins are of two types:
(i) The *extensive margin of cultivation*, where it is no longer profitable to bring additional land into use. Thus, in ◊ *agricultural location theory*, the extensive margin refers to the farthest locations from which agricultural products can profitably be shipped to commercial markets. Also termed the *no-rent margin*.
(ii) The *intensive margin of cultivation*, which refers to the amount of ◊ *factors of production*, such as labour and fertilizers,

that can be profitably used on a given area of land. The intensive margin is reached where it is no longer profitable to add additional units of the variable factors to the given area of land. ◊◊ *cultivation limit, physical margin of cultivation*.

economic overhead capital A type of public ◊ *investment* directly related to encouraging and supporting private productive investment. It usually takes the form of investment in ◊ *infrastructure*, such as power supplies, transport facilities and water supply, which are needed to facilitate the successful operation of private businesses. Many ◊ *development area* programmes concentrate on expanding economic overhead capital on the grounds that this will attract new industrial capacity. ◊◊ *capital, fixed capital, social overhead capital*.

economic planning The process of identifying a nation's future economic needs, together with the systematic management of the scarce resources available in as efficient a manner as possible to satisfy those needs. The means adopted form economic policy. ◊ *planning*. ◊◊ *indicative planning*.

economic rent A payment to a unit of any ◊ *factor of production* over and above the minimum amount necessary to bring that factor into production and to keep that factor in its present occupation, i.e. a surplus over and above ◊ *opportunity cost*. This modern definition of economic rent represents a refinement of the older classical concept which treated rent simply as the economic return that accrues to land in the production process. With this concept, economic rent is normally associated with the income received by land resources, but elements of economic rent can also be identified in the returns received by capital, labour and management. For example, a professional footballer may have a choice between clubs: if one club offers him £1,000/week for his services and a second £850/week the £150 surplus return may be identified as an economic rent to labour.

The concept of economic rent is of value in determining choice between alternatives in the use of resources. In particular, it underlies all questions of competition for the use of land, as well as providing the means whereby this competition is resolved to generate that pattern of land use which represents the ◊ *highest and best use* possible. The concept has been applied in a rather different way in certain ◊ *agricultural location theory* where, instead of distinguishing between competing land uses, it is used to explain why land is or is not used for production. Here economic rent is taken as the net income accruing to an area of land over and above the net income of land at the extensive ◊ *economic margin of cultivation*. The latter *no-rent margin* is usually determined by the additional transport costs involved in marketing with increased distance from the market. As ◊ Fig. 57 shows, net income

no economic rent: within the margin economic rent increases the nearer the land is located to the market (◊ *Ricardian theory of rent, von Thünen model*). The foregoing analysis relates to the special case of a single crop. More important is the use of the concept in analysing two or more crops competing for the use of land. Net income from producing different crops will vary from location to location owing to differences in the market prices, production costs and marketing costs of the crops concerned. ◊ Fig. 58 illustrates how crop patterns or land use zones are determined in such circumstances; note that economic rent, in terms of its modern definition, represents the surplus, at any location, between the net income of the most profitable crop and that of the next best crop. ◊◊ *location rent, rent*.

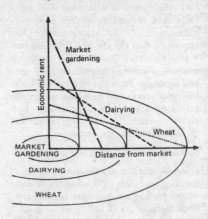

Fig. 58 Economic rent

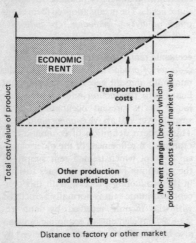

Fig. 57 Economic rent

at the extensive margin is just sufficient to bring the land into cultivation and there is

economic shadow A concept summarizing the relative ability of a region to supplement locally owned and controlled industry with external or foreign-owned capital and entrepreneurship. The economic shadow effect is composed of three major elements:

(i) *Interactance decay* (I_k). The number of subsidiary or ◊ *branch plants* established within a region by all parent companies in a city located beyond that region is directly proportional to the total number of firms in that city, and inversely proportional to its distance from the region.

(ii) *Sectoral affinity* (A_{ik}). A measure based on the number of subsidiaries located in the sector of the region lying between the parent company's location and the region's primary market centre.

(iii) *Sectoral penetration* (d_{ik}). The distance a parent company is prepared to penetrate into a region to locate a subsidiary is correlated with its distance from that region.

Thus,

$$\text{Economic shadow at } P_1 = \sum_k \frac{I_k + A_{ik}}{d_{ik}}$$

where I_k = number of industrial firms in a city beyond the region
  A_{ik} = measure of sectoral affinity and intervening opportunity
  d_{ik} = distance of the external city from P_1

economic space A symbolic space representing perceived economic interactions. It represents the application of economic variables on or in geographical ◊ *space* and can be described via a mathematical process, e.g. the time–cost dimension. Economic space need not be continuous or localized, e.g. the group of factories of a large corporation. ◊◊ *activity space*.

economic statistics ◊ *Statistics* concerned with ◊ *production*, ◊ *distribution* and ◊ *consumption*, with income and expenditure at the macroeconomic level. Such statistics are concerned with units of goods and services, and with financial aggregates. ◊◊ *economic indicators*.

economic system A way of organizing human activity to provide for the material needs of society against a background of scarcity. The basic functions of an econ-

omic system are to:
(i) match ◊ *supply* to effective ◊ *demand* for goods and services in an efficient manner,
(ii) determine what goods and services are to be produced, and in what quantities,
(iii) distribute ◊ *factors of production* among the industries producing the goods and services,
(iv) allocate the goods and services produced among members of the community.
(v) provide for the maintenance and expansion of ◊ *investment*,
(vi) ensure the full utilization of ◊ *resources*.

At first sight it might seem that the 'economic problem' could be solved in many different ways, but the solutions which have been adopted are just three, ◊ *bazaar economy*, ◊ *market economy* and ◊ *redistributive economy* (although these have been used in various combinations). ◊◊ *economy*.

economic union A type of international economic integration, which includes a ◊ *common market* and the harmonization and co-ordination of economic policies of the member countries.

economic welfare That part of ◊ *social welfare* which is concerned with material well-being (as distinct from bodily, moral or spiritual) and which can be brought directly or indirectly into relation by the measuring rod of money. ◊◊ *welfare geography*.

economics A social science concerned with how people, either individually or in groups, attempt to allocate scarce resources, each with alternate uses, to meet their unlimited wants through the processes of ◊ *production*, ◊ *substitution* and ◊ *exchange*. ◊◊ *neoclassical economics*.

economies of agglomeration ◊ *agglomeration economies*.

economies of environment One of a set of advantages an area or location may offer to economic activity. In this case the area is distinctive in some respect, e.g. the presence of plentiful, cheap raw materials or labour, that is attractive for a particular activity. The other set of advantages is ◊ *agglomeration economies*.

economies of localization ◊ *localization economies*.

economies of massed reserves An internal ◊ *economy of scale* related to the level of reserves of materials, equipment and spare parts to meet temporary shortages of supply, breakdown of machinery, etc. Larger plants hold a significant cost advantage over smaller ones in this respect. All production units must hold a certain level of such reserves, but the larger the plant the lower the proportion of its resources that need to be tied up to meet such contingencies. For example, a plant operating several machines of the same type needs to hold proportionately fewer spare parts than a plant with a single such machine, because there is a low probability that more than one will fail at the same time by virtue of the breakdown of the same part. Therefore, where supplies of a part or a component must be held, the bigger plants enjoy economies of massed reserves because these spares service the potential needs of more machines and the costs of holding them unused in stock is spread over more units of output.

economies of scale The gains, by way of reduced costs of production per unit of output, arising from large-scale production. As firm or plant size, and hence output, increases, average cost of production falls, i.e. total costs of production increase less than proportionately with output up to the point where *diseconomies of scale* set in.

Economies of scale derive from a firm or plant as a result of its own efforts; they are internal to the plant or firm concerned. Such *internal economies* are realizable by the individual firm as a result of:
(i) *Specialization economies*, which increase efficiency via improved ◊ *division of labour* in the organization of production.
(ii) *Equipment size economies*, which are based on ◊ *indivisibilities*: plant/machines are built to a certain capacity below which the average cost of production is higher than at full capacity. The cost of producing such equipment rises less rapidly than its capacity.
(iii) *Large-scale purchasing economies*, which are the result of large firms/plants being able to secure preferential terms from their suppliers of goods and services because of the size of their transactions.
(iv) ◊ *Economies of massed reserves*, which stem from the holding of stocks and spare parts.

The extent to which any firm or plant can enjoy economies of scale depends upon the size of its market, the variability of demand for its products through time, the level of technological knowledge and the skill of its managers. ◊◊ *agglomeration economies, external economies*.

economy The ◊ *system* of activities and administration through which a society uses its resources to produce wealth. ◊ *bazaar economy, closed economy, informal economy, market economy, open economy, peasant economy, reciprocal economy, redistributive economy, robber economy, space economy, subsistence economy.* ◊◊ *economic system*.

ecosystem An ecological ◊ *system* consisting of a set of interacting, interdependent, living organisms and their physical, biological and chemical environment. The term was originally coined to convey the idea of a group of organisms, the place or ◊ *habitat* they occupy and the way the two are linked together to form a working or functioning unit.

ecumene (oecumene) Broadly, the entire habitable world of people. On the global scale it involves dividing the continents into the permanently inhabited – the ecumene – as compared with the uninhabited, or *non-ecumene*. It is applied within a state to encompass the ◊ *core region*, which supports the densest and most extended population and has the closest-knit transport network.

ecumenopolis C. A. Doxiadis's term for the futuristic city that will eventually cover the ◊ *ecumene* as a continuous system forming a universal settlement. It envisages a massive increase in the functional linkages among presently separate urbanized regions and a related increase in the physical continuity of urban settlement as regions expand and coalesce. The spatial limits of ecumenopolis will be determined by the existence of reasonably flat land and the climatic conditions to support human settlement.

edge (1) In ◊ *network* geometry, the straight path or *link* (as it is known) between two ◊ *nodes*.
(2) In environmental appraisal, a linear element in a ◊ *landscape* or ◊ *townscape* which represents a distinctive physical break because dissimilar materials or features come together. The edge is a boundary. Common edges are skylines, land and water junctions, and, in the city, urban motorways. ◊◊ *landmark*, *path*.

edge effect An observation from recreation studies that recreational visitors to a site, such as picnickers, choose to locate along a boundary or ◊ *edge* between different homogeneous areas such that one gives a screening effect (behind), while the other affords a wide view (to the front), e.g. a crescentic beach backed by a cliff, or an extensive open area in a forest.

edge length variance A measure developed by B. Boots to classify the shape of areas.

$$\text{Edge length variance} = \sum_{i=1}^{n} (x_i - \bar{x})^2 / n$$

where n = number of edges
x_i = length of the ith edge
$\bar{x}$ = mean length of the n edges

A regular polygon gives a variance of zero.

Alternative indices are listed under ◊ *shape measures*.

Educational Priority Area (EPA) An approach, recommended in the Plowden Committee report *Children and their Primary Schools* (1967), to the problems faced by schools with substantial numbers of immigrants from the Commonwealth, which would introduce ◊ *positive discrimination* into educational policy by identifying Educational Priority Areas where schools would receive special help. The policy was not implemented in full.

EEC ◊ *European Economic Community*.

effective demand The total ◊ *demand* for ◊ *consumer goods* together with the total demand for ◊ *capital goods*.

efficiency of migration Between any two areas, the ratio of the net flow of migrants to the total gross flow in both directions. For example, if all migrants go in the same direction, the efficiency is 100% (in the sense that there is no cross-hauling of migrants: the net flow equals the gross flow). At the other extreme, if the flows in the two directions just balance, so that there is no net movement at all, the efficiency is said to be zero. The concept is useful in suggesting the degree to which a net migration figure can be misleading as an indicator of the amount of movement, but it has little to do with efficiency in any meaningful sense. ◊ *migration*.

EFTA ◊ *European Free Trade Association*.

eftopia A good place. A more specific term than ◊ *utopia*, since it does not suggest impossibility or unreality. Also spelt *eutopia*.

egocentrism The habit of ordering the world so that its components diminish rapidly in value away from the individual (self). ◊◊ *ethnocentrism*.

eigenvalue Eigenvalues in ◊ *factor analysis* are the characteristic or latent roots of the correlation matrix. An eigenvalue measures the relative importance of a factor, indicating the proportion of the ◊ *variance* in the original variables accounted for, i.e. the ability to summarize a high proportion of the variability in a smaller number of factors or dimensions. They may be thought of roughly as the length of the vector which passes through a scatter of points in multi-dimensional space in such a way as to reduce to a minimum the distance between the points and the vector.

Einzelhof A rural settlement type involving scattered farmsteads. ◊◊ *dispersed settlement*, *rural settlement location theory*.

ejido A Mexican communal farm operated by inhabitants of a village or commune on a co-operative basis. ◊ *collective farming*. ◊◊ *kibbutz, kolkhoz, kung-she, moshav, sovkhoz*.

ekistic logarithmic scale (ELS) A logarithmic scale for the classification of settlements according to their size, running from Man (unit 1) as the smallest unit of measurement to the whole Earth (unit 15). The fifteen units and areas occupied are: 1. Man (3 m²), 2. Room (15 m²), 3. Dwelling (50 m²), 4. Dwelling group (0·005 km²), 5. Small neighbourhood (0·03 km²), 6. Neighbourhood (0·2 km²), 7. Small town (1·2 km²), 8. Town (7·0 km²), 9. Large city (40·0 km²), 10. ◊ *Metropolis* (300 km²), 11. ◊ *Conurbation* (5000 km²), 12. ◊ *Megalopolis* (80,000 km²), 13. Urban region (0·8 m km²), 14. Urbanized continent (6 m km²), 15. ◊ *Ecumenopolis* (40 m km²). ◊◊ *G-scale*.

ekistic unit A distinctly separate settlement or a relatively homogeneous part of a settlement.

ekistics The science of human settlements. A term coined by C. A. Doxiadis to cover the quasi-discipline concerned with the integrative study of human settlements of all sizes and how they develop.

elasticity, income The response of the ◊ *demand* for a good to changes in the real income of consumers. *Income elasticity of demand* is calculated as

$$\frac{\% \text{ change in quantity demanded}}{\% \text{ change in income}}$$

elasticity of demand The sensitivity of the level of ◊ *demand* to a change in the ◊ *price* of a good. Elasticity of demand is calculated as

$$\frac{\% \text{ change in quantity demanded}}{\% \text{ change in price}}$$

Where the percentage change in quantity demanded is greater than the percentage change in price, demand is said to be *elastic*; where it is less than the percentage change in price, demand is *inelastic*. Elasticity of demand for a good depends on various factors such as the availability of close substitutes, the proportionate share of a good in a consumer's total expenditure, and whether the replacement of a good is deferable.

elasticity of substitution A measure of the ease with which ◊ *factors of production* can be substituted for each other in a production process. Where factors must be employed in fixed proportions, the elasticity of substitution is zero. ◊ *substitution*.

elasticity of supply The response of the level of ◊ *supply* to a change in the ◊ *price* of a good. Elasticity of supply is calculated as

$$\frac{\% \text{ change in quantity supplied}}{\% \text{ change in price}}$$

Where the percentage change in quantity supplied is greater than the percentage change in price, supply is said to be *elastic*, and where it is less than the percentage change in price *inelastic*.

electoral geography A geographical approach to electoral analysis concerned with the organization, conduct and results of elections. Election statistics provide material for a variety of geographical analyses:

(i) The spatial organization of elections, especially the delimitation of constituencies.

(ii) The spatial pattern and structure of voting choice as revealed by election results, including changes over time.

(iii) Spatial patterns of representation, dependent upon election systems for translating votes cast into seats in assemblies, etc.

(iv) Influence of environmental and cultural factors on voting decisions.

(v) The effect of voting decisions upon a constituent's environment, reflecting spatial variations in power and in policy representation.

The relationship of electoral geography to ◊ *political geography* as a whole appears confused: for some it is an integral part of that discipline, even the very core and substance of political geography, while for others it seems to be a discipline in its own right (belonging more to the realms of sociology than political geography). ◊ *districting algorithm, friends-and-neighbours effect, gerrymander, malapportionment, normal vote, pork barrel, proportional representation.*

electricity generation The generation of electricity, a ◊ *secondary fuel*, from ◊ *primary fuels* such as coal, oil, ◊ *hydroelectric sources* or ◊ *nuclear power*. It is usually carried out at centralized power stations. ◊ *energy.* ◊ *base load, base load plant, load factor, load following, peak load, pumped storage scheme.*

electricity transmission The distribution of electricity over long distances using overground power lines or underground cables. Large coal- and oil-fired power stations are usually located close to the source of supply of their ◊ *primary fuel* (coalfield or oil refinery), often some distance from areas of high demand. There is a requirement, therefore, for the large-scale distribution of electricity, and this is usually integrated into a national/regional transmission system or grid.

elementary family ◊ *nuclear family.*

ellipticity index A measure of the shape or form of a geographical area, based on the area and longest axis of the unit concerned.

$$\text{Ellipticity index} = \frac{L}{2\{A/[\pi(L/2)]\}}$$

where L = longest (major) axis
A = area

The more compact the geographical unit the lower the index, with a circle having a limiting value of 1·0.

Alternative indices are listed under ◊ *shape measures.*

elongation ratio A simple measure of the shape or form of a geographic area.

$$\text{Elongation ratio} = \frac{L_{\max}}{L'_{\min}}$$

where L = longest (major) axis
L' = secondary (minor) axis

The method is most useful when the boundary of the area in question can be approximated by an n-sided convex polygon. A ratio value of 1·0 denotes a circular-shaped area, increasingly greater values denoting an ellipsoid area shape and the limiting case being a straight line.

Alternative indices are listed under ◊ *shape measures.*

ELS ◊ *ekistic logarithmic scale.*

embourgeoisement The adoption of a characteristically middle-class way of life by the more affluent members of the working class.

emigration The departure of people from one ◊ *state*, usually their native land, to settle permanently in another. *Sponsored emigration* is where a person is assisted in leaving by landlords, charity or government. ◊ *migration*.

eminent domain The authority of a government to appropriate any property within its jurisdiction for necessary public use, subject to the payment of reasonable compensation. ◊◊ *compulsory purchase*.

emission standard An emission or *performance standard* specifies the amount of ◊ *pollutants* permitted to be discharged from a pollution source. Such standards deal with the objective to be accomplished, leaving the polluter to find the most cost-effective way of achieving the set emission standard. Emission standards for solid, liquid or gaseous pollutants are commonly set in terms of the mass of releasable pollutants over a certain time, or mass of pollutants per unit mass of material processed, or mass of pollutants per unit volume of discharged material. ◊ *ambient standard, specification standard.* ◊◊ *acceptable dose limit, pollution control.*

empiricism A philosophy of science based on the belief that knowledge is the result of experience and which, therefore, accords precedence to empirical questions, those with factual content. Empiricism makes certain assumptions about scientific observations: (i) that they are ontologically privileged, meaning that empirical statements are the only ones which refer directly to real world phenomena, and (ii) that they are epistemologically privileged, meaning that they can be declared true or false without reference to the validity of theoretical statements. Empiricism is a fundamental component of ◊ *positivism*.

employee density A measure, in conjunction with ◊ *employment density*, of the relative importance of production workers in a manufacturing establishment. Employee density is a ratio obtained as follows for each industrial site:

$$\frac{\text{Average (or normal) number of shift (or hourly paid) workers}}{\text{Occupied hectarage or groundspace of the site}}$$

◊◊ *density*.

employment, full A situation in which all those persons seeking jobs in a society are able to find suitable work fairly readily. The result is that a very high proportion of the ◊ *active population* is actually in work at that time. The level of full employment is reached when all offering themselves for work are in jobs, with the exception of those temporarily unemployed owing to switching from one job to another, i.e. frictional ◊ *unemployment*. In practice full employment requires the number of unfilled vacancies in a locality to be greater than the number of persons seeking work (since some vacancies may not be suitable for applicants). Since the end of the Second World War, the government has accepted responsibility for the maintenance of a high and stable level of employment. Lord Beveridge defined full employment as a situation in which the number of those unemployed did not exceed 3% of the active population.

employment density A measure of ◊ *density* of workers in industry obtained as follows for each workplace:

$$\frac{\text{Average (or normal) number of workers of all occupations}}{\text{Occupied hectarage or groundspace of the site}}$$

employment multiplier A multiplication factor used to calculate the total number of jobs in all sectors of an economy which will result from the creation of jobs in any one sector. ◊ *multiplier*.

empolder To reclaim land by the creation of ◊ *polders*. ◊◊ *reclamation*.

enclave (1) A small area or ◊ *territory* located within a ◊ *state* but which does not come under its jurisdiction. The enclave may be a micro-state, e.g. San Marino and the Vatican City in Italy, or it may be governed as part of another state, e.g. West Berlin as part of West Germany. In the latter case the terms enclave and ◊ *exclave* are used interchangeably; thus West Berlin is an enclave within East Germany and an exclave of West Germany.
(2) A type of ◊ *ethnic area*.

enclosed ports ◊ *Ports* where the docks are enclosed and the water level in them is maintained by a system of locks.

enclosure Enclosure in England was a technical term applied to the process by which ◊ *common rights* over an area of land were extinguished and scattered properties consolidated. As a result the land was turned into ordinary ◊ *freehold*, with recognizable boundaries (ditches, fences, hedgerows and walls) to demarcate the individual ownership. The conversion process could be by both legal (◊ *Enclosure Act, enclosure award*) and illegal means. There was a continuous enclosure movement on a small scale in England dating back to the 13th century but the two most important periods were in the 16th and 18th centuries. These have been studied in some depth by historical geographers.

Enclosure Act A legal provision for the alteration of a farm-holding system, with special reference to ◊ *consolidation* and ◊ *enclosure*, e.g. the Statute of Merton (1235) enabled a lord of the manor in England to enclose, provided he left enough land as pasture for his freehold tenants. Until the mid 18th century most enclosures were carried out by private agreement between the owners of the land in question, but after that date enclosure by private Act of Parliament was the normal procedure. The General Enclosure Act, 1801 (as amended 1836 and 1845), was passed as a result of demands to facilitate agricultural

improvements and to avoid specific references to Parliament on each occasion that an enclosure was proposed. ◊ *enclosure award*.

enclosure award An enclosure award, extinguishing historical land use and rights at the time of ◊ *enclosure*, went with each ◊ *Enclosure Act*. The award required a majority of signatures by value of acreage, and title owners. All land in the ◊ *common fields*, homesteads and ancient enclosures were surveyed and allotments made to the chief landowner and the vicar/rector in lieu of their titles. A new road system was laid out (◊ *enclosure roads*) and allotments made to other villagers.

enclosure roads The ◊ *enclosures* of the 18th and 19th centuries severed many tracks/paths connecting village to village, so that Parliament provided for new ◊ *roads*. Such enclosure roads were laid out in a regular pattern among the newly enclosed fields, often running straight for considerable distances before making a sharp change of direction. A minimum width of 40 ft (13 m) was stipulated.

endemic A term used to describe an infectious disease which is commonly found in, and normally restricted to, a particular area, e.g. yellow fever in West Africa. ◊ *epidemic, pandemic*.

endogenic change A change that takes place within a ◊ *system*, e.g. the growth or decline of population within a nation. ◊ *exogenic change*.

endogenous activities ◊ *non-basic activities*.

energy Energy is the physical ability to do work, the means of providing motive force or heat or light. Sources of energy have been divided into (i) capital (e.g. coal, oil) or income (e.g. sun) and (ii) commercial (e.g. fossil fuels) or non-commercial (e.g. fuel-wood, bagasse, dung). It is, however, more constructive to define the terms used to describe energy at the various stages as it flows through successive production

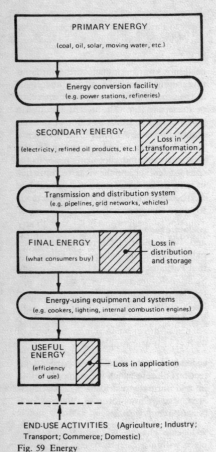

END-USE ACTIVITIES (Agriculture; Industry; Transport; Commerce; Domestic)

Fig. 59 Energy

equipment. ◊ *alternative energy sources, ambient energy sources, biological energy sources, fund energy resources, renewable energy sources.* ◊◊ *electricity generation, fossil fuels, geothermal energy, hydroelectric power, hydrogenation of coal, life sequence of fuel, nuclear energy, solar power, water power, wave energy.*

energy analysis A systematic method of tracing energy flows through an economic system or sub-system in order to identify the energy requirement of each commodity or service provided in that system. ◊ Fig. 60 illustrates the method.

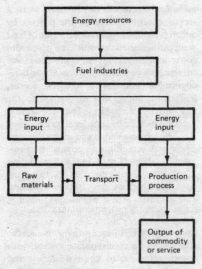

Fig. 60 Energy analysis

processes until finally consumed. The terms and relationships are summarized in ◊ Fig. 59. ◊ *Primary energy* is that in which each of the energy forms is considered according to its calorie equivalent terms. This energy passes through central conversion facilities (e.g. power stations, refineries) to produce ◊ *secondary energy* forms. *Final energy* is what consumers buy, that is, *secondary energy* less losses in distribution. *Useful energy* is that which is finally delivered through energy utilization

energy coefficient The relationship between ◊ *economic growth* and ◊ *energy* consumption in any country.

$$\text{Energy coefficient} = \frac{\text{Energy consumption growth rate}}{\text{Economic growth rate}}$$

When evaluated from data over several decades, variations in the energy coefficient give some indication of the effect of the development process on the relation between energy demand and economic growth. Generally the energy coefficient is greater than unity during the early stages of ♢ *industrialization* but less than unity during the later stages of development.

energy congruence The economically and socially efficient balance between energy supply and demand in a nation. Energy congruence entails not only a physical balance but also a pattern of procurement, conversion and consumption that assists in the attainment of national goals. Where congruence exists the pattern of energy conversion and use is well adapted to the current and prospective pattern of energy supply, quantitatively and qualitatively. A country lacking fossil fuels but with virtually unlimited access to hydroelectric power which made no use of electricity for rail transport would, for example, be considered out of balance.

Enforcement Notice When a local planning authority believes a landowner has carried out ♢ *development* without permission or in a manner which ignores conditions attached to the permission granted, it may serve an enforcement notice to compel compliance. ♢ *development control, planning permission, Stop Notice.*

Engel's Law A generalization of the relationship between the ♢ *demand* for a good and the income of a consumer. Basically, as a person's income rises, the proportion of income spent on food declines (proportionately more being spent on other consumer goods and services).

engrossing The accumulation under the ownership of one person/family of agricultural holdings sufficient for the maintenance of more than one family. ♢ *deserted village.*

entail To leave land or an estate for inheritance purposes in such a way that none of a line of heirs can give it away or sell it.

enterprise ♢ *entrepreneur.*

enterprise zone The original idea of enterprise zones was as ♢ *free trade areas* within cities which were thrown open to all kinds of initiative, with minimal governmental interference or control, involving the free movement of ♢ *capital*, in an attempt to improve the economy of the ♢ *inner city*. The idea was taken up in 1980 in the United Kingdom in a less extreme form: the intention being to put ♢ *derelict land* and vacant urban land to good use and to stimulate commercial and industrial activity in the private sector. The range of incentives which were introduced (i) provided for a tax holiday in the form of remission of local property taxes (with any loss to local revenues made good by central government grant), 100% capital allowances against corporation tax for commercial and industrial buildings, and reduced capital gains taxation, and (ii) simplified various administrative procedures by reducing zoning and planning regulations to a minimum and exempting firms from industrial training board requirements (so that only basic pollution, health and safety standards applied). Such enterprise zones were open to manufacturing and service industries, wholesale and storage warehouses, commercial offices, retail distribution outlets, hotels and motels. However, these enterprise zones do not offer deliberate encouragement in the form of grants to outside entrepreneurs to come in and establish new businesses.

entopia A place that is practicable, that can exist. ♢ *eftopia.*

entrepôt A specialized ♢ *port* with external ♢ *trade* relations of a re-export form. It acts as an intermediary centre for trade between foreign countries to which goods in transit are brought for temporary storage (without having to pass through customs) before re-export. Entrepôt functions have been assisted and encouraged in many instances by the creation of ◊ *free ports*. Entrepôts are less dependent than other types of port on their ◊ *hinterland*. ◊◊ *export processing zone*, *integrated port*.

entrepreneur A business organizer (either an individual or a group such as a board of directors) who co-ordinates and controls the ◊ *factors of production* and who takes the non-insurable risks through production in order to gain ◊ *profit*. The tasks of the entrepreneur are popularly regarded as embracing the initial establishment of an enterprise, piloting it through the difficult formative period, and subsequently making decisions that affect the type of business it is and its future prospects. Decisions have to be made about what goods and services will be produced, how the factors of production will be combined for this purpose, the scale of production and the marketing of the products. Such entrepreneurial functions are regarded as a factor of production – *enterprise* – but merge imperceptibly into the functions of management. ◊ *boss nexus*, *free man nexus*, *hobby nexus*. ◊◊ *firm*.

entropy Entropy is often referred to as a measure of disorder or disorganization in a ◊ *system*. As a concept it relates directly to ideas of ◊ *probability* and ◊ *uncertainty*, being a measure of the degree of uncertainty in a probability distribution or a system subject to constraints. As such it is a measure of the relationship between a macro-state and the possible micro-states that correspond to it. Take, for example, the distribution of forty workers, who can reside at various distances from their city-centre workplace, across five concentric residential zones. A micro-state is a specific, individual level allocation of workers to residential zones: the first worker to the nearest zone, the second worker to the furthest zone, and so on. A macro-state is an aggregate frequency distribution of

workers across zones. More than one micro-state may correspond to the same macro-state, e.g. different workers go to different zones: the first worker to the furthest zone, the second worker to the nearest zone, and so on, but the frequency distribution remains the same. While certain macro-states (e.g. all forty workers in the nearest zone) have only one associated micro-state, most macro-states (e.g. eight workers in each of the five zones) correspond to large numbers of different micro-states. The number of micro-states corresponding to a macro-state is, therefore, a measure of entropy and is given by W, the likelihood of which is calculated as:

$$W = \frac{N!}{\prod_i n_i!}$$

where N = total number of individuals (workers)
n_i = number of individuals (workers) in each area (zone).

In the example, W thus gives the total number of distinct ways that a specific spatial allocation of workers to residential zones can occur. ◊◊ *entropy-maximizing model*, *Theil's entropy index*.

entropy-maximizing model A mathematical model for identifying the most likely state of a ◊ *system* subject to constraints. An approach now used extensively by geographers in spatial allocation and interaction modelling. The system constraints determine what macro-states are possible, and the idea of ◊ *entropy* is to find some assignment of probability of occurrence to all the micro-states that make up a possible macro-state. Since no information is available about particular micro-states it is assumed that all are equally likely to occur. On the basis of this assumption of equal probability of occurrence of all micro-states, the entropy-maximizing approach can justify, on frequency grounds, the choice of the macro-state with the most micro-states as the most likely state of the system. This most likely state is the maximum entropy state because it corresponds to positions where we are most uncertain about the micro-state of the system (for which there is the largest number and no grounds for choosing between them).

entry rate, entry ratio In the analysis of manufacturing plants in a region, an entry rate is the ratio of the number of new plants opened during a certain period to the total number of plants existing in the region at some time in the period. ◊ *exit ratio, survival ratio.*

entry zone An extension of the ◊ *threshold* concept of ◊ *central place theory* whereby the threshold of any function is taken as the mid-point of its entry zone. The zone is delimited by an upper population size above which all settlements have the function and a lower population size below which no settlements have the function.

enumerated population ◊ *de facto population.*

enumeration district The smallest basic spatial unit on which the collection of data for the ◊ *Census* of Population in the United Kingdom is based.

environment Generally, the total of the external conditions that surround an organism, community or object. This is the most inclusive view of environment, since it embraces the whole objective or ◊ *phenomenal environment* which is external to the organism. The term has also been used in geography in a more limited way. In some cases it has been used to denote the *natural environment* – the landscape before people arrived – or the *physical environment* which includes all phenomena apart from human beings and the things they have created. In others the *geographical environment* has been viewed as a unified milieu of people and environment, embracing both the phenomenal environment and the ◊ *be-*

havioural environment, in which relationships are considered in terms of spatial location. The distinction between the impersonal/objective environment and the personal/subjective one is valid and important. ◊ *affinity environment, built environment, congruent environment, daily-life environment, decision environment, functional environment, habitat, incongruent environment, operational milieu, perceptual environment, social environment.*

environmental archaeology That part of ◊ *archaeology* which deals with all the physical and biological components of people's ◊ *environment.* It includes research into the geological and geographical factors affecting people, as well as the study of the environment as a source of raw materials.

environmental area As used originally, in the Buchanan Report *Traffic in Towns*, an area having no ◊ *extraneous traffic* and within which considerations of environment predominate over the use of motor vehicles. It is now used in a more generalized manner to describe any area of sufficient aesthetic quality or unity to merit it being considered as a whole. ◊ *conservation area.*

environmental behaviourism ◊ *cognitive behaviourism.*

environmental blight ◊ *blight.*

environmental capacity In relation to the ability of the environment to absorb, without damage, ◊ *pollutants*, environmental capacity is the rate of introduction of a pollutant which, at equilibrium, will result in a rate of exposure of the 'target' per unit of time equal to that defined by the ◊ *ambient standard.* ◊ *acceptable dose limit.*

environmental determinism The doctrine that the ◊ *environment*, in particular the physical environment, is the primary causal or determining factor in human activity. Also referred to as *geographical* *determinism* and, sometimes, as *physical determinism*.

Geographical research in the late 19th century, influenced by the work of Charles Darwin, was primarily concerned with recognizing the laws of nature. In human geography this approach led to a rather deterministic view of struggle and survival – people's achievements were to be explained as consequences of natural conditions. The formalization of this doctrine is commonly traced back to F. Ratzel, but is primarily associated with the work of E. C. Semple, E. Huntington, E. Demolins and G. Taylor. Crude environmental determinism quickly fell into disrepute, representing a retreat from a situation in which determinate solutions are available to all problems and a recognition that the overall system is far too complex for determinate answers to be expected in all cases. Modified approaches were sought in ◊ *possibilism* and ◊ *probabilism*. ◊◊ *determinism, environmentalism*.

environmental hazard ◊ *natural hazard*.

environmental impact assessment Resource use/development decisions have, in the past, been made largely on a trial-and-error basis. Moreover, the decision to develop a resource in one location has implications, often unintended, for surrounding places. During the 1960s, in North America and Western Europe, increasing public concern was expressed about the likely consequences on the quality of the ◊ *environment* of major new resource developments being proposed, particularly in non-urban locations. ◊ *Cost-benefit analysis*, which had been used in a number of cases, was seen as too narrow a method of appraisal, hence environmental impact analysis emerged as a response to the call for a broader ranging procedure to assess resource development proposals.

Environmental impact assessment is a process of carrying out a balanced appraisal of the potential total effects (or impact) of a major proposed development on the physical environment, taking economic and social effects into account. The history of impact assessment is quite recent, stemming specifically as a formal procedure from the US National Environmental Policy Act of 1969, which required *environmental impact statements* to be prepared by federal agencies for all their major developments before approval would be given to the developers. Such statements would detail:

(i) a complete technical description of the proposed activity, including its location,

(ii) an analysis of the likely positive and negative impacts on the natural and human environments,

(iii) a description of possible alternative solutions and variations, including alternative locations,

(iv) a description of all the adverse impacts which cannot be avoided or minimized,

(v) an examination of scarce resources which would be irreversibly committed.

Similar procedures have been adopted subsequently in other countries, e.g. Australia, Canada and Spain, and for World Bank projects.

environmental perception A person's image of the ◊ *phenomenal environment*. That image is formed by a filtering of information from their experiences or consciousness of the phenomenal environment and reveals their ◊ *intentionality* towards it. Such perception conditions a person's attitudes and influences their taking decisions. ◊ *lifeworld, perception, perceptual environment*.

environmental planning That set of processes and procedures which regulate the distribution of ◊ *land uses* and which is responsible for policies covering the ◊ *development*, ◊ *conservation* or change of human-made or natural features of the land surface. In Britain frequently described as 'town and country planning', 'town planning' or simply ◊ *planning*.

environmental possibilism ◊ *possibilism.*

environmental quality standard ◊ *ambient standard.*

environmental recovery A term used to describe the ◊ *rehabilitation* of complete districts or ◊ *neighbourhoods.* It involves selecting an area of housing and other mixed uses where the properties are still structurally sound although lacking certain amenities. An assessment is made of which properties are to be retained and which must be demolished. Some demolition is usually inevitable in order to secure space for play areas, landscaping, etc.

environmentalism A doctrine which stresses the influence, rather than strict control, of the ◊ *environment* on human behaviour. ◊ *Environmental determinism* is an extreme form. ◊◊ *possibilism.*

environmentally sensitive area An ◊ *ecosystem* whose natural characteristics and processes are to be maintained, preserved and protected. It is a natural ◊ *landscape* containing features such as ◊ *aquifer recharge*, headwaters, breeding or overwintering animal habitats, vital ecological functions, rare or endangered species, unusual landforms, or combinations of habitat and landform which could be valuable for scientific research or conservation education. ◊◊ *nature reserve, Site of Special Scientific Interest.*

eotechnic A term used by Lewis Mumford to denote the first of three technological phases of urban-industrial development (◊◊ *neotechnic, paleotechnic*). The eotechnic phase is characterized by immobile power sources (dominated by wood, wind and water), primitive technology and undeveloped transportation means. Manufacturing is organized on a household/ ◊ *cottage industry* basis, using ubiquitous raw materials, having a high labour input, and with a scattered spatial pattern.

epidemic An outbreak of an infectious disease which spreads rapidly to affect a large number of people in a community at the same time. ◊◊ *endemic, pandemic.*

epidemic diffusion ◊ *diffusion.*

epidemic models Originally developed to study the spread of various diseases through human populations, epidemic models have been applied by human geographers to the ◊ *diffusion* of ◊ *innovations.* There are two basic types:
(i) The *simple epidemic model*, in which the population of the area is divided between susceptibles ($\equiv$ potential adopters) and infectives ($\equiv$ adopters). This model describes a birth process in which everyone who becomes an adopter continues to transmit information indefinitely. Eventually the total population of potential adopters is informed. The main object of this type of model is to study the evolution of the system to this limiting state.
(ii) The *general epidemic model*, which involves a division of the population into susceptibles, infectives and removals. Removals comprise adopters who, after some period of time, cease to pass on information about the innovation. They are passive adopters compared to the active (transmitting) adopters in the infectives category. A birth–death process is involved and the general epidemic model allows the spatial and temporal extent of the diffusion to be determined, as well as the notion of thresholds for an innovation to be explored.

epistemology A branch of philosophy which is concerned with the study of the nature of knowledge, the source and possible forms of knowledge, and the criteria of knowledge (the conditions in which valid knowledge may be achieved). ◊◊ *ontology.*

epoche A tool of ◊ *phenomenological reduction* which enables the phenomenologist to look at human experience in a

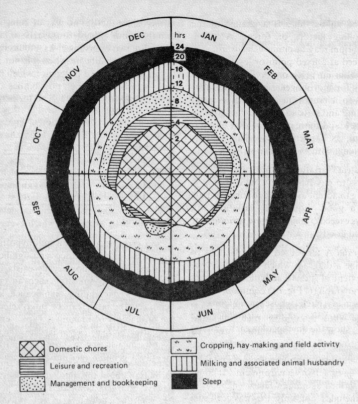

Fig. 61 Ergograph: hypothetical dairy farmer

Legend:
- Domestic chores
- Leisure and recreation
- Management and bookkeeping
- Cropping, hay-making and field activity
- Milking and associated animal husbandry
- Sleep

new light. Epoche is the suspension of belief in the experience or experienced thing. Through epoche the phenomenologist attempts to disengage himself from the ⟡ *lifeworld* in order to re-examine its nature. While the phenomenologist does not reject the world or his experience of it, he does begin to question these things, as well as all concepts, theories and models designed to describe and explain them.

equalizing differentials A situation in which money wage or income differentials between regions are balanced by cost of living differences, e.g. a labour market where living costs are 10% above average

and wages 10% above average, so that real wages there would be the same as anywhere else.

equation of time The difference in value between ⟡ *apparent time* and mean ⟡ *solar time.*

equifinality A ⟡ *systems* analytic term indicating that different initial conditions can lead to similar end structures.

equilibrium A theoretical state of stability or balance. It implies that there is a normal state with respect to both internal balance in a ⟡ *system* and its external relationships which will not be altered with the passage of time unless there is a change in the controlling factors or forces. A stable equilibrium may be either *homeostasic*, i.e. balanced at a fixed point or level, as with an equilibrium price, or *steady-state*, which allows for morphogenesis, a process that leads to changes in a system's form, structure and state so that it comes to exist at a new and more complex level of equilibrium, as happens with urban systems complying with the ⇨ *rank–size rule*.

equivalent variation A measure of willingness to pay based on what a person is willing to accept as a bribe to forgo or part with a good. Equivalent variation will always exceed ⇨ *compensation variation* for normal goods.

ergograph A term used by A. Geddes to describe a diagram which shows the type and extent of human activities by season. An ergograph (⇨ Fig. 61) commonly takes the form of a circle, whose circumference is divided into 30° sections, with concentric arcs to show the time spent in each activity.

ergonomics The scientific study of the relationship between human beings and their working or activity environments. It could be described as human factor engineering and includes not only the physical surroundings but also tools and equipment, and work organization and methods. The object is to increase efficiency.

error A term used in ⇨ *statistics* to convey the idea that perfect accuracy cannot be expected in statistical data. The concept of error includes mistakes in data collection, such as those due to lapses in the collector's concentration, misassignment of observations, miscalculation and double-counting, limitations in measuring equipment, or to a sample being taken. Errors may be constant, affecting all observations in the same direction, or random, in which case they cannot be entirely eliminated.

Error can also arise in ⇨ *significance testing*, since there is no way of being certain that a null ⇨ *hypothesis* is true or false. There are two opposing risks – to accept a difference as significant when it is not and to fail to recognize a difference which is of real significance: the possibilities are summarized in ⇨ Fig. 62. The former, or

		NULL HYPOTHESIS: True	NULL HYPOTHESIS: False
OUR DECISION	Reject	ERROR (Type 1)	CORRECT
	Accept	CORRECT	ERROR (Type 2)

Fig. 62 Error

Type 1 error, is to reject a null hypothesis when it is true and so discover a significant relationship where none really exists. The seriousness of committing such an error leads to a demanding significance level being set: the latter can be interpreted as the probability of making a Type 1 error. The latter, or *Type 2 error*, accepts the null hypothesis when it is false and fails to identify a genuine relationship where one actually exists. The likelihood of a Type 2 error is greater the more demanding the significance level. ⇨ *response error*, *sampling error*, *standard error*.

essential traffic ⇨ *traffic*.

establishment An identifiable unit of business under single legal ownership engaged in manufacturing, retail or service activity at a distinct physical location. It is usually a building, such as a shop, office or factory, within which a single business may conduct a range of functions. Newsagent–confectioner–tobacconist shops or meat-packing factories with technical units or departments producing lard, cured bacon and canned meat are examples of single establishments. An establishment may be one of a number owned by a ⇨ *firm*. Also referred to as a *plant* in the case of ⇨ *manufacturing* industry.

estancia A large farm in South America, especially Argentina, used for ◊ *ranching* on an extensive scale. Many have been broken up into smaller holdings.

estate (1) Landed property, of varying extent but with a greater part leased to tenants. The estate of a particular landowner need not necessarily comprise a contiguous spatial unit but could involve a large number of holdings scattered over a wide area.
(2) More generally the rights and interests a person holds in the ownership, possession or control of property.

estate village ◊ *planned village.*

estovers ◊ *common rights.*

ethnic area Ethnic areas are the result of ethnic ◊ *residential segregation*, the most pronounced form of segregation within urban areas. They have been classified by F. Boal as:
(i) ◊ *Colony*: an ethnic area which is temporary in character, providing a foothold in new societies for groups likely to experience little difficulty in achieving behavioural or structural ◊ *assimilation.*
(ii) ◊ *Enclave*: an ethnic area which persists over some time but which is primarily based on choice and a preservation function in particular.
(iii) ◊ *Ghetto*: an ethnic area which persists because it is based on constraints and discriminatory action of the ◊ *charter group.*

ethnic group A term referring to vertical divisions in a society where a group, which is part of a larger population, possesses a distinct ◊ *culture* of its own. The members of such a group feel a common origin, real or imaginary, and are frequently set apart by ◊ *race*, religion or national origin, or some combination of these. The existence of such ethnic groups has been determined in large part by ◊ *migration*, and the processes of ◊ *assimilation* and ◊ *integration* are closely connected with the distinctiveness and persistence of ethnic ties. ◊ *charter group.* ◊◊ *ethnic area, ethnocentricity.*

ethnobotany The study of the relationships between human groups and the plant species they utilize.

ethnocentricity The awareness of one's own ◊ *ethnic group.*

ethnocentrism Collective ◊ *egocentrism*. Individuals are members of groups, and all have learned to differentiate between 'we' and 'they', between real people and people less real, between home ground and alien territory. 'We' are at the centre.

ethnography The science which deals with the distribution of the ◊ *races* of mankind, with their customs, habits and points of difference. Now dealt with as part of ◊ *anthropology.*

ethnology The scientific study of the ◊ *races* of mankind, now subsumed within ◊ *anthropology.*

ethology A behavioural approach to the study of environmental attitudes deriving from the biological study of animal behaviour. People–environment relations are studied from within, in an attempt to understand how both individuals and groups perceive their surroundings and hence, within the limits of their technology, how they act.

European Economic Community (EEC) The EEC, or 'Common Market' as it is popularly known, was formed on 1 January 1958 as a result of the Treaty of Rome signed by the 'Six' (Belgium, France, Italy, Luxembourg, the Netherlands and West Germany) some nine months earlier. It was extended in 1973 when Denmark, Eire and the United Kingdom became active members, in 1980 with the inclusion of Greece, and again in 1986 when Portugal and Spain joined. The EEC is thus a supranational organization, membership of which requires a partial surrender of state ◊ *sovereignty.* Early emphasis was designed to encourage trade within the EEC group at the expense of more general trade by the formation of a ◊ *customs union* and ◊ *common market*, but the Treaty of Rome also provided for common external and transport policies and the co-ordination of the countries' social, financial, commercial and economic programmes. While progress has been made in some areas, e.g. with a Common Agricultural Policy (CAP), achievements in other directions have been slower than anticipated, e.g. with economic union.

European Free Trade Association (EFTA) A trade group seeking to eliminate ◊ *tariffs* on a wide range of industrial products between its members. EFTA came into being in May 1960, its founder-members being Austria, Denmark, Norway, Portugal, Sweden, Switzerland and the United Kingdom. Finland became an associate member. ◊ *Free trade* was achieved by December 1966. Iceland joined EFTA in 1970, while Denmark and the United Kingdom left in 1973 on joining the ◊ *European Economic Community*.

European peasant farming ◊ *Peasant farming* is still found throughout large parts of Europe and is distinguishable from ◊ *mixed farming* (which in some ways it resembles) in being largely ◊ *subsistence*-oriented, with only a very limited dependence on the market. Peasant holdings are commonly small, often fragmented and under-equipped. They yield only a small livelihood and, today, are giving way to commercially organized mixed farming.

eutopia ◊ *eftopia*.

even-aged forest A ◊ *forest* composed of trees of the same age.

event-tree analysis Event-tree analysis considers a variety of events relating to a particular activity or production process which could lead to an accident. It is commonly used in the case of likely ◊ *pollution* accidents, e.g. the failure of a pump

in a nuclear power station or the collision of a tanker with a jetty at an oil terminal. An assessment is then made of the likely consequences of each event. The analysis is helpful in deciding what precautionary measures can be taken and in estimating the risks of an accident. ◊◊ *fault-tree analysis*.

evidence account ◊ *countertrade*.

exceptionalism The view that ◊ *geography* (and history) do not share the methodology of the other sciences because of the peculiar nature of their subject matter – the study of unique places or regions.

exchange A transaction between two economic units (e.g. family and firm) in which one offers a good or service for another product and the other accepts and offers the latter product for the former good or service. Usually the term is now taken to mean a transaction in which money is involved.

exchange-production sector ◊ *basic activities*.

exclave Part of a ◊ *state* which is separated from the main territorial unit and entirely surrounded by the territory of a neighbouring state. Most exclaves are the relics of historical political patterns, e.g. Llivia, an exclave of Spain within France, or Baarle, an exclave of Belgium in the Netherlands, but some are modern, e.g. West Berlin. The same territory is an ◊ *enclave* in respect to the state within which it is physically located. ◊◊ *pene-exclave*.

exclusive economic zone A ◊ *maritime zone* which may extend for 200 nautical miles (370 km) beyond the ◊ *baseline* from which the ◊ *territorial sea* is measured. Within this zone the coastal ◊ *state* has sovereign rights for the purpose of the exploration, exploitation, conservation and management of the natural resources of the seabed, subsoil and superjacent waters. Natural resources include both living and non-living resources and the use of the seas and winds for the production of energy. No foreigner can conduct any economic enterprise, such as fishing or mining, without the permission of the coastal state, although they do have rights to navigate vessels through the zone, to lay submarine cables and to overfly. The relationship between the exclusive economic zone and the other maritime zones (◊ *contiguous zone*, ◊ *continental shelf*, ◊ *internal waters* and ◊ *territorial sea*) is illustrated in ◊ Fig. 29. ◊◊ *high seas*, *zone of diffusion*, *zone of exclusive fisheries*.

exile A person compelled by circumstances to live outside their native land. It is important to distinguish the exile, who is compelled, from the ◊ *expatriate* and the ◊ *refugee*.

existential insideness A situation in which a ◊ *place* is experienced without deliberate and selfconscious reflection yet is full of significance. ◊◊ *insideness*.

existentialism A philosophical doctrine holding that human beings are responsible for making their own nature. It stresses personal freedom, personal decision and personal commitment in a world in which there are no absolute values outside people themselves. Existentialism has, therefore, a particular concern with the quality and meaning of human life in the everyday world. Its value in geography has been the focus on human beings as the subjects of past, present and future experiences, in contrast to the view of human beings as rational decision-makers. Within ◊ *historical geography* an existentialist approach has been used in an endeavour to reconstruct a ◊ *landscape* in the eyes of its occupants, users and explorers. ◊◊ *humanist geography*, *lifeworld*.

existing use value The market value or price of land or real property, based on a continuation of the current use because there are no proposals or prospects of the land being developed or the property redeveloped to a more profitable use. Existing use value is then the ◊ *net present value* of the stream of future net benefits from the present use of the land or property. ◊◊ *development value*.

exit ratio In the analysis of manufacturing plants in a region, an exit ratio is the ratio between the number of plant closures during a certain period to the total number of plants existing in the region at some time in the period. ◊◊ *entry rate*, *survival ratio*.

exogenic change The shaping of conditions in a ◊ *system* by external factors, e.g. foreign trade on a nation's manufacturing industries. ◊◊ *endogenic change*.

exogenous activities ◊ *basic activities*.

exonym ◊ *conventional name*.

expanded towns, expanding towns Towns selected for expansion under the provisions of the 1952 Town Development Act. Such towns were a second instalment, after ◊ *new towns*, of the ◊ *overspill* plan to deal with the planned relocation of population and activities from major metropolitan centres. The 1952 Act was designed to facilitate town expansion by local authorities and to encourage them to meet the overspill problem themselves by agreement and co-operation. Large cities wishing to provide for their surplus populations (the exporting authority) would do so by voluntary agreements with neighbouring or more distant towns (the receiving authority). Actual development can be undertaken by the receiving authority; or by the exporting authority acting either as an agent for the receiving authority or on their own account; or by the county council in whose area the receiving authority is situated. Certain financial help was available from the central government in the form of a grant towards the cost of main sewerage, sewage-works and waterworks required for the development, as well as the normal housing subsidy. The exporting authority could also make available financial and technical assistance. ⟡ *concentrated decentralization*.

expansion diffusion ⟡ *diffusion*.

expansion investment ⟡ *investment*.

expansive diffusion ⟡ *diffusion*.

expatriate An individual who voluntarily chooses, especially for personal reasons, to live outside their native country. Expatriate should be distinguished from ⟡ *exile* and ⟡ *refugee*.

expectation of life ⟡ *life expectancy*, *life table*.

expectation of life at birth Also called the *mean length of life*, it is the average of the years lived by a birth ⟡ *cohort*. ⟡ *life expectancy*.

expected distance In an analysis of distances between points in an area, that distance which occurs most frequently, given that many pairs of points are randomly chosen within an area. Minimum expected distance occurs with a circular-shaped area. It assumes straight-line distances and that transportation is possible in all directions.

experiential space ⟡ *phenomenal environment*.

explanation A statement or fact that accounts for something. ⟡ *cognitive description*.

exploitation-history projection A method of forecasting the amount of a mineral resource available in any area on the basis of a ⟡ *discovery–depletion cycle* or exploitation curve based on the history of production. The method has been used extensively in the case of oil and natural gas. ⟡ *geologic-analogy projection*.

exploratory data analysis Classical ⟡ *statistics* were developed to meet the requirements of the natural sciences and therefore reflect the more deductive nature of ⟡ *hypotheses* developed in those sciences. Such statistics have offered the social scientist little in the way of techniques for exploring messy data in the context of incomplete theories. Exploratory data analysis, pioneered by J. W. Tukey, is directed towards the problem of finding hypotheses and provides techniques to search for patterns and exceptions to patterns. ⟡ *confirmatory statistics*. ⟡ *descriptive statistics*, *inferential statistics*.

export base theory ⟡ *economic base theory*.

export concentration A term used to describe the situation where one or a few goods account for the bulk of a nation's ⟡ *exports*. More commonplace than ⟡ *import concentration*, it is typical of many countries and is a function of their trade access to the ⟡ *First World* – the lesser the access the greater is export concentration. ⟡ *commodity concentration*.

export processing zone Or *investment promotion zone*. An area of a ⟡ *port*, approved by the national Customs, where factories can be built to produce goods for export without incurring the various forms of local taxation that would add to the cost of the goods, e.g. as at Kaohsiung, Taiwan's major port. ⟡ *entrepôt*, *free port*.

exports Goods, surplus to a country's requirements, which are sent abroad in ⟡ *trade*. From the national standpoint they may be regarded as goods exchanged for ⟡ *imports* (⟡ *balance of payments*, *balance of trade*, *terms of trade*). Normally the goods have been produced in the exporting country, but sometimes they are re-exports of goods originally purchased abroad. ⟡ *export concentration*, *invisible exports*.

export theory of growth ⟡ *economic base theory*.

exposure index ⟡ *isolation index*.

extant dereliction ⟡ *derelict land*.

extended environment ⟡ *real environment*.

extended family A composite ◊ *family* structure, which may consist of several generations of basic family units (◊ *nuclear family*), related by descent, marriage or adoption, living together. Anthropologists have used the term in a more restricted sense to mean a group consisting of a number of brothers living with or near their father and managing a common patrimony under his authority. Sociologists apply it in the wider sense of any household group which includes kin outside the nuclear family. Sometimes also referred to as *joint family*.

extensive agriculture An ◊ *agricultural system* characterized by low levels of inputs, especially labour, per unit area of land. With low inputs, yields per unit area are also low and depend largely on inherent ◊ *land capability*. Farm sizes must therefore be very large to secure a reasonable profit.

extensive margin of cultivation ◊ *economic margins of cultivation.*

external diseconomies Factors outside the control of the individual firm that cause inefficiencies in the firm's manufacturing and other operations. External diseconomies generally result from too-large concentrations of competing activities in a particular area. ◊ *diseconomies.* ◊◊ *external economies.*

external economies External economies represent cost advantages obtained by a firm through no direct effort on its own part, i.e. scale economies from sources external to the individual firm. These lower costs arise from:
(i) Labour supply advantages such as the local availability of skilled labour, workers familiar with the industry in question, local colleges geared to provide training.
(ii) Locational association of firms promoting ◊ *specialization* between firms and inter-firm ◊ *linkages* in the supply of materials, components, equipment and technical services.
(iii) Infrastructure benefits, including the provision of ancillary services such as banking and transportation.
(iv) Research and development opportunities, not forgetting the spin-off of ideas from competitors.

External economies typically develop in a localized concentration of firms engaged in a particular activity and their extent is a function of the number of firms present. Such external economies are especially important to small firms. ◊ *economies of scale, localization economies.*

externalities An externality is said to exist when one firm's production (or an individual's consumption) affects the production process (or standard of living) of another firm (household) in the absence of any market transaction between them. Thus one activity generates certain unpriced and usually unintended effects upon others. Hence an alternative term occasionally used is *third-party effects.* Externalities may be positive (confer benefits) or negative (impose costs) and may also be unidirectional (where A imposes an externality on B but B does not on A) or reciprocal (where A imposes an externality on B and B likewise on A). Many externalities have a spatial dimension because they relate to effects of one land use on neighbouring locations, e.g. the noise problem experienced by residential areas located near an international airport. ◊ *externality field.*

externality field The spatial field or extent over which an ◊ *externality* is experienced.

extractive industry ◊ *Primary activities* involved in the extraction of ◊ *non-renewable resources*, e.g. mining, quarrying.

extraneous traffic ◊ *Traffic* which has no reason to be in a particular locality apart from having been directed there, or come there of its own accord because no other route is available, or in response to congested conditions or lack of parking space elsewhere. Extraneous traffic is therefore not functionally related to the land uses in the area it is using. ◊ *environmental area.*

extrapolation A simple method of projection which involves extending the known values of a variable beyond the limit of observations by continuing the trend shown in the observed values, e.g. future population trends based on extending past rates of natural increase.

extraterritoriality Rights awarded to one ◊ *state* in the ◊ *territory* of another. Most cases concern provisions made for the trading activities of landlocked states.

exurban A term describing the zone beyond the continuous urban ◊ *built-up area* within which ◊ *commuters* to the urban area are dominant. These commuters have been referred to as *exurbanities.* ◊◊ *rural–urban fringe.*

ex-works pricing ◊ *f.o.b. pricing.*

F

F-ratio test, *F*-test ◊ *analysis of variance*.

fabrication-in-transit ◊ *in-transit privilege*.

fabric effects In an urban area, the effect of inherited ◊ *morphology* on modern land use, e.g. ◊ *gentrification* is affected by the location of housing types most amenable to renovation and upgrading.

facies triangle ◊ *ternary diagram*.

factor analysis A multivariate technique whose single most distinctive characteristic is its data-reduction capability, since it replaces the original ◊ *variables* by a new set of uncorrelated components, the leading ones accounting for relatively large shares of the original ◊ *variance*. There are, however, fewer factors than original variables, because factor analysis ignores the unique aspects of each variable (those not correlated with any other), leaving some of the variance to be accounted for by an error term.

Given a matrix of ◊ *correlation coefficients* for a set of variables, factor analysis seeks to determine whether some underlying pattern of relationships exists such that the data may be 'rearranged', 'reordered' or 'reduced' to a smaller set of factors that may be interpreted as source variables accounting for the observed interrelationships in the data. Factor analysis thus identifies the characteristics which the variables have in common and which result in their interconnection. ◊ *factor loadings*. ◊◊ *principal components analysis*.

factor loadings In a ◊ *factor analysis*, a factor loading represents the degree to which a given ◊ *variable* is attached to a factor, in the sense of co-varying with the family of variables that most contribute to that factor. Each variable has a factor loading for each factor, and where variables are strongly correlated they will have similar factor loadings of high value on several factors. The factor loading is the value of the square root of the sum of the common variances (that proportion of total ◊ *variance* that correlates with other variables) for each variable.

factor mobility The degree to which ◊ *factors of production* can move from region to region or occupation to occupation in response to differences in factor prices and other measures of benefits and opportunities.

factorial ecology The application of ◊ *factor analysis* in ◊ *urban ecology* to the study of ◊ *areal differentiation*. It is most often applied at the intra-urban scale, using demographic, housing and socio-economic data from censuses, and is based on the assumption that the differentiation of residential areas can be accounted for by a much smaller number of factors than the original variables. ◊ *Social area analysis* provides the usual approach.

factors of production The various agents or resources which are combined to produce goods and services. ◊ *Land*, ◊ *labour* and ◊ *capital* are the traditional categories, the first two being primary factors of production whereas capital is a derived factor of production. Organization or enterprise is sometimes added as a fourth category (◊ *entrepreneur*). Factors may be classified as *specific*, of a specialized type which cannot easily be adjusted to serve an alternative purpose, or *non-specific*, which can readily be put to alternative uses. From the geographical point of view factors of production have to be assembled at one place before production can begin. Socialist economics uses the concept of ◊ *productive forces* rather than factors of production.

factory The building or unit in which goods are manufactured, i.e. where the ◊ *form utility* of raw materials is changed in the production process. ◊◊ *firm*.

factory farming The technique of ◊ *capital intensive* animal-raising in an artificial environment, used for chicken, egg, turkey, beef, veal and pork production. Animals are restrained in a controlled indoor environment and their food is brought to them. The buildings take on the appearance of industrial units. ◊◊ *agricultural system*.

factory system A method of organizing manufacturing which gathers workers together in one place, the ◊ *factory*, to perform their tasks based on the principle of ◊ *division of labour*. Early factories were generally established to take advantage of a single power source that could drive many machines simultaneously. ◊◊ *cottage industry*, *domestic industry*, *mass production*.

factory village ◊ *planned village*.

fairs A periodical gathering for the sale of goods, often with side-shows and entertainments. A certain kind of merchandise was often associated with a particular fair, e.g. cheese fairs. Fairs appear to have their origin in the gatherings of people in prehistoric times and later in the religious assemblies at holy shrines or on the wake or feast of a saint. During medieval times fairs were frequently held in churchyards on saints' days. ◊◊ *market*.

fairway The main navigable channel, usually buoyed and lighted, which is the usual course or passage of a vessel entering or leaving a ◊ *port* or a ◊ *harbour*.

fallow The practice of letting certain ◊ *arable land* remain without cropping for a season or more to allow it to recover its fertility without manuring. The soil is rested after some crops have been taken and the soil cleaned of weeds by leaving it unused; the latter is most successfully accomplished during a long dry spell, hence it is also known as *summer fallow*.The soil is ploughed several times and harrowed during the fallow period, so aerating the soil, whose nitrogen content is also improved by the decaying weeds. It is an ancient practice (◊ *triennial fallow*) but an expensive and uncertain one. The period varies between areas, being longer on heavier soils. In semi-arid areas fallowing is commonly practised to allow the soil to build up in moisture (◊ *dry farming*). ◊◊ *social fallow*.

familial space ◊ *activity space*.

family A social group of two or more persons based on marriage and united by ties of ◊ *kinship*, with a common culture and living together in a common household. The simplest form is the ◊ *nuclear family* (or *conjugal family*, or *elementary family*, or *minimal family*, or *primary family*) which comprises father, mother and immature children. ◊ *extended family*, *problem family*. ◊◊ *completed family size*, *family cycle*.

family cycle Every ◊ *family* with children passes through various stages in the family cycle, with corresponding changes in its housing needs, etc. The first, pre-child, stage commences with marriage and ends with the birth of the first child. Stage two is that of family building, childbearing and child-rearing, and stage three that of dispersal, child-launching, as children leave home. At the last, post-child, stage the couple are living alone again. At stage two there is an *expanding family* and at stage three a *declining family*. Stages two and three may overlap in a very large family or where births are exceptionally widely spaced. These stages may also witness the emergence of a *one-parent family* where, because of death, desertion or divorce, the remaining parent has to bring up the children while at the same time attempting to earn a living with or without assistance from public funds.

Family Expenditure Survey The continuous sample survey of some 10,000 households per annum to obtain information on personal expenditure and income. The information is used in a regular revision of the weighting system for the index numbers of retail prices, as well as in a more general social way.

family farm ◊ *farm*.

family planning ◊ *birth control*.

family reconstitution A method of historical demographic analysis based on the identification of all the ◊ *vital events* (baptisms, marriages, burials) of individuals in a given ◊ *family* which can be extracted from parish registers.

farm The modern usage of the term is as a synonym for ◊ *agricultural holding*, an area of land, which may vary enormously in size, and its buildings, owned or rented by one management and used for growing crops and/or raising livestock. Originally the term meant food, but by the 15th century it had come to mean ◊ *rent*, in money or kind, for a landholding and later any area of land occupied by a ◊ *tenant* for farming.

A *family farm* has been a common unit, which, ideally, supports a single ◊ *family*. It differs from a traditional peasant holding in the employment of outside labour in addition to family labour and is organized as a commercial enterprise. ◊> *ladder farm*, *residential farm*, *second farm*.

farm fragmentation The situation in which the fields of a ◊ *farm* are scattered over an area so that the ◊ *agricultural holding* of each farmer is not composed of a single contiguous unit of land. Fragmentation results from partible inheritance practices, the fossilization of former ◊ *open field* systems, piecemeal land reclamation, and the commercial amalgamation of non-contiguous holdings. ◊ *Land consolidation* schemes have been promoted by many governments in order to overcome the inefficiencies associated with farm fragmentation. ◊> *morcellement*, *parcellement*.

farm rent A *contract* ◊ *rent* paid by a tenant farmer to the landlord on a regular basis for the use of an ◊ *agricultural holding*. The level of rent, where determined on the open market, reflects the varying capability of the land, the size of holding and location. Length of ◊ *tenancy* and responsibility for the provision of ◊ *landlord and tenant capital* will also be reflected in the rent payable.

farmer A person who makes a living from ◊ *agriculture* by managing and cultivating a ◊ *farm*, whether as tenant or owner. ◊> *hobby farmer*, *sidewalk farmer*, *suitcase farmer*.

farming ◊ *agriculture*.

farmscape A ◊ *landscape* dominated by ◊ *agriculture*: crops, ◊ *pasture*, orchards, i.e. improved land, not rough grazings. While farmland is clearly the major element in farmscape it is not the only element, since non-agricultural uses may be included as long as these are neither of the type, nor of the extent, to preclude agricultural dominance. Thus agricultural villages are part of farmscape (and not of ◊ *townscape*).

fast reactor A nuclear reactor (◊ *nuclear energy*) which uses plutonium as a fuel. The plutonium is sufficiently concentrated for the fission reaction to be sustained by fast neutrons and no moderator is necessary. Without a moderator the reactor core can be compact and have a high heat rating provided an efficient coolant is used to transfer heat to the water that drives the steam turbine to generate electricity. Liquid sodium is the coolant used. The number of neutrons produced per fission is higher than in a thermal reactor so there are more 'spare' neutrons available for absorption by the common uranium isotope U-238 and, by suitable design, this conversion gain can be chosen so that more fissile material is produced than is consumed. Reactors of this latter type are *breeder fast reactors*.

fauch Part of the ◊ *outfield* which was occasionally cropped but never received any manure.

fault-tree analysis An approach to the analysis of circumstances which could lead to a ◊ *pollution* accident. It seeks to identify the faults which could occur in an activity or production process and so cause an accident. Fault-tree analysis then seeks to determine the conditions which allow the fault to develop in order to plan for prevention or to improve safety procedures. ◊ *event-tree analysis.*

'favoured nation' status ◊ *Trade* patterns are heavily dependent upon political relationships between the governments of different countries. A country which is given preferential treatment in access to the market of another country while other countries face higher ◊ *tariffs* or ◊ *quotas* is referred to as having 'favoured nation' status.

fecundity A biological term expressing the physiological capacity (the reproductive potential) of a female or a population to produce live born children. ◊ *fertility.*

federal state A political system involving a two-tier form of government in which there is a clear division of powers between the all-union, central ◊ *state* government and the governments of the component provinces or states. This power division is protected by constitutional arrangements, hence both central and local governments derive their powers from the constitution and enjoy autonomy within their allocated sphere of responsibility. Central government is usually responsible for matters such as defence and foreign policy which affect the country as a whole, leaving the lower-tier governments to handle more domestic matters such as planning.

Federal states or *federations* were formed by the merging, on an equal footing, of states in what were originally sparsely populated areas, e.g. Australia, Canada, the USA, the USSR. *Federalism* was seen as a means of preserving regional diversity while at the same time allowing the benefits of co-operation in wider matters of international concern. ◊ *unitary state.*

fee simple ownership The ownership of land held without restriction on inheritance, embracing the philosophy that individuals could do as they wished with their land. It is the broadest and most complete concept of property ownership. ◊ *freehold, owner-occupation, property rights.*

feedback A term widely used in ◊ *general systems theory* and in computing. It refers to the ability of an organism, activity or machine to adjust itself or correct itself as it proceeds through time. The feedback is the information given to the control of the organism, activity or machine to regulate itself and produces a reaction which may be *positive* or *negative*.

feeder route ◊ *route.*

felled at roadside The basis on which timber is offered for sale: trees are felled by the landowner and extracted from the forest to an access or sales point on a public road.

felling licence The felling of growing trees in Great Britain is subject to licence from the Forestry Commission. Private woodland owners must obtain a felling licence before commencing felling operations. Such controls were originally imposed during the Second World War with the object of controlling the quantities of timber cut each year and also to improve the rate of replanting after ◊ *clear-felling*, since felling licences could impose conditions requiring the land to be replanted. Since the late 1960s felling licences have generally been freely granted subject to the replanting condition, and, because the felling of trees can conspicuously change the appearance of the countryside, the Forestry Commission have improved consultations with local planning and other authorities before granting approval.

There are certain exceptions to the need for a felling licence, the main ones being:
(i) Trees in gardens and orchards.
(ii) Any trees below 3 in (7·6 cm) in diameter, measured 5 ft (1·65 m) from the ground.
(iii) Underwood below 6 in (15·2 cm) in diameter, measured 5 ft from the ground.
(iv) Thinnings below 4 in (10·3 cm) in diameter, measured 5 ft from the ground.
(v) Dedicated woodlands (◊ *dedication scheme*).
(vi) In cases where the amount of timber felled for the landowner's own use is less than 825 hoppus ft in any quarter of a calendar year.
◊◊ *tree preservation order*.

ferling A quarter of a ◊ *yardland*.

fermtoun A small group of farms or ◊ *hamlet* in lowland Scotland. ◊◊ *clachan, kirktoun*.

fertility A term which refers in a general context to all aspects of human reproduction leading to live births, but in a narrow sense to the achieved number of live births, in contrast to ◊ *fecundity*, the potential number. ◊ *fertility rate*. ◊◊ *cohort fertility, marital fertility*.

fertility rates Since the only persons likely to give birth to children are women between certain ages, fertility rates are measured as the ratio of the number of live births per thousand women of childbearing age.

$$\text{General fertility rate} = \frac{\text{No. of live births} \times 1{,}000}{\text{No. of women aged 15–49 years}}$$

This measurement is to be preferred to the crude ◊ *birth rate* as an index of ◊ *fertility*. However, the general fertility rate does not allow for variations in the childbearing capacity, as the proportion of women at different ages changes; therefore fertility probabilities are calculated for ◊ *cohorts* of women within the childbearing age range to give *age-specific fertility rates*.

Fertility rates are a function of the characteristics of (a) potential mothers, such as their age and occupation, whether they are married and if so their age at marriage; (b) the family unit, including the number and age of existing children, the social class of the parents, their income and religion; (c) the geographical area, such as urban or rural, and general standards of housing and environment; and (d) society at large, including the extent of urbanization, education, medical know-how and fashion in family size. ◊ *reproduction rate*. ◊◊ *cohort fertility, completed family size, total fertility rate*.

fertility schedule A table or set of age-specific ◊ *fertility rates*.

fertilizer Material (natural or artificial) which is added to the soil to increase its productivity by supplying those chemical elements (in particular nitrogen, phosphorus and potassium) that are necessary for plant growth. ◊◊ *manure cycle*.

Fetter's model An early contribution to the ◊ *locational interdependence theory of industrial location* dealing with the highly simplified context of ◊ *duopoly*. F. A. Fetter considered some of the ways in which firms might compete to control as much of the market as possible. His market penetration model assumed two firms producing identical goods at fixed locations on a uniform plane where ◊ *freight rates* are proportional to straight-line distance. The boundary between the market areas of the two competing firms forms an ◊ *indifference* curve along which prices quoted by both firms are equal and potential consumers are indifferent as to which firm they buy from. The market boundary is a hypercircle determined by the equation

$$P_1 + T_{1x}D_{1x} = P_2 + T_{2x}D_{2x}$$

where P = market price at firm locations 1 and 2
T_x = freight rate between firm location 1 or 2, and a given consumption point, x
D_x = distance between firm location 1 and 2, and consumption point x

◊ Fig. 63 illustrates three alternative forms of the boundary: in (a) factory prices and freight rates are the same for both firms; in (b) firm 1 has a lower factory price than firm 2; and in (c) firm 1 enjoys lower freight rates.

feu The principal form of land ownership in Scotland, where land is held on a perpetual lease for a fixed annual service or payment, the *feu-duty*.

feudalism A pre-capitalist ◊ *mode of production* common in Europe during the Middle Ages in which land was held by giving one's services to the owner. Thus neither labour nor the products of labour were marketable commodities. The peasant, the immediate producer, was bound to the land by serfdom, a specific social relationship. The land was controlled by a class of feudal lords who extracted a surplus from the peasants by means of politico-legal compulsion, forcing them to work on the ◊ *demesne* and restricting their spatial mobility.

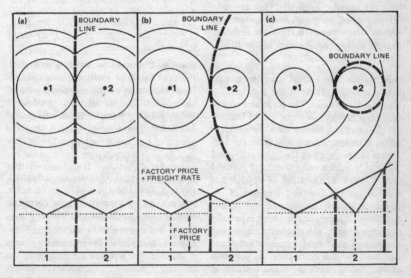

Fig. 63 Fetter's model

ffridd, ffrydd The Welsh equivalent of ◊ *in-by land*: ◊ *rough grazing* enclosed from the mountain and used as common pasture.

field (1) A piece of land, cleared of natural vegetation and specifically bounded, for use as ◊ *arable* or ◊ *pasture*. Sizes and shapes of fields vary enormously depending on the geological structure of an area, its farming history and practices. New ◊ *Stone Age* fields were small circular clearances of about 1·0 acre (0·4 hectare). ◊ *Celtic fields* were small and rectangular, mainly on chalk uplands, and surrounded by small banks. The Saxons, with the advantage of heavier ploughs, had ◊ *open fields* with longer furrows in strips separated by ◊ *balks* of turf or stone. Typical ◊ *enclosure* fields are rectangular with regular hedgerows. ◊ *field system*.
(2) The spatial extent of a characteristic or range of a centre's influence, e.g. ◊ *information field, mean field*.

field drainage The removal of excess surface and sub-surface water from the land. Originally, until the 18th century, farmers relied on ◊ *ridge and furrow* and gravity, but new methods, such as brush drains, hollow drains and tile draining, have been introduced.

field system The formal arrangement or layout and utilization of the ◊ *fields* of a farming community. The form and size of fields is a product of three sets of factors: (a) physical conditions such as geology, relief, drainage, climate and soils, (b) biological factors, such as the crops cultivated and the livestock raised, and (c) cultural factors, such as the state of agricultural technology, the law and customs of inheritance, and the pressure of population. ◊ *Historical geography* has been especially concerned with the reconstruction and analysis of past field systems. Emphasis has been on the cultivation of common arable fields, with a basic distinction drawn between a field system that had no communally organized cropping scheme, ◊ *open field*, and those that did, ◊ *common field*.

Practices varied widely both with regard to the ◊ *crop rotations* over the arable area and to the type and length of ◊ *fallow*. ◊◊ *three-field system, two-field system*.

filter-down theory of industrial location A theory propounded to explain the spatial ◊ *diffusion* of manufacturing activity within an ◊ *urban system* in terms of the relocation of existing firms from innovating areas. New manufacturing firms are started in the largest urban areas because of their need for the entrepreneurship, capital, infrastructure and, above all, the skilled labour which is available there. Once successfully established the firm seeks to improve its profitability by improving its production process and, after a time, with the aid of changing production technology that process becomes standardized and mechanized. From this point the large urban area becomes, increasingly, a high-cost location. Firms therefore seek alternative locations in smaller cities where low-cost unskilled labour is available. ◊ *industrial location theory*. ◊◊ *stage model of industrial location*.

filtering A process by which a change in the real value of existing houses allows their occupation by different social groups. In practice, filtering involves obsolescent housing being handed down the social hierarchy. The concept implies that the ageing of housing brings a relative decline in a house's attractiveness and value because of ◊ *obsolescence*. It also assumes that new (quality) housing is produced only for the highest-income groups.

As the housing formerly occupied by the highest-income households moving into newly built property is vacated and becomes available to lower-income groups a chain effect is created throughout the housing market. Successively lower-income groups, it is argued, can improve their housing conditions by moving into houses vacated by the next higher-income group. In so far as whole ◊ *neighbourhoods* may be affected filtering is a special case of ◊ *invasion-succession* and was viewed, especially in the inter-war period, as a means of improving the housing conditions of the lower-income groups. This latter is by no means certain, however, since property may have deteriorated below an acceptable level and the rate of filtering may be inadequate to meet the demand because some vacated housing is converted to non-residential use, while other vacated housing, with poor public transport, is locationally unsuitable for lower-income households.

Emphasis in the above process has been on houses, but there is also the view that households, not houses, filter. This view recognizes that housing utility can be improved either by staying put and using financial and social power to increase the flow of housing services through neighbourhood ◊ *rehabilitation* (◊ *gentrification, incumbent upgrading*), or by moving location to obtain a preferred bundle of housing services. The former is referred to as *passive filtering*, the latter as *active filtering*.

final energy ◊ *energy*.

financial capital ◊ *capital* (*2*).

financial linkage ◊ *linkage*.

fire agriculture ◊ *shifting cultivation*.

fire ecology The influence of fire on ◊ *ecosystems*. Fire has been a significant factor in ecosystem development and some major vegetation types have been caused or maintained by it. Fires may be natural, e.g. from lightning strikes, or caused by human beings, deliberately or accidentally. ◊ *muirburn*.

firm A self-governing economic unit that organizes resources to produce goods and services in response to consumer demands. As a basic unit of management it operates under a trade name and may be engaged in either the extraction of minerals, the production or manufacturing of goods, or the selling of goods and services (or in any two or all three of these activities simultaneously). A firm may be constituted as a sole proprietorship, a partnership, a private or public ◊ *limited liability* company, or a state-owned enterprise. ◊ *establishment*.

first law of geography Spatially located data generally exhibit ◊ *spatial autocorrelation* and geographers fully appreciate that the statistical concept of independence cannot be sustained for spatial data. Hence W. R. Tobler's first law of geography: Everything is related to everything else, but near things are more related than distant things.

First World A euphemism for the non-Communist, richer countries of the world, which set the relative standard of affluence, based on ◊ *industrialization*, for other countries to follow. The First World is one of three major worlds of ◊ *development* recognized in a global generalization of economic patterns (◊ *Second World, Third World, Fourth World*). It is dominated by the United States, Western Europe and their satellites and is characterized by an economic system based on ◊ *capitalism*, with its attendant emphasis on private ownership, corporate wealth and a ◊ *market economy* with a minimum of ◊ *planning*. To this commercial-exchange system the First World has added political, social and military systems in which parliamentary democracy exists (with strategy rather than ideology differentiating the main political parties), a liberal mass education is provided based on middle-class values, and a professional military class (with low political involvement) has emerged. The First World is also highly urbanized, is highly bureaucratized, and has a high level of mass consumption and increasing time for leisure activities.

fish acreage ◊ *ghost acreage*.

fish farming The technique in which fish are bred and raised in specially constructed tanks or ponds. Since a controlled environment is provided, in which the competition for limited food supplies found in nature is removed, fish grow more rapidly in these conditions than they would in a natural state. To date it has proved most successful with the more expensive fish such as trout.

fisheries Catching fish ranks as one of society's oldest ways of exploiting the sea but, in spite of a wide range of edible marine fish, only a few species support really large *commercial fisheries*. Such fisheries belong to one of two groups: one catching demersal (bottom-living) fish, e.g. cod, haddock, plaice, sole; the other catching pelagic (surface-living) fish, e.g. anchovy, tuna, herring. Pelagic fishing can take place anywhere around the oceans where sufficient fish are found, but demersal fishing can operate only in shallow seas such as the ◊ *continental shelf* area and where great banks rise up from the sea bottom. Demersal fishing predominates in the temperate regions of the northern hemisphere because a greater proportion of the continental shelf is found there, while pelagic fishing is more important in the tropics and the southern hemisphere. ◊◊ *drift net, fish farming, mariculture, longline fishing, seine net, trawl fishing*.

fishy-back principle A freight transportation practice which combines the advantages of land transport for short hauls with water transport for longer hauls, i.e. a co-ordinated service based on the use of containers/trailers to facilitate inter-modal transfer. ◊◊ *containerization, LASH, piggy-back principle*.

fixation lines Certain limits established in the process of urban growth act, by their significance, as fixation lines. Such lines

structure the ◊ *town plan* and growth takes place in an annular fashion in relation to them, i.e. as a series of ◊ *fringe belts*.

fixed capital ◊ *capital* (*2*).

fixed costs Manufacturing ◊ *costs* which do not vary with volume of output within a certain range or scale. Costs of ◊ *fixed capital* and certain ◊ *overhead costs* must be met irrespective of level of output. ◊◊ *variable costs*.

flash A term, specially used in Cheshire, for a pool created by subsidence due to the working of rock-salt and the pumping of brine.

floating capital ◊ *capital* (*2*).

floating population Persons, such as gipsies, tramps and others, who move around more or less continuously and who may, therefore, elude ◊ *census* enumeration.

floating value The speculative or potential value of land. At any given time there is a certain demand for land for ◊ *development* purposes and many parcels of land may be available for development, but until the decision is made to develop a particular site the potential value can be viewed as 'floating' over all the sites being considered. ◊ *development value*.

flood irrigation ◊ *irrigation*.

floor price The minimum price which a potential seller is prepared to accept when selling a particular real property interest. Floor prices are subjective valuations and are influenced by the present value of the income or satisfaction the seller is enjoying, by the selling prices of comparable properties and, in the case of an occupier, by the cost of equivalent reinstatement. Sellers' subjective valuations, even of comparable properties, are therefore likely to differ. ◊ *ceiling price*.

floor space index An alternative to ◊ *plot ratio* as a means of controlling building ◊ *density* in non-residential areas. The floor space index is established by dividing the total floor space of a building or buildings proposed for a particular site by the area of the site, including half the areas of any adjoining roads.

flow line A line drawn on a map between the origin and destination points of a trip following the best route available. ⟡ *desire line*.

flow resource ⟡ *natural resources*.

flyover ⟡ *grade-separation*.

f.o.b. pricing *Free-on-board pricing*, or *ex-works pricing* or *source pricing*, whereby a ⟡ *price* is quoted at the point of production. The term is used when the price of goods to be shipped does not include ⟡ *transport costs* or insurance charges: the producer will deliver the goods, without charge, to a transportation carrier and place them on board, and from then on the buyer must be responsible. Thus the cost of transport to the consumer's location must be added to the factory price. An f.o.b. price is therefore a non-discriminatory price in the sense that each consumer pays a price in exact accordance with his/her location relative to the point of supply (i.e. the factory price plus transport cost) and it allows the ⟡ *frictions of distance* to play their full part in framing the geographical pattern of the productive activity concerned. F.o.b. pricing appears to be the natural and most logical system of allocating transport costs and has been assumed as such in most location theory. ⟡ *c.i.f. pricing, basing point pricing, blanket rate pricing, uniform pricing*.

foggara Underground channels, slightly inclined, to bring water for ⟡ *irrigation* from aquifers near the base of mountains to neighbouring lowland areas, especially in the Sahara. ⟡ *ganat, karez, levada*.

fold An enclosure for sheep, made of hurdles. Its purpose was to assist 'tathing' or manuring and trampling of the soil.

fold course, foldland An area of land originally allotted to each ⟡ *manor* upon which its sheep were kept. It comprised ⟡ *open field* arable, heaths, marsh and enclosures, so that both summer and winter pasturage was available. Also referred to as a *sheepcourse*. The practice of feeding sheep in movable ⟡ *folds* on such land was termed *foldage*.

folk society A term used by R. Redfield to convey an ideal or abstract type of society studied by anthropologists. Folk societies are small, scattered and isolated, dominated by personal and ⟡ *kinship* relations, in which secular values are outweighed by magic and religious ones. Each folk society is an integrated unit, is static and uses a simple technology. ⟡ *Gemeinschaft*.

folly A structure or extravagant building with no apparent function other than to enliven the ⟡ *landscape* to satisfy the whim of the owner. Such follies usually date from the 18th and 19th centuries and were inspired by the landowner's classical education or sights seen during European travels.

footloose industry ⟡ *Manufacturing* industry which has no strong locational preference, being neither resource- nor market-oriented. Firms in such footloose industries can locate anywhere they please within certain broad ⟡ *spatial margins* because they enjoy greater freedom and flexibility of choice deriving from the relative unimportance of transport costs to their activities and from technological advances in the use of raw materials.

footpaths Legally protected rights of way providing the pedestrian with, usually, a pleasant route, in town or country, between two places. Footpaths shown on the definitive statutory maps that county councils are required to prepare are maintainable by the highway authorities.

forced technology transfer ⟡ *countertrade*.

foreign direct investment theory Foreign direct investment theory has evolved from studies of the behaviour of ◊ *multinational corporations* and is based on a neoclassical model of the profit-maximizing firm which develops a direct investment policy in response to product prices, factor prices and tax rates that affect profits. Thus a multinational firm that has been exporting to a particular foreign market area may be confronted with rising ◊ *tariffs*, imposition of ◊ *quotas*, increasing ◊ *distribution costs* or other barriers that restrict the least-cost supply of its product to the foreign country. The firm may therefore decide that these marketing restrictions can be overcome by locating a production facility inside the foreign country, i.e. by making a direct investment.

An alternative explanation is based on the international movement of ◊ *capital* as a ◊ *factor of production*. The basic postulate is that capital moves from country *A* to country *B* because the long-term return on capital is higher in country *B* than country *A*. A third possibility views foreign direct investment as belonging to the theory of industrial organization and market imperfections, especially in its concentration in a few very large firms that possess monopolistic advantages. A fourth explanation links such investment to the ◊ *product life cycle* concept which builds on the dimension of monopolistic advantage.

foreign trade zone The US equivalent of ◊ *free port*.

foreland ◊ *Ports* have ◊ *hinterlands* and forelands. Whereas the hinterland is the area served on the landward side of the port, the foreland is the seaward trading area, the area served for the import and export of goods on the water side of the port. Forelands therefore lie beyond the port's ◊ *maritime space* and are connected to the port by ocean transport. Forelands are rarely exclusive to a particular port but are shared with other ports. ◊◊ *port space*.

forest A continuous and extensive area of land dominated by trees of any size, which may represent the natural cover of the land or have been specially planted and which is capable of producing timber or other forest products (but not necessarily exploited for such).

Alongside this modern connotation, which is usually regarded as synonymous with *woodland*, the term forest continues to have historical meaning. In the United Kingdom an area of former forest, now largely cleared for agriculture and settlement, while retaining only small vestiges of woodland, may still use its 'forest name', e.g. Ashdown Forest. More specialized was the use of the term from Anglo-Saxon times to denote waste or uncultivated heath or moorland used for hunting and stalking. Technically there was a legal distinction between forest and ◊ *chase*: the former belonged to a king, the latter to a nobleman. The royal hunting forest was outside the common law, being subject to forest law. In practice the distinction between forest and chase was usually lost because many chases were granted by the king, who retained jurisdiction and required that forest law be observed. ◊ *closed forest, high forest, normal-aged forest, open forest.*

forest park A forest park comprises a group of ◊ *forests*, part of a forest or a whole forest designated by the Forestry Commission as an area open to public access in which a variety of recreational facilities, including camping and touring caravan sites, are provided. The idea of forest parks was stimulated by the 1931 Report of the Committee on National Parks and the first – the Argyll Forest Park – was operative from 1936. By 1947 a further five had been opened: Glentrool, Glenmore, The Dean, Snowdonia and Hardknott (the latter has since been dropped). The Trossachs, which became known as the Queen Elizabeth Forest Park, was designated in 1951 and the Border Forest Park in 1955. The New Forest is managed as a forest park in all but name.

To begin with, forest parks required little recreational management but with the increase in countryside visitors in the 1960s specialized recreational management measures were adopted, including the control of car parking, the provision of picnic places and toilets, the creation of information centres, guided walks and nature trails, and the zoning of competing uses in different parts of the forest.

forestry The farming of trees to ensure a continuing supply of timber and other forest products, i.e. it conveys an idea of economic management which woodland management need not. Foresters care for existing trees, protecting them from fire, pests and diseases, and felling where trees are overcrowded or dying and when ready for cropping. They also plant new areas (◊ *afforestation*) and replant felled areas (◊ *re-afforestation*). Such planting may rely on natural regeneration or use transplanted seedlings, which have been raised in a forest nursery from seed from selected trees. Recently planted forests are usually composed of softwood trees, quick-growing conifers. ◊◊ *clear felling*, *normal-aged forest*, *selective logging*, *silviculture*, *thinning*, *yield class*.

form ratio A simple measure of the shape or form of a geographic area. Calculated as:

$$\text{Form ratio} = \frac{A}{L^2}$$

where A = area
L = longest (major) axis

A circular area produces a maximum value, 0.78 ($\pi/4$), whereas a value of zero is associated with a line.

Alternative indices are listed under ◊ *shape measures*.

form utility A change in the form of a raw material or good which increases the ◊ *utility* of the original resource, e.g. iron ore into pig iron, metal into a machine or timber into furniture. ◊◊ *place utility*, *time utility*.

formal region ◊ *uniform region*.

fortified town A town, of medieval origin or earlier, enclosed by walls, moats or other defences.

forward linkage ◊ *linkage*.

fossil fuels A collective term for all fuels derived from fossilized organic material, including peat, coal, petroleum and natural gas, and related materials such as tar sands and oil shales. ◊ *energy*, *fund energy resources*.

Fourier series analysis Fourier series analysis, or *harmonic analysis*, is a mathematical technique for analysing cyclic phenomena, involving the calculation of the regular periodicities in a time series by fitting sets of sine–cosine waves. Emphasis is on the periodicity of the series of events, i.e. the same pattern of events is repeated both forward and backward in time, e.g. seasonal unemployment, which implies no overall trend in the data. The basis of Fourier analysis is the decomposition of a given set of data into a series of simple waves (cycles or periodicities), each of which goes some way towards describing the form of the compound curve (data set). It thus breaks down the total ◊ *variance* in the original data into harmonics of different frequencies, each of which accounts for some proportion of the total variance. Fourier analysis is deterministic, with the number of cycles and their duration fixed in respect of time. Since the fluctuations dealt with in human geography are frequently non-periodic, a more robust technique, ◊ *spectral analysis*, is needed.

Fourth World A term increasingly used to denote the poorest group of developing countries, comprising (for the United Nations) the twenty-five least developed

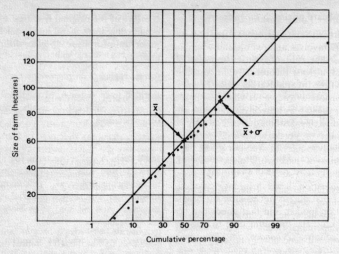

Fig. 64 Fractile diagram

countries. ◊ *least developed countries.*
◊◊ *First World, Second World, Third World.*

fractile diagram A method of testing the
normality of a ◊ *distribution* by plotting the
original individual observations on probability paper (which has cumulative percentage frequency on its horizontal axis).
The individual observations are ranked,
cumulative percentages are worked out
and then plotted against the values of the
observations they represent. The resultant
curve is measured, on the fractile diagram
(◊ Fig. 64), against the appropriate ◊ *normal distribution.* The normal distribution is
represented on the fractile diagram by a
straight line, i.e. if there are twenty-five
observations each observation represents
4% of the total, so the cumulative percentage of the first, lowest, observation is 4,
of the second 8, and so on until the last,
highest, reaches 100. Comparing the actual
cumulative percentages against this theoretical distribution shows precisely how the
distribution departs from normality.

fragmentation ◊ *farm fragmentation.*

frame ◊ *core-frame concept.*

framework agreement ◊ *countertrade.*

frankpledge The system by which the
householders of a ◊ *manor* or a ◊ *village*
were grouped into tithings (◊ *tithes*) in order
that each tithing could be held corporately
responsible for the good behaviour of its
members.

free city ◊ *free port.*

free energy A measure of a ◊ *system's*
capacity to perform work.

free goods ◊ *Goods* which are not scarce in
relation to the ◊ *demand* for them. They do
not, therefore, command, or could not
command, a ◊ *price* or exchange value, although they may still yield ◊ *utility* in use.
◊◊ *common property resource.*

free man nexus A term used by P. S. Florence to denote the psychological motive
of an ◊ *entrepreneur* to be free from the
control or power of others. The existence
of such a motive helps to explain the reluct-
ance of an entrepreneur to accept a ◊ *merger*
at the price of a loss of autonomy. ◊◊ *boss
nexus, hobby nexus.*

free-on-board pricing ◊ *f.o.b. pricing*.

free port In the strictest sense a free port or *free city* involves an area of land wherein merchandise is not subject to customs facilities and, at least theoretically, to customs jurisdiction. Invariably it is a ◊ *port* or zone within a port (a *free zone*) at which ◊ *imports* and ◊ *exports* may be received and shipped without paying customs duties. The system encourages the port to act as an ◊ *entrepôt*.

The advantages of free ports are simplification of paperwork as a result of customs concessions, a secure and protected location, lower insurance charges, the fact that duty is not payable on goods wasted or spoiled, and that goods can be stored until the optimum time to import into a country. ◊◊ *bonded, duty free zone, foreign trade zone, special economic zone*.

free trade ◊ *Trade* which is unimpeded by ◊ *tariffs*, import and export ◊ *quotas* and other measures which obstruct the free movement of goods and services between ◊ *states*. ◊ *free trade area*.

free trade area Or *duty free area*. A group of ◊ *states* that have agreed to abolish all ◊ *tariffs*, ◊ *quotas* and preferences on ◊ *trade* between themselves but at the same time maintaining their individual tariffs and restraints on trade with the rest of the world. ◊ *European Free Trade Association, Latin American Free Trade Association*. ◊◊ *common market*.

free zone ◊ *free port*.

freehold The outright or absolute ownership of land. ◊ *land tenure, owner-occupation*.

freeway A common term for interstate highways in the United States. They are usually four or more lanes in width, with separated carriageways, and may therefore be regarded as the equivalent of ◊ *motorways*.

freight absorption A situation in which the seller of a product pays all ◊ *transfer costs*.

The seller discriminates in favour of more distant buyers in order to extend a location's market area. Normally a price is set that covers average delivery costs plus the producer's other costs. ◊ *c.i.f. pricing, uniform pricing*.

freight rates The charges made by a transporter for loading, moving and unloading goods. For many goods, freight charges are a major element in ◊ *transport costs*. Freight rates discriminate between goods on the basis of their ◊ *transferability*. ◊ *class rates, commodity rates, line-haul costs, terminal costs*. ◊◊ *freight-rate territories, in-transit privilege, rate-group principle*.

freight-rate territories ◊ *Freight rates* regulated on a regional basis to reflect differing volumes of traffic. ◊ *rate-group principle*.

frequency distribution An empirical frequency distribution represents a series of figures or scatter of observations ranked according to magnitude if measured on a continuous scale (e.g. wheat yields/unit area for different locations) or to frequency of occurrence where discrete categories (e.g. manufacturing firms in each industrial group) are involved. Most often the data, even for continuous scale measurement, are presented as a grouped frequency distribution in order to bring out the pattern more clearly. This involves tabulating the number of occurrences per class of the values of the variable. This tabulation is often displayed in the form of a ◊ *histogram*. Theoretical frequency distributions (◊ *binomial distribution, normal distribution, Poisson distribution*) indicate the number of occurrences per class to be expected according to some algebraic formula.

friction of distance Geographical space is perceived as a barrier or obstacle to movement. There is no such thing as perfect ◊ *accessibility*; thus friction of distance or friction of space is a measure of the retarding effect of ◊ *distance* on human interaction. Without such friction there would be no ◊ *transport costs* and all locations would be perfect, but since there is friction of distance, movement costs show an increase with increasing distance of movement. This frictional effect is measured and incorporated in the ◊ *gravity model*.

frictional blight ◊ *blight*.

frictional unemployment ◊ *unemployment*.

Friedmann model ◊ *spatial structure and national economic development*.

friends-and-neighbours effect In ◊ *electoral geography* a type of ◊ *contextual effect*, with voters favouring candidates of local origin.

fringe belt A belt-like zone of mixed land uses at the edge of a town's ◊ *built-up area*. The mixed character reflects the clustering of land use units seeking peripheral locations, having been forced out of town by ◊ *centrifugal forces*. A fringe belt describes the growth of a town in relation to ◊ *fixation lines* and, being recognized as a major plan division of a town, is the basis of M. R. G. Conzen's methodology of ◊ *town plan* analysis. Fringe belts comprise two sections: a *proximal* or *inner margin*, where development is closer and more continuous, and a *distal* or *outer margin*, where growth is more sporadic and development more dispersed in character.

Over time, significant changes in population and economic base cause intermittent acceleration, deceleration or standstill in the outward growth of a town, as well as pronounced changes in the admixture of land uses in the fringe belt. The geographical result is often a series of broadly concentric fringe belts separated by other, relatively homogeneous, residential areas. Each belt is self-perpetuating, passing successively through initiation, expansion and consolidation phases. Thus a first or *inner fringe belt*, one or

more *middle fringe belts*, and a most recent or *outer fringe belt* may be recognized. ◊ *rural–urban fringe*.

fringe benefits Or *supplementary labour costs*. The various supplementary payments made by employers in respect of their ◊ *labour force*. These include contributions to pension and insurance schemes, sick pay benefits, provision for holidays and vacations, and amenities at the plant such as canteens, work clothing, medical care and sports facilities. All form part of the total labour costs of an employer. Fringe benefits account for around one-fifth of total costs of labour in advanced industrial countries.

front-and-fixture alterations The modernization of internal services and of the external appearance of well-located older buildings by commercial users while the building shell remains intact.

frontalier A trans-frontier commuter or *frontier worker* or *Grenzarbeitnehmer*. A person who lives in one country and works in another and who therefore commutes daily across the international ◊ *boundary*.

frontier Frontiers are zonal areas at the margins of the settled ◊ *territory* of a ◊ *state* and their existence is indicative of a particular stage in the expansion of the effective area of the state, since frontiers are areas into which expansion may take place. A distinction is made between *political frontiers*, where the de facto limits of the state advance hand in hand with the advance of its frontiers but its de jure boundaries lag behind, and *settlement frontiers*, which mark stages in the expansion of the state ◊ *ecumene* within preexisting de jure boundaries.

Political frontiers are often confused with ◊ *boundaries*, largely because international boundaries have frequently been drawn in frontier zones. As the sovereign state replaced earlier forms of political region so it became essential that the exact extent of sovereignty should be known: the very necessity for a boundary implies that the frontier is under pressure from both sides and may not be claimed as legitimate territory of either one or other of the states in contact with the boundary line. The expansion of Russian settlement into Kazakhstan and Soviet Central Asia took place within political frontiers. Today such frontiers are found only along the southern margins of Saudi Arabia.

Settlement frontiers, as illustrated by the colonization of the interior of Australia after the territory was already claimed, may be divided into primary and secondary categories. *Primary settlement* frontiers exist when a state is taking possession of its territory for the first time and disappear when the legal limits of the state are reached, e.g. the western expansion of United States' sovereignty through its territory in North America. As the primary settlement frontier advances, certain areas will be by-passed because adverse physical environment or inadequate techniques hinder settlement. *Secondary settlement frontiers* mark the subsequent colonization of these enclaves of unsettled territory left behind. ⟡ *march*.

frontier-mercantile model ⟡ *mercantile model*.

frontier thesis A rather romanticized theory, advanced by F. J. Turner, to explain American development in terms of the availability of an area of free land which permitted the westward advance of American settlement. The ⟡ *frontier* provided the opportunity for the rapid Americanization of the population for, as it moved westwards via a series of colonization waves, it moved steadily further away from European influence and led to the creation of a society of resourceful individuals. As successively new environmental challenges were faced with each new phase of colonization society was revamped and democratic beliefs enhanced.

fuel poverty A situation in which low-income consumers may not have sufficient resources to meet the cost of the fuel they need for heating, lighting and cooking.

fuelling station A specialized ⟡ *port* supplying either coal or oil to ocean-going vessels which are unable to carry sufficient fuel for their complete voyage in their bunkers.

full car ownership The situation in any area when the ratio of private cars to population ceases to show a material annual increase. Also known as a *saturation level*.

full employment ⟡ *employment, full*.

full-search shopping A type of consumer behaviour involving lengthy search procedures and full comparative shopping before costly and/or highly socially visible ⟡ *durable goods* are purchased. ⟡ *limited-search shopping*.

function In ⟡ *central place theory*, a separate type of business. There can be more than one function performed in a single ⟡ *establishment*. ⟡ *functional index of urban centres*.

functional approach ⟡ *functionalism*.

functional blight ⟡ *blight*.

functional boundary ⟡ *boundary*.

functional classification of cities Cities have developed to serve a variety of functions, but as they grow they usually accumulate a range of other functions. The economic structure of a particular city will therefore consist, at any point in time, of a complex amalgam of functions of varying strength. Since most cities display significant imbalances in their functional bases, various attempts have been made to classify them in terms of their functions.

The earliest attempts were qualitative, involving primarily intuitive typologies based upon functional specialization, e.g. cities were divided into administrative, defensive, cultural, productive, communication and recreation types by M. Aurousseau. The imprecision involved in such classifications led to a search for quantitative methods of classification, most using employment or occupational data, e.g. attempts to classify cities by measuring their ◊ *economic base*. In recent years the aim has changed from attempting to distinguish cities in terms of their particular functions to one of grouping together cities with the greatest functional similarity.

functional diffuseness A concept, cited by B. F. Hoselitz, as a pattern variable in distinguishing levels of economic ◊ *development*. Societies with widespread obligations and work patterns are functionally diffuse and contrast with societies at the other extreme where obligations are well-defined and roles specific and limited, i.e. *functional specificity*.

functional distance A broader concept than ◊ *social distance* which assesses in a single measure all the factors impeding ◊ *migration* between a given pair of places. Functional distance can be evaluated by comparing actual migration flows with the flows that would be expected to occur on the basis of the populations of the places in question. ◊ *distance*.

functional environment A basic unit of cultural ◊ *landscape evaluation*. The functional environment concept was developed to express those visual–cultural characteristics which describe dominant land uses. Each functional environment is a general landscape class determined by a prescribed proportion of open, forest and urban land uses, population distribution and population density. For example, in the S E N E (South-East New England) Study a forest–town clustered functional environment consists of at least 5% open land, at least 60% forested land and 0–25% developed land, with at least half the development clustered rather than dis-

persed and less than 2,590 people per km² (1,000 people per square mile).

functional index of urban centres An index, suggested by Webb, to indicate the importance of a particular function in a given city relative to the general importance of that function in the urban system being studied. It is calculated as the percentage of a city's labour force employed in a particular occupation divided by the average proportion of the labour force employed in that occupation throughout the urban system.

$$\text{Index} = \frac{\begin{array}{c}\text{\% of city's labour force employed} \\ \text{in particular occupation}\end{array}}{\begin{array}{c}\text{average \% of labour force} \\ \text{employed in that occupation in} \\ \text{all urban settlements in the system}\end{array}}$$

◊ *specialization index of urban centres*.

functional interdependence ◊ *interdependence*.

functional paradigm A major sociological ◊ *paradigm* concerned with social ◊ *systems* comprising interdependent parts which may be considered to be in a stable ◊ *equilibrium*.

functional region ◊ *nodal region*.

functional regionalism A situation in which a national or central government establishes regions but denies those regions any policy-making capability as a political or institutional entity.

functional specificity ◊ *functional diffuseness*.

functionalism Functionalism is concerned with the analysis of the functions of activities and artifacts in society as parts of larger ◊ *systems* of behaviour and belief. It is based on the view that knowledge of the way in which things work or function provides the key to understanding and explaining them, i.e. that scientific analysis and explanation must be teleological (◊ *teleology*). Major developments of functionalism as a scientific model of social systems are associated with the work of E. Durkheim, B. K. Malinowski, A. Radcliffe-Brown, T. Parsons and R. Merton in sociology and anthropology.

Functional explanatory models are common in geography, e.g. of the location of activities. A functional explanation of the location of, say, a town or factory is not however usually a sufficient explanation where there are several equally good locations for performing the function in question. In most cases therefore the functional approach demonstrates only the *necessary* conditions for a town or factory to flourish – it will seldom indicate which conditions are *sufficient* to make any one location the only possible location. The functional approach is useful in isolating some of the conditions necessary for a phenomenon to function within a given system, but it must be remembered that there is no certainty that that explanation is unambiguous and fully tenable. ⟐ *genetic approach*.

fund energy resources Non-renewable energy resources, such as peat, lignite, coal, petroleum, natural gas, oil shale and tar sands. ⟐ *fossil fuels*. ⟐ *renewable energy resources*.

fundamental circuit A ⟐ *circuit network* comprising the minimum number of ⟐ *links* to create a completely connected circuit. ⟐ *alpha index, cyclomatic number, Hamiltonian circuit*.

furlong (1) A measure of length, standardized by the end of the Anglo-Saxon period, equal to 220 yds (200 m). It was thought to derive from the distance that an ox team could plough before resting.
(2) A subdivision of an ⟐ *open field*, being an area of strips or ⟐ *selions*, of varying shapes and sizes, all of which ran in the same direction. The strips belonged to different owners. Such furlongs may have been original units of clearing from the waste or woodland incorporated into an open field. ⟐ *assart*.

G

G-scale A standard geographical measurement, proposed by P. Haggett, R. Chorley and D. Stoddart, in an attempt to simplify the multiplicity of conventional standards by substituting a scale of natural values. It was based on the area of the earth's surface (G_a) and its scale of measurement – the G-scale – was derived by successive subdivisions of this standard area by the power of 10. ⟡ *ekistic logarithmic scale.*

game theory A framework for determining an optimal strategy for behaviour in a situation where there is an element of conflict and choice, i.e. an interdependent decision situation. Decisions are made under conditions of ⟡ *risk* and ⟡ *uncertainty*, with two or more decision-makers (players) having to choose a course of action (strategy) in ignorance of the other players' choices but with the knowledge of the costs and benefits (pay-offs) of the alternative strategies. Game theory assumes that players will act rationally, the opposing players each attempting to select the optimum strategy which enables them to reap the best reward, i.e. one which promises to give the best return in the light of what future actions an opponent might take.

The principal method of analysis is to consider the various possible choices open to the rival players and to tabulate the results of possible choice in a *pay-off matrix*. The matrix shows which strategies will benefit which player. Within this framework games fall into a number of categories:

(i) Games with perfect or imperfect information. With perfect information each player knows what choice the other has made as the game proceeds (as in chess). In games with imperfect knowledge chance plays a part.

(ii) Zero-sum or non-zero-sum games. In the former one player's gains are the other's losses (so that there is no net profit or loss when the game ends), whereas non-zero-sum games are not limited in that way.

(iii) Games negotiated or non-negotiated according to the presence or absence of co-operation between players.

(iv) Games categorized according to the number of players, e.g. a two-person game.

PAY-OFF MATRIX FOR A

		PLAYER B		
		Strategy 1	Strategy 2	Strategy 3
PLAYER A	Strategy 1	-4	3	-2
	Strategy 2	4	6	SADDLE 2 POINT
	Strategy 3	3	-3	-1

Fig. 65 Game theory

⟡ Fig. 65 illustrates a possible pay-off matrix for player A in a two-person zero-sum game (the pay-offs for B are simply the reverse of A's). A can choose from strategies 1, 2 or 3 and will clearly choose strategy 2 because, whatever B does, A will get the maximum pay-off. B will choose strategy 3 knowing, as *B* does, that *A* will choose the rational course, strategy 2 (i.e. for *B*, − 2, − 6 or − 4). This is a *minimax* solution, which indicates that each player has a 'best' strategy) and occurs in games which have a *saddle point* in the pay-off matrix. A saddle point is defined as the cell in the matrix in which the value is at the same time the row minimum and the column maximum, or vice versa. Not all games have saddle points, but in those which do the saddle point is the unique solution to the game which is best for both players.

Game theory derives from a study of games in which strategy is an essential element and has been applied in geography to conflicts in location decision-making, as well as to situations in which one 'player' is the environment (although the latter are not strictly game theoretic situations since only one of the players is actively striving to win). Game theory promotes an understanding of some of the complexity underlying decision-making, largely because of its explicit focus on uncertainty and decision-makers' attitudes towards uncertainty. It forms a bridge between the behaviourally rigid approach of normative location theory and the more flexible approach of the behavioural viewpoint. However, given its assumption of optimizing behaviour, game theory is still essentially normative, presupposing that decision-makers have high levels of information and computational abilities to set up pay-off matrices.

gamma The measure of association in a ◊ *contingency table* which makes no adjustments for either ties or table size.

$$\text{Gamma} = \frac{P - Q}{P + Q}$$

where *P* = concordant pairs
   Q = discordant pairs
Gamma has a positive value if concordant pairs predominate, negative if discordant

predominate, and zero if they are equal. ◊ *Kendall's tau.*

gamma index The measure of the degree of ◊ *connectivity* in network geometry, being the ratio of the number of observed ◊ *links* between ◊ *nodes* on a ◊ *network* to the maximum number of links possible on that network.

$$\text{Gamma index} = \frac{e}{\frac{1}{2}n(n - 1)}$$

where *e* = number of links (edges or routes)
   n = number of nodes
Note: $\frac{1}{2}n(n - 1)$ gives the maximum number of links.

Values of the index range from 0·0 to 1·0, with 0·0 representing no connections between any nodes and 1·0 the maximum number of connections where there are direct links between all the nodes. Also referred to as the *connectivity index.* ◊ *alpha index, beta index, cutpoint index, cyclomatic number, detour index, König number, Shimbel index.*

ganat An underground channel which carries water for ◊ *irrigation* from the mountains, where precipitation is plentiful, to the drier areas below in Iran. ◊ *foggara, karez, levada.*

gap town A town situated in, or at the entrance to, a gap and which therefore commands important passages used by modern ◊ *routes* through physical barriers such as ridges and ranges of hills. ◊ *confluence town.*

garden An enclosed piece of land, especially attached to a house, used for the cultivation of flowers, fruit and vegetables. ◊ *allotment.*

garden city A settlement, carefully designed and built according to a master plan, with the object of providing a spacious, high-quality environment for living and working. The garden city movement drew upon the various 19th-century philanthropic concepts and efforts to develop utopian communities for factory workers. The formal exposition of the garden city idea was undertaken by Ebenezer Howard in his book *A Peaceful Path to Social Reform* published in 1898 (reissued in 1902 as *Garden Cities of Tomorrow*), in which he advocated the garden city as a ◊ *satellite town* incorporating the best of both urban and rural environments, in contrast to the congestion and squalor of the 19th-century industrial town.

Howard's garden city would accommodate some 32,000 inhabitants on a site of some 6,000 acres (2,429 hectares), planned to a concentric land use pattern with a central built-up area of 1,000 acres (405 hectares), using individual housing plots of 20 ft × 130 ft (6 m × 40 m), and with a gross residential density of thirty persons per acre (seventy-five/hectare), i.e. ten houses per acre (twenty-five/hectare). There would be six ◊ *boulevards*, 120 ft (36 m) wide, extending radially from the centre, which would assist in forming six wards to provide the basis of local government and community services. The garden city would be self-sufficient in terms of employment, possessing its own light industry, commerce, shops and agriculture. When the planned capacity was attained a further garden city would be developed. Such garden cities would be clustered around a central city of 50,000 people, tied to that city and each other by efficient road and rail links. Open space and the extensive planting of trees would be provided within the town in the form of wide streets, low-density housing and ◊ *public parks*, and beyond by open farmland and ◊ *green belt*.

These ideas were put into practice. In 1899 Howard formed the Garden City Association (which became the Town and Country Planning Association in 1918), and a company called Garden City Pioneer Company was registered in 1902 with the express purpose of finding a suitable site.

A site at Letchworth was obtained in 1903 and the First Garden City Ltd was in business. Letchworth represents the first successful modern attempt at such a development, although progress was slow because of financial constraints due to the venture being entirely privately financed. A second garden city was begun at Welwyn in 1920 but its growth was also hampered by financial stringency. The garden city movement was a forerunner of the postwar ◊ *new towns* programme.

garden suburb, garden village A planned and landscaped residential area, originally derived from the ◊ *garden city* concept, where overall control is exercised by a ground landlord (usually in the form of a property company), e.g. Hampstead Garden Suburb, whose plan was drawn up by B. Parker and R. Unwin, the architects for Letchworth Garden City. ◊◊ *suburb*.

Garin–Lowry model ◊ *Lowry model*.

garth A small plot of enclosed land, usually by a house or cottage. ◊◊ *garden*.

Gastarbeiter ◊ *guest worker*.

gatekeepers ◊ *urban managerialism*.

gateway city A settlement which links one area or region to others and manages the area's commerce with the outside world. Gateway cities arose at the entrance points, usually favourable physical locations, to producing regions and functioned as collecting centres for the basic products from surrounding settlements and as distribution points for manufactured goods brought in from outside the region. The gateway function therefore involves such bulk assembly, break-of-bulk, trans-shipment activities as are normally associated with ◊ *ports*. Also known as *portal city*.

gathering ◊ *primitive gathering*.

gauge, railway The distance between the inner edges of the rails on a railway track. Gauges vary between countries, and are classified as broad, standard or narrow. Broad gauges include those of 5 ft (1·52 m) or more; the *standard or international gauge*, as used in the United Kingdom, is 4 ft 8½ in (1·43 m); and the narrow gauges include the metre gauge, the 3 ft 6 in (1·06 m) and smaller gauges.

Gaussian distribution ◊ *normal distribution.*

gavelkind A system of tenure whereby land could be divided equally among the sons of the last landholder. If there were no sons the daughters would inherit. Gavelkind or *partible inheritance* therefore led to ◊ *farm fragmentation. Disgavelling* was the procedure by which the inheritance rules were changed so that property could descend via ◊ *primogeniture.*

gazetteer An index of places and named geographical features, such as rivers and mountains, with references to their absolute ◊ *location.* It may also include brief descriptions or notes.

GDP ◊ *Gross Domestic Product.*

Gemeinschaft Several attempts have been made to construct a continuum of ◊ *community* life, ranging from the small isolated village to its antithesis in the big city. The best-known basis for such a continuum was put forward by F. Tönnies, who identified two ideal types whose essence would be found in all kinds of social systems – these polar opposites are usually referred to as Gemeinschaft and ◊ *Gesellschaft.* Gemeinschaft describes the more traditional type of society in which relationships are personal, intimate and often enduring. These relationships are often ends in themselves and are functionally diffuse, having more than one purpose. The society in which they occur is homogeneous and immobile, with relatively few cleavages or clashes of interest. Every member knows and accepts their place, and the moral code of society is clearly defined and generally upheld. ◊◊ *folk society, rural–urban continuum.*

general age group A term used to describe the ages of people at particular life stages. *Infant* or *baby* may mean a child who has not yet reached its first birthday or a very young child. A *child* is a person who has not yet reached puberty, a pre-school child being one who has not yet reached compulsory school age. An *adolescent* is a person who, having attained puberty, can no longer be regarded as a child, yet is not old enough to be considered as an adult. *Young people* are commonly those below the age of 30–35. The term *middle-aged* describes those between 35 and 55. The term *elderly* describes the period before and after the age of retirement. *Retired people*, *senior citizens* or *pensioners* are those above the retirement age. *Old people* may mean those over the formal retirement age or, more commonly, those over 70–75.

With most of these general age groups there is some disagreement on the exact age span which they cover.

general aviation Business executive, club and private flying. ◊◊ *aviation, commercial aviation.*

General Development Order A General Development Order identifies 'permitted development'. If a proposed ◊ *development* falls within any of the classes recognized by the General Development Order (e.g. agricultural buildings, works and uses; forestry buildings and activities; the enlargement of dwelling-houses within prescribed limits, etc.), no application for ◊ *planning permission* is necessary – the General Development Order itself constitutes permission. The purpose is to remove from the system the relatively mundane matters that might otherwise clog the planning machinery. The deemed permissions of the General Development Order can be withdrawn in specific areas by the issue of an ◊ *Article IV Direction Order.* ◊ *development control.*

General Household Survey Introduced in 1970 in response to the government's increasing need for regular information on a variety of characteristics of households, the General Household Survey covers family composition, housing, unemployment, illness and medical attention, long-distance journeys and educational qualifications.

General Improvement Area A major example of the pursuance of an area approach within housing policy and part of the attempt to co-ordinate in spatial terms the improvement of housing. Introduced under the 1969 Housing Act, General Improvement Areas could be designated by local authorities in areas of fundamentally sound houses capable of providing good living conditions for many years ahead and which were unlikely to be affected by known redevelopment or major planning proposals. The approach involves both the comprehensive improvement of houses by the concentration of ◊ *improvement grant* effort and the improvement of neighbourhood amenities by the local authority through a series of environmental works, such as pedestrianization, landscaping, and the provision of play space and off-street parking. The areas so designated usually have low population turnover and a majority of owner-occupiers, ensuring the voluntary improvement of housing through a high take-up of improvement grants. ◊ *housing policy.* ◊ *housing action area.*

general systems theory Essentially a general theory of organization that aims at the unification of science, i.e. a scientific doctrine of 'wholeness'. It was first put forward in the late 1930s by the biologist L. von Bertalanffy, who argued that scientists would not really understand the laws which govern the life of an organism until they studied the individual organism as a ◊ *system* of many associated parts. He soon realized that the idea could be extended to non-biological systems and that all these systems had many common characteristics

over a wide range of science, e.g. ◊ *allometric growth*, ◊ *entropy*. The development of a general systems theory which gave the same analytical framework and procedure for all sciences was therefore possible.

While there is a fair measure of disagreement about the validity of such a general discipline there is little doubt that the concept of a system and ◊ *systems analysis* has added to our understanding of how our complex world works. This accords with the position in geography, in which the hopes prevalent in the 1960s that general systems theory offered the prospect of fusion between human and physical geography have given way to studies of particular systems and the interfaces between them. ◊ *Macrogeography* has made the most explicit commitment to general systems theory.

generation (1) A group of persons all born about the same time (group of years) and therefore of the same age. Analysis of the experiences of a generation is a type of ◊ *cohort* analysis.
(2) The average period, regarded as about thirty years, in which children grow up and take the former place of their parents.

generative city A city that, according to B. F. Hoselitz, acts as a centre of change and stimulates ◊ *economic growth.* ◊ *heterogenetic city.*

generic boundary ◊ *boundary.*

genetic approach An approach to explanation which is based on the belief that knowledge of the way in which things originated, and then developed through time, provides the key to understanding them. The genetic approach describes the sequence of events that produced the phenomenon being explained and therefore focuses on the unique. There is no hint of generality in any of the statements of a *genetic explanation*, nor is there any explicit reference to any law or theory which could make those statements more general. ⟡ *functionalism*, *temporal analysis*.

genre de vie A concept denoting the set of social facts that intervene between geographical conditions and people's behaviour. Each group or culture has its own genre de vie, a unified functionally organized way of living, made up of habits, techniques and social, economic and psychological structures.

gentrification A process whereby the social character of a ⟡ *neighbourhood* is changed by the infiltration of professional/higher-income groups seeking central city locations. While gentrification is socially important in attracting some middle- to high-income residents back to central areas it is not numerically significant among urban population flows. Gentrification is selective not only of the population it can attract but also of the conditions under which it can occur. Its spatial incidence depends on the locations of house types most amenable to renovation and upgrading: such types are the larger, older, but structurally sound properties. The upgrading of the old housing stock represents a positive investment in inner-city environments and converts dilapidated, subdivided dwellings, even slum neighbourhoods, into expensive single family homes. This normally involves the transfer of privately rented accommodation to owner-occupation, a transfer frequently aided by the promotional efforts of estate agents. Upgrading has also been helped in the United Kingdom by the availability of ⟡ *improvement grants* and the ability to designate ⟡ *general improvement areas*. In essence gentrification is the reverse of ⟡ *filtering* and has therefore, to an extent, led to a reduction of low-cost housing and the displacement of those at the bottom of the housing class ladder. ⟡ *incumbent upgrading*.

geodesic distance Geodesic or *real distance* is the shortest path between two places measured on an absolute scale of length (kilometres or miles). ⟡ *distance*. ⟡ *social distance*.

geographical association ⟡ *areal association*. ⟡ *coefficient of geographical association*.

geographical concentration, coefficient of ⟡ *coefficient of geographical concentration*.

geographical determinism ⟡ *environmental determinism*.

geographical environment ⟡ *environment*.

geographical inertia ⟡ *industrial inertia*.

geographical market fragmentation The division of the ⟡ *market* for a product into geographical areas in which some producers have strong locational advantages over other producers.

geographical mile ⟡ *nautical mile*.

geographical mobility ⟡ *mobility*.

geographical momentum ⟡ *industrial momentum*.

geographical name The proper name or geographical expression for a place in the form used in the country concerned, e.g. Athínai (Athens), Beograd (Belgrade), Firenze (Florence). ⟡ *Conventional names* are given in brackets.

geographical region J. F. Unstead's term to describe ⟡ *regions* where there is a high degree of homogeneity in both the physical environment and human activity. ⟡ *uniform region*.

geography Geography has undergone progressive evolution over the course of several centuries, but particularly in the 20th century. It may now be viewed as the study of the earth's surface as the ⟡ *environment* and ⟡ *space* within which human beings live. Geography is therefore concerned with the structure and interaction of two major systems – the ecological system that links human beings to their environment and the spatial system that links one area of the earth's surface with another. The essential elements in geographical study are: (a) ◊ *spatial analysis*, with an emphasis on ◊ *location*; (b) ecological analysis (◊ *ecology*), with an emphasis on people–environment relationships; and (c) regional analysis, with an emphasis on region-building and ◊ *areal differentiation* (◊◊ *regional science*).

Lying athwart both the physical and social sciences, different branches of geography have proliferated, each concerned with a limited research area. ◊ *agricultural geography, anthropogeography, applied geography, behavioural geography, cultural geography, economic geography, electoral geography, historical geography, human geography, industrial geography, Marxist geography, mathematical geography, medical geography, macrogeography, microgeography, necrogeography, political geography, population geography, radical geography, regional geography, rural geography, social geography, systematic geography, time–space geography, transport geography, urban geography, welfare geography.* ◊◊ *quantitative revolution in geography.*

geolinguistics The geographical study of languages and their change over space and time.

geologic-analogy method A method of estimating undiscovered mineral reserves involving projections based on rates of production at deposits currently worked to similar geological structures in other areas. It is applied particularly to oil and gas reserves using either (1) the average oil-in-place content of productive sedimentary masses, or (2) the average number of barrels produced per unit rock volume in productive basins, or (3) the finding rate per unit of exploratory footage drilled in productive environments, to estimate the reserves of potentially productive prisms of sedimentary rock. ◊◊ *exploitation-history projection, reserves.*

geometric mean A measure of ◊ *central tendency* which is used only infrequently. The geometric mean is the preferred mean when relative changes or ratios in some variable quantity are to be averaged, i.e. where the values of the variable represent a series that tends to grow geometrically, e.g. in geography it could be used to estimate the population of a town for years mid-way between censuses. The geometric mean is defined as the Nth root of the product of the values of the variable in question from the 1st to the Nth:

$$\text{Geometric mean} = \sqrt[N]{X_1 \times X_2 \times X_3 \times \ldots \times X_N}$$

where $X_1, X_2, X_3 \ldots X_N$ = the observed
values of X
N = number of
values of X
◊◊ *arithmetic mean, harmonic mean.*

geonomic efficiency G. T. Renner's term to denote the degree to which a firm's or industry's location corresponds to its optimum location.

geonomics A term, not generally adopted, for ◊ *economic geography*, suggested by G. T. Renner.

geopacifics A term used by T. Griffith Taylor to denote the study of geography to promote peace.

geopiety A term coined by J. K. Wright to describe the special complex of relations between a person and nature. 'Geo' means earth, and 'piety' means reverence and attachment to one's family and homeland and to the gods who protect them. Geopiety therefore covers a broad range of emotional bonds between a person and nature and a person and their home. The concept was adapted by Yi-Fu Tuan (◊ *topophilia*).

geopolitics A term first used in 1899 by R. Kjellen in developing F. Ratzel's organic view of the ◊ *state* to mean the science of the state as a realm in space. Geopolitics or *Geopolitik* is, however, a much abused, indeed disreputable, term because of its close identification with Hitler's Third Reich. Kjellen's ideas, based on the view that competition for power would lead to the concentration of that power in the hands of a very few, large states, gave a quasi-scientific justification to the rights of strong states to expand by any means possible. The growth of such states was assumed to be inevitable, the result of 'natural laws'.

Geopolitik was avidly taken up by extreme nationalists, associated with the soldier and geographer K. Haushofer, in Germany and, in the aftermath of the humiliation imposed on that country at the end of the First World War, was developed as the geographical conscience of the state in order to enlist support for the supposed German right to ◊ *Lebensraum*. As such, geopolitics is essentially a body of thought developed in a given state which seeks the maximization of its own ends. This was viewed by many as a perversion of geographical science and brought the term into disrepute.

It has been suggested that ◊ *political geography* suffered as a result of the general reaction against Geopolitik, but those who used the term loosely as a synonym for political geography were poorly informed, since the distinctions between the two are clear: geopolitics is concerned with the spatial *requirements* of a state while political geography examines only its spatial *conditions*. L. D. Kristof's suggested revival of the term for the geographical study of politics at the interface between political geography and political science is probably premature in view of the earlier associations of the term.

Georef system A world-wide system of locational referencing which combines the advantages of both cartesian and spherical grid co-ordinate systems. Georef is short for *World Geographic Reference*. It sim-plifies locational references based on latitude and longitude by omitting the north, south, east, west degrees, minutes and seconds.

Georef divides the global surface into 288 segments based on the intersection of 15° meridional and latitudinal bands, each of which can be defined by index letters. Each segment (◊ Fig. 66) can be uniquely defined by a two-letter code, in which the letter of the meridional is given first. Segments, in turn, are divided into 225 quadrangles, each $1° \times 1°$, with a similar lettering system. Within each quadrangle the final location is given by the number of minutes of arc at which the place lies east and north of the south-west corner of the quadrangle.

geosophy A term introduced by J. K. Wright for the study of geographical knowledge. Wright pointed out that geographical knowledge of one kind or another is universal among human beings. Geographical knowledge therefore extends beyond a core of professionally systematized knowledge and includes the geographical ideas of all manner of people (farmers, taxi-drivers, artists and so on). Wright conceded that the study of such wide-ranging geographical knowledge was subjective but claimed that it provided indispensable background and perspective to professional geographical work.

geostatistics ◊ *centrography*.

geostrategic regions Macro-regions which reflect groupings of ◊ *states* within the international system as a result of supra-national forces. Such groupings are united by a measure of complementarity in behaviour and outlook and may have potential for further integration. Geostrategic regions are sufficiently large to exert a world-wide influence and are units over which certain elements of power could be applied and with certain minimal levels of unity in outlook and trading activity. Also referred to as *international regions*.

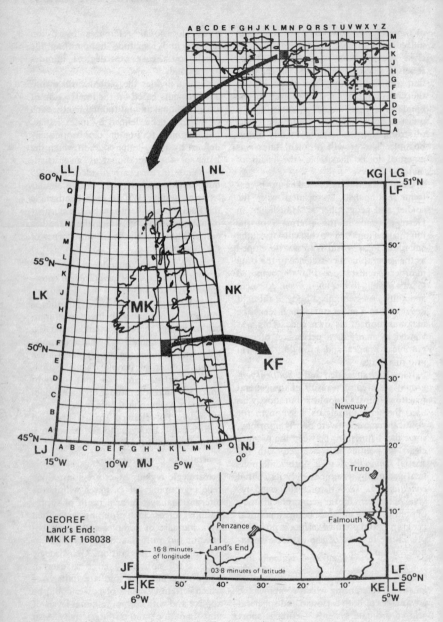

GEOREF
Land's End:
MK KF 168038

16·8 minutes
of longitude

03·8 minutes of latitude

Fig. 66 Georef

geothermal energy ◊ *Energy* available as heat emitted from within the earth's crust, usually as hot water or dry steam. Geothermal energy can be exploited only in particular areas where geological formations lead to high temperature gradients, localized at attainable depths. Potential areas are classified according to the temperatures encountered as either *hyperthermal areas*, confined to regions of seismic activity, or *semi-thermal areas*. On a global scale the present use of geothermal energy is relatively insignificant, with commercial exploitation restricted to hyper-thermal fields. The latter have been used for either local direct heating supply, as in Iceland (including horticultural applications) and North Island, New Zealand, or for electricity generation, as at Lardarello, Italy. Although geothermal energy as a whole may be treated as an inexhaustible resource, a single bore will have a limited life.

gerrymander The deliberate redrawing of constituency boundaries to maximize the electoral advantage of one party and diminish that of another party. The result is electoral bias, allowing the favoured party to elect more representatives than would be possible under a 'fair' system. The term is derived from Governor E. Gerry of Massachusetts, who manipulated boundaries in his party's favour in the early 19th century. Two contrasting strategies may be used in deciding constituency boundaries – opponent containment or opponent dispersion. The former, an excess-vote strategy, concentrates as much of the opposing vote as possible in a small number of constituencies where the massive support produces only a few successful candidates. The latter, a wasted-vote strategy, spreads opposition votes over a large number of constituencies so that they always remain in a minority in any constituency.

Electoral bias can occur without any gerrymandering and the use of the term has sometimes been extended to cover a number of these situations, e.g. a *silent gerrymander*, where constituency boundaries are not changed to coincide with population change. ◊ *districting algorithm*, *electoral geography*.

Gesellschaft Gesellschaft describes the industrial society which is at one pole of F. Tönnies' continuum of social systems. It typifies a society where relationships are selected and used for their rationality and efficiency in achieving specific ends. ◊ *Mobility* is high, both socially and spatially. Life is dominated by impersonal and contractual ties, often of a transitory and superficial nature, and there is an absence of traditional morality. ◊ *Gemeinschaft*, *rural–urban continuum*.

Gestalt psychology A 'school' of psychology, originating in Germany in the early 20th century, whose basic tenet is that the whole is greater than the sum of its parts. Psychologists of this school believe that behaviour and experience should be studied in a way which emphasizes the organization, patterning and wholeness of human behaviour, rather than any of its atomistic elements. They therefore reject the stimulus–response approach of ◊ *behaviourism*. *Gestalt* is the German for shape or form.

Gewanndorf A nucleated ◊ *village* with strip fields. ◊ *Haufendorf*.

ghetto A small residential district in an urban area distinguished by the extreme concentration of an ethnic or cultural group. Historically the term ghetto described the quarter of the medieval city, especially in Italy, to which the Jews were legally restricted for residence. As a term to describe the immigrant districts of American cities it was first used at the end of the 19th century, when large numbers of east European Jews settled in the inner areas of north-eastern and mid-western cities. In that context, the word very quickly lost its exclusive association with Jewish settlements and acquired more general meaning to describe the residential segregation of newly arrived immigrants. In American cities today ghettos are particularly associated with black populations: their occurrence in the worst inner-city districts is a reflection of the black population's inability to achieve structural ◊ *assimilation*, and their restriction to limited areas for expansion indicates the barriers presented by ◊ *charter group* attitudes and discriminatory practices in the housing market.

In effect, the term is now applied to any highly clustered ethnic or cultural group irrespective of whether they are materially deprived, socially disorganized or concentrated in the inner city. Such extreme segregation results from the psychological and political desires of the ethnic group and/or the constraints and discriminatory action of the charter group. Ghettos are not necessarily ◊ *slums* or low-income areas, and some urban geographers have distinguished *temporary ghettos*, through which immigrant populations become adjusted to new ways of life, from *permanent ghettos* (the more normal usage), in which a cultural group can actively resist being weakened and lost in the larger community of which it is a part. ◊◊ *ethnic area, gilded ghetto, natural area.*

ghost acreage A concept suggested by G. Borgstrom to convey the dependence of modern industrial farming on imports from the underdeveloped countries. Ghost acreage is that amount of land which would need to be worked by a given country in order to produce an equivalent nutritional output in the absence of protein imports. It is subdivided into *fish acreage* and *trade acreage*. The former represents the amount of land required to produce an animal protein output equivalent to that provided by fisheries via food and feeding stuffs; the latter the amount of land needed to replace the net imports (exports) of agricultural products traded.

Gibbs–Martin index of diversification An index developed to measure the ◊ *diversification* of industrial employment in an area.

$$\text{Index} = 1 - \frac{\sum_{i=1}^{n} x_i^2}{\left(\sum_{i=1}^{n} x_i\right)^2}$$

where x_i = number of employees in the ith industrial category in an area
n = number of industrial categories

The values of the index can range from 0·0 to 1·0: it is zero if the labour force is concentrated wholly in one industry for the area under study, and 1·0 if the labour force is evenly distributed throughout every industry in the area. ◊◊ *coefficient of specialization, location-quotient.*

Giffen goods Giffen or *inferior goods* are commodities of relatively low quality which form an important element in the diet of low-income households, e.g. bread, potatoes. More of such goods are consumed when their price is high because as their price rises it is equivalent to a fall in real income.

gilded ghetto Some ethnic groups move up the social scale and move residentially as a group, abandoning their original inner-city quarters and reconcentrating in well-defined suburbs where they have re-established their ethnic institutions. These suburban concentrations become so well established that they are as closely identified with the ethnic heritage of their residents as were their original inner-city clusters. They are described as gilded ghettos. ◊ *ghetto.*

gilds Gilds were of two types: (i) *Merchant gilds* were formed for the regulation of trade and the mutual protection of its members. Each gild rested on a ◊ *monopoly*, and outsiders were excluded from buying and selling wholesale, except to and from gild members. Such gilds came into existence in Britain soon after the Norman Conquest and were more important in small than large ◊ *boroughs*. (ii) *Craft gilds* developed in the 13th and 14th centuries to represent the common interests of craftsmen. Though subject to the general control of the borough, such gilds managed the affairs of their respective crafts within the town.

J. E. Vance has attributed the quartered and many-centred ◊ *preindustrial city* to the role and status of the gild. Gild membership was the standard means of entry to established urban life, the gild offering a place of security, social contact, religious orthodoxy, business and entertainment. Individual *gildhalls* were foci of interests, and members tended to live within their precincts, creating occupational districts.

gill net ◊ *drift net*.

Gini coefficient The Gini coefficient, or *index of concentration*, is a versatile and commonplace measure of the degree of correspondence between two sets of percentage frequencies. Where data on a number of different activities or conditions in an area are expressed as a percentage of the areal total they can be compared collectively with the proportions of the same activities or conditions in the wider region or nation to give a profile of the area's character, or they may be compared with some hypothetical norm.

$$\text{Gini coefficient } (G) = \tfrac{1}{2} \sum_{i=1}^{N} |X_i - Y_i|$$

where X_i and Y_i represent two sets of percentage frequencies in a set of areas $(1, 2, \ldots i, \ldots N)$

The vertical brackets indicate the modules or absolute values of the expression within,

i.e. the differences are summed irrespective of their sign. The value of G will be on a scale from 0·0 to 100, with 0·0 indicating exact correspondence between the two percentage frequencies (in which case the area would be typical of the nation) and 100 indicating they were as different as possible (the area would be atypical of the nation). The Gini coefficient is applicable to all socio-economic phenomena, and is especially useful as a measure of the equality of the distribution of something between different groups in a population. ◊ *Lorenz curve*.

glacis An extension of the territorial control of a state across a mountain divide.

glasshouse cultivation Hothouse ◊ *horticulture* in which the basic productive unit is the glasshouse or greenhouse. It is the purpose of the latter to protect plants against adverse weather conditions, at the same time allowing just as much light to reach them as if they were growing in the open. Glasshouses also act as a heat-trap and may, in addition, be artificially heated to allow crops to be grown outside their normal outdoor growing season. The modern glasshouse industry concentrates on growing tomatoes, lettuces, cucumbers, peppers, flowers and pot plants.

glebe land A term used in historical geography and land ownership to denote land which belonged to the parish church and which a clergyman or minister in a parish had a right to in addition to his stipend. By the 19th century glebe land had become redundant and disposal was facilitated by an 1866 statute.

global village A characterization of Western society following the creation of a general world-wide culture by the mass media which cuts across social classes and political boundaries. The mass media, particularly television and other electronic systems, are all pervasive transmitters of urban culture since they simulate the kinds of experiences and interaction that a city provides even though the person experiencing them may live in remote places. Some suggest that *global city* would be a more appropriate term. ⟡ *ecumenopolis.*

GMT ⟡ *Greenwich Mean Time.*

GNP ⟡ *Gross National Product.*

goaf The depth and width of area of coal extracted in a British coal mine.

goals-achievement matrix (GAM) An approach to the evaluation of alternative plans, projects and strategies based on an assessment of the extent to which each plan, project or strategy achieves each of the declared goals or prescribed objectives. The GAM approach was developed by M. Hill as an alternative to traditional ⟡ *cost-benefit analysis* and ⟡ *planning balance sheets* which, he argued, were not related to specific, well-defined objectives. It seeks to allocate benefits (i.e. movements towards achieving a goal: costs representing movement away from a goal) to groups within society and, by looking at the different mixes of goal satisfaction and achievement within each alternative, give guidance on the preferred course of action.

The preparation of a goals achievement matrix involves:
(1) The establishment and ordering of goals. Not only do goals need to be identified and defined operationally, i.e. expressed as objectives, but also their relative importance must be determined from an assessment of the community's problems and values, i.e. they are weighted.
(2) The identification of the different groups within the community who will be affected.
(3) The preparation of a goals compatibility matrix, since there may be conflicting goals.
(4) The examination of each alternative plan, project or strategy to see how far it satisfies each goal, i.e. the preparation

of a matrix with unweighted goals. This involves problems of ⟡ *discounting* because of the different timing of costs and benefits. Also costs and benefits cannot be expressed in the same terms for all goals: some can be assessed as monetary values, whereas others are expressed qualitatively.
(5) The preparation of a matrix with weighted goals for each plan, project or strategy.
(6) The formulation of final matrices with weighted indices of goal achievement across all alternatives. This allows the overall performance of each alternative in relation to all goals to be compared.

GAM therefore compares and ranks alternatives rather than testing each for absolute desirability. As with any sophisticated technique the preparation of a GAM is complex and expensive. Its conceptual framework does, however, contribute towards providing a more rational basis for decision-making, although its use in planning is not widespread. Among the disadvantages of GAM are that the achievements on individual goals cannot be summed and that interaction and interdependence between goals is not registered. The validity of its results is entirely dependent upon the weighting of objectives/goals: since the goals are identified and expressed at a point in time, the approach is static.

good Anything which satisfies a want, e.g. ⟡ *consumer good*, service. ⟡ *capital goods, convenience goods, durable goods, Giffen goods, high-order goods, low-order goods, shopping goods.* ⟡ *commodity.*

grade (1) Of a road, railway, etc., the degree of inclination of the track to the horizontal, i.e. the rate of ascent/descent or gradient.
(2) Of a metalliferous ore, the ratio of the amount of metal produced to the volume of rock which has to be processed in order to extract the metal, i.e. the percentage metal content.

grade-separation The use of different levels to separate two opposing or crossing streams of motor traffic in the interests of greater safety and/or to avoid delays inherent in at-grade intersections. Grade-separated interchanges are therefore necessary to connect a grade-separated road with its intersecting routes. A *flyover* is a road which passes over another road, whereas an *underpass* is a road passing under another road.

grain size Of cities, the dimensions of the areas/blocks between the main arteries of movement.

graph theory A branch of mathematics that treats ◊ *networks* on their simplest topological level as a system of ◊ *nodes* and ◊ *links*. In reducing networks to graphs some sacrifice of information is involved, as ◊ Fig. 67 illustrates, but the essential spatial elements in the form of termination or intersection points (the nodes) in the network and the routes (the links) between them are retained. Graphs may be (a)

directed (with a one-way only connection between two nodes) or undirected (where flow is possible between two nodes in both directions along a link); (b) planar (single plane or two-dimensional) or nonplanar; and (c) unitary (where all nodes are connected, however indirectly) or divided (comprising sub-graphs). The graph's information can be summarized in a ◊ *connectivity matrix* in which each row and each column represents a node and the cell entry in the binary form is 1 or 0 to record presence or absence of a link. Alternatively the matrix could be completed by recording the number of intervening links between pairs of nodes along the shortest path connecting them.

Within human geography, graph theory has been most commonly used to measure quantitatively the properties of transportation networks. The manner in which the number of nodes and links are interconnected can be measured by several indices developed within graph theory.

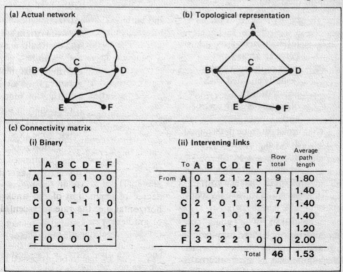

Fig. 67 Graph theory

These indices measure in a uniform and consistent way a network's attributes and structure. Such indices may measure centrality or ⟡ *accessibility* (e.g. ⟡ *König number*, *Shimbel index*), ⟡ *connectivity* (e.g. *beta index*, *cutpoint index*) or shape (e.g. *network shape index*).

grassland Land laid down to grass, either permanently or temporarily, for hay or pasture. Permanent grass lasts for between ten and twenty years before deterioration sets in. Reseeding is then necessary to maintain productivity. ⟡ *ley*, *meadow*, *pasture*.

gravity model An approach to summarizing in mathematical terms the essential nature of patterns of use of ⟡ *networks* which relates interaction to the attraction or generating power of the nodes and the length or friction of the routes between them. The gravity model is inductively based and so-called because of its analogy with the physical and conceptual ideas of Newton's law of gravitation. The earliest applications of the gravity model used a formulation in the form:

$$T_{ij} = G \frac{P_i P_j}{d_{ij}^b}$$

where T_{ij} = interaction or flow between areas i and j

P_i, P_j = mass of the two areas (usually equated with population)

d_{ij} = distance between areas i and j

G = constant to be determined at ⟡ *calibration*

b = distance exponent (measure of the frictional effect of distance and assumed to have a value of $2 \cdot 0$ in the original gravity model)

Such models were widely applied in migration and shopping studies from the late 1920s but, despite its inherent attractiveness, this simple formulation is very crude and planning applications revealed poor fits to real data sets. Further empirical work on interregional flows, particularly in transportation, has improved the definition of variables, e.g. the relationship with distance, and has produced better ways of fitting the model, e.g. adjustments to ensure that the total flow predicted by a model either from origins or to destinations, or both, coincides with observed flows. Thus, among the whole range of gravity models now available it is usual to distinguish three types:

(i) The *singly constrained gravity model*. This may be either *origin-constrained* or *destination-constrained*. If the level of activity generated from the origin zones is fixed, the gravity model is origin-constrained and the model is free to allocate and determine the level of activity in each destination zone. In essence this is an ⟡ *allocation-interaction model* and can be expressed by the equation:

$$T_{ij} = A_i O_i D_i F(c_{ij})$$

where $A_i = \left[\sum_j D_j F(c_{ij}) \right]^{-1}$

and with T_{ij} = interaction/flow between origin zone i and destination zone j

O_i = activity to be distributed from origin zone i (a fixed level)

D_j = an attraction index for destination zone j

c_{ij} = cost of travel between origin zone i and destination zone j

$F(c_{ij})$ = some function of travel cost, generally an inverse power function or a negative exponential function

A_i = competition term or balancing factor

The alternative form is the destination-constrained version:

$$T_{ij} = B_j D_j O_i F(c_{ij})$$

where $B_j = \left[\sum_i O_i \, F(c_{ij}) \right]^{-1}$

with D_j = the fixed level of activity to be allocated from destination zone j

B_j = competition term or balancing factor

O_i = index of attraction from origin zone i

while T_{ij} and $F(c_{ij})$ are defined as before.

(ii) The *doubly constrained gravity model*, in which the level of activity generated by origin zones and the level of activity attracted to destination zones are both fixed. This model is purely an interactance model; with trip ends O_i and D_j fixed, the model finds the trip pattern T_{ij} to satisfy these constraints. The equation is

$$T_{ij} = A_i B_j O_i D_j F(c_{ij})$$

where $A_i = \left[\sum_j B_j \, D_j \, F(c_{ij}) \right]^{-1}$

and $B_j = \left[\sum_i A_i \, O_i \, F(c_{ij}) \right]^{-1}$

and with T_{ij} = trips from origin zone i to destination zone j

O_i = trips generated from origin zone i

D_j = trips attracted to destination zone j

$F(c_{ij})$ as defined previously.

(iii) The *unconstrained gravity model*, which is the original equation in a more general formulation:

$$T_{ij} = G O_i D_j d_{ij}^{-\gamma}$$

where T_{ij} = interaction between origin zone i and destination zone j

O_i = measure of level of demand generated at origin zone i

D_j = measure of level of attraction at destination zone j

d_{ij} = distance between origin zone i and destination zone j

γ = parameter on distance function to be found at calibration

G = a constant to be determined at calibration

Gravity models have been widely used in geography to establish the basic characteristics of existing patterns of movement – migration, journeys to work, to shop, to school, etc. – and to predict future patterns. The models can be used for prediction by modifying the mass or distance terms in the equation or by extrapolating changes over time from the value of the distance component.

Such models have their limitations and operational problems. In particular gravity models are partial models simulating interaction for one activity, assuming all other parts of the system are held constant. Similarly they are static equilibrium models in that they simulate the situation at a point in time. Moreover they deal with closed regions, for all the interaction has to take place within the modelled area. Finally it must be noted that there is still a lack of behavioural theory and causal explanation underlying the models. ◊ *Lowry model, Reilly's law.*

green An open space which is a central feature of many ◊ *villages*, around which the main buildings are normally grouped. ◊ *Fairs* and ◊ *markets* were held on the green, which may have originally served a defence function as a place of safe keeping for the community's animals. Today the green is treated as a form of ◊ *common land*, open to all for lawful exercise. Greens vary considerably in size and shape. ◊ *green village, plaistow.*

green belt An area or zone of open, semi-rural, low-density land surrounding existing major urban areas, but not necessarily continuous. The zone is to be kept open by permanent and severe restrictions on new ◊ *development*.

The green belt concept, involving various interpretations by protagonists such as Ebenezer Howard, Raymond Unwin and Patrick Abercrombie, is of long standing in British planning. Two distinct views have emerged as to the basic purpose of green belts. On the negative side the green belt is seen as necessary for the containment of an urban area in danger of becoming too big, for the retention of the special character of a historic town, and for the prevention of the coalescence of neighbouring urban areas. This view dominated the early implementation of green belt policies and provincial cities were urged, from the mid-1950s, to follow London's example (where such policies had been applied since 1938 and the London green belt officially approved in the first development plan prepared for the region under the 1947 Town and Country Planning Act). Other authorities have included green belt proposals in their subsequent plan submissions, but not all of these have been officially approved.

The positive view argues the role of the green belt in providing land for recreational opportunities outside the town and in protecting agricultural land use.

Green belts have physically contained the areal size of many cities, but they clearly have not stopped urban growth, since development has leapfrogged the green belt.

green lane ◊ *greenway*.

Green Revolution A term applied to the introduction of new, more productive agricultural techniques, especially high-yielding varieties of grain, in developing countries. New high-yield or high-protein strains of food crops were the result of research in plant breeding: new hybrid wheats were first bred in Mexico in the 1950s and new rice varieties in the Philippines in the 1960s. Such new varieties have since spread to other ◊ *Third World* countries and have had considerable success, in some cases more than doubling the yields of traditional varieties. The new strains mature early and are relatively insensitive to the length of day, making ◊ *double-cropping* possible.

However, to realize their full potential these new strains require high ◊ *fertilizer* inputs, the production of which implies heavy capital investment. Abundant water supply is also necessary, as are pesticides and machinery for planting and harvesting. It is just those countries that need the crops most that are desperately short of capital to finance the infrastructural and fertilizer inputs.

Although high-yield agriculture is promising in this context it is unlikely that the Green Revolution will ever fulfil its original promise. Lack of capital, demand for fertilizer outstripping supply, lack of expertise, problems of water supply, lack of time and the will to act quickly, lack of cooperation on the part of farmers and consumer resistance to the new products (some new rice strains are unpalatable) all contribute to restrict its achievements. In addition there are uncertainties about how resistant the new strains are to attacks of insects and plant diseases and about the environmental consequences of such large-scale use of fertilizers. Thus in many Third World countries the Green Revolution has done no more than allow growth in food production to keep pace with population growth.

green village A village settlement with a ◊ *green* forming the core of its plan structure. The inhabitants have a customary right of grazing certain animals and using it for recreation. H. Thorpe distinguished *street green village*, where there is a central street bordered on either side by a narrow strip of green, from *broad green village*, where the green is of irregular shape but its breadth is more than a quarter of its length. The essential features of most green villages were established at the time of Anglo-Saxon colonization, although some may have originated with the re-grouping of former hamlets during the medieval expansion of the arable acreage. ◊ *Angerdorf, Runddorf.*

greenfield sites Undeveloped sites outside the existing built-up urban area which are favoured by large firms/organizations seeking locations for new developments, such as headquarter offices, housing and industrial estates. Greenfield sites have the advantage of being virgin sites uncluttered by any previous development and are normally available as extensive tracts in a single property deal, so facilitating land acquisition.

greenway Or *green lane.* A term applied to a variety of country roads which have been left without a metalled surface. Some may be local routes, e.g. giving access through fields to moorland grazing areas, but others are long-distance, such as pack-horse ways, prehistoric ridgeways, ◊ *drove roads* or abandoned turnpike routes.

Greenwich Mean Time (GMT) ◊ *Local time* on the line of longitude (zero meridian) which passes through Greenwich Observatory. It is used as ◊ *standard time* for the British Isles and as the basis for calculating time throughout the world, since nearly all countries choose their standard time so that they are an exact number of hours/half hours ahead or behind Greenwich Mean Time.

Grenzarbeitnehmer ◊ *frontalier.*

grey areas ◊ *intermediate areas.*

grid plan A term describing the layout of a town where every street crosses another at right-angles and at the same interval. Such towns are also called *Hippodamian settlements* and the street pattern *chequer board.* The term has also been used more loosely to mean any rectangular arrangement of streets. ◊ *town plan.* ◊ *radial–concentric plan.*

Gross Domestic Product (GDP) The total output of goods and services produced by a national economy in a given period, usually a year, valued at market prices. Intermediate products are excluded because their value is implicitly included in the prices of final goods. It is *gross*, since no allowance is made for the value of replacement capital goods. The use of market prices means the value of indirect taxes are included but subsidies excluded. Thus *GDP at factor cost* – representing total domestic factor incomes earned in producing the goods and services – equals GDP plus subsidies minus indirect taxes. ◊ *Gross National Product.*

gross material Assembled ◊ *localized materials* which lose much of their original weight when used in a manufacturing process. Only a portion or none of the weight of a gross material therefore enters into the weight of the finished product. In processing sugarbeets, for example, seven-eighths of the weight is lost in refining the beets to sugar. The extreme type of gross material is fuel, which does not enter into the weight of the product. Industries using gross materials with significant weight losses may be attracted to material locations. ◊ *pure material.*

Gross National Product (GNP) ◊ *Gross Domestic Product* adjusted for foreign transactions, i.e. to the figure for Gross Domestic Product must be added any income accruing to residents of the country arising from investment and other factor earnings abroad and from it must be deducted any income earned in the domestic market by factors owned by foreigners abroad. *GNP at factor cost* equals GNP net of indirect taxes and subsidies. GNP, expressed per capita, is commonly used as an indicator of a country's economic performance. But as a realistic guide to a nation's economic well-being it has its shortcomings because (a) it includes the value of 'non-productive' goods, such as expenditure on arms and the military, and (b) it includes the value of expenditure on pollution control and cleaning-up activities.

gross rateable value ◇ *rateable value.*

gross register tonnage A standard measurement of the capacity of merchant ships, relating to all the enclosed parts of the ship including its superstructures. The unit of measurement, 1 gross register ton = 100 ft³ (2·83 m³). Dry-dock charges are based on it. ◇ *deadweight tonnage, net register tonnage, tonnage.*

gross reproduction rate ◇ *reproduction rates.*

ground movement ◇ *subsidence.*

ground rent The ◇ *rent* paid to a freeholder for land that is leased for building. It therefore implies the separation of land ownership from the ownership of any building on the land. Such ground rents are generally payable for long periods of time, since leases are often of 99 years duration (many early ones are of 999 years) and the payment is a fixed sum unless the lease contains a rent revision clause which is operative at regular intervals.

growing season The growing season is a guide to crop growth prospects and relates to the number of days in the year with a mean temperature above 6°C. In general the growing season decreases in duration with distance from the equator: in equatorial forest the growing season is continuous throughout the year but in the tundra it lasts for only two to three months. ◇ *physical margin of cultivation.*

growth centre ◇ *growth pole.*

growth composition analysis A simple but commonly used method of ◇ *population forecasting.* It recognizes the factors of change in population to be births, deaths

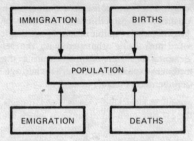

Fig. 68 Growth composition analysis

and migration and the magnitude of each of these factors is expressed in rates which represent probabilities (◇ Fig. 68). Refinement can be achieved by disaggregating the population into cohorts, with common age/sex characteristics to which specific rates can be applied. This works well for births and deaths, when the analysis becomes a ◇ *cohort-survival method.* Migration remains a difficult factor to forecast confidently, particularly its age and sex structure.

growth curve The generalized graphic or mathematical expression of an empirical or planned rate of growth of any phenomenon over time. It is applied particularly to ◇ *economic growth.* ◇ *logistic curve.*

growth industry An ◇ *industry* which is expanding faster than the national average for all industries. Employment is the normal unit of measurement, but output or value added are also used.

growth pole The term growth pole has been widely and loosely used. It was conceived by F. Perroux, who used *'pôle de croissance'* to mean a dynamic sector of an economy. In Perroux's terms therefore growth poles comprise industries or firms, i.e. an *industrie motrice* or ◇ *propulsive industry,* that exerts dominance through its inter-industry ◇ *linkages* over other manufacturing sectors. These interrelationships between the propulsive industry and other sectors are considered exclusively in abstract, functional economic space. A growth pole is capable of rapid growth and of transmitting that growth through ◊ *multiplier* effects to other sectors of the economy. Growth poles may therefore be represented as sectors in an ◊ *input–output matrix*, in which growth effects are transmitted through the rows and columns.

The idea of growth poles, as developed by Perroux, has been reworked within a much more explicit spatial framework. J. R. Boudeville argued that growth poles would appear as a geographical clustering of activities in response to ◊ *external economies* and ◊ *agglomeration economies*. The reworked concept is now generally, and more appropriately, known as a *growth centre*: it retains a number of characteristics associated with growth poles but is explicitly conceived in geographical space. A growth centre is based on an urban–industrial complex which experiences spontaneous and sustained growth that also influences the economic fortunes of surrounding areas. It consists of one or more urban areas which, together, provide or are likely to provide a range of cultural, social, employment, trade and service functions for itself and associated hinterlands.

The concept has been developed further in a policy context. Growth centres could be created, and regional planners were quick to appreciate the potential of the regionally differentiated growth such a spatial strategy might generate. Thus the growth pole approach to regional policy has called for propulsive industries to be attracted to specific growth point locations in depressed or stagnating areas. Implementation of the policy has not been without problems. There are difficulties in identifying propulsive industries in practice and there is a lack of understanding of the relationship between the infrastructural base to be provided and the needs of propulsive industries. Moreover a question arises as to the period of time over which the growth effects might be expected to spread out from the growth centre: evidence to date suggests that such spread effects are spatially restricted to the immediate vicinity of the growth centre or benefit higher-order centres in the urban hierarchy. Adherence to growth pole policy has, therefore, more often resembled religious belief than objective logic.

guaranteed prices A method of agricultural support used by governments in cases of uncertain agricultural markets and conditions to guarantee a certain minimum price for crop and livestock products regardless of world or regional price conditions. Guaranteed prices are usually manipulated so as to provide an adequate level of income in aggregate for the farming industry.

Such a system operated in the United Kingdom between 1947 and 1972 in respect of cereals, eggs, fatstock, milk, sugar beet and potatoes. Guaranteed prices were set annually in consultation with the farming industry, bearing in mind production trends, market requirements, levels of profit in the industry, increasing agricultural efficiency and cost of subsidies. Farmers sold their produce at freely determined market prices, and where the average market price was below the guaranteed price the difference was made good by a *deficiency payment*, e.g. a farmer paid a market price of £50 for a product which had a guaranteed price of £65 received from the government a deficiency payment of £15. With the United Kingdom's entry into the European Economic Community in 1972 guaranteed prices have been phased out (over the period to 1978), to be replaced by a system of ◊ *intervention prices*.

guest workers Guest or *transient workers* are persons who migrate to another country in search of permanent work but

203

who have no intention of settling permanently in that country. Such ◇ *migration* is therefore temporary and is normally directed up the economic development continuum of countries, especially to ones with labour markets where demand exceeds supply, e.g. West Germany (where such workers are called *Gastarbeiter*) and the Netherlands in the 1960s. The migrants are predominantly male, normally undertake low-paid, unskilled or routine assembly-line work, often congregate in the worst housing or have to be provided with special accommodation, and suffer the greatest insecurity of jobs. Although most mean to return home some eventually settle permanently. ◇ *frontalier*.

guild ◇ *gild*.

Guttman scale analysis An approach to the measurement of attitude used in social survey research which attempts to identify a single scale along which effective measurement of attitude in a given situation can be attained. The approach typically involves asking a set of questions, each of which requires a 'yes' or 'no' answer. The questions are so ordered that a positive answer by a respondent to any given question implies and requires for consistency a positive answer to all questions of lower position in the order. For example, if three questions were asked – (1) are you over 6 ft tall? (2) are you over 5 ft 9 in tall? (3) are you over 5 ft 6 in tall? – a respondent who answers yes to the first question must also answer yes to the second and third questions. Guttman scales are therefore unidimensional and cumulative. Where there are several respondents they can be ranked in order from those with the most positive attitude to those with the most negative.

H

H **test** ◊ Kruskal–*Wallis H test.*

habitat Although frequently used by geographers as a synonym for ◊ *environment*, a habitat is the kind of physical or natural environment in which a plant or animal is normally found. In a sense it is the home they occupy, and most of the organisms living in a specific habitat are affected in some way by the other organisms present. The role an organism plays in its habitat is called a *niche.*

habitat theory An expression introduced into ◊ *landscape evaluation* and design studies by J. Appleton in 1975. It postulates that aesthetic pleasure in landscape derives from the observer experiencing an environment favourable to the satisfaction of his/her biological needs. The aesthetic satisfaction stems from the spontaneous perception of landscape features which, in their shapes, colours, spatial arrangements and other visible attributes, act as sign stimuli indicative of environmental conditions favourable to survival.

hacienda A term used in Spanish-speaking countries for a large agricultural estate, often similar to a ◊ *ranch.*

ha-ha A sunk fence or concealed ditch acting as a boundary around parkland which does not interrupt the view, but prevents livestock from entering or leaving. Common in the 18th century.

half-life A measurement of the radioactivity of a substance. The half-life of a radioactive isotope is the time required for the intensity of the radiation to fall to half its original value.

half-year land Half-year or *Lammas land* was arable or pasture land which was occupied in severalty (i.e. individually) for part of the year but which after the crop was taken was opened to ◊ *common rights*, usually of pasturage. Half-year land was normally opened for grazing on Lammas Day (1 August) or Old Lammas (12 August).

halo effect A particular type of ◊ *boundary effect* in which locations close to a political border are seen as relatively unattractive places.

ham (1) Pasture-ground, usually near a river, especially rich ◊ *pasture* in southern England.
(2) Old English for home and, in this sense, very common as part of ◊ *place names* of Anglo-Saxon origin.

Hamiltonian circuit The sequence of ◊ *links* in a ◊ *transport network* which forms an unbroken chain through all the ◊ *nodes*, and in which the first and last nodes coincide. The shortest Hamiltonian circuit is the 'travelling salesman tour'. ◊ *circuit network, fundamental circuit, travelling salesman problem.*

hamlet A cluster of farmhouses, associated cottages and outbuildings in a rural area. It usually comprises six to eight farms and is therefore too small to have a church or parochial status. The term is imprecise, being used for any settlement too small to be called a ◊ *village*. ◊ *clachan, drubbel, fermtoun, kirktoun.*

Within ◊ *central place theory* the term hamlet has been used to describe a settlement with a population of 100–200 persons, serving approximately 2,000 people with everyday or ◊ *convenience goods* and services for which people will not travel for more than five minutes (3 m/5 km).

hammer-pond A pond formed by damming a river or stream to provide water power to drive mill wheels which operated heavy hammers in early iron works. Hammer-ponds were particularly a feature of the Weald and were in use until coal replaced charcoal in the 18th century.

harbour A stretch of coastal water, protected from the open sea, which affords shelter to sea-going vessels. Ships may lie at anchor in safety, hence the term *anchorage*, and, if necessary, undergo repairs and revictualling. Harbours may be formed naturally or artificially, or by the improvement of a natural feature. ◊◊ *port*.

hardwood A term used in the timber trade for wood produced by broadleaved trees. ◊◊ *softwood*.

harmonic analysis ◊ *Fourier series analysis*.

harmonic mean A measure of ◊ *central tendency* used to compute the mean of a series when the observations relate to rates of movement or growth such as vehicle speeds.

$$\text{Harmonic mean} = \frac{N}{\sum \frac{1}{x_i}}$$

where x_i = observed values of x, from x_1 to x_i

N = number of observed values of x

◊◊ *arithmetic mean, geometric mean*.

harmonic mean centre A centrographic technique (◊ *centrography*) which establishes the point of peak potential in a spatial distribution pattern.

Harrod–Domar model An approach in growth theory to the explanation of the ◊ *economic growth* of a nation, so named after the work of R. F. Harrod and E. S. Domar. The indispensable condition for economic growth is ◊ *investment*, since investment ultimately determines both the supply of and demand for goods. Growth theory seeks to determine the rate of investment which will bring supply and demand into equality. In the closed economy of the Harrod–Domar model that rate is determined by the propensity to save and yields a steady or equilibrium growth path. The model can be adapted to describe a regional system, but since the individual region must be treated as an ◊ *open system* the position is more complex because account has to be taken of import and export leakages.

Haufendorf A compact, nucleated ◊ *village*, with an irregular plan-form. ◊◊ *Gewanndorf, Marschhufendorf, Strassendorf, Waldhufendorf*.

haulage costs ◊ *line-haul costs*.

hazard assessment The formal, systematic appraisal of the nature and magnitude of the hazards associated with an installation, normally manufacturing plant. It involves consideration of a variety of potential accident sequences or events and the estimation of their frequency and potential consequences, i.e. forming a judgement of how real the danger is. Today increasing emphasis is placed on the assessment of hazards and risks in quantitative terms. ◊ *event-tree analysis, fault-tree analysis*.

hazard perception The assessment by an individual of the long-term potential of a given site for settlement or use relative to the variety of hazards, both natural and people-made, associated with the area, i.e. focus is on multiple hazards rather than on the spatial distribution of a single type of hazard. In general people pay more attention to what they perceive as the rewards of being in an environmentally hazardous place than they do to the risks, and they discount the unusual, suppressing and perceiving only vaguely the certainty that the unusual will recur. For example, about one-third of the United States population live in areas of chronic and periodically acute smog, and about one eighth in areas subject to periodic flooding.

Variation in hazard perception and estimation is a function of a combination of factors – the magnitude and frequency of the hazard, the recency and frequency of the experience, the importance to a person's livelihood and individual personality. ◊ *natural hazard, perception.*

hazardous installations An installation (factory, warehouse, etc.) in the United Kingdom which is officially identified as being hazardous as a consequence of the handling, at any one time, of quantities of dangerous materials in excess of certain specified amounts. There have been two categories – *major hazard installations* and *notifiable installations.* The major hazard categorization, introduced in 1972, operated until 1982, when it was replaced by the notifiable categorization. Installations in the notifiable category hold much smaller quantities of dangerous materials than those in the former major hazard category. The threshold value of dangerous quantities varies according to the material concerned. It has been estimated that there were some 500 major hazard installations in the United Kingdom, and that the number of notifiable installations is between 2,500 and 3,000.

hazardous pollutant A ◊ *pollutant* to which even slight exposures may cause serious illness or death. The United States Environmental Protection Agency has classified asbestos, beryllium and mercury as hazardous pollutants.

head-dyke A continuous feature in the form of a dry stone or turf wall built across the head of every farm along the edge of the moorland. Head-dykes generally predate ◊ *enclosure* and separated the hill

◊ *pasture* from the ◊ *arable* and ◊ *meadow* land.

head of navigation The farthest point upstream on a river that can be reached by vessels for purposes of trade.

headland ◊ *balk.*

headrights A system for granting land in the Southern colonies of North America during the early Colonial period which offered a formula for adjusting private land to the number of settlers able to work the land and for controlling settlement density.

headship rate analysis The use of headship rates – i.e. the proportion of each age group who are either married couples, lone parent, one person or other households – to aid the estimation of housing need. The approach concentrates on identifying a 'core' individual in a ◊ *household*, traditionally the head of household. By selecting the core individual it is possible to distinguish stable units (the continuing households) and to forecast new ones (the emerging households), and so predict housing need in an area. The number of potential or emerging households is a function of the age, sex and marital status structure of an area's population.

heaf A dialect word from northern England to describe the accustomed fell ◊ *pasture* of sheep.

hearth areas, hearthlands Regions or areas thought to have been the centres of certain agricultural and technological innovations and inventions, such as the selection of plant crops, and from which the practices and information diffused to surrounding areas. It was in these areas, between the 8th and 5th millennia, that the first ◊ *states* appeared. These centres of ancient civilization – Mesopotamia, Egypt, India and China – have much in common, such as a position on the banks of a great river like the Tigris–Euphrates, Nile, Indus and

Hwang Ho, whose flood waters and silt make for fertility; a knowledge of methods of ◊ *irrigation*; the cultivation of important food crops like rice and wheat, which led to a great increase in population; the early development of metallurgical and artistic techniques; the use of improved languages and means of expression, such as writing; and the rise of great religions. Similarly in the Americas the hearthlands of Mexico and Peru had developed a distinct form of civilization (which was arrested by the Spanish conquest).

heartland A term used in a geopolitical context to describe the rich interior lowlands of the Eurasian continent which formed a heartland or *pivot area*, the core of H. J. Mackinder's ◊ *World Island*. Mackinder advanced a world power theory based on the belief that land-based, rather than maritime-based, ◊ *states* held the potential key to world domination. The heartland is inaccessible to sea power, because it drains inland or, to the north, because the coast is beset by ice, and it will also guarantee self-sufficiency in food and raw materials. Hence, control of the heartland would allow domination of the World Island. ◊◊ *rimland theory*.

heath Open, flat, uncultivated lowland developed on sandy and gravelly soils and covered with low herbage and dwarf shrubs. It is largely waste land, although it may provide ◊ *rough grazing*. The term also applies to the vegetation itself. ◊◊ *moor*.

heavy industry A descriptive term for those ◊ *secondary industries* which use bulky machinery and handle large quantities of raw materials, usually necessitating water or rail transport, e.g. coal-mining, metal manufacture. It is also referred to as *basic industry*. Such industries are involved either in bulk-reduction processes, which are usually, though not invariably, mineral-based, or in the further processing of heavy products from these primary stages of manufacture. They require extensive sites, have low labour inputs relative to other factors of production and often have serious nuisance qualities, emitting dirt, noise or unpleasant odours.

Heckscher–Ohlin theorem A neoclassical explanation of the origins of ◊ *comparative advantage*, and hence export specialization. Two broad causes of comparative advantage are possible: (i) regional differences in technology, and (ii) regional differences in the availability of factors of production. The Heckscher–Ohlin theorem emphasizes differences in factor endowments and argues that countries/regions will specialize in the production and export of commodities that use their relatively abundant factor intensively. Regions with abundant supplies of labour therefore specialize in labour-intensive industries, raw-material-abundant regions in raw-material-intensive industries. In effect it is a factor price equalization theory implying that free trade in commodities will equalize factor prices even if factors are geographically immobile.

The theorem rests on highly restrictive assumptions: that trade is free from all obstructions (including transport costs), production functions are identical in all regions and exhibit constant returns to scale, there is perfect competition in both commodity and factor markets, each region's endowment of factors is fixed at any instant of time and supply is inelastic. These assumptions have been subject to extensive criticism.

Hedberg zone A maritime zone, advocated by the American geologist H. D. Hedberg, designed to allow each country to claim the offshore area within which there was a reasonable chance of finding hydrocarbon deposits. It is linked to the ◊ *continental slope* in that a line is identified which marks the junction between the continental slope and the continental rise and this line is used as a ◊ *baseline* of a zone within which the outer edge of the continental margin should be set. The width of the zone remains to be settled by international agreement. There are also problems of locating the contact between the continental slope and rise in many areas, but these should not prove insuperable. ◊ *contiguous zone, exclusive economic zone, territorial sea.*

hedge A line of closely planted bushes or shrubs, marking the boundaries of a ◊ *field.* The type of hedge varies between parts of the country, and its age can be dated from the number of species of tree and shrub present. In England many date from deliberate plantings at the time of the ◊ *enclosure* movement of the 18th century. Over the last thirty years hedgerow removal has had a marked visual effect on lowland agricultural landscapes. From the farmer's point of view, in areas of predominant arable or intensively managed grazing, there is little or no economic justification for retaining hedges: fixed internal boundaries deny the farmer flexibility, hedges take up valuable land space and absorb scarce time and money on maintenance, and even their usefulness in preventing wind erosion is now questioned.

henge A general term for circular earthwork enclosures of the late ◊ *Neolithic* in Britain, distinguished particularly by the bank being outside the ditch.

herding ◊ *primitive herding, nomadism.*

heritage coasts Outstanding stretches of high scenic quality along the remaining areas of undeveloped coast of Britain, designated since 1970 by the Countryside Commission as worthy of protection and effective public management. Heritage coasts may be within, or without, ◊ *National Parks* and ◊ *Areas of Outstanding Natural Beauty.* Heritage coast policies stem from a series of regional conferences on coastal preservation in the 1960s and are incor-

porated, where appropriate, into ◊ *structure plans* and ◊ *local plans,* embracing both ◊ *development control* and positive management. ◊ Fig. 2.

hermeneutics An approach which attempts to clarify the conditions in which understanding can take place. It tries to reveal expressions of the inner life of persons by understanding and empathy – in effect, putting oneself in another person's shoes. ◊ *cognitive description, idealism, Verstehen.*

heterogenetic city The city of technical order which, according to R. Redfield, is the bearer of rapid social change and gives priority to economic growth. In such cities new states of mind are developed, representing universalist, achievement-oriented value systems, and creating original modes of thought that have authority beyond or in contrast with the old, local cultures. ◊ *generative city.* ◊ *orthogenetic city.*

heuristic In problem-solving, an approach that depends on trial and error rather than a set procedure, such as an ◊ *algorithm.*

hidden economy ◊ *informal economy.*

hidden household Hidden or *concealed* or *potential households* are ◊ *families* who are living with relatives or with other people because they are unable to obtain a separate ◊ *dwelling.* Hidden households are identified to establish ◊ *housing need.* ◊ *household.* ◊ *composite household.*

hide A measure of land capacity equivalent to ◊ *ploughland* of eight oxen, commonplace in Anglo-Saxon times but probably of earlier origin. In essence it was the land which supported one family, or for fiscal purposes was deemed capable of supporting one family, i.e. it became a unit of assessment for the king's support (◊ *yoke*) and was imposed on ◊ *shires* and ◊ *hundreds.* In areas of Danish influence the ◊ *carucate* was the equivalent unit. Hides varied in size, being smaller where population was densest, but were normally between 100 and 120 acres (40–48 hectares) and subdivided into four ◊ *virgates* (or ◊ *yardlands*). ◊◊ *sulung*.

hierarchical diffusion ◊ *diffusion*.

hierarchy In general terms a hierarchy is a system with grades of status ranked one above another in a series, with the ranking usually reflecting some relationship of dependence of those in each rank to those in the rank above. In geography the term is most often used to refer to a hierarchy of settlements or urban areas.

In particular the concept is used in ◊ *central place theory* to describe the grouping together of urban areas (central places) and their trade areas into distinctive levels of functional importance. The individual consumer will travel to the many smaller, closer urban areas for convenience purchases and to the less numerous larger, more distant places for goods demanded less frequently. A definable hierarchy has been identified at a variety of spatial scales and in quite varied geographical conditions. There is a strong tendency for researchers to follow the framework laid down by W. Christaller rather than the more flexible hierarchy devised by A. Lösch, although in reality patterns may be closer to the more continuous distribution proposed by Lösch.

high farming A term used in the 19th century to describe the type of farming that developed in an attempt to offset falling prices by increased output. It was basically an extension of ◊ *mixed farming*, dependent upon increased inputs.

high forest system A silvicultural system which produces forest trees from seedlings rather than from ◊ *coppice*. All trees are allowed to grow to their full height and they close overhead to form a *closed canopy*. ◊ *forest*.

high-order goods ◊ *Goods* with extensive ◊ *ranges* and high ◊ *thresholds*, provided from high-order ◊ *central places*. ◊ *durable goods, shopping goods*. ◊◊ *convenience goods*.

high-rise building Multi-storey building, with more than four storeys, used primarily as offices or flats. ◊◊ *low-rise building*.

high seas The open sea lying outside the ◊ *exclusive economic zones* of states (◊ Fig. 29). All states have equal rights to navigate, to overfly, to lay submarine cables, to construct artificial islands, to fish, and to conduct scientific research within the high seas. ◊◊ *deep seabed*.

highest and best use A concept which states that ◊ *land* resources are at their highest and best use when they are used in such a manner as to provide an optimum return to their owners or to society. Land is ordinarily considered to be at its highest and best use when it is used for that purpose or that combination of purposes for which it has the greatest ◊ *comparative advantage*. For example, competition for the most accessible land in an urban area leads to its use by the activity/entrepreneur with the highest ability to pay for the land and produces the highest present land value. The highest and best use of any particular site is subject to change over time as levels of technology and demand alter.

highland clearances A general term for the destruction of ◊ *townships* and the eviction of tenants by landlords to make room for sheep which occurred in the Scottish Highlands particularly in the periods 1782–1820 and 1840–54.

highway A public ◊ *road*, forming the main or direct route between one town or city and another, which is open to all forms of traffic. With the advent of fast motor traffic certain changes have been necessary and types of road (◊ *motorway*) have been introduced with access restricted to certain types of vehicle.

hill and dale A term used to describe the principal form of dereliction left by ◊ *opencast mining* of the Jurassic ironstones in the East Midlands before 1951 as a

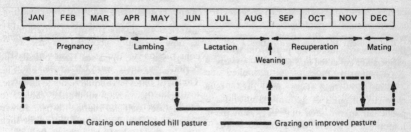

Fig. 69 Hill farming

result of mechanical excavators dumping the overburden behind the advancing working face. ⟡ *derelict land.*

hill farming A pastoral system by which natural hill vegetation is used. It has developed over the last 250 years following ⟡ *enclosure* of the lower, more fertile land. The system varies between parts of Britain but is essentially a ⟡ *ranching* system based upon sheep, though usually with some cattle. Such hill land was suited only to the rearing of livestock and not to their fattening, and gave rise to traditional hill farming in which the natural pastures are set-stocked, i.e. the stocking rate of breeding ewes is constant irrespective of seasonal variations in pasture growth. Sheep numbers are adjusted to a level which allows a certain minimum level of nutrition during the winter: the resultant stocking rate may range from 1 sheep/acre (2·5/ha) on high-quality pasture to 0·1 sheep/acre (0·25/ha) on the poorer vegetation. These low stock densities lead to severe undergrazing, even where cattle are used in summer to increase the grazing pressure. The major limitation on cattle numbers is usually the amount of winter feed that can be conserved.

Hill farming has received subsidy support since the Second World War and continues to receive special grants via the European Economic Community and help from the European Fund for Regional Development. This support has main-

tained the viability of the larger hill farms.

The principal shortcomings of traditional hill farming arise from the lack of grazing control and poor pasture quality. New sheep production methods have developed following upon modern techniques of reclaiming moorland to provide enclosed and improved pastures. Such enclosed grassland can be integrated with a much larger area of hill vegetation in a year-round grazing system (⟡ Fig. 69) which increases stock numbers considerably.

hill fort A hilltop fortified settlement. Hill forts vary considerably in shape and size, from under 1·0 to over 6·0 hectares (2–15 acres) and represent settlements surrounded by one or more earthen banks and ditches, with inner ramparts sometimes strengthened by timber or stone revetments. The earliest date from the beginning of the ⟡ *Iron Age*, but the practice appears to have been continued for about 1,000 years into the post-Roman era. Their distribution throughout the British Isles suggests that they served as strongholds for small groups rather than tribal centres.

hill grazing ⟡ *hill farming.*

hill station A tropical mountain resort, associated particularly with the period of British rule in India, where altitude results in a lowering of temperature.

hinterland From an early vague meaning of 'back country' the term hinterland became especially associated with ◊ *ports*. It is that part of ◊ *port space* (◊◊ *foreland*) which comprises the tributary area on the landward side of the port from which exports are collected and to which imports are distributed.

A port does not always have exclusive claim to all parts of its hinterland and a particular inland area may be within the hinterland of several ports. Indeed a port generally has a different hinterland for each commodity that enters into its trade. Hence reference is made to *primary hinterlands*, in which a single port has a dominant influence; *secondary* or *competitive hinterlands*, where no single port controls more than 70% of the area's traffic; and *commodity hinterlands*, based on the area of collection or distribution of a particular commodity or group of commodities. The use of the term has been extended to cover the ◊ *sphere of influence* of any settlement, i.e. its market or trade area (◊◊ *Umland*).

HIP ◊ *housing investment programme*.

Hippodamian settlement ◊ *grid plan*.

histogram A graphical representation of a ◊ *frequency distribution*, in which the number of occurrences are plotted against the appropriate class and a diagram drawn in the form of 'building blocks'. The areas of the blocks should be proportionate to the frequencies. ◊◊ *bar-graph*.

historic bay The historic bay concept was recognized, but not defined, by the first United Nations Conference on the Law of the Sea in 1958. Bays of whatever size may be claimed as historic waters providing (i) those waters have been used exclusively for a long time by the claimant ◊ *state*, (ii) a formal claim to ◊ *sovereignty* has been made and (iii) that claim is accepted by other countries. If these three conditions are satisfied a bay can be declared as ◊ *internal waters* and, in theory, the state's ◊ *territorial sea* is measured seaward from the closing line across the mouth of the bay.

historical analysis ◊ *temporal analysis*.

historical geography Historical geography is now generally accepted as the reconstruction of the geographies of past periods, but there were earlier meanings. The term has been applied, for example, to the history of geographical thought, to the history of exploration, discovery and mapping (a common 19th-century usage), and to the study of change in political boundaries and the extent of administrative divisions at different times. Other views of historical geography – as the operation of the geographical factor in history, as the evolution of the ◊ *cultural landscape* and as the study of geographical change through time – have more current substance and shade into the now orthodox view of historical geography as the reconstruction of past geographies. The latter is pursued either as a cross-section or a series of successive sections in time to build a comparative geography or as a spatial and retrospective appraisal of changes through time. The location in time of cross-sections is dependent upon available source material. Historical geography stood apart from mainstream geography in respect of the methodological changes of the ◊ *quantitative revolution*, but by the 1970s its reintegration with the mainstream was apparent with the increasing use of statistical procedures and the recognition of behavioural/humanistic approaches. ◊◊ *diachronic analysis*, *vertical theme*.

historicism An approach to social science which assumes that historical prediction is the principal aim and argues that the nature of a phenomenon can be entirely understood by reference to its development. By discovering the rhythms, patterns or trends that underlie events, historicism implies that a complete knowledge can be attained. ◊◊ *genetic approach*, *temporal analysis*.

hobby farmer A person whose main, full-time source of income is a job outside ◊ *agriculture* but who lives on a farm and operates this as a commercial venture, often using profits from the other job/business. Also called a *weekend farmer*. ◊◊ *part-time farming*.

hobby nexus P. S. Florence's term to describe the psychological motivation of an ◊ *entrepreneur* through love of work itself. ◊◊ *boss nexus, free man nexus*.

hodography The study of backroads and the human experience of travel. It has developed as an off-shoot of travel research, especially as a phenomenological reaction to the seeming excesses of quantitative travel research.

holding Land held by legal right by tenant or owner.

holding capacity The optimum level of use or design capacity of a people-made facility, e.g. the seating capacity of a football stadium or theatre. ◊◊ *carrying capacity, congestion*.

holding company A ◊ *firm* formed to hold shares of other companies which it then controls. The holding company acquires a majority or the whole of the equity capital (shares) of one or more other companies, known as *subsidiaries*. The names, local management and goodwill of the subsidiaries are normally preserved, with the holding company providing specialized managerial and financial services. Holding companies are likely to be created where the optimum size of financial unit or managerial unit or marketing unit is larger than the optimum size of production unit. ◊◊ *acquisition behaviour*.

holiday In recreation and tourist literature a holiday is defined as any period of one or more nights, up to a maximum of three months, spent away from home for any purpose other than business travel. The British Travel Association regard a *main*

holiday as four or more nights away from home.

home territory ◊ *territory*.

homelands ◊ *apartheid*.

homeostasic equilibrium ◊ *equilibrium*.

homeostasis The idea of self-regulation involved in the ability of a living organism to maintain a balance by adjusting itself to changes in its environment.

homestead As a general term homestead can be either the place of one's home or house, or a farmhouse with its dependent buildings and the land surrounding it. The term has been used by geographers to denote a rural settlement type of dispersed farms. The term is used in a particular sense in the United States as a lot of land adequate for the residence and maintenance of a family, especially the lot of 160 acres (65 ha) granted to a settler by the 1862 Homestead Act. In this latter context homestead is a real property concept to which special rights apply: *homestead rights* are usually defined as a proportion of the holding, limited both in area and value, owned and occupied by the family as their home, which they cannot be forced to sell even when in debt.

homogeneous region ◊ *uniform region*.

homoscedasticity The equal ◊ *variance* assumption. When comparing the means of two sample populations it is assumed that the variances of the two populations are equal. This may be checked by carrying out an F-test upon the ratio of the sample variances obtained from the two sets of observations (◊ *analysis of variance*).

hook and haul operations When a continuous ◊ *unit train operation* is not viable, it may still be practicable to move goods in train-load units from an origin to one or a few destinations before being split up. This is referrred to as a hook and haul operation.

horizontal combination ◊ *combination.*

horizontal disintegration ◊ *disintegration.*

horizontal diversification ◊ *diversification.*

horizontal expansion The expansion of a firm by extending the production and sales of its existing product into new markets or by capturing a larger share of an existing market. ◊ *integration.* ◊◊ *vertical expansion.*

horizontal linkage ◊ *linkage.*

horizontal mobility ◊ *labour mobility.*

horticulture A term that originally covered every form of gardening, whether scientific, recreational or commercial, but now applied especially to intensive agriculture. *Commercial horticulture* includes the production of fruit, vegetables and flowers, plant breeding, landscape gardening and the raising of plants in nurseries. ◊ *glasshouse cultivation, market gardening, truck farming.*

Hotelling model A ◊ *locational-interdependence* approach to the analysis of location decisions by two firms competing for market territory, developed by the economist H. Hotelling. The emphasis is on the impact of demand on location, with particular interest in the factors that cause firms to be attracted or repulsed by each other. This approach generally assumes that all firms have identical production costs and sell to a spatially distributed market where delivered price to consumers varies with the cost of overcoming distance from the factory. For simplicity Hotelling assumed a linear, evenly dispersed, market in which he demonstrated that the two firms would cluster at the mid-point of the linear market so that each firm could supply buyers located at the market extremities without surrendering locational advantage to its rival.

This conclusion has been, traditionally, explained in terms of two retail competitors, ice-cream sellers, in a bounded linear market. In ◊ Fig. 70 *A–B* represents a

(a) Socially optimal locations

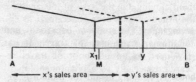

(b) Relocation extends x's market

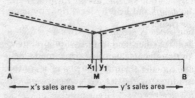

(c) Competitive equilibrium

Fig. 70 Hotelling model

given length of beach supplied by two ice-cream sellers each selling the same brand (i.e. without product differentiation) of ice cream at the same price. People are evenly spread along the beach, all purchase the same amount of ice cream (i.e. inelastic demand) and choose their seller on the basis of which one is nearer to them (i.e. purchasers bear the cost of delivery in the sense that they go to the seller's location). Locations at x and y in ◊ Fig. 70(a) would provide each seller with half the beach from which to draw customers: respective sales areas are split at the point where delivered prices from the two sellers are the same. However, assuming that firms are perfectly mobile, each firm could improve its position by moving nearer to the centre of the beach: in ♢ Fig. 70(b) x has moved to x_1 and extended his market area at y's expense; y must therefore also move nearer to the centre to protect his share of the market. The equilibrium solution is shown in ♢ Fig. 70(c), where the two sellers are located side by side at the mid-point of the beach with each seller retaining one-half of the market. This is a stable equilibrium, since neither firm can gain any advantage from moving. On the basis of this analysis the argument has been generalized to explain industrial ♢ *agglomeration* under conditions of infinitely inelastic demand. ♢ *Fetter's model.*

house A building meant for human habitation, usually by one ♢ *family*, but the term is not specific about form and size. ♢ *dwelling.*

household A group of persons who wish to live together and therefore share living quarters and their principal meals. The commonest form is the *family household* or *private household.* An *institutional household* comprises a larger number of people living together in an institution such as a boarding school. ♢ *composite household, hidden household.*

household density ♢ *occupancy rate.*

household fission A process whereby ♢ *composite households* split into smaller, separate units of parents and children, of old people living alone, of single people maintaining a flat, of groups of young people who share flats instead of living with their parents or who become lodgers in someone else's house. Generally household fission leads to a decline in household size but an increase in number of households.

household industry ♢ *cottage industry.*

Housing Action Area An ♢ *area-based policy* designed to stimulate both housing and environmental improvement or rehabilitation in compact districts within British cities. Housing Action Areas, which were officially introduced in the 1974 Housing Act, were to be declared by local authorities in areas of ♢ *multiple deprivation* or social stress, measured by such indices as overcrowding, shared accommodation, etc. The aim therefore was to upgrade not only the physical qualities of the area but also the related social conditions. Householders within Housing Action Areas were given preferential access to grants for improvements and these were more generous than any previous legislation had allowed. ♢ *general improvement area.*

housing association A non-profit-making organization formed by various groups to build new houses or convert old houses for people to rent unfurnished, i.e. to provide an alternative supply of rented accommodation. A group is often formed with special tenants in mind.

housing class A group of people/households occupying a particular housing type. Access to housing is gained either by obtaining a tenancy in the public or private sector or by having access to capital and credit to facilitate purchase. In developing the concept J. Rex recognized seven housing classes:
(i) Outright owners of good-quality housing in fashionable areas.
(ii) Mortgagees who are buying similar homes to (i).
(iii) Tenants of purpose-built housing.
(iv) Tenants of other publicly acquired housing (usually ♢ *slum* properties awaiting demolition).
(v) Tenants of private landlords.
(vi) House-owners who sublet to finance loan repayments (often immigrant households borrowing capital for short periods at high interest rates).
(vii) Lodgers.

Entry to a particular housing class depends upon certain 'eligibility' rules, designed and operated by the various organizations active in the housing markets – building societies, local authorities, etc., i.e. ◊ *urban managers and gatekeepers.*

housing demand The effective, market ◊ *demand* for houses at current price levels. ◊◊ *housing need.*

housing investment programme (HIP) A system, introduced in 1978/9, designed to enable local authorities to present co-ordinated analyses of housing conditions in their areas and to formulate coherent policies and programmes of capital spending on public housing. Local authorities draw up, annually, four-year housing investment programmes covering all their capital expenditure in the housing field and receive, each November, financial allocations from central government. The system is supposed to give local authorities more discretion in the way they allocate their housing funds, for they receive block grants to spend as they see fit.

housing mobility Housing or *residential mobility* measures the number of changes of residence which occur in a given period of time between particular areas, relative to the total number of households within the areas. A change of residence is defined as the movement of one ◊ *household* from one ◊ *dwelling* to another. ◊◊ *mobility.*

housing need An assessment of the deficiencies in the existing housing stock, compared to a housing stock which would provide socially acceptable standards of accommodation. The factors taken into account are the internal space standards and levels of domestic equipment, the suitability of the house plan for a wide variety of household activities, the quality of design of the housing and its surrounding environment. Since society's views change as to what is desirable, assessment of housing need changes over time but, at its most fundamental, it relates to an individual's basic need for shelter. ◊◊ *housing policy.*

housing policy Central government has a long-standing concern with the collective and individual needs of households for accommodation and, over the past fifty years, has assumed increasing responsibility for housing. Through legislation it can provide the powers and often the financial means that are necessary if objectives are to be achieved. Housing policy is that series of measures, enacted by central government and applied by local authorities, designed to maintain a housing stock which is generally acceptable, both in terms of quantity and quality. ◊ *general improvement area, housing action area, housing investment programme, housing need, rent control, slum clearance, support lending scheme.*

housing retirement A term used to describe the removal of houses, usually substandard units, from the housing stock.

hubit A unit of measurement of information transmitted between individuals. A hubit, according to R. L. Meier, is a bit of meaningful information received by a single human being.

huerta A small, highly cultivated, lowland area in the Spanish provinces of Valencia, Murcia or Granada which, by virtue of prolonged high temperatures, produces two or more crops per year with the aid of ◊ *irrigation.* Huerta polyculture yields abundant fruit (e.g. oranges, pomegranates, figs) as well as vegetables (e.g. lettuce, haricot beans, pimento), with wheat, maize, hemp and sugarbeet also included in rotations. The irrigation system, formerly dependent on streams from the mountains, has been improved this century by drawing upon underground water raised by mechanical pumps. ◊◊ *vega.*

human behaviour ◊ *cycle of human behaviour.*

human capital migration theory Migrants invest time, effort and money in an attempt to achieve greater returns in the form of economic rewards. The human capital migration theory argues that migrants respond to differences in real income between places but take into account the costs likely to be incurred in the relocation process. ♢ *Migration* behaviour is therefore seen as economic in rationale with costs and benefits evaluated as though on a balance sheet and decisions made so as to maximize the stream of net financial gains.

In its simplest form the human capital migration theory assesses the net present value (PV) of a migration investment for the average migrant as:

$$PV = \left(\frac{I_j - I_i}{rd_i}\right) - C_{ij}$$

where I_j and I_i = average real incomes in places j and i respectively

rd_i = ♢ *discount rate* applied to future real income in i

C_{ij} = costs of migrating from i to j including opportunity costs

human ecology The study of the mutual relationships of people and their environment, both natural and social, using ecological concepts. The idea of geography as human ecology was advanced in the 1920s as a path towards synthesis within geography. The idea was revived in the 1960s with recognition of the value of the ecosystem concept and a systems analysis interpretation of human ecology. However, some argued that this view placed people in too subordinate a role and the approach loses significance in respect of people's ability to manipulate nature. ♢ *urban ecology.*

human geography ♢ *Geography* has traditionally been pulled in two directions: on the one hand – physical geography – towards the study of the natural environment and on the other hand – human geography – towards the study of people

and their activities. The scope of human geography has expanded considerably this century, from a rather restricted view of people–environment relations (♢ *environmental determinism*) to its present all-encompassing coverage of all those aspects of geography not directly concerned with the physical environment, nor with technical matters in such sub-fields as cartography. The umbrella term human geography includes the major systematic fields of ♢ *behavioural geography*, ♢ *cultural geography*, ♢ *economic geography* (♢ *agricultural geography*, *industrial geography*), ♢ *historical geography*, ♢ *political geography* (♢ *electoral geography*), ♢ *population geography*, ♢ *rural geography*, ♢ *social geography* (♢ *medical geography*), ♢ *transport geography*, and ♢ *urban geography*. In addition ♢ *regional geography* is included. Like geography as a whole, human geography covers three related themes: (i) spatial analysis – the recording and description of human phenomena around the earth's surface, with special attention to the significance of space as a variable; (ii) the study of the interrelationships between human beings and their environment, both natural and socio-economic; and (iii) a regional synthesis which combines the first two themes in specified localities. All can be pursued on a variety of spatial scales.

human resources ♢ *resources.*

humanism A viewpoint that emphasizes the distinctively human value, quality, subjectivity and even spirituality of events in people's lives. In geography it has been associated with ♢ *humanistic geography.*

humanistic geography A perspective in human geography, based on ♢ *humanism*, which emphasizes human awareness, values and experience. Humanistic geography seeks to achieve an understanding of the human world by studying people's relations with nature and their spatial behaviour in terms of their feelings and ideas about ◊ *space* and ◊ *place*. The style is highly empirical, attempting to focus on the complete human being in order to identify the ideas which direct and stimulate people's acts. Such approaches were to the fore in human geography in the 1970s and are best understood as a form of critical reaction to the overly mechanistic and abstractive tendencies of the scientific geography developed during the ◊ *quantitative revolution*. Such scientific approaches tend to minimize the role of human awareness and knowledge. Humanistic geography, by contrast, tries specifically to understand how geographical actions reveal the quality of human awareness – a concern for the social organization of space rather than the spatial organization of society, i.e. the emphasis is on the social constructions of space and the relations between them and the ◊ *lifeworlds* which give them meaning. Many of the early efforts in humanistic geography draw upon ◊ *existentialism*, ◊ *idealism* and ◊ *phenomenology*.

hundred An ancient subdivision of a ◊*shire*, dating from Anglo-Saxon times, which continued in use until the late 19th century. The hundred is thought to have originated either as a measurement of land area, denoting 100 ◊ *hides*, or as a group of 100 families, and then became the district occupied by those families. In shires where the Danish influence was strong the equivalent term was ◊ *wapentake*.

husbandry An alternative term for ◊ *farming*, but today restricted to pastoral farming, i.e. animal husbandry.

hydroelectric power Electricity generated by harnessing the potential ◊ *energy* of water. The energy available from stored water is proportional to the mass of the water and the height through which it falls. The conversion efficiency of hydroelectric generating plant is high – over 85%. While it is possible to use flowing water directly, it is usual to modify the natural flow by

means of a ◊ *dam*. Capital costs of hydroelectric schemes depend on geographical location but, since the water is usually treated as 'free', the running costs are very low and, if sufficient water is available, the plant may be used for ◊ *base-load* generation. Hydroelectric plants are also very flexible and can be brought on-stream in a very short time (minutes), making them suitable for meeting peak demands (◊ *pumped storage scheme*).

Hydroelectric power is a renewable source of energy which currently provides about 2% of the world's primary energy needs. ◊ *electricity generation*.

hydrogenation of coal The production of synthetic gas or oil from coal. It does not represent a new ◊ *energy* source. Moreover the conversion process represents an overall loss of energy, which, in part, is offset by efficient use of the product. Processes for the production of *syncrude* (oil) are less advanced than for gas production: economic assessments suggest that the widespread use of syncrude is not presently feasible and would not be economic until some time after the introduction of synthetic natural gas.

hydroponics The soil-less cultivation of crops, using a solution of chemical and organic elements.

hypermarket A form of retailing designed to offer the motorized shopper a car-oriented centre where a wide range of goods can be purchased unhindered by weather or traffic. Hypermarkets offer retailers reduced overheads by simplifying store designs and allowing diversification into durable sales (clothing, household and electrical goods, etc.). They are usually located at the edge of or outside towns.

The term hypermarket has been used interchangeably by some with ◊ *superstore*, but when defined on the grounds of floorspace and operational characteristics, a hypermarket is a large-scale, free-standing store of over 50,000 ft² (4,650 m²) floorspace, with the ratio of sales to storage area of the order of 2/3:1/3 and with the sales area given over to non-food retailing greater than 50%.

hypothesis A proposition or postulate which is as yet unproven but which is tentatively accepted in order to test its accord with facts or relationships to be determined. A hypothesis specifies the direction and strength of the relationship between two or more ◊ *variables* and is amenable to empirical testing. The approach involves stating clearly the hypothesis that is to be tested. This hypothesis is known as the *null hypothesis* (H_0) and is expressed in such a form that there is no significant difference between the variables being compared. The null hypothesis is thus the opposite of what the researcher would like to believe. An *alternative* or *research hypothesis* (H_1) is also set up which states that there is a significant difference between the values of the variables being compared. ◊◊ *law*.

I

IATA ⬦*International Air Transport Association.*

iconic model ⬦ *model.*

iconography The study of the meaning of ⬦ *images.*

IDC ⬦ *Industrial Development Certificate.*

idea-area chain ⬦ *unified field theory.*

idealism A philosophy which makes a fundamental distinction between the explanation of human and natural events: any event involving human decisions must, according to idealism, be explained in terms of the thoughts contained in it. Idealism therefore regards reality as mental or mind-dependent – the activity of the mind is the foundation of human existence and knowledge. Idealism comprises two separate philosophical positions:
(i) *Metaphysical idealism*, which maintains that mental activity has a life of its own and is not controlled by material objects and processes.
(ii) *Epistemological idealism*, which limits human understanding to knowledge based on an individual's perceived experience of the world. There is no 'real' world that can be known independently of the mind.

In the 1970s, L. Guelke advocated epistemological idealism as the foundation of a ⬦ *hermeneutic* approach to human geography. The *idealist approach* in this context provides a method by which the academic scholar can rethink or reconstruct the thoughts contained in a human action, i.e. what the decision-maker believed (not why he believed it). This mode of explanation is referred to as ⬦ *Verstehen.* Idealism therefore underpins a type of ⬦ *humanistic geography* that seeks to understand the development of the earth's ⬦ *cultural landscapes* by elucidating what the earth means to its people and showing how the landscape is related to the way people have construed their situations.

ideological space The spatial context of ⬦ *community*, the ⬦ *nation state* and ⬦ *nationalism.* It is the symbolic ⬦ *space* shaped by the ⬦ *ideology* of an individual or group.

ideology A pattern of beliefs, values and concepts which together form the basis of a complete view of human life and society.

idiographic approach A method which stresses the individuality and uniqueness of phenomena, as opposed to their similarities (⬦ *nomothetic approach*). Traditional ⬦ *regional geography* has been represented as idiographic because of its concern for how areas and regions differed from each other.

image An individual's personal assessment or 'picture' of reality, i.e. perceived reality. Such mental pictures are formed from memory or by imagination and provide, within ⬦ *behavioural geography*, a mediating link between environment and people. ⬦ *iconography, imageability, perception.* ⬦⬦ *landmark, mental map, perceptual environment.*

imageability That quality in a physical object which gives it a high probability of evoking a strong ⬦ *image* in any observer. It has also been called *apparency* and *legi-*

bility. It is the shape, colour or arrangement which promotes the making of vividly identified, powerfully structured, mental images of the environment.

immigration The process whereby a person (the *immigrant*) enters a foreign country for the purpose of permanent settlement. Immigration policy may be enacted by the receiving country in order to control the rate of immigration, as well as the nationality and/or the ethnic and other characteristics of the immigrants who are allowed to enter. ◊ *migration*. ◊◊ *conscripted immigrant, second-generation immigrant*.

imperfect competition A general term for ◊ *market* situations in which neither ◊ *monopoly* nor ◊ *perfect competition* prevails. It represents conditions closest to real life and is characterized by (a) the ability of sellers to influence demand by ◊ *product differentiation* and advertising (◊ *monopolistic competition*), and/or (b) the restriction of entry of new firms either because of the size of the initial investment required or because of restrictive practices (◊ *cartel*, *oligopoly*), (c) the existence of ◊ *uncertainty*, with imperfect knowledge of competitors' positions, and (d) an absence of price competition in varying degrees. ◊◊ *locational interdependence theory of industrial location*.

imperialism An ideology that justifies the acquisition or control of foreign ◊ *territory* by a ◊ *state* in order to exploit its resources. A dependent relationship is therefore created between the dominant, imperial state and the other territories. These territories need not be contiguous with the imperial state. The purpose of an *imperialistic policy* is to create a system in which the economic and political bases of the imperial state are enhanced by drawing on their ◊ *colonies*. To maximize the advantages, the imperial power must bind its colonies to itself through various forms of dependency while avoiding undue dependence upon them. This relationship is based upon ◊ *mercantilism*, involving the monopoly of the external trade of the colonies, the fostering of their trading dependence upon the imperial power and the discouragement of their production of goods also produced by the imperial power.

The term has often been used interchangeably with ◊ *colonialism*, although some would distinguish imperialism as the occupation of land and domination of an indigenous population and colonialism as the occupation of virtually uninhabited territory.

An imperial system represents an inherently unstable political condition. The most influential theory of its break-up was advanced by V. I. Lenin, who deduced that in an imperialistic capitalist system power was transferred from industrialists to financial institutions, for whom colonies provided excellent investment outlets, constituting not only captive markets but also sources of cheap raw materials. Lenin predicted that the struggle for the control of colonies would bring rivalry between the great powers, so destroying the stability of the capitalist bloc, and that the exploitation of native labour in the colonies created a new revolutionary class. A systems-based framework for the analysis of imperial disintegration was provided by R. L. Merritt, who demonstrated that the colonies (the dependent sub-system) could succeed in forging commercial and other connections with powers outside the imperial one (the dominant sub-system). ◊◊ *economic imperialism, neocolonialism*.

import concentration A term used to describe a situation in which one or a few goods account for the bulk of a nation's ◊ *imports*. ◊ *commodity concentration*. ◊◊ *export concentration*.

import replacement, import substitution The investment in plant and capacity to produce goods which were formerly imported into a country or region.

imports Goods which are brought into a country in ◊ *trade*. From the national standpoint they may be regarded as goods obtained in exchange for ◊ *exports*. Normally the importing country finds the goods impossible, difficult or uneconomic to produce for itself. ◊◊ *balance of payments, balance of trade, import concentration, invisible imports, terms of trade.*

improvement grant A government grant, available through local authorities, to encourage house-owners/occupiers to introduce modern amenities in sound older houses (i.e. installation of bathrooms, hot water systems, etc.) or to convert for modern housing old houses and other buildings. Improvement grants are part of general ◊ *housing policy* and aim to raise the standard of the older housing stock. Although improvement grants were first introduced in Britain in 1949 they represent 'permissive' legislation in the sense that reliance is placed on the house-owner taking the initiative. The spatial pattern of improvement is therefore likely to be piecemeal. Rates of grant have been varied through time, and from the late 1960s an attempt was made to concentrate the take-up of improvement grants into particular areas by introducing higher rates of grant in ◊ *General Improvement Areas* and *Housing Action Areas.*

imputed risk ◊ *subjective probability.*

in-by, in-bye Enclosed land of relatively high quality usually adjacent to the farmstead of a hill or upland farm. Formerly these were the fields which received the manure from the farm's livestock, making them suitable for ◊ *arable.* ◊◊ *infield, out-by.*

incidence matrix A square or rectangular table or matrix used in ◊ *graph theory* and ◊ *Q-analysis* to indicate relationships between two sets. The rows and the columns represent the elements of two sets and the entry in each cell (i.e. row/column intersection) is recorded as 1 or 0, to indicate where an element in one set is (1) or is not (0) related to an element in the other set.

incidence rate (of disease) The ratio of the incidence of a disease, that is the number of new cases which are diagnosed in a given time period, to the population under consideration. The incidence rate gives a rough probability of any individual's developing a disease in a given year. ◊ *prevalence rate.*

incivisme The acceptance or encouragement of an attitude of indifference towards public obligation and responsibility.

inclosure ◊ *enclosure.*

income elasticity of demand ◊ *elasticity, income.*

income energy ◊ *renewable energy sources.*

income substitutes Goods, services or other benefits received without the expenditure of household money income.

incommutation Reverse ◊ *commuting.*

incompatibility A term used to describe a situation in which competing land uses repulse each other and therefore seek locations protected from each other. Incompatibility arises because of the adverse effect of the operation of one use on the other or of each use on each other, e.g. the effect of an obnoxious industry on residences or on an industry with a high hygiene standard. ◊◊ *compatibility.*

incongruent environment An ◊ *environment* that impedes people in following their desired ◊ *life style.* ◊◊ *congruent environment.*

incubator hypothesis A term used by E. M. Hoover and R. Vernon to describe the concentration of births of new firms in central cities. More commonly referred to as ◊ *seedbed growth.*

incumbent upgrading A sub-type of residential change involving the voluntary ◊ *rehabilitation* of obsolescent buildings and areas in the city. Incumbent upgrading does not involve a change of population in a ◊ *neighbourhood* because it is commonly associated with lower-status groups who have enough confidence and pride in their residential community to wish to check its physical decline. The buildings and environs have to be in reasonable condition to encourage long-term investment by ◊ *owner-occupiers*. ◊◊ *filtering, gentrification*.

index numbers Figures or indices providing a measure of the relative change in some ◊ *variable* or group of variables over a specified time period. A fixed period or point is chosen – the base year – and figures for all other years are expressed as percentages of the figures for the base year. The percentage change can be weighted where the index includes several components, e.g. the ◊ *index of retail prices*. The advantage of using index numbers is that they are independent of the initial magnitude of the data, and of the units in which they are measured. A limitation is that index numbers do not show the proportional change between any two years in a time series, but only between one year and the base year.

index of centrality ◊ *Central place theory* explains variations in the size and spacing of towns in terms of their ◊ *centrality*, the functions provided for the population of their surrounding complementary region or market area. Since population tends to measure the overall importance of a town rather than its centrality alone, W. Christaller devised an operational measure of centrality based on the relative concentrations of telephones of a region into particular towns:

$$\text{Centrality } (C) = T_p - E_p \cdot \frac{T_R}{E_R}$$

where T_p = number of telephones in the particular town
   E_p = population of the particular town
   T_R = number of telephones in the region
   E_R = population of the region

The measure was reasonably appropriate to the time that Christaller was working in southern Germany, but it was still imprecise in that it assumed telephone concentration was an indicator of service status.

An alternative measure, *Preston's centrality index*, compares total retail and service sales in a town with the expenditure on those items of persons resident in the town to provide an index of the town's importance in serving persons resident elsewhere. In mathematical terms,

$$\text{Centrality } (C) = R + S - \alpha M_t F_t$$

where R = total sales in retail establishments (\$)
   S = total sales in selected service establishments (\$)
   α = average percentage of median family income spent on retail goods and selected services
   M_t = median family income in town t (\$)
   F_t = total number of families in town t

index of circuity ◊ *detour index*.

index of circularity A measure of shape or form of a geographic area:

Index of circularity $(M_c) = 100A/\pi(D/2)^2$

where A = area of spatial unit
   D = length of longest (major) axis

The maximum value of M_c is 100, representing a circle, and as M_c tends towards zero so the degree of elongation of the spatial unit increases. Alternative indices are listed under ◊ *shape measures*.

223

index of concentration ◊ *Gini coefficient*.

index of contact possibilities A modification of the ◊ *population potential* concept proposed by G. Törnqvist. The index of contact possibilities is based upon the number of hours of personal contact that can be had in a single day by people based in one region with people working in another region, averaged over all regions. It is calculated as:

$$P_i = \sum_{j=1}^{n} (Tij - Dij)Kj$$

where P_i = measure of ◊ *accessibility* from region i to potential contact sources in the other n regions

Tij = length of time in a single working day it is possible to remain in region j after a journey from region i

Dij = travel time by the shortest route from region i to region j

Kj = total number of persons employed in region j in contact-intensive job functions, weighted by the national average daily hours of contact for each job function

index of dispersion A measure of the extent to which a spatial distribution is concentrated or dispersed around its centre of gravity or ◊ *mean centre*. The index of dispersion is the mean of all the distances of points in the distribution from the mean centre. The more dispersed the distribution the greater will be the index. By comparing the index of dispersion for a particular activity, say employment in a given industry, with the index of all activity, employment in all industry, an *index of relative dispersion* is obtained, a value of 1·0 indicating that employment in a given industry is dispersed in the same pattern as all employment. ◊ *standard distance*.

index of dissimilarity A simple index of the extent to which two spatial distributions differ. The index of dissimilarity is calculated from data giving for both spatial distributions the percentage of the total present in each areal sub-unit. The index is then one-half of the sum of the absolute differences between the two distributions, taken area by area, i.e.

$$I_D = \frac{1}{2} \sum_{i=1}^{k} |x_i - y_i|$$

where x_i = the percentage of the x distribution in the ith areal sub-unit

y_i = the percentage of the y distribution in the ith areal sub-unit

with the summation being over all the k sub-units making up the given area.

The value of the index may range from 0·0 (complete similarity) to 100 (complete segregation). It may be interpreted as a measure of net displacement showing the proportion of one population which would have to move into other areas in order to reproduce the percentage distribution of the other population. The basic form of the index of dissimilarity has been applied to a wide variety of geographical phenomena, but especially to the study of residential segregation. It has also formed the basis for further measures: ◊ *index of redistribution, index of residential differentiation, index of segregation*.

index of diversification Conceptually similar to the ◊ *coefficient of specialization*: in effect the corollary of the latter. ◊ *Gibbs–Martin index of diversification*.

index of diversity A method of classifying cities, developed by E. L. Ullman and M. F. Dacey, which is based on the ◊ *minimum requirements technique*. Cities are classified by reference to the extent to which a city departs from various minima for employment in given sectors. The index is calculated as:

$$D = \frac{\Sigma_i \left[\frac{(P_i - M_i)^2}{M_i} \right]}{\frac{(\Sigma_i P_i - \Sigma_i M_i)^2}{\Sigma_i M_i}}$$

where i = each of the employment groups

P_i = percentage employed in each of i groups

M_i = minimum requirement for each group

Σ_i = sum of all the groups

The higher the index the more specialized the city.

index of independence A measure of the degree of self-sufficiency of an urban centre in terms of employment for their resident populations. The index is expressed as the ratio of daily work-trips within an urban administrative area to the total volume of cross-boundary movement into and out of that area. The higher the index value, the greater the degree of self-containment.

index of labour cost An index used by Alfred Weber to measure the importance of ◊ *labour* for any particular industry. The index for an industry was the average cost of labour to produce one unit of output. The higher the index, Weber argued, the greater the industry's susceptibility to diversion from the least-transport cost location. However, Weber regarded the ◊ *labour coefficient* as a more satisfactory measure. ◊ *Weber's theory of industrial location.*

index of localization ◊ *coefficient of localization.*

index of primacy An elementary measure of the importance of the largest town in a nation or region. Its ◊ *primacy* is established as:

$$\text{Index of primacy} = \frac{P_1}{P_2}$$

where P_1 = population of the largest town

P_2 = population of the second largest town

◊ *primate city distribution.*

index of racial affinity ◊ *blood-group indices.*

index of redistribution A version of the ◊ *index of dissimilarity* which compares the spatial distribution of a given activity at two points in time. The index of redistribution indicates the net percentage of population that would have to change its area of residence/occurrence in any given year in order to reproduce the distributional pattern of an earlier year. The formula is the same as for the index of dissimilarity, but x_i represents the percentage of the population contained in the ith areal sub-unit in a given year, and y_i represents the percentage of the same population in the ith unit in an earlier year. It has been used particularly in the analysis of intra-urban migration.

index of regional specialization ◊ *coefficient of specialization.*

index of relative dispersion ◊ *index of dispersion.*

index of residential differentiation An extension of the ◊ *index of dissimilarity* designed to summarize the distribution of more than two groups of population in a single index. The index of residential differentiation (RDI) measures the extent to which the distribution of the population groups departs from an even distribution. It is calculated as:

$$\text{RDI} = \frac{0.5 \sum_{i=1}^{r} \sum_{j=1}^{c} |N_{ij} - (N_{.j} N_{i.}/N_{..})|}{\sum_{j=1}^{c} |N_{.j} - (N_{.j^2}/N_{..})|}$$

where r = number of areal sub-units

c = number of social/population groups

N_{ij} = number of households of type j in sub-area i

$$N_{.j} = \Sigma_i N_{ij}$$
$$N_{i.} = \Sigma_j N_{ij}$$
$$N_{..} = \Sigma_i \Sigma_j N_{ij}$$

The index may be interpreted as the number of households who have to change residence for the c groups to be evenly distributed, standardized as a proportion of the number who would have to move out if, at the outset, the c groups were totally segregated. ◊ *index of segregation.*

index of retail prices Popularly referred to in the United Kingdom as the *cost of living index*, the index of retail prices measures monthly changes in the level of retail prices. It is a weighted ◊ *arithmetic mean* of price relatives based upon ten main groups of items – food, alcoholic drink, tobacco, housing, fuel and light, durable household goods, clothing and footwear, transport and vehicles, miscellaneous goods and services. The basis of the weighting is provided by regular inquiries into household expenditure (◊ *Family Expenditure Survey*).

index of rural settlement form Much early work on rural settlement was concerned with the identification of the predominant form of settlement within different regions and sub-regions. Such work was criticized for its failure to distinguish settlement types sufficiently precisely, there being no agreed standard of division between large and small ◊ *villages,* ◊ *hamlets,* etc. In an attempt to overcome this weakness various indices of rural settlement form have been developed which measure either the distance between habitations or their relative degree of concentration and dispersal. For example:

(i) J. Bernard's index measured concentration:

$$C = \frac{HA}{s^2}$$

where C = degree of concentration
H = number of habitations

A = area
s = number of settlements

(ii) J. A. Barnes and A. H. Robinson considered separation distance:

$$D = 1 \cdot 11 \sqrt{\frac{A}{N}}$$

where D = average distance of a farm to nearest six farmhouses
A = area
N = number of farmhouses

(iii) K. H. Stones measured the continuity of settlement:

$$R = Nh + Nr$$

where R = continuous or discontinuous settlement
Nh = pattern of permanent habitations within 3 miles (4·8 km) along 1–6 major directions from any one permanent residence
Nr = number of interregional and local transport routes within 10–20 miles (16–32 km) of each residence

All such indices suffer from subjectivity, particularly in the selection of vital size and distance thresholds. Moreover they are not truly comparable because their underlying bases differ and their use has been largely confined to their country of origin. ◊ *Kant's index of concentration.*

index of segregation The measure which results when an ◊ *index of dissimilarity* is computed between a sub-group of a population and the remainder of the population (i.e. total population minus those in the specified group). It is a measure which has been used particularly to assess the degree of residential segregation of a sub-group within the wider population. The formula is:

$$I_S = \frac{I_D}{1 - \frac{\Sigma x_{ai}}{\Sigma x_{ni}}}$$

where I_D = the index of dissimilarity
Σx_{ai} = the total number of the sub-group in the city
Σx_{ni} = the total population of the city

The value of the index can range from 0·0 (complete mixing) to 100 (complete segregation). ◊ *index of residential differentiation*.

index of spatial efficiency An index which assesses the relative suitability of any location within an area compared to the area's ◊ *mean centre*. The index of spatial efficiency is calculated as:

$$E = \frac{M_G}{M_B}$$

where M_G = ◊ *moment of inertia* calculated for points around an area's mean centre
M_B = *moment of inertia* calculated for some other point in the area, e.g. an actual administrative centre

If $E = 1·0$ then the actual administrative centre would be located at the area's mean centre. As the value of E decreases so the distance between the actual centre and the theoretic centre increases.

index of surplus workers ◊ *minimum requirements technique*.

index of tourist irritation An attempt to assess the social impact of tourist development on the resident or host population of the area/resort visited. Irritations have their origins in the number of tourists and the threats which they pose to the way of life of permanent residents. The responses of residents in different destinations will vary and resident responses will change through time in a predictable sequence comparable to that of the ◊ *resort cycle*. Tourist destinations pass successively through:
(i) The *stage of euphoria*: Residents are

enthusiastic about tourist development, visitors are welcomed and there is a mutual feeling of satisfaction. Opportunities are created for locals and money flows in with the tourists.
(ii) The *level of apathy*: As the tourist industry expands, visitors are taken for granted, contacts become more formal and the tourist is a target for profit-taking.
(iii) The *level of irritation*: Irritation begins as the industry nears saturation point or is allowed to pass the level at which the locals cannot handle the numbers without the expansion of facilities.
(iv) The *level of antagonism*: Irritations are overt and the tourist is associated with all that is bad. The tourist is 'ripped off'.
(v) The *final stage*: People have forgotten that what they cherished in the first place was what drew the tourist. In the wild scramble to develop they have overlooked this and the environment has been destroyed. The area may still be able to draw tourists, though of a very different type from those welcomed in early years, and if it is large enough to cope with mass tourism it will continue to have an economic future.

The level of irritation arising from contacts between the hosts and the tourists will be determined by the mutual compatibility of each, though, even with seemingly compatible groups, sheer numbers may generate tension. Differences in race, culture, economic status and nationality are complicating factors. ◊ *tourist function*.

index of variability ◊ *coefficient of variation*.

index of vitality A demographic index, combining age-structure with ◊ *fertility* and ◊ *mortality*, which measures the growth potential of a population. It is measured as:

$$I_V = \frac{\text{Fertility rate} \times \% \text{ aged 20–40}}{\text{Crude death rate} \times \text{old-age index}}$$

◊ *death rates, fertility rates, old-age index.*

indicated reserves ◊ *reserves.*

indicative planning A form of ◊ *economic planning* in which central government establishes general targets for the major sectors of the economy, to serve as guidelines and inducements to firms' decentralized economic decision-taking.

indifference analysis An approach developed by economists to help construct a more satisfactory theory of consumer behaviour. Consumers consciously or subconsciously compare various possible purchases and finally express a preference for one article by buying it. This preference may be for a combination of ◊ *goods*, e.g. ten apples and two oranges rather than nine apples and four oranges. The reason why more ◊ *utility* is apparent in the first combination to a particular consumer is not discussed in economics, but it is accepted that consumers can place goods in order of preference or priority. If consumers can express preferences, they are also able to express indifference.

To understand consumer behaviour, indifference analysis seeks to establish which combination of goods yields the consumer the same satisfaction or ◊ *utility.* For example, all possible combinations of

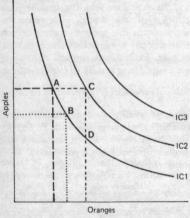

Oranges

Fig. 71 Indifference analysis

two commodities, say apples and oranges, to which a consumer is indifferent can be plotted as an *indifference curve* (◊ Fig. 71). Thus the combination of apples and oranges represented by point *A* on indifference curve 1 has exactly the same utility for a given consumer as the combination represented by point *B* on the same curve, i.e. all combinations of two goods which represent the same utility for a consumer lie on the same indifference curve. For each consumer it is possible to construct an infinite series of indifference curves, with curves further from the origin representing higher levels of utility – point *C* on indifference curve 2 yields a higher utility than point *A* (because it has the same number of apples but more oranges than *A*) and also a higher utility than point *D* (because it has the same number of oranges but more apples than *D*).

Indifference curves are convex to the origin because of diminishing marginal utility, i.e. the more of a good a consumer has the lower is the satisfaction from each additional unit obtained. Hence the consumer is less willing to give up apples for one orange as his consumption of oranges in relation to apples increases.

Since consumers want to maximize their utility they will choose combinations of goods that lie on the highest indifference curve compatible with their income.

indigenous A term used to describe not only plants and animals but also population and human activities which originate and remain in a specific place.

indirect contact space A component of ◊ *action space* which refers to the ◊ *space* about which an individual has knowledge but which lies outside the ◊ *activity space* (direct contact space) where their activities are normally carried out. Indirect contact space is defined in terms of information received at second hand from such sources as acquaintances' experiences and the mass media.

indirect integration ◊ *integration*.

individual distance The characteristic spacing of species members, such as human beings. Individual distance can exist only when two or more members of the same species are present. It depends on ◊ *population density* and territorial behaviour. Individual distance interacts with ◊ *personal space* to affect the distribution of persons: individual distance can be outside the area of personal space (as in a conversation between two persons sitting in chairs on opposite sides of a room) or it may be within the bounds of personal space (as in the case of someone standing close to other people in a crowded tube train).

individual goods ◊ *Goods* which by their nature could be made available for purchase by individuals and which are paid for by individuals. ◊◊ *public goods*.

indivisibility A term used of ◊ *factors of production*, especially fixed ◊ *capital*, where the inputs come in single whole units with a given capacity for output, i.e. those units cannot be subdivided. This is particularly true of plant and machinery which must be used on a large scale, or not at all, if it is to fulfil its functions. The minimum size of the unit is determined by the state of technology at the time, and there is also a minimum threshold of production before such indivisible inputs can be profitably employed. ◊◊ *economies of scale*.

induced invention ◊ *invention*.

induction A method of reasoning from the part to the whole, i.e. from particular cases to general conclusions. Induction provides a method by which truths of scientific value are inferred but which are not directly deducible from principles already known. Inductive method begins by observing and recording specific cases and proceeds, via the ordering and classification of data, to reveal regularities which, being based on a large number of cases, have the status of ◊ *laws*, so allowing the

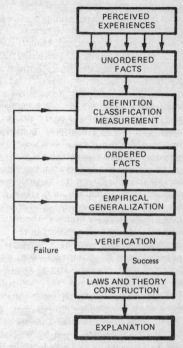

Fig. 72 Induction

construction of ◊ *theory*. ◊ Fig. 72 provides a summary of the inductive method. ◊ *scientific method*. ◊◊ *deduction*.

industrial action space ◊ *action space*.

industrial archaeology Technically industrial archaeology should include the archaeological study of industry in all periods of the past, but in practice it has been restricted to the period beginning with the start of the ◊ *Industrial Revolution*. This is because archaeologists of prehistoric, classical and medieval periods have included the industries of those times within their studies. ◊ *archaeology*.

industrial compensation ◊ *countertrade*.

industrial complex A geographically localized set of specific industries subject to important production, marketing and other interrelationships, gaining ◊ *external economies* from agglomeration and communicating innovations. Usually each industry makes significant purchases from the others, i.e. uses the others' outputs as inputs. *Local industrial complexes*, where the constituent industries of a complex are located in a single urban area, have been distinguished from *regional industrial complexes*, where constituent industries are dispersed throughout a region. The industries present can be subdivided into *complex-forming industries* about which the complex develops (◊◊ *key industry*) and *complex-serving industries*. ◊ *industrial complex analysis*. ◊◊ *growth pole, territorial production complex*.

industrial complex analysis A method of analysing the ◊ *linkages* between industries in an ◊ *industrial complex* with the objective of identifying the type of industrial complex which would be most suitable for a given development programme or region. Industrial complex analysis is a hybrid technique, developed by W. Isard and his associates, which retains the more important inter-industry relations of ◊ *input–output analysis* in combination with the strengths of ◊ *comparative cost analysis*. The technique has proved most successful in analysing modern industry, such as petrochemicals, where there are well-defined and limited chains of linked manufacturing processes.

industrial concentration A term which expresses the proportion of a particular economic activity which is accounted for by a specific number of business enterprises. At the level of manufacturing industry as a whole the leading 50, 100 or 200 firms are generally used; at the level of an individual industrial sector, concentration is usually measured by the share of output, sales or employment which is held by the leading four to eight enterprises in that sector.

industrial decentralization ◊ *decentralization*.

Industrial Development Certificate (IDC) A selective form of locational clearance and control used in British ◊ *industrial location policy*. IDCs were introduced under the 1947 Town and Country Planning Act and were required by any industrial building, new or extension, having more than a certain floorspace. New industrial building had to be officially approved by central government as consistent with the 'proper' distribution of industry; thus IDCs were a major policy instrument used to restrict development in the prosperous regions and to divert it to areas of high unemployment. The floorspace limits have been varied from time to time and there has also been some variation in the areas where IDCs were necessary. Since 1979 IDCs have not been required in any of the ◊ *assisted areas* and have been readily granted in non-assisted areas where they apply only to the very largest factories.

industrial geography A branch of ◊ *economic geography* which deals with the spatial distribution of manufacturing or ◊ *secondary activity*. Much of the early work in industrial geography concentrated upon the description of individual manufacturing activities – their spatial pattern and its historical development, with an explanatory emphasis on the influence of raw material and power sources. From the 1960s, drawing from economics, industrial geography developed an explicit interest in ◊ *industrial location theory*, especially the normative approaches embodied in ◊ *variable cost* and ◊ *variable revenue analysis*. Subsequently more original contributions have come from geographers as a result of dissatisfaction with traditional location theory and the emergence of an alternative behavioural perspective which shifted the emphasis to the study of location decision-making in practice. This line of research has been further expanded into processes of locational adaptation and of ◊ *linkage* adjustment by firms in response to both internally initiated and environmentally initiated (including government policy) change. This research is complemented by studies of the geography of enterprise which concentrate on the organizational and corporate aspects of manufacturing industry.

industrial growth ◊ *law of industrial growth.*

industrial inertia The tendency of particular industries or groups of industries to remain in an existing location after the original factors for their localization have weakened or disappeared. Industrial inertia is generally associated with the development of ◊ *external economies* and ◊ *agglomeration economies*, i.e. the local advantages that are built up by the industries concerned. Also, the relative immobility of the large investment in existing physical structures and resources militates against radical change. Consequently present location has an influence on future patterns, in so far as previous experience generates decisions which strongly reinforce existing spatial patterns. Many established industrial regions therefore survive by the contraction and adaptation of existing industries *in situ* and by the development of new industry. Industrial inertia is the most commonly used term, but it is also referred to as *geographical inertia* or *locational inertia* and sometimes as *geographical immobility.*

industrial linkage ◊ *linkage.*

industrial location policy A course of action adopted by a government in order to influence the location of industrial activity. In a ◊ *mixed economy*, industrial location policy usually forms an integral part of ◊ *regional policy* and is aimed at the revitalization of ◊ *declining regions*. In underdeveloped countries it can have a role to play in initiating ◊ *industrialization.*

Industrial location policy normally relies upon area-based measures, both negative, to control the level of industrial development in certain areas, and positive, to provide incentives to attract industries to other areas. ◊ *Industrial Development Certificate.*

industrial location theory A generic term for those formal, abstract and deductive solutions to the problem facing the firm that wishes to locate a new plant (◊ *spatial elasticity of locational choice*). It might, therefore, more aptly be described as the theory of location of the firm. Industrial location theory seeks to derive the optimum location for the individual manufacturing firm, and the major work has been carried out by economists attempting to integrate location into the mainstream of economic theory. Three approaches can be distinguished:
(i) The *least-cost approach*, which attempts to explain location in terms of minimization of factor costs, especially transport costs. Implicit in this approach is the assumption of ◊ *perfect competition*. The least-cost theory is traditionally associated with the work of Alfred Weber (◊ *Weber's theory of industrial location*), which dominated much early 20th-century thinking and provided the basis for ◊ *variable cost analysis.* (◊ *comparative cost analysis.*)
(ii) The *locational interdependence approach* (◊ *locational interdependence theory of industrial location*), which focuses on the rivalry and interrelationships between firms, especially under conditions of ◊ *imperfect competition*. The particular concern with demand or market factors provides a basis for ◊ *variable revenue analysis.* (◊ *Fetter's model, Hotelling model.*)
(iii) The *profit-maximization approach* which attempts the integration of the other two approaches, as in the work of M. L. Greenhut, W. Isard and A. Lösch. (◊ *spatial margins.*)
Subsequent work has questioned the

extent to which firms maximize profits, and has attempted to extend the analysis from the single-product, single-plant firms assumed in the above approaches to multi-product, multi-plant firms, as well as replacing the static concepts of traditional analysis with dynamic and process-oriented theories of location and corporate growth. ⟡ *filter-down theory of industrial location, foreign direct investment theory, seedbed growth, stage model of industrial location.*

industrial migration The actual physical transfer or *relocation* of productive capacity to a new location by an existing manufacturing firm. The establishment of a ◊ *branch plant* is included in some uses of the term. ⟡ *industrial movement.*

industrial mix A term describing the composition of a place's industries. It is usually measured by employment structure.

industrial mobility An individual's potential, by virtue of occupation, to be employed in more than one type of industry. ⟡ *occupational mobility.*

industrial momentum A concept similar to ◊ *industrial inertia* in that it relates to an area which has lost, or has had appreciably altered, its original locational advantages, but the term momentum implies an ability of established industries in the area to increase their importance.

industrial movement The opening of new manufacturing plants, the origin of which can be attributed to some other location. Two basic categories are distinguished:
(i) ◊ *Industrial migration*: the complete relocation or transfer of a firm, which involves the closure of previously occupied premises and the opening of a new establishment.
(ii) ◊ *Branch plant* creation, which involves the opening of a new establishment without the closure of existing premises.

industrial noise measurement The meas-urement of the disturbing effects of ◊ *noise* from industrial premises. In the United Kingdom industrial noise is measured by the ◊ *corrected noise level*, based on the ◊ *decibel A-scale*, with corrections for definite continuous tones, e.g. hum, irregularities, e.g. bangs, and the proportion of time the noise lasts. ⟡ *noise control.*

industrial organization The administrative–managerial structure responsible for the control, decision-making and hence operation of one or more manufacturing units. Significant changes have been witnessed in the complexity of industrial organization, especially this century. While small single-plant enterprises are still the most common type of firm, they are no longer the most important type of enterprise when measured in terms of employment, production, sales or financial resources. With increasing scale of industrial production and expansion of the spatial extent of operations, multi-product, multi-plant corporations, in which decision-making functions are more dispersed, have come to dominate manufacturing industry. Such developments have recently been recognized in ◊ *industrial location theory*, with attention being paid to why and how firms develop and grow and the consequent changes in spatial organization which occur. Generally such complex business firms have evolved a hierarchical structure of control which is mirrored in a hierarchical structure of spatial organization.

Industrial Revolution The process of ◊ *industrialization* which converted a fundamentally rural society into an industrial one in late-18th-century and 19th-century Europe and North America. It was initially a technological revolution in which new machines, new techniques and new processes, associated especially with new power sources, greatly increased the production and range of manufactured goods. The Industrial Revolution was spread over at least a century after about

1750, Great Britain being the first country to undergo such a change. It might be suggested that the changes took place too slowly to be accurately called a revolution, even allowing for the accelerated changes after 1800, but the effects on every aspect of human life were certainly revolutionary. Thus the term Industrial Revolution is in common use and, as long as the time dimension involved and the nature of the change is understood, it is a convenient descriptive term.

industrial specialization model An explanation of ◊ *urbanization* and the evolution of urban systems based on North American urban experience and associated with the work of economic historians, e.g. E. E. Lampard, geographers, e.g. A. Pred, and urban economists, e.g. W. R. Thompson. The explanation tends to equate urbanization with ◊ *industrialization* and to associate urban growth with industrial growth. Regional cities were converted into national metropolitan status by the development of a powerful and integrated industrial economy, while many smaller towns grew substantially as a direct result of the location of factories. Industry thus imposed a new urban pattern on top of the existing structure.

The explanation is largely aspatial and does not account for the location of manufacturing activities within any given region.

industrial splashing A term suggested for the simultaneous establishment of a main plant and ◊ *branch plants* within a state, usually an underdeveloped country, by a foreign ◊ *multinational firm*. It is a locational strategy that contrasts with the sequential development of branch plants throughout a national market area.

industrial symbiosis G. Renner's term for industrial clustering or agglomeration. *Disjunctive symbiosis* occurs where there are advantages for unlike industries to group together, and *conjunctive symbiosis* when the industries in an area are organically linked to each other.

industrialization The process whereby ◊ *manufacturing industry* comes to occupy the predominant position in a national or regional economy. The process may be spontaneous but nowadays is likely to be induced by some form of ◊ *planning*. As societies began to demand more products than individuals could make at home, they came to appreciate the advantages of having specialist producers of various goods. In its spontaneous form industrialization therefore involved the replacement of small-scale ◊ *cottage industry*, supplying limited local markets, by a ◊ *factory system*, dependent on the use of inanimate power and machines in large units to produce uniform goods in large amounts at lower unit costs than previously possible. (◊◊ *Industrial Revolution*.)

The spatial impact of industrialization was tremendous, leading to (i) the exploitation of previously unvalued mineral resources, (ii) the concentration of population in cities, (iii) clusters of manufacturing towns, (iv) a sharper distinction between prosperous and poor regions, and (v) increased spatial extent of trading. In the early stages of industrialization ◊ *primary industries* tend to be dominant, but as society becomes more affluent ◊ *secondary industries* take precedence. Industrialization within a capitalist system also brings significant changes in the social relations of production as market forces come to dominate the supply and allocation of labour.

Industrialization was seen as a means of escape from poverty in underdeveloped countries, but both the shortage of capital and the primary producer role assigned by the world economy to these countries constrains its likely effectiveness. However, planned industrialization figures as part of the development strategy in most ◊ *Third World* countries, although, other than in oil-rich countries, it is dependent upon external capital, often available only through ◇ *multinational corporations*, which implies dependency (◇◇ *economic imperialism*). Besides these negative effects society is increasingly aware of the environmental consequences of industrialization in the form of rates of resource exploitation and ◇ *pollution*.

industrie motrice ◇ *growth pole, propulsive industry.*

industry In English-speaking countries the term has been used in both a broad and a narrow sense. In the broadest sense industry refers to any business activity, e.g. the tourist industry, covering all the activities involved in the transport, accommodation, marketing and entertainment of tourists. In the narrow sense industry relates to factory activity in which materials are processed or transformed by mechanical or chemical means into more valuable products. To avoid confusion many social scientists term the latter ◇ *manufacturing industry*. ◇◇ *cottage industry, extractive industry, footloose industry, growth industry, heavy industry, infant industry, lag industry, lead industry, light industry, parasitic industry, primary industry, service industry, tertiary industry, ubiquitous industry.*

industry protection policies Measures introduced by national governments to support home-based industry against foreign competition. Such measures may give protection to established industry (in form of ◇ *tariffs* or ◇ *quotas* on imported products) or seek to promote new industry (◇ *infant industry*).

inertia ◇ *industrial inertia.*

infant industry An ◇ *industry* that is new to a particular country and which has little chance of success unless it is protected from competition. Such industries, often in underdeveloped countries, have difficulty in competing with imports of similar industries abroad during their early years because the latter enjoy benefits of economies of scale. As a consequence governments usually impose ◇ *tariffs* and ◇ *quotas* on the competitive imports in order to protect the infant industry.

infant mortality The number of infant deaths, normally expressed per 1,000 live births. The *infant mortality rate* is therefore an age-specific ◇ *death rate* and is computed as the ratio of infant deaths (children who die before their first birthday) in a given year to the total number of live births registered during the same year.

Infant mortality is regarded as one of the most important indicators of the demographic structure of the population because of its sensitivity to social and environmental conditions. A distinction may be made between *neonatal mortality*, those infant deaths occurring within the first four weeks of life, and *post-neonatal mortality*, those deaths occurring within the remainder of a child's first year. The causes of infant mortality may be categorized as *endogenous mortality*, deaths from congenital malformations or delivery complications, and *exogenous mortality*, deaths from infections and poor care.

General reductions in infant mortality usually precede overall mortality decline and stem from improvements in modern medicine and health services and better nutrition, which reduce exogenous mortality. ◇◇ *mortality, perinatal mortality.*

infantile towns ◇ *age of towns scheme.*

inferential statistics A distinction is normally made between ◇ *descriptive statistics*, which summarize observations, and inferential statistics, which use observations as a basis for making estimates or predictions, i.e. inference about a situation which has not yet occurred. Inferential statistics allow probabilistic statements to be made about the truth of ◇ *hypotheses* and about the characteristics of a population from which a ◇ *sample* is drawn.

◊ *confirmatory statistics, exploratory statistics.*

inferior goods ◊ *Giffen goods.*

inferred reserves ◊ *reserves.*

infield That part of a farm, usually a hill farm, around the farmstead. It was the best land because it received all the winter manure, which was put on about one-third of the infield and ploughed three times before sowing with barley, the remainder being ploughed once and sown with oats. The infield was approximately one-third of the extent of the ◊ *outfield.* ◊ *in-by.*

infield–outfield system A system of cultivation in which the ◊ *infield* was manured and cropped continuously and the ◊ *outfield* was cultivated in temporary breaks, with parts being cultivated for as many years as they would produce a reasonable yield and then abandoned in favour of another part. The system was associated especially with Scotland and northern England from the 16th century, representing an adaptation where the population requiring support exceeded the area of potentially cultivable land.

infilling The ◊ *development* of sites initially by-passed in the expansion of an urban area. ◊ *repletion.*

informal economy, informal sector That part of a national economy, a sub-set of the secondary labour market (◊ *dual labour market*), which undertakes necessary and productive labour without formal systems of control and remuneration and which operates outside official recognition. The value of the informal economy is not measured by official statistics of ◊ *Gross National Product* because of non-reporting and under-reporting. It gives concern to governments because it is outside the net of the tax authorities. The informal economy may be subdivided into a legal set of activities, e.g. house-painting, carwashing, and an illegal set, e.g. prostitution, drug-peddling.

It is also known as the *black economy, cash economy, hidden economy, irregular economy, moonlight economy, parallel economy, submerged economy, twilight economy, underground economy, lavoro sommerso, Schattenwirtschaft* or *travail noir.*

information field The mental information that an individual has about the spatial distribution of a specific set of environmental elements. Most information fields display ◊ *distance-decay* characteristics, i.e. the individual has more information about nearer places than ones further away. Such *private* or *spatial information fields* will be the areas an individual knows best and within which his/her activities will be located (◊ *action space*).

information theory The mathematical analysis of the way in which messages and signals (i.e. information) are stored, processed and transmitted. Developed by C. E. Shannon in the late 1940s, information theory focuses on quantifying the 'commodity', information, treating it as a physical entity. The meaning of the message is unimportant since the emphasis is on the capacity of the channel to pass information, how fast it can be transmitted and how interference or distortion can be eliminated.

infrasound Low-frequency ◊ *sound*, e.g. from heavy transport engines, in frequencies below 100 hertz. Infrasound is not catered for on the ◊ *decibel A-scale*, which is weighted to represent the response of the human ear. It can cause disturbance through resonance and the only effective way to cut down infrasound is to eliminate it at source.

infrastructure The installations and facilities that provide a fundamental framework for an economy and which, therefore, facilitate industrial, agricultural and other forms of economic development. It includes the provision of transport, communications, power supplies and other public utilities. ⟡ *economic overhead capital, social overhead capital, transport infrastructure.*

initial advantage An advantage accruing to a location, region or nation through its being the first to introduce a new product or process and to establish a market area. ⟡ *comparative advantage.*

in-migration field Areas/regions from which a city draws its in-migrants.

inner city A loosely defined area close to the city centre. Present usage relates to the area that used to be referred to as the ⟡ *transition zone* or ⟡ *twilight zone*, i.e. an area of obsolescent and dilapidated housing in multiple occupation, often performing a reception function for new immigrants to the city.

The term has also been used in the United States as a synonym for ⟡ *central city* and, in the context of historical urban geography, to describe the historic urban centre, which was that part of the town formerly enclosed by walls. ⟡ *red-line areas.*

inner fringe ⟡ *rural–urban fringe.*

inner range ⟡ *range.*

innovation The use of an idea or an ⟡ *invention* to lead to change in individual behaviour or in a production process. Thus the initial introduction of a new product or the first utilization of a new production process or organizational technique. Within the production process an innovation always rests upon an invention, being the commercial adoption of the latter. ⟡ *borrowing innovation, innovation wave.* ⟡ *diffusion.*

innovation ratio The proportion of the population with an introduced item.

innovation wave The analogy of innovation ⟡ *diffusion* as a wave arising from an origin and moving outward, with the changing form of the wave, describing the pattern of acceptance of the ⟡ *innovation* at any distance and time from the origin (⟡ Fig. 73). The crest of the wave, the zone of most active acceptance, moves outward from the origin, and the overall probability that people either accept the innovation or tell others about it falls with both increasing distance from the origin and the passing of

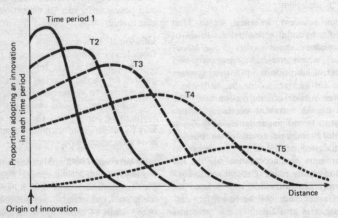

Fig. 73 Innovation wave

time. Hence the final level of acceptance of an innovation often declines slowly with increasing distance from the origin and, as T. Hägerstrand has suggested, the passage of the wave can be characterized as a four-stage model involving ($\diamond$ Fig. 74):

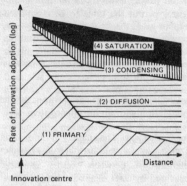

Fig. 74 Innovation wave: stages of spread

(1) A *primary stage*, marking the beginning of the diffusion process by the establishment of adoption centres and by a strong contrast between the innovating centre and more distant areas.
(2) A *diffusion stage*, in which powerful centrifugal effects accompany the creation of adoption centres in more distant locations and which is marked by a reduction in the strong areal contrasts typical of the primary stage.
(3) A *condensing stage*, in which the relative rate of adoption is similar in all locations.
(4) A *saturation stage*, indicating a slowing and eventual cessation of the diffusion process, as well as a general but slow asymptotic increase to a maximum acceptance.

Over time the acceptance of the innovation at any point in space will follow an *s*-type logistic curve ($\diamond$ Fig. 75), since the rate of acceptance will be low when the innovation is still far off, i.e. early innovators will be comparatively few. As the

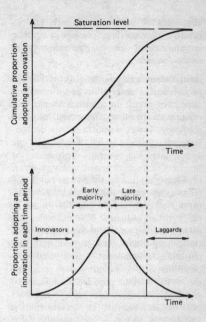

Fig. 75 Innovation wave: cumulative adoption

innovation takes hold in that place the proportion of adopters quickly rises as a group called the early majority comes in. Their example is followed by the late majority and the rate of new acceptances falls off because most people who will adopt the innovation have already done so, leaving a few laggards at the end. The concept of innovation waves has proved a useful device for thinking about certain types of diffusion process, particularly contagious diffusion, and has been applied successfully to the diffusion of agricultural practices and consumer goods.

innovative migration $\diamond$ *migration.*

innovative planning An approach in $\diamond$ *planning*, suggested by J. Friedmann, which attempts to mobilize and channel resources to new or neglected uses, achieving in the process the legitimization of new social objectives or a major realignment of existing objectives. The innovative planner therefore acts as a public entrepreneur. ◊ *advocacy planning*. ◊◊ *allocative planning*.

input–output analysis A quantitative approach to the description of an economy which brings out the interdependence that exists between all sectors/industries of an economy. Input–output analysis demonstrates the ways in which the inputs of one sector are the outputs (products or services) of another sector and vice versa, i.e. for each industry it shows its purchases from every other industry and how the output of each industry is distributed to every other industry. For example, the manufacturing sector requires inputs from the mining (metal ores), agricultural (raw materials), commercial (finance) and various other sectors, including itself (machine tools), in order to produce manufactured goods. These products in turn form inputs of other sectors, such as tractors for the agricultural sector, office machinery for the commercial sector and so on.

Sector producing \ Sector purchasing	Agriculture	Mining	Manufacturing	Services	Households	(Exports)	Total gross output
Agriculture	0.4	0.1	0.3	0.2	0.4	0.4	1.8
Mining	0.1	0.1	0.6	0.0	0.0	0.3	1.1
Manufacturing	0.6	0.3	0.9	0.3	0.5	0.5	3.1
Services	0.3	0.1	0.4	0.8	0.4	0.2	2.2
Households	0.2	0.2	0.4	0.6	0.1	0.1	1.6
(Imports)	0.2	0.3	0.5	0.3	0.2	*	1.5
Total inputs	1.8	1.1	3.1	2.2	1.6	1.5	11.3

* Cell left vacant because transactions with other regions are external to the area under study

Fig. 76 Input–output analysis: hypothetical matrix (in £m)

The pattern of purchases and sales among sectors is normally represented as an input–output table (◊ Fig. 76). Sectors are arrayed in the same order horizontally and vertically. Receipts or sales figures allow the table to be completed on a row-wise basis, with the final entry in a row representing the value of the gross output of the sector. Expenditure or purchasing figures permit the table to be completed column-wise, the final entry in a column representing the total cost of inputs to that sector. Whichever way the table is completed the result must be the same: this identity must follow since every sale is at the same time a purchase. Such a table is a flow or transactions matrix for a given period of time and is obviously a very useful descriptive device when a fine industrial classification is used.

The strength of the ◊ *linkages* or interrelationships between sectors can be measured by a set of production or interindustry coefficients, which indicate the number of inputs from an input sector which must be used to produce one unit in the output sector. These coefficients are obtained by dividing the total value of output in a sector into each of the inputs listed in the sector column, e.g. ◊ Fig. 77 shows coefficients obtained from the in-

Sector producing \ Sector purchasing	Agriculture	Mining	Manufacturing	Services	Households	(Exports)
Agriculture	0.22	0.09	0.10	0.09	0.25	0.27
Mining	0.06	0.09	0.19	0.00	0.00	0.20
Manufacturing	0.33	0.27	0.29	0.14	0.31	0.33
Services	0.17	0.09	0.13	0.36	0.25	0.13
Households	0.11	0.18	0.13	0.27	0.06	0.07
(Imports)	0.11	0.27	0.16	0.14	0.13	–
Total	1.00	1.00	1.00	1.00	1.00	1.00

Fig. 77 Input–output analysis: coefficients table

formation contained in Fig. 76. These coefficients may be used to predict the total volume of growth generated by expansion in a particular sector (though this assumes that the relationships represented by the coefficients are constant, which may not be justified in view of scale economies, technological advance and changes in the relative prices of inputs and outputs).

Input–output analysis has been used as a basis for ◊ *economic planning* in many countries and has been used at urban, regional, national and even international levels.

insideness The key to the identity of ◊ *place*, insideness is the degree to which a person belongs to and associates himself/ herself with a place. ◊ *existential insideness*.

installed capacity The total potential capacity or output of a plant or machine (as distinct from the utilized capacity). In the energy industry in particular the percentage relationship between utilized and installed capacity indicates the ◊ *load factor*.

instrumentalism A conception of science which accepts that theories can never be validated conclusively and which therefore adopts a pragmatic set of standards, evaluating theories according to the success of their predictions against the real world, i.e. it is only the end result that matters. Even if it is not possible to prove that geographical phenomena are subject to universal ◊ *laws*, there is still value in treating them as if they were. Models and laws are therefore seen as instruments of manipulation rather than as explanatory devices. An instrumentalist approach underlies much ◊ *neoclassical economics* and was carried over into geography during the ◊ *quantitative revolution*, where it became virtually indistinguishable from ◊ *positivism*.

intake A temporary ◊ *enclosure* made from the waste, often illegally.

integrated port A ◊ *port* where provision is made for the quayside processing of a commodity moved in bulk and even the subsequent export of the product. This provision reduces transport costs, eliminates payment of import duty, and minimizes pilferage and documentation. ◊ *entrepôt, free port*.

integration (1) A process by which sub-groups within a society come to participate fully in the wider life of the community while retaining some aspects of their individual identity and cultural awareness. It is distinguished from ◊ *assimilation*, which implies the gradual disappearance of culture differences.
(2) The carrying-out within the same ◊ *firm*, often the same ◊ *establishment*, of successive stages or operations in a production process, e.g. an integrated iron and steel works comprises coke ovens, blast furnaces, steel-making furnaces and rolling mills. The firm improves its efficiency by controlling directly either, or both, the backward and forward ◊ *linkages* in the production process, hence the terms *vertical integration, backward integration* and *forward integration*. Firm growth incorporating integration only may be a result of either ◊ *vertical expansion* or ◊ *combination*. (◊ *acquisition behaviour*.)

The term *indirect integration* has sometimes been used to describe firms/industries with complementary labour demands, but this is better viewed as a form of ◊ *linkage*.

intensive agriculture Systems of ◊ *farming* characterized by high levels of factor inputs, especially ◊ *capital*, ◊ *labour* and ◊ *fertilizer*, per unit area of land and generating high gross, and usually high net, yields per unit area of land. Such systems keep land continually in use, often producing several crops per season, employing ◊ *irrigation*, ◊ *crop rotations*, etc. as necessary. ◊ *extensive agriculture*.

intensive margin of cultivation ◊ *economic margins of cultivation.*

intentionality The view that objects are experienced in their meaning; that meaning is conferred by the consciousness a person has of an object in their ◊ *behavioural environment.* People have intentions and cannot be understood as objects from the outside: their behaviour has to be studied and described in terms of their orientation to a situation or object, and this reflects acquired, experimental and culturally determined attitudes and assumptions.

interaction ◊ *spatial interaction.*

interaction breaking point ◊ *breaking point.*

interaction potential Interaction is postulated as a function of ◊ *distance* from an activity and the drawing power of that activity. The likelihood of interaction between one place and another can be estimated using ◊ *gravity models.* ◊ *intervening opportunity, isolation index.*

interactive space ◊ *social space.*

intercommoning The practice whereby a ◊ *manor,* ◊ *vill* or ◊ *parish* with a shortage of common pasture shared a tract of land with a neighbouring manor, vill or parish. Many such areas were subdivided between vills in the 13th century.

interculture ◊ *intertillage.*

interdependence A term used to describe the mutually interlocking relations of ◊ *economy* and ◊ *society.* Such *functional interdependence* arises from the joint roles a person plays in the operation of the different sub-systems of society, e.g. the same person operates in economic, family, social and political arenas – as worker, father, club member, voter. It is therefore a concept which emphasizes the 'wholeness' of components of a system.

interdependence trap A central phenomenon of urban ◊ *blight.* Neighbouring property owners are interdependent, but neighbours are trapped by the ◊ *uncertainty* of each other's behaviour into a position where the optimum strategy for each acting independently produces a lower return than it would have if each was constrained to follow a strategy that would maximize the yield to the group. A property owner therefore sees little point in improving or maintaining his property if all his neighbours are allowing their properties to fall into decay. A coalition is only possible where each property owner understands the pay-off to the others as well as to himself. The result is most likely to be that no one acts.

interest group A group of persons sharing a common interest, such as drama, athletics, an environmental cause or a trade-union matter. ◊ *peer group.*

interest rate The price paid by a borrower to a lender for the use of ◊ *capital funds,* usually expressed as a percentage of the capital per annum. The *classical theory of the rate of interest* argues that, under the interplay of market forces, the rate of interest comes to rest at the level where the amount of investment equals the amount of savings, whereas *Keynes' liquidity-preference theory* emphasizes the function of the interest rate in bringing about a balance between the supply of and demand for money, i.e. the interest rate is a payment to persuade an individual or firm to part with their liquidity for a period of time. There are various interest rates in existence at any given time, varying with the nature and term of the credit.

interface A surface or boundary lying between two ◊ *systems.* The term has frequently been used of the boundary, especially if poorly defined, between academic disciplines.

intermediate area Intermediate or *grey areas* were introduced by the 1970 Local Employment Act following the recommendations of the 1969 Hunt Committee Report. The Hunt Committee's terms of reference were 'to examine in relation to the economic welfare of the country as a whole and the needs of the ⟡ *development areas*, the situation in other areas where the rate of economic growth gives cause (or may give cause) for concern, and to suggest whether revised policies to influence economic growth in such areas are desirable and, if so, what measures should be adopted'. While there is no clear-cut and well-defined category of intermediate areas, they are regions in which economic difficulties are not necessarily reflected in high ⟡ *unemployment* but in which symptoms of concern (e.g. sluggish or falling employment, slow growth of personal incomes, low earnings, serious outward migration, low proportion of women at work, etc.) are evident. The areas designated, which have been varied through time, qualify for some but not all of the normal Development Area aid, and firms could obtain ⟡ *industrial development certificates* with comparative ease. Intermediate areas thus form part of a three-tier area-based approach to ⟡ *industrial location policy*. ⟡⟡ *special development area*.

intermetropolitan circulation of élites A form of ⟡ *migration*, within and between developed nations, involving the movement of highly paid professionals, such as managers, bankers and academics, from city to city, and country to country, in pursuit of career advancement. ⟡⟡ *mobility transition*.

internal colonialism An explanation, advanced by M. Hechter, for the rise of ethnic–regional separation as an antecedent cause of regional inequality. Expanding ⟡ *nation-states* incorporate not only overseas ⟡ *colonies* but also 'internal' colonies, equivalent to ethnic enclaves, within their boundaries. Continued economic exploitation of the ethnic periphery results in a clear-cut division of labour on predominantly cultural lines: the inequalities within the nation reflecting the monopoly of credit and capital exercised by the wealthy core and this is reinforced by selective recruitment, discrimination on the basis of language, race or religion, the control of political decision-making and the concentration of research and innovation at the centre. ⟡⟡ *core–periphery model*.

internal economies ⟡ *economies of scale*.

internal waters The ⟡ *maritime zone* closest to the shore (⟡ Fig. 29), not necessarily continuous, lying on the landward side of the ⟡ *baseline*. Internal waters exist because straight baselines are drawn along indented coasts or across the mouths of bays and estuaries. Such waters are legally treated as part of the land territory of the country. ⟡ *historic bay*. ⟡⟡ *contiguous zone, exclusive economic zone, territorial sea*.

International Air Transport Association (IATA) A ⟡ *cartel* comprising most of the international airlines which sets international passenger fares and licenses scheduled services. The practice was to charge fares at high rates per kilometre on high-density routes, such as the North Atlantic, and award licences for such lucrative routes only where the airline was prepared to take on less lucrative routes as well, the latter being cross-subsidized by the former. Competition from non-IATA airlines offering stand-by or bus-stop services at lower rates has forced some changes in practices.

International Coffee Agreement Coffee is a crop that has experienced periods of surplus and deficit, hence sharply changing prices and returns for producers. The stockpiling of coffee in Brazil and the initiation of artificially high prices encouraged coffee production elsewhere. As producers competed for markets in the 1950s, prices fell, competition increased

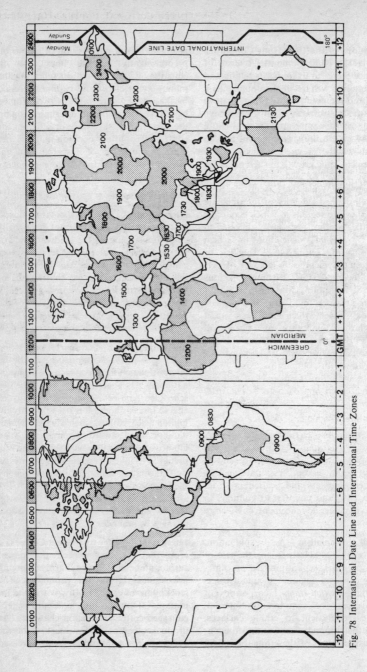

Fig. 78 International Date Line and International Time Zones

and the ◊ *terms of trade* deteriorated for coffee producers. As a consequence the International Coffee Agreement was signed within the United Nations whereby exporting countries accepted export ◊ *quotas* and importing countries accepted a floor on coffee prices and agreed to limit purchases from those nations not signing the agreement.

International Date Line Places immediately west of longitude 180° are twelve hours ahead of ◊ *Greenwich Mean Time*, places just east twelve hours behind. To compensate for this, the International Date Line, an imaginary line, internationally accepted, has been devised. It generally follows longitude 180°, but adjustments are made for convenience sake to avoid cutting through land areas or island groups (◊ Fig. 78). The line compensates for the accumulated time-change of one hour in each 15° longitude time zone, such that travellers crossing the line from east to west must add twenty-four hours (i.e. a day is omitted) and travellers crossing the line from west to east must subtract twenty-four hours (i.e. a day is repeated). ◊ *International Time Zones.*

international region ◊ *geostrategic region.*

International Sugar Agreement An agreement to regulate world free market supplies of sugar to keep the price above a certain minimum. The primary measure was export ◊ *quota*, but the pact was largely defective and attempts are being made to renegotiate it.

International Time Zones The world is divided for convenience into International Time Zones, blocks of territory between specified longitudes (◊ Fig. 78). In each time zone the ◊ *local time* at a central meridian is accepted as the ◊ *standard time* throughout the zone.

International Wheat Agreement An agreement signed in 1948 by wheat-growing

nations to share the existing world market for wheat rather than for any one of them to glut the market during a highly productive year. It was only partially successful, as signatories started dropping out from 1949.

inter-neighbour interval The average distance between neighbours in a given area. ◊ *interpersonal space, nearest neighbour analysis.*

interpersonal space A measure of relative location, being the linear distance separating an individual, household or other group from their neighbours. ◊ *personal space.*

interpolation The insertion of (estimated) values between known (measured) values. Since the inference concerns unknown areas within the distribution of known values, it is likely that the degree of error will be small compared to ◊ *extrapolation.*

inter-quartile range A crude index of ◊ *dispersion* in a ◊ *frequency distribution* based on the use of percentiles, in this case the 25th and 75th, i.e. upper and lower, ◊ *quartiles.* The upper quartile is found by taking the 25 per cent highest values and finding the mid-point between the lowest of these and the next lowest value. Similarly the lower quartile is found by taking the 25 per cent lowest values and finding the mid-point between the highest of these and the next highest value. Thus 50 per cent of the values in the distribution lie between the upper and lower quartiles and the difference between the values of these two quartiles is in the inter-quartile range. In ◊ *exploratory statistics* it is referred to as the *midspread.*

interregional income inequality model A model which attempts to explain the existence, development and persistence of regional disparities within a nation. The most important such model is probably G. Myrdal's ◊ *cumulative causation* one.

interregional input–output analysis A form of ◊ *input–output analysis* that accounts for transactions between ◊ *regions* as well as between sectors within regional economies.

intersubjective verification An approach used in ◊ *phenomenology* to establish generalizations about human experience which involves the corroboration of one person's subjective accounts with another persons's accounts.

intertillage Or *interculture*. A practice of mixed cropping whereby two or more different ◊ *crops* are grown together on the same area of land. Sowing and harvesting are often staggered, with plantings timed so that as one crop matures another is getting started. ◊ *catch crop*.

interval scale, interval data A form of measurement in which each observation is allocated a precise numerical value along a continuous scale. An interval scale has the property that the distances between the categories are defined in terms of fixed and equal units, i.e. the direction and magnitude of position on the scale are known, but the choice of the unit of measurement and of the zero point is arbitrary. For example, measured on the centigrade scale the freezing point of water is zero, but this corresponds to 32 on the fahrenheit scale. The concept of ratio is meaningless on an interval scale because of the arbitrary zero; thus it *cannot* be stated that 20°C is twice as hot as 10°C (if converted to fahrenheit they become 68°F and 50°F respectively). ◊ *nominal scale*, *ordinal scale*, *ratio scale*.

intervening opportunity The idea that the presence of closer opportunities greatly diminish the attractiveness of even slightly better but more distant ones. The concept was developed in ◊ *migration* theory by S. A. Stouffer and, in formal terms, states that the number of movements from an origin to a given destination is directly proportional to the number of opportunities at that destination and inversely proportional to the number of intervening opportunities between origin and destination. The concept has since been applied to a wide variety of other flows, e.g. shopping behaviour. Intervening opportunity also forms one of the three basic factors in E. L. Ullman's typology of spatial interaction. (◊ *complementarity*, *transferability*.) ◊ *gravity model*.

intervention prices An alternative to ◊ *guaranteed prices* as a method of agricultural support used by governments to iron out price fluctuations of agricultural products in the short run and to raise the level of farm incomes. As a system of price support it is based on direct intervention buying by the government in the domestic market in order to maintain a minimum price to home-based farmers and on the imposition of tariffs/levies on imported agricultural products. Intervention or *threshold prices* are set at a percentage of the *target price* (an annually set price which allows farmers an adequate profit). Price on the home market cannot drop below the level of the intervention price for a commodity, since the government, as intervention agency, must buy all the produce offered by home farmers at that price, while tariffs ensure that imported commodities cannot be available at lower prices.

The European Economic Community's Common Agricultural Policy is based on such a system of intervention prices and provides evidence for those who argue that such a support system encourages overproduction.

in-transit privilege Applied to ◊ *freight rates*, the quotation of a single, through rate from material source to market, even though the materials are stopped and processed somewhere *en route*. The object of the in-transit privilege or *fabrication-in-*

transit is to remove the disadvantage of intermediate locations, which would generally involve the combined greater costs of two short hauls, by quoting a long haul rate. In-transit privileges tend to equalize freight rate burdens between locations.

intransitive choice An individual's inconsistent preference for or ranking of different items. For example, a person who ranks *A* higher than *B* and *B* higher than *C* may, unexpectedly, rank *C* higher than *A*. Intransitive choice may be due not only to the unpredictability of human nature but also to the fact that a good can be evaluated in different ways (e.g. apples by weight, taste, texture, storage properties, etc.).

introduced capital ◊ *capital*.

invasion-succession concept An ecological process of sequential change at the ◊ *neighbourhood* level which is part of the process of urban growth. It involves more intensive land uses outbidding existing uses for buildings in a formerly homogeneous neighbourhood or ◊ *natural area*. Occupancy of some buildings by new groups or putting them to new uses tends to make the area unsuitable for the original group or use, which moves out to new locations – a process of group or land use displacement and replacement.

Speculation precedes invasion by the more intensive use and, as some existing buildings are put to new uses, they tend to deteriorate faster, with consequent effects for adjacent buildings whose use has not yet changed. With housing the process can be likened to an areal version of ◊ *filtering*, as the new uses represent a lower-income group prepared to live at higher densities than the previous occupants and often with different cultural or ethnic characteristics which hasten the exodus of the original households. The first entrants from the new group may bid property prices up since they must outbid competing existing uses, but where successful their presence

depreciates the value of surrounding properties and the long-run effect is of price fall as the neighbourhood declines. Succession, when the new use has taken over the neighbourhood, marks the end product of invasion. ◊ *neighbourhood evolution, residential cycle succession, tipping-point*.

invention The addition of new products, techniques and production processes to the existing stock of knowledge. Invention may be:

(i) *Autonomous invention*, a long-term, spontaneous and apparently randomly generated contribution of those occasional geniuses who invent things, i.e. the extension of the existing stock of knowledge by intuitive thought.

(ii) *Induced invention*, which involves the deliberate expenditure of effort, resources and time for the purpose of generating new technical knowledge. Today induced invention is the most important element in the expansion of technical ability and is internalized in the research and development activities of large firms.

The commercial application of an invention is referred to as ◊ *innovation*.

investment An increase in the stock of physical assets (machinery, factories, roads, bridges, houses, etc.) over a given period of time, i.e. new ◊ *capital* goods. *Expansion investment*, the increase in stock of fixed capital goods by a firm in order to attain a higher production level, may be distinguished from *replacement investment*, the acquisition of new capital goods to make up for the wear and tear on old capital goods. Such *directly productive investment* has been separated from ◊ *economic overhead capital* and ◊ *social overhead capital*.

investment capital ◊ *capital*.

investment promotion zone ◊ *export processing zone*.

invisible exports, invisible imports Invisible exports are services rendered to a foreign country (in contrast to normal ◊ *exports* which involve the actual transfer of goods), for example, trade conducted for foreign countries by national shipping lines, or expenditure in the country by foreign tourists, or interest earned by national capital invested abroad. Invisible ◊ *imports* are similar movements in the reverse direction. ◊◊ *balance of payments*.

Iron Age That major phase of prehistoric culture following the ◊ *Bronze Age*, in Britain extending from about the 6th century BC to around AD 43. During this period iron replaced bronze as the metal for tools and weapons and for artwork. The Iron Age saw the strengthening of agricultural communities, although tribal warfare was widespread, an aspect typified by fortified settlements, such as ◊ *hill forts*, and centres of tribal government, ◊ *oppida*.

Iron Curtain By the end of the Second World War the USSR was an established world power and a new (communist) regime in eastern Europe developed behind a heavily fortified western boundary which also served as an invisible barrier of secrecy and restriction, preventing free passage of people and information between the USSR and its satellites and the Western world. This 'boundary' became known as the Iron Curtain, a term used by Winston Churchill as early as 1946 when he said 'an iron curtain has descended across the continent' (of Europe).

irredentism The claim by a government of a country that a minority living across its boundary with a neighbouring state belongs to it historically and culturally. That claim may be backed by a propaganda campaign and even the declaration of war, e.g. the Sudeten Germans, whose imagined grievances against the Czechoslovakian government were inflamed by Nazi propaganda to provide Hitler with a pretext for the invasion of Czechoslovakia and the annexation of the Sudetenland in 1938.

irregular economy ◊ *informal economy*.

irrigation The artificial distribution and application of water to arable land to initiate and maintain plant growth. The practice dates from the early civilizations of the Middle East. Irrigation is essential to farming if the annual rainfall is less than 30 cm (12 in), and is desirable where rainfall is less than 50 cm (20 in). However, irrigation is used not only in arid and semi-arid conditions but may also be needed in areas of higher rainfall at drier times of the year, as in the United Kingdom to rectify summer soil-moisture deficits. Irrigation water can be more effectively used than the equivalent amount of rainfall because a regular supply can be ensured when most needed. Two main types have been recognized:
(i) *Basin or flood irrigation*, associated with water brought by a river in flood (as used to be the case with the Nile in Egypt and Sudan). Flood waters are led off into specially prepared basins, whose size varies from a few hectares to several square kilometres, separated by earth banks. Basin irrigation has been progressively replaced by:
(ii) *Perennial irrigation*, whereby the land can be watered, via permanent irrigation canal networks, as needed at any time of year. This may be achieved by (a) lifting water onto the land from the low-level stage of a river by means of primitive devices, such as ◊ *sakiyeh* or ◊ *shaduf*, or, more likely now, by modern pumps; (b) lifting water by similar means from wells; and (c) by building ◊ *dams* or ◊ *barrages* across a river to create an artificial lake by ponding back the flood or high-water level of the river. Sprinkler systems are increasingly used today for the final application.

Irrigation using brackish waters over long periods can eventually render soils unfit for crop growth owing to the accumulation in the soil of dissolved solids as a residue from plant evapo-transpiration which acts as a distillation process. ⬦ *foggara, ganat, huerta, karez, levada.*

isarithm ⬦ *isoline.*

isobase ⬦ *isoline.*

isochrone A line of equal travel time from a given starting point. ⬦ *isotachic map.* ⬦ *isodistante.*

isodapane A line joining all points that have equal additional transport costs for a given production unit, drawn around the point of minimum total transport cost. The concept is associated, originally, with ⬦ *Weber's theory of industrial location.*

isodistante A line joining places of equal ⬦ *distance* from a point.

isogram ⬦ *isoline.*

isoikete A line joining places with an equal degree of habitability.

isolation index A measure of ⬦ *spatial interaction*, also called the *exposure index*, which assesses the average probability of persons in a sub-group interacting within some larger population. It is based on the distribution of persons by sub-areas and assumes that interaction is with someone in the same sub-area.

$$\text{Isolation index} = a P_{*a} = \sum_{i=1}^{n} \left(\frac{a_i}{A}\right)\left(\frac{a_i}{t_i}\right)$$

where a_i = number in sub-group a in sub-area i

A = number in sub-group a in all sub-areas

t_i = total population in sub-area i

isoline Any line drawn on a map connecting places of equal data value. Also called *isarithm, isobase, isogram, isometric line, isontic line* or *isopleth.*

isometric line ⬦ *isoline.*

isontic line ⬦ *isoline.*

iso-outlay line A line, sometimes called a *price-ratio line*, which shows all possible alternative combinations of goods or factors of production that can be obtained for a given total expenditure or outlay. Where such iso-outlay lines relate to purchases of goods by consumers they are increasingly known as *budget lines* or *consumption-possibility lines.* The term *isocost line* has been used to describe all those combinations of factor inputs which can be bought by a producer for the same total outlay.

isopercept A line joining all places having similar preference ranking or percept by a set of individuals.

isophor A line connecting points with equal freight rates from a given centre.

isopleth ⬦ *isoline.*

isoproduct curve Or *isoquant.* ⬦ *production possibilities curve.*

isostade A line joining places with the same significant dates, e.g., in the colonization of a frontier region, settlements which were founded during the same year.

isotachic map A rate of travel or travel-speed map derived from ⬦ *isochrone* maps. Each isochrone map is drawn for a specific place. By measuring rates of travel speed at a set of locations on a series of isochrone maps covering a given area, data sets can be assembled for each location from which average travel speed can be calculated and the isotachic map drawn.

isotante The locus of points where the ⬦ *delivered prices* from two producers are equal.

isotim A line connecting points about each material or product source where procurement costs on factor inputs or delivery costs on finished products are equal.

isotropic surface A surface which exhibits the same physical properties in all directions. An isotropic land surface (i.e. one

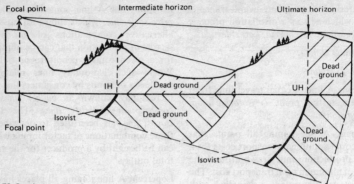

Fig. 79 Isovist

that is completely flat and homogeneous) is a basic assumption in many location theories.

isovist A term used in ◊ *landscape evaluation* to denote a line of equal vision or, more strictly, a 'limit of vision' line. It is measured from a focal point chosen by the observer, using the full 360° circumference of vision, and is drawn on a map to delineate the horizon. The latter may be any feature of the landscape (e.g. nearby buildings, trees, ground ridges) beyond which there is an area of ◊ *dead ground* out of view of the observer. Where nearby objects only partly limit the view they may be marked as an intermediate horizon, with the ultimate horizon depicted beyond (◊ Fig. 79). The use of isovists on a map allows the observer to take away a permanent record of the view which would otherwise depend either upon memory or on a large number of annotated photographs.

issue–attention cycle A descriptive model, suggested by A. Downs, which charts the rise and fall of public concern with a problem. The cycle is rooted in both the nature of certain national problems and the way major communications media interact with the public. There are five stages:

(1) *Pre-problem.* Although interest groups may be aware of a highly undesirable condition, it has yet to be drawn to the attention of the general public.

(2) *Alarmed discovery.* A series of dramatic events focuses public attention on the problem. There is belief in society's ability to solve the problem and, invariably, clamour for the government to take action.

(3) *Realization of cost.* There is a gradual appreciation that the economic, social and political cost of eliminating the problem is high and that a solution requires major sacrifices elsewhere.

(4) *Decline of public interest.* As the instant solutions wanted by the public are not forthcoming, the public become discouraged or get bored.

(5) *Post-problem.* The issue has lost its position at the centre of public attention and receives only spasmodic references in the media. Most people are not strongly enough motivated by the severity of their own suffering to take action.

There are no fixed time periods for the stages and an issue may be rediscovered, in which case the cycle is repeated.

iteration A repetitive process of successive approximations in an ◊ *algorithm*.

J

jackal principle A term used in ◊ *political geography* to describe the situation in which a ◊ *state*, having proved itself unable to resist territorial encroachment, becomes the victim of territorial losses to several of its neighbours. This most often occurs after a country has suffered defeat in war.

job ratio The ratio between the ◊ *night population* of an area (i.e. the occupied resident population) and the ◊ *working population* of that area during the day, multiplied by 100. A ratio of over 100 indicates an excess of jobs over resident workers.

joint action space The area within which ◊ *agglomeration* of manufacturing firms is feasible as a consequence of overlapping critical ◊ *isodapanes*. ◊◊ *action space, operational space*.

joint demand A situation in which the satisfaction of a want involves two or more separate ◊ *goods* being used together (e.g. motor cars and petrol). ◊◊ *demand*.

joint family ◊ *extended family*.

joint products Two or more products produced by a single production process, e.g. meat and hides from rearing cattle. The products may be of equal importance, but more frequently one product is the primary commodity, the chief object of the production, while the other is considered a ◊ *by-product*. ◊◊ *complementary products, supplementary products*.

journey to work Strictly the trip from home to workplace, but the term is also used in a wider context to cover the reverse work–home trip as well, since these two systems of movement dominate local (urban) travel patterns in advanced societies.

jugerum ◊ *centuria*.

June Returns In Great Britain the *4 June farm returns* each year provide the basis for what is, in effect, a census of agriculture carried out by the Ministry of Agriculture, Fisheries and Food. The resultant agricultural statistics are a primary source of agricultural data and cover: the area under crops; numbers of livestock; production/yields; number, size and distribution of holdings; numbers of agricultural workers; farm machinery; horticulture; prices and incomes.

jurisdiction The limits within which a power may be exercised, such as the territory within which a government exercises its authority.

juvenile towns ◊ *age of towns scheme*.

juvenility The proportion of children in a population.

K

k-value (1) In ♢ *central place theory*, the number of settlements at a given level in the hierarchy served by a central place at the next highest order in the system.

(2) As used by G. Alexandersson, the minimum requirement value of an industry when establishing its locational character (♢♢ *minimum requirements technique*). *K*-values reflect the number of employees in an industry required to satisfy local demands. Industries with low *K*-values relative to the average were regarded as ♢ *footloose* by Alexandersson.

Kaldor–Hicks compensation test A test or principle, associated with the economists N. Kaldor and J. R. Hicks, of the economic worthwhileness of any action. It recognizes that some people will be made worse off and compares the level of benefits to those carrying out an action with the losses suffered by third parties as a consequence of that action. The action is only worthwhile from society's view if the level of benefits exceeds the level of losses and those benefiting compensate those who lose. Compensation must be to the full extent of the losses and can take the form of transfers between individuals, as a result of which the action may also meet the criterion of ♢ *Pareto optimality*.

kampong A form of rural settlement typical of Malaysia comprising a small, clustered village and its associated mixed gardens or horticulture. The latter includes coconuts, fruit trees and vegetable gardens as well as ponds for breeding fish and growing water hyacinth.

Kant's index of concentration An ♢ *index of rural settlement form* designed by E. Kant

for use in reducing a map showing distribution of habitations by means of non-quantitative dot symbols to one in which the dispersion and concentration of settlement is more precisely reflected in terms of the distance between the habitations. It was calculated as:

$$X = \frac{1}{M} \sqrt{\frac{A}{D}}$$

where X = interval between two
           habitations

$\dfrac{1}{M}$ = scale of map

    A = area under consideration

    D = density of habitations

kappa effect A perceptual response to a journey made in two parts. The kappa effect describes the situation in which the two parts take the same length of time, but because a greater distance is covered in one part, that part appears to take longer than the other. ♢ *tau effect*.

karez An underground channel bringing water for ♢ *irrigation* from the foothills to the arid plains in Baluchistan. ♢♢ *foggara, ganat, levada*.

Kendall's tau A simple ♢ *non-parametric* index describing the direction and degree of association between two ♢ *ordinal scale* variables, i.e. it is a rank correlation test. It measures the disorder of the ranks of one variable when the other is placed in natural (numerical) sequence. The test concentrates on changes in rank, each pair of observations being checked to see if the relative order is the same, i.e. concordant, on the first variable as on the second.

Discordance is therefore assessed by counting the number of inversions in ordering pairs of observations in the two rankings. An inversion exists between any pair of observations when one has a higher rank than the second on one variable and a lower rank than the second on the other variable. Kendall's tau compares the actual number of inversions with the maximum possible numbers. The higher the actual number of inversions compared to the possible, the weaker is the correlation between the two rank orders.

The formula for the coefficient tau is:

$$\tau = 1 - \frac{2n_{inv}}{N(N-1)/2}$$

where n_{inv} = number of inversions observed
N = number of observations or pairs of ranks

The denominator gives the total number of possible inversions for that number of observations.

Certain modifications have been suggested to take account of tied rankings, and different formulae are suggested for data that can be presented as a square ◊ *contingency table* (tau b) and as a rectangular one (tau c).

kernel A term used for the original centre of a town formed by the earliest development of functional units. Also referred to as the *old town*.

key industry ◊ *propulsive industry*.

key settlement, key village A modern, widely used concept in ◊ *rural planning* in which certain villages are designated as rural service centres where activities will be concentrated as part of a programme of rural settlement reorganization or rationalization. Such a concentration is seen, in the long run, as more economic than the dispersion of facilities through all villages. It does assume, however, that the focusing of services in one key village will also

satisfy the essential needs of surrounding villages and hamlets, and the formulation of policies in practice has not always been related effectively to ◊ *thresholds* for the provision of services, nor to the problems of mobility of rural populations. In many cases key settlement policies have been widened to include residential and industrial developments. Such settlements have also been referred to as *king villages*.

key workers' scheme A government scheme, operated in Great Britain, to induce labour migration of skilled personnel into ◊ *depressed regions*. The purpose of the scheme is not to reallocate labour but to make it less costly for firms to move to the depressed areas by meeting the financial costs of bringing key personnel with them. ◊◊ *labour mobility, labour transference policies*.

Khoisanoid One of the primary ◊ *races* of people, including the Hottentots and Bushmen of southern Africa, whose characteristics are shortness of stature, yellowish-brown skin and sparse body hair. ◊◊ *Australoid, Caucasoid, Mongoloid, Negroid*.

kibbutz An Israeli form of rural settlement based on ◊ *collective farming* and communal villages. Kibbutzim have an agricultural base, the land is communally owned and decisions on economic and social organization are taken collectively. More recently some kibbutzim have diversified into industrial production. ◊ *moshav*. ◊◊ *ejido, kolkhoz, kung-she, sovkhoz*.

kilocalorie One thousand ◊ *calories*. In nutrition the term is used to indicate the useful energy contained in food, and in this context it is normally referred to as just 'calorie'. Food needs measured only in terms of kilocalories are an incomplete way of presenting ◊ *nutritional requirements* because the human body also needs protein and other nutrients.

kinetic sensation ◊ *serial vision.*

king village ◊ *key village.*

kinship The social recognition of a blood relationship or network of ◊ *family* ties. Kinship is one of the most fundamental structures of society, creating a network of rights and obligations and generating social cohesion.

kirktoun Lowland Scots ◊ *fermtoun*, consisting of a group of farms with a church. ◊◊ *clachan.*

kiss-and-ride ◊ *park-and-ride.*

kitchen midden Formerly a popular term to describe any deposit thought to represent the domestic activities of prehistoric man. ◊ *shell mound.*

knock-on effect A term used for negative ◊ *multiplier* effects, especially the consequences of the run-down of a major firm on job opportunities in an area.

kolkhoz Large-scale Soviet ◊ *collective farm.* Land is state-owned but leased permanently to the collective as a unit. The kolkhoz is farmed as a single unit under the direction of a committee elected by the shareholder farm workers of the collective, with profits distributed to all who participate in production. ◊ *sovkhoz.* ◊◊ *ejido, kibbutz, kung-she, Volksgüter.*

Kolmogorov–Smirnov tests A general class of 'goodness-of-fit' tests, appropriate for deciding whether data are consistent with a continuous distribution. The tests are associated with the name of A. N. Kolmogorov, and the modification which enables two samples to be compared with a view to deciding whether they come from the same parent population with the name of N. V. Smirnov. Such tests provide a quick check on the significance of the difference between two sets of frequencies expressed as cumulative proportions. The Kolmogorov–Smirnov statistic is simply the maximum difference between the observed and theoretical cumulative probability distributions.

Kondratiev cycles Long-term, approximately half-century, fluctuations in the behaviour of the world economic system, associated with the name of the Russian economist N. D. Kondratiev, but popularized in the English-speaking world by J. Schumpeter. Some prefer to call them *long waves.*

Great controversy still surrounds Kondratiev cycles, many economists doubting their existence and some historians using them only as a convenient form of periodization. The cycles have been analysed in terms of a number of economic indicators, especially movements of prices and interest rates, but also production figures for such basics as coal and iron. Each Kondratiev cycle involves the rise of new technologies, major infrastructure investments, changes in the international location of industry and technological leadership, and other structural changes, e.g. in the skills and composition of the labour force.

Four cycles have been experienced during the industrial epoch (◊ Fig. 80). The first of these, *c.*1785–1842, the original ◊ *Industrial Revolution* based on steam power, was almost entirely a British phenomenon. The second, *c.*1843–97, was dominated by the steel industry and the railways; the third, *c.*1898–1939, by the development of electrical power and the chemical and automobile industries; and the fourth, beginning *c.*1940, by the aerospace, electronics and computing industries. There is now the suggestion that the 'microchip' is about to herald the onset of the fifth Kondratiev.

Such changes are brought about primarily through bursts of innovative activity by entrepreneurs. During the recession phase of a long wave inventions remain dormant, but these begin to find commercial applications at the beginning

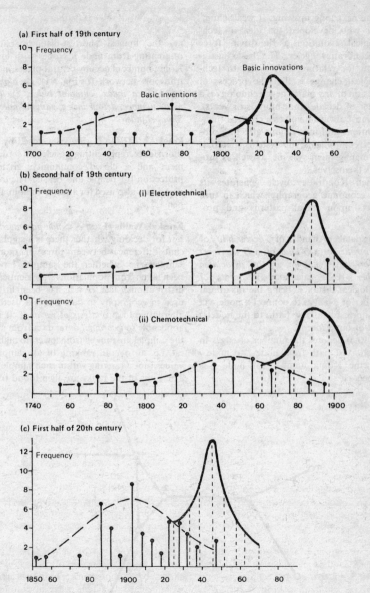

Fig. 80 Kondratiev Cycles

of the next long upswing. It was Schumpeter who developed the idea of technological revolutions as the driving force of Kondratiev cycles. The basic justification for relating such cycles to technological change is that the process of diffusion of any major new technology is a matter of decades (not months or years). It almost always involves a cluster of new inventions and innovations affecting processes, components, sub-systems, materials and management systems, as well as products themselves.

Each Kondratiev cycle generates its own economic geography, which in turn reflects upon social patterns and processes.

König number An index of ◊ *accessibility* or ◊ *centrality* of a ◊ *node* on a ◊ *transport network*, also known as the *associated number*. It is calculated in terms of topological distance, being the maximum number of ◊ *edges* to connect a node, via the shortest available path, to the node(s) most distant from it.

If $s(i,j)$ denotes the number of edges in the shortest path from node i to node j then the König number for node i is defined as:

$$\underset{j \ne i}{\text{Max}} \{s\,(i,j)\}$$

i.e. the longest shortest-distance path originating from node i. Nodes with low König numbers occupy central places in a transport network (◊ Fig. 81). ◊◊ *alpha index, beta index, cutpoint index, cyclomatic number, detour index, gamma index, Shimbel index.*

kraal An African ◊ *village*, enclosed by a thorn fence, representing a nucleated settlement and a closed community, giving protection for people and beasts. The expression is also used for a cattle- or animal-pen.

Kruskal–Wallis H test A ◊ *non-parametric test* for deciding whether there is a significant difference between three or more samples, i.e. whether the samples have been taken from populations with identical distributions. The H test has been little used in geography to date but is a useful alternative to ◊ *analysis of variance*. It is applicable to ◊ *ordinal* data: data from all the samples are ranked from lowest to highest, i.e. an overall ranking of all sample values (not a ranking within each sample). The sums of the ranks are then found for

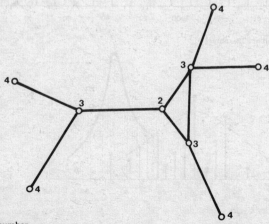

Fig. 81 König number

each sample and this information is used to calculate the *H statistic*:

$$H = \left[\frac{12}{N(N+1)} \times \Sigma \frac{R^2}{n} \right] - [3(N+1)]$$

where
N = total number of observations in all samples
R = sum of ranks within a sample
n = number of observations in that sample

The term $\Sigma \dfrac{R^2}{n}$ means that the sum of all the values of $\dfrac{R^2}{n}$ (one for each sample) have to be found.

Kuczynski rate ◊ *net reproduction rate.*

Kulturlandschaft ◊ *cultural landscape.*

kung-she A ◊ *collective farm* in the People's Republic of China. ◊◊ *ejido, kibbutz, kolkhoz, sovkhoz, Volksgüter.*

kurtosis A measure of the peakedness in a ◊ *frequency distribution*, i.e. the extent to which values are concentrated in one part of the distribution. It provides an indication of how the shape or spread of an observed distribution differs from a ◊ *normal distribution*. The measure of kurtosis involves the ratio of the fourth moment measure about the mean to the fourth power of the ◊ *standard deviation*:

$$K = \frac{\Sigma(x - \bar{x})^4}{n\,\sigma^4}$$

where
$(x - \bar{x})$ = fourth power of the deviations of the values about their mean
σ = standard deviation
n = number of values

A normal distribution has a value of K equal to 3·0. In a *leptokurtic* distribution, with a high degree of kurtosis and a K-value greater than 3·0, one class or group of adjacent classes in a frequency distribution contains a large proportion of all observations in a distribution. A *platykurtic* distribution, with a low degree of kurtosis and a K-value less than 3·0, occurs where each class contains a similar proportion of all observations. Leptokurtic, mesokurtic and platykurtic curves are illustrated in ◊ Fig. 82. ◊◊ *skewness.*

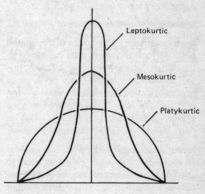

Fig. 82 Kurtosis

L

labour One of the ◊ *factors of production*. It includes all exertions – manual, physical or mental – by individuals, directed towards the production of wealth. There is both a quantitative aspect to labour, i.e. amount, effort and time, and a qualitative one, i.e. intelligence and skill. The availability of particular types of labour can influence the location of economic activities. ◊ *complementary labour*. ◊◊ *division of labour, dual labour market, fringe benefits, index of labour cost, labour intensive, manpower forecasting*.

labour, division of ◊ *division of labour*.

labour coefficient A measure of the spatial sensitivity of an industry to variations in the cost of ◊ *labour* as an input factor. It is the ratio of the labour cost per unit of product to the ◊ *locational weight* of that unit (i.e. the sum of the required weights of materials and product). ◊◊ *index of labour cost, Weber's theory of industrial location*.

labour displacement The need for workers to move from one job or occupation to another. Displacement may be internal to a nation, resulting from the substitution of ◊ *capital* for ◊ *labour*, or external, as when a worker is dismissed because of cheaper imports. The shift over from one job to another is not instantaneous, hence ◊ *unemployment*.

labour force ◊ *active population*.

labour intensive A form of production in which a high proportion of ◊ *labour* is used relative to the amount of ◊ *land* or ◊ *capital* employed.

labour market area ◊ *laboURshed*.

labour-mix The proportion of salary-earners to wage-earners in a business enterprise.

labour mobility A term encompassing the ability and willingness of an individual to change employer, occupation and residence and the act of doing so. ◊ *industrial mobility, mobility, occupational mobility*. ◊◊ *key workers' scheme, labour transference policies*.

labour productivity ◊ *productivity*.

labour theory of value ◊ *value, theories of*.

labour transference policies Government measures which seek to move (unemployed) workers to places where there are jobs available. They are often advocated as ◊ *regional policy* measures, but are rarely practical. ◊ *key workers' scheme*.

labour turnover The number of workers who leave a job, or are replaced, in a given period, expressed as a percentage of the average number of workers employed during the period. It is usually calculated on a firm, plant or regional basis. The actual change in total employment is equivalent to the number of additions to employment (engagements or hires) minus the number of terminations of employment (separations or discharges). Terminations may be classified into *voluntary separations* – sometimes referred to as *natural turnover* – which are initiated by the employee (e.g. in order to change jobs), and *involuntary outflows*, which may be further subdivided into *natural wastage* (through retirements, deaths, etc.), redundancies, and other lay-offs and dismissals. Redundancies, lay-offs and dismissals are employer-initiated. Additions can be subdivided into new hires (i.e. workers not previously employed) and rehires (i.e. recruitment takes place from among the unemployed and new entrants to the labour force and from among existing workers who change jobs).

labourer Specifically an *agricultural labourer*: a landless rural worker, sometimes with a specific skill, such as ditching or hedging. The position of such labourers in the rural hierarchy has changed over time. ◊ *peasant*.

labourshed The zone or *labour market area* from which workers commute to a city or to an individual plant. ◊ *commuting, daily urban system, journey to work*.

ladang ◊ *shifting cultivation*.

ladder farm A descriptive term for a farm with a succession of small ribboned fields. Also known as *striped farms*.

lag industries Industries which do not experience autonomous expansion but which depend for growth on expansion elsewhere in the economy. ◊ *lead industries*.

laissez-faire A French term meaning 'leave alone' adopted by French economic thinkers in the 18th century to signify a policy of non-intervention by the government in economic affairs. The underlying philosophy is that people are motivated predominantly by self-interest and that there exist certain immutable laws which produce a natural harmony. The principle of laissez-faire governed the conduct of economic affairs throughout the 19th century and remained a powerful influence in free-enterprise economies until after the Second World War. ◊ *market economy*.

lambda A measure of association for ◊ *cross-tabulations* involving ◊ *nominal data*.

Lammas land ◊ *half-year land*.

land As a ◊ *factor of production*, land is the sum total of the natural and human-made resources over which possession of the earth's surface gives control. It includes all of the earth's surface, not only the ground but also water and ice. In addition to building sites, farm soil, growing forests, mineral deposits and water resources, it also includes such natural phenomena as access to sunlight, rain, wind and changing temperatures and location with respect to markets and other areas. Furthermore, it includes all those human-made improvements, e.g. drainage systems, which cannot be easily separated from the earth's surface. Land is necessary for any productive activity, and orthodox economic analysis asserts that it is relatively fixed in supply. In absolute terms, land is considered irreplaceable, for no one piece of land is exactly like any other. Its immobility, or fixed location, also distinguishes it from other factors of production. Geographers frequently use the term to refer, however, only to the solid part of the earth's surface. ◊ *land system, land tenure, land use*.

land absorption coefficient For any city or region, the rate at which vacant land is being brought into urban use as a result of an increase of population or employment. Land absorption coefficients therefore relate increases in population and employment to increases in developed land and can be used to estimate future land needs. The reciprocal of the coefficient may be considered the *marginal density*, i.e. the density at which new development is occurring.

land capability Or *land evaluation*. An estimate of the potential or usefulness of land for ◊ *agriculture* or ◊ *forestry*, based solely on physical environmental factors. The appraisal is heavily dependent upon soil survey, although other factors such as aspect, rainfall, gradient and temperature are also taken into account. The main concept used is that of 'limitations' – the restrictions or constraints known, or reasonably assumed, to act upon the type of agriculture or forestry concerned. Temporary restraints are distinguished from permanent limitations. Present land use or agricultural productivity is ignored. Results may be expressed in qualitative terms, i.e. suitability for use, or in quantitative terms, i.e. predicted crop yields, or in economic terms, i.e. as gross or net cash output.

Attempts have been made to extend the principles to other types of land use, e.g. recreation, building land. Land capability can be used as a basis for ◊ *land classification*. ◊ *Canada Land Inventory*, *potential production unit*.

land classification The classification of ◊ *land* into categories according to its quality for a particular purpose, most usually agriculture. The results are presented as a land classification map and can be used as a basis for ◊ *land use planning* decisions. Land classification involves two distinct approaches. The first, which views land as the sum of purely physical characteristics, generates a ◊ *land capability* or physical classification based on an assessment of the physical quality and agricultural potential of the land. The second, adopting a more comprehensive definition of land to include socio-economic conditions such as farm structure and management, factor combinations and commodity prices, produces an economic classification and relies heavily on the mapping of actual production data. As compared with the physical character of the land, farm structure and management is generally regarded as being a changeable feature and the problem is to combine the two approaches. ◊ *land use*.

land consolidation Land consolidation or *agricultural consolidation* is an aspect of ◊ *land reform* aimed at the amalgamation of scattered plots of farmland by re-parcelling to form compact holdings around farmsteads. The process is often government-sponsored and farm enlargement may also be involved. Schemes vary in scope from simple exchanges of parcels of land to very ambitious programmes of rural management in which consolidation is just one element along with fertilization, building new or improved roads, water management and even industrial development. Called *remembrement* by the French, and *ruilverkaveling* by the Dutch. ◊ *farm fragmentation*.

land conversion process The conversion of agricultural land on the urban fringe can be represented as an evolutionary sequence of states and decisions, from an initial condition of non-urban uses through several stages of ◊ *development* to a state of active residential use by a household. The land conversion process or *residential development sequence* is illustrated in ◊ Fig. 83. Such land can be considered as passing through the following stages:

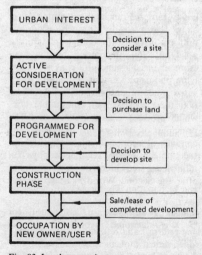

Fig. 83 Land conversion process

(1) A state of urban interest when, at some point in time, a person recognizes that the land has a potentially more valuable, higher-order use than for agriculture.

(2) The land is actively considered for development, as landowners offer sites for sale and developers/builders advertise for land.

(3) The land is programmed for development after purchase by a developer/builder.

(4) A construction phase, as the land is actively developed.

(5) The completed development is purchased and occupied by a household.

The complete process may take between two and ten years. ⟡ *parcelling-out*, *precession wave*.

land economics The social science which deals with the economic utilization of the surface resources of the earth and with the physical and biological, economic and institutional factors that affect, condition and control people's use of those resources. While the chief focus of interest in land economics centres around one particular type of resource, ⟡ *land*, the land economist can never give exclusive attention to the land factor for the simple reason that land has little economic value until it is related to other ⟡ *factors of production*. The subject is often subdivided into rural and urban sub-fields. Ideas from *urban land economics* strongly influenced ⟡ *urban geography* during the 1960s.

land evaluation ⟡ *land capability*.

land nationalization The act of bringing all land ownership, and hence rights to use land, under the (permanent) control of the government.

land reclamation The process of bringing desert, marsh, sea coast or other waste or unproductive land into use or cultivation.

land reform Land reform involves a social and political movement for changing the nature of ⟡ *land tenure* in a country. Land reform programmes have been stimulated by a variety of factors, including undesirable tenure conditions, anti-landlord sentiment, a desire for the wider distribution of ownership rights and a need to resettle large displaced populations. Most commonly such programmes have involved the expropriation of lands held in large estates and its redistribution, usually on an owner-occupier basis, to small farmers or peasant proprietors. In such cases land reform is usually part of a wider programme of ⟡ *agrarian reform* and rural development.

Programmes for the collectivization of agriculture may also be seen as land reform, although no effort was made to compensate the expropriated owners and much of the expropriated land was shifted to collective farms. ⟡ *collective farming*. ⟡ *land consolidation*.

land rent ⟡ *rent*.

land rotation Land rotation or *rotational bush fallowing* or *rudimentary sedentary tillage* is a subsistence type of agriculture in which land is cultivated for a few years until its natural fertility is exhausted, then allowed to rest for a considerable period during which the natural vegetation regenerates itself, before it is again cleared and the land recultivated. The farms or settlements from which cultivation takes place are fixed and, as the population increases, so the length of the fallow period is likely to be reduced. ⟡ *shifting cultivation*.

land tenure The manner in which ⟡ *land* is owned and possessed, i.e. of title to its use. Systems of land tenure embody legal, contractual or customary arrangements whereby individuals or groups gain access to economic and social opportunities through the ownership and use of land. The precise form of tenure is fashioned by the rules and procedures (incorporated in land law in advanced societies) which govern the rights and responsibilities of both individuals and groups in the use of and control over the basic resource, land.

The concept of ◇ *freehold* (individual ownership of land) is comparatively modern. Primitive peoples regard land as 'owned' by the ◇ *community* (as is also the case in certain collectivist societies): here the individual has use rights to occupy and cultivate a share of the land and a part interest in areas of uncultivated and potentially useful land, but long-term land ownership is of no significance since land is neither saleable nor bequeathable to heirs. In Europe, land tenures have evolved from a medieval system, ◇ *feudalism*, by which land was held for a variety of services and dues in kind, which came eventually to be commuted for a money payment. Modern European and New World systems are now, principally, ◇ *owner-occupation*, cash ◇ *tenancy* and ◇ *share-cropping*. Certain tenure systems may involve a combination of owner-occupation and tenancy types, e.g. ◇ *latifundium*.

land use, land utilization As defined by R. H. Best, the term land use deals with the spatial aspects of all human activities on the land and with the way in which the land surface is adapted, or could be adapted, to serve human needs. This definition implies that it is the human adaptation of the land surface which is important. Some geographers extend the definition to include types of vegetation as land use categories. A conflict of definition arises, since two distinct concepts are involved: the *functional use of land* to meet people's needs (e.g. agricultural, recreational, residential) versus the *form of ground cover* (e.g. trees, houses, crops). Where the two coincide, e.g. residential use/houses, there is no problem, but if they do not there is the possibility of confusion, e.g. trees and moorland can be recognized as a form of cover without establishing whether the land is used for agriculture,

forest, recreation or some other purpose. In the strict sense land use should apply to the activity on and not to the appearance of the land surface. ◇ *land use classification*, *land use survey*.

land use classification The classification of land according to the use made of it. The problem is to develop a classification in which the categories recognized are both exhaustive and mutually exclusive. While this is generally possible within a country, it has proved much more difficult to agree a world-wide classification. Most classifications have concerned the use of rural land, with categories for woodland or forest, cropland, improved permanent pasture, unimproved grazing, horticulture and agriculturally unproductive land. In urban areas categories for residential, open space, industrial, commerce, office, retail and public uses are usually distinguished. ◇ *land use survey*.

land use competition A principle which recognizes that a given piece of ◇ *land* can normally be put to several uses. It is assumed that the landowner or decision-maker can evaluate or rank the alternative uses on the basis of the average returns or ◇ *economic rent* that each can generate in a given time period. A decision-maker striving to maximize net income will choose the use or uses yielding the highest economic rent. ◇ *highest and best use*.

land use planning ◇ *physical planning*.

land use regions Or *type of farming areas*. Agricultural regions may be categorized on the basis of land use specialization. A type of farming or land use region is a spatially contiguous grouping of areal units which exhibit a degree of uniformity in land use type and intensity, associations of crops and livestock, and mechanization. Thus, 'corn belts', 'cotton belts', 'wheat belts', 'tobacco areas' and 'fruit belts' have been recognized in a number of cases. Problems arise in transitional areas of land use change or farming systems involving several crops and livestock. Recent trends in types of farming analysis have concentrated on standard man-day units (in which all farm production is expressed in terms of standardized labour inputs) and on the proportion of total farm income derived from each farm product.

land use survey An inventory of ◊ *land use*, especially agricultural, the results of which are presented in map form. Such a survey is descriptive of land use at a point in time. The major land use surveys in the United Kingdom – the *First Land Utilization Survey* (1931–9) and the *Second Land Use Survey* (1961–9) – were essentially concerned with land cover, e.g. they recorded the extent of heath and rough grassland rather than the use being made of that land. This work was pioneered in the 1930s by L. D. Stamp. Such early surveys involved field-by-field recording of information, but aerial photography and remote sensing imagery may now be used. ◊◊ *land classification*.

land use theory Apart from ◊ *von Thünen*'s work on agricultural land use, most emphasis has been on the development of theories to explain urban land use. Two contrasting approaches may be noted. Urban geographers and sociologists emphasize *use value* characteristics and have evolved a variety of land use theories which focus on patterns of land use, e.g. ◊ *concentric zone theory*, ◊ *multiple nuclei theory*, ◊ *sector theory*. Such approaches have been carried further by ◊ *factorial ecology* and have also produced statistical generalizations of macro-urban land use patterns such as the negative exponential model of population density decline (◊ *density gradient*). An alternative approach, based on neoclassical microeconomics, focuses on *exchange value* and analyses the ways in which individuals trade off quantity of housing, accessibility and all other goods, within an overall budget con-straint, e.g. ◊ *the Alonso model*. This latter approach may be thought of equally as generating ◊ *land value theory*.

land use–transportation study ◊ *transport study*.

land value A term with two interdependent meanings: (i) the actual or potential contribution which ◊ *land* makes in the production process, or (ii) the ◊ *price* one receives or would expect to receive from the sale of one's interest in land. The value of land from a production viewpoint is the ◊ *net present value* of the sum of all future incomes which the land will yield. ◊ *development value, existing use value, floating value*. ◊◊ *economic rent*.

land value theory A theory concerning the basis and pattern of ◊ *land values* or prices. The value of a given piece of land depends on far more than its intrinsic qualities, especially upon its ◊ *location* and ◊ *accessibility*. The foundation of present-day land value theory remains the ◊ *Ricardian theory of rent*, which was developed to explain differential prices paid for agricultural land and is now associated especially with the neoclassical micro-economic approach to ◊ *land use theory*.

landlocked state A ◊ *state* lacking direct access to the sea. Including the European micro-states there are, at present, twenty-six landlocked states, nearly half of them in Africa. In an attempt to explain their origin, W. G. East emphasized common factors other than their lack of sea frontage, especially the economic and political weakness of such states and their function as ◊ *buffer states*. His model of a hypothetical circular continent envisages a centrally located landlocked state whose existence is seen as advantageous to the surrounding maritime states, in that it avoids the convergence of boundaries of powerful neighbours at the centre of the continent.

The concern of every landlocked state is

to secure guaranteed access to the sea for purposes of trade. This may be achieved by the use of a major river, backed by international convention (rights of land-locked states to innocent passage), by bilateral agreement or by a political settlement involving a ◊ *corridor*.

landlord capital and tenant capital In agricultural tenancies a distinction is made between assets provided by the landlord and those supplied by the ◊ *tenant* farmer. *Landlord capital* consists of fixed assets, including the land, farm roads, buildings and drainage systems, whereas *tenant capital* covers movable equipment, machinery, stock and seed. The distinction is not clearcut and the dividing line can vary depending on the type of tenancy. The specialization of function in the provision of ◊ *capital* assets does allow two sources of funding to be tapped, one by the landlord and the other by the tenant. ◊◊ *land tenure*.

landmark A feature or point-reference in a ◊ *landscape* or ◊ *townscape* which can be observed but not normally entered or passed through. Such landmarks are well-defined physical objects – buildings, mountains, etc. – which are easily identifiable and easily remembered. They act as ◊ *images* structuring a ◊ *mental map*. ◊◊ *district, edge, node, path*.

landscape The term landscape can be interpreted in a number of ways (which are not mutually exclusive, although of differing emphasis). The Centre for Urban and Regional Research at the University of Manchester distinguished ten concepts of landscape:
(i) As a total regional environment, e.g. the landscape of the Fens.
(ii) As countryside.
(iii) As land use, e.g. agricultural landscape, polder landscape.
(iv) As topography or landform, e.g. downland landscape.
(v) As an ecosystem in which ecological

relationships are realized as different types of landscape, each the product of the interaction of edaphic and climatic factors with the effect of people and animals.
(vi) As scenery – probably the most commonplace usage, being the overall visual appearance of a stretch of countryside. In reality, a portion of land which the eye can comprehend in a single view.
(vii) As heritage or historical artefact, where there is an association with cultural influences, e.g. the Potteries, Thomas Hardy country.
(viii) As a composite of physical components, i.e. landscape classified according to the presence or absence of components, e.g. wooded landscape, urban landscape.
(ix) As an art form – the original use of the term was by artists to denote rural scenes, i.e. landscape describes the composition and unified arrangement of the parts.
(x) As a resource, e.g. landscape attractive to tourists.
◊ *landscape evaluation, Landschafts-geographie*. ◊◊ *cultural landscape, farm-scape, townscape*.

landscape architecture Initially a skill of classical times, landscape architecture – as *landscape gardening* – was rediscovered in the Renaissance. Since that time its scope has broadened to cover the planning and management of ◊ *landscapes* created by human activities. The role of the landscape architect is to understand the interaction between ◊ *ecology* and landscape, and their dependence on geological, economic, climatic and cultural factors, in order to assess the possible consequences of any changes on the landscape. The landscape architect can then advise how proposed changes can be absorbed into the existing ecological situation or form the basis of a new one. The object is to plan the land-scapes created as both functionally and aesthetically satisfying units. Much work has performed a cosmetic role, e.g. the rehabilitation of derelict land or the screening of motorways or pylons, but increasingly today landscape architects play a creative role at the design stage, e.g. in the choice of motorway route or the pattern of afforestation.

landscape classification ◊ *landscape evaluation*.

landscape evaluation Landscape evaluation seeks to assess ◊ *landscape* or scenic resources in some objective and, increasingly, quantitative fashion. Within the range of assessment techniques that has evolved three general approaches may be noted:

(A) *Landscape consensus studies*. Such studies reflect the earliest approaches and involve an informal process, lacking in systematic base, by which experts strive for a consensus about the landscape attributes of an area. This approach was extensively used in Great Britain to delimit ◊ *National Parks* and ◊ *Areas of Outstanding Natural Beauty*.

(B) *Landscape description studies*, which attempt to describe landscape in terms of its different components or its overall character. Emphasis is placed on identifying and measuring critical landscape variables. Where these are simply measured (e.g. the presence or absence of water, the amplitude of relief), with no judgement of quality or value imputed in the process, an inventory of landscape types is produced and the process frequently referred to as *landscape classification*. Where the relative importance of the variables is considered, descriptive studies lead to an assessment of the relative quality of landscapes against some standards or criteria, e.g. L. B. Leopold's attempt to calculate how nearly unique a particular site or landscape was.

(C) *Landscape preference studies*, which seek to determine which landscapes and which aspects of the environment are seen as attractive or unattractive, i.e. a personal appreciation of landscape. Preferences

may be established through (i) a direct approach in which individuals are interviewed and asked to indicate their preference for actual landscapes or for landscapes depicted upon photographs; or (ii) an indirect approach which infers preferences from evidence such as literature, art and comparable sources.

While landscape evaluation, involving as it does aesthetic judgements, is inevitably subjective, it does have a contribution to make to planning, development and conservation. ◊ *habitat theory*.

Landschaftsgeographie *'Landscape geography'* associated particularly with the inter-war era of ◊ *regional geography*, but which has its origin in the late-19th-century German view of geography as 'landscape science'. *Landschaft*, literally analogous to the English 'landscape', also means a 'scientifically defined geographical region' in German – either a specific unit area or a type of area. The fundamental concern of Landschaftsgeographie was with landscape morphology, involving the examination of all that was visible on the earth's surface and the investigation of the characteristic associations of phenomena which existed in a specific region.

lapse rate ◊ *distance decay*.

LASH (lighter-aboard-ship) A lift-on/lift-off method of moving cargo in which flat-bottomed lighters, with a capacity of about 250 tons, are loaded in ◊ *port* and towed out to be hoisted aboard specially designed vessels anchored offshore. The ship wastes no time entering ports, heavy loads can be taken aboard or discharged in a very short time and, in addition, no deep-water berths or approach channels are needed. A similar principle involves *BACAT* – barge-aboard-catamaran. ◊ *fishy-back principle*.

lateral commuting ◊ *commuter, commuting*.

lateral linkage ◊ *linkage*.

latifundium (plural: *latifundia*). A large

landed estate, found originally in southern Europe, though the term is now commonly applied to similar estates in South America. It is a partly feudal, partly capitalistic institution. The estate may either be managed centrally and run with a number of hired labourers (formerly slaves or serfs); or be held by an absentee landlord and the estate split into small parcels rented out to individual peasants who use primitive farming techniques. The latter type has increased in relative importance since the 19th century.

Latin American Free Trade Association (LAFTA) The world's largest ◊ *free trade* association, established by the 1960 Treaty of Montevideo as part of the Latin American countries' attempt to promote mutual co-operation and integration among themselves and lessen their dependence on industrial nations. LAFTA member countries are Argentina, Bolivia, Brazil, Chile, Colombia, Ecuador, Mexico, Paraguay, Peru, Uruguay and Venezuela. Although trade between the countries has been increasing, progress has been slow, in part because of problems of transport between member countries, in part because the products each country has to offer are in greater demand outside Central and South America than within it, and in part because of internal disagreements on the extent to which ◊ *tariffs* should be reduced.

law In ◊ *scientific method* laws are ◊ *hypotheses* which have been tested and confirmed as being valid. A law takes the form of a general statement concerning a specific association, relationship, connection or interaction between two or more ◊ *variables* or classes of things. Scientific laws have universal validity and may be invariant or probabilistic. Invariant law enables statements to be made about individual members of a class of things; such law is ◊ *deterministic* and holds without exception. Probabilistic law does not permit deterministic statements about individual

events, since there is only a certain chance that the relationships will hold. Laws allow past and present experience to be explained and enable predictions to be made about future events.

law of diminishing returns ◊ *diminishing returns.*

law of industrial growth Individual industries tend to pass through a common cycle of development, beginning with a period of experimentation, followed by a period of rapid growth, then diminished growth, and ending with a period of stability or decline. This cycle has been characterized as the law of industrial growth and reflects the interplay between scale of output and rate of technological progress within industrial firms. The idea is developed more fully in the ◊ *product life cycle concept.*

law of peripheral neglect The potential decay of a government's awareness of regional problems is encapsulated in L. Kohr's law of peripheral neglect, which states that the concern of the ◊ *capital* for its surrounding political space decreases with the square of the distance from it.

law of retail gravitation ◊ *Reilly's law.*

law of variable proportions ◊ *diminishing returns.*

laws of migration ◊ *migration.*

lazy-bed A small arable plot, used especially for growing potatoes, in the West Highlands of Scotland, the Hebrides and other parts of the Celtic fringe. The method, traditional where soils are very thin, involves placing seed potatoes in a row on the ground and covering them with soil or turf dug from either side. The potatoes grow on these raised spade-built ridges, 2 to 8 ft wide (0·6 to 2·4 m), divided by trenches, 1 to 3 ft wide (0·3 to 1·0 m), which aid drainage especially where they run lengthwise down any slope. Lazy-beds are therefore easy to prepare and look after with the minimum of labour. Seaweed is frequently used as a fertilizer. Lazy-beds are sometimes also used to grow cereals and cabbages.

lead industries A term used in a similar context to ◊ *propulsive industry*. In any economy, lead industries, in contrast to ◊ *lag industries*, are those industries with growth-inducing impacts or *lead effects* on other industries, i.e. through their demand for inputs. Lead industries have a higher rate of product growth and a higher rate of productivity increase than the average for the nation or region. The idea is also applied to firms, i.e. *lead firms*. ◊◊ *dominant industry*.

lead-lag model A model which identifies differences in timing – leads and lags – in the transmission of fluctuations through the components of a system. Lead-lag models have been used in regional economics to analyse the relative timing of peaks and troughs in ◊ *regional cycles* and in the study of spatial ◊ *diffusion* of ◊ *epidemics*.

leading farm ◊ *farm*.

league A free association of ◊ *states* to form an international organization for a particular, often political, purpose, e.g. the Organization of American States to foster American solidarity, the Arab League to foster co-operation among Arab, especially Muslim, nations.

leap year A ◊ *year* of 366 days. Leap years were devised to compensate for the fact that the duration of the earth's orbit about the sun is approximately 365·25 days. Therefore the addition of a complete day to the normal year every fourth or leap year ensures the correction necessary for the seasons to fall in the same months every year. This adjustment was first made as part of the Julian ◊ *calendar*. A further adjustment, introduced in the Gregorian calendar, is that century years are not leap years unless divisible by 400 (i.e. AD 2000 will be a leap year). This compensates for the fact that the earth actually takes 365·2422 days to orbit the sun (not 365·25).

learning theory Learning refers to the process whereby an individual or group develops a behavioural pattern in response to situations through time. All human behaviour, including spatial behaviour, involves a learning process, facilitated by decisions that have to be made most frequently. Psychologists have been responsible for most of the developments of learning theory, although geographers and economists have shown a concern with specific aspects.

Learning may be a conscious process, as when individuals seek to improve decisions through problem-solving behaviour which eliminates certain alternatives as unsatisfactory on the basis of experience, or it may occur imperceptibly, almost unknown to an individual.

Learning is closely related to adaptive ◊ *decision-making*. Consider an immigrant settling in an unpopulated area. His initial search behaviour (assuming an absence of communications links) will involve a trial-and-error procedure. He will select crops randomly to discover useful ones. This represents *hypothesis behaviour* or first try. After the first crop year, future decisions will be expected to reflect the learning process, i.e. he will concentrate on crops that grew well in the first year but continue to experiment with further new ones. By the end of the second crop the settler has learned more, and conclusions are reinforced about the returns from various crops. In the crop years that follow crop decisions consistently yielding good results are reinforced and those crops are grown with increasing confidence, a process referred to as *statistical learning*. After some time a fairly constant cropping pattern is established, reflecting stabilized behaviour, and the settler then appears as a creature of habit, following a ◊ *principle of least effort*. ◊◊ *S–R theory*.

265

lease A contract by which the owner of land or property (the *lessor*) allows another person (the *lessee*) to use that land or property for a specified time, usually in return for the payment of ◊ *rent*. *Leasehold* therefore is the holding of land or property by means of a lease. ◊ *land tenure, tenancy*.

leaseback ◊ *sale-and-leaseback*.

least cost theory of industrial location ◊ *Weber's theory of industrial location*.

least developed countries A term used by the United Nations for those countries with severe long-term constraints on ◊ *development*. Such countries are identified as having (i) a ◊ *Gross Domestic Product* per capita of $100 or less in 1970 (a figure updated to $250 in 1976–8); (ii) a share of ◊ *manufacturing* in gross domestic product of 10% or less; and (iii) a literacy rate of 20% or less of the population aged fifteen years or over. ◊ *Fourth World, underdevelopment*.

least effort ◊ *principle of least effort*.

leat An open watercourse built to conduct water for use especially in mills but also for household purposes, for mines and to feed reservoirs.

Lebensraum The 'living space' or area occupied by any living thing, from plants to people. The term was associated especially with German geopoliticians in the 1920s and 1930s, who advanced the supposed German right to Lebensraum, i.e. living room for the state, to enlist support for Nazi aggression. ◊ *geopolitics*.

legal spaces ◊ *bounded spaces*.

legibility ◊ *imageability*.

leisure A generic term comprising activities primarily in the arts, ◊ *sport*, ◊ *recreation* and socializing, and ◊ *tourism*. Leisure is a 'state of being', in which the activity is performed for its own sake or as its own end. It therefore consists of relatively self-determined activity-experience which is psychologically pleasant (in anticipation and recollection also) and which provides the individual with entertainment, amusement, improved knowledge or skill, increased voluntary participation in community life, or just rest and relaxation.

Largely as a consequence of changing work patterns due to industrialization, the concept of leisure has taken on a time-related meaning. It was gradually equated with 'free time' and now customarily refers to a period of discretionary time during which the individual is free to do as he/she pleases. There are various interpretations of *leisure time*, but it is usual to define it as a residual – the time available after work, sleep and necessary personal and household chores have been completed.

leisure lack The chronic or temporary absence of the experience of ◊ *leisure* as a result of either personal or societal factors and/or their interaction.

leptokurtic ◊ *kurtosis*.

levada An ◊ *irrigation* canal which leads down from high ground to the small, cultivated, terrace plots on the lower slopes in Madeira. ◊ *foggara, ganat, karez*.

level of living ◊ *standard of living*.

lex parsimoniae ◊ *principle of least effort*.

ley Land in a farming rotation sown with grass or clover. The practice dates back to medieval times, but ley farming still forms an essential part of management on many farms. It involves ploughing up the old grass, growing normal field crops for a number of years and then sowing down to grass or clover, etc. The length of time the grass is left down varies: a *short ley* of up to four years often consists of one grass only – usually a rye-grass – although it may also include red clover and sainfoin, whereas a *long ley*, lasting on average about seven years (although sometimes up to twenty years), often contains about five grass species with three or four strains of clover.

life cycle The process of change experienced by an individual over their lifespan, from childhood, through adolescence to adulthood and, ultimately, old age. This sequence is repeated from generation to generation and each stage is marked by characteristic forms of social, economic and political behaviour, e.g. mobility, earning potential, housing needs, leisure activities. ⟡ *family cycle*.

life expectancy The average number of years a person can expect to live, usually expressed at birth (although it can be expressed for any age-cohort). A distinction is usually made between male and female expectation. ⟡ *Expectation of life at birth* is usually less than at the end of a person's first year because of ⟡ *infant mortality*, but thereafter, as ⟡ *life tables* show, the decline in life expectancy is steady. Life expectancy has improved dramatically this century – the number of years a new-born baby may expect to live has risen from fifty to seventy or more in the West. This improvement is almost entirely due, however, to a reduction in ⟡ *death rates* in childhood or early adult life (since life expectancy at the age of eighty is virtually the same now as it was a hundred years ago – five years for men and seven years for women).

life sequence of a fuel A descriptive generalization which recognizes three phases in the use of a fuel:
(i) A substitution phase, during which a new fuel is developed and accepted in a national energy market. During this phase other fuels are replaced at such a rate that it is the ⟡ *substitution* factor (rather than the expansion of aggregate demand) which underlies the increasing sales of the new fuel, e.g. the replacement of wood by coal as an industrial and household fuel in 19th-century USA. During this phase cyclical economic fluctuations have little effect upon the demand for the fuel concerned.
(ii) A dominant phase, in which the fuel concerned satisfies a much larger share of the total energy demand than any competing fuel, e.g. coal in the British economy until the 1960s. Variations in the overall size of the market, reflecting economic cycles, are then the primary determinant of changes in the output of the fuel.
(iii) A decline phase, during which the fuel is replaced by another fuel or fuels. Replacement takes place over a relatively long period and the decline in demand is irregular, being most rapid in times of economic recession.

life space ⟡ *daily-life environment*.

life style The aggregate pattern of day-to-day activities which make up an individual's way of life. This pattern is shown overtly by an individual's manner of dress, place of residence, choice of expenditure on goods and services, etc. and reflects in particular ⟡ *social class*, age and personality.

life table Or *mortality table*. A life table shows the probability of a person surviving from any given age to any subsequent age, based on the age-specific ⟡ *death rate* currently applicable to the area concerned. A life table normally contains five common coefficients: (a) the life table death rate, which indicates the probability of dying during a given age interval; (b) a survival table, depicting the number of persons surviving at each age; (c) a death table, giving the number of deaths at each age and for each sex; (d) the average ⟡ *life expectancy*, being the number of years of life expected by each of the survivors at any given age; and (e) the probable or median life, which is the duration necessary to reduce by half the population in any age category. Life tables are usually published after a ⟡ *census* and are used by demographers in ⟡ *population projection* to 'age' populations forward as well as for actuarial purposes such as the calculation of life assurance premiums.

lifeworld A phenomenological term describing the spatial–temporal setting of a person's everyday life. It is the world of the ◊ *natural attitude*, being the sum total of a person's routine involvement with the geographical world in which he or she typically conducts a day-to-day existence. The lifeworld thus represents a taken-for-granted pattern and does not have to be an object of conscious attention. ◊ *behavioural environment, lived space, place*.

light industry A loose, descriptive term for those ◊ *secondary industries* which, in contrast to ◊ *heavy industry*, are characterized by high space-use intensity, producing goods of high ◊ *value added* and of high value relative to bulk and weight. Such industries are usually engaged in the secondary stages of ◊ *manufacturing*, transforming small quantities of inputs (usually in the form of semi-finished products) with the aid of large amounts of, often skilled, labour.

light water reactor (LWR) A type of nuclear reactor in which ordinary (light) water is used as the heat transfer medium. There are two main types, the *pressurized water reactor* (PWR) and the *boiling water reactor* (BWR). The major difference is that in the BWR the primary coolant water is allowed to boil and produce steam from the reactor core which is used directly to drive a steam turbine to generate electricity, whereas in the PWR heat is first transferred to a secondary circuit to produce steam. Together these types account for *c*. 80% of the current world nuclear power reactors. ◊ *nuclear energy*.

lily-whiting An overt tactic used by realtors in North American cities which involves directing and controlling the growth of black residential areas by steering white buyers away from any area that contains even a few blacks. ◊ *blockbusting*.

limes A Latin word for ◊ *frontier*.

limited liability A concept, authorized by statute in Britain since 1855, whereby an investor in a business cannot lose more than the amount he has paid for his shares if the business fails. Limited liability has been one of the most important developments encouraging modern industrial organization, since it makes investors more willing to lend money and provides a means of financing large-scale projects. Limited liability companies are of two types: ◊ *private company* and ◊ *public company*.

limited-search shopping A type of consumer behaviour involving limited spatial search and comparative shopping before purchase of goods. It is subdivided by L. P. Bucklin into:
(i) *Limited-search* (*casual*) *shopping* for inexpensive items in everyday use which need to be replaced frequently and which are obtainable from many retail outlets at low price. For these the consumer turns to the nearest shopping centre.
(ii) *Limited-search* (*directed*) *shopping* for goods in frequent use but which are more costly, less frequently obtained and more socially visible than the ◊ *convenience goods* purchased via casual shopping. While price is a major consideration, the goods are standard ones and search is limited to known stores of a certain perceived image. ◊ *full-search shopping*.

lineage A social group the membership of which is based on a proven relation to a common ancestor.

linear city A planned urban area whose structure is determined by a main axis or thoroughfare, on both sides of which development takes place. The idea of linear development along a high-accessibility corridor is a common feature of many metropolitan regional plans.

linear programming A mathematical technique used increasingly in the social sciences to determine the optimal solution to allocation problems. In general the objective of linear programming is to maximize or minimize some linear function (the *objective function*), subject to certain constraints expressed as linear equalities or inequalities. The method of solution is based on a series of linear equations which intersect each other and the intersection points can be used to calculate the optimal solution. The procedure is iterative (i.e. converges on the optimal solution by a series of adjustments to an initial solution). What is to be maximized or minimized? The choice of objective represents a ◊ *value judgement*, e.g. maximization of profit, minimization of costs, minimization of aggregate distance to be travelled for some purpose. What are the constraints on achievement of the objective? Basically the resources or inputs available, and it is a requirement of the method that these 'production functions' are linear.

The principles involved may be illustrated via a graphical solution of the simplest linear programming problem. Consider an urban community which wishes to maximize its total income from the production of goods and services subject to the two constraints of capital and labour availability. The possible output combinations of goods and services can be shown in a graph. In ◊ Fig. 84 the constraint or resource limitation line for capital, *GS*, indicates the various com-

binations of production levels of goods and services which just use up the total amount of capital available: at one extreme, *G*, the maximum amount of goods is produced if all the capital is channelled into the production of goods and, at the other extreme, *S*, the maximum amount of services if all the capital is used to produce services. The constraint on the total capital available means that any solution above and to the right of line *GS* is not feasible, whereas any solution below and to the left of *GS* uses less than the amount of capital available. Similarly, ◊ Fig. 85 demonstrates the resource limitation line for labour,

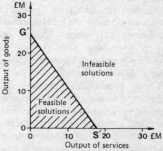

Fig. 85 Linear programming: resource limitation line for labour

G'S'. A solution requires that the two resources are considered jointly and in ◊ Fig. 86 the individual resource limitation

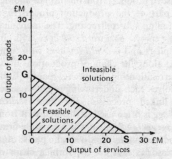

Fig. 84 Linear programming: resource limitation line for capital

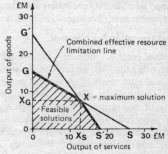

Fig. 86 Linear programming: combined effective resource limitation line

269

lines for capital and labour are super-imposed. This shows that some solutions are not feasible because of capital constraints, others because of labour constraints, and yet others for both reasons. All efficient solutions lie on the combined effective resource limitation line, GXS', which is referred to as a *convex hull*, and the combination of goods and services generating the maximum income is at X (representing X_G of goods and X_S of services).

Consideration of further constraints would mean that the convex hull will have more sides, but it could still be represented in two-dimensional space. However, the introduction of additional productive activities would mean the hull is located in multi-dimensional space. Hence most linear programming problems use the $\diamondsuit$ *simplex algorithm* as a general means of finding a solution.

All linear programming problems have an alternative formulation: in cases where the primal problem is, say, minimization, there exists a dual problem which is to maximize some mathematical equation, e.g. a transport cost minimization solution is also one that maximizes location rent.

Linear programming has proved a useful tool in a number of geographical contexts, including the study of agricultural production, manufacturing and warehouse location, the delimitation of various administrative districts and transport movements. $\diamondsuit\!\!\diamondsuit$ *transportation problem*.

linear regression $\diamondsuit$ *regression*.

line-haul costs An element of $\diamondsuit$ *transport costs*, being the costs incurred in the actual physical movement of goods and passengers. Line-haul or *haulage costs* are the costs of the journey proper, excluding $\diamondsuit$ *terminal costs* and handling charges, and depend on the costs of operating vehicles plus, where appropriate, the costs of maintaining the track. $\diamondsuit\!\!\diamondsuit$ *freight rates*, *transfer costs*.

line-haul route $\diamondsuit$ *route*.

lingua franca An auxiliary language used as a common means of communication between people of an area where several languages are spoken, e.g. Swahili is the lingua franca in East Africa. English is the world's most common lingua franca, followed by French.

link $\diamondsuit$ *edge*, *route*.

linkage Operational connections between firms, in the form of flows of materials, goods and information, within a relatively restricted geographical area. Links between firms exist because they take part in a similar kind of process or in a sequence of operations which involves a number of firms. The concept has been most fully developed in $\diamondsuit$ *industrial geography*, where linkage signifies $\diamondsuit$ *interdependence* among firms and has implications for locational choice, since it is through linkages that $\diamondsuit$ *external economies* are transmitted to individual firms. The concept is thus sometimes referred to as *transfer economies*. Linkages between manufacturing firms have been categorized in a number of ways, with some emphasis being placed on the distinction between *material* and *information linkages*, but the most generally recognized types are:
(i) *Process or production linkages*, involving the physical movement of semi-finished products from one firm to another as part of the production process, and including sub-contracting. The individual firm enjoys *backward linkages* with its suppliers and *forward linkages* with firms next along the chain of production. If the interrelationship between separate firms involves each undertaking one of a series of linked processes, the term *vertical linkage* is often used to distinguish it from *convergent linkage*, in which separate firms produce many individual parts and accessories that do not form a chain of processes but feed an assembly firm producing the finished product ($\diamondsuit$ Fig. 87).

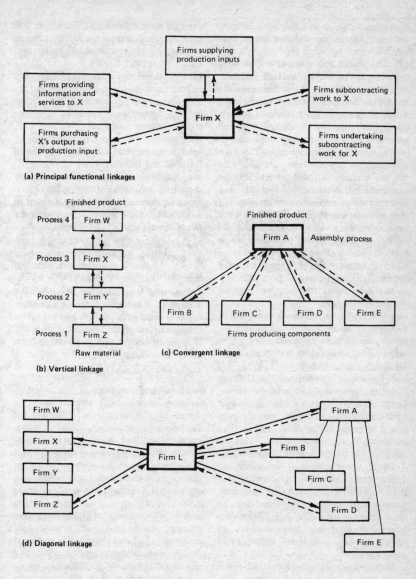

(a) Principal functional linkages

Firms supplying production inputs

Firms providing information and services to X

Firm X

Firms subcontracting work to X

Firms purchasing X's output as production input

Firms undertaking subcontracting work for X

(b) Vertical linkage

Process 4 — Firm W — Finished product

Process 3 — Firm X

Process 2 — Firm Y

Process 1 — Firm Z — Raw material

(c) Convergent linkage

Finished product

Firm A — Assembly process

Firm B   Firm C   Firm D   Firm E

Firms producing components

(d) Diagonal linkage

Firm W

Firm X

Firm Y

Firm Z

Firm L

Firm A

Firm B

Firm C

Firm D

Firm E

———▶ Movement of goods/materials/services/information

----▶ Money flows

Fig. 87 Linkage

271

Convergent linkage has also been referred to, less aptly, as *horizontal* or *lateral linkage*.

(ii) *Service linkages* connect a firm to a different set of sub-contractors and suppliers, namely those whose functions are to supply services ancillary to the production process itself. These include supplying machinery, equipment and ancillary parts such as tools and dies, as well as meeting the repair and maintenance requirements of such items. Included also are the supplies of more general services like cleaning, printing, accountancy and other financial and advisory services (although some would distinguish these latter separately as *financial and commercial linkages*). Since firms providing these services deal with firms in a number of different industries or at different stages in the production process of a given industry, it has also been described as *diagonal linkage* (◊ Fig. 87).

(iii) *Marketing linkages* with firms whose business it is to distribute and sell the goods of a particular producer, e.g. packaging firms, wholesalers, transport undertakings.

It should be emphasized that linkage concerns associations between firms. Large firms, however, can internalize within the production unit itself the provision of many of the goods and services obtainable through linkage. This is achieved via the process of ◊ *integration*.

The term *complementary linkage* or, less appropriately, *indirect integration* has been used in industrial geography in cases where firms/industries are complementary in their demands for labour, e.g. food industries with a strong preponderance of female workers and metal industries of male workers.

The concept has also been used in ◊ *urban geography* in the study of business clustering. Four types of linkage have been recognized in this context:

(a) *Competitive linkages*, reflecting the tendency of similar firms to cluster near one another when competing for a common market, e.g. comparative shopping outlets.

(b) *Complementary linkages*, arising when related firms cluster together because they are supplying the same market with different but interlocking demands, e.g. speciality clothing shops.

(c) *Commensal linkages*, in which two or more firms depend on the common use of facilities and infrastructure.

(d) *Ancillary linkages*, describing the clustering of unlike firms supplying a common area, e.g. the variety of shops in a neighbourhood centre. ◊ *dependency ties, product cycle.*

linkage, coefficient of ◊ *coefficient of geographical association.*

linkage analysis ◊ *cluster analysis.*

linkage tree A graphical or diagrammatic summary of the groupings or classifications at various scales of generalization through to complete generality (◊ Fig. 24). It is produced, for any given set of data, via ◊ *cluster analysis.*

linked trip ◊ *multipurpose trip.*

listed building Buildings of special architectural or historical interest may be 'listed' by the Secretary of State for the Environment and such listed building status gives that building special protection under the planning system. There is a strong presumption, upon listing, in favour of preservation, and before any such building can be demolished or altered *listed building consent* is required. The criteria for selecting listed buildings have changed with time and now include buildings which are regarded as works of art, as architectural curiosities, as part of a chain of architectural development, or are important because they illustrate technological developments or past ways of living, or are associated with famous people or great events. The first listing, which took place between 1945 and 1968, concentrated upon pre-1840 buildings, but the second listing, still underway, included pre-1914 buildings and, now, pre-1939 ones. ◊ *building preservation notice*. ◊ *conservation area*.

live birth rate ◊ *birth rates*.

lived space For the phenomenologist the ◊ *space* in which a person typically lives and dwells, being an environment of familiar objects and ◊ *places*. ◊ *lifeworld*.

livestock ranching ◊ *ranching*.

load duration curve A curve which shows the proportion of time that the demand for electricity exceeds any given value. It may be constructed for an entire year or for any shorter period. An example is shown in ◊ Fig. 88, from which two features, which apply in most real situations, can be noted:
(i) There is a minimum below which demand never falls – this is the ◊ *base load*.
(ii) Demands close to the peak are exceeded for only a very small fraction of the time.

The load duration curve can be used to determine the way in which an electricity supply system should be operated to minimize costs. The most economic way to operate the supply system is to use plant

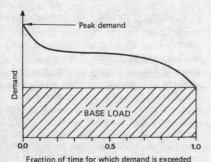

Fig. 88 Load duration curve

with low operating cost, e.g. nuclear power stations, as near continuously as possible to meet the base load demand. Demand immediately above the base load is met by fossil fuel plant, using the most efficient first (◊ *merit order*). Demands very close to the peak are met by older, small generating units used only for short periods, or by gas turbines, or ◊ *pumped storage schemes*. ◊ *load factor*, *system load factor*.

load factor The ratio, expressed as a percentage, of the number of units actually produced by a plant during a given period (e.g. a year) to the amount it could have produced during that period if it had been operating continuously at its maximum ◊ *installed capacity*. The concept is used particularly in respect of ◊ *electricity generation* (◊ *base load*, *load duration curve*, *peak load*, *system load factor*). It is also used in connection with transport systems, e.g. the actual use compared to the capacity of ◊ *pipelines*, the extent to which seats are taken up by passengers (◊ *seat load factor*).

load following A term used to describe variation in the output of a power station to match the changing demands of an electricity distribution system. ◊ *base load*.

load line The load line is a compulsory inscription on the hull of every cargo vessel which must not be submerged. Its aim is to prevent the overloading of ships. It is a line drawn through a circle (christened the *Plimsoll line* or *mark*) to show the amount of the hull the ship must have above water when loaded (◊ Fig. 89).

The original mark served as the load line for every ocean and all seasons, but conditions in the North Atlantic in winter require a greater margin of safety than, say, those in the Caribbean. The world's seas and oceans are therefore divided into zones according to the severities of wind and sea that might be expected and an appropriate scale added alongside the

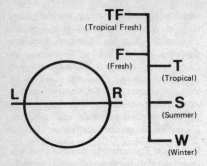

Fig. 89 Load line

load line. Since the 1930s, when these adjustments were made, there has been some revision in the case of the more weathertight vessels, such as tankers and bulk carriers, which are allowed to show proportionately less hull above the water.

lobbying Since governments have substantial powers to influence private socio-economic decisions, a common response of organizations and places has been lobbying – activities and processes intended to persuade government to take particular kinds of decisions. ⟡ *political representation effects, pork barrel.*

local activities ⟡ *non-basic activities.*

local plan The other major element, along with the ⟡ *structure plan,* in the system of ⟡ *development plans* introduced under the 1968 Town and Country Planning Act. Local plans are intended to:
(i) apply the general policies and proposals of structure plans to particular areas in a detailed way,
(ii) provide a detailed basis for ⟡ *development control* and give better information to developers,
(iii) provide a framework within which public and private development in a particular area may be co-ordinated,
(iv) draw the attention of the public to detailed issues in local planning and provide for ⟡ *public participation.*

While there is no standard form of presentation or procedure for implementation of local plans (since they are locally approved and represent an elaboration of policy proposals contained in the structure plan already approved by the Secretary of State for the Environment), all local plans are based on survey and must contain a map (showing any land allocation boundaries as precisely as possible), as well as diagrams, illustrations and a written statement which includes an explanation of structure plan policy as it affects the local area. Three types of local plan may be drawn up:
(1) An *action area plan,* for the comprehensive planning of small areas, indicated in the structure plan, for improvement, development or redevelopment, starting within the next ten years. The leading instrument of short-term action.
(2) A *district plan,* intended for the comprehensive planning of relatively large areas where change is expected to take place in a piecemeal fashion over a long period of time.
(3) A *subject plan,* dealing with highly specific and systematic land use within the structure plan in advance of a district plan or where the latter is not necessary, e.g. a plan to reclaim derelict land within an area.

local time Local or *apparent time* is the time at any given place on the earth's surface calculated from the position and movement of the sun. Noon or 12 o'clock midday local time occurs when the sun reaches its highest point in the sky at that place, i.e. the sun crosses the meridian and shadows are at their shortest. Given the rotation of the earth on its axis, places lying on the same meridian will have the same noon and the same local time, but for places to the east and west of that meridian noon will occur one hour earlier or one hour later respectively for every 15° of longitude. ⟡ *standard time.*

localization As a concept localization refers to the variation in relative frequency with which an event or object occurs across a set of subdivisions of some spatially delimited area. It is particularly important in the study of industry, where it is used to signify the local concentration of an industry in a certain area or areas. ◊ *coefficient of localization, localization curve.* ◊ *concentration and centralization.*

localization curve A simple graph, based on the ◊ *Lorenz principle*, which depicts the tendency of activities to concentrate in certain areas. Localization curves are usually constructed to summarize the geographical pattern of industry at any given point in time. To draw the graph, the regions or areal subdivisions have to be ranked according to their ◊ *location quotients* for the industry in question. Then the cumulative percentages for that industry (usually based on employment data) are plotted against the cumulative percentages for all industry. The kind of result obtained is illustrated in ◊ Fig. 90. The 45° diagonal from the origin indicates perfect correspondence between the cumulative percentages for the particular industry and all industry. The greater the degree of deviation of the localization curve from this diagonal the greater is the degree of ◊ *localization*. The ◊ *coefficient of localization* measures, in fact, the equivalent of the area between the localization curve and the diagonal. Also termed *diversification curve* and *specialization curve*.

localization economies A form of ◊ *agglomeration economies*, equivalent to ◊ *external economies*, which arise from the ◊ *localization* of firms in a single industry.

localized material A ◊ *raw material* obtainable from only one geographically well-defined source, or from relatively few such sources. According to Alfred Weber localized materials exerted a specific influence on manufacturing location. They may be either ◊ *pure materials*, contributing their full weight to the product, or ◊ *gross materials*, contributing only part or none of their weight to the product. ◊ *locational weight*.

location An area or ◊ *place*, commonly recognized and defined, where something is situated. It is normally treated as a point at the scale of observation used. In a narrow sense the term has been used as equivalent to ◊ *site*, and in a wider context to indicate ◊ *situation* or even ◊ *region*.

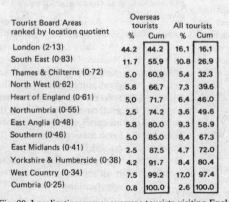

Tourist Board Areas ranked by location quotient	Overseas tourists %	Cum	All tourists %	Cum
London (2·13)	44.2	44.2	16.1	16.1
South East (0·83)	11.7	55.9	10.8	26.9
Thames & Chilterns (0·72)	5.0	60.9	5.4	32.3
North West (0·62)	5.8	66.7	7.3	39.6
Heart of England (0·61)	5.0	71.7	6.4	46.0
Northumbria (0·55)	2.5	74.2	3.6	49.6
East Anglia (0·48)	5.8	80.0	9.3	58.9
Southern (0·46)	5.0	85.0	8.4	67.3
East Midlands (0·41)	2.5	87.5	4.7	72.0
Yorkshire & Humberside (0·38)	4.2	91.7	8.4	80.4
West Country (0·34)	7.5	99.2	17.0	97.4
Cumbria (0·25)	0.8	100.0	2.6	100.0

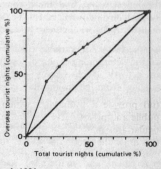

Fig. 90 Localization curve: overseas tourists visiting England, 1981

Absolute or *primary location* can be distinguished from *relative* or *secondary location*. *Absolute location* gives the exact position, in terms of spatial co-ordinates, of an object or place in relation to a conventional grid reference system designed solely for locative purposes. *Relative location* considers where an object or activity is located in terms of the advantages and disadvantages of a particular location measured with reference to all competing locations. ◊ *optimum location, space.*

location-allocation models Mathematical models designed to find the ◊ *optimum location* for centralized facilities, such as factories, warehouses, hospitals and schools, which have to satisfy the demand of consumers spread in geographic space. Such models must determine simultaneously the location of facilities and the allocation of patrons to them. Given the location of consumers, the demand of consumers, the capacities of facilities, the costs of operating the facilities and transport costs between consumers and facilities, a location-allocation model can be used to find the number, size and location of facilities, the allocation of consumers to facilities and the least-cost transport flows. Two types of location-allocation model exist: those dealing with location on a continuous surface, commonly used in locating public sector facilities and in theoretical work, and those considering location on a network, in which case more realistic transport costs can be used.

location factor Any variable which is significant in determining choice of location for an activity. Such factors are diverse, ranging from environmental considerations, such as climate or water availability, through the supply of all the individual ◊ *factors of production*, to the characteristics of space itself, i.e. problems of overcoming distance, and including the influence of government and matters of scale, agglomeration, technology and markets.

Where a single factor dominates the choice of location the term ◊ *orientation* is used.

location leader A pioneer firm, or firm exercising technical leadership, which, having chosen its own location, attracts through its ◊ *linkages* numerous other firms to locate nearby. ◊ *active locators.*

location quotient A simple coefficient for comparing an area's percentage share of a particular activity with its percentage share of some basic aggregate. It therefore shows the extent to which that area departs from the norm. Location quotients were developed, and have been most commonly used, to provide a measure of the concentration of a particular industry in a particular area. Employment figures provide the usual data base.

Where the base data is in percentage form then the location quotient for a given activity in any area j is

$$LQ_j = \frac{X_j}{Y_j}$$

where X_j = (variable) area percentage in the activity
Y_j = (constant) percentage in the nation (or whatever areal base is being used)

For absolute data the location quotient is given by:

$$LQ = \frac{X_i/X}{Y_i/Y}$$

where X_i = number (employment) in a given activity i in an area
X = total number (employment) in all activity in the area
Y_i = number (employment) in activity i in the base area (nation)
Y = total number (employment) in all activity in the base area (nation)

The higher the value of the location

quotient the greater the degree of concentration of the activity in question. A value of 1·0 means that the activity is represented in the area in exactly the same proportion as for the nation (base area); less than 1·0 shows the activity to be under-represented in the area against the norm; and over 1·0 that the area has more than its fair share. ◊ *minimum requirements technique*.

location rent Location rent has been viewed as a particular interpretation of ◊ *economic rent*, representing an evaluation of the ◊ *comparative advantage* accruing to a user of a particular location because of its geographical position alone. Location rent is not the same as a ◊ *rent* payment, being for a given land use at a given intensity in a specific location the difference between the returns flowing from the use of that land and the costs involved in its use (where costs include a ◊ *normal profit*). Assuming a single central market the location rent for any location growing a particular crop is given by:

Location rent $= Y(P - C) - YD(F)$

where $Y =$ crop yield/area
  $P =$ market price of crop/ton
  $C =$ production cost of crop/ton
  $D =$ distance (km) to central market
  $F =$ transport rate/ton/km

Calculated for a series of locations such rents can be represented as a ◊ *rent gradient* or surface. ◊ *bid rent, highest and best use*.

location theory Location theory has developed in response to the need to explain and predict the location of economic activities. It tends to single out the transport factor, seeking to expose the spatial aspects of production and of other economic activities and to examine the emerging spatial structures as objects of interest in themselves. The need to economize on transport expenditures creates a particular logic of spatial relationships,

and emphasis is placed upon this facet of location because it is amenable to equilibrium analysis. Thus location theory is concerned with the micro-economics of space, with allocation and equilibrium as achieved by the price mechanism, while the macro-economic aspects of location and regions is the province of ◊ *regional science*.

Historically location theory evolved via a study of agricultural land use (◊ *agricultural location theory*) and of the location of manufacturing plants and of industry (◊ *industrial location theory*) to a more inclusive analysis of the spatial pattern of all economic activities. While this evolution is associated especially with economics, generally economists placed more emphasis on the analysis of time than of space. Although some interest in location was apparent in 17th- and 18th-century political economy it ended with the ◊ *von Thünen model* (1826) and for much of the 19th and early 20th centuries location theory was relegated to a residual status. The exception was the German school of location theory, where the contributions of Alfred Weber, 1909 (◊ *Weber's theory of industrial location*), Walter Christaller, 1933, and August Lösch, 1944 (◊ *central place theory*), are most important. It was not until after the translation of Weber's book in 1929 and the publication of Christaller's work in 1933 that geographers began to take an interest in deductive and abstract modes of analysis and not until the early 1960s that location theory was formally and widely known to geographers. Meanwhile location theory continued to draw on the theoretical base of ◊ *neoclassical economics* to develop general theories of the space economy, e.g. that of Walter Isard (1956), and to refine the partial equilibrium models dealing with specific economic activities.

Three levels of analysis can be distinguished: (a) the location of the individual firm or activity unit, (b) the location of a group of firms or activity units in stable competitive situations vis-à-vis each other, and (c) the location of sets of activities, such as urban land use structures, in which all activities have a stable competitive relationship.

Location theory provides both an ex-post rationalization of location patterns on a trial-and-error basis within an adoptive economic system and a basis for adaptive economic action whereby entrepreneurs can make rational decisions regarding the location of their firms. Initially concerned with the spatial behaviour of ◊ *economic man*, controlling a single-plant, single-product firm in abstract competitive space, location theory has developed in a way which recognizes more realistic behavioural situations (◊ *behavioural geography*) and the complexity of business or corporate structures, as well as explicitly acknowledging its historical origins in the space economy of ◊ *capitalism*.

locational adjustment In ◊ *industrial geography*, re-organization undertaken by a ◊ *firm* in which the number of plants remains the same or is reduced but their capacities, products or linkages are changed.

locational costs ◊ *Costs* incurred by manufacturers in addition to ◊ *basic costs*. Locational costs derive from the need to transport an input to some point away from its cheapest source. ◊ *assembly costs*.

locational inertia ◊ *industrial inertia*.

locational interdependence (theory of industrial location) An approach, especially in ◊ *industrial location theory*, which recognizes that the location decision of an individual firm is influenced by the locations chosen and policies pursued by its competitors. It stresses the importance of ◊ *demand* or market factors in attracting (repelling) firms to (away from) each other and analyses the strategies devised by firms to ensure a degree of ◊ *spatial monopoly* in respect of the market area. Locational interdependence is closely associated with

the theory of ◊ *imperfect competition*, and typically assumes ◊ *oligopoly* as the market structure. It may lead to the ◊ *agglomeration* of firms even in the absence of ◊ *economies of scale*, significant spatial differences in production costs, or marked spatial variations in demand. ◊ *Fetter's model*, *Hotelling model*.

locational pull The force of attraction exerted by a place or an area when alternative locations for an activity are being considered.

locational triangle In ◊ *industrial location theory* a simple diagram, devised by Alfred Weber, to illustrate the derivation of the least-transport-cost location in the case of fixed locations of materials and markets and where movement was possible in any direction at the same cost per unit distance.

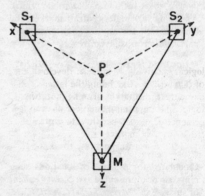

Fig. 91 Locational triangle

If, in ◊ Fig. 91, two materials are produced at S_1 and S_2 and the product is consumed at M, where will P, the point of production, be located? The optimum or least-transport-cost location is the point at which the total ton-distance involved in assembling materials at the point of production and distributing the finished product is at a minimum. Each corner of the triangle exerts a pull on P measured by the weight to be transported to (or from) that corner. *P* will usually be found somewhere within the locational triangle. This point can be found by geometric means, by a physical analogue model (◊ *Varignon's frame*), by computer ◊ *algorithm*, or, where costs of transport are known, by constructing ◊ *isodapanes*. ◊ *Weber's theory of industrial location*.

locational utility ◊ *place utility*.

locational vulnerability The degree to which the well-being of a place depends on decisions and actions taken in other places.

locational weight The total weight to be moved per unit of product. A product made only from ◊ *ubiquities* would have a locational weight of 1·0 because only the product itself has to be moved, whereas if it is made of ◊ *pure material* the locational weight is 2·0 because both the product and an equivalent weight of materials have to be transported. ◊ *material index*. ◊ *weight-loss ratio*.

logical positivism A modern development of ◊ *positivism*, extending the latter's fundamental principles by arguing that formal logic and pure mathematics, as well as evidence of the senses, provide sure knowledge.

logistic curve A time series curve which shows an accelerating growth rate (i.e. a lower concave upward portion), then a point of inflexion, followed by a decelerating growth rate (i.e. an upper convex upward portion) leading to a saturation or steady state level (◊ Fig. 92). It is applied, for example, to population growth.

log-linear modelling A method used in the analysis of cross-classification tables where both independent and dependent ◊ *variables* are measured at the ◊ *nominal* level.

lognormal distribution A ◊ *distribution* of data in which the logarithm of the values is used.

long barrow ◊ *barrow*.

long house An early dwelling, typical of the highland zone of England and Wales, incorporating house and byre under one roof. ◊ *black house*.

long-line fishing A type of commercial ◊ *fishing* using a long weighted line with side branches (as many as 500) ending in hooks. It is used to catch mainly demersal and mid-water fish, e.g. cod, haddock, tuna.

long-lot farm system A system of land ownership of ◊ *farms* and ◊ *fields* laid out at right angles to rivers and streams. Each farmer thus receives a variety of land and soil types and also has access to the river 'highway'.

long waves ◊ *Kondratiev cycles*.

longitudinal analysis ◊ *cohort-survival method*.

longwall mining A common European method of underground mining, especially of coal, in which the complete seam is worked and no pillars or supports are left behind. There are two principal forms: (1) *long-wall advancing*, which proceeds out from the shaft bottom to the outer limits

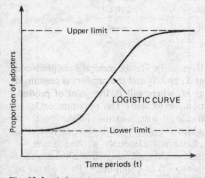

Fig. 92 Logistic curve

of the mining concession, and (2) *long-wall retreating*, which works from the outer limits of the concession back to the shaft or main haulage road. All the coal is removed as the face advances, leaving voids equal to or even greater (where thin seams are mechanically mined) than seam thickness. Some support may be provided by loosely packed waste and the lining of haulage roadways in the ◊ *goaf*, but this is to facilitate working and does very little to minimize ◊ *subsidence*. Therefore as mining proceeds a trough of subsidence is created at the surface. ◊◊ *adit mining, advance mining, bord and pillar, drift mining, pillar and stall.*

look-out techniques Planning techniques which assist the structuring of thoughts about the future and which allow the making of wide-ranging and unconstrained predictions. The most common forms are scenario writing and panelling, particularly the Delphi form.

Lorenz curve A mathematical curve which provides a visual comparison of the extent to which a given distribution of data differs from a uniform distribution. It is drawn by expressing the frequency in each category as a percentage of the total frequencies and then plotting the result

graphically in the form of a cumulative frequency curve (◊ Fig. 93). The uniform distribution is represented as a straight line at an angle of 45° across the graph. The visual effect of concentration is shown as the area contained between the curve and the line of even distribution increases in size. Additionally a precise index of the difference may be derived from the graph as the ratio of the right-angled triangle with the base line of uniform distribution and the area contained by the Lorenz curve (◊◊ *Gini coefficient*). ◊ *localization curve.*

lost village ◊ *deserted village.*

lotting The periodic reallocation of tillage, meadow and pasture.

low-order goods ◊ *Goods* with low ◊ *ranges* and low ◊ *thresholds*, provided from low-order ◊ *central places*. ◊ *convenience goods.* ◊◊ *high-order goods.*

low-rise building A building of one, two or three storeys, usually for residence. ◊◊ *high-rise building.*

Lowry model A general model of the generation and spatial allocation of urban activities and land uses, developed originally by I. S. Lowry in 1964 and reformulated by R. A. Garin in 1966 – hence,

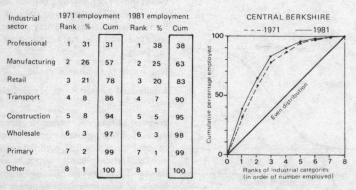

Fig. 93 Lorenz curve: employment by industrial sector in central Berkshire, 1971 and 1981

also, *Garin–Lowry model*. It comprises two ◊ *gravity models*, one for residential location and one for service location, coupled together through the ◊ *economic base* mechanism. It assumes that the settlement structure of an area can be described in terms of population and employment and the interaction between them, in both a functional and a spatial sense. Employment is split into basic and service categories and it is assumed that other activities can be determined from a given level of basic employment.

In the model the spatial allocation of basic employment is assumed to be given by zones, and the households of these workers are allocated around these basic workplaces by a residential location model using the ◊ *population potential* concept. The total population dependent on basic jobs in residential zones is derived via a ◊ *multiplier*, the ratio of population to total employment. This population generates a demand for services and opportunties for service employment. Service employment is estimated by the application of a further multiplier, the ratio of service employment to total population. Demand in residential zones having been estimated, service employment is allocated to service centres with the aid of a service location model according to the market potential offered. Service workers also need to be housed, so they are returned to the residential location model and allocated to their place of residence. This whole procedure is then recycled until the system converges to equilibrium.

lumber camp A temporary or semi-permanent settlement functioning as a residence for workers and an assembly point for outbound timber freight.

lynchet A step or terrace on a slope formed during the cultivation of prehistoric and medieval hill ◊ *fields*. Lynchets are found especially in chalk country, at elevations between 90 and 180 m (300 and 600 ft), on slopes between 6° and 27°. Topsoil, loosened by ploughing, gradually moves downslope under the influence of gravity and the resulting accumulation of topsoil at the foot of a sloping field is a *positive lynchet*, while a depression at the top of such a field caused by the loss of topsoil is a *negative lynchet*. Where they occur as a flight ascending a slope a series of *strip lynchets* is created.

M

machair A zone of fertile coastal sand plain on the windward coasts in the Outer Hebrides. It offers the best agricultural environment.

macroeconomics The study of the totals of economic activity in a nation, e.g. national income, investment. ⟡ *microeconomics.*

macrogeography The study of empirical regularities in aggregate spatial distributions, using techniques of ◇ *centrography.* Its origins lie in the work of the ◇ *social physics* school and its core concept of ◇ *population potential* was shown in the 1960s to be related to a large number of other patterns in the social and economic geography of the United States. ⟡ *microgeography.*

macroscopic A term used to describe a level of investigation or study that concentrates on large-scale patterns.

Magnox (reactor) The generic name applied to the power stations of the UK's first nuclear power programme. These used a gas-cooled graphite moderated reactor with Magnox-clad natural uranium metal fuel. Magnox, an alloy of magnesium, was developed for this purpose: it does not react with the carbon dioxide coolant (hence the name – 'magnesium, no oxidation'). Carbon dioxide gas is heated by passing it over the fuel in the core and transfers its heat to water in a steam generator. ◇ *nuclear energy.* ⟡ *AGR.*

malapportionment Where supporters of various political parties are spatially segregated, a given party can further its own electoral purposes by drawing up constituencies which differ significantly in the number of voters they contain, i.e. small constituencies for one's own party and large ones for the opposition. Such an electoral abuse is termed malapportionment. ◇ *electoral geography.*

malnutrition The lack or inadequacy of particular (or several) essential nutrients in a person's food intake, particularly protein, which can lead to various deficiency diseases, such as beri-beri and rickets. Malnutrition should be distinguished from ◇ *undernutrition* (i.e. lack of calories or hunger). However, most persons who suffer undernutrition also suffer from protein malnutrition.

Malthusian theory of population A body of doctrines derived from the writings of Thomas R. Malthus, who published *An Essay on the Principle of Population* in 1798. Malthusian theory argues that ◇ *population pressure* on the means of ◇ *subsistence* available to a given population is inevitable. The fundamental thesis is that, in an enclosed area with no trade or technological change, population would soon outstrip the means of feeding it, since population, if unchecked, increases at a geometric rate while food supplies increase only at an arithmetic rate. It is argued that population always increases up to the limits of the means of subsistence.

For example, any amelioration in the conditions of life leads to a temporary fall in the ◇ *death rate* while the ◇ *birth rate* remains consistently high. As population increases the conditions of life become more severe so that the death rate rises once more, until it again equals the birth rate, and population equilibrium is reached when the standard of living has fallen back to subsistence level. This is the Malthusian or *primitive population cycle.* If the death rate rises above the birth rate for a period, the size of the population may fall back to its original level. However, if the amelioration which initiated the change is a technological innovation, rather than a temporary bounty of nature, then the equilibrium population will be set at a higher level. Population equilibrium is maintained by the so-called positive, Malthusian checks of famine, misery, pestilence and war. In second and subsequent editions of his book Malthus recognized the possibility of preventive checks, such as the postponement of marriage, sexual abstinence before marriage or outright celibacy, as a possible solution to the population problem. Malthus's ideas have been criticized for confusing moralist and scientific approaches and especially because his theory has proved a poor predictor of events. Marx, for example, argued that poverty was the result of capitalism, not population growth. With the possible exception of Ireland, no European or North American country has exhibited a Malthusian population cycle. However, his ideas still hold some influence today (◊ *neo-Malthusianism*).

managed economy ◊ *state socialism.*

management agreements General powers under the National Parks and Town and Country Planning Acts enable public authorities to enter into management agreements. These are formal, written, voluntary agreements between the authority, often the local planning authority, and the owner or occupier of land who undertakes to manage land in a specified manner to satisfy a particular public need. Usually the owner receives some form of financial compensation in return for what he agrees

to do, allow or give up. Management agreements have been used to secure a public interest in the way in which rural land is used, e.g. to provide access for recreation or conserve wildlife.

managerial matrix Individual decision-makers are constrained by an institutional framework and by a value system. The kinds of managerial decisions reached in a ◊ *market economy* can be outlined in a managerial matrix. The matrix represents on its two axes two commonly identified motivations in a commercial environment: the desire for ◊ *profit* and the desire for some other entrepreneurial satisfaction (◊ Fig. 94). Task management describes decision-makers seeking to achieve production objectives and to maximize profits. At the other extreme such objectives are incidental to satisfaction in the country club approach, where factors like prestige and leisure opportunities are important. The matrix is of value to geographers seeking to understand locational decisions. ◊ *behavioural matrix.*

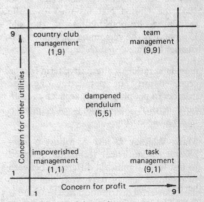

Fig. 94 Managerial matrix

managerialism A framework for study, used especially in ◊ *urban geography*, which emphasizes the role of an intermediate level of decision-makers or managers in resource allocation, particularly within the public sector. Whatever the social formation, these managers exist between central government or central institutions and the public. While they work according to agreed principles or rules they are capable of exercising some discretion. Their allocative decisions, reflecting institutional constraints and their discretion, affect social and spatial distributions. The fact that discretion exists means that the managers are key figures to be studied in their own right. The managerialist thesis has been most strongly developed in the context of government and has focused on those managers concerned with finance and housing supply.

mandate, mandated territory A ◊ *territory*, formerly part of the German or Turkish empires, which was transferred after the First World War to the League of Nations to be governed, under mandate from the League, by one of its member ◊ *states*. Such territories were administered by the mandatory state only until such time as they were able to govern themselves. From 1945 the United Nations took over the mandatory responsibilities of the old League and the remaining mandated territories became ◊ *trusteeships*.

man–land ratio An alternative term for the crude density of population, i.e. the number of people per unit area. ◊◊ *agricultural density*, *population density*, *population–resource ratio*.

Mann–Whitney *U* test A robust ◊ *non-parametric* statistical technique designed to test for a significant difference between two sample sets of data. It is one of the most powerful distribution free tests and is applicable to ◊ *ordinal data*. It determines whether a difference in the median of two independent samples is statistically significant. The Mann–Whitney *U* test provides an alternative to the ◊ *student's t-test* when

the assumptions required for the latter are not fulfilled. ◊◊ *Wilcoxon test*.

manor Originally a basic unit of English territorial organization held by feudal tenure (◊ *feudalism*) but later equivalent to a landed estate. Manors were of variable size, most containing a single village, and were held in ◊ *fee simple* so that they passed automatically from the lord of the manor to his heir. They were the smallest unit of feudal government: each possessed its own court dealing with petty offences. The lord of the manor retained a large tract of land, ◊ *the demesne*, around his house and beyond this the arable land was normally divided into three fields (◊ *three-field system*) which were cultivated on a strip pattern (◊ *open field*). Originally tenants rendered services to the lord of the manor and paid ◊ *tithes*, but later money rents were substituted. The heyday of the manorial system in England was from the 11th to 14th centuries, but it began to break up with ◊ *enclosure*.

manpower forecasting The estimation or prediction of the future demand for and supply of ◊ *labour*. Demand may be established by inquiry methods (such as surveys of employers' expectations) or by statistical methods (for example, the extrapolation of past and present trends). Supply can be estimated by projecting ◊ *activity rates* and applying these to the population aged fifteen or over as predicted by ◊ *population projection*.

manufacturing industry That branch of ◊ *industry* (in its broadest sense) which transforms the ◊ *commodities* from ◊ *primary industry* into fabricated articles or ◊ *products*. The term implies the opposite of its literal meaning – 'made by hand' – i.e. the making of articles on a large scale by machines. Also referred to as the *production sector* and *secondary industry*. ◊◊ *footloose industry*, *heavy industry*, *light industry*.

manufacturing stocks district A concentration of ◊ *wholesalers*, usually near the city centre, supplying a relatively standardized product for a highly diversified manufacturing process, e.g. paper for printing. Access to the customer is an important consideration. ◊◊ *produce district, product comparison district, will-call delivery district*.

manure cycle The process by which waste materials from plants, animals and human beings are returned to the soil to restore nutrients consumed in plant growth.

march, marchland A medieval word for a district within a ◊ *frontier* zone, i.e. debatable land between two states.

margin line A line, used by E. M. Hoover, to show how ◊ *delivered prices* at the edge of a firm's market vary as the spatial extent of the market itself varies. In ◊ Fig. 95 a good is produced at point *O* and *L*, *M* and *N* represent possible edges to the firm's market area in one direction. If area *OL* is supplied, production costs per unit are represented by *Ol* on the ordinate, and the line *ll'* – a transport-gradient line – shows how delivered price increases away from *O* as transport costs are added. If the market

is extended to *M* the production cost, assuming decreasing returns to scale, rises to *Om* and a new transport gradient *mm'* is introduced. Extending the market to *N* produces a similar effect. The margin line is formed by joining *l'*, *m'*, *n'* with the delivered price at all other possible edges of the market area.

margin of cultivation ◊ *economic margins of cultivation*. ◊◊ *cultivation limit, physical margin of cultivation*.

margin of profitability The limit of profitability, below which a firm operates at an economic loss. ◊◊ *profit surface*.

margin of transference In the ◊ *von Thünen model* the boundary between two zones of land use. On one side the ◊ *economic rent* from one agricultural practice exceeds that of any other practice and on the other side that from a different agricultural practice exceeds all others.

marginal analysis In economic analysis, an approach which stresses the borders, margins or limiting areas of an activity or problem, rather than the entire range of the phenomenon. Marginal, for the economist, means 'extra'. Marginal analysis is therefore concerned, for example, with the utility of successive units of a good or service consumed or with the costs of successive units of a good produced, in order to identify conditions of ◊ *equilibrium*, disequilibrium or processes of change.

marginal cost The additional ◊ *cost* of producing each successive unit of output. The cost of producing the last unit of output equals the cost of producing $n + 1$ units minus the cost of producing n units.

marginal cost pricing A method of determining the ◊ *price* at which goods are offered for sale whereby the price asked for all units sold is equal to ◊ *marginal cost* (the cost of producing the last unit).

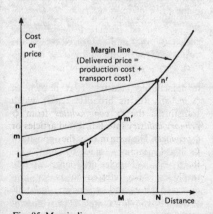

Fig. 95 Margin line

marginal land ◊ *Land* which just yields an average return sufficient to cover the cost of production. It is the last land to be brought into, or the first land to be taken out of, a particular line of production and does not afford an opportunity for earning ◊ *economic rent*.

marginal product The amount added to total product by the use of one more unit of inputs.

marginal productivity The ◊ *productivity* or additional output of the last unit of a ◊ *factor of production* used.

marginal revenue The revenue received from the sale of an additional unit. It equals the total revenue from $n + 1$ units minus the total revenue from n units. Under conditions of ◊ *perfect competition* the marginal revenue is constant and equal to ◊ *price*.

marginal sea ◊ *territorial sea.*

mariculture The farming of the sea. ◊◊ *fisheries.*

marina A purpose-built ◊ *harbour* providing moorings and parking areas for leisure craft, along with associated facilities.

marine belt ◊ *territorial sea.*

marital fertility Live births to married women. Thus the marital fertility rate is the number of legitimate live births per 1,000 married women. ◊ *fertility rates.*

marital status The legal status of an individual in relation to marriage. A population can be divided into two classes: (a) the *never-married* (consisting of bachelors and spinsters) and (b) the *ever-married* (including not only married people but also those formerly married – divorced and separated people, widows and widowers). ◊◊ *marriage rate.*

maritime industrial area A large industrial site with a deep-water frontage. Development of such areas has been a response to the economics of bulk-handling and ◊ *transshipment*. Such sites are normally provided with public utilities on a large scale and are linked to main road and rail networks. They attract capital-intensive industries using bulk material inputs.

maritime space The area of water or ocean separating ◊ *ports* from their ◊ *forelands*. It is therefore part of ◊ *port space* and is of interest with regard to the distances involved.

maritime zones Areas of sea or ocean which are or will be subject to national or international authority (◊ Fig. 29). Various maritime zones are claimed by ◊ *states* seeking exclusive access to the resources of the sea and the seabed: ◊ *archipelagic waters*, ◊ *contiguous zone*, ◊ *continental shelf*, ◊ *exclusive economic zone*, ◊ *historic bay*, ◊ *internal waters*, ◊ *territorial sea*. Beyond the limits of national jurisdiction are the ◊ *deep seabed* and the ◊ *high seas*. ◊◊ *Hedberg zone.*

mark ◊ *march.*

marker crude Saudi Arabia light oil ◊ *f.o.b.* from Ras Tanura in the Persian Gulf. The price of oil set by OPEC refers to this marker crude and the prices of other oils from other sources are adjusted in relation to the price of marker crude. ◊◊ *Organization of Petroleum Exporting Countries.*

market A place or location where goods and services are bought and sold. ◊◊ *central place theory*, *periodic market.*

market area The spatial area in which the consumers of an enterprise's goods or services are located. Also termed *trade area*. ◊◊ *catchment area*, *service area.*

market area analysis An approach, based on the work of A. Lösch, which demonstrates how the market area of the firm is determined. It is applicable to both industrial location and the provision of services. A simple example is provided in ◊ Fig. 96, where plant X, with given pro-

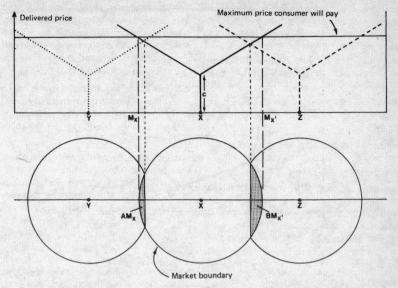

Fig. 96 Market area analysis

duction cost per unit (c), is located at the centre of an isotropic plain, with the horizontal axis representing a transect. Customers buy the commodity at a ◊ *delivered price*, which covers production cost and transport costs, and there is a maximum price they are prepared to pay to obtain a unit of the commodity. The boundary of the market area of the plant at X is shown in ◊ Fig. 96 by M_x and $M_{x'}$, i.e. where delivered price is equal to the maximum the customer will pay. On the isotropic surface, in the absence of competitors, plant X will have a circular market area.

If competing plants Y and Z are introduced on either side of X, then assuming homogeneous products, customers purchase from the cheapest supplier and plant X will lose customers in area AM_x to Y and in $BM_{x'}$ to Z. As further firms enter the industry the space will be filled and shared, via a process of competition, until the market areas of plants are reduced to the minimum size consistent with a normal level of profits (◊ *central place theory*).

Where customers are unevenly spread, market area analysis depicts optimal location of the plant as occurring where the largest market area is monopolized, i.e. where sales potential and total revenue potential are maximized. In practice, market areas need not be separated out in this way but may overlap because of consumer behaviour and preferences, pricing policies and competitive practices (◊ *locational interdependence*).

market cycle ◊ *Periodic markets* characterize rural settlements in which the purchasing power of the population is insufficient to maintain a continuous urban function. Such periodic functions in a set of locations may form a market cycle in time and a ◊ *market ring* in space. Periodic markets may be fitted into a ◊ *central place theory*

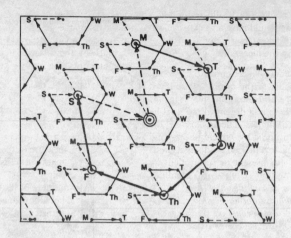

Fig. 97 Market cycle

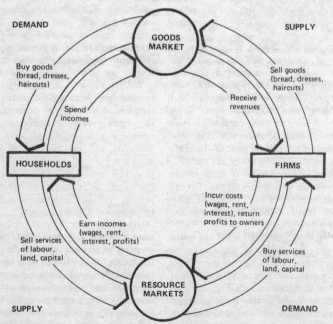

Fig. 98 Market economy

framework, and ◊ Fig. 97 illustrates how a market trader could have a weekly cycle in a $k = 7$ settlement hierarchy at either of two levels in the hierarchy.

market economy An economic ◊ *system* in which the bulk of the output is produced for exchange and the economic decisions are freely taken at a decentralized level by firms and consumers. The ◊ *market* is the central institution by which buyers and sellers come together to exchange goods for money, for present or future delivery and consumption. Commonly identified with private ◊ *capitalism*. ◊ Fig. 98. ◊ *bazaar economy, informal economy, laissez-faire, reciprocal economy, redistributive economy, subsistence economy*.

market garden A British term, introduced in the 19th century, for the commercial growing of plants for their produce, i.e. the intensive production of vegetable crops, soft fruits and flowers for sale. The equivalent term in North America is ◊ *truck-farming*. The market garden is distinguished from the ◊ *nursery*, although both are covered by ◊ *horticulture*.

market orientation The location of an economic activity at or near its ◊ *market*. The market is most likely to influence location when the cost of transporting the product to the consumer is a significant proportion of the total cost or when consumers will travel only short distances to obtain a service. Market orientation may operate at various spatial scales, from the small-scale producer supplying a highly localized market, to the regional or national scale where it is a factor in the ◊ *agglomeration* of industry in metropolitan areas.

market penetration A largely non-spatial concept describing a firm's share of a ◊ *market*.

market potential A method, closely related to the ◊ *gravity model*, of describing spatial variations in the intensity of demand. The market potential or estimated value of sales attainable at any location, i, is obtained by dividing the retail sales of each jth place by the distance between i and j and summing the result, i.e. in general form by

$$MP_i = \sum_{j=1}^{n} \frac{M_j}{d_{ij}}$$

where MP_i = market potential at i
  M_j = measure of the size of the market at j (usually retail sales)
  d_{ij} = measure of the distance between i and j (usually transfer costs)

Where market potential is calculated for all places in a region or a nation, an ◊ *isopleth* map representing a *market potential surface* can be constructed. Market potential provides an indication of the general proximity of a location in relation to the spatial distribution of total demand: peak values on the isopleth map give an approximation of the maximum sales location. ◊ *population potential*.

market principle ◊ *central place theory*.

market ring The spatial pattern of ◊ *periodic markets*, whose regular occurrence forms a ◊ *market cycle* (◊ Fig. 97).

market socialism An ◊ *economic system* in which the means of production, distribution and exchange are socially owned, but decision-making is performed mainly at the decentralized level of firms and households.

market town Generally, any ◊ *town* which has a permanent or periodic ◊ *market* serving as a place of trade for the surrounding district. In Britain a market town normally received a charter granting the right to hold a weekly market and an annual fair. Such charters were often purchased from the Crown by lords of the manor for political reasons. This was the first step in the growth of a settlement from a purely rural status, and, in time, ◊ *borough* status was granted.

marketing The processes of physical movement, storage and ownership of ◊ *goods* involved in the transfer of those goods from producer to consumer. As these processes operate so goods change their locations. Marketing is part of the ◊ *tertiary sector*. ◊◊ *direct marketing*.

marketing geography The separation of consumption and production which is the reason for ◊ *marketing* is essentially a spatial concept and marketing geography is concerned with the problems of overcoming this separation, i.e. with marketing a product efficiently. Marketing is a complex, composite and open ◊ *system*, the basic product movements of which are summarized in ◊ Fig. 99 – goods are transported from the production point, to be assembled, sorted, reassembled, distributed and displayed by one or several middlemen, e.g. wholesalers, brokers, agents, retailers, before the good is finally consumed.

Geographers have contributed to the theory of marketing systems by (a) extending marketing theories to include the spatial dimension, and (b) demonstrating how geographical theories may be of value to the market researcher. The spatial processes in the marketing system involve the study of (i) consumer behaviour, (ii) retail, and to a lesser extent wholesale, location decisions, (iii) the effectiveness of transport in the market system, as well as (iv) market research in terms of information flow.

marketing linkage ◊ *linkage*.

Markov chain A type of ◊ *stochastic* process, comprising a sequence of possible states, in which the ◊ *probability* of being in a given state at time t is wholly dependent upon the state at some preceding time. Such a Markov process has a chain of actors connected by decisions which are thus the result of both chance and systematic influence. The systematic influence is derived from the preceding time period(s): where only the immediately preceding period $(t - 1)$ is considered it is termed a first-order Markov chain, but higher orders can also be modelled.

The complete set of probabilities, p_{ij}, for a Markovian process are represented on a transition probability matrix, p, of the form

$$
p = p_{ij} = \text{Initial states } (t) \quad
\begin{array}{c}
 \\
s_1 \\
s_2 \\
\vdots \\
s_n
\end{array}
\overset{\text{Outcome states } (t + 1)}{
\overset{s_1 \quad\ s_2 \quad\ \cdots\cdots\cdots \quad\ s_n}{
\begin{bmatrix}
p_{11} & p_{12} & \cdots\cdots\cdots & p_{1n} \\
p_{21} & p_{22} & \cdots\cdots\cdots & p_{2n} \\
\multicolumn{4}{c}{\cdots\cdots\cdots\cdots\cdots\cdots} \\
p_{n1} & p_{n2} & \cdots\cdots\cdots & p_{nn}
\end{bmatrix}}}
$$

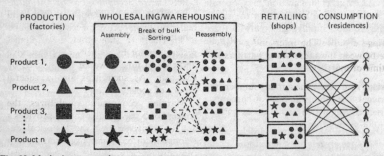

Fig. 99 Marketing geography

			State at $(t + 1)$	
		Owner-occupied	Private rented	Public housing
State at t	Owner-occupied	0·95	0·03	0·02
	Private renting	0·10	0·65	0·25
	Public housing	0·20	0·20	0·60

Each p_{ij} represents the expected proportion of initial states assigned to each outcome state. For example, movement of households by tenure could be modelled by the matrix above.

Thus, between time t and $t + 1$, 95% of owner-occupiers who move purchase another owner-occupied property, only 3% renting privately and 2% going into public housing. A similar interpretation applies to the second and third rows. The main diagonal of the matrix, $p_{11} \ldots p_{nn}$, estimates the probabilities of repeated decisions or no change of state. The repeated operation of such a process results in a stable distribution which is independent of the way in which the former state was achieved. Markov chains have been used by geographers to study the growth of firms, the relocation of firms and households, and urban travel patterns. ◊ *mover–stayer model*.

mark-up The percentage of ◊ *profit* added to the cost ◊ *price* of goods by traders in order to determine selling price. In retailing, mark-up refers to the difference between wholesale and retail price.

marriage distance The intervening ◊ *distance* between the addresses of partners at the time of marriage.

marriage rate Either the annual number of marriages, or the number of persons married, during a year expressed as a rate per 1,000 population, i.e.

$$(1) \text{ Marriage rate} = \frac{M}{P} \times 1,000$$

$$(2) \text{ Marriage rate} = \frac{2M}{P} \times 1,000$$

where M = number of marriages in the year

P = total population at mid-year

Such measures are crude rates because they relate to total population and not to the number of marriageable persons. ◊ *marital status, nuptiality.*

marriage-standardized reproduction rate ◊ *reproduction rates.*

Marschhufendorf A term of German origin for a linear or stringlike ◊ *village* found in marsh environments. ◊ *Gewanndorf, Haufendorf, Strassendorf, Waldhufendorf.*

Marxian economics An approach in ◊ *economics*, with its origins in the conditions created by the ◊ *Industrial Revolution*, that seeks to provide an understanding of how an economy functions. Developed from the political economy of Karl Marx and Friedrich Engels, Marxian economics offers an alternative interpretation to ◊ *neoclassical economics* on how ◊ *capitalism* operates. It adopts a historical materialist perspective on economic affairs in an effort to show that the capitalist system cannot by its very nature survive and that in time it would be replaced by socialism. As such it is also a general theory of society.

Marxian economics emphasizes the concept of ◊ *value*. Value theory provides a key to understanding the historical development of economic organization in a capitalist society. While the neoclassical economist regards value as market-determined, the Marxian economist uses the concept in respect of class struggle. Social classes take shape in response to their share in, and control of, wealth production. Thus at any time the class which has the greatest economic power has the greatest political power. Such social relations of production underpin the inequalities which are commonplace under capitalism.

The economic base or ◊ *mode of production* is critical in determining a society's pattern of development. Mode of production comprises both the capacity to produce (◊ *productive forces*) and the 'relations of production' (the way in which people participate). Four modes of production precede socialism – primitive communal, slave, feudal and capitalist. With any increase in productive forces conflict arises within the relations of production, a conflict resolved historically by replacing one mode of production by another. With the rise of capitalism not only was the status of labour changed but workers were divested of the means of production (e.g. tools, land) which would have allowed them to command a greater share in the new wealth.

Conventional approaches view the sale of labour as part of the exchange system, but the Marxian approach suggests an exploitative social relationship which is masked by commodity transactions. The basis of the argument is that ◊ *surplus value*, the difference between the use and exchange values of labour, accrues to the capitalist. This interpretation relies on the labour theory of value, which defines exchange value of a good in terms of the amount of labour time required to produce it. That labour is socially necessary labour. The idea applies to labour itself, the exchange value of labour being determined by the cost of producing and reproducing workers, i.e. the socially necessary labour for subsistence. Theoretically, then, the exchange value of labour is decided

independently of the specific job a worker might do but, once sold to capital, labour power may be used to produce goods that can be sold at a price greater than the cost of labour reflected in that price in the form of wages paid. The use value of labour exceeds its exchange value and the surplus value accrues to the capitalist as the basis of profit. Ownership of the means of production therefore enables the capitalist to appropriate part of the value of the product of labour, and this extraction of surplus value from labour is the starting point of the process of capital accumulation.

The prophecy that capitalism will eventually be destroyed by the internal conflicts it creates has not been fulfilled and contemporary Marxist approaches concentrate on exposing the limitations of the operation of the capitalist system. ◊ *Marxism, Marxist geography.*

Marxism The body of thought developed by Karl Marx which claims that the state, through history, has been a device for the exploitation of the masses by a dominant class and that class struggle has been the main agent of historical change.

Marxist geography ◊ *Marxism* provides geographers with an opportunity to develop the potential of ◊ *geography* as a truly synthetic science, to transform geographical thought and practice. While Marxist geography may be narrowly viewed as the application of Marxist philosophy to the interrelationship between social processes on the one hand and the natural environment and spatial relations on the other, it must be remembered that Marxist science is a 'whole science' and geographical studies will be fused with social sciences and natural sciences under the umbrella of historical materialism. The aim is not merely to understand the world but to change it.

Marxist science starts from a material analysis of society, proceeds via a critique of the capitalist control of the material base of society ($\Diamond$ *Marxian economics*), to propose solutions in terms of social ownership of the material (economic) base. It therefore rests on the foundation of its assumptions about the importance of material production in the social formation – social processes deal essentially with the production and reproduction of the material basis of life. Such social processes occur in $\Diamond$ *environments* comprising elements of the natural world and various types of relationship across space: different processes operate in different places, and the same process may operate differently under different environmental conditions. Such geographical variation in the operation of social processes leads to the recognition of spatial processes. These are originally social processes whose spatial manifestations have become so strong that they are co-dominant features of the process, e.g. the social contradiction between $\Diamond$ *capital* and $\Diamond$ *labour* is implanted into space, in one form, as the spatial contradiction between the $\Diamond$ *First* and $\Diamond$ *Third Worlds*; or the social process of the transfer of surplus value reveals itself as a spatial process of transfer of surplus value from the peripheral to metropolitan regions of capitalism. Spatial form then becomes an input into the continuing social process, altering the shape and speed of development, which, in turn, is expressed in a variety of local forms. Thus there exists a dialectic interaction between social process and spatial form.

Marxist geography therefore considers one area of the set of interactions surrounding social processes but, like other Marxist sciences, it is aimed at changing the fundamental operation of social processes by changing the social relations of production. To date, Marxists working in geography have focused on the role of the market system in determining land use, on residential, industrial and commercial location, and, especially, on regional and international development – seeking, in each case, to identify the class character of the processes involved. $\Diamond$ *radical geography*.

Marxist theory of rent Under a Marxist approach rent is that part of $\Diamond$ *surplus value* paid to landowners. It arises from the existence of monopoly control over land conferred by the institution of private property, i.e. rent is a social relationship derived from particular property arrangements. Marx defined three categories of rent with reference to the form of that social relationship.

(i) *Differential rent*, which is of two types. The first reflects directly the differing qualities of land ($\Diamond$ *Ricardian theory of rent*). Values and prices are determined by the labour required to produce crops on the worst-quality land in use. Production on more fertile or more accessible land requires less labour and produces more surplus value, some of which can be extracted by landowners in the form of rent, since farmers compete for the better land. The second type reflects the varying amounts of capital invested by the user to generate more surplus value. In this case the landowner will not necessarily be able to extract extra rent, since there will be no competitive bidding as improvements are built into the selling price. The landowner's opportunity to get extra rent comes when rent revisions and leases are negotiated.

(ii) *Monopoly rent* is received by landowners who lease land for the production of goods sold under $\Diamond$ *monopoly* conditions. Since land is an essential element the landowner can claim some of the surplus profit as a monopoly rent.

With differential and monopoly rents the landowner intercepts the surplus profits which would otherwise have gone to users and, for both types, the rent level will be set by the difference between the production and market prices of the goods produced on the land. These rents therefore have no effect on prices.

(iii) *Absolute rent* arises from the monopoly power of landed property which allows landowners to manipulate the supply of land to maintain scarcity and so force up rents. Absolute rent is the rent derived from this ability to create and increase rent payments and it does have an effect on prices.

mass-production The large-scale manufacture of a standardized product at a fast rate, and hence at a low cost per unit. Mass-production rests on the use of specialized ◊ *labour* and ◊ *capital* equipment.

massed reserves ◊ *economies of massed reserves.*

master industry ◊ *propulsive industry.*

material goods ◊ *Goods* which can be produced in increasing quantities and consumed without loss of quality. ◊◊ *positional goods.*

material index An index, devised by Alfred Weber, used in industrial location to show the extent to which the optimum location for a particular manufacturing industry will be ◊ *material-oriented* or ◊ *market-oriented.* It is calculated as the proportion of the weight of ◊ *localized materials* to the weight of finished product:

$$MI = \frac{\text{weight of localized materials used in the industry}}{\text{weight of the product}}$$

An M I greater than 1 indicates a tendency towards a material location (because of the weight loss characteristics of the localized material). In cases where ubiquitous materials are used as well, the product may have a weight greater than the localized material, i.e. M I is less than 1, and there is a tendency towards a market location.

◊◊ *locational weight, orientation index, weight-loss ratio.*

material orientation The location of an economic activity at or near the source of a material used in producing a good. This is most likely to occur where the cost of materials varies considerably with location and material costs form a significant proportion of total costs for the industry concerned, e.g. in primary metal manufacturing and agricultural product processing. ◊◊ *market orientation, material index, orientation, transfer orientation.*

materialism The doctrine that reality is matter (everything that exists is material). Mind and consciousness are only manifestations of such matter and are reducible to its physical elements. The opposite of ◊ *idealism.*

mathematical geography A division of ◊ *geography*, recognized in the 18th century (alongside physical geography and historical or political geography), dealing with the shape, size and motions of the earth.

mature town ◊ *age of towns scheme.*

maturity A term applied to a stage in the economic ◊ *development* of a country characterized by a broad and balanced industrial structure, the existence of skilled human resources and a substantial ◊ *infrastructure.* ◊ *Rostow model.* ◊◊ *development stages theory of growth.*

maximum sustainable yield The maximum yield that can be obtained from a renewable ◊ *resource* in any given period if it is to maintain the same future productivity. Maximum sustainable yield is a biological concept and the yield is determined by reducing the size of a stock, e.g. a fish population, from its natural equilibrium population to the point where maximum net growth in population is achieved (◊ Fig. 100). A stock of this size

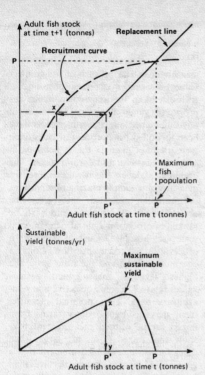

Fig. 100 Maximum sustainable yield

can be considered in equilibrium as long as the annual catch/harvest equals the net growth.

meadow Strictly a term for a field of permanent grass used for hay, but also applied to rich, waterside grazing areas that are not suitable for arable cultivation. Often used loosely to refer to any piece of ◊ *grassland*. ◊ *pasture*.

mean ◊ *arithmetic mean*.

mean age The average age of a population, i.e. the total of all the individual ages divided by the number of people.

mean centre The simplest measure of the centre of a spatial ◊ *distribution*. It is the

exact equivalent of the ◊ *arithmetic mean* of conventional statistics and is the 'balancing point' or centre of gravity of the distribution. The mean centre can be calculated using several methods, but the most convenient depends on the use of grid co-ordinates (◊ Fig. 101). If each point in the spatial distribution is not given equal weight a *weighted mean centre* is calculated, e.g. if each point is a factory weighted by its output. ◊ *median centre*, *standard distance*.

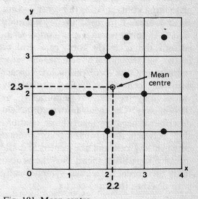

Fig. 101 Mean centre

mean deviation A measure of the ◊ *dispersion* of a data set, being the average extent to which individual values deviate from the ◊ *arithmetic mean*. It is calculated by summing the absolute deviations of all values of the original data from the arithmetic mean and dividing by the number of values, i.e.

$$\text{Mean deviation} = \frac{\Sigma|x - \bar{x}|}{n}$$

where $|x - \bar{x}|$ = the absolute difference between each value x and the mean, $\bar{x}$

Σ = sum of all these absolute deviations

n = number of values

mean distance deviation A measure of the average distance separating the points of a spatial distribution from the ◊ *mean centre*.

mean field A term used to describe a town's or centre's range of influence for economic and other social interactions. The mean field is the area nearest to the centre accounting for one half of the interactions. ◊ *sphere of influence*.

mean information field The operational definition of an area containing probabilities of receiving information from, or making contact with, the central point in that area. It is used in ◊ *simulation modelling* to represent a ◊ *distance decay* pattern and takes the form of a grid or matrix in which each cell has a value representing the probability of contact with the central cell. The probability values may be derived empirically or theoretically. The mean information field describes a negative logarithmic relationship between the probability of contact between any cell and the centre and the distance separating them; thus the probability of contact declines symmetrically with distance from the centre.

mean length of life ◊ *expectation of life at birth*.

mean percent angular distortion A measure of shape, devised by B. Boots, to assist the classification of areas. The formula is

$$\text{MPAD} = \sum_{i=1}^{n} \left(\frac{|\theta_n - \theta_i|}{\theta_n} \times 100 \right) \Big/ n$$

where n = number of sides of the polygon

θ_i = value, in degrees, of the ith internal angle

θ_n = value for a regular polygon of n sides where θ_n is given by $(2n - 4)$ right angles

Values range from 0, a regular polygon, to 100, a straight line. Alternative indices are listed under ◊ *shape measures*.

mean square deviation ◊ *variance*.

measured reserves ◊ *proved reserves, reserves*.

measurement The process of assigning a value or score to observed phenomena. Rules defining the assignment of an appropriate value determine the level of measurement. Four ascending levels have been identified for purposes of classifying types of data, namely the ◊ *nominal*, ◊ *ordinal*, ◊ *interval* and ◊ *ratio scales*. The nominal scale is the weakest level of measurement, simply placing observations in mutually exclusive categories; the ordinal scale allows observations to be ranked in order of magnitude; the interval scale uses absolute values to indicate an observation's precise position along a continuous scale; and the ratio scale, the highest level of measurement, assigns values relative to some objective and non-arbitrary base. Thus nominal measurement may distinguish dairy farms from mixed farms, ordinal measurement may show that mixed farms are larger than dairy farms, interval measurement that a given mixed farm has n more hectares than a particular dairy farm, and ratio measurement that mixed farms are twice as large as dairy farms.

The distinction between levels of measurement is important since particular statistical techniques can be applied only to data measured on a particular scale.

median A simple measure of central tendency, being defined as the middle value in a data set when the values are arranged in order of magnitude, i.e. an equal number of values occur above and below it. The median is the appropriate measure of central tendency to use in skewed distributions (◊ *skewness*), since it is not affected by the extreme values and is the value about which absolute deviations are minimized. ◊ *arithmetic mean, mode*.

median centre A measure of central tend-

(a) Locating the median centre

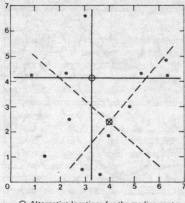

O Alternative locations for the median centre
(3·3, 4·1) (4·0, 2·4)

(b) Centre of minimum travel

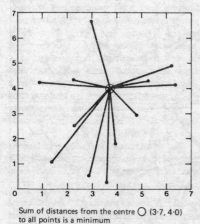

Sum of distances from the centre O (3·7, 4·0)
to all points is a minimum

Fig. 102 Median centre

ency in point patterns, the counterpart to the ◊ *median*. It is located at the intersection of two axes at right angles to one another such that each axis has an equal number of points on either side. It is difficult to identify a unique median centre because several pairs of axes, each intersecting at a different point (◊ Fig. 102a), may fulfil this

definition. One interpretation of the 'true' median centre, referred to in North America as the *centre of minimum travel*, is the point of minimum aggregate travel (◊ Fig. 102b), i.e. the location from which the sum of the distance to all points in a distribution is a minimum.

median distance The radius of a circle which encloses one half of the points in a distribution around a ◊ *mean centre* or any given location. ◊ *mean field*.

medical geography The geographical study of human health, including the provision of health care. It covers the description of the spatial distribution of ◊ *morbidity* and ◊ *mortality* and considers possible causative relationships between sickness, disease and death and local variations in environmental conditions. A more recent interest is with the spatial aspects of the organization of health services, especially the identification of optimum locations for health care facilities.

Mediterranean agriculture A distinct ◊ *agricultural system* that has changed little in 2,000 years and takes its name from the lands encircling the Mediterranean Sea. The three environmental characteristics fundamental to its evolution were the comparatively mild, moist winters, the hot, sunny summers with associated drought, and the terrain. Mediterranean agriculture involves particular sets of winter crops (cereals), of summer crops (trees) and of animals (sheep and goats). Cereal crops are sown in autumn after the rains have begun and reaped at the beginning of the dry season (◊ *dry farming* is practised in the drier areas). Since spring-sown crops are excluded by the summer drought, summer crops are heavily dependent on tree crops – olives, figs, vines and dates. In some areas ◊ *irrigation* permits intensive cultivation through the summer of such crops as cotton, maize and vegetables. ◊ *huerta*, *latifundium*, *vega*.

297

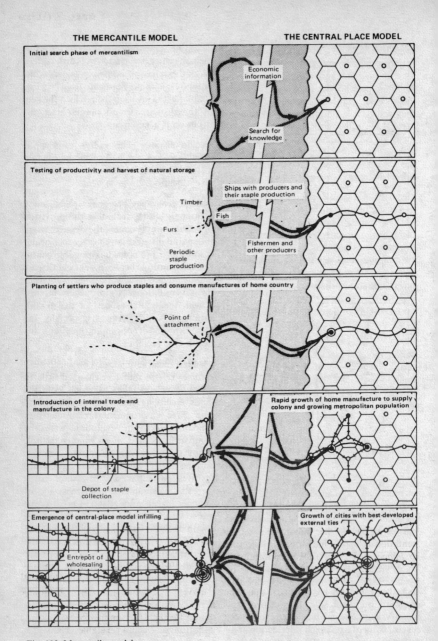

THE MERCANTILE MODEL   THE CENTRAL PLACE MODEL

Initial search phase of mercantilism

Economic information

Search for knowledge

Testing of productivity and harvest of natural storage

Ships with producers and their staple production

Timber

Fish

Furs

Fishermen and other producers

Periodic staple production

Planting of settlers who produce staples and consume manufactures of home country

Point of attachment

Introduction of internal trade and manufacture in the colony

Rapid growth of home manufacture to supply colony and growing metropolitan population

Depot of staple collection

Emergence of central-place model infilling

Growth of cities with best-developed external ties

Entrepôt of wholesaling

Fig. 103 Mercantile model

megalith A general term for any large stone arranged in some way by people, usually as a monument and dating from the ◊ *Neolithic* period. Megaliths are frequently left in their natural, irregular shape and they can be free-standing (individually, in a circle or in a row or some other alignment) or part of a larger structure such as a megalithic tomb. Single standing stones are also referred to as ◊ *menhirs* and megalithic tombs as ◊ *dolmens*.

megalopolis A term applied by J. Gottman to the highly urbanized seaboard of the north-eastern United States, but used in a wider context for any overgrown or outsize urban area which has developed by the gradual merging of many ◊ *metropolises* and cities to operate as one polynuclear urban system. It is distinguished, according to C. Doxiadis, from the metropolis either because its population exceeds 10 million people or because it has incorporated more than one metropolis.

melting-pot concept A term used to describe the merging of many ethnic heritages to produce a new type of person, e.g. the emergence of the 'American' in the late 19th and early 20th centuries. ◊◊ *acculturation, assimilation*.

menhir From the Breton for 'long stone', a tall, upright stone of ◊ *Neolithic* origin, probably of religious significance, e.g. marking a burial place. ◊◊ *megalith*.

mental map A mental map is a representation of the spatial form of the ◊ *phenomenal environment* which an individual carries in his or her mind. The representation is of the individual's subjective ◊ *image* of ◊ *place* (not a conventional map) and not only includes knowledge of features and spatial relationships but also reflects the individual's preferences for and attitudes towards places.

Such mental maps are derived via ◊ *environmental perception*: the cognitive mapping process involved comprises a series of psychological transformations by which an individual obtains, codes, stores, recalls and decodes information about the relative locations and their attributes. The product of this process, at any point in time, is a mental or *cognitive map* and can be shown cartographically as a perception surface.

Thus, for the individual, mental maps serve (1) like a real map as a means of organizing data, (2) as a mnemonic device by which locations of places, people and things are remembered, (3) as an aid to decision-making in rehearsing spatial behaviour and organizing spatial routines, (4) as an imaginary world which, interpreted in terms of spatial desirability, may tempt people from habitual routines and (5) as a reference framework for giving directions to strangers. ◊◊ *landmark, topophilia*.

mercantile model A model of urban systems evolution, put forward by J. E. Vance, Jr, based on the geography of ◊ *wholesaling* and the fact that settlement developed in the 'New World' was prompted by external forces in the form of trading impulses from the 'Old World'. The establishment and growth of urban centres is initiated externally by investment decisions from a previously developed urban sub-system, and the evolving pattern of urban places in an area is heavily influenced by competition between merchants located outside the area, i.e. the concern is with external markets and does not reflect competition for internal markets between the urban centres. Stages in the evolution of a mercantile pattern are illustrated in Fig. 103. The mercantile model therefore contrasts with ◊ *central place theory*, which is based upon internal forces as being dominant in evolving urban patterns.

mercantilism A school of economic thought, dominant in the 17th and early 18th centuries, which aimed to involve the

299

power of the state in the regulation of economic life so as to increase national wealth and power. Foremost amongst mercantilist principles was the belief that the wealth of a country was determined largely by the extent to which it gained wealth from other countries, i.e. a nation became richer the more it exported and the less it imported.

merger The amalgamation or merging of two or more ◊ *firms* into a single undertaking. The usual motive is to make more efficient use of available resources. A *horizontal merger*, between firms producing similar goods, will reduce competition and bring benefits of ◊ *economies of scale*, whereas a *vertical merger*, between firms at different stages of a production process, will assure supplies and markets. A *diversified merger*, between firms producing very different products, leads to the formation of a *conglomerate*. ◊◊ *take-over*.

merit goods Goods and services the quantities of which supplied through the market are deemed by society to be unsatisfactory. Markets and usable prices do or could exist for merit goods, but there is some part of the national need which is not satisfied. Merit goods are consumed on an individual basis and there is an advantage in standardizing the good, at least in terms of a minimum (or adequate) level of provision, since the benefits to society greatly exceed the 'market price'. Examples are housing, health and education services. Standards are a function of government and where provision is also by government a merit good may be a ◊ *public good* also.

merit order The rank order of increasing running costs among the power stations of a grid-linked electricity generating system. Not all power stations are needed all the time (◊ *load duration curve*); those that are lowest in the merit order are brought into use only at times of peak demand, while those highest in the merit order supply the continuing base load needs (◊ *base load plant*).

merkland A term, used in the arable parts of Scotland between the 12th and 18th centuries, for the land which gave full employment to one plough and one family.

mesocephalic An intermediate head-form that is neither broad nor long: defined by anthropologists as a skull with a ◊ *cephalic index* between 76 and 83·1.

mesokurtic ◊ *kurtosis*.

Mesolithic An archaeological term (from the Greek for *middle stone age*) used to describe the ◊ *culture* of the early postglacial period when people had largely given up the herd-hunting practices of the ◊ *Palaeolithic* and moved to semi-permanent settlements but had not yet discovered ◊ *agriculture*. ◊◊ *Neolithic*.

mestizo A half-caste person, now primarily the offspring of Spanish and American Indian parents. ◊◊ *mulatto, zambo*.

métayage A system of ◊ *land tenure*, formerly widespread in Western Europe (especially France) and the United States, in which the farmer pays a certain proportion of the produce (usually half) to the landlord as rent. The landlord normally provides all or part of the stock and seed. ◊◊ *share-cropping*.

métropoles d'équilibre The metropolises or *counterweight cities* designated under the Fifth French Plan, 1966–70, to act as major ◊ *growth poles* in the decentralization of economic growth to less privileged regions, to counterbalance the attraction of Paris, and to create a more balanced urban hierarchy. The eight métropoles d'équilibre were Bordeaux, Lille–Roubaix–Tourcoing, Lyons–St-Étienne–Grenoble, Marseille, Nancy–Metz, Nantes–St-Nazaire, Strasbourg, and Toulouse.

metropolis A term applied loosely to any large city (◊ *metropolitan area*), but specifically to that city in a country which is the seat of government, of ecclesiastical authority, or of commercial activity. In ◊ *central place theory* a metropolis represents a level in the urban hierarchy which is a controlling centre of the modern economy, with a population of at least one million people and dominating a region containing 5–30 million people.

metropolis–satellite hypothesis A theory of economic underdevelopment, propounded by G. Frank, which is based on ◊ *conflict theory*. Conflict and tension build up between the capitalist metropolis and its exploited satellites. Contemporary underdevelopment in any country is thus part of the wider capitalist economic system and is a historical product of past and continuing economic and other relations between the satellite underdeveloped and the developed metropolitan countries. Frank's theory contains three hypotheses: (i) There is unlimited potential for the development of the world metropolis. In contrast the development of subsidiary metropolises is limited by their satellite status. (ii) Satellites experience their greatest economic development when their ties to their metropolis are weakest. (iii) The most underdeveloped regions and countries are those that had the closest ties to the metropolis in the past.

Frank tested his theory in respect of Latin American experience.

metropolitan area An American term for a very large urban settlement, or extended urban area. The concept was first given operational definition by the United States Bureau of the Census in delimiting '*Metropolitan Districts*' in 1910. These districts attempted to group large cities with their contiguous suburbs as single data-reporting units. The term was changed to *Standard Metropolitan Area* in 1950, a concept based on the functional urbanized area, and this became the ◊ *Standard Metropolitan Statistical Area* in 1960. ◊ *Census Metropolitan Area*.

Metropolitan Economic Labour Area (MELA) An attempt by the Political and Economic Planning group to develop a new set of definitions for urban areas in Great Britain based on journey-to-work and employment from the 1961 census. The MELA is an employment core together with its commuting hinterland and is spatially more extensive than the ◊ *Standard Metropolitan Labour Area*, with the inclusion of an outer metropolitan ring of local authorities which are less strongly integrated with the core although the largest proportion of their out-commuters head there. The concept of the *metropolitan labour area* or ◊ *daily urban system* is now well established in many countries.

metropolitan village An alternative term to ◊ *dormitory settlement* for a ◊ *village* within commuting distance of an urban centre which is socially and economically no longer rural.

mezzadria A system of leasing vineyards in southern Italy whereby the farmer offers his services to the landlord in return for half the crop plus payment on a day-wage basis for half of the work he does. The cost of chemicals is also shared equally between the owner and the mezzadro. ◊ *share-cropping*.

microeconomics Study of the behaviour of individual economic units, e.g. household, firm. ◊ *macroeconomics*.

microgeography The detailed study of geographic patterns at the level of sub-areas and small-scale regions. The emphasis is on individual and small-group behaviour as related to the local environment and the social, cultural and economic workings of the group are outlined in depth. ◊ *macrogeography*.

middle-run migration The movement of people between places for a period of more than a season but less than a lifetime, e.g. because of a shift in a person's occupation or position in the hierarchical structure of a firm. ◊ *migration*.

midspread ◊ *inter-quartile range*.

migrant A person who moves voluntarily from one country to another for purposes of permanent residence. That person is an ◊ *emigrant* from their native country and an ◊ *immigrant* into their new country. Contrasts with ◊ *exile* and ◊ *refugee*, where movement is involuntary. ◊ *migration*. ◊> *expatriate*, *passive migrant*.

migration The permanent or semi-permanent change of a person's place of residence. Elements of time and space are integral to the concept, and the definition of migration requires the specification of both a time scale and a set of boundaries within which and across which movement takes place. A basic distinction is drawn between ◊ *circulation*, involving repetitive reciprocal movements which begin and end at a person's home, and migration, involving change of location of a person's home. Complex geographical ramifications are involved in migration associated with the characteristics of the place of origin and the place of destination, intervening obstacles, whether there are legal constraints, the cost of moving (◊ *migration costs*) and most of all the personal factors affecting the decision of whether and where to move.

Migration is probably a more important element in determining population structure and change in an area than ◊ *fertility* and ◊ *mortality*. The volume of migration or *gross migration* includes all migration flows into and out of an area, whereas *net migration*, the balance of migration, is the difference between the in- and out-flows for an area. (◊> *migration change component*.)

Patterns of migration have been classified in various ways. From a geographical view spatial scale is important – migration may be intra-urban, rural to urban, urban to urban, interregional, international, etc. *Centripetal migration*, in which people move towards population centres from the surrounding countryside, has been distinguished from *centrifugal migration*, in which people disperse outwards from central cities into the surrounding towns and villages. In this latter context, a further distinction may be important (◊ Fig. 104) between *partial displacement migration*, in which change in location of a person's home disturbs only part of their reciprocal movement pattern because their place of work remains the same, and *total displacement migration*, in which a completely new pattern of reciprocal movement is established. On a time scale, migration may be temporary or permanent. Temporary movement may take the form of *seasonal migration*, usually of agricultural workers, to meet a demand during labour-intensive seasons, or *periodic migration*, of workers away from their permanent homes for several years during which they send home remittances, and in more developed societies ◊ *middle-run migration* and the ◊ *inter-metropolitan circulation of elites* may be important.

In addition migration movements may be classified on the basis of the reasons behind the movement, e.g. voluntary or forced, sponsored or free, for conquest or colonization, whether impelled by idealistic or economic factors. Thus in *innovative migration* people migrate as a means of achieving something new, whereas in *conservative migration* they move in response to a change in conditions in order to retain what they had. *Betterment migration* is similar to innovative in that a person moves to improve their position, but suggests that push factors at the place of origin are less important than the pull

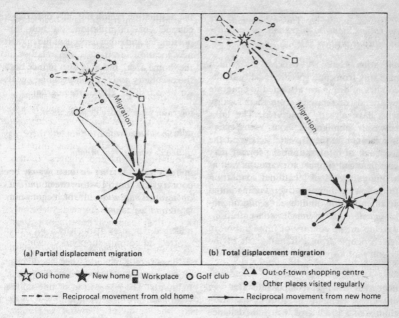

(a) Partial displacement migration   (b) Total displacement migration

☆ Old home   ★ New home   ▣ Workplace   ○ Golf club   △▲ Out-of-town shopping centre
                                                            ○ ● Other places visited regularly
— – ← – — Reciprocal movement from old home   ————→ Reciprocal movement from new home

Fig. 104 Migration

of the destination. It contrasts with *subsistence migration*, in which a person moves away from poor economic conditions, i.e. push factors are more important than pull factors. A distinctive geographical pattern is associated with *retirement migration*, the change of residence by people at or shortly after retirement, since origin areas are spatially restricted and the destinations even more focused, i.e. there is a strong environmental preference in the flow.

Migration research has built on the pioneering study of E. G. Ravenstein in the 1880s who derived '*laws of migration*', namely: (1) most migrants move only a short distance; (2) there is a process of absorption, whereby people immediately surrounding a rapidly growing town move into it and the gaps they leave are filled by migrants from more distant areas, and so on until the attractive force is spent;

(3) there is a process of dispersion, which is the inverse of absorption; (4) each migration flow produces a compensating counter-flow; (5) long-distance migrants go to one of the great centres of commerce and industry; (6) natives of towns are less migratory than those from rural areas; (7) females are more migratory than males; (8) economic factors are the main cause of migration.

Although migration is recognized as a response to social, political, economic and cultural changes there is no overall theory of migration. Geographers have concentrated on the relationship between migration and distance, and increasingly on migration as a process involving information flows and people's behavioural responses (✧ *migration elasticity*). ✧ *active migrant, efficiency of migration, emigration, human capital migration model, immigration, in-migration field, perverse migration, return migration, selective migration, stepwise migration.* ⟐ *mobility, mobility transition.*

migration chain A process by which migrants from one specific locality in the country of origin are attracted to emigrate by friends or relatives from their locality who have already emigrated. The links between immigrants and prospective immigrants frequently extend beyond the feedback of information: the former may give financial support for fares, as well as acting as agents of locational adaptation for following migrants by providing initial accommodation and even securing employment. As a result concentrations develop in the country of immigration in which people from different parts of the country of origin are grouped together. ⟐ *chain migration, migration stock effect.*

migration change component The *net migration* element in total population change of a given area, being the balance between ◊ *immigration* and ◊ *emigration.*

migration costs The costs to a migrant of moving. These include money costs – the costs of household removals, the costs of buying and selling non-movable assets, income forgone temporarily while searching for a job in the new location – as well as non-pecuniary costs associated with the uprooting of families and the difficulties of settling into an unfamiliar location.

migration elasticity The relative length of time for which impulses or stimuli from the environment must be transmitted to a potential migrant before he/she makes the desired move.

migration field ◊ *in-migration field.*

migration stock effect A similar idea to ◊ *migration chain*, i.e. the tendency of migrants to follow in the footsteps of previous generations of migrants. The existence of a community of earlier migrants in

the destination region not only opens up a channel of information on job opportunities and other aspects of life in their new location for friends and relatives in the 'home area', but may also reduce both the pecuniary and the non-pecuniary costs for new arrivals. ⟐ *passive migrant.*

migratory husbandry ◊ *nomadism.*

mile ◊ *nautical mile, statute mile.*

milieu ◊ *operational milieu.*

military zone A zone or base which one country may control within the boundaries of another as a result of negotiation. ◊ *occupation zone.*

milkshed The area from which an urban centre's liquid milk supply is drawn.

millionaire city A term used to describe any large city with over one million inhabitants. The population of one million is an arbitrary size definition.

milpa ◊ *shifting cultivation.*

mine A term used to describe excavations for working fossil fuels, metalliferous ores and certain non-metalliferous minerals. A distinction is usually made between *mining*, involving underground working, and ◊ *quarrying*, based on surface working, although the terms *deep mining* and *surface mining* are also used. ◊ *adit, advance mining, bell pit, bord and pillar, drift mining, pillar and stall, pit, retreat mining, strip mining, solution mining.* ⟐ *national mining cycle.*

minerals classification Minerals, in the context of economic geography, are ◊ *resources* exploited by mining and therefore include any solid inorganic deposit. Minerals are normally subdivided on the basis of several criteria, hence the categorization may not always be mutually exclusive. Criteria used have included physical/chemical characteristics, end-use, locational characteristics, unit values,

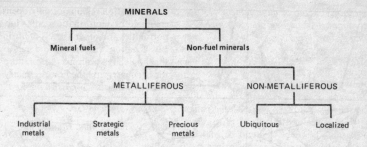

Fig. 105 Minerals classification

degree of processing and scale of working. ◊ Fig. 105 provides a summary classification. *Mineral fuels* (e.g. carbons and hydrocarbons such as coal, oil, natural gas) differ from other minerals in that they are not incorporated in the final product, but (with the obvious exception of petrochemicals) are consumed to provide ◊ *energy*. Within the non-fuel category a further distinction can be made between *metalliferous* and *non-metalliferous minerals*. *Metalliferous minerals* have been subdivided into *ferrous* and *non-ferrous metals* but an alternative division is into *industrial metals* (e.g. iron, copper, aluminium, tin, lead, zinc), *strategic metals* (e.g. antimony, cadmium, cobalt, tungsten, uranium, zirconium) and *precious metals* (e.g. gold, silver, platinum). *Industrial metals* can be further subdivided into the *older major metals* (e.g. copper, tin, lead, zinc), the *light metals* (e.g. aluminium, magnesium, titanium) and the *steel industry metals* (e.g. iron, manganese, nickel).

The term *strategic mineral* is increasingly used of those minerals needed to supply the military, industrial and essential civilian needs of a country during a national emergency which are not available within that country in sufficient quantities to meet that need, and for which substitution possibilities are limited. While many *strategic metals* figure as strategic minerals for any country, the latter can include other minerals, depending on the country's resource base and the nature of its import dependency. For example, during the Second World War, asbestos, mica, graphite and quartz (oscillator quality) were regarded as strategic minerals by the United States.

minifundia Very small peasant subsistence holdings, especially in Latin America.

minimal family ◊ *family*.

minimax ◊ *game theory*.

minimum cost path That route location for which the total cost of a particular layout is the lowest possible between two locations, i.e. the least-cost choice between alternative routes or paths.

minimum distance network A topological approach to the problem of building the 'shortest-distance' route between several centres. There are a number of possible solutions to the problem, as illustrated in ◊ Fig. 106:
(a) The minimum distance network for starting at a particular point and visiting all the other places by the shortest route – the 'Paul Revere' type of network.
(b) The ◊ *travelling salesman* route, which is the shortest cyclic path around all the places.
(c) For a hierarchy, connecting one point directly to each of the other places.

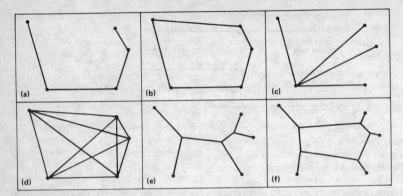

Fig. 106 Minimum distance network

(d) The shortest complete network connecting any point to all other points. This is the least cost solution from the user's view and includes all lines in the previous three solutions.

(e) The shortest set of lines joining all the places (it does not contain any of the previous elements and is the least cost solution from the builder's view).

(f) The general topological arrangement suggested by M. Beckman (the two previous cases are special, limiting cases of this).

minimum noise route The channelling of aircraft departing from and arriving at major international airports along restricted flight paths in order to minimize nuisance from aircraft ⟡ *noise*. It would be more accurate to term such paths minimum population overflown routes. ⟡ *noise and number index*.

minimum requirements technique A method in ⟡ *economic base* analysis, proposed by J. Mattila and W. Thompson, for determining the level of employment in ⟡ *basic activity* in an area. It is a modification of the ⟡ *location quotient* approach, in which base employment is determined as a surplus of actual employment compared to some national proportion, hence its

alternative name – *index of surplus workers*.

Each area has a minimum requirement for every industry which is needed to satisfy local demand. Therefore, in employment terms, a certain proportion of the labour force of each industry in the area would be engaged in producing for local needs and any employment in excess of this can be equated with producing for export. This minimum requirement is found by calculating the number of workers in each industry who are surplus to those necessary to produce for local consumption. The latter ratio is generally assumed to be the share of the industry in the total employment of the nation. Alternatively, a number of areas of similar population size may be examined to establish a norm of employment for an industry (the minimum requirement or smallest representation). The formula to compute surplus workers in a particular industry in one area is:

$$S = e_i - \frac{e_t}{E_t} \times E_i$$

where S = minimum requirement
  e_i = employment in industry i in the area
  e_t = total employment in the area

E_i = employment in industry i in the nation

E_t = total national employment ⬦ *K-value* (2).

minimum user requirements In the study of ⬦ *recreation*, the identification of minimum thresholds or characteristics required of a site before a recreational activity can take place on the site.

minority A group of people resident in a country but different from the majority of the inhabitants by reason of race, religion, language, social customs and national sympathies.

mixed cultivation The ⬦ *cultivation* of two or more different ⬦ *crops* intermingled in the same field, e.g. a mixture of tree and ground crops.

mixed economy An ⬦ *economy* which has some of the characteristics of both ⬦ *capitalism* and ⬦ *state socialism*.

mixed farming A commercial ⬦ *agricultural system* involving the production of both crops and livestock on one farm. The system places a premium on intensive production and emphasizes the maximization of diversity and flexibility but with a high degree of interdependence between crops and livestock. ⬦ *high farming*.

mobility (1) The capacity a person possesses for movement in their daily life. There is a distinction between *potential mobility* (the ease with which a person could travel should they wish to do so) and *actual mobility* (which describes movements undertaken in visiting other people and facilities). Compared to ⬦ *migration* it implies that a definitional boundary has not been crossed even though movement has taken place.
(2) The ease with which ⬦ *factors of production* can be transferred from one type of employment to another. This is specifically ⬦ *factor mobility*.
(3) In the case of ⬦ *labour* the ease of movement between areas has been termed *geographic* or *horizontal* or *lateral mobility*, and between jobs as *vertical* or ⬦ *occupational mobility*. ⬦ *social mobility*.

mobility transition A model, postulated by W. Zelinsky, which parallels ⬦ *demographic*

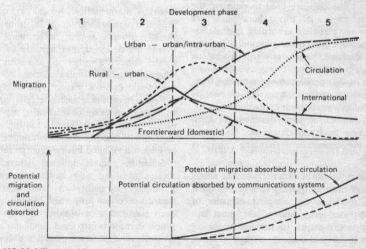

Fig. 107 Mobility transition

transition and considers the whole process of movement in history. It hypothesizes a relationship between different types of movement and general processes of ◊ *urbanization*, ◊ *industrialization* and ◊ *modernization*. Its main components refer to the volumes of international and internal ◊ *migration* (◊ Fig. 107), which vary as society progresses towards its final stage of ◊ *development*. Then, as a result of technological advance and the associated ◊ *time-space convergence*, much of the former volume of migration will be replaced by ◊ *circulation* and communications. ◊◊ *intermetropolitan circulation of elites*.

modal split Or *modal breakdown*. The varying proportions of the total freight and passenger traffic carried by the competing modes of ◊ *transport*.

The various methods used to estimate modal split are all based on the competitiveness of each mode with the others available. This competition depends on (i) the characteristics of the journey to be made, (ii) the characteristics of the person or freight making the journey and (iii) the characteristics of the transport system. Various models are used to estimate the modal choice of trip-makers: these are normally classified according to their relationships with other components of the trip decision, particularly trip generation and trip destination. *Trip generation modal split models* predict trip generations from origins by mode whereas *trip destination modal split models* aim to predict, by mode, the number of trips destined for each location. Such models are used to analyse the consequences of changing transport costs.

mode A statistical term for the value which occurs most frequently in a set of data. The mode is the simplest measure of central tendency and is the most appropriate measure to use when dealing with ◊ *nominal data*. ◊◊ *arithmetic mean*, *median*.

mode of production A central concept of ◊ *Marxian economics* which describes the way productive activities are organized and social life thereby reproduced by society. Four modes are normally recognized:

(i) *Primitive communist*, in which factors of production are owned communally and there is an equal distribution of work and of the products of labour.

(ii) *Slave labour*, in which the slave worker is the means of production to be bought, sold and owned by the slave owner.

(iii) *Feudalism*, in which the peasant is legally tied to the land. The latter, along with a set portion of the produce, is the property of the feudal landowner.

(iv) *Capitalism*, in which the wage-labourer, free to sell his/her labour power for a wage, is separated from ownership of all means of production.

Each mode of production comprises both ◊ *productive forces*, which include the physical means of production, and the social relations of production, the way in which people participate in the productive process.

model A mathematical, logical or mechanical representation of a relationship, theory, process, system or sequence of events, so designed that a study of the model functions either as a means of summarizing the complex relations of the real world or as a way of illustrating a ◊ *theory*. In each case the model is designed to focus on relevant or interesting aspects of the theory or real-world situation and to eliminate incidental information, i.e. to provide a simplified but rational picture.

Scientific model-building therefore creates idealized and structured representations of reality in order to demonstrate certain properties. Models have been classified in a number of ways. A simple division is into *iconic*, *analogue* and *symbolic models*. *Iconic models* are simple scale representations of reality, *analogue models* represent people, events or places as points or lines on maps or diagrams and *symbolic models* convert the original properties of the real world into abstract mathematical expressions.

Alternatively models may be classified as *natural models*, e.g. the wave theory of urban expansion uses a natural physical process to demonstrate the dynamics of urban growth patterns, *experimental models*, e.g. the use of the Varignon frame to determine industrial location, or *mathematical models*, e.g. the mathematical expression of a distance-decay function to represent a spatial pattern.

Descriptive models replicate selected features of an existing situation and attempt to show how it operates; *predictive models* rearrange the structure of a descriptive model so that variables of interest at the end of a causal sequence can be predicted from variables earlier in the sequence; while *planning models* allow alternative courses of action to be evaluated.

Theoretical or *conceptual models* have a high degree of abstraction, while *empirical* or *operational models* are the reverse, with a low level of abstraction and a basis in empirical considerations. Operational models are also predictive models and are either deterministic or have some stochastic element built in. ⟡ *paradigm*, *stochastic process*.

model village ⟡ *planned village*.

modernization A process of ⟡ *social change*, relating ⟡ *economic growth* to ⟡ *social structure*, by which social systems evolve and become more complex. It involves both the application of science and technology to enhance productive efficiency, and changes in social structure and values necessary to support a more sophisticated organization of production. As a temporal process it represents a spatial ⟡ *diffusion* of the characteristics of the Western (apparently more advanced)

societies through less developed societies. The changes inherent in modernization are similar to the preconditions for take-off in the ⟡ *Rostow model*. ⟡ *development*.

modification order ⟡ *revocation order*.

moiety One of two parts into which an estate was divided: not necessarily a half.

mole A jetty or breakwater constructed in the sea so as to protect a ⟡ *harbour* from storms.

moment measures A term used in ⟡ *statistics* to describe the characteristics of a ⟡ *distribution*. There are four moment measures about the ⟡ *arithmetic mean*: the first is the average deviation, which always equals zero, the second is the ⟡ *variance*, the third is the ⟡ *skewness* and the fourth the ⟡ *kurtosis*.

moment of inertia A measure of the dispersion of matter around a point. For any point j in an area the moment of inertia is defined as the sum over the area of each minute segment of area multiplied by the square of the distance separating it from point j, i.e.

$$M = \sum_{i=1}^{n} d_{ij}^2 m_i$$

where d_{ij} = distance between j and the ith point
m_i = the weight (e.g. number of consumers) at point i
n = number of points

In a geographical context it can be used as a ⟡ *shape measure* or an ⟡ *index of spatial efficiency*.

money capital ⟡ *capital* (2).

Mongoloid One of the primary ⟡ *races* of people, accounting for some three-quarters of the world's population. Mongoloids include the peoples of South-East, East and Central Asia and all the American Indians. The characteristics of Mongoloid people are straight black, coarse, hair; a moderately broad nose with low bridge; broad cheekbones; and dark eyes, covered by a flap of skin (epicanthic fold) in the part nearest the nose which gives them their characteristic slant-eyed look. ⬦ *Australoid, Caucasoid, Khoisanoid, Negroid.*

monoculture The ⬦ *cultivation* of a single crop species exclusively. Monoculture can lead to a build-up of soil-borne disease, as ⬦ *crop rotation* is not practised, and to an increase in insect pests. ⬦ *agricultural system.*

monogamy The legal marriage of one man to one woman. ⬦ *polygamy.*

monopolistic competition A market form characterized by a substantial number of buyers and sellers whose products are similar but not perfect substitutes for each other because of ⬦ *product differentiation* and/or ⬦ *geographical market fragmentation.* It is a form of ⬦ *imperfect competition.*

monopoly A market form characterized by a single seller, who has exclusive control over the provision of a good or service. In practice the term is used when a firm produces a sufficiently large proportion of the total output of a good to enable it to control the price at which the good is sold. ⬦ *natural monopoly, spatial monopoly.*

monopoly rent ⬦ *Marxist theory of rent.*

monsoon agriculture A special case of ⬦ *tropical peasant agriculture* characterized by intensive, irrigated cultivation of rice during the hot, wet season. It is common for a dry-season crop to be taken after the rice harvest. ⬦ *agricultural system.*

Monte Carlo method A ⬦ *simulation* technique based on ⬦ *stochastic* processes. It involves setting up a stochastic model of a real situation in which change is simulated by random sampling from a known probability distribution function. Both

spatial and time aspects are included as variables, and each stage in the evolution of a spatial pattern over time is dependent on the preceding stage, with an allowance for the operation of chance factors. The method is used by geographers mainly in solving problems of spatial ⬦ *diffusion,* e.g. migration studies, the progress of epidemics, flows in networks. ⬦ *Markov chain.*

moonlight economy ⬦ *informal economy.*

moor, moorland Terms applied to any tract of unenclosed, waste land, usually found at higher elevations and covered in heather. Moorland provides ⬦ *rough grazing* and is often held in common. The term is also used for similar land which is strictly reserved for shooting. ⬦ *heath.*

moor-burning ⬦ *muirburn.*

morbidity rates Statistics of the diseases and illnesses of a living population. There is no overall index of morbidity (ill-health), but for any disease/illness ⬦ *prevalence rates* and ⬦ *incidence rates* may be calculated.

morcellement The acute fragmentation of agricultural holdings, in which each holding may be made up of a number of scraps of land scattered through many fields. ⬦ *farm fragmentation, parcellement.*

morphological system ⬦ *systems analysis.*

morphology ⬦ *urban morphology.*

morphometry, morphometric analysis The scientific measurement of shape. The emphasis in human geography is on the cognitive description of spatial form, e.g. the shape and pattern of urban areas. Measurements are developed from a geometric, spatial co-ordinate system. ⬦ *shape measures.*

mortality The occurrence of deaths, which along with ⬦ *fertility* and ⬦ *migration* is a determinant of population structure and change. Geographical study has emphasized the spatial pattern of mortality, its role in population change and its relationship to environmental as well as economic and social conditions. ◊ *death rates.*

mortality rates ◊ *death rates.*

mortality table ◊ *life table.*

moshav The first type of Jewish rural settlement in Israel in modern times. Essentially an agricultural village in which organization is co-operative but where the family remains the basic social and economic unit and each farmer owns his own land. ◊ *kibbutz.* ◊ *ejido, kolkhoz, kung-she, sovkhoz, Volksgüter.*

mother settlement In tracing the pattern of settlement expansion in an area a mother settlement is a centre from which a group establishing a new or *daughter settlement* originates. Strong links are maintained between such settlements. ◊ *clone colonization.*

motivation The force that leads people to seek certain goals in relation to their needs.

motorway A ◊ *road,* reserved for certain classes of motor traffic only, which is specially designed to carry heavy volumes of traffic over long distances at high speeds. Motorways have slight gradients, gentle curves and long sight distances with no visual obstructions. Opposing flows of traffic are completely separated by a continuous central reservation and access to the motorway is widely spaced and provided by one of the various forms of motorway interchange which give complete ◊ *grade-separation.* ◊ *classified road.*

movement space The perceived part of the ◊ *environment* in which ◊ *movement* takes place. For the individual it may be subdivided into a core area of frequently travelled space (i.e. in which regular journeys are made), a median area representing

occasionally travelled space, and an extensive cosmological space which is conceived or concept-learnt.

movements Trips made by people. Movements may be classified according to purpose as *essential* (e.g. work trips) or *discretionary* (e.g. leisure trips); or in relation to time as *temporary* (e.g. shopping trips), or *transient* (e.g. going on holiday), or *permanent* (involving change of residence). ◊ *mobility.*

mover–stayer model A generalization of the ◊ *Markov chain* model in which two types of individual are assumed to exist in the population under consideration. The stayer who remains in the same category for the entire period of time (i.e. there is a probability of $1·0$ that there will be no change) and the mover whose changes over time can be described by a Markov chain with a constant transition probability matrix.

moving average Or *running mean.* A method of reducing irregular fluctuations and thereby producing an estimate of the trend in time series data. The moving average is calculated by finding the ◊ *arithmetic means* for successive and overlapping groups of time periods and assigning them as trend values to the midpoint in each time period, as in the table below, for a three-year moving average:

Year	Observation	Three-year moving average
1	a	—
2	b	$\dfrac{a + b + c}{3}$
3	c	$\dfrac{b + c + d}{3}$
4	d	$\dfrac{c + d + e}{3}$
5	e	etc.

muirburn (moor-burning) The deliberate practice of periodically burning off the above-ground vegetation of heather-dominated ◊ *moorland* in Britain with the aim of maintaining it in as nutritive and as productive a condition as possible. For heather the burning is essential to renew the stand before it reaches a mature state. Regeneration after burning is most rapid if the stand is less than twelve to fifteen years old and the fire temperature does not exceed 500°C. Both criteria are met by a ten-year burning cycle.

mulatto A person who is the offspring of one white and one Negro parent. The term is also used loosely for any half-caste resembling a mulatto. ◊ *mestizo, quadroon*.

multicollinearity A statistical term describing the situation in which some or all of the independent variables are very highly intercorrelated.

multi-dimensional scaling A technique developed by psychologists for the analysis of attitude measurement and pattern identification. In addition to its original purpose it has been used by geographers in ◊ *classification* because it provides a procedure for simplifying, yet maintaining, the rank order in a matrix where cell values represent the 'distance apart' of each pair in a set of observations. ◊ *Guttman scale analysis*.

multifinality A systems term that denotes that similar initial conditions can lead to different end effects. ◊ *systems analysis*.

multilateral trade ◊ *Trade* involving several countries, as when a country sells goods in a second country and uses the proceeds to purchase goods from a third country. ◊ *bilateral trade*.

multinational firm A ◊ *firm* that manufactures goods or provides services in several countries while directing operations from a headquarters based in one of the countries. The overseas plants are often established to avoid ◊ *tariff barriers* imposed on ◊ *imports* into the countries concerned, or to take advantage of cheap labour, raw materials and energy. These subsidiary plants are usually incorporated in the country of location. Also referred to as *transnational firms*. ◊ *multiplant firm*.

multinational state A ◊ *state* in which the population includes at least one ethnic ◊ *minority*. The relationship between the national minority and the state can vary from almost complete harmony to a situation where the minority is discriminated against. Thus, for a multinational state to achieve and maintain stability, justice must be seen to be done to the minority group.

Spatial factors, such as the dispersion of the minority throughout the state or whether the minority has a historic homeland absorbed by the larger state, will influence the state–minority relationship. In most multinational states there is an element of ◊ *segregation* in the distribution of national groups, due to historical, social or political causes, which isolates and disadvantages the minority. R. Muir has categorized the forms this segregation can take as: (i) *historical segregation*, as in 'French' Canada, (ii) *community conflict segregation*, as in Northern Ireland and Cyprus, (iii) *socio-economic segregation*, which often shows in ◊ *ghetto* formation, (iv) *institutionalized segregation*, as with ◊ *apartheid* policy in South Africa, and (v) *expulsion and extermination*, involving attempts to get rid of the minority, e.g. the expulsion of Ghanaians from Nigeria in 1984.

multiplant firm A ◊ *firm* which operates production, administration, research and distribution activities at more than one geographical location. Where the locations are in more than one country the multiplant firm is also a ◊ *multinational firm*.

multiple-cropping A technique of growing

two, or three, successive ◊ *crops* on the same plot of land each year. The first crop is harvested before the second is sown. ◊ *catch-crop, double-cropping, polyculture.*

multiple deprivation A measure of an area's or a group's disadvantage in terms of several socio-economic indicators. ◊ *deprivation.*

multiple land use The joint use of a plot of land for two or more purposes, e.g. the use of an area of forest for timber production, recreation and watershed protection. There is a need to distinguish such multiple land use from situations in which there is a mosaic of complementary small units of land specialization and from ◊ *sequent occupance*, i.e. there is a measure of simultaneous use in the time period involved in the concept. The opportunity for and success of multiple land use depends on the ◊ *compatibility* of the different uses and upon the level and quality of ◊ *resource management.* The possibilities of joint use can be extended by ◊ *time zoning*, a practice

which is commonplace where recreational activities are one of the uses. ◊ *common use, land use, multiple use, parallel use.*

multiple nuclei theory One of the three major models of urban land use (◊ *concentric zone theory, sector theory*). The multiple nuclei theory, postulated by C. D. Harris and E. L. Ullman, observes that urban areas have more than one focal point which influence the location of land uses. Thus the land use pattern in many urban areas is built up, not around a single centre, but around several discrete nuclei (◊ Fig. 108). In some urban areas these nuclei existed from the beginning, as subsidiary settlements were swallowed up by the growth of a large urban area. In other cases additional nuclei have appeared as the growth of the urban area has stimulated increased specialization.

Separate nuclei arise because of the differing access requirements of activities, the grouping of complementary activities, the mutually repellant nature of certain

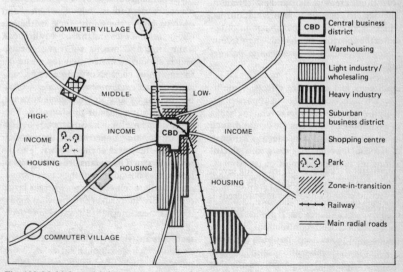

Fig. 108 Multiple nuclei theory

land uses, and the fact that some users cannot afford the rents for the most desirable sites. The number of nuclei depends on the size of the urban area and, besides the ◊ *central business district*, may include heavy and light industrial areas, cultural and entertainment concentrations, suburban business districts and ◊ *science parks*. The residential use of land develops in response to the various nuclei.

multiple occupation A term used of a ◊ *dwelling*, or any part of a dwelling, which is let in lodgings or occupied by members of more than one ◊ *family*. It covers a wide variety of domestic situations, from the well-equipped bed-sitters let to professional people to the communal occupancy of a house by an ◊ *extended family* group.

multiple regression ◊ *regression*.

multiple use In ◊ *resource management*, the planned, shared use of a ◊ *factor of production*, primarily land (◊ *multiple land use*) but also capital in the form of facilities, by several different activities and interests. The shared use may be simultaneous, where there is perfect ◊ *compatibility* between the activities, or phased, where ◊ *time zoning* is practised. ◊◊ *common use*, *parallel use*.

multipliers and multiplier effects A multiplier is a numerical coefficient applied originally in ◊ *macroeconomics* to relate a change in a component of aggregate demand, such as investment, to a consequent change in ◊ *national income*. It shows how fluctuations in, say, the amount of investment, although small in relation to the national income, are capable of generating fluctuations of much larger magnitude in total employment and income. It applies equally to expansion and contraction. The application of the concept has been extended to other spatial scales, and multipliers have become increasingly important as a tool of regional analysis for summarizing the

intended and unintended consequences of an action.

A multiplier is the ratio of the direct, indirect and induced changes of an action on a regional or national economy to the direct initial change itself. Its measurement may be either in terms of jobs created/lost, i.e. an *employment multiplier*, or in terms of the increased/decreased money value of the changes in economic activity, i.e. an *income multiplier*. For example, the opening of a new manufacturing plant in a region creates directly new jobs in that plant. Indirect effects also occur in industries supplying components and other inputs to that plant. As these other firms increase their workforce (i.e. indirect employment) there will be further rounds of expenditure by their new workers, generating more jobs elsewhere in service activities, etc. (i.e. induced employment). Multiplier effects describe this cumulative process whereby a given change sets in motion a chain reaction of further growth (or decline).

In regional analysis simple *regional multipliers* are derived from ◊ *economic base analysis* but, increasingly, they are based on ◊ *input–output analysis*. Multipliers summarize and predict short-run effects, and it should be noted that the value of the multiplier changes over time for a given area, e.g. an *employment multiplier* would be affected by any technological advance which improved labour productivity. The value of the multiplier also depends on the size of the area under study: the smaller the area the lower the multiplier. This is not unexpected because more of the effects leak across boundaries in the case of small areas and are felt elsewhere, whereas large regions are more likely to provide many more services internally. ◊◊ *knock-on effect*.

multipurpose trip A single ◊ *trip* made by a person which accomplishes two or more purposes. Such trips, also called *linked trips*, are likely to have more than one destination. They yield savings in time and distance travelled and provide a basis for the ⟡ *agglomeration* of certain functions in particular centres.

multivariate analysis The statistical analysis of the relationships between more than two variables. ⟡ *factor analysis, principal components analysis.*

N

nation A group of people who are conscious of their own ◊ *nationality*, are closely associated with each other by common cultural characteristics, values and aspirations and are identified with a specific ◊ *territory*. Such a group wishes to maintain its cultural unity free from political domination and is usually organized as a separate independent ◊ *state*. However, a state may constitute two or more national groups. Each nation is unique, with the characteristics held in common, e.g. language, racial origin, religion, varying from case to case. ◊ *nation-state, nationalism*.

nation-state An independent ◊ *state* in which all (or most) of the inhabitants share a general sense of national cohesion, subscribing to a set of common values. Typically, the nation-state occupies a clearly defined ◊ *territory* and is the ultimate geographical realization of ◊ *nationalism*. ◊ *nation*.

national income The value of the flow of goods and services becoming available to a nation during a given period of time, usually one year. National income is measured in three ways: (i) by the *expenditure approach*, i.e. the total expenditure on ◊ *consumer goods* and on ◊ *investment goods* during a year; (ii) by the *income approach*, i.e. the total of all incomes (wages, rent, interest, profits) derived from working in the production of goods and services during a year; and (iii) by the *product approach*, i.e. the total ◊ *value added* of all goods and services produced during a year. ◊ *Gross Domestic Product, Gross National Product*.

national mining cycle A five-stage model generalizing the pattern of mineral production within nations:
(1) The development of mining to maximize the export of crude ore.
(2) Maximum production in terms of the number of mines in operation.
(3) The development of secondary processing and the operation of the maximum number of smelters.
(4) The maximization of metal production from domestic ores.
(5) The further expansion of metal production and/or exhaustion of domestic ores, bringing a reliance on imported ores as the main source of supply to the smelting industries.

This model was developed at a time, the 1920s, when countries such as the United Kingdom had reached stage 5 but could still control the resources of colonies at stages 1 and 2. Today importing countries are much less able to control the mineral resources of exporting countries and, therefore, a further stage is proposed:
(6) The use of advanced technology to exploit deep and perhaps low-grade indigenous deposits.

National Park National Parks vary in status from country to country but, generally, they are extensive tracts of ◊ *landscape* of great natural beauty and interest which are set aside for the protection and ◊ *conservation* of scenery, flora and fauna, largely for public enjoyment (open-air recreation) but also because of their scientific and historic importance. Once designated, National Parks are placed under some form of legislative or regulatory control.

Thus in England and Wales (◊ Fig. 2),

under the 1949 National Parks and Access to the Countryside Act, a National Park was defined as 'an extensive area of beautiful and relatively wild country, in which, for the nation's benefit and by appropriate national decision and action: (a) the characteristic landscape beauty is strictly preserved; (b) access and facilities for public open-air enjoyment are amply provided; (c) wild life and buildings and places of architectural and historic interest are suitably protected; and (d) established farming is effectively maintained'.

At the international level the definition suggested by the International Union for the Conservation of Nature requires a relatively large area which contains one or several ◊ *ecosystems* not materially altered by human occupation and exploitation, where plant and animal species, geomorphological sites and habitats are of special scientific, educative and recreational interest, or which contains natural landscape of great beauty. It also requires that the highest competent authority of the country has passed legislation to prevent or eliminate exploitation or occupation and to protect the ecological, geomorphological and aesthetic features of the park. Visitors are allowed only under carefully controlled conditions for inspirational, educative, cultural and recreational purposes. ◊◊ *country park, forest park*.

national plan A government economic plan which lays down the proposed pattern of economic development (investment, production and consumption levels) over a number of years to come. India and the USSR use a succession of national plans covering five-year periods. Such plans suffer the disadvantage of rigidity, proving to be not easily adapted to changing circumstances. ◊ *planning*.

national product ◊ *Gross National Product*.

national road network A primary ◊ *network* of trunk ◊ *roads*, whose function is to provide for long-distance, high-speed, interurban traffic, and a secondary network of principal through roads, which provide for easy access between neighbouring towns.

nationalism The political expression of nationhood or aspiring nationhood, which reflects the consciousness of belonging to a ◊ *nation*. R. Muir has proposed a classification of types of nationalism: (i) *Ante-state nationalism*, in which a group develops a strong national consciousness before the establishment of its own ◊ *nation-state*, e.g. the Basques. (ii) *Post-state nationalism*, which has developed from the integration of diverse cultural strands in an arbitrary political state, e.g. Switzerland. (iii) *Third World nationalism*, in which peoples who have come together to resist ◊ *colonialism* have then continued to work to create a new state, e.g. most black African countries. (iv) *Pan-nationalism*, in which groups, larger and less integrated than nations, have come together to promote a common objective, e.g. the Organization of African Unity. (v) *Community conflict nationalism*, in which internal conflict divides a nation, with a measure of cultural cohesion, into subgroups, e.g. the Ulster Catholics. (vi) *Totalitarian nationalism*, in which a party, often a minority, seizes power and claims to embody the will of that nation, e.g. dictatorships.

nationalization The act of taking land, property, industry, etc. into ◊ *state ownership*. ◊◊ *public sector*.

natural area A natural area is conceived as a spatial unit, limited by natural boundaries enclosing a homogeneous population with a characteristic moral order, which is the result of unplanned urban growth. It is distinguished by its physical individuality and internal uniformity and by the social, economic and cultural characteristics of its residents. Its existence stems from the fact that households with similar characteristics are treated similarly by the economic process of competition. The outcome of that process is a pattern of ◊ *segregation* in the form of a mosaic of natural areas, each delimited by de facto boundaries such as main roads, railways, parks and rivers, which relate local social organization to the physical structure of the urban area. ◊◊ *ghetto*.

natural attitude Phenomenological term to describe an individual's unquestioned acceptance of the things and experiences of his/her daily living. ◊◊ *attitude*.

natural change component ◊ *natural increase*.

natural environment ◊ *environment*.

natural hazard A natural event, e.g. earthquake, volcanic eruption, flood, avalanche, lightning, high wind, which is perceived by people as a ◊ *risk* to life and property. The risk cannot be conceived independently of the people afflicted. For example, floods would not represent a hazard if people did not use floodplains. Natural hazards can be short-term in duration, e.g. a bolt of lightning, or a continuous component, e.g. ultra-violet light in high-altitude areas. In recent years there has been a recognition of another group of *environmental hazards* created or exacerbated by the action of people in polluting the atmosphere, rivers, lakes and oceans. ◊◊ *disaster preparedness, disaster prevention, hazard perception*.

natural increase (of population) The rate of natural increase of a population in a given area is the excess of births over deaths. Natural increase (or its reverse natural decrease) forms the *natural change component* in the ◊ *population equation*.

natural monopoly A situation in which competition among producers, although possible, is deemed undesirable for technical reasons or reasons of public safety, e.g. the provision of potable water. ◊ *monopoly*.

natural rate of unemployment ◊ *unemployment*.

natural region A ◊ *uniform region* based on features of the physical environment (topography, climate, vegetation). The area contains within its borders relatively uniform and distinctive structural and climatic features. ◊◊ *pays concept*.

natural resources ◊ *resources*.

natural subsidy A concept in ◊ *resource management* which argues that people are the continuing beneficiaries of a subsidy in the form of work performed by natural forces of which they take advantage. How large a subsidy people derive depends on their ability to use the results of the work of nature. The natural subsidy is not uniformly distributed throughout the world.

natural turnover ◊ *labour turnover*.

natural wastage ◊ *labour turnover*.

naturalization (1) The procedure by which a foreigner or alien is admitted to the position and rights of citizenship of the country in which they now reside permanently.
(2) The process by which plants and animals, introduced to places where they are not indigenous, adapt and flourish under conditions similar to their native ones.

nature conservation order Under the 1981 Wildlife and Countryside Act the Secretary of State for the Environment in England (in Scotland the Secretary of State for Scotland and in Wales the Secretary of State for Wales) has the power to make a nature conservation order in respect of land for the purpose of ensuring the survival of certain plant and animal species, of complying with an international obligation or of conserving species or features of national importance. An order will specify those operations which are likely to cause damage and on which the Nature Conservancy Council's agreement is required. Compensation is payable where there is any depreciation in the value of agricultural land as a result of making such an order. ⟡ *Site of Special Scientific Interest.*

nature reserve An area of land and/or water designated as having protected status for purposes of preserving certain botanical, zoological, geological or physiographical features. Reserves are managed primarily to safeguard these features and provide opportunities for research into the problems underlying the management of natural sites and of vegetation and animal populations. Regulations are normally imposed controlling public access and disturbance.

In Great Britain it is one of the duties of the Nature Conservancy Council to establish and manage *national nature reserves* and it has powers to acquire land or to enter into agreements with landowners in order to establish such reserves. In addition, *local nature reserves* may be designated by local authorities and *forest nature reserves* by the Forestry Commission, both in consultation with the Nature Conservancy Council; and there also exist many, smaller, private nature reserves established by voluntary conservation bodies. ◇ *conservation.* ⟡ *Site of Special Scientific Interest.*

nature trail A guided trail, designed to explain to the general public a piece of countryside, the type of soil, flora, fauna, etc. Such trails may be self-guiding, using either explanatory notices set up at intervals or numbered boards referring to a printed leaflet: in other cases parties may be led by a demonstrator or warden.

nautical mile A unit of measurement used in navigation, theoretically equal to the length of one minute of arc on a great circle drawn on a sphere having the same area as the Earth. It equals 1·1516 ◇ *statute miles.* Since the earth is a geoid, a sphere with flattening at the poles, a minute of latitude varies. The British Admiralty and merchant marine have standardized on one minute of arc at 48° latitude, i.e. the 6,080 ft (1,853·18 m) nautical mile, whereas all other countries use a nautical mile of 1,852 m (6,076·12 ft) based on one minute of arc at 45°. 1 English nautical mile = 1·00064 international nautical miles.

nearest neighbour analysis A statistical test developed by the ecologists P. J. Clark and F. C. Evans to describe plant patterns and used by geographers as a method of comparing an observed point pattern with theoretical random patterns. The method consists of measuring the straight-line distance between every point and its nearest neighbour in the study area, and then calculating the mean nearest neighbour distance as:

$$\text{Observed mean nearest neighbour distance} = \bar{d}_o = \sum_{i=1}^{r} \frac{d_i}{r}$$

where d_i = distance between point i and its nearest neighbour

r = number of points

$\bar{d}_o$ is then compared with an expected mean nearest neighbour distance, $\bar{d}_e$, for an infinite number of points in a randomly distributed pattern, i.e.

$$\text{Nearest neighbour statistic} = R = \frac{\bar{d}_o}{\bar{d}_e}$$

The nearest neighbour statistic or index can vary in value from 0 (completely clustered), through 1·0 (random) and 2·0 (uniform grid), to 2·149 (uniform triangular). ⟡ *inter-neighbour interval, quadrat analysis, reflexive nearest neighbour analysis.*

necrogeography The geographical study of cemeteries, including the size, shape, number, site, situation and internal design, as well as the analysis of headstone data.

necropolis Literally the 'city of the dead', but the term is sometimes applied to cemeteries.

negative binomial distribution A compound and generalized ◊ *frequency distribution* used as a norm for assessing whether a given distribution could have been the result of a clustering process that includes a random element, i.e. negative binomial ~ Poisson ∧ logarithmic (or gamma). Thus the negative binomial distribution is given by a ◊ *Poisson distribution* as the basic probability law governing the spacing of observations within each quadrat and the logarithmic (or gamma) term is the generalizing distribution or the way in which the density at which the Poisson process is operating from quadrat to quadrat. The negative binomial distribution has been used in modelling ◊ *diffusion* processes where true contagion exists, e.g. where the original settlers in an area locate at random and later settlers choose locations near to the earlier settlers.

negentropy A measure of the order or organization in a ◊ *system*. Open systems tend to be negentropic, decreasing in ◊ *entropy* and increasing in the complexity of their structure.

Negroid One of the five primary ◊ *races* or people. Their characteristics are: a dark brown to black skin pigmentation, which serves as a protection against the sun; a broad nose with a low bridge; thick everted lips; dark eyes; tight curly hair; and long limbs. The majority of Negroes have their origins in Africa. ◊◊ *Australoid, Caucasoid, Khoisanoid, Mongoloid.*

neighbourhood (1) A district, normally in a city, identified as a social unit by the face-to-face relationships between its residents. It represents a spatially bounded ◊ *community* and, while its boundaries are imprecise, outsiders are more aware of its existence than the residents. ◊◊ *balanced neighbourhood.*
(2) As a physical planning unit, ◊ *neighbourhood unit.*

neighbourhood centre The lowest order recognized among urban shopping centres. It serves a local area, providing mostly day-to-day requirements such as ◊ *convenience goods*, hence the alternative term *convenience centre*. Typical functions include a ◊ *supermarket*, launderette, barber, dry cleaner, greengrocer, etc., involving 2,750–9,290 m² (30,000–100,000 ft²) of retailing space and serving a catchment area of 5,000–50,000 people. ◊◊ *community centre, regional centre.*

neighbourhood effect That local social influence which is the result of a person's attitudes and activities being conditioned by his/her local ◊ *social environment*. Thus an individual's behaviour is conditioned not only by perceived self-interest but also by the opinions and images of other people in their ◊ *neighbourhood* with whom they interact. The idea has been used by geographers in the analysis of a wide range of distance-contact relationships, especially in the ◊ *diffusion* process, e.g. the spread of innovations and information, the distribution of benefits from a centrally provided public good (◊ *tapering*) and the explanation of voting behaviour. It has also been extended to account for the mutual support and decline of property values in a neighbourhood. Thus the greater the proportion of obsolescent buildings in a neighbourhood the less desirable is that district as a location for new activities and the more difficult it is to sustain the value of sound buildings or redevelop individual sites.

neighbourhood evolution Urban ◊ *neighbourhoods* exhibit a cyclical pattern of change in which five stages have been recognized:
(1) Rural land is converted to residential use, with development in the form of single-family houses (◊ *land conversion process*). A long period of stability follows.
(2) There is further building, particularly multi-family structures, to meet increased

demand. Higher densities of development are more profitable.

(3) As population and density continues to increase the conversion and downgrading of use of existing buildings takes place. The residential status of the neighbourhood declines as a consequence.

(4) A process of thinning-out reduces population and density. There is a decrease in demand for accommodation, with only the elderly heads of families staying put.

(5) Buildings are demolished and the area is redeveloped. ⟡ *invasion–succession concept*, *residential population cycle*.

neighbourhood space ⟡ *activity space*.

neighbourhood unit A concept in modern town planning, attributed to C. Perry, of a residential area which has been planned as a wholly or partly self-contained unit, often with some degree of architectural unity in its design. It is based on both sociological ideas of ⟡ *community* and the efficient provision of services. Neighbourhood units provide an ⟡ *environment* for family and community life in which all residents are within convenient access of a primary school, a local shopping centre (⟡ *neighbourhood centre*) and open playspaces. Typically such a unit has its own network of distributor roads and pedestrian ways and is insulated from the main through traffic of a town. ⟡ *Radburn layout*.

nemoriculture A primitive stage of human culture – food-gathering (fruit, roots, etc.) from forest glades, etc.

neobehaviourism A perspective on behaviour which views a human being not as a simple, reflex machine but as a person with an active cognitive capacity who seeks out information. ⟡ *behaviourism*.

neocapitalism The form of ⟡ *capitalism* dominated by corporations, conglomerates and ⟡ *multinational firms*, and also involving large-scale government intervention.

neoclassical economics A refinement and extension of the ideas of the formative, classical school of ⟡ *economics* and their application to the current operation of the market mechanism in guiding economic activity in modern capitalist society towards optimal resource allocation in terms of maximization of social welfare.

neocolonialism A pejorative term describing the tendency of the powerful ⟡ *states* with developed economies to retain or gain influence over the economies and societies of independent developing countries (often former ⟡ *colonies*). The domination is achieved in a variety of ways and, although the motives are often political, the weapons are economic, involving trade and investment, e.g. foreign industrial and finance capital, special commercial arrangements. ⟡ *colonialism*, *economic imperialism*.

Neolithic An archaeological term (from the Greek for *new stone age*) used to describe the culture of the middle post-glacial period when people had extended their ability to make stone implements to include grinding and polishing. In addition, a major feature of the Neolithic was the development of an economy wholly or partly dependent on the cultivation of crops and the domestication of animals – described by V. G. Childe as the *Neolithic Revolution* – as well as the beginnings of various home crafts, e.g. pottery. In Britain the Neolithic lasted from approximately 5200 BP until the ⟡ *Bronze Age*, c.4000 BP (2000 BC). ⟡ *Mesolithic, Palaeolithic*.

neo-Malthusianism The up-dating of the doctrines of the ⟡ *Malthusian theory of population* and their application to present-day conditions.

neonatal mortality ⟡ *infant mortality*.

neoplantation A highly mechanized ⟡ *plantation*.

neotechnic A term used by Lewis Mumford to denote the last of three technological phases of urban–industrial development (✧ *eotechnic, paleotechnic*). The neotechnic phase is characterized by technical innovations in industry, agricultural and energy resources, and transportation (e.g. electricity, internal combustion engines, alloys and synthetic materials). Manufacturing is organized along the lines of corporate ✧ *capitalism* and there is ✧ *mass-production* for mass markets.

nesting A topological term used to describe the way in which ✧ *networks* of different modules can fit one into another, e.g. in ✧ *central place theory* the tendency for hexagonal market areas of lower-order centres to 'nest' or be included in the larger hexagonal market areas of higher-order places. The term is also used to describe sampling within the designated subdivisions of a network.

net present value method A commonly used method for evaluating an investment project whereby future costs and benefits are discounted to present-day values in order to determine whether or not the project is worthwhile. ✧ *discount rate*.

net register tonnage A measure of the passenger- and cargo-carrying and, therefore, earning capacity of a ship. It is the ✧ *gross register tonnage* less deductions for crew living space, stores, engines and ballast. Harbour and docking charges are normally assessed on net register tonnage. ✧ *deadweight tonnage, displacement tonnage, tonnage*.

net reproduction rate A population index, originally known as the ✧ *Kuczynski rate*, which compares the number of female births with the number of potential mothers in a population (i.e. women aged fifteen to forty-nine) and which is weighted to allow for the chances of female babies surviving to the reproductive years. It therefore measures the average number of daughters who would be born to a female during her reproductive years if, throughout her lifetime, she were subject to the age-specific ✧ *fertility rates* and the ✧ *life table* death rates of the period under consideration. A net reproduction rate greater than 1·0 will mean that ultimately the population will increase, and less than 1·0 that it will ultimately decrease. ✧ *reproduction rate*.

network The actual physical system of links between points along which movement can take place. Such networks may be visible or invisible, tangible or intangible. In human geography the term is most commonly used to denote a ✧ *transport network*, either of permanent track (roads, railways, canals) or of scheduled services (airline, bus, train). It can be extended to cover other types of line pattern, such as telephone links.

Whatever their physical nature, all networks may be represented in the form of a graph (✧ *graph theory*). Such graphs simply indicate the existence of links without reference to their true length and direction. The three important elements in any network are its ✧ *nodes*, its ✧ *edges* and its sub-graphs (independent or unconnected parts). These serve as a basis for calculating summary measures of ✧ *connectivity*. ✧ *accessibility index, alpha index, beta index, cyclomatic number, dispersal index, gamma index, König number, Shimbel index*. ✧ *branching network, capacitated network, circuit network, minimum distance network, network density, network deviousness, network shape index, spanning tree, tree*.

network density The length of route per unit area. It has implications for ✧ *accessibility*.

network development model ✧ *transport network development*.

network deviousness The discrepancy between the lengths of the actual routes in a ◊ *network* and the straight-line distance between the places linked up. For any pair of places on the network it can be measured by the ◊ *detour index*.

network shape index A measure of the extent of a transport ◊ *network*.

$$\text{Network shape index} = \pi = \frac{M_T}{M_d}$$

where M_T = total mileage of the transport network
M_d = total mileage of the network's diameter (i.e. length of edges in the shortest path between the most distant nodes)

In practice the values for the index vary considerably and it is sensitive to the economic state of transport networks. For their railway networks, developed countries may have indices approaching 30, underdeveloped countries about 1·0.

Neustadt ◊ *bastide town*.

neutral zone A part, or even the whole, of a country which has imposed on it, either voluntarily or by an external power, restrictions on the freedom of action of the ◊ *state* in matters of foreign policy and defence. Certain states, e.g. Sweden, have freely adopted a policy of neutrality (except where their own ◊ *sovereignty* is threatened), while other countries are required to be neutral as a condition of their continued existence, e.g. Austria since 1955 under the terms of the Allied peace treaty. Where only part of a country is involved, a neutral zone is often a *demilitarized area*, which acts as a buffer between antagonistic neighbours. A neutral zone may also exist in the special case where two neighbouring states cannot agree on a ◊ *boundary* between their two territories.

new town A free-standing urban centre planned on a completely new site. While such developments have taken place for many centuries, e.g. the ◊ *bastide* towns of the 12th–14th centuries, and have been attempted in many countries, e.g. the USA since the late 1920s, the term new town is primarily associated with post-1945 developments in Great Britain. These developments, part of a wider policy for the distribution of population and employment, were a response to the problems of urban congestion and represented a logical extension of the ◊ *garden city* concept. British new towns were conceived as self-contained, socially balanced towns planned to receive ◊ *overspill* population and employment.

Changes in the planning philosophy underlying the British new towns are reflected in a three-fold classification – Mark I, II and III developments – based on differences in plan form. The *Mark I* new towns comprise the first fourteen to be designated, between 1946 and 1950 (e.g. Crawley, East Kilbride, Stevenage), and they most epitomize the garden city ideals. The plan-form emphasizes a nucleated but spacious urban area, with residents allocated to distinct ◊ *neighbourhood units*, developed with low-density housing. Industry is concentrated in one or two locations and well segregated from the neighbourhoods. There is generous provision of open space, and the road system is designed with curvilinear primary distributor roads. Planned size varied from 25,000–80,000 (although some targets have been raised).

The *Mark II* new towns, designated between 1955 and 1966 (e.g. Cumbernauld, Washington), reflected adjustments in plan-form to cater for the impact of the motor car. There was a tendency towards the use of a more compact, linear shape, implying higher densities, and greater emphasis on the transport network because of the greater centralization of facilities. Target populations ranged from 80,000–120,000.

The *Mark III* new towns, designated since 1967 (e.g. Milton Keynes, Peterborough), are distinctive in their plan-forms because of the large urban fabric that existed before their designation. Again prominence is given to the development of the transport network, but all, except Milton Keynes, have oriented their activity patterns around existing town centres. Target populations are generally of the order of 250,000, but 'starting' population varies from 75,000 to 150,000. ⬦ *expanded town*.

New World A term commonly applied to that part of the world not discovered by Europeans before 1492. It comprises the western hemisphere, i.e. the continents of North and South America and the islands of the Caribbean. ⬦ *Old World*.

nieuwstad ⬦ *bastide town*.

night population In city centres which have lost their residential population, the small population of caretakers, night watchmen and other nightshift workers who are the only people remaining there at night. ⬦ *day population*.

night-soil Manure or excrement, especially human excreta. The term is derived from the old custom of removing it from cesspits under cover of darkness, which is still the practice in some eastern towns.

no-rent margin ⬦ *economic margins of cultivation*.

nodality Property conferred on a location by the convergence of established routes. ⬦ *centrality*.

nodal region An area under the economic and social domination of an urban centre. Nodal regions are delimited on the basis of ⬦ *spatial interaction* and emphasize functional ⬦ *interdependence* between the different locations within the area. In terms of links between locations:

$$\frac{\text{Internal (within region)}}{\text{External (between region)}} = \text{maximum}$$

Boundaries are not always clear-cut, and nodal regions may overlap and interpenetrate. Also known as *functional region* or *polarized region*. ⬦ *uniform region*.

node (1) A topological term for a termination or intersection point on a ⬦ *network*. Also known as a *vertex*. Nodes are connected by ⬦ *edges*.
(2) In urban imagery, a strategic point into which an observer can enter and which is an intensive focus to or from which he/she is travelling. ⬦ *landmark*.
(3) A term used generally to describe any cluster of social, economic or political activity which functions as a focus for activities at other locations.

noise (1) Unwanted ⬦ *sound*. Sound may be socially undesirable because it intrudes on, disturbs or annoys people, or medically undesirable – very high levels of sound can cause hearing damage. Noise is therefore regarded as a form of ⬦ *pollution*. ⬦ *decibel*, *noise control*, *noise indices*.
(2) A term carried over from communication theory into statistics to describe the uncontrolled natural or random variation in a data set. It is used to explain ⬦ *variance* after the effects of the known variables have been accounted for.

noise and number index (**NNI**) An index of air traffic ⬦ *noise*. Aircraft noise, consisting of a build-up to a peak level and then a fall-off, occurring at intervals, is claimed to be a most pervasive and disturbing source of noise. In social surveys around London (Heathrow) Airport the annoyance caused by air traffic was found to depend on the peak perceived noise levels and the number of aircraft heard in a given period. The Noise and Number Index is based on these two factors:

$$NNI = \overline{PNdB} + 15 \log N - 80$$

where $\overline{PNdB}$ = logarithmic average of aircraft noise in perceived decibels
N = number of aircraft heard on an average summer day between 06.00 and 18.00 hours GMT

80 is the estimated zero annoyance level and the justification of 15 log N to allow for the effects of the number of aircraft on annoyance is purely empirical. Representative levels of N N I are:

60: close to airports where there are many overflights at low altitude, interfering with sleep and conversation in ordinary houses.

45: very busy flight paths from airports, interfering with conversation in houses.

35: overflying, typically irregular, at noise levels which are noticeable and occasionally intrusive in houses.

Maps of exposure to aircraft noise, based on N N I, have been used to find ♢ *minimum noise routes*. ♢ *noise indices*.

noise control The adoption of measures to reduce the incidence and impact of ♢ *noise*. Noise control can be attempted in any one, or all, of three areas: (i) at the source of noise generation (e.g. the fitting of silencers to motor vehicles or mufflers on pneumatic drills), (ii) along the path between the source and the listener (i.e. noise screening via the erection of noise barriers and the use of sound insulation such as double glazing), and (iii) at the listener (e.g. the use of ear protectors to avoid noise-induced hearing loss).

Laws, regulations setting standards and zoning have been the major instruments of noise control to date. ♢♢ *pollution control*.

noise indices Measures which relate the disturbing qualities of ♢ *noise* (loudness, variation over time, etc.) to the average subjective response of individuals. Various indices have been suggested, some specific to particular types of noise. All, with the exception of aircraft noise, are related to the ♢ *decibel A-scale*, which has gained wide acceptance as giving reasonable correlations with subjective estimates of the loudness of many sounds. Such indices are used in planning residential developments, motorways, airports, etc. Indices such as the ♢ *noise-rating number* and the ♢ *speech interference level* have gained a measure of general acceptance; the ♢ *corrected noise level* is used for industrial premises; the ♢ *noise and number index* for aircraft noise; and various ones for road traffic (♢ *traffic noise index*).

noise-rating number A ♢ *noise index* used in ♢ *environmental impact assessment* to indicate acceptable standards under a variety of conditions, e.g. the level of noise that can be tolerated in a library is much lower than that in a factory. The noise-rating number varies with frequency, but at 1,000 hertz it is equal to the noise level expressed in ♢ *decibels* with respect to that level which represents the threshold of human hearing.

noise zone, noise abatement zone A zone which enables planning authorities to maintain a satisfactory ♢ *noise* climate by preventing gradual additions to the ambient noise level. In such zones, defined along heavily trafficked roads, no building may be allowed (or special planning permission may be required). In noise abatement zones, designated under the 1974 Control of Pollution Act, the problem of an existing noise nuisance can be tackled by serving an abatement notice (once it has been established that a nuisance exists). ♢♢ *noise control*.

nomadism A wandering form of life in search of subsistence, both of food (in the form of fruit and roots) and of ♢ *pasture* for livestock, with little or no reliance on sedentary ♢ *cultivation*. Nomadism therefore involves the repeated shifting of the nomads' habitat, the essence normally being movement due to the needs of their livestock. Nomadic societies are usually found in the natural grasslands of arid and semi-arid regions where conditions are too harsh to support settled agriculture and pasture for livestock has to be sought in different places at different times of year. It is basically a self-sufficient system, movement often exhibiting a regular circular pattern. Nomads travel in small groups based on tribal or ⬦ *extended family* units. Nomadism supports about 0·4–0·8 persons/km² (1–2/mile²).

True nomads, who build no dwellings and practise no agriculture, should be distinguished from semi-nomads, who move only during the dry season, and from mere wanderers, who may be collectors, like the aboriginal Australians, or practise some special craft, like the gipsies. ⬦ *pastoralism*. ⬦ *transhumance*.

nominal scale, nominal data A form of ⬦ *measurement* in which each observation is placed into one of a number of different categories depending on the presence or absence of recognizable attributes. Hence also referred to as *categorical data*. A nominal scale has categories which are mutually exclusive and also exhaustive: all observations within each category are treated the same, e.g. a person's sex is either male or female. It is therefore a qualitative, non-parametric scale. Observations in each category may be counted and the tally represented by a number, hence also *counted data*. Much geographical data is in this form. ⬦ *interval scale*, *ordinal scale*, *ratio scale*.

nomograph ⬦ *ternary diagram*.

nomothetic approach A law-seeking method concerned with the establishment and verification of generalizations about phenomena. In human geography it has been the basis of the generally accepted ⬦ *paradigm* since the ⬦ *quantitative revolution*, in which repeated patterns are sought and attempts made to develop universal statements of ⬦ *law* and explanation in terms of general theories. ⬦ *idiographic approach*.

non-basic activities ⬦ *Economic base theory* divides the economic activities in a region into two groups – ⬦ *basic activities* and non-basic activities. Non-basic activities are those economic activities whose final product is used within the region, i.e. that proportion of activities in the region dependent upon markets internal to the region. Such activities facilitate the circulation of money within the region. Two components are sometimes recognized – consumer-serving activities and producer-serving ones. Also known as *city-filling activities*, *city-serving activities*, *endogenous activities*, *local industries*, *passive industries*, *residentiary activities*, *service activities*.

non-conforming use The allocation of land for specific purposes under a planning system can be achieved via ⬦ *zoning*. Where zoning is applied to an area of mixed development and the permitted uses relate only to certain activities found in the area, the other activities are non-conforming uses. Thus, if an area of mixed industrial–residential development is zoned for future residential use, existing industrial premises become non-conforming uses, which, in time, will need to be relocated.

non-cryophilous crop ⬦ *cryophilous crop*.

non-ecumene ⬦ *ecumene*.

non-parametric statistics A set of procedures used in distribution-free ⬦ *significance tests* and not dependent on the form of the ⬦ *frequency distribution* of the data or statistical population, distribution-free meaning that they ignore information on the pattern or scatter of observations which reflect the distribution displayed by the population. They test whether the populations are identical. Non-parametric statistical tests are essential for use with data obtained at ⬦ *nominal* and ⬦ *ordinal scales* of measurement and may be advisable in other cases of higher-order measurement where there is uncertainty as to whether the parent population is normally distributed. Such tests have a lower-power efficiency than ◇ *parametric tests*, i.e. they are less sensitive in detecting the effect of an independent variable on the dependent variable. Examples of such tests include ◇*chi-square test*, ◇ *Kendall's tau*, ◇ *Kruskal–Wallis H test*, ◇ *Mann–Whitney U test*, ◇ *phi coefficient*, ◇ *sign test*, ◇ *Spearman rank correlation coefficient*, ◇ *Wilcoxon test*.

non-place community, non-place realm A non-place community or *urban realm* is a heterogeneous group of people interacting from widely scattered places throughout the world. Conventional ◇ *distances* are unimportant and ◇ *accessibility* rather than proximity is the necessary characteristic of ◇ *place*. As accessibility and communication improve, so cohabitation of the same place is not necessary for interaction, and consequently random and apparently untidy and unexpected arrangements of work and homes can really be very efficient. Specialized professionals, particularly, maintain intimate contact webs with fellow specialists wherever they may be (◇ *inter-*

metropolitan circulation of elites). ◇ *place community*.

non-renewable resources ◇ *resources*.

non-specific capital ◇ *capital* (2).

non-specific factor ◇ *factors of production*.

non-utilitarian resource A ◇ *resource* which has social rather than practical value, e.g. a society enjoying a relatively high standard of living will generally place greater value on the need for clean air and water and access to unspoiled recreation areas than a society faced with food shortages, widespread unemployment and lower material standards of living.

Norfolk system ◇ *alternate agriculture*.

normal-aged forest A ◇ *forest* composed of trees in a series of age classes in proportions which allow ◇ *sustained yield* felling under any given forest management system.

normal deviate For any observation, the deviation from the ◇ *mean* expressed in terms of the ◇ *standard deviation*.

normal distribution A hypothetical ◇ *frequency distribution* which possesses perfect symmetry about the three measures of

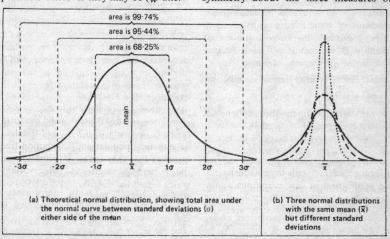

(a) Theoretical normal distribution, showing total area under the normal curve between standard deviations (σ) either side of the mean

(b) Three normal distributions with the same mean (x̄) but different standard deviations

Fig. 109 Normal distribution

central tendency (its ◊ *arithmetic mean* = ◊ *median* = ◊*mode*). The normal distribution or Gaussian curve, when plotted (◊ Fig. 109), is a regular bell-shape, indicating the infrequent occurrence of extreme values (large or small) and the more frequent occurrence of values relatively close to the mean, i.e. the probability of occurrences within a given distance of the mean is known. The normal curve is described by the mathematical function:

$$f(X) = \frac{1}{\sigma\sqrt{2\pi}} . e^{-\frac{(x-\mu)^2}{2\sigma^2}}$$

where $f(X)$ = frequency with which any value of X occurs

μ = mean

σ = ◊ *standard deviation*

π and e (base of natural logarithms) are mathematical constants, 3·1416 and 2·7182 respectively.

Distributions for a wide variety of natural and socio-economic phenomena approximate to the normal distribution, which is central to statistical analysis. The known properties of the distribution enable the reliability of estimates made by sampling to be judged. The normal distribution is sometimes known as the *normal law of error*, as repeated measurements of some fixed quantity tend to show a normal distribution about that quantity. ◊ *binomial distribution*, *Poisson distribution*. ◊◊ *kurtosis*, *skewness*.

normal law of error ◊ *normal distribution*.

normal profit ◊ *profit motive*.

normal science In the revolutionary model of science a period of normal science is one where, in any discipline, a particular school of thought is dominant (◊ *paradigm*) and researchers concentrate on adding further knowledge to the accepted model, retesting, verifying and extending its laws.

normal vote A concept used in explaining electoral behaviour. The pattern of voting of any group within an electorate can be split into two components: (i) a baseline or normal vote to be expected, all other things being equal, from that group, and (ii) deviations from that norm which reflect the issues of a particular election and the group's reaction to those issues. The concept implies that an electorate can be divided into relatively homogeneous groups based on characteristics which strongly influence their voting behaviour.

normality A fundamental assumption of many statistical ◊ *significance tests*, i.e. that the population or process generating the data approximate a ◊ *normal distribution*. ◊◊ *normalization*.

normalization The processing or transforming of a set of data which departs considerably from a ◊ *normal distribution* into a normal state (or near enough) to enable statistical procedures assuming ◊ *normality* to be used. Normalization can be achieved by using any function of the variable which is found to be normally distributed, but the two most common methods are to replace the original data by their logarithms or by their square roots. ◊◊ *transformation*.

normative theory A ◊ *theory* of what ought to be, rather than what actually occurs (◊ *positive theory*). The method of inference is ◊ *deduction* as normative theory seeks to construct what is rational or optimal according to some given criterion and is derived as a logical outcome of the integration of sets of postulates (e.g. physical, economic and behavioural in the case of normative geographical theories of location). Normative theory is deterministic and serves as a norm or standard, which enables experiences to be compared in a precise way. Most classical ◊ *location theory* is normative in character.

North Atlantic Treaty Organization (NATO) An ◊ *alliance*, established in 1949, between certain European nations and the USA and Canada for purposes of mutual defence. The members promise to maintain and develop their individual and collective capacity to resist armed attack and to consult each other if any one of the countries is threatened politically. The original European members were Belgium, Denmark, France, Iceland, Italy, Luxembourg, the Netherlands, Norway, Portugal and the United Kingdom. Greece and Turkey joined in 1952, and West Germany in 1955. The relationship between the countries is hegemonical, with the superpower, the USA, serving as a nucleus.

nosology The classification of diseases.

Notice of Intention Regulations concerning ◊ *National Parks* in England and Wales, and sometimes other protected areas, require that permitted ◊ *development* should not take place without the submission to the planning authority of a Notice of Intention to build. The procedure was introduced in 1950 by the Landscape Special Development Order and the planning authority has fourteen days within which to call in the development, otherwise planning permission is deemed to have been agreed.

notifiable installation ◊ *hazardous installation*.

nova villa ◊ *bastide town*.

novus burgus ◊ *bastide town*.

nuclear energy ◊ *Energy* which originates in the nucleus of an atom and which is released as a result of the regrouping or rearrangement of the nuclear particles. Potentially there are two principal processes for obtaining nuclear energy: (i) *fission*, which uses energy released in a controlled nuclear reaction in which an isotope, uranium-235, is split by the capture of neutrons, and (ii) *fusion*, which depends on energy released when a heavier element is formed by the fusion of lighter ones.

It is the fission process which is the basis of current, commercial nuclear power

stations. There are two basic types of nuclear power reactor – *thermal reactors* and ◊ *fast reactors*, named after the speed of the neutrons. Thermal reactors have a moderator to slow down the neutrons so that a sufficient number react with uranium-235. The choice of moderator leads to two families of thermal reactors: (a) graphite-moderated (◊ *magnox*, ◊ *AGR*), and (b) water-moderated (◊ *light water reactor*). Fast reactors use plutonium fuel, produced initially as a ◊ *by-product* from thermal reactors.

Use of such methods of energy generation creates problems of safety and radioactive waste disposal (◊ *nuclear reactor waste*). ◊ *nuclear fuel cycle, nuclear fuel services*.

nuclear family ◊ *family*.

nuclear fuel cycle The stages involved in finding and processing uranium for use in nuclear reactors and the subsequent stages of reprocessing and waste disposal. ◊ Fig. 110 illustrates the cycle for ◊ *light water reactors*. The stages are:

(i) Mining and concentration. Deposits of uranium with concentrations of 3% down to 0·05% are economically exploitable. The ore is mechanically crushed and the uranium (in the form of an oxide U_3O_8), which is chemically extracted, is known as 'yellow cake'.

(ii) Conversion and enrichment. There is further chemical purification before conversion to uranium hexafluoride (UF_6). Enrichment is then carried out by the centrifuge or gas diffusion methods to ensure the fuel contains the 2·7–3·3% uranium-235 required by the reactor.

(iii) Fuel element fabrication. Conversion to uranium dioxide (UO_2), a ceramic material which is formed into pellets and inserted into fuel rods, which in turn are assembled into fuel crates for insertion into the reactor core.

(iv) Reactor loading and the use of fuel to produce heat and give power output.

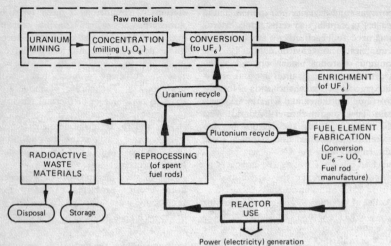

Fig. 110 Nuclear fuel cycle

About one-third of the core of a light water reactor needs replacing annually.

(v) Spent fuel handling and reprocessing. On discharge from the reactor, spent fuel is highly radioactive and always handled by remote control. It is initially stored on the reactor site in water-filled cooling ponds (metal-lined concrete containers) as the shorter-lived fission products decay.

(vi) Reprocessing. Some fuel rods are reprocessed – chopped up mechanically and chemically treated to separate out the uranium and plutonium from fission products. The latter go to temporary storage in heavily shielded cooled steel tanks. The uranium and plutonium are recycled via the enrichment process.

(vii) Waste disposal and storage. Spent fuel rods are disposed of entirely. The fission products from reprocessing, along with intermediate and low-level radioactive wastes, need to be stored or disposed of (◊ nuclear reactor wastes).

nuclear fuel services A term used to describe the enrichment and reprocessing activities in the ◊ nuclear fuel cycle.

nuclear reactor wastes Radioactive wastes are produced at various stages of the ◊ nuclear fuel cycle. Up to the fuel element fabrication stage of the cycle, the radiation levels from the uranium do not require extensive shielding procedures and standard industrial procedures, with extensive quality control, suffice. The most important radioactive wastes are produced in the nuclear reactor and the spent fuel rods, once removed, require special treatment. Where the fuel rods are sent for reprocessing, radioactive wastes are a by-product, and this is now the most important source of radioactive wastes. Three categories of radioactive waste are recognized:

(i) High-level: radioactivity greater than 1 curie/gallon.

(ii) Intermediate-level: radioactivity between 1×10^{-6} and 1 curie/gallon.

(iii) Low-level: radioactivity less than 1×10^{-6} curie/gallon.

Procedures for storage and/or disposal vary and may be summarized as follows:

(a) For high-level wastes (from reprocessing plants) the waste management

policy is to *concentrate and contain*. These wastes present a very substantial hazard and need to be effectively isolated from the biological environment. Current methods of storage in steel–concrete tanks are only temporary until a more satisfactory and permanent solution is found.
(b) For intermediate wastes (largely gaseous wastes of shorter-lived isotopes) the policy is to *delay and decay*. They are therefore compressed and stored on site until releasable.
(c) For low-level wastes the policy is to *dilute and disperse*, i.e. they are diluted by air or water and immediately released.

nucleated settlement A term used to describe a ◊ *rural settlement* with a compact morphology and consisting of homes and farmsteads clustered around a church and/or green. ◊◊ *dispersed settlement*.

null hypothesis ◊ *hypothesis*.

nuptiality The degree to which a population marries, usually measured as a ◊ *marriage rate*. Marriage and marital practices are major determinants of ◊ *fertility* – the absolute and relative ages of spouses at marriage, the degree to which celibacy is encouraged or condoned, the prevalence of plural as opposed to single marriages, customs regarding divorce or remarriage of the divorced and widowed, forms and prevalence of ◊ *contraception*, etc. Especially important therefore are the intensity of nuptiality (the proportion of population in certain age groups remaining single at any given time) and the precocity of marriage (expressed, for both sexes, as age at first marriage). ◊◊ *polygamy*.

nursery A commercial garden growing plants either for sale as plants, or to produce seed for direct sale or for sale to wholesale seed merchants.

nutritional requirements Five categories of nutrients are necessary for human life and health – carbohydrates, fat, protein, minerals and vitamins. No one food contains all these nutrients and a satisfactory diet can be obtained by regularly eating foods from four groups: (i) milk and dairy products, soybeans and whole small fish (protein, minerals, vitamins), (ii) meat, fish, poultry, eggs (protein, fat, vitamins), (iii) cereals and starchy vegetables (carbohydrates, vitamins, some protein), and (iv) fruits and vegetables (carbohydrates, minerals, vitamins, some protein). Carbohydrates provide the body with energy, as do fats, while protein provides for the growth and repair of body tissue as well as energy; minerals are required for growth and repair and, along with vitamins, for the regulation of body processes.

The energy value of food is measured in ◊ *calories* and the daily calorie requirements of humans vary according to age, body size and structure, physical activities engaged in and environmental temperature. For example, a twenty-five-year-old man, weighing 70 kgm, living in a temperate environment and engaging in moderate physical activity requires some 2,880 kcal/day, compared to a woman, at 58 kgm, who needs about 2,100 kcal/day. Calorie intake is a sound quantitative indicator of diet adequacy, but is not a good indicator of quality. Protein intake is the key indicator of diet quality.

O

oasis A place in a desert where water availability is sufficient to support plant growth. The water may reach the surface naturally or be raised from deep-bored wells. The size is variable, ranging from a clump of palm trees to a fertile area some hundreds of kilometres². The latter form isolated communities where people settle.

oast-house A stone or brick building containing a kiln for drying hops. It is usually circular (the most efficient shape for retaining heat), with a conical roof topped by a wooden ventilation cowl driven round by a wind vane. Most were built in the 19th century.

objective sampling ◊ *sampling.*

'obo' vessel Or *universal bulk ship.* A multipurpose cargo ship – oil/bulk/ore carrier – designed and built to carry a variety of dry and liquid cargoes in bulk. The object is to increase the ◊ *payload–distance ratio.*

obsolescence (1) Generally, the loss in value of physical assets due to technological change rather than to physical deterioration. For example, in the case of a building such obsolescence results from the ageing and dating of the internal structure and facilities as well as architectural and design changes.
(2) Geographers also use the term in respect of *site obsolescence* (where the introduction of undesirable land uses on neighbouring sites reduces the value of the original use of a site) and of *locational obsolescence* (where changes in access conditions mean an area is no longer a favoured location for the activity originally located in the area). ◊ *blight, decay, economic life of a building, filtering.*

occupancy cost The total expenditure incurred in occupying a site, including land cost and building cost, mortgage or rent, insurance, licences, utility costs, maintenance and land taxes.

occupancy rate An index of both urban density and accommodation density which relates the number of people occupying a dwelling to the number of habitable rooms (i.e. a room normally used for sleeping or living in). It is one of the most sensitive measures of housing conditions and is used to gauge the level of overcrowding or under-occupation, one person/habitable room being widely accepted as the threshold above which overcrowding exists. Also referred to as *household density, persons per room, room density.*

occupation zone An area of a ◊ *state* which remains occupied by foreign troops for a limited time following the cessation of warfare. ◊ *military zone.*

occupational mobility An individual's ability to change occupation by virtue of his/her level of acquired skill. ◊ *labour mobility, mobility* (2).

ocean shipping International trade in goods/commodities carried by ship. ◊ *coastal shipping.*

O-D survey *Origin-and-destination survey.* A method of obtaining data on the origins and destinations of trips of motor vehicles and their passengers. The object is to identify all traffic that (i) passes through an area having both origin and destination outside, (ii) travels to the area having an origin outside and a destination inside, (iii) travels from the area having an origin inside and a destination outside and (iv) travels within the area having both origin and destination inside. Data are normally obtained by questioning a random sample of travellers, either via a household interview survey or from a traffic survey in which vehicles are stopped along a *cordon line* around the survey area (◊ *cordon survey*) and along one or more *screen lines* bisecting it.

oecological time Time which is related to the environment, its vagaries and its seasonalities. ◊ *structural time*.

oecumene, oikoumene ◊ *ecumene*.

offensive diversification ◊ *diversification*.

office activity A category of ◊ *tertiary activity* which deals with the transactional and administrative duties associated with the collection, processing and exchange of information. Office organizations may range from international headquarters of firms involved in finance, insurance, commerce and industry to field offices of organizations such as building societies, to independent single offices of solicitors and accountants, as well as a range of government institutions.

office decentralization ◊ *decentralization*.

office development permit Central government concern over the potential congestion likely to result from office development pressures in Central London led to the imposition in 1964 of a ban on office development in the metropolitan London area. Developers wishing to build offices, initially involving more than 280 m² (3,900 ft²) of space (the threshold has changed), first had to obtain an office development permit from the central government as well as normal planning permission from the local authority. The system was extended to the Birmingham conurbation in 1965 and to other parts of the South-East and West Midlands regions in 1966. In applying for a permit, the developer had to demonstrate that the prospective occupier of the proposed office was tied to London (or Birmingham) and could not operate efficiently elsewhere. The aim was not only to limit office development to firms with an operational necessity for such locations but also to encourage the redirection of excess office development pressure to locations in the peripheral regions in order to redress the imbalance in office employment in those regions.

off-road recreation activities Those ◊ *recreation activities* that can take place away from public roads and even tracks, e.g. rambling, cross-country skiing, snow-mobiling, trail-bike riding, canoeing, horseback riding, camping, fishing, bird-watching, etc.

offset ◊ *countertrade*.

offshore assembly A particular form of export activity in some developing and centrally planned economies which involves the processing and assembly of components imported from developed, industrialized countries. It normally takes place under offshore assembly provisions whereby the industrialized country charges no customs duties on components imported by the developing country. It can be likened to international sub-contracting, often within the ◊ *multinational firm* to gain increased competitiveness of products by relocating ◊ *labour-intensive* processes abroad.

ogive A cumulative (percentage) ◊ *frequency distribution* curve.

oil–finance cycle A commodity–finance relationship which today influences the operation of the world economy. The oil–finance cycle begins with an excess demand for oil, bringing a sharp rise in the price of oil because it is in inelastic supply and is essential for industrial activity. This sharp rise in oil price leads to the accumulation of large financial surpluses in relatively few countries, with corresponding deficits in many other countries around the world. Countries react to their financial deficits by cutting back their balance of payments deficits, through domestic deflationary action, export promotion or import-saving. The deflationary effects drive down world activity and with it the demand for, and hence the price of, oil. In turn this has the effect of reducing drastically the surplus of the ◊ *OPEC* nations, as the world economy oscillates beyond what might be termed an equilibrium. The reduced OPEC surplus is matched by a corresponding balance of payments strength of industrialized and other oil-using countries, which, together with the relatively low price of oil, leads to a marked rise in the demand for oil. At this point the cycle starts again. Two cycles have been experienced to date: the first began in 1973, the second in 1979/80.

old age A term applied to the final and declining stage in the economic ◊ *development* of a country. It is characterized in the industrial development cycle by a deterioration of ◊ *infrastructure*, immobility of labour and fixed skills, and a declining industrial mix. ◊ *Rostow model*, ◊◊ *development stages theory of growth*.

old-age index A measure of the importance of senior citizens (◊ *general age group*) in a population. It is calculated as the ratio of those persons over retirement age to those adults of working age:

$$\text{Old-age index} = \frac{\text{Aged (over 60 or 65 years)}}{\text{Adults (15–60 or 65 years)}}$$

◊◊ *age*, *demographic ageing*.

Old World A term applied to Europe, Asia (as far as the Malay archipelago) and Africa (including Madagascar). It therefore includes those parts of the world known to Europeans before the discovery of the Americas and Australia. ◊ *New World*.

oligopolistic reaction In the process of international expansion by ◊ *multinational firms* the location of a branch plant by one firm in a particular country may prompt a response from competing firms in the ◊ *oligopoly*. Oligopolistic reaction is the locational response of a firm to a rival's decision to locate a production unit in a new country.

oligopoly An industry in which production is controlled by only a few firms. The firms are few enough in number to recognize the impact of their actions on rivals and the impact of their rivals' actions on them (◊ *oligopolistic reaction*). To avoid the potential dangers in such competitive actions oligopolists often collude, e.g. in price fixing agreements (◊ *cartel*). ◊◊ *duopoly*, *monopoly*.

one-field system ◊ *field system*, *open-field*.

one-parent family ◊ *family*.

one-tailed test ◊ *tail*.

onomastics The study of the human habit of naming things.

on-site costs ◊ *Costs* in ◊ *manufacturing industry* which are not related to the transport of materials and products but occur at the site. These commonly include rent, labour and those costs directly attributable to ◊ *economies of scale* and to environmental features. ◊◊ *basic costs*.

ontology Branch of metaphysics (study of reality) concerned with the nature of being – a conception of what exists or what can be known. ◊◊ *epistemology*.

OPEC ◊ *Organization of Petroleum Exporting Countries*.

open-cast mining A British term for ◊ *strip mining*.

open economy An exchange ◊ *economy* in which transactions occur both within the system and with economic systems external to it. ◊ *closed economy*.

open field A historical agrarian term, often used synonymously with ◊ *common field*, to describe fields in the system of arable farming that existed throughout much of Europe prior to ◊ *enclosure*. The ploughland of each village or ◊ *manor* was divided into two or three large open fields (◊ *two-field* and *three-field systems*) which were subdivided into long narrow strips a few metres wide. Each farmer was allocated a number of strips, which were seldom together, on the principle that no one should have all of the best or all of the worst land. Open fields were worked either in common or severalty by the tenants under the direction of the manor court, i.e. the crop rotation, usually triennial, was compulsory. ◊ *field system*.

open forest A ◊ *forest* where the canopy is not closed, possibly a consequence of lack of trees over a large area. ◊ *closed forest*.

open-pit mining ◊ *strip mining*.

open port A tidal ◊ *port* which is open to the sea or to an estuarial river.

open space A loosely employed term which refers to all land used for purposes which do not require many buildings and which enable it to be left substantially in its natural state or to be treated in a visually pleasant way. The term is often prefixed by 'private' or 'public'. Typical examples are parks, playing fields, cemeteries and allotments. ◊ *plaistow*.

open system A ◊ *system* exists in relation to an environment, i.e. what surrounds it. In relation to that environment a system may be either *open* or *closed*. An open system is not isolated from its environment (contrast ◊ *closed system*) but exchanges materials or energy with it. Under such conditions the system regulates and adjusts itself and may attain a steady state. Virtually all geographic systems are open. As a tool of

analysis, open systems have the advantage of being less deterministic, allow random effects to occur, and are applicable to a wide variety of situations.

operating reserves ◊ *reserves*.

operational milieu Or *operational environment*. The environment or milieu within which people operate, i.e. which influences behaviour in some way or another, and which is interposed between the decision-maker and the objective reality of the geographical ◊ *environment*. The operational milieu contains the ◊ *behavioural environment* and the ◊ *perceptual environment* and nests, itself, within the geographical environment (◊ Fig. 111). While the geographical environment is the same for everyone, the operational milieu differs from individual to individual, group to group and nation to nation, since it consists of such interrelated elements as a value system, cultural factors, economic systems, environmental factors, etc. The operational milieu is a common environment in human geographical studies.

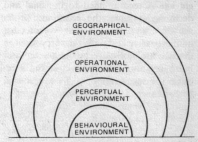

Fig. 111 Operational milieu

operational space The ◊ *action space* of a manufacturing firm defined by the set of locations that represent its operational ◊ *linkages*, both material and information. Each firm has an *industrial action*/operational space from which it derives inputs and within which it undertakes production, and a *commercial action*/operational space within which it markets its products.

oppida Fortified lowland sites of the most advanced ◊ *Iron Age* group, the Belgae, who imposed their rule over much of south-east England. These settlements possessed quasi-urban functions, being the centres of power from which tribal government was conducted.

opportunity cost A neoclassical economic term for the real cost of satisfying a want in terms of the cost of the sacrifice of alternative activities, i.e. the forgoing of the next best alternative good or service in favour of the good or service actually used.

opportunity set A term used in geographical studies of ◊ *retailing* to denote the location of all shops that each customer could have visited.

optimization model A ◊ *model* which provides an optimal solution to a problem. Derived from mathematics and operations research, optimization models were introduced first into ◊ *economic geography*, where they have been applied to problems of industrial, agricultural, retail and public services location; transport flows and network development; regional and urban growth; and spatial subdivision for administrative and political purposes. The models are normative in character and many are also deterministic, since all require the specification of an operational performance criterion or objective function which details the quantity/ quantities to be maximized or minimized subject to constraints. Many such models accept the ◊ *operational environment* as predictable, although those based on ◊ *game theory* accept that certain elements in the system being modelled are uncertain.

optimizer An individual or group who attempts to attain the best outcome they think possible from an action, i.e. the optimal outcome. The most common use of this concept is in the context of the entrepreneur seeking to maximize profits (◊ *economic man*). ◊◊ *satisficer*.

optimum firm Given the level of technical knowledge and managerial ability, that size of ◊ *firm* which minimizes the costs of production per unit of output. Expansion up to this size is accompanied by falling average costs as a result of ◊ *economies of scale*.

optimum population Generally the ◊ *population* that achieves a given aim (economic, military, social) in the most satisfactory way. More specifically from the economic point of view, that size of population which permits the full utilization of the natural resources of an area and hence maximum per capita output under given technical and socio-economic conditions, i.e. gives the highest possible per capita standard of living. Emphasis is placed on the balance between population size, available resources and prevailing socio-economic structures, and the concept is applicable at national or global scales (◊ Fig. 112a). Optima vary in time and space according to a wide range of factors – physical size of an area, its geography, social structure, technical progress, quality

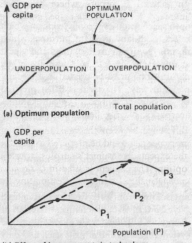

(a) Optimum population

(b) Effect of improvements in technology

Fig. 112 Optimum population

of communications, etc. ($\diamond$ Fig. 112b). $\diamondsuit$ *Ackerman formula, carrying capacity, overpopulation, underpopulation*.

optimum size of city That size of city, usually measured in population terms, at which the gains from $\diamond$ *agglomeration* are greatest. The concept is derived from the idea that as urban growth takes place the net benefits associated with the concentration of population vary with the size of the city. Up to a point – the optimum size of city – the benefits outweigh the costs imposed by growth, but beyond that point increasing population yields dysfunctional urbanism due to negative agglomeration effects, i.e. the city becomes a less efficient and less desirable place in which to live and carry on economic activities.

option demand, option value A willingness to pay for the possibility of consumption of a good or service in the future, even if that possibility is, in fact, never exercised. Option demand becomes important only in a situation where there is the likelihood of the removal of supply in the future, e.g. failure to preserve a natural environment. In general it occurs where the costs involved in re-providing the goods or services curtailed are prohibitive, i.e. current supply enters positively into the utility functions of prospective future users. The presence of identifiable option values in addition to conventional $\diamond$ *consumer's surplus* depends on there being uncertainty about the future. Option value is essentially a risk-aversion premium, the difference between the maximum option price people would be prepared to pay and the expected consumer's surplus from the option. The concept is used in $\diamond$ *resource management* as a means of estimating the additional cost attributable to any action that forecloses future options because of the irreversibility of the original action, e.g. when a natural environment is destroyed by development. $\diamondsuit$ *vicarious benefit*.

optional cargo A term applied to cargo shipped on a $\diamond$ *bill of lading* that provides for discharge at alternative $\diamond$ *ports*, e.g. 1,000 bales of wool may be shipped from Fremantle to London, option Hamburg, Bremen or Antwerp. It enables the shipper to take advantage of changing market conditions because he can sell his merchandise while it is still at sea. The option must be taken up by the purchaser within a stated time otherwise the cargo will be landed at the port of first option.

optional traffic $\diamond$ *traffic*.

ordinal scale, ordinal data A form of $\diamond$ *measurement*, one step up from the $\diamond$ *nominal scale*, in which observations are placed in order, being ranked according to some criterion (hence also known as *ranking scale*). Each observation has a unique position relative to the others on the scale, even though absolute values are not known. Ordinal measurement has proved especially useful in geography in perception and preference studies. $\diamondsuit$ *interval scale, ratio scale*.

ore-dressing The process of crushing an ore and separating the metalliferous minerals from the waste. In the past this separation was achieved by methods exploiting the higher specific gravity of the metals. These were generally cheap but not particularly efficient. More recently chemical methods, e.g. the flotation process, have been used to dissolve and remove the desired minerals, which are then recovered from the solution.

Organization of African Unity (OAU) A political $\diamond$ *alliance*, formed in 1963, which now links some forty independent African $\diamond$ *states* having common interests in regard to development. Its aims are to promote African unity and solidarity, to put an end to $\diamond$ *colonialism* in Africa, and to co-ordinate members' political, economic, defence, health, scientific and cultural policies. A subsidiary organization is the *African Development Bank*.

Organization of American States (OAS) A political–military ◊ *alliance*, established in 1948, involving some twenty Latin American countries in a hegemonial relationship with the United States. Its aims are to foster American solidarity, to aid collaboration between members, to protect their independence, sovereignty and boundaries, and to settle disputes peacefully. Originally directed towards mutual military support against communist interference, since 1960 the OAS has been mainly concerned with economic and social development.

Organization of Petroleum Exporting Countries (OPEC) A commodity ◊ *cartel* formed in 1960 by the major oil-exporting countries (outside the communist bloc). The founder members – Iran, Iraq, Kuwait, Saudi Arabia and Venezuela – have been joined by Qatar and the United Arab Emirates (1961), Indonesia and Libya (1962), Algeria (1969), Nigeria (1971), Ecuador (1973) and Gabon (1975). Besides being major oil exporters they were all developing countries relying on oil revenue to finance their development projects, and they also had a common interest in remedying the concessions originally granted to international oil companies to exploit their oil resources. Dominated by the Arab countries, which control most of the world's oil reserves, OPEC operates the most powerful of all commodity agreements, meeting periodically to fix prices at which oil will be supplied (◊ *marker crude*).

orientation A term used to describe the locational tendencies of manufacturing industry – at markets (◊ *market orientation*), at resource sites (◊ *material orientation*) or in response to transport factors (◊ *transfer orientation*).

Origin and Destination survey ◊ *O-D survey*.

orthogenetic city The city of the moral order which, according to R. Redfield, was derived from the basic unitary folk culture. The first cities in early civilizations were of this kind and they combined a developmental cultural function with political power and administrative control. From their dependence on the old culture stems a resistance to change or reorganization of the social order. The economy of such cities stagnates as they maintain the particular value system of the old culture. ◊ *parasitic city*. ◊◊ *heterogenetic city*.

out-by ◊ *outfield*.

outdoor recreation Any type of human behaviour that falls within the definition of ◊ *recreation* and takes place out of doors, e.g. camping, fishing, hunting, nature study, pleasure driving, sailing, sunbathing, swimming, walking, etc.

outer fringe ◊ *rural–urban fringe*.

outer range ◊ *range*.

outfield In ◊ *hill farming* areas, the extension of arable cultivation beyond the ◊ *infield* but still within the ◊ *head-dyke*. Referred to as *out-by* in northern England and Scotland. The land was cropped only occasionally and for a restricted period, since it received no manure and was fallowed to regain its natural fertility. ◊ *fauch*.

outline planning permission ◊ *planning permission*.

outport A subsidiary ◊ *port* at the mouth of an estuary which is auxiliary to a main, older-established port further upstream. Outports are a product primarily of the increased size of ships, although in some cases they may also be a response to the progressive silting-up of the main port or the requirement of passenger transport for speedier rail transport to its destination. Thus in order to prevent a loss of trade the original port undertakes the development of new facilities to the seaward – the outport – in order to attract larger vessels. ◊ *anyport, port–outport model*.

outrun Grazing land held in common by a ◊ *crofting* community and found beyond the ◊ *head-dyke*.

outstep well ◊ *appraisal well*.

outwork Minor productive operations carried out in private homes for factories. Outwork is paid for on the basis of output.

ouvriers-paysans ◊ *worker-peasant*.

overbounded city In the spatial delimitation of towns and cities for statistical and administrative purposes, the case where the administrative unit includes not only the physical urban aggregate but also part of the surrounding rural area. ◊◊ *underbounded city*.

overgrazing, overstocking In animal husbandry, the putting of too many animals on to the land to graze so that the vegetation cover is depleted and/or destroyed. The process is operative in two ways: (i) the density of grazing animals is such that first the more nutritive plant species are depleted at the expense of the poorer, less nutritive ones so that the feeding value of the ◊ *pasture* is decreased, and (ii) the density of the selective grazing animals may be such that forage plants are cropped at a faster rate than they can grow so as to be completely eaten out. Such removal of surface organic material can foster soil erosion.

overhead capital ◊ *economic overhead capital, social overhead capital*.

overhead costs ◊ *Costs* which do not vary with output and which, therefore, cannot be charged directly to any unit produced. Overhead costs include rent of premises, salaries of sales and research staff, salaries of directors and all other similar general expenses. Also called *supplementary costs*. ◊ *fixed costs*. ◊◊ *prime cost*.

overpopulation A state of imbalance in which there is an excess of ◊ *population* over utilized or potential ◊ *resources* in an area at a given time. The condition may result from a natural increase in population, a decline in resources, a decline in the demand for labour or a combination of these factors. The marginal product of labour is less than the existing average output and a high proportion of the population exists at ◊ *subsistence* level. A decrease in the area's population would therefore yield economic and social benefits to the remainder. ◊ *optimum population, population pressure*. ◊◊ *demographic relaxation theory*.

overpressing ◊ *surcharging*.

overspill The planned dispersal of population and employment from large cities as a consequence of the ◊ *redevelopment* of inner-city areas. The redevelopment is planned to relieve congestion and overcrowding and is rarely able to provide as much accommodation as formerly existed because it is planned to a lower gross ◊ *residential density*. This arises not only where the pattern of land use is to be changed but also where the type of use remains unaltered because of the need to provide more land for ancillary uses now considered to be socially and functionally essential or desirable, e.g. open space and children's playgrounds in residential areas. The displaced population and activities that cannot be rehoused in the redevelopment area form the overspill to be accommodated elsewhere, e.g. in a ◊ *new town*.

owner-occupation A common form of absolute ownership of property in which the owner does not pay rent and has complete control over his/her property, subject only to legal controls (including planning), to the rights of adjoining property owners, and subject, in certain cases, to ◊ *easements* such as the right to run underground services under the land.

Where the owner-occupier has borrowed money on the security of the property he/she is a *mortgagor*, owing money to the *mortgagee* under the terms of a *mortgage*.

The term is also applied to a building owner who leases the land on which his/her building stands, under the terms of a *ground lease* from the absolute owner of the land, the *ground landlord*. ◊ *fee simple ownership, freehold*. ◊◊ *land tenure*.

oxgang A term generally synonymous with ◊ *bovate* (as much land as one ox could plough in a year) and half as much as a ◊ *yardland*.

P

package tourism Holidays sold on an inclusive basis covering transport and accommodation, and frequently also meals, entertainment and sightseeing. Two types are distinguished on the basis of the travel patterns involved: (i) the *circuit* package – the traditional form – which follows a multiple-stop itinerary with sightseeing as the major activity and (ii) the *stayput* package, which involves travel to a single resort, usually associated with recreational activity in the mountains (e.g. an all-in skiing holiday) or at the coast. ◊ *tourism*.

packet port, packet station A rarely used term for *ferry* ◊ *port*.

packing theory Packing theory is concerned with the efficient subdivision of areas into discrete non-overlapping units, e.g. the subdivision of a national territory into local administrative units. Efficiency may be measured in two ways: (i) efficiency of movement, as measured by distance from the centre to outlying parts of an area, and (ii) efficiency of boundaries, as measured by length of an area's perimeter. Certain geometrical principles are important in applying these minimum energy criteria to the subdivision of an area, e.g. regular polygons are more economical shapes than irregular ones (hexagons allow the greatest amount of packing into an area consistent with minimizing movement and boundary costs). ◊◊ *contact number, shape measures*.

paddock A small enclosure under ◊ *pasture*.

paddy farming Another name for ◊ *wet-rice cultivation*, derived from the *paddies* or small fields in which rice is grown.

Palaeolithic An archaeological term (from the Greek for *old stone age*) used to describe the earlier human culture during the Pleistocene period when people made simple stone implements (*palaeoliths*), especially from flint. ◊ *Mesolithic, Neolithic*.

pale A now obsolete term referring to a district or territory within prescribed bounds, or subject to a particular jurisdiction.

paleotechnic A term used by Lewis Mumford to denote the middle of three phases of urban–industrial development (◊◊ *eotechnic, neotechnic*). The paleotechnic phase is characterized by the use of coal as a power source and the development of the iron and steel industry. The transportation system was primitive and therefore costly. Urban settlements were compact, with manufacturing organized on a ◊ *factory system* based on private ◊ *capitalism*, using localized raw materials (especially heavy weight-losing minerals) and serving fairly localized markets.

pandemic The world-wide or continent-wide distribution of an infectious disease, i.e. an ◊ *epidemic* affecting many countries at the same time. ◊◊ *endemic*.

panel studies A term describing studies that collect data from the same set of people at two or more points in time. Often used for measuring change or trends.

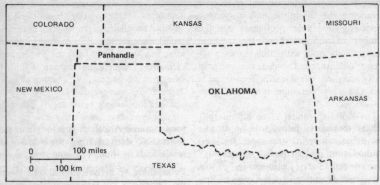

Fig. 113 Panhandle

panhandle An American term for a long narrow extension of a state or territory between two others or between one other and the sea (◊ Fig. 113).

pannage (1) The pasturage of swine or the right to feed swine in the ◊ *forest* or woods or on the waste of the manor. Pannage time lasted from 14 September to 18 November.
(2) The payment made to the landowner for the *right of pannage* (◊◊ *common rights*).
(3) The acorns, beechmast and other woodland produce on which swine feed.

pan-nationalism ◊ *nationalism*.

paracmastic process A process, the reverse of ◊ *diffusion*, which involves adopters disinnovating or divesting themselves of an ◊ *innovation* because it is no longer a good idea to have it. Two processes, based on the structural characteristics of the disinnovation, may be recognized: (i) *hierarchic paracme*, in which disinnovation occurs at successively larger or smaller centres; (ii) *contagious paracme*, in which the spread of information from a 'teller' causes an innovation to be abandoned.

paradigm A term, derived from T. S. Kuhn, which describes the stable pattern of scientific activity that holds within a discipline during a period of ◊ *normal science*. It is a 'supermodel' which provides intuitive and inductive rules about the kinds of phenomena scientists in that discipline should investigate and the best methods of investigation. A paradigm therefore represents the universally recognized scientific achievements within a discipline which, at the time, provide model problems and solutions for the community of scholars, so regulating research in that discipline.

According to Kuhn, the growth of knowledge depends on *paradigm shift*. Normal science proceeds unquestioned as long as new problems are solved: research improves the basic constructs, extends the situations to which they are applicable and improves methods of testing theories. Periodically a discipline fails to make progress – new questions throw up anomalies, predictions of existing theories prove false and accepted methodologies fail to solve new problems. There is an accumulation of unsolved problems and a situation of *paradigm crisis* prevails. Minority groups in the discipline propose alternative approaches and there follows vigorous and protracted debate on the new concepts and ideas between the advocates of the new and the defenders of long-held beliefs. During this period of *extraordinary science* the new approach wins converts, primarily new entrants to the discipline, where it demonstrates its real chance of advancing the discipline and answering previously insoluble problems. As the number of supporters of the original paradigm dwindle with time through retirement, death, etc. the ideas become generally accepted, the scientific revolution is over and a new paradigm is established in that discipline.

The Kuhnian model of paradigm shift has been widely used to examine the evolution of human geographic thought. While the concept of paradigm shift has been criticized for its simplicity and is now recognized as only one perspective on the development of science, the term paradigm continues to serve as a convenient description for the pattern of thought prevailing in a discipline or part of a discipline.

parallel economy ◊ *informal economy.*

parallel use A type of ◊ *multiple land use.* Land within a given area is treated as a single management unit and is used for two or more primary purposes, although the latter are kept spatially separate by zoning.

parameter (1) A statistical term for any summary measurement of the characteristics (or attributes) of a ◊ *population*, i.e. the true values of the mean, standard deviation, etc. which are computed from all observations in a population. The corresponding quantity based on a sample of measurements is known as an estimate of that parameter.
(2) A numerical constant in a mathematical model.

parametric tests 'Classical' statistical tests whose derivation involves assumptions about the ◊ *parameters* of the population ◊ *frequency distribution*, i.e. distribution-dependent ◊ *significant tests* which can only be applied to data on ◊ *interval* or ◊ *ratio scales* of measurement. These classical tests generally have a greater power efficiency than ◊ *non-parametric tests*, but the assumptions they make about the background populations from which ◊ *samples* are drawn are not always warranted and certainly should not be taken for granted. The most frequent assumption is that the background population is normally distributed (◊ *normal distribution*) and, the smaller the sample being tested, the more nearly normal must the background population be for most parametric tests to be valid (although some may be quite robust to violations of their assumptions). Examples of such tests include the F-test (◊ *analysis of variance*) and the ◊ *t-test*.

parasitic city A ◊ *city* that, according to B. F. Hoselitz, dominates the economic, social and political activities of an area to the extent that it has a dampening effect on economic growth. It contrasts with the ◊ *generative city.* ◊ *orthogenetic city.*

parasitic industry An industry (or firm) which depends on another industry (or firm), e.g. a parasitic industry may utilize the ◊ *by-product(s)* of the parent industry.

paratransit A term encompassing the full range of small vehicles which are available for public hire on a trip basis and which form an important adjunct of the total metropolitan transport system.

parcellement The subdivision of individual ◊ *fields*, e.g. as a result of ◊ *gavelkind.* ◊◊ *farm fragmentation, morcellement.*

parcelling-out The subdivision of land for ◊ *development* into individual building plots. It includes the layout of access roads, etc. and is a critical stage in the ◊ *land conversion process.* ◊◊ *residential development sequence.*

Pareto optimality A criterion of economic efficiency involving maximum ◊ *social welfare*, suggested by V. F. D. Pareto. Pareto optimality represents an equilibrium situation in which no change can be made to make any one person better off without making others worse off. Changes that satisfy this criterion are Pareto approved changes. ◊ *Kaldor–Hicks compensation test.*

paring and burning A method of preparing peatlands for cultivation. The top layer of peat was pared off, dried and burnt. Crops were then grown in the underlying peat or soil enriched by ash. The method was formerly widespread in Britain.

parish In Britain originally an ecclesiastical division superimposed on the basic pattern of ◊ *townships*. Each parish had its own church and clergyman to whom ◊ *tithes* and dues were paid. Parishes varied in extent according to the number and size of townships, ◊ *manors* or other units of landholding contained. The number of parishes increased, largely by the division of existing ones as populations grew and wealthy families built and endowed new churches. From the 16th century, parishes began to acquire certain civil (administrative) functions, e.g. the care of the poor, the maintenance of roads. These duties were transferred to new units of local government in the early 19th century, but later in the century the parish was re-established in England and Wales as the civil authority responsible for such matters as street lighting, ◊ *allotments*, burial and recreation grounds, footpaths and other rights of way.

park A term originally used to describe an enclosed tract of land, held under royal grant or prescription, for hunting. During the 18th century it was used for any large ornamental piece of ground, usually comprising pasture and woodland, which was laid out around country houses or mansions. In the 19th century it also came to be applied to enclosed areas of land in towns used for public recreation (◊ *public park*).

park-and-ride A method of ◊ *commuter* travel which combines the use of private cars to assemble (disperse) passengers at (from) suburban stations with the use of frequent bus or train services to the city centre. Extensive ◊ *parking* facilities are normally provided at the stations. A variant, termed *kiss-and-ride* by British Rail, involves the commuter being taken to and fetched from the station so as to leave the family car available for shopping, school and other trips during the working day.

parking The storage of an unattended motor vehicle. *On-street parking* is distinguished from *off-street*. *Short-term parking* is commonly defined as periods up to two hours, *medium-term* as longer periods up to a day and *long-term* for more than a day.

parking control area A controlled zone, normally in a town centre, where restrictions are imposed on ◊ *parking* except in defined places for limited periods of time. On-street parking will be prohibited or controlled by meters or discs and parking regulations are legally enforceable.

parking standard The number of ◊ *parking* spaces required to be provided by the developer of a new building. Standards are normally expressed in relation to the size of the building and the type of activity carried on.

parkway A specially designed, controlled-access ◊ *highway* with landscaped margins which serves a recreational function for ◊ *pleasure driving*. Parkways provide a scenic drive together with facilities for camping and other overnight accommodation, eating and picnicking, walking, etc. A toll is often charged to drive on a parkway. ◊ *scenic drive.*

partial compatibility ◊ *compatibility.*

partial correlation A method of measuring the ◊ *correlation* between two ◊ *variables* while a third variable, on which both the others depend, is controlled. Partial correlation therefore allows the effect of one variable upon the relation between two other variables to be eliminated and is a particularly helpful tool in locating spurious relationships. A spurious correlation is defined as a relationship between two variables, *A* and *B*, in which *A*'s correlation with *B* is solely the result of the fact that *A* varies along with some other variable, *C*, which is the true predictor of *B*. In this case, when the effects of *C* are controlled, *B* no longer varies with *A*.

partible inheritance ◊ *gavelkind.*

participation rate The proportion of an eligible population (national, age group, etc.) engaging in an activity. The concept has been applied to workers in the labour market (◊ *activity rate*) but has been most fully developed in the field of ◊ *recreation.* A participation rate represents an actual or revealed level of behaviour, i.e. what people do: it should not be interpreted simply as what they want to do, since the rate also reflects what people are able to do and must be interpreted in terms of both demand and supply variables (◊ Fig. 114). Observed levels of participation may conceal frustrated demand which can only be satisfied by the creation of new opportunities or increased capacity at existing facilities.

Participation rates, in recreation activity, are a function of demographic (e.g. age, sex, marital status) and socio-economic (e.g. education, income) characteristics of the population, and of their situational characteristics (such as time, mobility), as well as of resource-related characteristics (i.e. opportunities). In recreation studies attention has also focused on the frequency of participation in an activity by an individual and considered this in relation to site specific situations, in which case the participation rate is viewed as the number of user-unit use-periods per capita per annum.

particularism A ◊ *pattern variable* put forward as an index of economic ◊ *development* by B. F. Hoselitz. A particularistic society is inward-looking and chooses among alternatives according to the interests of the local group. Contrast ◊ *universalism.*

partnership In property development an arrangement between a local authority and

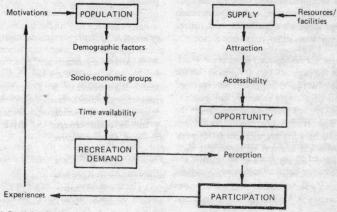

Fig. 114 Participation rate

345

a private developer whereby the local authority may use its powers to acquire and amalgamate freeholds of sites for ◊ *development*/redevelopment. The local authority retains the freehold in order to participate in ownership and profit-sharing, with the private developer responsible for the building development.

part-time farming Or *spare-time farming*. A type of ◊ *agriculture* in which farmers also have a regular non-farm occupation. Definitions of part-time farmers are usually based on either the amount/proportion of time devoted to or the amount/proportion of income derived from the off-farm job, or both. Farming may be combined with a wide range of other occupations and part-time farming may arise in two contexts: (i) Where a previously full-time farmer takes up an additional non-farm job. This is common throughout much of central and Western Europe, where worker-peasants run a ◊ *smallholding* alongside an industrial job. In this case part-time farming may be a transition stage out of full-time farming. ◊◊ *sidewalk farmer*, *suitcase farmer*. (ii) Where farming is added to an existing non-farm occupation. In much of North America and Western Europe such farmers are often ◊ *hobby farmers* and are very much less dependent on agriculture as a source of income than other part-time farmers.

passenger car unit (p.c.u.) A measure which enables the capacity of a ◊ *highway*, or the volume of actual ◊ *traffic*, to be expressed in terms of a single number, independent of the type of vehicles comprising the traffic flow. It allows for the different types of vehicle by considering them in terms of the equivalent number of passenger cars: commonly, private cars and light vans = 1 p.c.u., motor cycles = 0·75 p.c.u., medium and heavy goods vehicles = 2 p.c.u., buses and coaches = 3 p.c.u. ◊◊ *traffic capacity*.

passive filtering ◊ *filtering*.

passive industry R. Vining's term for ◊ *non-basic activity*.

passive locator A firm which is unwilling to risk new locations and which practises imitative (i.e. adoptive) behaviour. Locationally passive firms cluster around successful ◊ *active locators* or ◊ *location leaders*.

passive migrant A ◊ *migrant* who responds to information stemming from persons of their acquaintance who have already made successful moves. ◊ *migration chain*, *migration stock effect*.

pastoral drift Long-term, long-distance movement of pastoral nomads from one area to another. ◊◊ *nomadism*.

pastoral farming, pastoralism The practice of breeding and rearing certain herbivorous animals, whether for meat, milk, wool or hides, to satisfy human needs for food, clothing and shelter. Pastoral farming ranges from large-scale, highly scientific systems, such as commercial ◊ *ranching*, to small-scale, primitive systems, as with pastoral ◊ *nomadism*.

pastoral nomadism ◊ *nomadism*.

pasture ◊ *Grassland* used for the grazing of domesticated animals. Pasture is not usually used for hay and is not as good as ◊ *meadow*. ◊ *ley*. ◊◊ *common rights*.

path (1) One of five elements recognized by K. Lynch in the image of the city's physical structure (◊◊ *district*, *edge*, *landmark*, *node*). Paths are the channels along which people move in the city. Since a basic problem for anyone in a city is how to get from *A* to *B* and movement stimulates observation, paths are the primary feature remembered and they tend to predominate in urban imagery.
(2) The set of links or ◊ *edges* in a network to get between two given ◊ *nodes*.

pattern planning The process of determinining future geographic patterns as policy objectives, including the evaluation of alternative patterns and the selection of appropriate policy instruments. ⟡ *regional planning*.

pattern variable A factor or index which highlights the type of choice open to individuals and groups. Pattern variables are dichotomous, e.g. ⟡ *universalism*/⟡ *particularism*, achievement/ascription, functional specificity/functional diffuseness. The side of a pattern variable chosen by an individual determines the meaning of a situation for that person. Pattern variable analysis has been used to identify similarities and differences between cultures and between levels of economic development.

pay-off matrix ⟡ *game theory*.

payload–distance ratio That proportion of an overall journey length during which freight/cargo is being carried, e.g. a tanker sailing between two ports which hauls crude oil in one direction and ballasts back in the other has a ratio of 50%.

pays concept *Pays* is a French word meaning country and was used by the French school of geographers in the early 20th century to describe a small-scale ⟡ *region* of considerable historical unity, e.g. one of the old provinces of France, and of individual geographic personality deriving from its physical unity. Such *pays* were viewed as having a distinctive way of life, characterized by vernacular building styles, particular methods of farming and patterns of settlement – all representing adjustment of each society to the local physical environment. The term has been used by some geographers in preference to ⟡ *natural region*.

paysage The French equivalent of ⟡ *Landschaft*: rural ⟡ *landscape*.

peak hour index A measure of the concentration of passenger traffic into the actual busiest hour of each of the morning and evening peak periods (07.00 to 09.59 hours and 16.00 to 19.59 hours respectively in Britain). It is measured for public transport systems, especially rail. The peak hour index is measured as the number of passengers arriving at or departing from a station or terminus during the two busiest hours of the peak periods expressed as a percentage of total daily passengers. ⟡ *peak period index*.

peak land value intersection (PLVI) The street intersection in a town's ⟡ *central busi-*

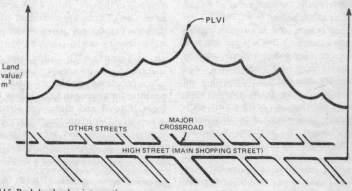

Fig. 115 Peak land value intersection

ness district where land values are at their highest (◊ Fig. 115).

peak load The highest load borne by electricity or gas supply systems, usually occurring in extreme weather conditions. It is sometimes referred to in the case of electricity as *simultaneous maximum demand*. Storage facilities are installed to help meet peak loads, e.g. ◊ *pumped storage*, but even so *peak load shaving plant* may be required, especially in the case of electricity, to satisfy demand. Shaving plant, e.g. gas turbines to generate electricity, has a low capital installation cost but is expensive to run. ◊ *load duration curve.* ◊◊ *base load, load factor.*

peak period index A measure of the concentration of passenger traffic into the peak periods (07.00 to 09.59 hours and 16.00 to 19.59 hours in Britain). It is usually applied to public transport, especially rail. The peak period index is measured by the number of passengers arriving at and departing from a station or terminus during the two peak periods expressed as a percentage of total daily passengers. ◊◊ *peak hour index.*

Pearson's correlation coefficient ◊ *product–moment correlation coefficient.*

peasant, peasant economy/farming A peasant works on the land, either as a small farmer or as a labourer, in a form of ◊ *agricultural system* and economic organization in which the ◊ *family* is the basic unit of production and social organization. The term has a very wide and general usage and usually indicates a standard of living at little more than ◊ *subsistence* level. Peasant farming is small-scale, technologically simple and dependent upon family labour. It produces a limited surplus over and above the basic needs of the family, which constitutes the basic group for consumption purposes. Any surplus is used to pay rent or is disposed of on the open market to buy goods the

farm cannot provide. Such peasant economies are usually pre-industrial or, at best, partly industrialized, rurally oriented, and attached to the land, local ◊ *community* and tradition. ◊ *European peasant farming, tropical peasant farming.*

pedestrian area An urban area from which ◊ *traffic* is wholly excluded or in which service vehicles are allowed only at certain times of day for loading or unloading. Also called *pedestrian enclave, pedestrian street,* and, especially where retail uses are involved, *pedestrian precinct* or *pedestrian mall.*

peer group A group of persons of similar age and common interests and outlook. ◊◊ *interest group, reference group.*

pene-exclave An area which, though not physically detached from the parent country, can be conveniently approached by road or rail only through the territory of a neighbouring ◊ *state.* ◊ *exclave.*

penny rate product The amount produced by imposing a ◊ *rate* of a penny in the pound which equals one-hundredth of the local ◊ *rateable value.* The penny rate product is a useful way of showing the cost of any new policy.

penthouse effect The phenomenon of high rents for the uppermost floors of ◊ *high-rise buildings* in the city centre. High rents are a function of both site amenities, such as the view, and certain psychological values attributed to being 'on the top'.

perambulation A term used in Britain in old documents to signify the official action or ceremony of walking round a ◊ *territory* for the purpose of examining and recording its ◊ *boundaries* so as to preserve the rights of possession. *Beating the bounds,* originally a religious ceremony to bless the coming agricultural year, had by the 16th century assumed a similar role.

perceived noise decibels (PNdB) A frequency band-weighted ◊ *noise* unit used in the measurement of aircraft noise. ⟡ *noise and number index*.

perception The process by which an individual acquires information as a result of visual, tactile, verbal, olfactory and auditory contacts with his/her ⟡ *environment*, and then organizes and interprets the data available in the light of his/her experiences and attitudes. It is therefore a cognitive or psychological process that enables an individual to convert sensory stimulation into organized and coherent experience, i.e. to evaluate and become aware of reality.

The term is also used, especially by geographers, to refer to the product – the *percept* – of this process, i.e. the individual's subjective assessment or conception of reality (⟡ *image*). Such assessments are viewed as being formed by (i) *operational perception*, the awareness due to the use of reference points in a person's everyday life, (ii) *responsive perception*, that immediate reaction to distinctive or unusual features, and (iii) *inferential perception*, that awareness drawn from past experiences and parallel situations. In human geography perceptual studies are concerned with identifying the social and cultural determinants of images in response to both physical and socio-economic environments and have concentrated on the perception of landscape quality, on hazards and environmental stress, on location decision-making, and the formation of areal, especially urban, images. ⟡ *appraisive perception, designative perception, environmental perception, hazard perception*. ⟡ *perceptual environment, stimulus–response theory*.

perceptual environment That part of the ⟡ *operational milieu* of which a person is aware, either because of an organic-sensory sensitivity that exists owing to a lack of body adaptation or because of a sensitivity that derives from a person's learning and experience. The perceptual environment therefore has both sensory and symbolic dimensions. Its relationship to both the ⟡ *behavioural environment* and the operational milieu is shown in ⟡ Fig. 111.

perceptual region ⟡ *vernacular region*.

perennial irrigation ⟡ *irrigation*.

perfect competition A concept, used in classical economic analysis, to demonstrate the basic forces common to all ⟡ *markets*. On the ⟡ *supply* side perfect competition requires (i) that many firms compete against each other, each firm supplying such a small proportion of total output that it is unable to influence ⟡ *price* by changing its output, (ii) that resources or ⟡ *factors of production* are perfectly divisible and mobile, so that each firm is able to increase output without forcing up the level of wages, etc., (iii) that firms have complete freedom to enter or leave an industry and (iv) that each firm has complete knowledge about the activities of its rivals. On the ⟡ *demand* side a similar set of assumptions prevail: (i) that there are many buyers, with no customer able to influence price by varying the amount they purchase, (ii) that each buyer has complete knowledge of the quantities offered for sale and the prices involved in all transactions, (iii) that transport costs are absent, so that no buyer is prevented from taking full advantage of different prices in different parts of the market, and (iv) that the products of firms are homogeneous, so that the product of any one firm in an industry is a perfect substitute for the product of any other firm.

The classical economists always assumed perfect competition when they argued that the ⟡ *price mechanism* ensured satisfactory results in the allocation of factors of production and in the use of scarce resources. ⟡ *imperfect competition, monopolistic competition, monopoly, oligopoly, pure competition*.

performance standard ◊ *emission standard.*

perinatal mortality Death which occurs during the period of prenatal existence after the foetus (unborn baby) has reached viability, during labour, or in the early part of extra-uterine life. ◊ *infant mortality.*

periodic market A ◊ *market* that operates at a particular location only occasionally, e.g. on one or more fixed days every week or month. The retail functions provided may be the only ones present in the settlement, as in many less developed countries, or they may be in addition to permanent facilities, as in market towns in Western Europe.

   Periodic markets have been explained, at least partially, in terms of a modified ◊ *central place* framework in which traders move from place to place to accumulate sufficient business to meet their ◊ *threshold* requirements. This generates the type of ◊ *market cycle* illustrated in ◊ Fig. 97. The *trader hypothesis* suggests that markets are synchronized in time and space to allow traders to follow routes which minimize their travel costs. An alternative, *consumer hypothesis* suggests that the synchronization is to allow dispersed rural populations easy access to markets through the week. The two hypotheses are compared in ◊ Fig. 116. Neither has general validity and a commodity hypothesis may be more acceptable. This suggests that market schedules are arranged so that adjacent market locations, supplying different types of goods, meet on different days and that these locations will normally be at different levels in the central place hierarchy.

periodic migration ◊ *migration.*

periodicity The relatively regular oscillation in a time series of events. The time interval between occurrences, which is approximately equal, is referred to as the *return period.*

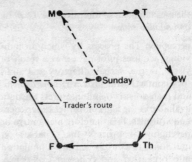

(a) Trader hypothesis
Trader based in higher-order centre visits each of the 6 lower-order centres in sequence, using seventh day for restocking, etc.

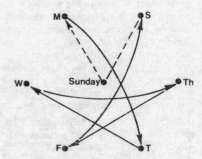

(b) Consumer hypothesis
Markets held in lower-order centres so that a consumer has access to market in nearest centre and the two neighbouring centres at intervals of one or two days.

Fig. 116 Periodic market

peripheral firms, periphery firms ◊ *dual economy.*

peripheral neglect ◊ *law of peripheral neglect.*

peripherality The condition experienced by individuals, firms and regions at the edge of a communication system, where they are away from the core or controlling centre of the economy.

permanent capital ◊ *capital (1).*

permanent necessitarian A person who lives, of necessity, permanently in a ◇ *slum*. Such persons may be social outcasts, adjusted poor, or indolent. ◇◇ *temporary necessitarian*.

permanent opportunist A person who lives and remains in a ◇ *slum* area largely because of the opportunities it provides, e.g. a fugitive (from the law, debt), an 'unfindable'.

person-trip A complete one-way journey made by a person from initial origin to ultimate destination for a specific purpose. One or more modes of travel may be involved. ◇ *trip*.

personal construct theory A methodology originally intended as a framework for personality assessment and psychotherapy that has been extended by geographers and others to examine the content and structure of personal ◇ *cognitions* of the everyday environment, i.e. to person–place interactions. It is based on the postulate that behaviour is guided by people's efforts to anticipate events and assumes that people act purposefully to achieve desired outcomes and to avoid undesirable consequences of their actions.

Constructs describe the perceived similarities and contrasts among events. They are expressed as bipolar adjectives that describe psychological rather than logical opposites. In general, one pole – the emergent or preferred pole – of a construct is preferred. Constructs are based on experience and describe the repeated similarities and contrasts among events that have proved useful for distinguishing between the desirable and undesirable consequences of one's actions. Thus they emerge from an individual's personal history.

Personal constructs are used to interpret and structure the experience of events. Methods of personal construct theory are designed to provide data describing the nature and organization of each person's constructs, the latter elicited from the individual by self-reporting.

personal probability ◇ *subjective probability*.

personal services Services supplied to individuals on a personal basis, e.g. by hairdressers, tailors. ◇ *tertiary industry.* ◇◇ *professional services*.

personal space An invisible area surrounding a person's body into which other people may not come. It is not necessarily spherical in shape, nor does it extend equally in all directions, e.g. people will tolerate the closer presence of a stranger at their sides than directly in front. Personal space is violated only in close emotional relationships or else involuntarily, such as in crowded places. Personal space is thus an emotionally charged zone around individuals which interacts with ◇ *individual distance* to regulate the spacing of people. Also referred to as *body territory, portable territory* or *spatial envelope*. ◇◇ *interpersonal space, proxemics*.

persons per room ◇ *occupancy rate*.

perverse growth A form of economic growth that undermines rather than enhances the potential of an area's economy for long-term growth.

perverse migration ◇ *Migration* which flows from prosperous to less prosperous regions. It occurs both because labour is not a homogeneous factor and as a result of ◇ *return migrants* (retirees, unsuccessful migrants).

petroleum refining The treatment of crude petroleum to separate out the fractions suitable for specific uses such as transport fuels, heating oils, feedstock. The two processes which characterize oil refining are distillation and 'cracking'. Progressive distillation (vaporization) results in the initial separation of the lighter petroleum products; cracking (involving the application of heat and pressure) of the lighter hydrocarbons from the heavier.

Oil refineries are now commonly located close to consumption centres, rather than at the supply source, although in the early days of the industry and up to the 1940s it was usual to refine petroleum at the point of production of the crude oil. The change was a function of the economics of oil production and refining, especially the need to transport large quantities of crude oil in tankers of ever-increasing size long distances to huge, modern refinery complexes.

phenogram ◊ *linkage tree*.

phenomenal environment An extension of the usual concept of geographical or physical ◊ *environment* to include modifications and alterations to the natural environment which are the result of human activity. Also known as *experiential space*. The phenomenal environment contains the ◊ *operational milieu*. ◊◊ *real environment*.

phenomenological reduction The change in attitude via which the phenomenologist seeks to make the ◊ *lifeworld* a focus of attention, such that acts, which in the ◊ *natural attitude* are simply lived, are thematized and made topics of reflective analysis.

phenomenology A philosophical approach, associated with E. Husserl, that emphasizes the study of phenomena as perceived by individuals and the general patterns of consciousness and experience of individuals. It attempts to suspend all presuppositions and to observe and describe the world of conscious phenomena,

particularly in connection with such problems of ◊ *perception* as space, time, colour, movement, sight and touch. For a phenomenologist there is no objective world independent of people's experiences, i.e. all knowledge proceeds from the world of experience and cannot be independent of that world.

Observation and description in this context are not the simple matters that conventional forms of science assume them to be. Phenomenology thus provides a powerful critique of ◊ *positivism* and, throughout the 1970s, was an important perspective in ◊ *behavioural geography* (and the latter's criticism of geography as a spatial science). ◊◊ *epoche, intersubjective verification, lived space, phenomenological reduction.*

phi coefficient A ◊ *non-parametric test* to determine the strength of association between two binary variables. It is a special case of a more general method known as the correlation of attributes. The phi coefficient is computed for 2×2 ◊ *contingency tables*, which may be set up as in the table below. Using this notation

$$\text{phi}(\varphi) = \frac{AD - BC}{\sqrt{(A + B)(C + D)(A + C)(B + D)}}$$

and ranges in value from $+1$ for a perfect positive association to -1 for a perfect negative association between the two variables. Where a ◊ *chi square* value is already known, phi can be obtained from

$$\varphi = \sqrt{\frac{\chi^2}{N}}$$

		Variable 1		
		Category 1	Category 2	Totals
	Category 1	A	B	$A + B$
Variable 2	Category 2	C	D	$C + D$
	Totals	$A + C$	$B + D$	N

phi coefficient

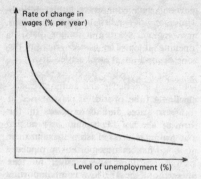

Fig. 117 Phillips curve

Phillips curve A negative exponential relationship between ◊ *unemployment levels* and rate of change in money wages, established by A. W. Phillips as a result of a study of wage rate changes in the United Kingdom between 1861 and 1957. As ◊ Fig. 117 illustrates, the higher the proportion unemployed the lower the increase in wages, because as unemployment increases the labour market becomes more favourable to the purchaser.

physical blight ◊ *blight*.

physical determinism ◊ *environmental determinism*.

physical environment ◊ *environment*.

physical margin of cultivation The limit at which the ◊ *cultivation* of a given crop becomes physically impossible. ◊ *cultivation limit*. ◊◊ *economic margins of cultivation*.

physical planning A general term, often used synonymously with *land use planning*, *spatial planning*, *town and country planning*, *territorial planning* and even *urban and regional planning*, for the process of ◊ *planning* an area's physical environment (◊ *land use*, communications and transport, utilities, etc.). Its origins lie in the regulation and control of town development. It involves a recurring cycle of operations for preparing and controlling the implementation of plans for changing systems of land use and settlement.

physical quality of life index (PQLI) A straightforward index, developed by the Overseas Development Council, designed for use in ◊ *development* studies to measure progress in physical well-being among countries. The aim was to produce an index that was more effective than ◊ *gross national product* or other monetary indicators. The PQLI is based on three apparently universal concerns:
(i) ◊ *Infant mortality*: people prefer to have few deaths among children born to them.
(ii) ◊ *Life expectancy* (measured at the age of one): people prefer to live longer rather than shorter lives.
(iii) Basic literacy (measured as the proportion of the population aged fifteen years or over who are literate): a surrogate measure for social participation.

The calculation of PQLI involves a simple indexing system. For each of the above indicators the performance of individual countries is fitted to a 0–100 scale, where 0 equals the 'worst' performance and 100 the best. The composite index is then calculated by averaging for each country the three indicators, giving equal weight to each of them. The resultant PQLI value is thus automatically scaled on an index of 0–100.

There is no basic theory underlying the PQLI, but it provides an unethnocentric measure, avoiding problems of culture relating to housing, clothing and nutrition. It also has the advantage of using data that is generally available for all countries.

A 'basic human needs' PQLI has been set at seventy-seven, but some two-thirds of the world's population are currently below this level. ◊◊ *quality of life*.

physiological density Population per unit of cultivable land. ◊◊ *agricultural density*, *comparative density*, *man–land ratio*.

pictogram A distribution map using pictorial symbols (e.g. aircraft, barrels, bricks, missiles) located over the area of occurrence to represent commodities or activities. The symbols may be drawn to scale or repeated to give some impression of the quantities involved.

piecemeal development ◊ *Development* or ◊ *redevelopment* which takes place by the building or rebuilding of single buildings on individual sites (as and when the market suggests the operation will be appropriate). The infrastructural arrangements of the area – layout of roads, public utilities, property boundaries, etc. – remain unchanged. ◊ *comprehensive development*.

pie graph A popular, descriptive name for a ◊ *divided-circle* graph.

piggy-back principle A freight transportation practice which combines the advantages of road transport for short hauls with that of rail transport on longer hauls. A co-ordinated service is offered whereby trailers/containers are driven to the nearest rail terminal, where they are loaded onto a rail flatcar for the journey to the rail terminal nearest the destination, at which they are unloaded to be driven the last stage of the journey. Also referred to as *trailer-on-flatcar*. ◊ *containerization*, *fishy-back principle*, *LASH*.

pillar and stall A method of coal-mining most commonly used up to the late 19th century which involved partially working a coal seam to the boundary of the mining concession, leaving pillars of coal to support the roof at predetermined intervals. In many coalfields it was then the practice to mine the pillars, working back to the shaft and causing abandoned galleries to cave in. Surface ◊ *subsidence* was minimal during the initial phase of mining, but substantial when the pillars were removed. ◊ *adit mining*, *advance mining*, *bord and pillar*, *drift mining*, *longwall mining*.

pioneer A person (explorer, hunter, settler) who is one of the first to enter or settle a new region, playing a major part in 'opening' it up. The *pioneer-fringe* is the zone beyond the present settled area.

pioneer boundary ◊ *boundary*.

pipeline A tube, of steel or plastic, used to transport gases, liquids or solids (in the form of 'slurries'). Petroleum, natural gas and products derived from them are the main substances transported by pipeline. Laying pipelines is expensive, but the operating costs are low compared with those of road or rail transport. ◊ *load factor*.

piscary ◊ *common rights*.

pit A term used to describe open workings in 'soft' or unconsolidated deposits such as clays, sands and gravels, and originally related to their shallowness. ◊ *mine*, *quarry*.

Pittsburgh plus system A ◊ *basing-point pricing* system operated in the marketing of steel in the United States, under which all steel consignments, irrespective of where they were produced, were charged to the consumer as if they originated from Pittsburgh. It developed in the late 19th century and persisted until the mid-1920s, when it was replaced by a multiple basing-point system. It was a device that protected Pittsburgh steel manufacturers from competition from locations with lower production costs.

pivot area ◊ *heartland*.

place A small part of geographical space occupied by a person or thing. It is a common formulation in ◊ *humanistic geography*, where places are regarded as centres of 'felt value' (Yi-Fu Tuan) and as fusions of human and natural order which act as 'significant centres of our immediate experiences of the world' (E. Relph). ◊ *geopiety*, *placelessness*.

place ballet An interaction of many ◊ *time-space routines* and ◊ *body ballets* rooted in space, which can occur in all types of environment (indoor, outdoor, streets, neighbourhoods, cities, etc.). It therefore describes the interlocking of people and their activities, especially regular, repeated patterns, at a ◊ *place*. The concept is of value in ◊ *behavioural geography* because it brings people together and joins them with environmental time-space.

place community A metropolitan community in which the interests and activities of the members, both at work and leisure, are largely contained within the community and have limited or no participation in wider urban realms (◊ *non-place community*).

place names The ◊ *geographical names* of places which, for the original settlers, usually had meanings describing the character of the area or settlement. Place-name studies have been used to provide evidence of stages in the settlement of an area, e.g. in Britain place names ending in *-ing* (*ingas*, group of people), *-ham* (homestead or estate), *-tun* (enclosure, farmstead or cottage) and *-ingtun* (*-ing* and *-tun* combined) are representative of stages in Anglo-Saxon settlement earlier than that characterized by names terminating in *-ley* (*-leah*, forest, wood, glade or clearing), *-worth* (enclosure), and *-field* (cleared land). The names of most British cities, towns and villages originate in Celtic, Anglo-Saxon, Scandinavian and Norman names. ◊ *conventional name*.

place utility (1) The value or measure of satisfaction an individual derives from a location or ◊ *place* relative to their goals. It is occasionally termed *locational utility*. The use of the term originated in migration studies but is now applied generally to many types of human movement. It is a measure of the attractiveness of a place, and an individual's assessment of the environment can generate a situation of satisfaction or stress, the latter occurring where there is a difference between actual circumstances and goals/aspirations. Stress can initiate ◊ *search behaviour* to find an alternative location.

(2) Applied to resources or goods, the ◊ *utility* achieved by transportation which, by overcoming the friction of distance, can bring materials or goods to places where they are both needed and absent. Such resources or goods have place utility (◊ *form utility*, *time utility*). More commonly described as ◊ *complementarity*.

placelessness The destruction of distinctive ◊ *places* and their replacement by standardized landscapes. It is the result of vastly increased personal mobility, the enhanced power of mass communications, and increasing uniformity in technology and equipment which allow people to transcend easily physical space and readily compare and switch places. People's ties with places are greatly weakened and relatively few people in modern Western societies feel the close identity with place that was automatic with their grandparents. Global similarity results, exemplified by the lack of planning and monotony of suburban development.

plaistow An open space for recreation, once used to describe what is now known as the village ◊ *green*. The term is of Anglo-Saxon origin and survives in various place names.

plan (1) A drawing, made by projection on to a flat surface (usually a horizontal plane), showing the relative position and size of buildings, boundaries, etc.

(2) A scheme of action, a method of proceeding thought out in advance (◊ *planning*). ◊ *development plan*, *local plan*, *national plan*, *structure plan*, *town plan*, *transport plan*.

planned economy ◊ *state socialism*.

planned village A term used to describe a ◊ *village* laid out in the 18th century in which architectural, economic and social considerations were interrelated. The *planned village movement* was most commonplace in north-east Scotland. Such villages were often *estate villages*, developed by a landowner, or *factory villages*, built to house workers at a water power site. The latter evolved by the middle of the 19th century into *model villages* for factory workers and these were the prototype for the later ◊ *garden villages*.

planning A general term with many meanings, all of which imply an ability to scheme or arrange beforehand. In practice planning is a highly formalized and disciplined activity through which society induces changes in itself, involving the development of policies and procedures for a decision-making unit, including the establishment of goals, i.e. it is a goal-directed decision-making process requiring the systematic provision of information and the evaluation of alternative courses of action, including the consequences of present choices for alternative goals in the future. Planning therefore involves (a) an ability to anticipate future events, (b) a capability for analysing and evaluating situations and (c) a capacity for innovative thinking to derive satisfactory solutions. As practised by government institutions it represents collective social action, a continuing process of strategic choice. Stages in the process are illustrated in ◊ Fig. 118.

Of particular importance to the geographer is the distinction between *spatial planning*, where the geographical dimension is explicit (◊ *environmental planning*, *pattern planning*, *physical planning*, *regional planning*), and *non-spatial planning*, where it is not (◊ *central planning*, *economic planning*, *social planning*). The latter can, however, generate spatial consequences which are of interest to geographers. ◊◊ *advocacy planning*, *allocative planning*, *innovative planning*.

planning appeal An appeal by an unsuccessful applicant for ◊ *planning permission*, stemming from a local planning authority's refusal to permit a ◊ *development* or the imposition of conditions on a proposed development. The applicant must appeal to the Secretary of State for the Environment under Sections 36–7 of the 1971 Town and Country Planning Act within six months of receiving the decision. The Secretary of State may reject or allow the appeal, or may alter the terms of the conditions, but before doing so he must afford both sides the opportunity of either a private (informal) hearing or a local public inquiry before a staff inspector of the Department of the Environment. To save the expense of a hearing, appeal proceedings may be conducted by way of

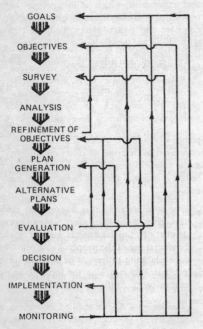

GOALS

OBJECTIVES

SURVEY

ANALYSIS

REFINEMENT OF OBJECTIVES

PLAN GENERATION

ALTERNATIVE PLANS

EVALUATION

DECISION

IMPLEMENTATION

MONITORING

Fig. 118 Planning

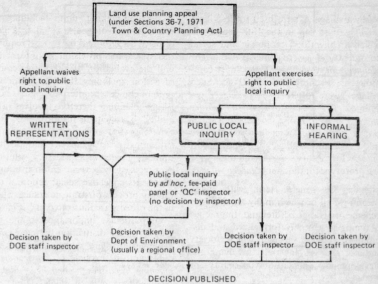

Fig. 119 Planning appeal

written representations. ◊ Fig. 119 outlines the various routes to an appeal decision. All appeal decisions by the Secretary of State are final except on a point of law.

planning balance sheet A technique of plan evaluation developed from ◊ *cost-benefit analysis* which systematically records in a set of accounts all the disadvantages (costs) and advantages (benefits) to affected parties. The essence of the method is to clarify to the planner the balance between monetary and physical costs with intangibles, as well as identify their incidence on different groups in the community.

The community is considered not only as a whole but also by main sectors: the most commonly used approach distinguishing between producers/operators and consumers. For each sector a list is made of all the advantages and disadvantages that will accrue from a plan in order to assess which plan yields the maximum net advantage. Measurement is not wholly in money terms but includes the un-measured analysis of intangibles, which are assessed on a points system. The results are presented in a descriptive table – a form of ◊ *social account* – which shows the implications of alternative plans both for the community as a whole and various groups within the community.

planning blight A term used to describe the adverse effect of long-term planning proposals or the consequences of planning indecision on the value of property affected by those proposals. As a result a landowner may be unable to sell the property at all or only at a depreciated price and, given time, the property may appear derelict. If the landowner cannot make beneficial use of the property as a result of such planning proposals he/she can serve a ◊ *purchase notice* on the local planning authority. ◊◊ *blight, worsenment.*

planning gain A term applied whenever, in connection with a grant of ◊ *planning permission*, a local planning authority

357

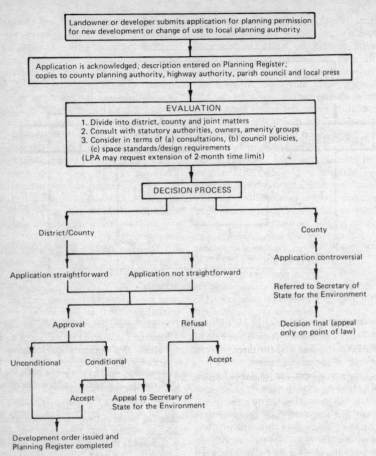

Fig. 120 Planning permission

seeks to impose on a developer an obligation to (i) carry out works not included in the ◊ *development* for which permission had been sought, or (ii) make some payment or confer some extraneous right or benefit in return for permitting the development to take place. Planning gain sometimes arises from the terms in which development is permitted, e.g. from a condition of the planning permission, and sometimes from an agreement made in association with it. In some cases the developer may offer such works or payment when applying for planning permission or in subsequent negotiations.

planning permission All ◊ *development*, since the 1947 Town and Country Planning Act, requires application for planning permission to be made to the local planning authority. The process of dealing with applications for planning permission is called ◊ *development control*. It is emphasized that permission must be secured before development commences. The applicant (developer) can make either an *outline application*, which is concerned only with the general principles of the proposed development, or a *detailed application*, which may either follow a successful outline application or be the first application made and which has to state the case for the development and illustrate the proposal in depth. Planning applications are normally determined by the local planning authority using the procedure outlined in ◊ Fig. 120. Decisions should be made, unless there is prior agreement, within two months of receipt of the application. Planning permission may be granted *unconditionally*, when the developer's proposals are agreed in full, or *conditionally*, when the local planning authority imposes conditions regulating the development. When permission is refused or the conditions imposed are unacceptable to the applicant, there is a right of appeal to the Secretary of State for the Environment (◊ *planning appeal*). When permission is granted it lasts for five years in the case of detailed permission and for three years in the case of outline permission.

Certain developments, as defined under the ◊ *General Development Order* and the ◊ *Use Classes Order*, are classed as permitted development and do not have to go through the above procedure. Where development takes place without the grant of planning permission the local planning authority can serve an ◊ *Enforcement Notice* and a ◊ *Stop Notice* to bring an immediate halt to the activity in question. To ensure that work is completed on a development which has started but been suspended, the authority has powers to issue a ◊ *Completion Notice*. When a site is incapable of beneficial use as a result of the refusal of planning permission or the imposition of onerous conditions, the landowner can serve a ◊ *Purchase Notice* on the local planning authority.

planning, programming and budgeting systems (PPBS) An approach to the implementation of policy decisions by an organization which embraces the corporate planning concept, emphasizing a holistic view of the objectives of that organization and the resources available to it. PPBS combines both established and new techniques, integrating these into a coherent method of decision-making and moving in a four-stage sequence which reduces goals to actual budgeting decisions:

(i) The specification of management objectives, involving a clear and explicit definition of the overall purposes of the organization, and of any specific actions it proposes.

(ii) The identification of resources and of alternative ways of marshalling them to meet these objectives. Alternatives are formulated in budgetary terms, with resource requirements structured on an annual basis.

(iii) The evaluation of the ◊ *cost-effectiveness* of the alternative courses of action to allow the optimum combination of alternatives to be selected.

(iv) Decision-taking.

PPBS originated with US industrial corporations. Its use was ordered throughout all Federal Departments in 1965 and its establishment at state and local levels was also encouraged. In Britain experimentation with the technique is more recent, but it has been employed both by central government and a range of local authorities.

planning region A legally ◊ *bounded space* delimited on an *ad hoc* basis for the purposes of government decision-making, i.e. a ◊ *region* which is a direct result of society's need to administer space. The planning regions delimited in any country need not completely exhaust the area but may be confined to only part of it. Also referred to as *development region* (J.

359

Friedmann) and *programming region* (J.-R. Boudeville).

plant ◊ *establishment*.

plantation (1) A settlement in a new or conquered country (◊ *colony*). The settlements of English and Scottish people on forfeited lands in Ireland during the 16th and 17th centuries were also called plantations.
(2) An estate, especially in a tropical country, on which the large-scale production of ◊ *cash-crops* takes place. ◊ *plantation agriculture*.
(3) An area which has been afforested, usually with quick-maturing conifers.

plantation agriculture An ◊ *agricultural system* for the commercial production of tropical and sub-tropical crops. The system originated under ◊ *colonialism*, when ◊ *plantations* were established using European organization, skill and capital and chiefly servile labour (sometimes native, sometimes imported). As such it marked the invasion of Western needs and capitalist organization into tropical agriculture. Plantation agriculture now generally operates via large-scale, scientific methods, under centralized management and with a large force of paid labour. Plantations specialize in the production of one, or possibly two, crops. Typical crops are sugar-cane, coffee, tea, cocoa, cotton, copra, bananas, oil palm, pineapple, sisal and rubber, most of which have fairly rigid requirements, so that plantation agriculture is scattered in favoured areas. It is also tied to coastal access because of the overriding need to export the crops. ◊ *neoplantation*.

platykurtic ◊ *kurtosis*.

pleasure driving, pleasure motoring Leisure travel by private car, undertaken both for the enjoyment derived from driving and from sightseeing *en route*. ◊ *parkway*, *scenic drive*.

Plimsoll line ◊ *load line*.

plot A parcel of land representing a land use unit defined by property boundaries on the ground.

plot ratio A means of controlling the building ◊ *density* of a non-residential development. The plot ratio is calculated by measuring the total floor area of a building and relating this to the area of the land within the curtilage of the building site, e.g. a four-storey building covering the whole site has a plot ratio of 4:1, as has an eight-storey building covering half the site. Plot ratio is similar to the ◊ *floor space index* but excludes any part of the road width and provides a more consistent standard for controlling development on individual sites, especially corner ones.

ploughland A unit of land mentioned in the Domesday book. Its exact extent is obscure, although there is some suggestion that it was equivalent to the amount of open arable land that would occupy an eight-ox plough team throughout the year – hence it varied widely in extent from parish to parish depending on soil conditions.

plug-in city A term used by architects to signify that anywhere within the ◊ *urban field* a person can connect his/her home to an elaborate and efficiently managed network of highways, telephones, radio and television outlets, as well as electricity, water supply and other public utility systems.

plural society A society in which two or more distinct cultures or social groups (with different languages, religious beliefs, kinship systems) live side by side without mingling in one political unit. These groups constitute the different levels of ◊ *social stratification*.

pluralism A philosophy about the structure of society which holds that no single dominant elite group exerts ubiquitous power over the entire political structure. Power is not held exclusively in a centralized monolithic governing body, but a certain degree of decision-making autonomy exists in localized political sub-systems. Political power is dispersed among a wide variety of groups. Potentially every decision can be made on the basis of all the group interests affected by that decision, and it is the function of government to co-ordinate and harmonize these different interests. Most Western democracies are pluralist. ◊ *plural society*.

point biserial correlation coefficient A variation on the ◊ *product-moment correlation* technique which can be used if one variable is measured on an ◊ *interval* or ◊ *ratio* scale and the other on a dichotomous scale. Arbitrary numbers are assigned to measurements on the dichotomous or ◊ *nominal* scale, then the product moment calculation is followed.

point of attachment The site of origin of a city or town.

Poisson distribution A hypothetical ◊ *frequency distribution* which is used to describe rare events and which is based on the natural law of growth called the exponential law. It describes a ◊ *stochastic process* and applies when the ◊ *probability* of an event occurring is much lower than the probability that it will not occur. In dealing with isolated, independent events in a continuum of time or space, while it is possible to specify the number of times an event did occur, it is not possible (or sensible) to say how often the event did not occur. The data are therefore always discrete, the frequency distribution is positively skewed and truncated (with most values low but a few extremely high) and there is a limit to the possibilities in one direction because of zero values and perhaps in the other because of magnitude. The implication is that the process generating the pattern is a random one. The formula for the Poisson distribution is given by

$$p(X) = \frac{\lambda^x e^{-\lambda}}{X!}$$

where $p(X)$ = probability of X events occurring in a given sample

P = probability of an event occurring

N = total sample size

λ = NP = mean and variance of the Poisson distribution

e = mathematical constant (2·71828 . . .) which forms the base of natural logarithms

It has been used by geographers to describe the distribution of events over spatial units, especially in the ◊ *quadrat analysis* of point patterns, as well as over time. ◊ *binomial distribution*, *normal distribution*.

polarization A term, first used by A. O. Hirschmann, to denote the tendency for uneven regional development to be intensified as a result of economic energy flowing to a ◊ *growth pole*. Inequality is increased by a process of circular and ◊ *cumulative causation*. ◊ *backwash effects*, *polarized development*.

polarization effects ◊ *backwash effects*.

polarization reversal A term coined by H. W. Richardson to describe the turning point when ◊ *polarization* trends in the national economy towards the ◊ *primate city* give way to dispersion.

polarized development A model, proposed by J. Friedmann, which views economic growth in a ◊ *development* context as a process of cumulative ◊ *innovation*, whereby innovations become organized into clusters and then into complex systems. Innovation is most likely in cities. The leading city and its region will constitute the core or centre of a national ◊ *urban* *system*, the rest of the system being a periphery dependent upon the core.

Innovation is diffused from the core to the periphery through exchanges of people, goods and services. Cities maintain power over their peripheries, in the sense that they alone possess real autonomy in decision-making and are recognized as the legitimate authority. The elite groups of the core population maintain their authority via the ◊ *backwash effect* (resource transfer to the core), the information effect (innovation), a production effect (scale economies) and a psychological effect. Cores and peripheries form a hierarchy of spatial systems ranging from world-wide to local. The hierarchy of cores transmits innovative impulses downwards from higher- to lower-order cores and outward from cores to dependent peripheries. Up to a point growth of a core aids development of the whole system around and below it, but in so far as development leads to a clash between the values of core elites and peripheral elites, a shift of power is inevitable in favour of the core. ◊◊ *core–periphery model, spatial structure and national economic development*.

polarized region ◊ *nodal region*.

polder A Dutch term for flat tracts of coastal or riverine land, at or below sea-level, which have been reclaimed from the sea, lake or river by endyking and draining, and kept clear of water by pumping. The work of creating them is referred to as *empoldering*. ◊◊ *reclamation*.

pôle de croissance ◊ *growth pole*.

political frontier ◊ *frontier*.

political geography The study of the effects of political actions on ◊ *human geography*, involving the spatial analysis of political phenomena. Traditionally political geography was concerned with the study of ◊ *states* – their groupings and global relations(◊ *geopolitics*)and their morphological characteristics, i.e. their ◊ *frontiers* and ◊ *boundaries*. In the last twenty years increasing interest has been shown in smaller political divisions, i.e. those within states, involving an appreciation of the interaction between political processes and spatial organization, e.g. the nature and consequences of decision-making by urban government, the relationship between public policy and resource development, the geography of public finance (◊ *political representation effect*) and ◊ *electoral geography*. ◊◊ *power analysis*.

political representation effect In the allocation of government expenditure, where areas with political representatives on key committees receive higher levels of government support than might be expected given their needs and resources. ◊ *pork barrel*.

pollard A broadleaved tree whose trunk is cut across (*polled*) about 2 m (6 ft) from the ground to produce a close crown of young branches. As the young shoots are well clear of the ground they are safe from grazing cattle or deer. Repeated pollarding gives successive crops of small poles suitable for fencing, basketry or firewood. The term derives from the Norman-French *poll*, meaning head. ◊◊ *coppice*.

pollutant A substance or effect introduced by people which adversely alters the ◊ *environment*, e.g. changes the growth rate of animal or plant species; interferes with the food chain; is toxic; or is harmful to human health and reduces the comfort, amenity or property values of people. A polluting substance may be a solid, semi-solid, liquid, gas or sub-molecular particle. A polluting effect is some kind of waste energy (heat, noise, vibration). Pollutants are normally introduced into the environment by some form of human activity, e.g. sewage and waste disposal, accidental discharge (◊ *pollution*). Pollutants may be classified in various ways:

(i) By whether they are conservative or non-conservative. *Conservative pollutants* remain largely unchanged when introduced into the environment. They are often toxic and tend to accumulate in biological systems. *Non-conservative pollutants* will eventually be assimilated into biological cycles via processes such as biodegradation.

(ii) By origin. They may be (a) biological, e.g. faecal contaminants; (b) chemical, e.g. sulphur dioxide emissions; (c) physical, e.g. noise, radioactivity, refuse.

(iii) By controllability – the ease with which a pollutant can be removed from or prevented from reaching the environment.

'polluter-pays' principle The principle which requires that the costs of ◇ *pollution*, whether incurred in preventing the release of a potential ◇ *pollutant* or in repairing pollution damage, should be 'internalized' and met by whoever causes the pollution.

pollution The introduction by people, directly or indirectly, of a ◇ *pollutant* into the ◇ *environment* which results in deleterious effects of such a nature as to endanger human health, harm living resources and ecosystems, and impair the use and amenities of the environment. It is the result of the release of substances and energy in the wrong places in quantities that are too large for the capacity of environmental systems either to neutralize or disperse them to harmless levels. From an economic viewpoint pollution is regarded as a consumption of environmental quality. Three main types of pollution are recognized on the basis of the environmental medium concerned:

(i) *Air pollution*, resulting from the emission of aerosols (minute suspended particles) derived largely from the combustion of fossil fuels.

(ii) *Water pollution*, with a distinction often made between *freshwater pollution* – the result of disposing of effluents, of the use of economic poisons in the form of pesticides, etc., and including *thermal pollution* due to the return of water used for cooling purposes – and *marine pollution* – the result of oil spillages at sea and of sewage and industrial waste disposal.

(iii) *Land pollution*, including the deliberate dumping of solid wastes and the occurrence of toxic metals in soil.

In addition *noise pollution* (from aircraft, road vehicles, industrial premises, etc.) is treated separately, as is *visual pollution*, caused by intrusive development and desecration of the landscape. ◇ *background concentration, environmental capacity, pollution control, pollution factor, pollution load.*

pollution control Legislative and administrative procedures aimed at reducing the harm of a potential ◇ *pollutant*. In formulating an effective pollution control strategy it is necessary to focus on the damage caused by emissions rather than just their volume. Emphasis is on the control or prevention of emissions (◇ *ambient standard, emission standard, specification standard*). Pollution control programmes are normally based on human-oriented ◇ *acceptable dose limits* (◇◇ *critical group*). Responsibilities for pollution control in England and Wales are shown in ◇ Fig. 121. ◇◇ *noise control, smoke control zone.*

pollution factor The amount of a ◇ *pollutant* or a combination of pollutants released into the environment by an industry per unit of output or per unit of raw material consumed. ◇◇ *pollution load, waste factor.*

pollution load The total amount of a ◇ *pollutant* or a combination of pollutants released into the environment by an industry or group of industries in a given area during a certain period of time. ◇◇ *pollution factor, waste factor.*

polyculture ◇ *Multiple cropping* on individual farms, or even in particular fields.

	Central Government		Regional or Local Authorities	
NOISE	Department of Trade	Aircraft noise	District Councils	Neighbourhood noise
NOISE	Department of Transport	Vehicle noise	District Councils	Neighbourhood noise
NOISE	Department of the Environment	Noise policy	District Councils	Heavy vehicle routes
NOISE	Health and Safety Executive	Noise in works	District Councils	Heavy vehicle routes
AIR	Health and Safety Executive	Emissions from registered works; radioactive discharges into air	District Councils	Emissions from domestic and commercial premises and non-registered works
AIR	Department of the Environment	Air policy	District Councils	Emissions from domestic and commercial premises and non-registered works
SOLID WASTES	Department of the Environment	Land wastes	District Councils	Collection of domestic and trade wastes
SOLID WASTES	Department of the Environment	Radioactive wastes	County Councils	Disposal of domestic and trade wastes; licensing of disposal sites
WATER	Department of the Environment	Water pollution	Regional Water Authorities	All water services
MARINE	Ministry of Agriculture, Fisheries & Food	Dumping and discharges at sea	Regional Water Authorities	Discharges from land
MARINE	Department of Energy	Offshore oil and gas installations	Harbour Authorities	Remedial action in harbours
MARINE	Department of Trade	Oil and chemical pollution	County & District Councils	Cleaning of beaches, etc.

Fig. 121 Pollution control

polygamy Compound marriage. There are two forms: *polygyny* – the marriage of one man to two or more women – and *polyandry* – the marriage of one woman to two or more men. ⟡ *monogamy, nuptiality*.

popular region ⟡ *vernacular region*.

population (1) In general a term for the number of people living in an area at a particular time. ⟡ *closed population, day population, de facto population, de jure population, dependent population, floating population, landward population, night population, optimum population, stable population, stationary population, working population, zero-growth population*.
(2) In statistics, every member or object of a group possessing the same basic and defined characteristic (which may vary in amount and quality from one member to another). Strictly speaking, a *statistical population* is a population of measurements, but the term is used to describe the entire set of people, places or other objects to which the measurement refers. It is the *target population* (the conceptual or ultimate total population) to which a study relates or which a survey attempts to cover, in contrast to the *sampled* or *survey population* which is actually covered. ⟡ *sampling*.

population, dependent ⟡ *dependent population, dependency ratio*.

population accounts A method of spatial demographic analysis applied to multiregional systems which takes into full consideration ⟡ *migration* between regions, as well as ⟡ *fertility* and ⟡ *mortality*. ⟡ *population projection*.

population-carrying capacity For a given area, at a certain level of ⟡ *development*, available resources will be able to support a maximum number of people. This is the population-carrying capacity. Also termed *population ceiling*. ⟡ *man–land ratio, population–resources ratio*.

population ceiling ⟡ *population-carrying capacity*.

population census ⟡ *census*.

population cycle The regular pattern of change in an area's population over a period of time. The best-known cycle is that of ⟡ *demographic transition*, based on European experience, but a *primitive* or *Malthusian population cycle* (⟡ *Malthusian theory of population*) and a *future* or ⟡ *baby boom population cycle* have also been recognized.

population density The number of people relative to the space occupied by them. ⟡ *density*.

population equation An equation identifying the components of population change:

$$P_{t+1} = P_t + (B - D) + (I - E)$$

where P_t and P_{t+1} = population size of the same area at two different times

$B - D =$ ⟡ *natural change component* in that area over the same time span from births (B) and deaths (D)

$I - E =$ net migration over the same time span from immigration (I) and emigration (E)

The equation is applicable to any area over any period of time (although the migration term is dropped if considering the global situation).

population forecasting ⟡ *population projection*.

population geography The study of the relationship between spatial variations in the distribution, composition, migration and growth of ⟡ *population* and the geographic character of places. It is concerned with:

(i) the description of the location of population, its numbers and characteristics;
(ii) an explanation of the spatial configurations of these numbers and characteristics;
(iii) the spatial analysis of population phenomena, e.g. births, deaths, ◊ *migration*;
(iv) ◊ *population policy*.

population implosion A term coined by P. Hauser to describe the large-scale movement of population out of the rural areas and into urban areas which was characteristic of 19th-century Western Europe and is now a feature of much of the Third World. ◊◊ *migration*.

population policy Government measures, and the principles on which they are based, to influence ◊ *population* change. Thus an expansionist policy may seek to increase the rate of population growth or check actual or incipient population decline, while a restrictionist policy checks population growth and reduces the rate of population increase. Measures favouring ◊ *fertility* include family allowances, marriage loans, restriction of availability of ◊ *birth control* appliances, declaring ◊ *abortion* illegal and the provision of ante- and post-natal care. Anti-natal measures usually comprise the legalization of abortion, birth control propaganda and sterilization.

population potential The population potential of a point is a measure of the nearness of people to that point, i.e. of the intensity of the possibility of interaction between that point and all other points in a system. In general the potential exerted at a point (PP_i) is defined as

$$PP_i = \sum_{j=1}^{n} \frac{P_j}{d_{ij}}$$

where P_j = population of the jth point
d_{ij} = distance between points i and j

n = number of points in the system

Each individual contributes to the total potential at any point an amount equal to the reciprocal of their distance away – the population potential at point i being the sum of the ratios of populations at all points to the distances those points are away from i. The term d_{ij} may be raised to some power to take into account friction of distance.

If the calculation is carried out for every point in the system and the resulting values are mapped using isopleths, a *potential population surface* results (◊ Fig. 122).

The term originates in ◊ *social physics* and the concept parallels that of the ◊ *gravity model*.

population pressure The growth of ◊ *population* in excess of the provision of economic and social facilities, leading to a deterioration in the quality of the human and physical resources of an area. Average standards of living and, in particular, food supply per capita decline. ◊◊ *demographic coefficient, overpopulation*.

population projection Or *population forecasting*. The estimation of the size and composition of a ◊ *population* at a future date, based on a particular set of assumptions concerning trends in ◊ *fertility*, ◊ *mortality* and ◊ *migration*. The various methods of estimating future populations may be classified as *direct* or *indirect*. *Direct methods*, which generate a population projection, are based on the extrapolations of past and current demographic trends (◊ *cohort-survival method, growth composition analysis*). *Indirect methods*, which are based primarily on ◊ *regression* and ◊ *correlation* analysis, produce population forecasts and take into account economic, social and political indices (such as employment, income, investment, etc.).

population pyramid ◊ *age/sex pyramid*.

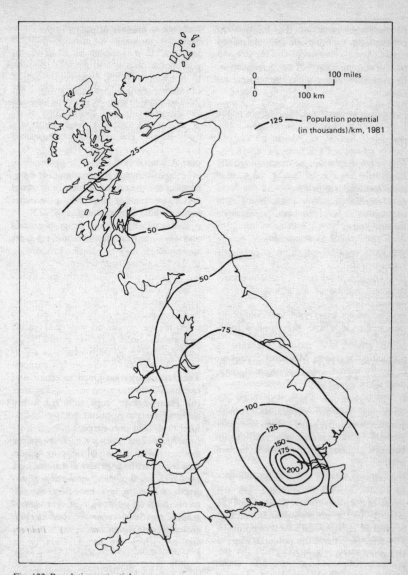

Fig. 122 Population potential

population–resource ratio The relationship between the quantity and quality of an area's natural ◊ *resources* and the size and technical competence of its ◊ *population*. ◊◊ *man–land ratio*, *population–resource regions*.

population–resource regions Regions of the world classified according to ◊ *population–resource ratios*. E. A. Akerman's classification recognized five types of region:
(i) The *United States type* – technologically innovative regions of low ◊ *population potential* resource ratio.
(ii) The *European type* – technologically innovative regions of high population–resource ratio.
(iii) The *Brazil type* – technologically deficient regions of low population–resource ratio.
(iv) The *Egyptian type* – technologically deficient regions of high population–resource ratio.
(v) The *Arctic-desert type* – technologically deficient regions with very limited food-producing resources.

population theory A theory designed to explain population growth. Such theories may be classified as:
(i) *Biological*, in which the laws determining human population growth parallel those influencing animal and plant growth, e.g. there is an inverse relationship between human fertility and protein intake.
(ii) *Cultural*, which emphasize the influence of people's culture and character on their fertility, e.g. the idea that the declining fertility of advanced industrial countries is associated with a desire for higher social and economic status.
(iii) *Economic*, which recognize the importance of economic forces in social change, especially the idea that the demand for labour determines its supply.

pork barrel An American term used to describe spatial bias in government resource allocation/expenditure programmes in order to appease political interests. It may occur at all levels of government and is frequently a response to lobbying by elected politicians on behalf of their constituencies, the government recognizing that the selective disbursement of benefits can critically influence its electoral support. ◊ *political representation effect*.

port A transport ◊ *node* – a place where land and water transport modes interconnect for the regular exchange of cargo and passengers. It is a point of contact between land and ◊ *maritime space* and provides services to both the ◊ *hinterland* and the maritime organization (◊◊ *port space*). Ports may be classified according to the functions they perform:
(i) *Terminal ports*: These are multifunctional, handling a wide variety of general cargo, various bulk imports and exports, and even passenger/ferry traffic and, as a consequence, command wide and varied hinterlands. Such ports are normally the final destination of ships which, as a general rule, expect to take on full cargoes. They are usually equipped to repair and overhaul ships.
(ii) *Ports-of-call*: Ships sailing between *terminal ports* may call at ports-of-call to load or unload part-cargoes.
(iii) *Specialized ports*, e.g. ferry ports, fishing ports, industrial loading places (concerned with the export of a single bulk product), naval ports. ◊ *enclosed port*, *entrepôt*, *integrated port*, *open port*, *outport*, *treaty port*. ◊◊ *anyport*, *port development model*, *port–outport model*, *port piracy*, *sustained port dominance*.

port area That part of ◊ *port space* comprising the physical site of the port installations and the contiguous water areas, i.e. the ◊ *harbour* and the port approaches (◊ *fairway*) leading in from the open sea.

port capacity The measure of a ◊ *port*'s size,

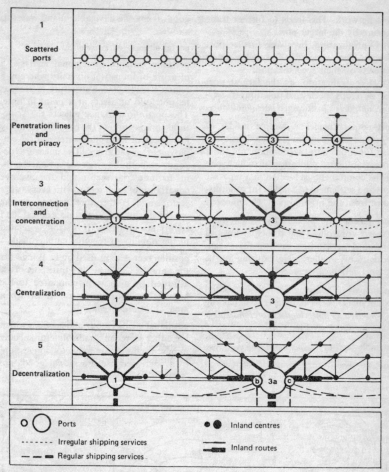

Fig. 123 Port development model

either in terms of the number of berths and total length of quay or the total tonnage of ships using the port during a year.

port development model A model, proposed by P. J. Rimmer, describing the growth of ◊ *ports* and their ◊ *hinterland* and ◊ *foreland* connections (◊ Fig. 123). It envisages five phases:

(1) Scattered ports – dispersed along a coast, each with limited hinterland and an irregular service.

(2) Landward penetration, in which some ports develop as foci of separate route networks at the expense of other ports (◊ *port piracy*).

(3) Interconnection and concentration, as feeder routes continue to develop and separate ports are linked by a landward trans-

369

port network. This leads to further trade capture by the larger ports.

(4) Centralization, involving further port piracy. The survival of smaller ports depends on their specialization.

(5) Decentralization, as the largest port also develops specialized functions (◊ *anyport*, *outport*). ◌ *sustained port dominance*.

port–outport model A simple model of ◊ *port* development involving a division of port functions into two components and a process of port relocation in which one of the components is located in a separate port and settlement (◊ *outport*) at some distance from the original port. ◌ *anyport*.

port piracy The process by which those ◊ *ports* controlling the principal lines of landward penetration capture the ◊ *hinterlands* of smaller, neighbouring ports. ◌ *port development model*.

port space The geographical or spatial extent of a ◊ *port*'s activities encompassing ◊ *port area*, ◊ *hinterland*, ◊ *foreland* and ◊ *maritime space* (◊ Fig. 124).

portable territory ◊ *personal space*.

portage The transporting of boats and goods from one navigable inland water to another.

portal cities ◊ *gateway cities*.

portfolio variance In regional analysis, a measure of industrial diversity whereby a region's employment structure is seen as its portfolio of assets at a point in time. The portfolio variance reflects the structural composition of the regional economy in respect of intra- and intersectoral employment covariation. The measure depends on both the observed variance within an industrial sector and the average covariance of each sector with every other sector, and is therefore defined as the weighted sum of the time-sectoral and covariance measures. It is strongly related to the stability of regional employment.

position rent A term used by L. Wingo for the annual savings in transport cost afforded by a location compared to the highest cost location in use in an urban area. ◌ *location rent*.

positional goods Goods and services which are either scarce in an absolute or socially imposed sense or are liable to 'congestion' from increased use. Positional goods are

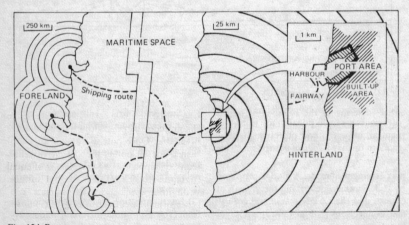

Fig. 124 Port space

often also ◊ *merit goods* and/or ◊ *public goods* and enjoyment or satisfaction from their consumption is affected by how many other people have access to the good. Contrast ◊ *material goods*.

positive discrimination A form of ◊ *social engineering* involving government policies designed to favour the most disadvantaged groups and areas. The objective is to reduce inequalities, both spatial and sectoral, by a redistribution of financial, technological and labour resources to the benefit of the most deprived. Such positive discrimination tends to treat the effects of inequality rather than removing its causes. ◊◊ *area-based policies*.

positive theory A ◊ *theory* which explains observed phenomena against which it has been, or could be, empirically tested. The method of inference is ◊ *induction*, as the procedure is to take a set of observations and develop a system of relationships that is accepted as a satisfactory explanation of the observed pattern. Contrast ◊ *normative theory*.

positivism A philosophy whose central thesis is that science can only deal with empirical questions, i.e. those with a factual content. It originates from A. Comte's early 19th-century attempt to distinguish science from metaphysics and religion. Genuine knowledge is restricted to facts that can be observed and to the relationships between those observations. Thus our sensory experiences are the sole source of valid information about the world. The philosophy proclaims the unity of science, which (ideally) is value-free, neutral, impartial and objective. Its more modern form is ◊ *logical positivism*. ◊◊ *empiricism*.

possibilism A philosophical view that the physical ◊ *environment* offers human beings a range of opportunities from which they select according to their cultural needs and norms. It is a branch of ◊ *environmentalism* and does not deny that there are finite, natural limits to human activity (◊ *environmental determinism*), but emphasizes the significance of freedom of choice for individuals. Spatial patterns of human activity are therefore the result of people's choices within an inert or permissive environmental frame. This viewpoint was stressed by the French school of geography (e.g. Vidal de la Blache, J. Brunhes) in the early 20th century.

possible reserves ◊ *reserves*.

postage stamp pricing A term for ◊ *uniform pricing*.

post-neonatal mortality ◊ *infant mortality*.

potential household ◊ *hidden household*.

potential production unit A measure of the relative output of different types of land proposed by L. D. Stamp. A potential production unit of 1 represented the average output of good farmland.

potential reserves ◊ *reserves*.

potential surface A method of transforming a set of discrete observations into a spatially-continuous distribution, in effect equivalent to a 'density' surface. The idea of 'potential' derives from the gravity concept and can be applied to a variety of economic and social phenomena. The influence at any point, with reference to any other point, is proportional to the mass exerting the influence and inversely proportional to the distance between the points: the sum of all influences at a point is termed the 'potential'. All points in space have a 'potential' value, determined by interpolation (if necessary) from the magnitudes at points for which data are available. Once potential has been established for all points the spatial variation can be mapped, using ◊ *isopleths* of equal potential to generate a potential surface. Common applications in human geography involve the calculation of ◊ *market potential* and ◊ *population potential*. ◊◊ *gravity model*.

poverty ◊ *cycle of poverty*.

power analysis Power is viewed as the driving force of the international system. ◊ *States* are engaged in a struggle for power, their command of which is demonstrated by an ability to obtain the best terms in their external relations. The power of one state must therefore be seen in relation to the power of other states. Political geographers' interest in power stems from the fact that the power of states is based, in part, on their geographical characteristics, as well as from its influence on state behaviour. Power analysis provides one approach in political geography. It begins by recognizing several bases of a state's power:

(i) *Morphological power*, deriving from the geographical characteristics of the state, such as size, shape, location and physical features.

(ii) *Demographic power*, reflecting the numerical strength of population, as well as its quality, morale and national characteristics.

(iii) *Economic power*, stemming from the commercial resources of the state, its technological and business acumen, and its trading relationships, especially import dependency.

(iv) *Organizational power*, reflecting the quality and stability of government and administration.

(v) *Military power*, depending on the size and equipment of a state's armed forces.

(vi) *Power from external relationships*, reflecting a state's international prestige and acknowledging its role in international organizations and alliances.

Relatively unsuccessful attempts have been made to measure state power in order to produce an international ranking.

pragmatism A philosophy which defines the meaning and knowledge of an action or idea in terms of its practical consequences, i.e. its role in experience. Pragmatism emphasizes the importance of 'concrete' or individual situations in obtaining scientific knowledge and for understanding human behaviour – the method of reasoning is by ◊ *induction*. Thus the meaning attached by a pragmatist to space or movement in space stems directly from the practical consequences of that space.

precession wave A dynamic feature of land use at the built-up edge of the metropolis, representing the period of penetration or urban land preparation during which changes in land ownership, plot size and roads are laid over the original rural pattern to make the area ready for urban occupancy. ◊◊ *land conversion process*.

precinct A term originally applied to land around a religious institution but now used more widely in town planning and urban geography to describe a specialized and defined area within a town – one which is easily recognizable, within which certain characteristics exist and whose boundaries are clearly distinguishable, especially a *shopping precinct* or other *pedestrian precinct* (◊◊ *pedestrian area*) from which all motor vehicles are excluded.

pre-compensation ◊ *countertrade*.

predisposition In the explanation of consumer behaviour a ◊ *consumer* is predisposed towards the purchase of a particular good when the motivation to buy is reinforced by knowledge that the good will satisfy a need. Predispositions reflect an individual's characteristics at the time the choice is made, i.e. factors such as values and beliefs, past experiences, etc. Final choice may be distorted even where the consumer is thus predisposed by other factors, e.g. high price, lack of availability. ◊◊ *product attribute*.

preference space Within ◊ *awareness space* that set of locations or areas which meet a household's or businessman's needs for ◊ *accessibility* and contact.

preindustrial city A generalization, suggested by G. Sjoberg, about the form of society and urbanization before the modern era – preindustrial cities were found prior to the ◇ *Industrial Revolution.* Cities are products of their societies, and at that time society was 'feudal', embodying a ◇ *social stratification* system with a small elite and a much larger lower class. The preindustrial city was controlled by this elite, which derived its power from non-economic, often extra-urban sources. Society, at that time, was also dependent on animate energy. Such cities were small, with less than 50,000 population, and each contained only a very small proportion of the national population.

Preindustrial cities were multifunctional, performing largely military and political roles but with economic, religious, administrative, educational and cultural functions in a supportive role. This was reflected not only in the power structure but also in the urban morphology: the key feature was the compact form – a distinct urban nucleus bounded by walls, which served as defences and as a means of controlling the entry of migrants and traders. The internal morphology was

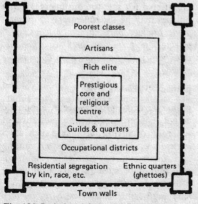

Fig. 125 Preindustrial city

characterized by narrow streets and a lack of functional differentiation of land use since, with separation of workplace and residence uncommon, most plots were put to multiple uses. Sjoberg, however, suggested a broad zonal pattern with the elite group residing close to the prestigious central core and the artisans and poor living in progressively less prestigious areas away from the core (◇ Fig. 125). Outside the central core some residential differentiation, in the form of quarters, could be distinguished on ethnic, occupational or kinship grounds.

The concept has been much criticized (i) because a single type of city is unlikely to have existed in all parts of the world over a time span of some 5,000 years; (ii) because of the use of the term 'feudal' to describe all societies before the Industrial Revolution; (iii) because the division of preindustrial society into elite and lower classes was considered too simple, and (iv) because not all such cities were unplanned and disorganized.

pressure group A primarily voluntary body which seeks to influence policy outcomes from the government decision-making process without becoming involved in that process to the extent that members adopt formal governmental roles. Several types of pressure groups may be distinguished: (i) *Partial* or *exclusive* groups. With the former, exerting political pressure is secondary and supportive of another more general aim, whereas an exclusive group exists in order to pressurize government. (ii) *Private* or *public* groups. Generally pressure groups are wholly private, established outside the realm of formal government, but there are examples of bodies within government circles (e.g. the Nature Conservancy Council) which act in the same fashion. (iii) *Interest* or *promotional* (*cause*) groups. Members of interest groups explicitly pursue political aims, in contrast to those in promotional groups, who have more altruistic goals, i.e. 'cause' or 'principle'. ◊ *public participation*.

pressurized water reactor (PWR) A type of ◊ *light water reactor*.

pre-urban nucleus A non-urban ◊ *settlement*, e.g. a castle or church, about which a town was formed. ◊ *point of attachment*.

prevalence rate (of disease) The total number of cases of a disease expressed as a percentage of the population. It depends on the incidence (◊ *incidence rate*) and duration of the disease and is the probability of an individual having the disease.

price The exchange ◊ *value* of a commodity or good or service in terms of money. *Equilibrium price* is determined in the ◊ *market* by the forces of ◊ *demand* and ◊ *supply*. ◊ Fig. 126. ◊ *index of retail prices*, *price mechanism*.

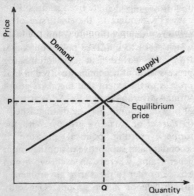

Fig. 126 Price

price funnel The selling price of a commodity increases with distance from the point of production by the cost of the freight and, on an ◊ *isotropic surface*, the trend in price in all directions about the production point describes a price funnel (◊ Fig.127). Price funnels are character-

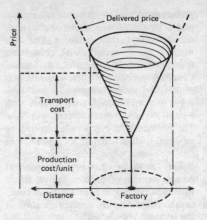

Fig. 127 Price funnel

istic of industry located at restricted places selling to areally spaced customers. ◊ *demand cone*.

price mechanism The economic system used in a competitive society to allocate scarce resources through the agency of ◊ *price*. Equivalent to the ◊ *market economy*.

price–ratio line ◊ *iso-outlay line*.

pricing policies The principles and practices of determining the prices at which goods are offered for sale to consumers. Pricing policies may be *discriminatory* (◊ *basing-point pricing*, *blanket rate pricing*, *c.i.f. pricing*, *uniform pricing*) or *non-discriminatory* (◊ *f.o.b. pricing*). ◊ *transfer pricing*.

primacy ◊ *primate city*.

primary activity, primary sector Economic activity concerned with the exploitation of naturally occurring resources, such as ◊ *agriculture*, ◊ *fisheries*, ◊ *forestry*, mining and quarrying (◊ *extractive industry*). The output of such primary production often needs further processing. ◊ *quaternary activity*, *secondary activity*, *tertiary activity*.

primary energy ◇ *Energy* contained in primary power sources, i.e. energy provided by the material itself, such as coal and petroleum, or derived from renewable sources, such as the sun, waves and wind. All energy used comes from these primary sources, although it may well be delivered in the form of secondary energy, such as electricity, coke or manufactured gas. ◇ *primary fuel.*

primary family ◇ *nuclear family.*

primary fuel Fuels which provide ◇ *energy* directly without undergoing any manufacturing or conversion process, e.g. coal, natural gas, wood. ◇ *secondary fuel.*

primary group A group of people, such as a ◇ *family* or ◇*extended family*, that has intimate, face-to-face social relationships.

primary hinterland ◇ *hinterland.*

primary industry ◇ *Manufacturing industry* specializing in basic processing or the conversion of ◇ *raw materials*, e.g. food and agricultural processing, canning and freezing, as well as firms refining ores into pure metal. Firms engaged in primary industry tend to show ◇ *material orientation* in their choice of location.

primary location ◇ *location.*

primary product A ◇ *product* that has not been fabricated, e.g. a foodstuff or raw material such as wood or wool. ◇ *secondary product.*

primary recovery The recovery of oil and gas from a reservoir using the natural confining pressure and pumping. The pressure on the hydrocarbons in the reservoir rock must be greater than that at the lower end of the well for oil and gas to flow out as a gusher. As oil is withdrawn the reservoir pressure decreases and ◇ *secondary recovery* may be employed. ◇ *recovery factor.*

primary territory ◇ *territory.*

primary town A long-established English ◇ *town* which was a settlement in Saxon or earlier times, was associated with early routes, had a minster church and an unusually large ◇ *parish*, was an early administrative and pre-Conquest trading centre and which best survived the economic stress of medieval times.

primary urbanization ◇ *Urbanization* originating within a country.

primate city (distribution) The *law of the primate city* is one of the earliest generalizations concerning the size-distribution of cities propounded by M. Jefferson. The primate city is a country's leading city and is disproportionately larger than any others in the system: it dominates all others not only in population size but also in its role as a political, economic and social centre for the country. It is usually the ◇ *capital city.* Thus a primate distribution (◇ Fig. 128) has a stratum of small towns dominated by one very large city, with an absence of intermediate sized centres. Primacy is a product of the small size of a country, of simple economic and political organization, of export orientation, a recent colonial history and a short history

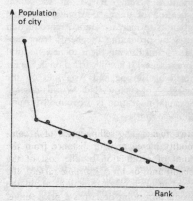

Fig. 128 Primate city distribution

375

of urbanization. ◊ *index of primacy.* ◊◊ *city-size distribution, rank–size rule.*

prime costs All ◊ *costs* which can be assigned to any single unit of a product. Prime costs include all ◊ *variable costs* and some ◊ *fixed costs,* e.g. administration.

primeur An 'out-of-season' or early vegetable crop grown in France.

primitive cultivation A crop-based subsistence agricultural system, also referred to as a *rudimental cultivation.* Three types may be recognized: ◊ *shifting cultivation,* semi-shifting cultivation and ◊ *sedentary agriculture.* It is a step up the economic ladder from ◊ *primitive gathering* since plants have been domesticated.

primitive gathering The lowest order of economic activity, involving the collection of food and other materials close at hand and supplied by nature (plants and animals). Palaeolithic peoples, like the few primitive groups in the world today, adopted three elementary modes of life – gathering, hunting and fishing. All these modes are migratory and nomadic in the long run and are limited to a ◊ *subsistence* level barely above the minimum for survival. ◊◊ *nomadism.*

primitive herding Based on the domestication of animals, primitive herding attempts to increase animal reproduction rates by protecting the herds from predators and driving them to new, natural forage areas. It is still carried on in the far north of Europe and Asia and on the margins of many Old World deserts. Seasonal migration is a common feature. ◊◊ *nomadism.*

primitive population cycle ◊ *Malthusian theory of population.*

primogeniture The system by which an eldest son inherits all his parents' property. Inheritance based on this system works towards the concentration of wealth.

principal components analysis A multivariate statistical method of analysing a matrix of correlation coefficients for three or more variables. The approach replaces the original set of intercorrelated variables $(x_1, x_2 \ldots x_n)$, via an orthogonal transformation, by a new set $(y_1, y_2 \ldots y_n)$ of components which are correlated with the original variables but uncorrelated with each other. As many components are derived as there are original variables, and the original total ◊ *variance* associated with $(x_1, x_2 \ldots x_n)$ is preserved exactly in the total variance of the components $(y_1, y_2 \ldots y_n)$. The solution is such that the leading components account for relatively large shares of the original variance, i.e. y_1 accounts for the highest proportion of this total variance, y_2 for the second largest and so on. The correlations between the original variables and the components are referred to as *component loadings,* and the interpretation of the principal components is done mainly with reference to these loadings – the variables having high correlations or loadings on a component serve to identify that component.

Principal components analysis is used as an empirical procedure seeking related groups of variables and as a method of data reduction. In geography its most frequent use has been for areal and urban classification. ◊◊ *factor analysis.*

principality A ◊ *state* over which a prince has jurisdiction or from which he obtains his title.

principle of least effort Or *lex parsimoniae* or *law of minimum effort.* A rather vague principle which is considered as guiding much human activity. If a job or activity can be done in more than one way a person will do it the way that requires the least effort, that is money, energy or time. For the geographer minimizing effort usually means minimizing distance and movement.

priority areas Areas designated to receive aid as part of government policy aimed at various regional and metropolitan problems. Such areas are frequently defined on the basis of having the 'worst' conditions, e.g. highest unemployment, poorest housing conditions. ◊ *positive discrimination.* ◊◊ *area-based policies.*

priority neighbourhood Basically an area which is suitable for treatment as a ◊ *housing action area* or ◊ *general improvement area* but where this is, for the time being, impracticable. Local authorities normally declare priority neighbourhoods adjacent to existing housing action areas in order to prevent the housing position in or around the stress area from deteriorating further and to stop stress from spreading out from areas which are subject to concentrated action.

pristine state A ◊ *nation-state* which developed out of purely local conditions. ◊◊ *secondary state.*

privacy The selective control of access to the ◊ *place* occupied by an individual or a group. Privacy is a goal in the human use of micro-space.

private company A ◊ *limited liability* company that is not allowed to offer shares to the general public on the stock market or to have more than a small number of shareholders (twenty in the United Kingdom). It is the major form of ownership for small businesses, enabling the owner(s) to put into a company only as much money as they wish. The company's existence as a legal organization is separate from that of the owner(s). ◊◊ *public company.*

private costs and benefits Costs and benefits of an action that are borne by/accrue to the decision-maker, e.g. production outlays of a firm, costs paid by consumer for a good, sales revenue received by a firm. Such costs and benefits are 'internal'

to the person or organization undertaking the action. ◊◊ *social costs and benefits.*

private sector That part of a national economy which is not subject to direct government ownership and control. The constituents of the private sector are ◊ *public companies*, ◊ *private companies*, partnerships, sole proprietorships and non-profit-making organizations. ◊◊ *public sector.*

probabilism A philosophical view which, although rejecting ◊ *environmental determinism* and recognizing the range of possibilities (◊ *possibilism*) afforded by the physical environment, argues that some outcomes are more likely than others.

probabilistic A term describing a viewpoint which holds that relationships between phenomena need not be invariant, even if conditions are held constant. This may be expressed as: if x, then either w or y or z, i.e. if a particular event x occurs then any one of the events or event sequences w, y or z may occur. Probabilities of occurrence are usually stated for the subsequent events. ◊◊ *deterministic.*

probability A basic statistical concept, the likelihood or chance of occurrence of a particular event, i.e.

$$\text{Probability of outcome} = \frac{\text{Number of times outcome occurred}}{\text{Number of events}}$$

Probability theory, a branch of pure mathematics, developed from the formal study of random phenomena which, on any single observation, may result in any one of a number of possible outcomes. The particular outcome of a single observation is dependent on chance and cannot be predicted ahead of time, but over repeated observations the outcomes will show some statistical regularity. Given a very large number of observations the relative frequency of a random event will approach a stable or fixed value – the probability of that event. Probabilities may take on any value between zero (meaning impossible, it cannot occur) and 1 (meaning certain, it must occur). ◊ *subjective probability*.

probability sampling ◊*sampling*.

probable reserves ◊ *reserves*.

problem family A ◊ *family* which is ill-adjusted to the social values and customs of the society in which it lives and is, therefore, not integrated into that society.

process linkage ◊ *linkage*.

process-response system ◊ *systems analysis*.

processing cost ◊ *production costs*.

procurement costs ◊ *assembly costs*.

produce district A traditional ◊ *wholesaling* district or market quarter, located in the core of the city at the edge of the shopping district, and dealing in fresh foodstuffs. The location was originally dependent on access by customers (restaurateurs, hoteliers, retailers). ◊◊ *manufacturing stocks district, product comparison district, will-call delivery district*.

producer An organization or ◊ *firm* responsible for converting ◊ *factors of production* into useful goods and services.

producer goods Goods that satisfy wants only indirectly as factors in the production of other goods. Contrast ◊ *consumer goods*. ◊◊ *capital goods*.

product The finished output of an industry in the ◊ *secondary sector*. It is distinguished from ◊ *commodity* and ◊ *good*. ◊◊ *primary product*.

product attributes The physical properties of the objects or services wanted by consumers. The concept is distinguished in the explanation of consumer behaviour because product attributes convey certain meanings to consumers, including an estimate of the object's potential to satisfy wants. ◊◊ *predisposition*.

product comparison district The grouping of wholesalers for whose customers comparison of goods is important, particularly characteristic of the clothing and furniture trades. It is usually located adjacent to that part of the central business district where out-of-town buyers come together in hotels. ◊ *wholesaling*. ◊◊ *manufacturing stocks district, product district, will-call delivery district*.

product cycle ◊ *product life cycle*.

product differentiation The methods by which goods of a particular producer are given real or imagined differences in the eyes of consumers, e.g. branding, packaging, advertising. ◊◊ *monopolistic competition*.

product life cycle A concept based on the development of total ◊ *demand* for a firm's or an industry's product over the lifetime of that product. Five periods are recognized: (i) A long introductory period during which sales of the product fluctuate as test purchases are made and sales therefore increase only slowly. (ii) A period of rapid growth in sales (and profit levels) as market penetration increases. (iii) Maturity, reached when profit levels peak (and even begin to decline) although sales volumes continue to rise. Competitive products appear by the end of this period. (iv) Market saturation, signalled when sales volume peaks (and profits decline further). (v) A period of declining sales, as the product's market penetration is eroded. The cycle may be interrupted or rejuvenated at any stage.

The product life cycle is associated with changes in a firm's expansion/investment programme. During phase (i), when the product commands a high price, the firm incurs high unit costs because production is labour-intensive, with a high proportion of scientific and technical inputs. Growth sees the adoption of ◊ *mass production*, and distribution methods and production processes become more capital-intensive. By maturity product specifications and production methods have been standardized and the firm's competitive position has derived the maximum advantage from available ◊ *economies of scale*, with unskilled and semi-skilled workers accounting for an increasing share of the labour employed. Saturation sees market penetration strategies replaced by product development ones in an attempt to stave off contraction in the face of competitive substitutes. Decline is met by attempts at ◊ *diversification* or even by closure, depending on the size and organization of the firm. ◊◊ *foreign direct investment theory*.

product-moment correlation coefficient A ◊ *parametric test* of the relationship between two ◊ *variables* measured on an ◊ *interval* or ◊ *ratio scale*. It measures the degree to which a change in direction and magnitude of one variable is associated with comparable changes in the other, taking into account the amount by which each value differs from the ◊ *arithmetic mean* of its own distribution, the ◊ *standard deviations* of the two distributions and the number of pairs of values. The notation of the formula can vary, but the product-moment correlation coefficient may be calculated as:

$$r = \frac{1/n \, \Sigma (x - \bar{x})(y - \bar{y})}{\sigma x \cdot \sigma y}$$

where Σ = sum of the product of the total variations from the means, $\bar{x}$ and $\bar{y}$

n = number of pairs of values

$\sigma x, \sigma y$ = the standard deviations of the two distributions

The term product-moment derives from the fact that each of the terms in the numerator of the formula represents an element of the first moment about the mean. ◊◊ *point biserial correlation coefficient*.

production (1) The process by which goods and services are provided through combining ◊ *factors of production*. The process generates ◊ *place utility* and ◊ *form utility*. (2) Total output measured in some absolute terms.

production capital ◊ *capital goods*.

production costs Or *processing costs*. The actual ◊ *costs* incurred in the ◊ *production* at a site. These are mainly attributable to capital and labour and exclude transport costs. ◊◊ *cost structure*, *on-site costs*.

production cycle A Soviet concept, associated with N. N. Kolosovsky, which denotes the sets of ◊ *linkages* that integrate particular industries into a complex. Eight production cycles are distinguished:
(i) The *iron–steel cycle* – from the mining of coking coal and iron ore, to smelting, rolling, metal working and heavy machinery fabricating.
(ii) The *nonferrous cycle* – the mining of metals such as copper and of fuels to smelt them, the production of cables, etc.
(iii) The *petroleum and petrochemical cycle* – the extraction and refining of oil and gases and the production of a variety of chemical products (plastics, fertilizers, artificial fibres).
(iv) The *hydroelectricity cycle* – industries (electro-chemicals, electrometals, etc.) dependent upon cheap electricity.
(v) The *lumber cycle* – lumbering, sawmilling, pulp and paper, wood chemicals.
(vi) The *labour and market cycles* – industries attracted to population centres.
(vii) The *agricultural–industrial cycle* – agricultural practices and the associated processing of leather, flour, tobacco, etc.
(viii) The *irrigation–agricultural–industrial cycle* – as (vii) but based on ◊ *irrigation*.
These energy–material–manufacturing cycles have been given spatial form in the planning of ◊ *territorial production complexes*.

production–depletion curve ◊ *discovery–depletion cycle*.

production function A quantitative expression of the relationship between inputs and outputs per unit of time, i.e. the level of production as a function of various combinations of ◊ *factors of production*.

production linkage ◊ *linkage*.

production possibilities curve, production possibilities frontier A curve representing a locus of the maximum combinations of two goods, *X* and *Y*, that can be produced with given resources and technology (◊ Fig. 129). The slope of the curve at any point can be interpreted as the marginal ◊ *opportunity cost* of *Y* in terms of *X* forgone, i.e. a substitution function. All combinations of goods lying above and to the right of the production possibilities curve are unattainable. Combinations to the left and below the line are attainable but use fewer resources or less efficient methods of production than the firm or society has available. Also known as *isoproduct curves* or *isoquants*. ◊ *transformation line*.

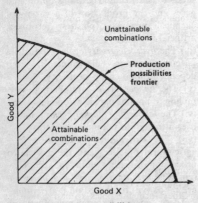

Fig. 129 Production possibilities curve

production sector ◊ *manufacturing industry*.

productive forces The basic elements of the production process, combining the means of production with labour power. Means of production are both objects of labour (the resources to which labour is applied) and instruments of labour (things used by labour in converting the objects of labour). For production to take place labour power (including scientific and other knowledge) has to be applied to the means of production. Productive forces, together with the relations of production, comprise the ◊ *mode of production*.

productive state The role played by government in actively providing goods and services which are either absent or not available to all in the workings of the ◊ *private sector*. The government's other major role is as a ◊ *protective state*.

productivity The efficiency with which inputs, i.e. labour, capital and land, are used to produce goods. It is usually measured by dividing the total output by the number of workers (*labour productivity*), or working hours, or the amount of capital required. ◊ *marginal productivity*.

professional services A group of ◊ *tertiary industries* including doctors, dentists, lawyers, teachers, architects, bankers and brokers. The services rendered are primarily on an individual basis and require face-to-face contact. ◊ *personal services*.

profit motive, profits Profits are the financial reward to a ◊ *firm* for taking non-insurable ◊ *risks*. They are a residual left over after wages, interest, rent, raw material and other contractual payments have been made by the firm. In economic analysis the profit motive is viewed as a general objective influencing the financial and investment decisions of firms. Profits allow payment of a return to investors who have risked their ◊ *capital*, provide a source of capital for further expansion (*retained profits*) and, in a competitive economy, are a measure of success.

Normal profit approximates the average rate of reward per unit of output in an industry over a period of time and is the minimum rate of profit necessary to ensure that a sufficient number of people will be prepared to invest, shoulder risks and organize production. Thus economists regard normal profit as a necessary cost of production in order to bring forth ◊ *entrepreneurs*. The rate differs from industry to industry depending on the risks involved, but generally industries in which the rate of profit is above normal will expand and those in which it is below normal will contract. Under ◊ *monopoly* and *oligopoly*, firms can continue to earn *abnormal* (high) *profit* in the long run.

profit surface A three-dimensional representation of the spatial variations in the ◊ *profits* to be earned at various locations from the sale of a good. The profit surface can be derived by subtracting the ◊ *cost surface* from the corresponding ◊ *revenue surface*. ◊◊ *margin of profitability*.

programming region ◊ *planning region*.

proliferation A term used to describe the spread of nuclear weapons, i.e. the acquisition by a non-weapon state of nuclear weapons, whether by its own research, purchase or treaty.

property rights In the legal sense property consists not of objects but of rights, i.e. an interest acquired by a person in an external object. Property rights comprise the set of laws, rules or customs which govern the relationships of people to each other in respect of the ownership and use of ◊ *land*. Certain basic rights relating to land ownership can be identified:
(i) A surface right, allowing the owner enjoyment of the current use of the land.
(ii) A productive right, allowing the owner to take a profit from the current use of the land.
(iii) A development right, allowing the owner to improve the property.
(iv) A pecuniary right, allowing the owner

to benefit financially from the ◊ *development value*.
(v) A restrictive right, effectively a right not to develop.
(vi) A disposal right, allowing the owner to sell or will the land.

Such property rights are exclusive, not absolute, always being subject to controls and limitations vested in the ◊ *state*. The most complete set of property rights pertaining to a parcel of land is ◊ *fee simple ownership*. ◊◊ *proprietary land unit*.

proportional representation The concept that each political party contesting an election should receive a number of seats proportional to the vote cast in its favour over the full set of constituencies. Electoral bias is said to exist where there are deviations from this norm. ◊◊ *electoral geography*.

proprietary land unit The basic decision-making unit with regard to land use, which includes the ownership of the necessary ◊ *property rights* and the physical area of land to which those rights pertain.

propulsive industry Also known as *industrie motrice*, *key industry* or *master industry* and similar in concept to ◊ *lead industry* and ◊ *dominant industry*. Propulsive industries are large-scale and fast-growing, enjoying a high income elasticity of demand for their products which are sold to national markets; they are highly innovative, with an advanced level of technology and managerial expertise; and they have a tendency to dominate because of a high intensity of input–output relationships with other industries. They play an important role in ◊ *growth pole* theory, as they form the poles around which the economy clusters, since they have marked ◊ *multiplier* and ◊ *polarization* effects. The concept is also applied at the level of the individual firm, hence *propulsive firm*.

prospect The view from a particular point or from a building.

prospect-refuge theory An expression introduced into ◊ *landscape evaluation* and design studies by J. Appleton. It postulates that, because the ability to see without being seen is an intermediate step in the satisfaction of many of a person's biological needs, the capacity of an environment to ensure the achievement of this aim becomes a very important source of aesthetic satisfaction in landscape evaluation. ◊ *habitat theory*.

prospecting The process of locating workable mineral deposits.

protected state, protectorate An internally self-governing ◊ *state* over which another country exercises some form of political control, especially in respect to foreign affairs and defence. The protected state is not formally annexed to the other country but has agreed by treaty or grant to the relationship.

protection The adoption by government of special measures to secure advantages for home-produced goods over ◊ *imports*, normally by imposing ◊ *tariffs* and ◊ *quotas*. Arguments used in support of protection include the need to make a country self-sufficient in respect of certain commodities, its use as a bargaining tool to induce other countries to lower their trade barriers and the desirability of giving temporary protection to new industry (◊ *infant industry*).

protective state The role played by government in most societies which involves the maintenance of law and order, according to society's prescribed rules. The government's other major role is as a ◊ *productive state*.

protoindustrialization A transition phase between peasant society and industrial capitalism. A term used by F. F. Mendels to describe the rapid but uneven growth of early industry – rural-based, traditionally organized but market-oriented.

proven reserves ◊ *reserves*.

proxemics The study of ◊ *personal space*, i.e. micro-spaces. Individuals possess a spatial envelope and a set of personal distances that may be regarded as extensions of their personality and expressions of their culture. Proxemics studies the invisible boundaries which protect and compartmentalize each individual, and the reactions of infringing on another's personal space or having your own personal space penetrated. ◊ *crowding*, *privacy*.

proximal margin ◊ *fringe belt*.

proximity A term used by D. Harvey to distinguish the effects of being close to something which people do not make any direct use of from ◊ *accessibility*, in which case they do want to make use of it. Proximity can impose costs, as when a household is proximate to a pollution source.

psychic distance ◊ *Distance* as perceived by people, especially businessmen. It represents a distortion of actual distance due to factors which prevent or interrupt information flows between firms and their potential commercial ◊ *action space*. Factors such as language, culture, level of industrial development and political systems act as barriers.

psychic income The non-monetary reward or satisfaction which an ◊ *entrepreneur* obtains from setting up his firm in a particular location. The concept is used in explaining the choice of non-optimal locations since, provided the location chosen is within the ◊ *margin of profitability*, the loss of ◊ *profits* compared to the profit-maximizing location is more than compensated for by the gain in enjoyment or satisfaction from the location, e.g. nearness to a favourite golf course.

psychological distance ◊ *social distance*.

psychological time Subjective time, which depends on how long people think an activity will take or took. Psychological time is useful in the explanation of observed behaviour at the activity-system and attitude-perception levels.

psychologism An approach which explains social phenomena in terms of facts and doctrines about the mental characteristics of individuals.

public company, public limited company A ◊ *limited liability* company that is allowed to offer shares to the general public on the stock market. In the United Kingdom such companies must have at least seven shareholders. The advantage to the company of 'going public' is that it can raise ◊ *capital* in the widest possible markets. Public companies are required to publish their accounts. The majority of large private businesses are public limited companies (PLC). ◊ *private company*.

public expenditure Spending by central and local government and by government agencies. It comprises expenditure on ◊ *public goods*, ◊ *quasi-public goods*, ◊ *transfer payments* and ◊ *subsidies*. The level of public expenditure has shown a tendency to increase on a world-wide basis, especially on social services, as the state has assumed a greater role in the life of the community. ◊◊ *tax*.

public facilities Government-owned installations, such as hospitals, schools and public housing.

public goods Goods which, because of their nature, cannot be subdivided for sale to individuals. There is no market and such goods are therefore provided for all the nation by the state, e.g. national defence, the administration of justice. A *pure public good* is characterized by:
(i) 'Joint supply', i.e. supply to one person allows supply of an identical quality good to all other people at no extra cost.
(ii) Non-rivalness, i.e. one person can consume the good without affecting another's consumption.

(iii) Non-excludability, i.e. if it is supplied to one person, it must be provided for everybody.
(iv) Non-rejectability, i.e. once supplied it must be fully and equally consumed by all.

The choice of which goods are provided, and which are not, is primarily a political, even ideological, decision. Thus the range of goods so provided includes not only pure public goods but also *impure public goods* (or ◊ *quasi-public goods*). The latter are not so much functions or goods that cannot be performed by the private market but rather functions or goods that can be more efficiently provided by public action, e.g. fire and health services, street lighting. The location of an impure public good means that the population does not enjoy exactly homogeneous quality and quantity as far as consumption is concerned (even though the same quality and quantity is available to them from the production view). Thus all localized public goods are impure. Also called *social goods*. ◊◊ *individual goods, merit goods*.

public interest An expression of what is best for the people of a region or country as a whole as perceived by politicians or professionals in government service (such as planners). The political reality is that general public interest is almost impossible to articulate.

public lands Lands owned by or held in trust by government organizations.

public overhead investment ◊ *economic overhead investment, social overhead investment*.

public parks ◊ *Open spaces* in towns reserved for general recreation purposes.

public participation Public participation implies a legal entitlement, a right of all citizens to be involved in the political decision-making process. In theory this requires public discussion of goals and alternative courses of action but, in practice, participation varies from voting for politicians at elections in a representative democracy to full citizen control. A distinction is made between *passive participation* – a general public awareness of issues which, by its very existence, influences decision-makers – and *pressure participation* – the actions of ◊ *pressure groups* attempting to influence policy outcomes. Participation is viewed as particularly valuable in increasing local accountability in those areas of government action which impinge on people directly, e.g. land use planning, housing.

public safety zone The zone beyond an ◊ *airport* perimeter and under the glidepath within which buildings must be low and consist preferably of warehouses with low employment characteristics, while houses and schools should not be allowed.

public sector That part of a national economy subject to direct government ownership and control. The constituents of the public sector are the departments of central and local government, various government agencies and the nationalized industries. The public sector is motivated by the welfare of the community as a whole. ◊◊ *private sector, public goods.*

public territory ◊ *territory.*

public transport The act or the means of conveying people in mass (by bus, train, etc.) as opposed to conveyance in private vehicles, especially cars, carrying very few people at a time. ◊◊ *paratransit, transport.*

public utilities Industries which supply essential services to the community, e.g. electricity, gas, water. Their common characteristic is that they are ◊ *natural monopolies,* competition being undesirable for technical reasons or reasons of public safety. Since public utilities are normally required to work in the ◊ *public interest* most are publicly owned in many countries. ◊◊ *statutory undertakers.*

pueblo A term applied to a group of North American Indians who live in Arizona and New Mexico and to the compact, communal settlements in which they live.

pumped storage scheme An ◊ *electricity generation* scheme designed to help meet sudden demand fluctuations and ◊ *peak loads.* Surplus power at periods of low demand can be converted into potential energy by pumping water from a low to a high reservoir in which it is stored. During peak periods the water is released, falling back to the lower reservoir via a hydro-electric turbogenerator. ◊ Fig. 130.

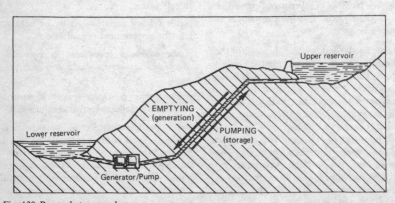

Fig. 130 Pumped storage scheme

purchase notice When ◊ *planning permission* is refused or onerous conditions are imposed which render land 'incapable of reasonably beneficial use in its existing state', the aggrieved landowner may, within twelve months of the decision, serve a purchase notice on the local planning authority requiring it to acquire the land affected by the decision. The notice requires ministerial confirmation. Normally, if an owner is refused planning permission or onerous conditions are imposed the decision must be accepted (or an appeal made to the Secretary of State for the Environment). Purchase notices can also be served in connection with ◊ *revocation,* ◊ *modification,* ◊ *discontinuance* and ◊ *tree preservation orders*, as well as in respect of control of advertisements, listed buildings and industrial premises.

pure competition A market situation similar to ◊ *perfect competition* in that there are many sellers acting independently to sell the same item (i.e. their products are undifferentiated) and they are so numerous that no seller acting alone can influence price. However, perfect knowledge does not hold for buyers and sellers. Pure competition is considered to exist in the markets for some agricultural products.

pure materials Assembled ◊ *localized materials* which do not suffer any weight loss during the manufacturing process. They therefore contribute their full weight to the weight of the product. Industries using pure materials are likely to be ◊ *market-oriented* in their location, especially where freight rates discriminate against finished products.

purposive sampling ◊ *sampling.*

Q

Q-analysis A methodology, based on general mathematical language, for describing and analysing structures. Central to its approach is the definition of sets and the exact representation of the relationships between sets.

Qanat ◊ *ganat.*

quadrat A basic unit or cell for areal sampling. ◊ *quadrat analysis.*

quadrat analysis A statistical technique for analysing point patterns. The area to be studied is divided into equal-sized cells or ◊ *quadrats.* The number of points falling in each quadrat is counted and a ◊ *frequency distribution* of quadrats containing zero, 1, 2 . . . *n* points is established. This observed frequency distribution is tested against a theoretical probability distribution generated by the particular set of processes thought to govern the distribution of points in space. It should be noted that the results are strongly influenced by the number and size of the quadrats used and also that differences in spatial patterns obvious to the eye (◊ Fig. 131) may not be

distinguished by quadrat analysis (unless arrangement is taken into account as well as distribution). ◊ *nearest neighbour analysis.*

quadroon A person who is the offspring of one white and one ◊ *mulatto* parent, i.e. has one-quarter negro blood.

qualitative variable ◊ *variable.*

quality of life Quality of life is largely a matter of individual preference and perception and overlaps the concept of ◊ *social well-being.* Generally the emphasis is on the amount and distribution of impure ◊ *public goods,* such as health care and welfare services, protection against crime, regulation of pollution, preservation of fine landscapes and historic townscapes. Operational attempts to define quality of life have involved composite measures covering health, environment, education, social order, recreation, etc. ◊ *physical quality of life index, social indicators.*

quantitative revolution A 'summary' term for the far-reaching changes which took

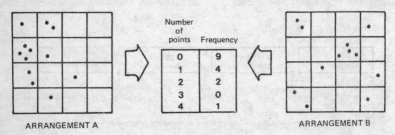

ARRANGEMENT A

Number of points	Frequency
0	9
1	4
2	2
3	0
4	1

ARRANGEMENT B

Fig. 131 Quadrat analysis

place in Anglo-American geography in the 1950s and 1960s. During this period the approach to geographical study underwent a significant change in its philosophy – the former emphasis on ◊ *areal differentiation* and ◊ *regional geography* based on an ◊ *idiographic approach* was replaced by a ◊ *nomothetic* one seeking to establish laws, models and theories of spatial structure.

Central to this change was the introduction of quantitative techniques whereby conventional statistical and mathematical methods were applied, modified and extended in geographical research. Much effort went into the development and demonstration of techniques, with the significance of the research problems often secondary. Within human geography the early applications of quantification were highly selective, concentrated in economic and urban geography.

The use of the term 'quantitative revolution' implies a ◊ *paradigm* shift, but that in a sense is misleading because the adoption of quantitative methods of analysis has been evolutionary (in that simple statistical techniques had been used earlier in geography). It also plays down the change in philosophical outlook which involved a commitment to ◊ *logical positivism*.

quantitative variables ◊ *variable*.

quarry A term used to describe open excavations, normally worked for building-stone, slate or other hard rock with no metalliferous or combustible content.

quartile deviation The ◊ *arithmetic mean* of the deviations of the first and third ◊ *quartiles* about the ◊ *median* (or half the ◊ *inter-quartile range*), i.e.

$$\text{Quartile deviation} = \frac{Q_3 - Q_1}{2}$$

It is the appropriate measure of dispersion or variability to use when the median is quoted as the most typical value.

quartiles The values which divide a ◊ *frequency distribution* or set of ranked observations into four equal parts. As ◊ Fig. 132 shows, there are three quartiles: Q_1, the first or lower quartile, which cuts off the lowest 25% of cases; Q_2, the second quartile, which corresponds to the ◊ *median*; and Q_3, the third or upper quartile, which cuts off the lowest 75% of cases. ◊ *inter-quartile range*.

quasi-public goods ◊ *Goods* which by their nature could be made available for purchase by individuals, but which the state finds administratively more convenient to provide for all the nation, e.g. education, roads. ◊ *individual goods, public goods*.

quaternary activity, quaternary sector Economic activity which specializes in the assembly, transmission and processing of information and in the control of other business enterprises. It includes the professions (e.g. solicitors, accountants, management consultants), finance (banking, insurance, etc.), intellectual services such as education, research and the media, as

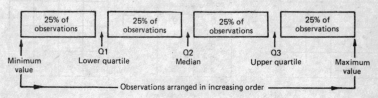

Fig. 132 Quartiles

well as public activities like central and local government. ⟡ *primary activity*, *secondary activity*, *tertiary activity*.

queuing theory A mathematical technique used to help solve 'bottle-neck' problems in a system. It makes use of ⟡ *probability* theory and ⟡ *linear programming* to determine the likelihood of a given input producing a given output in a given system on either a time-dependent or time-independent basis. Vehicle flows, e.g. at traffic lights, can be viewed as a queuing problem in which inputs or vehicle arrivals at the light-controlled junction are queued during a red-light phase and 'serviced' by the green-light phase. Queuing theory can be used to determine the optimum length of the green-light phase on each of the intersecting routes. ⟡ *traffic intensity index*.

quota An agreed or specified maximum or minimum level of production or ⟡ *trade* during a specified period, e.g. an *import quota* restricts the volume of a commodity that can be imported into a country during a period.

quota sampling ⟡ *sampling*.

R

race A major division of human population on the basis of common hereditary physical characteristics. Scientifically race is the final subdivision in the animal world of a series of biological classes beginning with the order Primates, and the classification of human races must rest on the same scientific basis as the remainder of the biological system. Classification of human populations into races used to be based on certain factors of appearance – skin colour; shape of head (◊ *cephalic index*), face, nose and eye; and type of hair – but now genetics and blood types make determination more exact. Three primary races, ◊ *Caucasoid*, ◊ *Mongoloid* and ◊ *Negroid*, are distinguished, although ◊ *Australoid* and ◊ *Khoisanoid* are usually added.

racial affinity, index of ◊ *blood-group indices*.

rack rent A term deriving from the situation in 18th- and 19th-century Ireland in which counterbidding by tenants in the face of limited alternative holdings and, especially, landlord greed forced ◊ *rents* up to a level where the return for the tenant's own inputs was reduced to a subsistence level. Such rents reflected the value of any improvements made by the tenant. Subsequently rack rent has come to be used for any rent which represents the full or maximum market value.

Radburn layout A particular physical layout for a residential area where pedestrian and vehicular circulation are planned

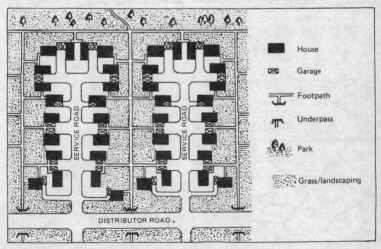

Fig. 133 Radburn layout

as segregated but related systems. This is achieved by keeping one side of a house (usually the front) free of vehicles and providing a 'rear' access road (usually in the form of a cul-de-sac off a distributor road) for servicing, garaging, etc. (◊ Fig. 133). The name derives from Radburn, New Jersey, planned as a satellite town for New York in the late 1920s.

radial shape index A measure, similar to the ◊ *coefficient of compactness*, of the shape or form of a geographic area. It is a measure of aggregate distance from the area's centroid and is calculated as:

$$\text{Radial shape index} = 100 \sum_{i=1}^{n} \left| \frac{d_i}{\sum_{i=1}^{n} d_i} - \frac{1}{n} \right|$$

where d_i = distance of ith point from the centroid of the area
n = number of points

Alternative indices are listed under ◊ *shape measures*.

radial–concentric plan A term describing the layout of a town where a number of roads radiate from a centre and are cut successively by a series of concentric circular roads (the centre of the radials and the circles being common). ◊◊ *grid plan*.

radical geography An umbrella term for several of the critiques of the established discipline, especially of the quantitative–theoretical approach, but also of the subjective–humanistic approach, which developed in the 1970s. Its origins in civil rights activities in the USA in the late 1960s reflected recognition of the 'unfairness' inherent in a market economy, the contradictions of participatory democracy, the conflicts between social groups and the like. Radical geography calls for both revolutionary theory and revolutionary practice, its mainsprings undoubtedly deriving from Marxism (although many geographers accept the validity of much of the critique without embracing fully the overall philosophy on which it is based). Stress is laid on the futility of disciplinary boundaries and the emphasis is on merging the work of geographers into the general ethos of the social sciences. ◊ *Marxist geography*, *structuralism*.

railway gauge ◊ *gauge, railway*.

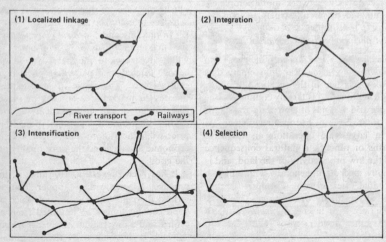

Fig. 134 Railway network evolution model

railway network evolution model A four-stage model of the spatial development of a railway network in a country (◊ Fig. 134):
(1) *Localized linkage*, the initial phase, characterized by four components – a prevalence of short links, isolated network segments, lines complementary to the previous ◊ *transport mode* and prevalence of branch links.
(2) *Network integration*, in which the isolated segments are linked into a more complete network, so by-passing the previous mode with which the railways now compete. There is an increase in ◊ *network density* and ◊ *connectivity*, although overall the form is still a ◊ *branching network*.
(3) *Network intensification*, which is characterized by the conversion of the branching structures that dominated the first two stages into ◊ *circuit networks*. Feeder lines are also built to serve peripheral regions.
(4) *Selection*. As railways face increasing competition from motor transportation the unprofitable lines are closed down. These are primarily feeder lines, but also include some duplicate lines in the main network. The pruning of the network that takes place leaves a network more completely dominated by circuit structures than before. ◊◊ *transport mode development stages*, *transportation network evolution model*.

ranching An ◊ *agricultural system* based on *commercial grazing*. Ranching emerged as a major system in the second half of the 19th century and is largely confined to the more arid margins of temperate grasslands in areas of recent European settlement. It is a large-scale operation on extensive farms or ranches, a natural consequence of the low productivity of the land, and is highly specialized, generally with only one product, beef or wool. Formerly the animals roamed on 'open' ranges, but now some are kept in enclosures, with alfalfa and other fodder crops being grown, with the aid of ◊ *irrigation*, as feedstuff. ◊◊ *range management*.

random numbers table A table of numbers used in random ◊ *sampling* and in ◊ *simulation* in which each digit has been generated by a chance or random procedure, i.e. the digits 0 to 9 each have the same probability of occurrence at each position in the table. The procedures vary in sophistication from drawing numbered balls from an urn to complex electronic devices.

random sampling ◊ *sampling*.

randomness (1) In a statistical sense a state in which there is an equal chance of any of a number of events or characteristics occurring at any moment or in any location. Randomness is also sought in many ◊ *sampling* contexts, i.e. each member of a population has an equal chance of being chosen in a sample. ◊◊ *stochastic process*.
(2) A term used in a geographical context to indicate that locational uncertainty or imprecision that results from the many small and unknown factors influencing locational decisions.

range (1) In statistics, the difference between the highest and lowest values in a ◊ *frequency distribution*. It is the simplest of all the measures of dispersion but is very sensitive to extreme values.
(2) In retailing and ◊ *central place theory*, the maximum distance a consumer is willing to travel to purchase a good or service offered at a particular price at a central place. The range of a good delineates the market area of a central place for that good and is dependent on the spatial distribution of population, the price-willingness of consumers, subjective economic distance and the price-quality of the good.
It has been suggested that range is, in practice, a zone with an upper limit – termed the *outer range* – beyond which a good can no longer be obtained from a centre, and a lower limit – the *inner range* – which is determined by the minimum amount of consumption which is necessary

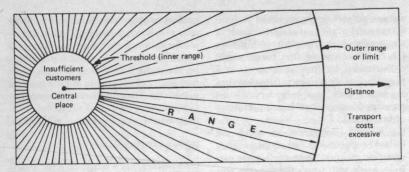

Fig. 135 Range

before production or offering the good for sale is profitable to the seller. This latter limit is more commonly termed ⟡ *threshold*. (⟡ Fig. 135.)

(3) In the public land system of the USA (⟡ *range, township and section method*) any series of contiguous townships, north or south of each other, between two successive meridian lines 9·65 km (6 ml) apart. (⟡ Fig. 136.)

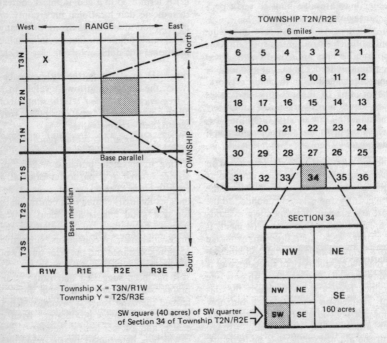

Township X = T3N/R1W
Township Y = T2S/R3E

SW square (40 acres) of SW quarter of Section 34 of Township T2N/R2E

Fig. 136 Range, township and section

range management Management practices in the settled grazing areas of the New World aimed at maximizing the forage available for livestock on a sustained and continuous basis. Range areas are relatively fragile ecosystems, easily degraded by overstocking, and it may be suggested that this problem has not been solved satisfactorily anywhere in the world. There is debate as to whether livestock numbers should be adjusted to actual forage supply each season or whether conservative stocking, based on feed supply in prolonged drought periods, is a better management system. ◊ *carrying capacity.*

range of tolerance A term used in ◊ *industrial location theory* for the set of locations around the optimal location which can be utilized at a profit. ◊ *spatial margin.*

range, township and section method A ◊ *cartesian* system of land division using a rectilinear grid as the basis of survey, which was adopted in the United States for most of the land west of the Appalachians and, in a modified form, in much of Canada.

The method divides land into 6 × 6 ml (9·65 × 9·65 km) square *townships* around a base meridian. Any series of contiguous townships, north or south of each other, comprise a *range*, and ranges are numbered east and west from the base meridian. Each township is subdivided into 1 × 1 ml (1·61 × 1·61 km) sections, i.e. 640 acres (259 hectares), numbered from 1 to 36. The section was the smallest unit whose out-boundaries were required to be surveyed by law, but the law also created imaginary boundaries which form quarter sections of 160 acres (65 h), each of which in turn was broken down into four squares of 40 acres (16 h) each. (◊ Fig. 136.)

This system, adopted in the USA in 1785 when the states ceded their western lands to the United States, provides a reference system that uniquely determines the position of each land unit.

rank–size rule An empirical regularity recognized in the city-size distribution of a country, whereby the product obtained by multiplying a city's rank by its size is equal to a constant, the population of the country's largest city. It is of descriptive rather than explanatory or predictive value.

If all cities in a country are arranged in rank order, beginning with the city with the largest population, then the size relationship between the towns of each rank is extremely regular. If the rank–size rule holds exactly, the population of the fourth-ranking city is one-quarter of the population of the first-ranking city, the population of the fortieth-ranking city is one-fortieth of the population of the first-ranking city, and so on. This may be expressed in a simple formula:

$$P_r = \frac{P_i}{r}$$

where P_r = population of the city ranked r
P_i = population of the largest city
r = rank of city P_r

i.e. the size of a city is inversely proportional to its rank.

The rank–size distribution approximates to the ◊ *lognormal distribution* and when represented on a double logarithmic graph is transformed into a straight line (◊ Fig. 137).

The rank–size pattern was considered to be characteristic of advanced, economically integrated countries, but evidence does not support the hypothesis that the progression of a country's city-size distribution from a state of primacy (◊ *primate city distribution*) to rank–size is directly dependent on the country's level of economic development. Lognormal distributions are produced by stochastic growth processes which result in a steady-state condition, i.e. a dynamic equilibrium. Thus the rank–size distribution is the pro-

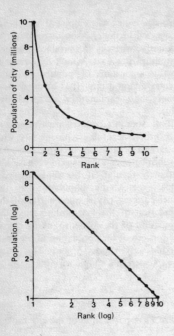

Fig. 137 Rank–size rule

duct of the operation of many factors over a long period of time, and once it is established change in any one of these factors produces only random and relatively minor deviations from the norm. Rank-size distributions are therefore not only found in advanced industrial countries, where they stem from the complexity of economic, political and social life, but may also be found in Third World countries with a long history of urban development, and in large developing countries with many resource-based cities. ◊ *urban system*.

ranking scale ◊ *ordinal scale*.

rate-group principle A practice, common among railways, in which ◊ *freight rates* are grouped in steps. Nodes along each route are divided into groups and all nodes in the same group have the same rate

for transporting freight over broad zones. Freight rates therefore rise in steps at the zone boundaries. ◊ *freight-rate territories*.

rate index An index, proposed by D. T. Herbert, for use in identifying that part of a town which could be termed the core of the ◊ *central business district*. It was calculated as:

$$\text{Rate index} = \frac{\text{Gross rateable value}}{\text{Ground floor space}}$$

rate support grant A general or block grant, initiated by the 1966 Local Government Act, to local government. It accounts for about 85–90 per cent of total central government aid to local authorities. The rate support grant has three parts:
(i) A *needs element* designed to compensate local authorities for the amount they spend per head of population. It is calculated according to a formula determined by central government and based on an analysis of past expenditure and indicators of expenditure needs that appear best to explain variations between local authorities in expenditure per head.
(ii) A *resources element* (which replaced the rate deficiency grant) paid to those local authorities whose ◊ *rateable value* per head falls below the national average level set by central government.
(iii) A *domestic element* designed to cushion domestic taxpayers from the full effect of local tax increases.

Central government is able to control the general level of local authority expenditure by reducing the total sum allocated to the rate support grant.

rateable value A value assigned to properties in Britain as a basis for the fixing of contributions towards local government finances (◊ *rates*). *Gross rateable value* is defined as 'the rent at which the hereditament might reasonably be expected to be let from year to year, if the tenant undertook to pay all the usual tenant's rates and taxes, and if the landlord undertook to bear the cost of repairs and other expenses, if any, necessary to maintain the hereditament in a state to maintain that rent' (Rating and Valuation Miscellaneous Provisions Act, 1955). Rateable value is therefore assessed as the ◊ rent of a building and reflects not only the physical condition of the building (including space, frontage and access) but also the site and locational advantages.

There is a standard scale of allowances to cover maintenance and insurance costs which are deducted from gross rateable value to give *net rateable value*, on which rates are actually paid.

rated capacity The maximum number of user-units that the agency or person operating a recreation facility allows to participate in the activity at one time on the site concerned. ◊◊ *recreational spatial capacity*.

rates A local tax paid in Britain by the occupiers of non-agricultural land and buildings in a local authority area as a contribution to local government finances. The amount paid by each occupier depends upon the ◊ *rateable value* of their property and upon the *rate poundage* fixed by the rating authority. The rate poundage is the number of pence in the pound which occupiers have to pay on the rateable value of their property. It is calculated by dividing the sum total to be raised by the estimated yield of a penny rate in the area of the rating authority. Thus, if a house has a net rateable value of £300 and the rate charged is £1·20, the liability for the year will be £360. ◊◊ *penny rate product*.

ratio of advantage The ratio or degree of advantage gained by producing one crop or commodity rather than another. ◊ *comparative advantage*.

ratio scale, ratio data The highest form of measurement in which measurements are made relative to some absolute and non-arbitrary base. The ratio scale is a parametric scale which measures precise differences (or distances) from a fixed or true zero and which preserves the ratio between numerical observations as well as between intervals. For example, distances of 5 and 10 miles form the same ratio ($\frac{1}{2}$ or 2) as their equivalents 8·045 and 16·09 kilometres. ◊◊ *interval scale, nominal scale, ordinal scale*.

rationalization A process of re-organization in an industry to achieve greater efficiency. It usually involves the concentration of economic activity into fewer units, e.g. factories, by means of ◊ *mergers* and occurs where an industry has excess capacity through a fall in demand. Production is concentrated at the most efficient factories, while the less efficient ones are closed down. The main advantage is the expected lower cost per unit of output through using fewer factories more intensively. Disadvantages include some unemployment and a reduction in the choice of product available to the consumer.

rational model (paradigm) of decision-making People who are goal-seeking are faced with a problem of choice in order to realize their goals. A rational decision occurs when this choice is made in a certain way:

(i) The decision-maker considers *all* of the alternatives or courses of action open to him/her.

(ii) The decision-maker identifies and evaluates *all* of the consequences which would follow from the adoption of each alternative.

(iii) The decision-maker selects that alternative whose probable consequences are most preferable in terms of his/her goals.

This approach has been applied by geographers to decision making in a locational context. ◊◊ *disjointed incrementalism*.

raw material A substance of an extractive nature (e.g. iron ore, stone, timber) which is intended for processing, fabrication or manufacture. ⟡ *resources*.

ray ⟡ *shifting cultivation*.

Rayleigh test A straightforward statistical test, named after the mathematician Lord Rayleigh, for the existence of a preferred orientation in a sample. It has been used as a directional statistic in geography when examining spatial distributions, e.g. in the study of migration directions and the orientation of houses.

reach of trade The distance over which transactions are carried on. Indirectly, it is a measure of the impulse to ⟡ *trade*.

reafforestation The correct term is ⟡ *reforestation*.

real capital ⟡ *capital*.

real distance ⟡ *geodesic distance*.

real environment The real or *extended environment* is the complete set of information assumed to be available to decision-makers in most classical theories and models. It is therefore similar to the ⟡ *phenomenal environment*. ⟡ *behavioural environment*.

realism A philosophical doctrine which views the world of physical things as existing independently of people's perception and cognition of those things. The empirical world is the result of the operation of processes that cannot be observed, although individual behaviour and the results of that behaviour can be observed and recorded in an objective manner, on universally agreed criteria. Realists seek to discover the relational cause-and-effect in nature and society, i.e. the natural necessity of the regularity. They argue that ⟡ *positivism* is unable to provide adequate explanations because it relies on logical – frequently mathematical – necessity. Positivists ask the question 'how' a spatial pattern is produced while realists ask 'why'.

reciprocal economy An ⟡ *economic system* dominated by reciprocal ⟡ *exchange*. Such reciprocity involves the exchange of goods, favours and services among individuals in a given group according to certain well-defined social customs and traditions. Reciprocity may be 'balanced' where mutual exchange is approximately equal or 'imbalanced', implying a constant movement from those who have to those without.

reciprocal movement A term used to describe a journey or movement made by a person which begins at their home, visits one or more other locations, and ends at home. A reciprocal movement cycle, which can be daily, weekly, monthly, etc. in duration, is established by aggregating all reciprocal movements of a person over a period of time.

reclamation The process by which flooded or waste ⟡ *land* is made usable, especially for agriculture. It includes the drainage of marshes and of lakes or a shallower part of the sea-floor, the improvement of heathlands and the restoration of ⟡ *derelict land*. ⟡ *empolder*.

reclamation bond A deposit, in the form of cash or sureties, made by a mineral extractor to cover the anticipated cost of restoration of mineral workings. The aim is to avoid dereliction of land. ⟡ *restoration levy*.

recovery factor The proportion of economically accessible ⟡ *reserves* that can be extracted, e.g. in the case of 'petroleum in place' the amount that can be extracted is related to the conditions of the reservoir, the composition of the crude oil and the method by which it is extracted.

recreation Any pursuit or activity, undertaken voluntarily, primarily for pleasure and satisfaction, during ⟡ *leisure* time (i.e. recreation is identified with activity, leisure with time). Such activity may be subdivided as (i) active/passive, reflecting the degree of physical exercise involved; (ii) formal/informal, depending on the degree of organization of participation; and (iii) resource-based/user-oriented, depending on the extent of reliance on the natural environment or people-made facilities. The implication is, for most recreation activities, that they take place away from the participant's home.

As an ideal, recreation implies the experience of re-creating oneself by restoring, refreshing or revitalizing the mind and the body. Indeed purists would argue that re-creation is, or should be, the culmination of recreation activity. ◊ *outdoor recreation activity, sport.* ◌ *off-road recreation activity, tourism, vacationist.*

recreation business district That section of an urban area that is an aggregation of restaurants, hotels, amusement businesses, and novelty and souvenir shops catering for a seasonal influx of tourists. The shape is elongated, centring on the point of convergence of incoming visitors and the attraction (beach, waterfalls).

recreation carrying capacity A concept which combines the notion of protection of a recreational resource base from overuse with, at the same time, assurance of enjoyment and satisfaction for the participant. Recreation carrying capacity is the level of recreation use a site can withstand without an unacceptable degree of deterioration of the character and quality of the resource or of the recreation experience. It can be expressed in terms of people per day or people-hours per day: thus *annual recreation carrying capacity* is the number of people-unit use-periods a recreation site can provide each year without permanent biological or physical damage to the site's ability to support recreation or appreciable impairment of the recreation experience. It therefore

implies an idea similar to the ◊ *sustained yield* principle. The (average) *daily recreation carrying capacity* is the annual carrying capacity divided by the number of days in the average season. Four separate types of recreation carrying capacity have been recognized:

(i) *Physical carrying capacity* (also *spatial capacity*), which is concerned with the maximum number of people (or boats, cars, activities, etc.) a site can accommodate. It corresponds to a design concept and also recognizes safety limits. ◌ *recreation spatial capacity, sustained yield capacity standard.*

(ii) *Economic carrying capacity*, which relates to ◊ *multiple use* situations and identifies the maximum level of recreation use that can be accommodated on a site (which is also used for some non-recreation purpose) before damage to the other activity becomes economically unacceptable. Since the aim is the right mix of uses economic ◊ *compatibility* might be a better term.

(iii) *Ecological carrying capacity* (also referred to as *biophysical* or *environmental carrying capacity*), which is concerned with the maximum level of recreation use, in terms of numbers and activities, that can be accommodated by a site or an ecosystem before irreversible ecological damage is sustained. This is not necessarily the point at which further recreation use will damage the site beyond its ability to restore itself by natural means, since sound management practices can stretch carrying capacity beyond so-called natural limits.

(iv) *Perceptual carrying capacity* (also known as *social* or *psychological* or *behavioural carrying capacity*), which relates to visitors' perception of the presence or absence of other people at the same time and the effects of crowding (or solitude) on the enjoyment of their recreation experience. It is defined as the maximum level of recreation use above which there is a decline in the quality of the recreation experience due to the presence of others, i.e. the number of people a site can absorb before the latest arrivals perceive the site as 'full' and seek their satisfaction elsewhere. Capacity in this sense is obviously a very personal affair and is also self-regulating. ⟡ *carrying capacity*.

recreation entity An area of land, with or without structures, which is used for recreation and considered as a single entity even though it may consist of a number of functional divisions, e.g. national forest, state park.

recreation spatial capacity A formal interpretation of the physical carrying capacity of a recreation site. It is defined as the ability of a site to provide recreation opportunities judged solely on the space available and the space required to make participation in the recreation activity concerned a satisfactory experience. It does not consider the possibility of detrimental effects on the site.

Momentary spatial capacity is the maximum number of user-units that can occupy a recreation site at one time and still provide a satisfactory experience for the majority of users. *Daily spatial capacity* is the maximum number of user-unit use-periods that can take place on the site in one day. ⟡ *rated capacity*, *recreation carrying capacity*.

recreationist In a continuum of holiday or vacation needs, recreationists are activity-oriented, e.g. day-trippers, weekend cottagers, sportspeople. They will spend less time travelling and be less concerned with the pleasure of the journey than ⟡ *vacationists*.

recycling The re-use of waste materials. Recycling allows materials to be reclaimed after their useful life is over and therefore contributes to resource conservation, the minimization of ⟡ *pollution* and the reduction of waste disposal problems. It takes three forms: (i) actual re-use, e.g. of returnable containers, (ii) direct recycling, e.g. scrap metal re-smelting, and (iii) indirect recycling, e.g. the incineration of refuse for district heating. The *recycling ratio* is the proportion of the original material or resource which is re-used: this varies considerably among materials, e.g. in the United Kingdom some 62% of lead is recycled but only 29% of aluminium. Recycling is currently economically unattractive for many wastes because of problems of collection from many scattered locations and problems of separation of mixed wastes after collection. It is possible for government to influence the extent of recycling by offering direct subsidies to firms, imposing disposal taxes on recyclable products, and virgin material taxes or levies on non-renewable resources.

recycling of funds The practice whereby a country earning exceptionally large amounts of foreign currency through trade returns funds to their country of origin by foreign investments.

redevelopment The demolition of an existing building and its replacement by a new building. ⟡ *development*. ⟡ *comprehensive development*, *piecemeal development*.

redistribution, coefficient of ⟡ *coefficient of redistribution*.

redistributive economy An ⟡ *economic system* dominated by a strong central agency which operates a closely controlled, co-ordinated and centrally planned process of decision-making governing the exchange of goods in order to fulfil well-defined goals in each sector of the national economy. Also known as a *command economy*.

red-lining A discriminatory practice in residential mortgage lending. It involves the demarcation by financial institutions, which lend money to would-be house purchasers, of residential areas, usually in the ⟡ *inner city*, in which they will not normally invest money. Red-line areas are viewed by mortgage controllers as being in social and economic decline and any property they contain is considered unsuitable as mortgage security. The practice originated in the USA, but has spread to some British building societies.

redundancy A term used in ◊ *network* analysis to describe the existence of surplus ◊ *edges* between ◊ *nodes*. Normally only one edge exists between any pair of nodes: this is the situation of zero redundancy. Any further edges to that node are termed redundant because they provide connections beyond the absolute minimum necessary.

reference group A group of persons taken into account by an individual in deciding what his/her standing, values and norms should be. The individual need not be a member of the group. ◊◊ *peer group.*

reflecting barrier ◊ *diffusion barrier.*

reflexive nearest neighbour analysis A refinement of ◊ *nearest neighbour analysis* which singles out first order reflexive nearest neighbours, i.e. reciprocal pairs of points where *i* is *j*'s nearest neighbour and vice versa. High values for the proportion of reflexive pairs indicate some uniformity of pattern.

reforestation The restocking or replanting of forests which have recently been cleared of trees by felling or natural causes (e.g. forest fire). ◊ *forestry.*

refraction A term used in transport geography to describe the bending of ◊ *routes*, usually involving the use of two transport modes, such that a shipment is made at the minimum cost. Lower-cost modes and routes are favoured in length, whereas distances shipped via higher-cost modes or along higher-cost routes are minimized (◊ Fig. 138).

refugee A person who leaves home to seek refuge in a foreign country to avoid religious, political or some other form of persecution. ◊◊ *exile, expatriate, migrant.*

region Any area of the earth's surface with distinct and internally consistent patterns of physical features or of human development which give it a meaningful unity and distinguish it from surrounding areas. There are almost endless criteria on which to base the delimitation of regions: physical attributes such as climate, land forms, soil, etc.; socio-economic characteristics, including occupational structure, economic activity, land use, language, etc.

The concept of region as a distinct part of the earth's surface was, for a long time, at the heart of the conception of geography itself as the study of ◊ *areal differentiation* (◊◊ *regional geography*). Although regional geography no longer holds the central stage, the regional concept remains fundamental to geography when ◊ *regionalization* is viewed as a classification problem (the region being one of the best means of organizing spatial information) and because of recognition of the ◊ *nodal region*'s importance in a planning context.

A variety of different types of region have been identified: ◊ *complementary region, congested region, core region, declining region, depressed region, downward-transition region, geographical region, geostrategic region, international region, land use region, natural region, planning region, resource-frontier region, specific region, underdeveloped region, uniform region, upward-transition region, vernacular region.*

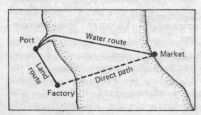

Fig. 138 Refraction

regional accounting The application of a system of ⬦ *social accounting* at the regional level, i.e. the process of measuring, systematically and quantitatively, regional income and output by sector. The purpose is to provide a better understanding of the state of a region's economy. Particular problems arise in establishing information about the external trade of a region.

regional centre The highest order of urban shopping centre outside the ⬦ *central business district*. Regional centres are frequently planned suburban or out-of-town centres catering for the purchase of a full range of convenience, comparison and specialist goods. Typical functions include at least one department store and a range of specialist stores, e.g. for furniture, electrical goods, records. They range in size from 27,500 to 92,900 m² (300,000 to 1,000,000 ft²) of retail space, provide up to 8,000 car-parking spaces and serve a catchment area of 150,000 to 500,000 people. ⬦⬦ *community centre*, *neighbourhood centre*.

regional convergence A process of adjustment through which any inequalities among regions are eliminated with the increasing economic development of the nation. The process implies that a national economy tends to reach an equilibrium state in which levels of regional performance will be equalized. Performance has usually been measured in per capita income terms and there is evidence to suggest the convergence of regional income differentials among regions. Such convergence would result from the development and maturation of regions once on the frontiers of settlement, the decreased importance of agriculture as a way of making a living, improved transport and communications and the associated increases in mobility of labour and capital, and the rise of more activities free from locational dependence on natural resources. Regional convergence in per capita incomes may not, however, be accompanied by regional convergence of opportunity, economic power and quality of life. ⬦⬦ *regional equality*.

regional cycles Short-term fluctuations in a region's level of economic activity which are the result of the dynamics of capitalistic development. Such cycles reflect in part the industrial composition of the region as well as the impact of national ⬦ *business cycles* on the region. Fluctuations are usually measured by changes in industrial output or unemployment, which in turn lead to changes in regional income, inducing changes in retail sales and service trades. The timing, duration and amplitude of regional cycles has been studied, alongside their relationship to national cycles and the spread effects of one region's cycles on other regions.

regional differentiation ⬦ *regionalization*.

regional employment premium A direct per capita subsidy on the employment of labour paid to firms in ⬦ *development areas* during the period 1967–77, as part of UK ⬦ *regional policy*.

regional equality The condition in which all regions within a nation have approximately equal values for a quantitative indicator of the ⬦ *standard of living*. It is frequently an objective of ⬦ *regional policy*. ⬦ *regional equity*.

regional equity A condition in which all regions within a nation have equivalent levels of opportunity, economic and social benefit, cost and risk. ⬦ *regional equality*.

regional geography The geographical study of ⬦ *regions* in their total composition and complexity. Regional geography has its origins in the consideration of empirical material and a reaction to ⬦ *environmental determinism*. It provided ⬦ *geography* with its own distinctive subject matter and was regarded as the core of the discipline. This view gained the widest acceptance between the two world wars and persisted until the 1950s.

Regions had to be identified and their boundaries defined, i.e. a process of ◊ *areal differentiation*. Each region was distinct, having its own personality, and regional geography presented a synthesis or integration of the physical and human phenomena of the area. Details of the physical environment of the region were presented before those on human occupance, implying some causal link. Where ◊ *systematic geography* existed its function was to provide basic information for regional geography. ◊ *Landschaftsgeographie*.

regional multiplier ◊ *multipliers and multiplier effects*.

regional planning A particular form of public ◊ *planning* action, embracing both economic and physical planning, applied at a sub-national but supra-urban scale. In Britain regional planning owes its origins to two quite separate conceptions: the problem of creating a better physical environment in the conurbations, and the problem of regions suffering serious economic problems, such as unemployment. ◊ *regional policy*.

regional policy National government policy influencing the distribution of mainly economic resources over part or all of the national space. Regional policy involves measures aimed at increasing the level of economic activity in an area where unemployment is high and growth prospects poor and at controlling the level of economic activity in areas of excessive growth. It is therefore an element of national planning and a means through which the spatial dimension has been introduced into national government decision-making. ◊ *Industrial Development Certificate*, *industrial location policy*, *labour transference policies*.

regional resilience A term describing the capability of a ◊ *region* to recover its economic health after some change in conditions, e.g. loss of ◊ *comparative advantage*, which is damaging to the viability of the region's economic structure.

regional science An interdisciplinary approach, involving economics, geography and planning, which focuses on the theoretical and quantitative analysis of spaces and systems of spaces, regions and systems of regions, locations and systems of locations. It provides a synthesis of the science of spatial systems with the art of planning and management. Its essence is the understanding of regional change and the projection (and planning) of regional futures.

Regional science had its beginnings in the late 1940s, when there was widespread dissatisfaction with the low level of regional economic analysis. It is largely the creation of the American economist W. Isard. The development of theory in regional science has reflected trends in economic theory, particularly the use of neoclassical equilibrium analysis, and its methodology relies heavily on quantitative techniques such as ◊ *input–output analysis*, ◊ *linear programming*, ◊ *game theory*, etc. Regional science came under criticism in the 1970s from ◊ *radical geography* and ◊ *Marxian economics*, but it has continued to flourish by developing econometric models of urban and regional systems, multi-goal programming, regional ecological/environmental impact modelling, etc.

regional specialization, index of ◊ *coefficient of specialization*.

regionalism (1) The feeling of distinctiveness, group consciousness or sectional identification and loyalty shared by people who live in a particular area.
(2) In planning, the attempt to define areas for a new, intermediate level of government and administration (between local and national) in order to make ◊ *regional*

planning more effective and efficient. ◊◊ *functional regionalism.*

regionalization Or *regional differentiation.* A special form of ◊ *classification* involving the delineation of ◊ *regions.* The method varies according to the purpose of regionalization, the criterion/criteria to be used and the data available. There are two main approaches: (i) aggregation, in which small areas are grouped together to form regions, and (ii) dissection, in which a large area is divided into regions. In both approaches the object is to minimize the internal variation within a region and to maximize its variation with respect to other regions.

The delineation of formal regions involves grouping together local units or subdividing larger areas according to similarity on certain clearly defined criteria. Where multi-criteria are used, weighted ◊ · *index number* or ◊ *factor analysis* approaches may be employed. Functional regions are delineated by grouping or division on the basis of flow analysis (what people do) or gravitational analysis (what people might do). ◊◊ *areal differentiation, synthetic regionalization.*

register tonnage ◊ *gross register tonnage, net register tonnage.*

registration ◊ *vital registration.*

regression A general parametric statistical technique which fits a precise mathematical function to the relationship between a single dependent ◊ *variable* and an independent variable or set of independent variables. Regression analysis relies on highly restrictive assumptions: the variables must be measured on the ◊ *interval* or *ratio scales* and the relationship(s) among the variables are linear and additive. Regression analysis determines the nature of a relationship (◊◊ *correlation*, which determines the strength of the relationship). It is a widely used technique in geographical research, especially as it allows predictions

to be made by ◊ *extrapolation. Simple* or *linear regression* is the term conventionally used for calculating the equation of a least-squares or best-fit (straight) *regression line* which represents the relationship between a dependent and an independent variable.

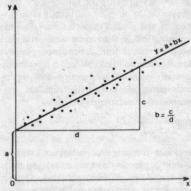

Fig. 139 Regression

The simple two-dimensional case is illustrated in ◊ Fig. 139 and gives a *regression equation* of the form:

$$y = a + bx$$

where x = independent variable
y = the dependent variable
a = intercept term (i.e. where the regression line crosses the y-axis)
b = slope term (i.e. measuring the steepness of the line)

There are several methods of calculating the *regression equation* or *line* but the most common is the least-squares method, which minimizes the sum of the squares of the deviations of the observed points (measured parallel to the y-axis) from the fitted line.

Multiple regression is used to examine the relationship between several independent variables and a single dependent variable. The general form of the equation becomes:

$$y = a + b_1x_1 + b_2x_2 \ldots + b_nx_n + e$$

where
$$y = \text{dependent variable}$$
$$a = \text{intercept term}$$
$$b(1, 2 \ldots n) = \text{constants of the independent variables } (x_1, x_2 \ldots x_n)$$
$$e = \text{a random error term}$$

Multiple regression may be used either as a descriptive tool to summarize and decompose the linear dependence of one variable on the others or as an inferential tool by which the relationships in a population are evaluated from the examination of sample data.

Sometimes a problem that was not originally one of fitting a straight line can be turned into one. In the case of *non-linear regression* certain relationships which are curvilinear are intrinsically linear and may be transformed (most commonly to logarithms), then subjected to regression analysis as above. It is the transformed data which must satisfy the assumptions of the regression technique. Where relationships between variables cannot readily be transformed to straight lines a curve may be fitted to the data. Regression methods for fitting a curve are called *polynomial regression* and the formula derived is of the form:

$$y = a + b_1x + b_2x^2 + b_3x^3 \ldots + b_nx^n$$

regret matrix An approach used to illustrate the importance of attitudes towards ◊ *uncertainty* in location decision-making. At some time or other, most people, having made a decision and observed its outcome, wish they had made a rather different decision, i.e. they suffer a degree of regret. The extent of this regret can be measured as the difference in the pay-off between the decision they made and the decision they would have made if they had known better. This *regret criterion* is analogous to the concept of ◊ *opportunity cost*. Its use in industrial location decision-making can be illustrated in the case of a manufacturer considering three locational choices between, say, expansion *in situ* in a growth region, a branch plant in a new town, and relocation in an assisted area, in relation to possible future states of the economy, for instance, continued growth, growth with curbs on expansion in prosperous areas, stagnation, and stagnation with a strengthening of regional aid to less prosperous areas. Hypothetical pay-offs are shown in the regret matrix (◊ Fig. 140). The manufacturer seeking to minimize regret adopts a minimax strategy (◊ *game theory*), identifying the largest regret value for each locational strategy, i.e. 100 for strategy I, 105 for II, and 120 for III, and choosing the lowest of these high values as the appropriate location decision, namely, 100 for strategy I in this example.

regular sampling ◊ *sampling.*

regulatory planning ◊ *allocative planning.*

MANUFACTURER'S LOCATIONAL STRATEGY	FUTURE STATES OF THE ECONOMY			IV Stagnation + incentives
	I Growth	II Growth + curbs	III Stagnation	
1. *In situ* expansion	100	95	60	45
2. New town branch plant	80	105	70	50
3. Relocation to assisted area	40	55	60	120

Fig. 140 Regret matrix

rehabilitation A term used, especially in housing policy, for the repair and improvement of existing structurally sound property to a standard compatible with modern requirements of health and amenity, for use for a period of up to thirty years. ◊ *general improvement area, housing action area.*

Reilly's law Also called the *law of retail gravitation.* A method to determine the relative amount of retail trade two cities attract from an intermediate place in the vicinity of the ◊ *breaking point.* It was developed by W. J. Reilly, an American market researcher, but has been widely used by geographers in studying shopping behaviour.

The law states that the two cities will attract trade from intermediate places in direct proportion to the populations of the two cities and in inverse proportion to the square of the distances of these two cities to the intermediate place, i.e.

$$\frac{R_a}{R_b} = \frac{P_a}{P_b}\left(\frac{d_b}{d_a}\right)^2$$

where R_a, R_b = retail trade from the intermediate place to cities a and b

P_a, P_b = populations of cities a and b

d_a, d_b = distances from the intermediate place to cities a and b

Generally the larger and nearer the city the greater the proportion of trade that city attracts. The method has the same basis as the ◊ *gravity model.*

relative deprivation ◊ *deprivation.*

relative dispersion, index of ◊ *index of dispersion.*

relative distance ◊ *distance.* ◊ *cost-distance, functional distance, social distance, time-distance.*

relative location ◊ *location.*

relativism The view that an individual's judgement is relative to place, time and value systems.

relevance Within geography, the question of 'if' and 'how' the discipline should contribute to the solution of societal problems. The debate was particularly prominent in the early 1970s and proved instrumental to the developing critique of ◊ *positivism* in geography. Positivist-based spatial science had been preoccupied with the study of the production of goods and the exploitation of natural resources and had neglected major social issues. The prosperity of the previous two decades had not been shared by all and important questions of human welfare and social justice were being raised. Geography could, and for many geographers should, provide the basis for a policy of resource redistribution (◊ *welfare geography*), but this could also necessitate a revision of geographical theory (◊ *Marxist geography, radical geography*).

reliability sampling ◊ *sampling.*

relict boundary Any ◊ *boundary* line which no longer serves a political purpose but which remains discernible in the cultural landscape.

relocation ◊ *industrial migration.*

relocation diffusion ◊ *diffusion.*

remembrement The French term for the regrouping and enlargement of agricultural holdings under ◊ *land consolidation* schemes.

remote sensing The acquisition and analysis of data relating to objects without being in physical contact with them. These data are normally in the form of electromagnetic radiation that has been reflected or emitted from the objects. A number of different *sensors* (electromagnetic scanning devices) have been developed, each acquiring energy measurements in a discrete portion of the electromagnetic spectrum. The distances from which these measurements are made vary greatly – from a metre or so to hundreds of kilometres. This capability has required the development of a wide range of sensor platforms: from ground-based booms to balloons, low- and high-altitude aircraft and, increasingly, earth-orbiting satellites.

Remote sensing is a relatively new term, introduced in the 1960s to replace the more limited *aerial photography* and *aerial photointerpretation*, which refer only to the acquisition and analysis of data acquired by conventional photographic processes. Remote sensing, however, covers the acquisition and analysis of data from all portions of the electromagnetic spectrum. Most current remote sensing systems operate in one of three regions of the spectrum the optical (visible/photographic), infrared and microwave.

The use of satellite techniques for earth surface remote sensing now gives frequent and repeated coverage of areas at increasingly detailed ground resolution scales and a widening range of applications can be noted in resource identification, pollution detection, land cover (vegetation) mapping, land use planning and land resource policy formulation, landscape conservation, the monitoring of natural hazards, sensitive ecosystems, crop growth, pastureland, and the enumeration of wildlife.

renewable energy sources Or *income energy sources*. Energy sources which are likely to be available as long as they are needed and which do not rely on finite reserves of fossil or nuclear fuels. They are directly or indirectly due to the sun (except for tidal energy, which arises from the earth's rotation) and include ◊ *solar energy*, wind energy, wave energy, tidal energy, hydro-electric power and photochemical energy stored in plants and animals. Fusion

energy and geothermal energy have also been included under this classification. Even though there is no theoretical limit on the total amount of energy people can get from a renewable energy source there is a limit on the rate at which they can draw energy from it at any time. ◊ *water power, wind energy.* ◊ *resources.*

renewable resources ◊ *resources.*

rent (1) In economic analysis, a surplus accruing to a factor of production. ◊ *economic rent.*
(2) A *contract rent* is a payment made by a person for the use of an asset, most commonly land or property, belonging to someone else. ◊ *clee rent, corn rent, farm rent, ground rent, location rent, position rent, rack rent.* ◊ *Marxist theory of rent, Ricardian theory of rent.*

rent control, rent restriction The statutory control of the rents of privately owned dwellings. Because of it, private landlords are unable to fix the level of rent according to demand and supply forces.

rent gradient The decline in rent (land value) with distance from a market or centre. Such decline is a function of the increasing transport costs that must be incurred the farther any given place is from the centre. As used in agricultural and urban land use theory it is a measure of the value to the landowner of the relative ◊ *accessibility* of a particular location. Because of competition for the more accessible locations, a ◊ *distance–decay* location rent gradient develops outwards from the central point of greatest accessibility. ◊ *bid-rent curve, transport gradient.*

repertory grid The method whereby individuals construct their personal models of reality, based on the theory of ◊ *personal constructs.*

replacement investment ◊ *investment.*

replacement rates ◊ *reproduction rates.*

replenishable resources ◊ *resources (renewable)*.

repletion The filling-up of an existing pattern of plots with secondary building development, mostly involving the subdivision of the original plots. ◊◊ *infilling*.

repopulation A term which has been applied particularly to the retirement to the countryside by people in a late stage of the ◊ *life cycle*, which has reversed the decline or rate of decline of rural population in certain areas.

reproduction rates Measures of the extent to which a ◊ *population* is reproducing or replacing itself (hence, also *replacement rate*), based on a consideration of female births in relation to the number of women of childbearing age.

The *gross reproduction rate* is a ratio obtained by relating the number of female babies (i.e. potential mothers) to the number of women of childbearing age:

Gross reproduction rate =

$$\frac{\sum \text{All age-specific } \Diamond \text{ birth rates of women aged 15-49}}{1,000} \times \begin{array}{l}\text{Proportion}\\\text{of female}\\\text{births}\end{array}$$

It expresses how many girls would be born to a newborn girl during the course of her life, supposing that she lived until fifty years of age. When the gross reproduction rate equals 1·0 there would be replacement of one generation by another.

The gross reproduction rate makes no allowance for deaths of female children before they reach the same age as the mothers they are due to replace, nor for deaths among the mothers themselves before they complete their childbearing period. Thus the ◊ *net reproduction rate* incorporates female mortality before age fifty by applying the appropriate survival rates to each age-specific birth rate. Net reproduction rate is the most commonly used replacement rate and measures the

average number of daughters produced by a woman during her reproductive lifetime, allowing for mortality. A rate greater than 1·0 means the population will increase, less than 1·0 that it will decline.

Because the net reproduction rate is based on fertility and mortality at a point in time it does not allow for variations due to the proportion of married women. A further refinement is to calculate a *marriage-standardized reproduction rate* on the basis of the number of women who would be married at each age and their marriage-duration specific birth rates. ◊◊ *fecundity, fertility*.

research and development (R & D) Two interrelated and essential stages in the promotion of technological inputs (new products and new processes of production). Most industries and many large firms maintain R & D establishments, although much R & D work is undertaken by or on behalf of government. *Fundamental research*, e.g. in chemistry and physics to understand how natural forces act, may be distinguished from *industrial research*, aimed at finding how to apply the results of the fundamental research to new products and more efficient production. *Development* is closely linked to industrial research, since it involves the translation of the research discoveries to the factory scale. Such technology-producing activity has developed its own location pattern, affected by the need to employ highly qualified scientists, engineers and technicians.

research park ◊ *science park*.

reserves The proportion of a ◊ *resource*, especially minerals, which can be exploited under existing economic conditions and with available technology. Reserves are developed from resources through the application of technology, capital and expertise in response to cost and price changes. Various reserve categories have been established (◊ Fig. 141). There is a

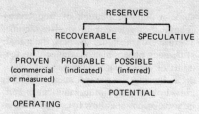

Fig. 141 Reserves

basic distinction between recoverable reserves and speculative reserves. *Recoverable reserves* cover the amount of a mineral likely to be extracted for commercial use within a certain time-span and level of technology. *Speculative reserves* are deposits that may exist in geologic basins or terrain where no exploration has yet taken place but the geologic make-up of the earth's crust is similar to that of regions that have yielded minerals. Recoverable reserves can be subdivided:

(i) *Proven reserves* (fossil fuels) or *measured reserves* (metallic ores) or *commercial reserves*. Essentially, what it has so far been in the commercial interest of an industry to discover. The amount and recoverability of the mineral has been measured within small margins of geological, geophysical and engineering error (less than 20%), e.g. by properly spaced drill-holes. Such reserves are virtually certain to be technically and economically producible and there is a 90% chance that the actual quantity extracted is greater than the amount estimated. The term *operating reserves* is used in coal-mining to describe reserves available in mines currently producing coal.

(ii) *Probable reserves* (fossil fuels) or *indicated reserves* (metallic ores) involve a greater element of risk, since their existence and quantity are estimated, on the basis of geologic information and judgement, partly from sample analyses and partly from reasonable geologic projections outwards from exploratory drill-holes into

or through one or more producing horizons. They are estimated to have a better than 50% chance of being economically and technically producible and there is a 50% chance that quantities recoverable will be greater than estimated.

(iii) *Possible reserves* (fossil fuels) or *inferred reserves* (metallic ores). Deposits in unexplored extensions of established areas of production, i.e. outside present production fields or mines but within formations proved to be productive. These are estimated by geologic projection and involve substantial risk, estimated to have a significant but less than 50% chance of being economically and technically producible.

Potential reserves are regarded by the oil industry as including probable, possible and speculative reserves but by metal mining as including only indicated and inferred reserves.

The relationship between *reserves* and resources is shown in ◊ Fig. 143. ◊ *recovery factor*. ◊◊ *exploitation-history projection*, *geologic-analogy method*.

reserves–production ratio (R/P ratio) The ratio between the annual production rate of a mineral and the proven or measured ◊ *reserves* remaining in the ground. It therefore indicates the number of years of production remaining at the current annual rate of production, assuming no other deposits are discovered. The R/P ratio may be calculated for an individual mine or field but is more commonly calculated at regional, national and global scales.

reservoir A natural or constructed storage capacity for water. Where the reservoir is artificially created, e.g. by building a ◊ *dam* at a suitable retaining point across a valley, the purpose is to remove fluctuations in the flow in order to provide for ◊ *hydroelectric production*, domestic and industrial consumption, and/or ◊ *irrigation*.

In respect of water supply, storage reservoirs may be of the *impounding* type, where a dam is constructed as above, or the *bunded* type, where a special (lowland) storage pond is constructed and water pumped to it from a nearby river. Impounding reservoirs may be *direct supply*, from which water is piped separately to the places of consumption, or *river regulating*, which provides an even flow to sustain downstream abstractions.

residential density A measure of the number of people (or houses) in a specified area of land. ◊ *Density* of residential areas is usually expressed in terms of persons/ hectare, rooms/hectare or dwellings/ hectare. *Overall residential density* or *town density* applies to a town as a whole, and is the residential population of the town divided by the number of hectares it occupies, irrespective of how the land within the town is used. *Gross residential density* applies to a residential area as a whole, and is the population of the area divided by the number of hectares of all land (including ancillary uses such as school sites, public open spaces, etc.). *Net residential density* applies to a particular housing layout or residential area, and is the population of that area divided by the number of hectares inclusive of dwellings and gardens and half the width of surrounding roads. ◊◊ *occupancy rate*.

residential development sequence ◊ *land conversion process, neighbourhood evolution*.

residential differentiation, index of ◊ *index of residential differentiation*.

residential farm A part- or spare-time ◊ *farm* operated at low productivity by an urban ◊ *commuter*.

residential mixing The inverse of ◊ *residential segregation* whereby an ◊ *ethnic group* is distributed evenly relative to the total population of a city.

residential (population) cycle A generalization of the pattern of population change in residential ◊ *neighbourhoods*. There are three stages: the first, the initial settlement phase, is characterized by the influx of young married couples with children. During the second stage, children grow up and leave home, families age and in some widows/widowers occupy single-family homes. Many houses are rented or converted into apartments and by the end of the stage most of the original inhabitants have left. The last stage witnesses either the growth of population as more flats replace single-family homes or further population decline and dilapidation of property and the eventual replacement of residential by higher-order uses. Such population changes mirror the process of ◊ *neighbourhood evolution*.

residential mobility ◊ *housing mobility*.

residential segregation The tendency of an ◊ *ethnic group* to cluster in particular residential areas. Any deviation from a uniform distribution relative to the remainder of the population in a city is an indication of residential segregation: the greater the deviation, the greater the degree of ◊ *segregation*. ◊ *natural area, residential mixing*. ◊◊ *index of residential differentiation, index of segregation*.

residentiary activities ◊ *non-basic activities*.

residual The difference or error between an observed and a computed value. In plotting a ◊ *regression* the residuals will be shown by the amount of deviation of some of the observations from the regression line, i.e. differences which are not accounted for or predicted by linear variation. In a descriptive context examination of residuals may provide useful information on special cases or reveal trends previously concealed, and in an inferential context residual values are inspected to determine whether they represent a truly random component about the systematic relationship identified by the regression line. ◊◊ *residual map*.

residual map When observations are made for contiguous areas or sample points in space, ◇ *residual* values may be plotted on a residual map, which is examined for any visual evidence of a non-random arrangement.

resort An urban community where ◇ *tourism* is a main or prime function, hence *tourist* or *holiday resort*. Study of the historical development of resorts in Western Europe show that four major types had emerged by the end of the 19th century:

(i) ◇ *Spas*, for health and entertainment, e.g. Baden-Baden.

(ii) *Climatic resorts*, for the treatment of tuberculosis and other diseases, e.g. Menton.

(iii) *Alpine resorts*, e.g. Chamonix.

(iv) *Seaside resorts*, for health cures and recreation, e.g. Brighton.

Classification of resorts has been proposed on the basis of function combined with extent of visitor hinterland – capital cities, select resorts, popular resorts, minor resorts, cultural/historic centres, winter resorts, spas/watering places and day-trip resorts, to which might be added the created or planned and integrated resorts. Some resorts would fit more than one category, while other resorts have progressed from one particular orientation to another (◇ *resort cycle*).

resort cycle ◇ *Resorts* go through a cycle of evolution:

(i) The *exploration stage*. Small numbers of tourists make individual travel arrangements and follow irregular visitation patterns. No specific facilities are provided for visitors and the physical fabric and social milieu of the area are unchanged by tourism.

(ii) The *involvement stage*. As numbers of visitors increase and assume some regularity, certain local residents begin to provide facilities primarily, or exclusively, for visitors.

(iii) The *development stage*. A well-defined tourist market area develops, shaped in part by heavy advertising. Some locally provided facilities disappear and are replaced by larger, more elaborate and more up-to-date facilities, particularly accommodation. Changes in the physical appearance of the area are noticeable.

(iv) The *consolidation stage*. Major franchises and chains in the tourist industry will be represented, but few, if any, additions will be made. The resort now has a well-defined recreational business district.

(v) The *stagnation stage*. The peak number of visitors is reached. Natural and genuine cultural attractions will probably have been superseded by artificial ones. Capacity levels will have been exceeded, with subsequent environmental, social and economic problems. The area will have a well-established image but it will no longer be in fashion.

(vi) The *decline stage*. The resort is no longer able to compete with newer attractions and so will face a declining market. Property turnover is high and tourist facilities may be replaced by other structures (e.g. retirement homes) as the area moves out of tourism. *Rejuvenation* is an alternative, but involves a complete change in the attractions on which tourism is based.

resource A resource is something material or abstract that can be used to satisfy some human want or deficiency, i.e. by definition the existence of a resource depends on its value to humans. What makes a thing a resource is not its intrinsically valuable properties but the fact that a given society expresses a desire for it and is willing to pay for it. Resources are therefore a cultural concept, and those things considered to be resources by one society may not be so considered by others who lack the knowledge or desire to use them, e.g. coal was not seen as a resource by Stone Age people. Resources (◇ Fig. 142) are usually divided into:

(i) *Natural resources*, which refer to those

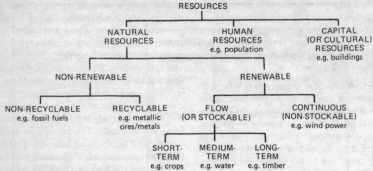

Fig. 142 Resource classification

parts of the environment that people find useful, including minerals and energy sources, climate, soils, natural vegetation, animal life, landscape, etc. They are identical with the formal economic concept of ◊ *land*. The total flow of a resource from its natural state through its period of human use to disposal (and perhaps re-use) is termed a *resource process*.

(ii) *Human resources*, which refer to the number and abilities, mental and physical, of people.

(iii) *Capital resources* (also *cultural resources*), which are people-made aids to production, e.g. machines and tools, and to living, e.g. houses. ◊ *capital*.

Strictly speaking all natural resources are renewable in the sense that they are part of natural cycles (e.g. geological, hydrological, atmospheric, biological), but they are usually subdivided according to their ability to renew or reproduce themselves at a rate meaningful to people:

(a) *Non-renewable resources* (also termed *non-replenishable*, *fund*, *stock*, *inventory* or *inorganic resources*) have been built up or evolved over a geological time-span and cannot be used without depleting the stock and raising questions of ultimate exhaustibility, since their rate of formation is so slow as to be meaningless in terms of the human life-span. There is no theoretical limit on the rate of use of a non-renewable resource – it depends on society's capacity to exploit it: the limit is one of quantity, i.e. the total amount that can ever be put to economic use. Non-renewable resources undergo physical and chemical changes during resource processes which change their form and allow further subdivision on the basis of recyclability. Ultimately only ◊ *fossil fuels* (◊◊ *fund energy resources*) are *non-recyclable*, being consumed in use, while other non-renewable resources, e.g. metals, are *recyclable*. ◊◊ *recycling*.

(b) *Renewable resources* have a natural rate of availability and yield a continual flow of services which may be consumed in any time period without endangering future consumption possibilities as long as current use does not exceed net renewal during the period under consideration (◊◊ *sustained yield*). They are replenished at a rate meaningful to people. A distinction has been made between *flow* (sometimes *stockable*) *resources*, which can be depleted, sustained or increased by human activity, and *continuous* (*non-stockable*) *resources*, which are always available and independent of human activity, e.g. solar and tidal energy (◊ *renewable energy sources*). Renewability need not be automatic and certain flow resources may be depleted, perhaps totally and irreversibly

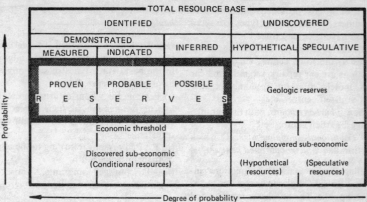

Fig. 143 Resources and reserves

by heavy use (e.g. overcropping, over-fishing) or misuse.

The relationship between resources and ◊ reserves is shown in ◊ Fig. 143. ◊◊ non-utilitarian resources, resource base.

resource base The sum total of all components of the ◊ environment that would become ◊ resources if they could be extracted from the environment.

resource-frontier region A peripheral area of new settlement where virgin territory is occupied and made productive. Of particular importance in this context is the non-contiguous resource frontier, which is an isolated pocket of development frequently based upon large-scale investment in mineral resources. ◊ region.

resource management A conscious process of decision-making whereby natural and cultural ◊ resources are allocated over time and space to optimize the attainment of stated objectives of a society, within the framework of its technology, political and social institutions, and legal and administrative arrangements. An important objective is the ◊ conservation of resources, implying a close and integrated relationship between the ecological basis and the socio-economic system. It is contrasted

with *resource development*, which is the actual exploitation of a resource to meet human needs. ◊◊ depletion policy, sustained yield.

resource process The total flow of a ◊ resource from its natural state, through a production process and period of human use to its disposal (either consumptively or in a form available for re-use).

response error In interview surveys, all errors due to the interviewer or the respondent or to the influence of one upon the other. The response that is recorded does not correspond exactly to the one given or to the one that would most nearly represent the truth.

restoration levy A levy per unit output of mineral production to finance a central reclamation fund in an attempt to avoid dereliction of land by mineral working. ◊◊ reclamation bond.

retail gravitation ◊ Reilly's law.

retail ribbon An element recognized in the spatial structure of urban retailing which serves demands originating from passing road traffic. Many trips to retail ribbons are single-purpose, often made on impulse, and there is little relationship between the order of goods provided and distances consumers travel. Three types of retail ribbon have been described:

(i) *Urban arterial ribbons*, along radial routes to the town centre. Characteristic functions are car repairs, second-hand car sales, motels, domestic appliance repairs, do-it-yourself centres, etc.

(ii) *New suburban ribbons*, with restaurants, garages, garden centres, etc.

(iii) *Traditional shopping streets*, which function like ◊ *neighbourhood centres*.

retailing Those marketing functions involving the sale of goods or services to the general public. The purchaser is motivated solely by a desire to satisfy his/her own personal wants or those of his/her family or friends through the personal use of the good or service purchased, i.e. it is not for resale. ◊◊ *marketing geography*.

retirement migration ◊ *migration*.

retreat mining A mining system in which extraction starts at the legal boundary of a deposit and works backwards to the ◊ *mine* shaft or point of entry. ◊◊ *advance mining*.

retrogressive approach In ◊ *historical geography*, the view that an understanding of the past landscape must begin with an examination of the present landscape. ◊◊ *retrospective approach*.

retrospective approach The view that the study of past landscapes is essential to the understanding of the present landscape. ◊ *Historical geography* would therefore be the foundation of all modern geography. The approach has much in common with ◊ *genetic explanation*. ◊◊ *retrogressive approach*.

return cargo Cargo carried on the return trip by a vehicle which has been hired to make a specific outward journey to deliver goods or freight. If the vehicle has to return empty from the outward journey ◊ *freight rates* would have to be high enough to cover the cost of the return journey. ◊◊ *back haul*.

return migration The return of ◊ *migrants* to the regions from which they had migrated in the past. Three types of such migrants have been recognized:

(i) Persons for whom return represents a logical progression in their career as a result of promotion or employment transfer.

(ii) Retired persons returning to the region of their birth or youth.

(iii) Discouraged migrants, whose expectations were not fulfilled. ◊ *migration*.

return period ◊ *periodicity*.

revealed preference analysis A statistical technique which uses actual choice decisions by individuals, i.e. what the public accepts or does in practice, as the basis for deriving an aggregate set of preferences between alternatives. Analytical procedures are based on ◊ *multi-dimensional scaling*, and the approach has been used in geography in a variety of contexts, especially those associated with the evaluation of environmental conditions. Its limitations include the assumption that behaviour is a valid guide to present (and future) preferences, the fact that revealed preferences are politically conservative as they reflect current economic and social arrangements, and the fact that it makes strong but often unsubstantiated claims about the rationality of decision-making. The alternative approach is to establish *expressed preferences* via some form of attitude survey.

revenue surface A three-dimensional representation of the spatial variations in the revenue to be obtained from the sale of a given volume of output. Distance is measured along the two horizontal axes and revenue, in money terms, on the vertical axis. ◊◊ *cost surface*, *profit surface*, *space revenue curve*.

reverse commuting ◊ *commuter.*

revocation order An order made by a local planning authority which withdraws or revokes a ◊ *planning permission* already granted. It is made when the ◊ *development* has not been undertaken (or before the change of use has taken place). The order requires ministerial confirmation and compensation is payable. This power has been used only infrequently. ◊ *discontinuance order.*

ribbon development A form of ◊ *urban sprawl* in which ◊ *development* takes place along one or both sides of main radial roads leading out of a built-up area. Such development is often only a single plot deep and may extend for considerable distances into the countryside. It is a line of least resistance, offering benefits in the form of good ◊ *accessibility* and cheap land. Since a ribbon development is commonly residential development, it is also known as a *residential ribbon.*

Ricardian theory of rent The theory of ◊ *rent* formulated by D. Ricardo early in the 19th century is generally accepted as the classical economic theory of rent. It explains rent largely in terms of differences in fertility, since Ricardo was concerned almost entirely with agricultural rents. It postulates that the rent of a plot of land is the excess of the yield of that plot over the yield of the worst land in cultivation.

Ricardo's analysis started by assuming a newly settled country, well endowed with fertile land, only a small proportion of which needed to be cultivated to support the population. He argued that only the most fertile land would be brought into cultivation and that no cost or rent would be associated with the use of that land. Rent could be charged for the most fertile land only when increased population increased demand to such a level that it was necessary to bring less fertile land into use. For example suppose that there are four grades of land with yields of 100, 90, 80 and 70 units of product for a given input of capital and labour (◊ Fig. 144). As long as only the first-grade land is needed, the market price of the product corresponds with the cost of production and no rent is paid. Before any second-grade land is brought into use product prices must rise to cover the higher unit-production costs incurred on those lands. Once prices rise to this level, second-grade land is brought into use and, at the same time, the value of the additional 10 units of product obtained on first-grade, compared to second-grade, land becomes an economic surplus. This surplus is unnecessary from the standpoint

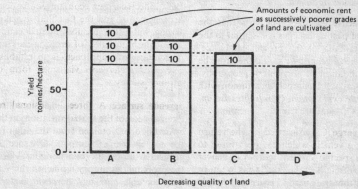

Fig. 144 Ricardian theory of rent

of continued production on first-grade land, but since it exists it goes as rent to the owners of the first-grade land because farmers would compete for the use of the most fertile land and the excess yield over that of no-rent land would be its rent. Thus the net return to farmers on a unit of land of any given fertility would tend to be the same. Since rent of land is a surplus, Ricardo held that it was price-determined, not price-determining. ⟡ *Marxist theory of rent*.

ride A grassed track through a forested area, formerly of importance for deer-hunting but now used for horse-riding or as a fire-break.

ridge and furrow Or *rigg and furrow*. A pattern of parallel ridges and furrows formed by ploughing. Soil from the furrow is thrown up by the plough to form a ridge. The earliest ridges were caused by teams of oxen constantly turning the soil in ◊ *open fields* in the same direction. The ridges varied in height, length and breadth, averaging 0·91 m (3 ft) high by 914·4 m (1,000 yds) long by 6·1–9·1 m (20–30 ft) broad according to the type of soil and plough, and the size of the plough team. It remains a feature of landscapes today, especially in the Midlands, where ridge and furrow patterns of former open fields can be discerned in present grassland.

ridgeway Tracks which ran along the line of watersheds used by prehistoric people to travel between ◊ *hill forts*. They were direct but not straight, keeping out of valleys and marshes and crossing rivers where there was the narrowest gap between hard dry banks.

riding Originally 'triding', meaning a third part and used in the 13th century to describe the subdivisions of certain ◊ *counties*.

rights of common ◊ *common rights*.

rimland theory A world power theory advanced by N. J. Spykman as a counter to

Mackinder's ◊ *heartland* thesis. Spykman argued that the control of Eurasia and ultimately of the world rested more logically in the rimland, the belt of nations surrounding the heartland (rather than in the heartland itself, as Mackinder suggested).

riparian doctrine A common law doctrine under which all landowners whose properties are bounded or traversed by a river, stream, spring or natural body of water have *riparian rights*. These owners have a right to use those waters to which they are riparian (situated on the banks) for domestic purposes, for watering their livestock, for navigation, for the generation of power and for fishing and recreational purposes. Strictly interpreted riparian owners have a right to have water flow by or through their property undiminished in quantity, undisturbed in time of flow, and unchanged in quality except for its use by upper riparian owners for domestic purposes and for the watering of livestock, i.e. they have usufructuary but not proprietary rights in the water that flows by their land.

ripening costs Costs incurred by a property developer when land or property interests are acquired well in advance of ◊ *development*, and which stem from the ripening or imagined ripening of properties from lower- to higher-order uses. Interest charges are the major element in ripening costs but can also include increased land tax or rate assessments. A parallel concept is ◊ *waiting costs*.

risk An estimate of the likely outcome(s) of some decision or future event in which the decision-maker's estimate is subject to error but the ◊ *probabilities* attaching to the outcomes are known. Risk is distinguished from ◊ *uncertainty* (under which the probabilities are not known).

In an environmental context people's perception of risk varies and a distinction is made between *voluntary* and *involuntary risks*, depending on whether or not a member of the public has a choice in bearing the risk. The public seems to accept risks from voluntary activities, e.g. skiing, driving, smoking, more readily than similar levels of risk arising from involuntary activities, e.g. the location of a nuclear power station.

riviera A term now used to describe an area of natural beauty along a coast where tourist ◊ *resorts* have developed. Derives from the Riviera, the region along the Mediterranean coast of south-east France, Monaco and north-west Italy.

road A term now generally reserved for a road suitable for motor vehicles, i.e. paved or surfaced with crushed rock. The term therefore excludes farm tracks, ◊ *bridle paths*, ◊ *footpaths*. Main or major roads (◊ *classified roads*, *freeway*, *motorway*, *turnpike*) are distinguished from local or minor roads (◊◊ *street*). A *public road* is a road maintained at the public expense and over which there is a public right of way which allows anyone to pass along it at any time. ◊◊ *enclosure roads*, *urban road hierarchy*.

road land Land occupied by ◊ *roads*, including, in addition to the carriageways for vehicles and any footpaths for pedestrians, cycleways, road embankments and cuttings, additional land reserved for road widening, and service areas, filling stations and picnic areas for road users.

roadstead, roads An open anchorage for ships, usually in a bay or estuary, which affords some degree of protection from heavy seas for ships unable to get into ◊ *harbour*.

robber-economy A term used to describe a particular approach to the extraction of various ◊ *resources* from the earth. Although it may include the working of minerals it is directed more pointedly at

the exploitation of renewable resources for immediate profit without concern for their future productivity.

robustness In statistics, the degree to which a technique is relatively insensitive to any violation of its assumptions, so that a ◊ *hypothesis* is accepted when it should be accepted and is rejected when it should be rejected.

room density ◊ *occupancy rate*.

R O-R O (roll-on-roll-off) system A system whereby road vehicles can be driven on and off specially designed ships.

Rostow model A model of economic and social growth which, although essentially non-spatial, is applicable at the national scale. It was suggested by the American economic historian W. W. Rostow, who generalized 'the sweep of modern history' in terms of a five-stage sequence of ◊ *development* through which all (capitalist) nations may pass. The five stages are:
(i) The *traditional society*, characterized by primitive technology (based on pre-Newtonian science), a static and hierarchical social structure, and behaviour conditioned by custom and tradition. These factors combine to place a low ceiling on the level of attainable production per head.
(ii) The *pre-conditions for take-off*, involving a process of transition, stimulated by primarily exogenous influences, in both the economy itself and the balance of social values, together with the establishment of a basis for an effective, centralized, national state. Economic growth is accepted as a necessary condition for general welfare, and there are the beginnings of a rise in productive investment, the installation of ◊ *social* and ◊ *economic overhead capital*, and the evolution of a new economically based elite. Agriculture and extractive industry play a key role at this stage.
(iii) *Take-off to sustained growth*, which is

the critical stage when, during a period of ten to thirty years, the economy and society are transformed in such a way that a steady rate of growth can be maintained. Forces making for economic progress come to dominate society – the rate of effective investment and saving rises, new industries expand rapidly as hitherto unused natural resources are tapped and the manufacturing sector is developed.

(iv) The *drive to maturity*, which sees the impact of growth and modern technology transmitted to all economic activities as the economy demonstrates its capacity to move beyond the original industries which powered its take-off. It is a long period of sustained if fluctuating growth, characterized by the diversification of most sectors, falling imports and the stabilization of productive investment at between 10 and 20% of national income.

(v) The *age of high mass-consumption*, which witnesses the leading economic sectors shifting towards consumer goods (especially durable ones) and services. Real income per head rises to a point where a large proportion of society has command over a level of consumption which transcends basic needs. Society ceases to regard further extensions of modern technology as the sole objective, and the ◊ *welfare state* emerges.

The Rostow model is essentially descriptive, since the underlying process of change is not explained. The stages therefore become little more than a classificatory system. Also referred to as the (*economic*) *stages of growth*.

rotation ◊ *crop rotation, land rotation.*

rotational bush fallowing ◊ *land rotation.*

rough grazing, rough pasture Unimproved grazing, including mountain, heath, moor and down land, saltmarsh, and other scrubland. In some cases the natural hill vegetation may be subject to some form of management, e.g. ◊ *muirburn.*

round barrow ◊ *barrow.*

round village ◊ *runddorf.*

roundwood Timber as harvested at the felling stage. ◊ *sawlogs.*

route A regularly travelled path or line of communication between different places. Travel or movement may be by road, rail, air, water, pipeline or some other means. Intersecting routes form a ◊ *network.* Many goods and passenger movements may be formalized as three-stage journeys involving:

(i) *Feeder routes*, which bring people and goods together at an assembly point relatively near to their places of origin.

(ii) *Line-haul routes*, along which people and goods are moved in bulk to a distribution point near to their destinations.

(iii) *Distributor routes*, via which people and goods reach their final destinations.

route development model ◊ *transport network development.*

route factor ◊ *detour index.*

routine decisions Decisions which are of a repetitive, habitual, minor, administrative or programmed nature. Since the need for such decisions occurs frequently, formal procedures are likely to be established to ensure they are taken as required. ◊ *decision-making.* ◊ *strategic decision.*

R/P ratio ◊ *reserves–production ratio.*

rudimental cultivation ◊ *primitive cultivation.*

ruilverkaveling ◊ *land consolidation.*

rule of intra-urban allometric growth An application of the concept of allometric growth (i.e. that the growth rate of a subsystem is proportional to the growth rate of the whole system) to the rate of growth of population density within an urban area. Thus the rate of growth of urban population density is seen as a positive exponential function of distance from the urban centre, i.e.

$$(1 + r_x) = (1 + r_o)e^{gx}$$

where r_x = proportional rate of growth of density at x

r_o = proportional rate of growth at the centre

e = base of natural logarithms

g = the growth gradient

rundale A form of joint occupation of land, found mainly in Ireland and also parts of Scotland in medieval times, characterized by the division of a piece of land of fixed extent into small strips, a number of which (not contiguous to each other) were cultivated by each of the joint holders. The system was associated with joint farms rather than ◊ *townlands* and may have developed from the subdivision of holdings among heirs. It disappeared in the 19th century whenever it became possible to rationalize holdings. The system was similar to ◊ *runrig*, but the strips were larger and the system more flexible and irregular.

runddorf, rundling A characteristic ◊ *village* type associated originally with the Slavonic peoples of eastern and central Europe. It is used as a representative term for *round villages*, in which farmhouses are grouped in a circle around a central ◊ *green* (◊ *green village*) with, originally, only one means of access.

running mean ◊ *moving average*.

runrig A system of land allocation in the Middle Ages, most common in Scotland but found also in parts of highland England and Wales, whereby field strips were periodically re-allocated among different proprietors and/or tenants. It may in fact mean no more than the division of land into strips, since at the earliest stage it implied ridges running in parallel within the same agrarian unit. However, in some places, it became associated with the system of lotting the strips (or rigs), either

annually or for a number of years. In the latter case two processes were involved: the division of the agrarian unit into a number of shares, and the allocation of those shares among tenants. The system largely disappeared as a result of 18th-century agricultural improvements and consolidation of holdings. ◊ *rundale*.

rural Although there is no agreed quantitative identification of 'rural', the term is used to describe those parts of a country which show unmistakable signs of domination by extensive uses of land, either at the present time or in the immediate past. The latter case should be emphasized, since, where the domination of extensive uses over an area has lapsed, the countryside and especially the settlements still appear rural to the eye although the settlements have become little more than an extension of the city as a result of the development of ◊ *commuting*. ◊ *urban*.

rural belt ◊ *country belt*.

rural community The smallest spatial group which encompasses the principal features of society, being a group of people interacting socially, with common ties or bonds with the geographically limited rural territory in which they live. It is also the smallest social group that is largely self-sufficient in terms of meeting its members' daily social needs. In geography rural communities have been considered from four perspectives: as settlements, as localities, as ecological systems and as social systems. ◊ *community*.

rural depopulation The decline in the absolute number of residents in a given area of countryside. It is the result of several processes. *Biological depopulation* occurs where the net immigration into an area is insufficient to compensate for an excess of deaths over births. Net out-migration also gives rise to depopulation: it may be non-occupational, i.e. the movement of young people away from a densely populated agricultural area at entry into the labour market because of the difficulty of finding any kind of employment in that area, or occupational, affecting only members of specific rural groups, e.g. landless labourers displaced by farm mechanization.

rural geography The study of the spatial aspects of human activities in ◊ *rural* areas. It is not a systematic study *per se* but is concerned with several realms of geographical knowledge, including the ◊ *economic geography* of agricultural production; the patterns, origins and functions of rural settlements; demographic changes in rural areas; the pattern of rural recreation and tourism; the impact of the growth of urban-dependent populations in rural areas; and ◊ *rural planning*.

rural planning ◊ *Planning* which is directed at the attainment of specified goals in the ◊ *rural* environment. Rural planning has developed in a rather fragmentary way, often with a land-fixed orientation, involving in the United Kingdom the twin objectives of urban containment and countryside protection. In particular, attention was paid to the planning of rural settlements (◊ *key village*), provision for recreation and tourism in the countryside, and the protection and management of rural landscape, but now there is an increasing awareness of a wider range of rural problems, including poor housing, lack of regular employment, and limited choice and opportunity.

rural settlement form, index of ◊ *index of rural settlement form*.

rural settlement location theory An explanation of the rural settlement process, put forward by J. C. Hudson, in terms of a spatial process analogous to that in ecology explaining the spread of plants and animals. Three components or phases are recognized: (i) *colonization*, associated with the dispersal of settlement as migrants enter a new territory, (ii) *spread*, representing an expansion in the number of settlements via secondary colonization (◊ *clone colonization*) as population density increases and gaps are infilled, and (iii) *competition*, through which limitations of the environment see weaker settlements forced out by their stronger neighbours as rural residents compete for space and respond to change. The result of competition is a more regular and stable pattern similar to that postulated under ◊ *central place theory*. ◊ *index of rural settlement form*.

rural–urban continuum A polar typological approach to the differentiation of rural from urban ◊ *communities*. In its original form the typology merely distinguished the extremes, but more recent interpretations have emphasized the gradual transformation which occurs from one pole to the other (i.e. paralleling the size continuum of settlements from ◊ *hamlet* to ◊ *city*). Rural societies (◊ *folk society*, *Gemeinschaft*) are close-knit, rigidly stratified, highly integrated and stable, whereas urban societies (◊ *Gesellschaft*) have a loose association, unstable membership, fluid social mobility and limited interactions between members.

rural–urban fringe, rurban fringe A zone or frontier of discontinuity between city and country in which rural and urban land uses are intermixed. The absence of a clear break between rural and urban conditions is a feature of the modern city. The fringe is defined in relation to the city and exists in the agricultural hinterland where land use is changing. It lies between the continuously built-up area and the ◊ *urban shadow* (◊ Fig. 145) and, ecologically, can be viewed as an area of invasion in which population density is increasing rapidly and land values are rising.

An *inner fringe* (sometimes *urban fringe*) is characterized by land in an advanced stage of transition from rural to urban land uses – land on which construction is taking

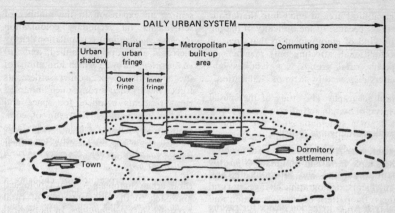

Fig. 145 Rural–urban fringe

place, land for which subdivision plans have been approved or planning permission granted. The *outer fringe* (sometimes *rural fringe*) is an area in which rural land uses continue to dominate the landscape, but the infiltration of urban-oriented elements is clear, e.g. urban uses which take up too much land to be easily accommodated elsewhere (airports, crema-toria, sewage works, hypermarkets, etc.). ◊ *fringe belt*, *urban sprawl*.

ruralization The process whereby an area becomes more dependent upon agriculture as a consequence of ◊ *rural depopulation*. The numbers of rural craftsmen and service workers fall proportionately more than the numbers employed in agriculture.

S

saddlepoint ◊ *game theory*.

saeter, seter A Scandinavian term for both the simple farm and mountain ◊ *pasture* used only in the summer months. ◊◊ *alp*, *shieling*.

sakiyeh An ◊ *irrigation* device for raising water from a river to land at a higher level, comprising a dipper at one end of a beam on a pivot. ◊◊ *shaduf*.

sale-and-leaseback A property or land transaction involving the disposal of the ◊ *freehold* or long leasehold in a development by the developer or landowner for a capital sum (usually to a financial institution) on condition of a ◊ *lease* being granted back to the original developer/landowner. There are a number of variations:
(i) *Horizontal* or *'top-slice' leaseback*, in which the developer is placed in a subordinate, unsecured position regarding rental income, i.e. the institution is assured of an agreed rental figure but the developer relies on the riskier (but potentially remunerative) top slice.
(ii) *Vertical* or *'side-by-side' leaseback*, in which the institution and the developer share the equity of the development in an agreed proportion.
(iii) *Reverse leaseback*, in which the institution purchases a long lease and sublets back, allowing the developer to retain the freehold (and, therefore, the assured and marketable bottom slice of the income).

sample A part or sub-set of a given total quantity or statistical ◊ *population*. Samples are normally selected deliberately in order to investigate the characteristics of their parent populations (◊ *sampling*).

sampling The procedure for choosing a ◊ *sample* (sub-set) of a defined statistical ◊ *population*. Thus samples are by definition only part of the parent population and cannot have exactly the same characteristics as the population from which they have been drawn. *Sampling theory* has been developed by statisticians to allow inferences or conclusions, derived from the investigation of a sample, about the characteristics of a population to be as precise as possible, i.e. within defined confidence limits. The population from which a sample is drawn is termed the *sampling frame*, and the ratio between the size of a sample and the size of its parent population is the *sampling fraction*.

A variety of *sampling methods*, i.e. the method of selection from the sampling frame, have been developed. Two general types of procedure may be distinguished:
(i) *Purposive* (or *subjective* or *hunch*) *sampling*, in which samples thought to be typical of the population as a whole are chosen, usually for convenience, arbitrarily and subjectively by the researcher, as in the use of the case study in geography, or *quota sampling*, in which a street interviewer has to complete a certain number of interviews. Such non-random sampling procedures do not ensure that every individual or unit has an equal chance of being included in the sample and are therefore more likely to be biased and unrepresentative.

(ii) *Probability* (or *objective*) *sampling*, in which samples are selected on the basis of rigorous statistical principles to be truly representative of the parent population, i.e. individuals or units are drawn from the population according to established rules. There is an elementary distinction between:

(a) *Random sampling*, where the choice of individuals or units for inclusion in the sample is left entirely to chance, i.e. every individual has an equal chance of inclusion in the sample throughout the sampling procedure (*independent random sampling*), and the selection of any particular individual does not affect the chance of selection of any other individual. Such random sampling may be with or without *replacement*. In the case of a finite population it is implicitly assumed that a given individual is chosen only once in any sample drawn, i.e. the individual drawn first is automatically excluded from being a further member of the sample, likewise for the second individual chosen, and so on. This is *sampling without replacement*. If the individual drawn first is replaced in the population after each selection this is *sampling with replacement* and that individual could appear more than once in the sample.

(b) *Systematic* (or *grid* or *regular*) *sampling*, where the choice of individuals or units is made in some regular way after selecting a random starting point. While it is generally quicker and easier than random sampling and gives a more even coverage of the sampling frame it should be used only if the units in the sampling frame are more or less randomly arranged. Systematic sampling should not be used if the data are ordered in any way.

There are also more elaborate methods of *stratified sampling*, involving multistage or hierarchical designs, in which the population is first stratified, i.e. divided into sub-sets or strata, certain strata may be randomly selected, and then within each

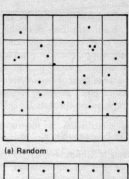
(a) Random

(b) Systematic or Grid

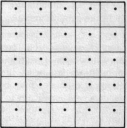
(c) Stratified random

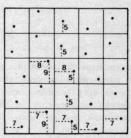
(d) Systematic stratified unaligned

Fig. 146 Sampling

strata individuals will also be randomly selected. Such stratified sampling procedures may often combine the random and systematic approaches to produce more complex sampling designs, e.g. *stratified systematic unaligned* or *nested/hierarchical*. Examples of point sampling designs used by geographers are illustrated in ◊ Fig. 146.

sampling distribution A theoretical distribution that would be obtained by randomly drawing all possible samples of a given size from a specified population.

sampling error The ◊ *error* attributable to the fact that a ◊ *sample* is taken, rather than a complete enumeration. It represents the difference between a sample estimate and a population parameter, and arises because sample estimates may be *biased* (with a tendency systematically to over- or underestimate the quantities being investigated) and/or *imprecise* (reflecting variation of the sample estimates around the population parameter). With random ◊ *sampling* procedures the error limits can be calculated.

sarvah An intensive, ◊ *subsistence* tillage system emphasizing the production of rice which is found in the deltas, plains and hill terraces of South and South-East Asia.

satellite town A term used in the years immediately after the First World War as an alternative to ◊ *garden city*. It subsequently developed a much wider meaning to include any town that is closely related to or dependent on a larger city yet is physically separate from it and has a corporate existence of its own. ◊◊ *new town*.

satisficer concept A model of decision-making that discards the rationality assumptions of ◊ *economic man* or ◊ *optimizer* and assumes that the objective of decision-making is to reach a level of utility or satisfaction that is acceptable. Decision-makers evaluate possible actions according to whether or not their expected

outcomes are satisfactory or unsatisfactory with reference to some threshold (◊ *aspiration level*). Satisficing behaviour is therefore non-optional behaviour in which decision-makers do not seek optimal solutions.

The satisficing concept has also been used in two other contexts: to describe forms of optimizing behaviour in which (i) criteria are personal or non-economic and (ii) decision-makers consider only a few pre-selected alternatives out of a larger set (◊ *bounded rationality*). ◊◊ *theory of administrative behaviour*.

saturation level (traffic) A term which has been used to describe two situations in traffic studies: (i) that in which the ratio of cars to population in any area ceases to show a material annual increase, and (ii) that in which no increase is possible in the number of vehicles on a road without traffic movement being brought to a standstill.

sawah The terraced rice farming of Indonesia, involving ◊ *irrigation* and open-field monocrop cultivation with a highly specialized regime. ◊◊ *paddy farming*.

sawlogs Timber considered suitable for producing sawnwood.

scale economies, returns to scale ◊ *economies of scale*.

scales of measurement ◊ *interval scale, nominal scale, ordinal scale, ratio scale*.

scalogram analysis ◊ *Guttman scale analysis*.

scattergram Or *scatter-diagram* or *scatter-graph*. A simple graphical device used as a first step in ascertaining the relationship between two variables (one plotted along the *x*-axis, the abscissa, and the other along the *y*-axis, the ordinate). If, when the values are plotted, they tend to lie along a diagonal line some degree of correlation is manifest.

scenic drive A ◊ *road* designed (or adapted)

primarily for ◊ *pleasure driving*, including the provision of associated recreation facilities. ◊ *parkway*.

scenic quality ◊ *landscape evaluation*.

scheduled monument consent The 1979 Ancient Monuments and Archaeological Areas Act introduced a system of scheduled monument consent whereby any alterations or demolitions of ◊ *ancient monuments* require permission from the Secretary of State for the Environment.

science park A term used to describe a variety of initiatives designed to promote innovation in industry via collaboration between academic researchers and businessmen, i.e. to increase the rate of technical progress. The purest form is the *research park*, located on or close to the campus of a university, where the key area of activity is academic/industry liaison in the leading edge technologies. The university usually plays a key role in the management of the research park and scientific advance is accorded greater priority than rental income from tenants. The *science park* covers not only basic research activity but also developmental work, including, possibly, prototype production facilities. A *technology park* accommodates firms engaged in the commercial application of high technology and may involve little or no academic participation.

Research/science parks have four main objectives: (i) to provide a mechanism whereby companies formed by academics can spin off from academic environments to form a focus for new enterprise development, (ii) to allow the transfer of technology/knowledge from academic to business environments at the least cost, (iii) to keep academic research aware of commercial priorities and (iv) to create a culture whereby academics and industrialists generate research and enterprise synergy within their own groups.

The impetus for science parks came from the USA, where they represented attempts to improve the exploitation of academic enterprise and research. American universities adjusted their administrative policies to create an environment which allowed individual academics to develop their own commercial ventures while remaining members of the university. The earliest research-based 'academic' companies were formed in the 1930s and 1940s in association with the Massachusetts Institute of Technology and Stanford University. In the UK, where the first science parks were not developed until the 1970s with the Cambridge and Heriot-Watt initiatives, some twenty-five such parks are now planned.

scientific method The processes and steps by which a science obtains knowledge. These normally include the identification of a problem; the formulation of a ◊ *hypothesis* to test; the collection of relevant data, their preparation and analysis against the hypothesis; and the interpretation of the results, i.e. the formulation of a conclusion with respect to the validity of the hypothesis. Results may form the basis for some generalization, and sufficient repetitions of the same patterns or tendencies may lead to the formulation of ◊ *laws*. Scientific method subsumes two main approaches: ◊ *deduction* and ◊ *induction*.

screenline survey ◊ *cordon survey*.

search behaviour The process by which an individual or organization, stimulated to take a decision in the face of a problem, decides which course of action to choose from a set of alternatives in order to bring about a satisfactory solution to the problem. Search behaviour ranges from the very systematic to the haphazard, depending on the ability of individuals and organizations to gather and use information. The geographical concern is with how people search space. This ranges from the study of geographical exploration to current location decision-making by firms and households in search of better economic and employment opportunities and people's search for information and social/recreational opportunities. Frequently the order of search is important, and this is emphasized in the distinction between ◊ *optimizers* and ◊ *satisficers* when viewing location decision-making and spatial behaviour as a search process. Emphasis is placed on people's highly restricted ◊ *perception* of space. Search behaviour therefore helps explain spatial patterns, relationships and processes.

search space The territory or space within which an individual or organization actively seeks alternatives. It is a sub-set of ◊ *awareness space* and is bounded according to the environmental and locational criteria of the individual's or organization's ◊ *aspiration region*.

search theory ◊ *search behaviour*.

season A period into which the ◊ *year* is naturally divided by the earth's changing position in relation to the sun and which is generally based on differences in the duration and intensity of solar radiation. Four seasons are recognized: *spring* – the sowing season; *summer* – the growing season; *autumn* (fall) – the harvest season; *winter* – the dormant season. Their duration varies according to latitude (in very high latitudes, the polar regions, the spring and autumn seasons are barely noticeable). In the northern hemisphere the seasons are defined astronomically as spring – 21 March to 21 June; summer – 22 June to 23 September; autumn – 23 September to 22 December; winter – 22 December to 21 March. The term is also used in respect of a time period in a calendar year during which a particular activity may be practised, e.g. the fishing season, cricket season, hunting season.

seasonal migration ◊ *migration*.

seasonal unemployment ◊ *unemployment*.

seat load factor The proportion of seats occupied on an aircraft flight compared to the total available. For most airlines the overall average tends to be around 60%. ◊ *load factor*.

seaway A term used to describe both a regular route for ships across the open oceans and a canal which is large enough for sea-going vessels. ◊ *ship canal*.

second farm An additional ◊ *farm* acquired by a ◊ *peasant* in an attempt to increase the agricultural potential of the main holding. Called *Zuhube* in the Austrian Alps.

second-generation immigrant A self-contradictory term which describes children born to immigrants in the country of their ◊ *immigration*.

second home A fixed property which is the occasional residence of a household that normally lives elsewhere (i.e. in a first home in a city). Second homes may be owned or rented on a long lease and are usually located in rural areas where they are used for weekend, vacation and recreational purposes. Hence also termed *vacation home* and *weekend cottage*.

Second World One of the three major worlds of ◊ *development* recognized in a global generalization of economic patterns (◊ *First World*, *Third World*, although a ◊ *Fourth World* is now also being distinguished). It comprises the Soviet Union, its allies and satellites. Countries of the Second World are characterized by a socialist system, which is dependent upon state ownership in a controlled exchange system, proletarian values and an emphasis on ◊ *secondary activities*, i.e. basically a redistributive economic system. The political system is based on the ideology of communism and socialism and is dominated by democratic centralism: usually there is only one political party. Second World countries, with a rapidly growing working class, are relatively highly urbanized, although a sizable peasant sector may still exist. Their societies are highly bureaucratized, enjoy a mass education emphasizing technical-scientific principles, high social welfare benefits and slowly increasing leisure time.

secondary activity, secondary sector An economic activity that adds ◇ *form utility* to the materials produced by the ◇ *primary sector*. It includes the ◇ *manufacturing* and construction industries. Several stages may be involved in the conversion of basic materials into more finely processed goods and more value is added at each stage. The term has also been used as a synonym of ◇ *non-basic activity*.

secondary fuel Fuels, such as electricity, coke and hydrogen, which are made by manufacturing or conversion processes from ◇ *primary fuels*.

secondary hinterland ◇ *hinterland*.

secondary industry ◇ *manufacturing industry*, *secondary activity*.

secondary labour force As usually defined, males aged fourteen to nineteen and over sixty-five together with all female age groups. ◇ *active population*.

secondary location ◇ *location*.

secondary recovery The recovery of oil from a reservoir using artificial techniques, e.g. water flooding and gas injection, after the 'natural drive mechanism' has been exhausted (◇ *primary recovery*). The terms *water drive* and *gas drive* are used to describe the action of water and gas in pushing oil out of a reservoir and into producing wells.

secondary state A ◇ *state* formed by the superimposition of a conqueror stratum. ◇ *pristine state*.

secondary territory ◇ *territory*.

secondary urbanization ◇ *Urbanization* within a country which is promoted as a result of exogenous forces.

sector principle A principle which is the

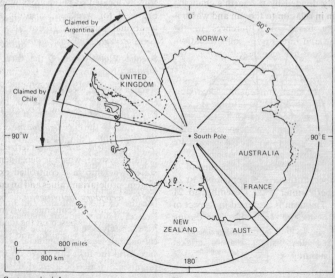

Fig. 147 Sector principle

basis of claims to land and sea made by several states in the Arctic and Antarctic. Subdivision is based on sectors which are defined from a base line or arc (e.g. the limit of existing national territory or even an arbitrary stretch of unclaimed coastline) with their apices at the pole, and jurisdiction is claimed over a triangular area (◊ Fig. 147). Originating at the beginning of this century, the principle has been generally accepted in the case of the Arctic Ocean but has proved more controversial in the Antarctic, where land rather than sea is at issue. Here claims overlap and agreement has proved difficult to reach – the 1959 Antarctic Treaty froze existing claims for thirty years, after which the territorial disputes will be considered afresh.

sector theory, sector model One of the three classic models of urban land use (◊ *concentric zone theory*, *multiple nuclei theory*). The sector theory, formulated by H. Hoyt on the basis of rent and housing data, is developed on the assumption that the internal structure of a city is conditioned by the disposition of routes radiating out from the city centre. The differential access associated with these radial routes attracts particular uses to certain radial sectors which emanate from the ◊ *central business district* (◊ Fig. 148). The key element is the high-status residential area which occupies the most desirable space, and other grades of residential area are aligned around the high-status one, leaving the lowest-status residential areas occupying the least desirable land, usually next to manufacturing industry.

sector theory of growth ◊ *development stages theory of growth.*

sectoral transformation The shift of ◊ *factors of production* among sectors of an economy in response to changing conditions and needs.

sedentary agriculture A form of ◊ *primitive cultivation* in which subsistence ◊ *agriculture* is practised in one place by a settled farmer. The term is used of primitive agricultural systems in Africa and Asia, where the same land is farmed indefinitely and covers a variety of subsistence crop combinations and intensities of cultivation (◊ *dryfield farming*, *sarvah*). Contrasts with ◊ *shifting cultivation*. ◊ *tropical peasant farming.*

seedbed growth, seedbed location Localized concentrations of specialized industry, based on ◊ *linkage* benefits of agglomeration, close to the ◊ *central business district*, which provide a suitable location for small, newly established firms. Such areas provide these firms with ready access to all the contacts they need to get going, i.e. services essential to their operation which, because of the small size and limited resources of firms, they are unable to provide for themselves, e.g. rentable space, physical capital, legal and financial services. If successful the firm can move on to larger premises outside the area, if unsuccessful it goes out of business and, in both cases,

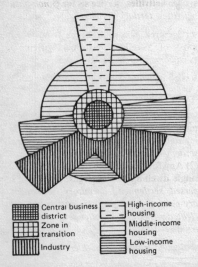

Central business district
Zone in transition
Industry
High-income housing
Middle-income housing
Low-income housing

Fig. 148 Sector theory

the premises are available to another firm. Such seedbed locations therefore have relatively high turnover rates (◊ *entry rate, exit rate*). The term *incubator hypothesis* is also used to describe this phenomenon.

segregation The separation of sub-groups within a wider population. It exists when members of a sub-group are not distributed uniformly relative to the remainder of the population. It is applied particularly in human geography to ◊ *residential segregation*. The degree of segregation may be measured by the ◊ *index of segregation*. ◊◊ *apartheid, natural area*.

seine fishing A method of fishing in which a long net is used to encircle shoals of pelagic fish. When the two ends of the net are brought together – or 'pursed' – the net is hauled aboard the fishing boat. ◊ *fisheries*.

selection system, selective logging A system of forest management in which mature trees are felled at intervals during the growth of a ◊ *forest* of mixed age structure. It is the method of management which approximates most closely to the dynamics of a natural forest, since it maintains the overall tree cover as well as providing a ◊ *sustained yield*. ◊ *clear felling, shelter belt system*.

selective migration ◊ *Migration* is selective from two points of view: (i) migrants select themselves physically on the basis of age, ability and other personal characteristics, and (ii) in the case of international migration, the host country lays down conditions concerning age, health, occupation, morality, etc.

self-production sector ◊ *non-basic activities*.

self-sufficiency The condition of economic independence whereby an ◊ *economy* – local or national – provides by itself for all its needs and demands.

selion The basic unit of ploughing in the ◊ *common field* system.

semi-quartile range ◊ *quartile deviation*.

senior citizen ◊ *general age group*.

sequent occupance D. Whittlesey's term for a succession of stages in the human occupance of an area.

sequential revelation ◊ *serial vision*.

serendipity The knack of making pleasant discoveries by accident, i.e. finding interesting items of information and knowledge when searching for something else.

serial autocorrelation ◊ *temporal autocorrelation*.

serial vision Also referred to as *kinetic sensation* and *sequential revelation*. A means of experiencing a view or skyline over time and from changing points of view. The important feature of this way of seeing views and skylines is that the observer is in motion, e.g. travelling in a motor vehicle.

sericulture The rearing of silkworms to produce raw silk.

service activities, service sector ◊ *non-basic activities, tertiary activity*.

service area The spatial area from which most of a seller's customers originate. ◊ *catchment area, market area*.

service industry ◊ *tertiary industry*.

service linkage ◊ *linkage*.

settlement (1) The opening-up and peopling (or colonizing) of a previously uninhabited or thinly populated area. ◊◊ *rural settlement location theory*.
(2) Any form of human habitation, from a single dwelling to the largest city. ◊◊ *dispersed settlement, dormitory settlement, dry-point settlement, key settlement, nucleated settlement, squatter settlement, wet-point settlement*.

settlement frontier ◊ *frontier*.

settlement hierarchy ◊ *hierarchy*.

settlement net The ◊ *settlement* structure of a region formed of a combination of rural and urban elements (their population, function and agglomerative form).

settlement pattern The spatial distribution of population clusters of varying sizes. ◊ *dispersed settlement, nucleated settlement.*

seven lives of downtown J. E. Vance's generalization of the stages of growth and change affecting the ◊ *central business district*:
(i) The *process of inception*, the original siting of the town.
(ii) The *process of exclusion*, as rent-paying ability sorts out activities able to command central locations.
(iii) The *process of segregation*, based on ◊ *linkages* between central business district activities.
(iv) The *process of extension*, involving the radial growth of the ◊ *downtown* area consequent upon increased mobility.
(v) The *process of replication and re-adjustment*, as the duplication of certain central functions outside the downtown area promotes a reappraisal of central business district functions.
(vi) The *process of redevelopment* of the physical fabric.
(vii) The *city of realms*, the end product in which the central business district is but one cell in a city of many cells without the strong hierarchical ranking that formerly held. ◊ *age of towns scheme.*

shadow effects A concept, similar to ◊ *backwash effects*, which recognizes that a particular action or decision, such as choice of location for an activity, introduces constraints, both in space and time, on other possible actions or decisions. ◊ *economic shadow.*

shadow price Or *accounting price*. A ◊ *price* which attempts to measure the benefits obtained or forgone by a society for goods not subject to ◊ *market* forces. Shadow prices are commonly used in ◊ *cost–benefit analysis* when valuing intangible items.

shadow site A site revealing traces of earlier cultivation or occupance which is observable from the air when the sun is low in the sky and casts oblique shadows which pick out slight undulations in ground form.

shaduf (shadoof, shadouf) A primitive device for raising water from a well. It consists of a long pole, weighted at one end and with a bucket at the other, which is mounted and hinged on a vertical pole in the ground. The bucket is dipped into the well, lifted, swung round and emptied into a trough or ◊ *irrigation* channel with a minimum of effort by virtue of the counterpoised weight.

shambles Stalls erected in medieval market towns and let out to townspeople or visiting traders on market days only, for the sale of fish and meat. Also slaughterhouses.

shanty town ◊ *squatter settlement.*

shape index ◊ *compactness ratio.*

shape measures Quantitative means of describing the shape of areas and map distributions. Various measures have been proposed, based on such characteristics as the area covered by a distribution, the perimeter of the area, the length of its longest axis. Commonly used measures are ◊ *circularity ratio,* ◊ *compaction index,* ◊ *compactness ratio,* ◊ *contact number,* ◊ *edge length variance,* ◊ *ellipticity index,* ◊ *elongation ratio,* ◊ *form ratio,* ◊ *index of circularity,* ◊ *mean percent angular distortion,* ◊ *network shape index* and ◊ *radial shape index.*

share-cropping, share tenancy A system of tenant farming in which the landlord is paid in the form of produce, rather than a money ◊ *farm rent*. The tenant pays a predetermined proportion of total production, usually between 25 and 50% of the crop, depending upon local custom and the landlord's contribution to the total inputs needed for production. Frequently the landlord contributes part or all of the farm stock and equipment. While the practice may allow tenants with little or no capital to farm on their own, it makes for inefficient farming since landlords attempt to maximize returns from minimum inputs and there is insecurity of tenure for the share-cropper. The arrangements stem from customary practice and many different versions occur around the world. Also referred to by the French term ◊ *métayage.* ◊ *landlord capital and tenant capital, land tenure, mezzadria, tenancy.*

shatterbelt, shatterzone A large, strategically located region occupied by a number of ◊ *states* and caught between the conflicting spheres of influence of greater powers, e.g. the Middle East, South-East Asia. International ◊ *boundary* disputes, minority problems and economic and political instability are characteristic of such regions.

sheep walk The area over which a lord of the ◊ *manor* exercised a right to feed sheep on the lands of the manor, including tenant land, at certain times of the year.

shell mound A prehistoric refuse tip, formerly known as a ◊ *kitchen midden.* It consisted chiefly of edible mollusc shells and bones of animals, along with some stone implements and other relics of prehistoric peoples.

shelter belt system A system of forest management in which groups of weaker trees are felled and the surrounding trees are allowed to seed into the gaps created. The parent trees provide shelter and are then felled when the new crop is well established. ◊ *clear felling, selection system.*

Shevkv-Bell model ◊ *social area analysis.*

shiel, shieling A term used in the Highlands and Western Isles of Scotland to refer to both the summer grazings (often hill pasture) and the rough, temporary huts of stone or turf erected by the herders, which are located at some considerable distance from the settlement to which the shieling belongs. ◊ *alp, saeter.*

shift–share analysis, shift ratio A descriptive technique for measuring regional shifts in industry and changes on a regional scale of the national share of an industrial group. Attention is focused on the significance of different components in regional growth (or decline) by comparing actual performances (usually in employment terms) with what would have happened if the region had followed some wider pattern. Thus the performance of an industry in a region is considered in relation to (1) the performance of that industry in the nation as a whole, (2) the performance of all industries in the nation and (3) the performance of all industries in the region.

The rate of change of employment in a given industry on a regional scale is first calculated over a given time period, assuming an overall or national base rate. This gives the *regional share component.* Then the difference or total shift is computed between the actual employment in the industry in the region and the employment that would have resulted had the region's rate of growth in the industry been the same as the national rate. A positive difference signifies a shift of industry into the region: a negative difference indicates a shift out. For the industry the *shift ratio* is calculated by summing, for all regions, the positive (or negative) shifts in employment and expressing the result as a percentage of total employment in that industry.

For a region, the growth of all industries may be due to a high concentration of industries growing rapidly at the national level or to locational shifts within industries unrelated to national growth rates. The total shift is therefore divided into a *proportionality shift* (or *composition effect* or *industrial mix component*), which accounts for the relative proportion of industries with above average growth rates, and a *differential shift*, representing the extra growth that may occur because the region is growing faster than the national average owing to locational changes within industries.

shifting cultivation Or *slash and burn cultivation* or *swidden*; less commonly *field-forest rotation, shifting field agriculture* or *fire agriculture*. A form of ◊ *agriculture*, most characteristic of primitive economies in areas of tropical rain forest, in which soil fertility is maintained by a cyclical process of field rotation. The attention that shifting cultivation has received from geographers is out of all proportion to its economic importance today. In practice there is a distinction between (i) the true shifting cultivation of nomadic tribes, (ii) the system of ◊ *land rotation* practised by peoples living in a permanent central village and (iii) the shifting cultivation associated with particular cash crops in which land is abandoned when yields fall below a certain minimum.

The essential feature is the rotation of fields rather than crops, with short periods of cropping alternating with long periods of natural fallow. An area is cleared of natural vegetation using slash-and-burn methods and is cropped until yields fall to some minimal level. This usually takes from one to three years, with yields dropping by around 30% in the second year and 50% in the third year. The area is then abandoned because of the exhaustion of the soil fertility. The natural vegetation will regenerate and soil fertility will recover, allowing the area to be cultivated again after some thirty years. Shifting cultivation is not a very productive system, being largely ◊ *subsistence*-oriented, sup-

porting between 13 and 65 persons/km² (5–25 persons/ml²).

Local names are used for the many variants found throughout the tropics, e.g. Barbecho and Coamile (Mexico); Conuco (Venezuela); Derrubadas e quemadas and Roça (Brazil); Milpa (Central America); Chitemene and Masole (Central Africa); Tavy (Madagascar); Bewar, Dahi, Dippa, Djum, Erka, Jara, Jhuming, Kumari, Parka, Podu and Prenda (India); Chena (Sri Lanka); Taungya (Burma); Tamrai (Thailand); Rây (Laos); Djuma (Sumatra); Humah (Java); Ladang (Malaysia); Kaingin (Philippines).

Shimbel index, Shimbel number A measure of the ◊ *accessibility* of a ◊ *node* in a ◊ *network*, being the number of ◊ *edges* needed to connect any node with all other nodes in the network by the shortest path. ◊ *alpha index, beta index, connectivity index, cyclomatic number, detour index, gamma index, König number.* ◊◊ *connectivity.*

ship canal A ◊ *canal* constructed to a depth and width which permits the passage of ocean-going vessels. Ship canals have been constructed either to shorten the voyage between two seas by cutting through an isthmus, e.g. the Panama Canal, or to convert an inland place into a ◊ *port*, e.g. the Manchester Ship Canal. ◊◊ *seaway.*

shires Administrative districts, formed for taxation purposes, into which the Anglo-Saxon kingdoms were subdivided. The term derives from the Old English *scir*, meaning a division. Shires were divided into ◊ *hundreds* in Anglo-Saxon areas and into ◊ *wapentakes* in the Danish areas. The shire system survived well into the Middle Ages in the North of England but further south it disintegrated after the Norman Conquest as the ◊ *county* became the basis for local administration (although the term was preserved in many county names).

shopping goods ◊ *High-order* ◊ *goods* (e.g. furniture), purchased at irregular and infrequent intervals by any one customer, which individually often represent a multiple of a person's weekly income, and for which choice is important – the purchase is delayable in order to 'shop around' and compare as wide a range of competing lines in different outlets as possible. Customers are therefore prepared to travel a great deal further than the nearest outlet supplying the good. ⟡ *convenience goods, durable goods.*

sidereal day A time interval based on motion in relation to the stars: the length of time – 23 h 56 min 4·09 sec – taken for the earth to make one complete rotation in relation to the stars and is some four minutes shorter than a mean ⟡ *solar day.*

sidewalk farmer In the USA a farmer who lives in an urban centre and cultivates a holding some distance away, usually less than 48 km (30 ml). Sidewalk farming is most commonly associated with specialist cereal growing, where day-to-day management is not needed. ⟡ *suitcase farmer.*

sieve mapping A technique used in land use planning to identify areas suitable for a particular type of use or development. It proceeds by eliminating or 'sieving out' all areas considered unsuitable for one reason or another. The result is obtained by using a series of overlays – maps printed as transparencies – each overlay representing a particular constraint on development.

sight distance The length of roadway visible to the driver of a motor vehicle at any given point on a road when the view is unobstructed by traffic.

sign test A simple ⟡ *non-parametric test* applicable to sets of paired observations and based on whether the observation in one set is greater (+) or less (−) than its paired observation in the other set. The null ⟡ *hypothesis* is that there is no difference between the two distributions – if true the same number of + and − signs

are to be expected, if not true one sign will dominate.

significance test In ⟡ *statistics*, a test carried out to demonstrate the degree to which a ⟡ *hypothesis* is acceptable, i.e. to indicate the ⟡ *probability* that the observed difference is large enough to signify a real difference and cannot be explained by chance. The probability level at which it is decided to reject the null hypothesis is termed the *significance level* $\propto$ (or *coefficient of risk*). The significance level indicates the proportion of times that the difference could be expected to occur by chance. The common practice is to refer to results as significant, highly significant or very highly significant respectively when significant at 5, 1 or 0·1% level (i.e. a 1 in 20, a 1 in 100, or a 1 in 1,000 probability of the given result occurring by chance). ⟡ *confidence limits.*

silage Green fodder (grass, clover, alfalfa, etc.) compressed, fermented and stored in a silo or silage-pit, for use as animal-feed.

silviculture The culture of forest trees, primarily for timber. ⟡ *forestry.*

similarity, coefficient of ⟡ *coefficient of geographical association.*

simplex algorithm A formal, general purpose, mathematical procedure to find the maximum or minimum values of a linear function which is subject to constraints. It begins with an initial feasible solution to the problem and continues via iteration (step-by-step instructions) to search for improved solutions until a final optimal solution is reached. It is the basis for all ⟡ *linear programming.* ⟡ *algorithm.*

simulation A method of representing real ⟡ *systems* or processes in an abstract form for the purposes of experimentation, and which maintains a close identity between the experimental and real-world situations. It may involve the construction of an

◊ *analogue*, which is usually employed to model a physical process, or *computer simulation*, in which a mathematical model is used. Simulation models may be either ◊ *deterministic* or ◊ *stochastic*. Simulation has been used in human geography to model the evolution of various spatial patterns and flows, e.g. ◊ *Monte Carlo methods* have been used especially to solve problems of spatial diffusion.

site The absolute ◊ *location* of an object or activity, being the ground or area upon which a town, factory, dwelling, etc. has been built or on which an activity takes place. A site is 'vertical', referring to the local relationship between a building or activity and its immediate physical environment. ◊ *situation*.

Site of Special Scientific Interest (SSSI) An area in the United Kingdom defined and listed by the Nature Conservancy Council as being of special interest because of its faunal, floral, geological or physiographical features. The Nature Conservancy Council notifies the local planning authority, since the latter must consult the Council before granting ◊ *planning permission* for any development affecting the site. While there is no legal obligation on owners or occupiers of such sites other than to provide a list of notifiable operations (actions potentially damaging to the site) the Nature Conservancy Council may propose ◊ *management agreements* with owners/occupiers to safeguard and enhance the scientific interest. Owners/occupiers may also take the initiative and seek such an agreement. ◊ *nature reserve*.

site value The value of the land on which a building stands, normally calculated as a residual by subtracting the reproduction cost of the building from the market value of the existing real property. ◊ *cleared-site value, economic life of a building*.

site value rating A form of land value taxation in which a local annual tax is levied on the ◊ *site value* and charged to the owners of land. It is not levied on any improvement to the land but is based on the optimum use to which land can be put. Site value rating has been suggested as an alternative to the system of local ◊ *rates* in Britain because it is claimed that it would encourage owners to make their land available for ◊ *development*, that it would reduce the profitability of owners holding land for speculative reasons and that it might retard the rise in land values.

situation The ◊ *location* of a place or activity with reference to the broad spatial system of which it is a part. Situation is 'horizontal' and functional, referring to regional interdependencies and ◊ *accessibility*. ◊ *site*.

skewness A measure of the degree to which a ◊ *distribution* approximates to a normal curve, i.e. its lack of symmetry or the

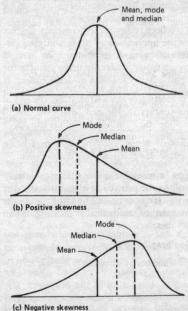

(a) Normal curve

(b) Positive skewness

(c) Negative skewness

Fig. 149 Skewness

extent to which the bulk of the values in a distribution are concentrated to one side or other of the ◊ *arithmetic mean*. In ◊ Fig. 149 a normal curve (a) is compared with *positive* or *right skewness* (b), where the bulk of the values are less than the mean, and with *negative* or *left skewness* (c), where most values are greater than the mean. Skewness is an important concept in geographical study because many of the variables measured have positively skewed distributions. It is the third moment measure about the mean. ◊ *kurtosis*.

skid row A term applied, in American towns, to a dilapidated street or district which has become the refuge of the 'down-and-out' – derelicts, drop-outs and petty criminals. ◊ *urban village*.

skinned land An area in the Hebrides stripped of peat over many generations. It forms a mosaic of bare rock and greyish till patches and is found especially along main roadways and tracks. In some cases it has been reclaimed to permanent pasture by the application of shell sand and fertilizer.

skyline The term was first used in the mid 19th century as a synonym for horizon, the meeting of sky and land. By the end of the century its use had been extended to include the outline or silhouette of a building or number of buildings or other objects against the sky. This new meaning was largely the result of the aggressive intrusion of skyscrapers. Attention is now paid to the protection of natural skylines from indiscriminate building and the creation of aesthetically pleasing urban skylines.

slag heap ◊ *tip heap*.

slash and burn cultivation ◊ *shifting cultivation*.

slum An area of sub-standard, overcrowded housing occupied by the poor, the unemployed, the unemployable and immigrants, who cannot afford to live elsewhere. Slums are judged by subjective criteria: a sub-culture with a set of norms and values reflected in poor sanitation, poor schools, fire hazards and shops retailing over-priced goods. Socially slums tend to be isolated from the remainder of urban society and exhibit pathological social symptoms (drug abuse, alcoholism, crime, vandalism and other deviant behaviour). The lack of integration of slum inhabitants into urban life reflects both lack of ability and cultural barriers. *Slums of hope* or temporary ghettos (◊ *urban village*), where integration may be expected eventually, are distinguished from *slums of despair* (or permanent ghettos or the urban jungle), where poverty and lack of ability are correlated.

slum clearance In the United Kingdom, usually the demolition of condemned dwellings, a *slum clearance scheme* being an official proposal to carry out slum clearance within an area defined in a ◊ *development plan* as a *slum clearance area*. The term has also been used in a more general context to include the improvement of substandard housing (◊ *slum dwelling*) to make it fit for human habitation. ◊ *housing policy*.

slum-dwellers, types of ◊ *permanent necessitarian, permanent opportunist, temporary necessitarian, temporary opportunist*.

slum dwellings A term used to describe both a condemned dwelling – judged on the basis of certain health criteria to be unfit for human habitation – and an obsolescent and sub-standard dwelling, whose defects can be remedied at reasonable expense to provide a further period of useful life.

small woods scheme A scheme designed to encourage the planting or restocking of small woods, generally those of less than 10 hectares (25 acres). The scheme was first introduced by the 1947 Forestry Act and was withdrawn in 1972, but owing to concern about the continuing loss of small woods, whose aesthetic, nature conservation and amenity value was increasingly recognized, it was reintroduced in 1977. Under the scheme there is grant aid for planting, but rates of grant do not distinguish between broadleaves and conifers, although special emphasis is placed on broadleaves where sites are suitable and the existing landscape is essentially broadleaved in character. The scheme is intended to meet the needs of woodland owners whose holdings do not qualify for aid under the ◊ *dedication scheme*.

smallholding Generally a small agricultural unit, intensively farmed on a family basis with no paid labour, often specializing in ◊ *market gardening*, ◊ *horticulture* or ◊ *glasshouse cultivation* and sometimes with pigs and poultry. The legal meaning of the term under certain British Agriculture Acts, e.g. 1947, is a holding of under 20 hectares (50 acres) and below a certain rental value.

smoke control area, smoke control zone Under the 1956 Clean Air Act, smoke emissions, particularly from domestic sources, were restricted. Local authorities are empowered to impose smoke control orders to create smoke control areas or

'*smokeless zones*', in which the emission of smoke from any chimney is prohibited. In combination with changes in domestic heating methods the effect has been a considerable lowering of atmospheric ◊ *pollution* levels in all urban areas and a great reduction in the frequency and duration of urban fogs. ◊◊ *pollution control*.

socage A form of tenure without servile obligation, dating from Anglo-Saxon times. The tenant normally paid a ◊ *rent*, although occasional services might be required. The tenure was free and partible (◊◊ *gavelkind*). ◊◊ *tenancy*.

social accounting A term given to the statistical classification of the activities of human beings and social organizations in the process of producing scarce goods and services and the compilation of accounts for those groups. It is applied at national (◊ *national income*) and regional levels (◊ *regional accounting*).

social anthropology The study of people in their social context, dealing with various aspects of social life, e.g. ◊ *kinship* systems and economic and political structures.

social area analysis A technique, developed by two American sociologists, E. Shevky and W. Bell, for deriving multivariate indices of residential differentiation in

CONSTRUCTS	CLASSIFICATION OF SOCIAL AREA TYPE according to		
	SOCIAL RANK (economic status)	URBANIZATION (family status)	SEGREGATION (ethnic status)
CENSUS MEASURES	Occupation Educational attainment	Fertility Female activity rate Proportion of single-family dwellings	Ethnic group Place of birth
DIFFERENTIATING CHARACTERISTICS	Job type Amount of schooling Condition and value of housing Car and durable goods ownership	Demographic characteristics Household size Family organization Tenure and housing type	Socio-cultural characteristics Religion Ethnic origins

Fig. 150 Social area analysis

order to classify standard census tracts within an urban area, together with the attempt to relate these indices to a more general theory of urban development. Shevky and Bell saw change in society through time as being mirrored in urban areas. Such change could be described as increasing societal scale, reflecting a continuum of change from a traditional primitive to an economically advanced system. This increasing scale could be summarized in three constructs (◊ Fig. 150):

(i) *social rank* or *economic status*, describing the changing division of labour and the associated ordering by social prestige,

(ii) *urbanization* or *family status*, reflecting the weakening of traditional family organization as society became more urbanized,

(iii) *segregation* or *ethnic status*, suggesting greater complexity of organization as population groups tended to form distinctive clusters.

Each of these constructs could be measured from available census data as a simple proportion for each census tract. For each construct a standardized score, ranging from 0 to 100, was defined:

$$S_t = X (r_t - O)$$

where S_t = the score for tract t
O = lowest value of the variable over all census tracts
r_t = value of the variable for tract t
X = 100 divided by the range of values for the variable

The final index for the construct is:

$$I_t = \sum \frac{S_t}{n}$$

where I_t = the index for tract t
S_t = as defined above
n = the number of variables forming the construct

Indices of social rank and urbanization are used to create a classification of census tracts (and thus of social areas), with segregation being added to the classification where the proportion of a census tract's total population in specified ethnic groups is above the average for the urban area as a whole.

Social area analysis has been criticized because of the weakness of the link between the technique and theory, but it did provide, throughout the 1950s, a stimulus to (urban) ◊ *social geography*, especially the evolution of residential differentiation studies. Since the 1960s it has been replaced by the more flexible and objective ◊ *factorial ecology*.

social benefits As defined by the economist, the total benefits deriving from any given action and comprising *private benefits* (accruing to the individual/group undertaking the action) and *indirect benefits* (which accrue to third parties). The latter are equivalent to positive ◊ *externalities*, and in planning circles these have sometimes been equated with the term social benefits. ◊◊ *social costs*.

social capital ◊ *social overhead capital*.

social change The process by which individuals evolve from a primitive traditional way of life to a more complex, technologically advanced and rapidly changing life style, as a result of which alteration occurs in the function and structure of a ◊ *society*. ◊◊ *spiralism*.

social class ◊ *class*.

social contact The implied agreement under which a ◊ *state* governs and its citizens consent to be governed.

social costs As defined by the economist, the total costs attributable to any given action and comprising *private costs* (borne by the individual/group carrying out the action) and *indirect costs* (which are borne by third parties). The latter are equivalent to negative ◊ *externalities* and, in planning circles, social costs have sometimes been equated with negative externalities. ◊◊ *social benefits*.

social Darwinism A philosophy, outlined by Herbert Spencer, that views human societies as closely resembling animal organisms and therefore needing to struggle against nature in order to survive in particular environments, much as animal and plant organisms do. In his general law of evolution Spencer claimed that all evolution is characterized by concentration, differentiation and determination. ◊◊ *environmental determinism*.

social distance ◊ *Distance* as perceived by individuals or small groups from themselves to other individuals or social groups. In practice it is a functional distance which involves the spatial separation of two or more distinct social groups for most activities. This may come about by mutual choice or by imposition by the more powerful group.

social engineering Given the premise that free market and mixed economies can never achieve an equitable equilibrium, social engineering is the philosophy which seeks to ameliorate the worst disparities and injustices of ◊ *capitalism* through piecemeal social and economic policies (rather than via the implementation of some utopian blueprint). ◊◊ *positive discrimination*, *social justice*, *spatial engineering*.

social environment Those characteristics which make up the social identity of an area and which reflect criteria of social differentiation such as ◊ *class* and ethnicity. The social environment mirrors the pattern of social relationships and serves as a major basis of ◊ *residential segregation*. ◊◊ *social network*.

social expenses That part of government expenditure which is not directly productive but is organized to maintain harmony and cohesion in society, e.g. welfare payments, support for the arts and for sport.

social fallow A term used to describe land left ◊ *fallow* by ◊ *worker-peasants* who continue to live on their farms but abandon farmwork in order to commute to industrial jobs in nearby cities.

social formation The particular distribution of ◊ *class* power characteristic of a ◊ *mode of production*. At any given time one mode of production tends to dominate in a society, although vestiges of past modes may still be discernible, and generally the social formation works to maintain its structure and reproduce itself.

social gatekeepers ◊ *urban managerialism*.

social geography The study of the patterns arising from the use which social groups make of space (as they see it), with the processes which underlie these patterns, and the ◊ *life styles* which evolve from them. As a sub-discipline social geography has largely evolved since the Second World War. Earlier, ◊ *cultural geography* and ◊ *human ecology* covered part of the subject matter. Given social geography's emphasis on urban areas there has been a major overlap with ◊ *urban geography*. Pattern identification benefited from the application of quantitative methods in geography, e.g. the use of ◊ *social area analysis*, ◊ *factorial ecology*. Since the 1960s the emphasis has been very much more on the nature of social problems and social geographers have been to the fore in adopting and promoting approaches associated with ◊ *radical geography*.

social goods ◊ *public goods*.

social indicator A measure or yardstick of social conditions or social well-being which is trans-economic and of direct normative interest. The objective is to develop integrated systems of social reporting in which such indicators are related to policies affecting the quality of life. ◊ *territorial social indicator*. ◊◊ *economic indicators*.

social justice A broad principle applying to the quality of outcome – both to the division of benefits and to the allocation of burdens – of an action. It is therefore concerned with the distribution and redistribution of income, public goods and other benefits and with the apportionment of burdens such as taxation and military service. ◊ *territorial justice*. ◊◊ *spatial democratization*.

social mobility The process whereby individuals move up or down the stratum of social ◊ *classes* in an open society as a result of changes in their income, educational attainment, etc. ◊◊ *spiralism*.

social network The web of social interactions, comprising relatives, neighbours and friends, in which an individual or family is enmeshed by shared values and goals. Where a network is spatially confined it may form the basis of a ◊ *community*. ◊◊ *social environment*.

social opportunity The life chances and opportunities for self-realization confronting an individual within the society of which he/she is part. Social opportunity varies with position in the social structure and location in the spatial structure.

social organization, social structure The pattern of the ways in which different age and sex groupings within any population relate to one another. The differentiations normally recognized are *sub-communities* (the presence of in-marrying groups) and *strata* (based on differing shares of resources such as income, education and power). ◊ *community, social stratification.* ◊◊ *social formation.*

social overhead capital (social capital) Assets, in the form of ◊ *infrastructure*, which belong to the community as a whole, rather than to private organizations or individuals, e.g. schools, hospitals, cultural amenities and other welfare facilities. The provision of social capital, it is argued, improves the rate of profit in private industry. This involves two facets:

(i) *Social investment* (the *constant capital* of Marx), comprising projects which improve private profits by increasing the productivity of labour via the provision of physical infrastructure such as transport facilities and industrial estates. This is more commonly referred to as ◊ *economic overhead capital.*

(ii) *Social consumption*, which involves projects aiming to improve the quality, and hence lower the costs, of labour, e.g. education.

social physics An approach to the study of human society as a phenomenon that is subjected to forces and processes analogous to those studied by physical scientists. Emphasis is on the analysis of aggregate human behaviour. In human geography the approach is best represented by the use of the ◊ *gravity model* to describe ◊ *spatial interaction* and the generalization of gravity concepts in ◊ *potential surfaces*, and underpins the work of J. Q. Stewart and W. Warnz in developing ◊ *macrogeography*.

social planning The deliberate interference by government with the structure and performance of society and the whole complex of social phenomena in order to improve the ◊ *quality of life* of the whole population. It includes measures initiated by government to influence both economic and social activity and to improve the physical environment. ◊ *planning*. ◊◊ *social engineering*.

social polarization The process by which people become segregated into ◊ *classes* or ◊ *ethnic groups*. For any geographical area it implies that either the proportion of the population at the two extremes of the class continuum increases or the proportion of the population at one point only on the continuum increases. ◊ *segregation*.

social rank ◊ *social status*.

social responsibility An obligation, assumed by or placed upon a business organization, to take into account the interests of society independently of consideration of its profit.

social space ◊ *Space* as perceived and used by members of a particular social group, and within which that social group carries on its interrelations (hence, also known as *consultative space* or *interactive space*). It is the framework within which the subjective evaluations and motivations of members of the group can be related to overtly expressed behaviour and to the external characteristics of the environment. ◊ *activity space*.

social statistics Data concerning people and the circumstances in which they are born, live and die. The coverage is not in fact complete in practice, for only those circumstances judged by government to be of sufficient public or policy interest and for which quantitative information can be obtained are covered. The main fields are crime and justice, education, health, housing, social security, population and ◊ *vital statistics*. They are required to provide indices of present social conditions.

social status The social position held by an individual, including its attendant rights and duties. Such status or *social rank* is subjective, judged in perceptive terms in relation to income, wealth, occupation, achievements, standard of living, kinship connections, education, associates, etc. Thus status groups are stratified according to their principles of consumption of goods as represented by distinctive ◊ *life styles*. ◊ *class, social stratification*.

social stratification The hierarchical ranking of individuals and groups in society

based on ◊ *class* and ◊ *social status*. The ranks or strata are those into which all members of a society may fall. Within a stratum all members are equal but between strata there exist recognized and sanctioned differences, which are the basis for placing one individual or group higher or lower than another in the social order. ◊ *dual society, plural society*.

social structure ◊ *social organization*.

social values The system of preferences that govern action in any society.

social visibility The symbols, common to a particular social stratum, which are clearly visible to other social ranks, e.g. ◊ *life style*, items of material culture including house types, language and dialects.

social welfare, social well-being A generic term for the family of overlapping concepts which includes level of living, ◊ *quality of life*, social satisfaction and ◊ *standard of living*. Such overall well-being takes into account social, cultural, environmental and aesthetic factors as well as conventional indicators of ◊ *economic welfare*. ◊ *welfare geography, welfare state*.

socialization The lifelong process by which individuals learn the principal values and beliefs of the social system and develop the behaviour patterns necessary for them to fit into their particular society. ◊ *acculturation, assimilation*.

society An organized ◊ *community* and the system of living within it. ◊ *transitional society*.

socio-ecological time A time dimension by which the activities of people and their co-ordination are measured. It is measured indirectly through the activities and events themselves and is the basis of the temporal organization of society, in which the clock and the ◊ *calendar* function as control devices. It defines the norms that society expects in roles such as work and educa-

tion. ⟡ *oecological time, structural time.*

socio-economic groups A social classification, based largely on occupation, introduced in the United Kingdom by the Registrar General in 1911. The original classification had only five groups – I Professional, II Intermediate, III Skilled, IV Partly Skilled, and V Unskilled. Because group III contained over half the gainfully employed population the classification was supplemented in 1951 by a more detailed breakdown into thirteen groups, since expanded to seventeen.

sociology The study of human society, which comprises the various forms, institutions and growth of social groups; the search for interrelationships between these phenomena in order to formulate laws of social growth and behaviour; and the interpretation of these laws in terms of their eventual connection with ethical theory.

softwood A term used in the timber trade for wood produced by conifers. ⟢ *hardwood.*

solar day The time interval between any two successive transits of the sun across a given meridian. The *mean solar day* or *civil day* is twenty-four hours. It varies slightly in length with latitude and at different times of the ⟡ *year* because the earth's orbit is ellipsoid and inclines towards the equator. ⟢ *sidereal day.*

solar energy, solar power While the term can apply to any form of ⟡ *energy* which has its origin in the sun, in practice it refers to the solar radiation falling on the earth's surface and its atmosphere. It originates from the thermonuclear reactions continually taking place within the sun.

The sun's radiant energy may be directly exploited in various ways. Most common is the development of *solar heating,* i.e. the use of solar energy for low-grade heat, in which the radiant energy is trapped and used to heat some suitable material. The typical method involves use of a *solar panel* or flat-plate collector (a black metal absorber, containing pipes for air or water to remove the heat, placed under one or more layers of glass). Direct conversion to thermal, electric or chemical energy is also possible. In the thermal case, focusing collectors are used to achieve high temperatures by concentrating direct radiation (sunshine) onto a small area to heat a fluid which then generates electricity through a conventional heat engine. *Solar cells* provide for the direct conversion of radiation to electricity by photovoltaic means (i.e. from light). Chemical and biochemical methods are still very much in the experimental stage.

Solar radiation offers a safe and inexhaustible source of energy (⟡ *renewable energy sources*) but in temperate regions its supply is unpredictable and out of phase with demands for heating.

solar year ⟡ *year.*

solution mining A method for recovering metals from low-grade mineral ores (and also from spoil heaps) in which the derived metal is leached *in situ* by the injection of an appropriate solution (e.g. dilute sulphuric acid in the case of copper ores) and then recovered from the leachate. The technique is likely to be increasingly adopted as reserves of high-grade ores are exhausted.

Somer's D A statistical measure of ordinal association in a ⟡ *contingency table.* There are two versions: (i) *symmetric D* – computed where no consideration is given to which variable is dependent and which independent; and (ii) *asymmetric D* – computed when one variable (which may be either the row or the column variable) is considered to be the dependent variable.

sough A level, drainage passage from a ⟡ *mine,* particularly in the Pennines lead-mining district.

souming In the ◊ *crofting* system the right of grazing on common pastures. A *soum* is the unit of stocking in common grazing and is expressed either as the amount of pasturage which will support one cow or a proportional number of sheep or other stock or as the number of sheep or cattle that can be maintained on a certain amount of pasture. The souming is then the number of livestock equivalents assigned to each crofter (and is therefore related to the estimated ◊ *carrying capacity* of the common pasture). ◊◊ *stint, stocking rate*.

sound Periodic wave-like fluctuations in air pressure as a result of a mechanical action which alternately compresses and rarifies air. The magnitude of the pressure variation is known as the sound pressure, the level of which is measured in ◊ *decibels*, and the rate at which the fluctuations occur is the frequency, measured in hertz. These physical properties of sound need to be related to the mental processes by which people hear and react to it.

source pricing ◊ *f.o.b. pricing*.

South East Asia Treaty Organization (SEATO) An ◊ *alliance* formed under American hegemony in South-East Asia after the Second World War in an attempt to contain the spread of influence of communist China. It was NATO's counterpart in Asia and involved Pakistan, Thailand and the Philippines along with the major capitalist powers. It broke up in the mid-1970s when China entered the United Nations and made overtures of friendship towards the USA.

sovereignty The supreme authority vested in the government of a ◊ *state* and exerted over the full extent of its ◊ *territory* and its citizens, against which there is no appeal. It is the most universally accepted of national rights.

sovkhoz A Soviet state farm, i.e. owned and operated by the state. The workers are paid employees, as in other state enterprises. A sovkhoz is a very large-scale farm, frequently covering over 20,000 hectares. ◊ *kolkhoz, Volksgüter.* ◊◊ *ejido, kibbutz, kung-she, moshav.*

spa A term used in general for mineral springs and watering places and deriving from Spa, the name of a watering place near Liège, Belgium, renowned for the curative properties of its mineral springs. In the 18th and 19th centuries belief in the medicinal properties of mineral waters for drinking or bathing stimulated health tourism and the growth of spas, but with the development of additional facilities for amusement and recreation the function of spa resorts has become more social than therapeutic.

space The term space, implying areal extent, is used in both absolute and relative forms in human geography. *Absolute space* (or *contextual space*) is objective – distinct, physical and real: a dimension which focuses on the characteristics of things in terms of their concentration and dispersion. The geographer's interest in space as a dimension can be traced back to the concern of early map-makers with the precise measurement of locational relationships and has subsequently influenced all forms of ◊ *spatial analysis. Relative space* (or *created space*) is perceptual – it is socially produced, being dependent on relations between events or activities and thus bound to process and time. It is a context, focusing on the characteristics of places, and is a descendant of the descriptions of unfamiliar areas by early travellers. *Relative space* is also continually changing its size and form in response to socio-economic demands and technological progress – hence the use of the term *plastic space.* ◊ *action space, activity space, awareness space, bounded space, cartesian space, cost space, defensible space, de jure space, development space, economic space, Euclidean space, experi-*

ential space, ideological space, indirect contact space, interpersonal space, joint action space, lived space, movement space, open space, operational space, personal space, preference space, search space, social space, virtual space. ⟨> *location, spatial fields, territoriality.*

space cost curve A section through a ⟨> *cost surface* showing spatial variations in production costs (⟨> Fig. 151).

space cost surface ⟨> *cost surface.*

space economy The ⟨> *spatial structure* of an economy.

space preference scale For any individual, the ranking, in terms of his/her values and goals, of the places he/she would prefer to live and work in. ⟨> *spatial preference.*

space revenue curve A section through a ⟨> *revenue surface* showing spatial variations in the revenue to be earned from a given volume of sales.

space standards In planning, the definition of the maximum (or acceptable) number of use units that can occupy or utilize available space. Where standards apply to an activity, e.g. recreation, they are set at levels which provide a satisfactory experience for the user. Such standards exist for a wide variety of land uses and activities, e.g. house floorspace, housing layouts, car parking, camping and caravan sites, etc. ⟨> *density.*

space–time autocorrelation A situation in which data display systematic variation through time and over space, e.g. measures of regional economic performance within a nation. ⟨> *spatial autocorrelation, temporal autocorrelation.*

space–time forecasting The modelling of a space–time process in order to forecast the change in variables over both time and space. The human geographer is particularly interested in urban and regional

forecasting, i.e. predicting levels of population, employment, recreation, spread of disease, etc. Various statistical models have been developed in response to the urgent problems facing society and the need to make spatial forecasts as a basis for policy and investment decisions. These models are of the general ⟨> *regression* form. The simplest is the auto-regressive model, where the forecast value of a variable at a future date is accounted for by regression on its own past values, but this has been extended to allow for spatial diffusion effects and exogenous or explanatory variables.

space zoning A solution to disputes over competing demands for land where the competing uses/activities are ⟨> *incompatible* and are therefore allocated to different sites. ⟨> *zoning.* ⟨> *time zoning.*

spanning tree In ⟨> *network* geometry, a set of $n - 1$ ⟨> *edges* joining n ⟨> *nodes*, such that any node can be reached from any other node. The *minimal spanning tree* is the shortest of all such spanning trees.

spare-time farming ⟨> *part-time farming.*

spatial analysis An approach to the study of geography which emphasizes the locational patterns of a variable or series of variables. It emerged as a dominant theme in Anglo-American geography in the post-Second World War period (⟨> *quantitative revolution*). Spatial analysis adopts a rigorous and systematic base for describing spatial patterns, and attempts to identify the factors controlling patterns of distribution and to demonstrate how those patterns can be modified to make distributions more efficient or more equitable (⟨> *location theory*). It therefore provides an alternative to the concept of ⟨> *areal differentiation* as the main concern of geography. Spatial analysis maintains an awareness of the interdependence of geography and geometry and the mathematics

(a) Cost surface or cost contour map derived from isocost lines on material distribution from A and market delivery to B

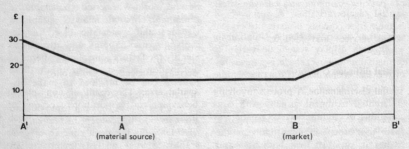

(b) Space cost curve

Fig. 151 Space cost curve

of space and therefore implies reliance on quantitative methods.

spatial archaeology The study of the interrelationships of sites with each other and with their ◊ *environments*, or the distribution of patterns of artefacts, using analytical methods derived from geography. ◊ *archaeology*.

spatial autocorrelation A systematic pattern in spatially located data (contiguous areas or sets of point locations) due to the set of values being related over space. The values display interdependence because events at one location influence outcomes at other locations owing to geographical proximity. In general, if high values of a variable at one location are associated with high values of that variable in neighbouring locations, i.e. a clustered pattern exists, the set of locations exhibits *positive spatial autocorrelation* with regard to that variable. Conversely, if high and low values alternate, *negative spatial autocorrelation* exists. Spatial autocorrelation is common in geographical data and its existence violates the independence assumption of many standard statistical tests regarding variates. ◊ *space–time autocorrelation, temporal autocorrelation*.

spatial covariation The study of the variation in two or more geographic distributions over the same area.

spatial democratization A process of planning for equality of access to critical social services and facilities. ◊ *social justice*.

spatial diffusion ◊ *diffusion*.

spatial discrimination A process involving differential treatment, usually with connotations of 'unfairness', i.e. spatial injustice. ◊ *positive discrimination*.

spatial discrimination effect In perception studies, the ability of an individual to discriminate more clearly between locations which are closer to them in space than between locations which are more distant. ◊ *spatial preference*.

spatial distribution A ◊ *distribution* or set of geographic observations representing the values or behaviour of a particular phenomenon or characteristic across many locations on the surface of the earth.

spatial efficiency The relationship between spatial location, spatial arrangement and ◊ *economic efficiency*. In particular the objective of maximizing or improving economic efficiency by adopting the optimal spatial arrangement for an activity.

spatial elasticity of locational choice The range of alternative feasible locations confronting a new or existing firm at a given point in time. Spatial elasticity of locational choice varies between manufacturing industries at any given time, and for a given manufacturing industry through time depending on the rate of economic growth, the share of new plants, the share of ◊ *footloose industry*, the share of larger plants and the importance of technological integration. ◊ *spatial margin*.

spatial engineering An approach to the amelioration of disparities and injustices which seeks to improve ◊ *social well-being* by altering the ◊ *accessibility* pattern. ◊ *social engineering*.

spatial envelope ◊ *personal space*.

spatial equilibrium A theoretical state of stability in an aggregate pattern of space usage, any deviation from which would decrease efficiency or profitability.

spatial error The result of non-optimal behaviour in the location decisions of individuals and firms. Where such 'mistakes' are made differences are discernible between actual spatial arrangements or decisions.

spatial field A conceptually ◊ *bounded*

space in which a set of locations are related by some aspect of spatial organization, e.g. ◊ *information field*, ◊ *in-migration field*, ◊ *urban field*.

spatial interaction The relationship or linkage between geographic areas. The term was originally used by E. L. Ullman (◊ *Ullman's bases for interaction*) to emphasize the interdependence of areas and implies the movement of commodities, goods, people, information, etc. between areas. In recent years the term has been used especially in respect of spatial flow studies (◊ *gravity model*).

spatial margin A locus of points delimiting the area within which a firm or industry must be located if profitable operation is to be achieved. At the margin the cost of producing a given volume of output (inclusive of ◊ *normal profit*) is equal to the total revenue from selling that output. The derivation of the spatial margin of profitability is shown in ◊ Fig. 152, its shape and extent varying according to the relevant ◊ *cost surface* and ◊ *revenue surface*.

The concept is widely accepted as a

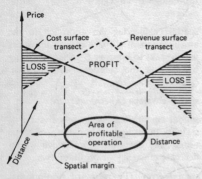

Fig. 152 Spatial margin

modification of the classical approach to ◊ *industrial location theory* – its significance being that it allows sub-optimal decisions to be incorporated in a theoretical framework. ◊ *Satisficer* locations are accepted

within the spatial margin and allowances can be made for differences in entrepreneurial ability and information availability. ◊◊ *range of tolerance, spatial elasticity of locational choice*.

spatial monopoly Monopolistic control exercised over a market by virtue of a producer's location. This is possible because distance from competitors provides protection. ◊ *monopoly*.

spatial organization The aggregate pattern of use of space by a society. It is, by and large, the outcome of people's attempts to use space efficiently. ◊◊ *space economy*.

spatial planning ◊ *physical planning*.

spatial preference The subjective evaluation, by individual or group, of the attractiveness or desirability of spatial alternatives, such as residential locations, holiday areas, shopping centres, migration strategies. Preferences may be ranked and can be summarized in the form of ◊ *mental maps* of areas.

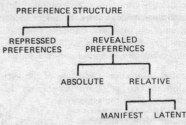

Fig. 153 Spatial preference

Preference structures may be categorized (◊ Fig. 153) into *repressed preferences*, involving situations which cannot be taken advantage of, and *revealed preferences*. The latter are either *absolute preferences*, in the sense that decision-makers do not perceive that they have or need choice, or *relative preferences*, where decision-makers do perceive their choice or need of choice. Relative preferences may be *manifest preferences*, where actions were undertaken because opportunities proved favourable, or *latent preferences*, where a person is aware of possible actions, but these lie dormant until a need arises. ⟡ *revealed preference analysis*.

spatial process The mechanism which produces the ⟡ *spatial structure* of a distribution.

spatial structure The result of a ⟡ *spatial process*, i.e. the way in which ⟡ *space* is organized by the operation of socio-economic and physical processes. It refers to the relative internal ⟡ *location* of the elements in a spatial distribution: the location of each element relative to each other element and the location of each element relative to all the other elements together.

spatial structure and national economic development (the Friedmann model) A simple model, suggested by J. Friedmann, of the stages of spatial organization a national economy passes through in its progress from a primitive pre-industrial society to industrial maturity (⟡ Fig. 154). There are four stages:
(1) A spatial pattern of separate cities, each in an enclave isolated from the others.
(2) At the time of incipient industrialization the pattern is dominated by a single strong centre or core, surrounded by an extensive periphery. The urban distribution is basically a ⟡ *primate city* one. External forces, particularly ⟡ *colonialism* in many countries, help explain evolution from stage 1 to 2.

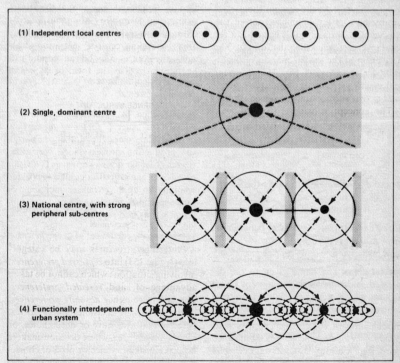

(1) Independent local centres

(2) Single, dominant centre

(3) National centre, with strong peripheral sub-centres

(4) Functionally interdependent urban system

Fig. 154 Spatial structure and national economic development

(3) The ◊ *core–periphery* situation is gradually transformed as strong peripheral sub-centres emerge alongside the single national centre. Inter-metropolitan peripheries now replace the previous national periphery. The sub-centres bring further resources into the national economy, so enhancing the growth potential of the economy.

(4) Finally a functionally interdependent system of cities appears: inter-metropolitan peripheries are completely absorbed and full integration of the economy is achieved, thus minimizing regional imbalances and maximizing the nation's growth potential.

Spearman rank correlation coefficient Or *Spearman's rho*. A ◊ *non-parametric* statistical test of the ◊ *correlation* between two sets of ◊ *ordinal* (ranked) data. The test was pioneered by C. Spearman in connection with experiments in psychology. The numerical value obtained when applying the test is the same as that obtained if the formula for the ◊ *product moment correlation coefficient* is applied to ranked data, instead of the original data, but Spearman's rho (ρ) is calculated as:

where d_i = difference in ranks for ith
        subject
   n = number of subjects

If there is complete agreement between the two rankings $\rho = +1$, whereas inverse rankings give $\rho = -1$. ◊ *Kendalls's tau.*

special areas The name given to the depressed, older industrial regions of Great Britain which were designated to receive central government aid under the 1934 Special Areas (Development and Improvement) Act. The areas originally designated were South Wales, North-East England, West Cumberland and Clydeside–North Lanarkshire. The act represented the first official attempt by central government to solve the problem of providing the unemployed with jobs in the ◊ *depressed regions.* Special areas were later replaced by ◊ *development areas.* ◊ *regional policy.*

special development areas In Great Britain, areas of special difficulty within ◊ *Development Areas.* Established in 1967, they were areas likely to suffer from exceptionally high and persistent unemployment as a result of the closure of coal mines. Because they faced the severest problems special development areas qualified for the highest levels of regional aid. The areas designated bore some similarity to the prewar ◊ *special areas.* ◊ *regional policy.*

special economic zones Selected areas established in China from 1979 in which foreign investors are offered tax concessions, labour supply advantages and access to the Chinese market. ◊ *free port.*

Special Scientific Interest ◊ *Site of Special Scientific Interest.*

specialization A situation in which a worker (or other ◊ *factor of production*) concentrates on one function or one part of the production process. Such specialization of ◊ *labour* is also known as ◊ *division of labour.* The situation can be replicated spatially so that particular locations or areas specialize in the productions of different goods and services.

specialization, coefficient of ◊ *coefficient of specialization.*

specialization curve ◊ *localization curve.*

specialization economies ◊ *economies of scale.*

specialization index of urban centres An index, suggested by Webb, for measuring the dependence of a given city on one or a few functions. It is calculated as the total of all the ◊ *functional indices* for all the occupations found in the city, divided by 100. The higher the value of the index the greater the degree of specialization of the city's economy.

specification standard In ◊ *pollution control*, a measure which specifies how an objective is to be accomplished (in contrast to an ◊ *emission standard*, which deals with the objective to be accomplished). Such standards normally require compliance with certain design specifications – hence they are also termed *design standards* – in order to reduce pollution at source, e.g. the 1956 Clean Air Act imposed restrictions on the design of industrial/commercial furnaces and chimneys. Specification standards are generally to be preferred when there are administrative difficulties in monitoring or enforcing emission standards.

specific birth rate ◊ *birth rates.*

specific capital ◊ *capital* (2).

specific death rate ◊ *death rates.*

specific factor ◊ *factors of production.*

specific region An area or ◊ *region* with a definite name and identity, e.g. East Anglia, Kempenland.

specific value Or *unit value*. The value to weight ratio for a firm's or industry's product. It has been used in industrial location analysis in the locational classification of industrial activity. Products with low specific values will be ◊ *market-oriented* in their location.

spectral analysis A mathematical technique for breaking down the total variance of a time series into the relative contributions made by different periodicities or cycles. It is an extension of ◊ *Fourier series analysis* and has been used in the analysis of ◊ *regional cycles.*

speculative building The construction of buildings by a property developer in advance of demand. It is most common in the case of houses for owner-occupation.

speculative reserves ◊ *reserves.*

speech interference level (SIL) A measure of ◊ *noise* nuisance. It is calculated as the ◊ *arithmetic mean*, in ◊ *decibels*, of the sound pressure levels of the noise in the three standard octave bands having centre frequencies of 500, 1,000 and 2,000 hertz. A SIL of up to 60 dB will permit normal conversation at a distance apart of 1 m. ◊ *noise indices.*

sphere of influence (1) In a political context a term of the colonial era referring to a territory (especially in Africa or Asia) which a particular nation had 'reserved' without annexation as of special interest and in which it was active. With the spread of ◊ *nationalism* this usage of the term has largely disappeared.
(2) In urban geography the term has been used to describe the extent of an urban area's influence over its surrounding countryside, but the term ◊ *urban field* is now more common.

spillover effects Spillover describes the mismatching of the area which bears the cost of providing a ◊ *public good* or service and the area which receives the benefit. Spillover is a direct result of the partitioning of space into administrative areas. *Benefit spillovers* occur when the benefits of public services provided in one local authority area are available to individuals living outside that area, e.g. when a town authority institutes a system of river pollution control from which places downstream also benefit. *Cost spillovers* (*spillins*) occur where an area has access to benefits from other areas. In the case of spillovers a local authority exports ◊ *externalities* and bears the cost of providing benefits to others, whereas with spillins the local authority imports externalities and enjoys benefits of expenditure by others.

spiralism, spiralist Spiralism is the mechanism by which individuals improve their job and ◊ *social status*. The term spiralist has been used particularly of those employees of large-scale organizations who are obliged to change their place of residence as they move through and up the status hierarchies of those organizations. ◊◊ *social mobility*.

sporadic activities A term used to describe industries which are distributed unevenly and whose location does not coincide with the distribution of the population or of the market. ◊◊ *ubiquitous industries*.

sport Any physical activity, in the form of structured games or play, which is undertaken for the purpose of ◊ *recreation* or *amusement* during ◊ *leisure* time. An element of competition or challenge against oneself, opponents or physical elements is an essential component.

sprawl ◊ *urban sprawl*.

spread city ◊ *dispersed city*.

spread effects The second of the sets of interdependencies (◊◊ *backwash effects*) recognized by G. Myrdal as characterizing the dynamic aspects of ◊ *core–periphery* structures in developing his ◊ *cumulative causation* theory of economic growth. Spread effects work to decrease the discrepancy between core and periphery, representing an expansionary momentum transmitted from the centre of economic growth to the surrounding regions via trading opportunities (especially the demand for natural resources) and more generally through the diffusion of ◊ *innovations*. Such effects are subject to ◊ *distance decay*, and generally come later and are weaker than backwash effects. Called *trickle-down effects* by A. O. Hirschman.

squatter settlement The dominant facet of ◊ *Third World* urban growth, comprising a concentration of makeshift dwellings, usually at the edge of the city, on public or private land which is neither owned nor rented by the builders/occupants. Such settlements or *shanty towns* have emerged because the formal housing market has been unable to cope with the rate of increase of population and especially immigration to urban areas. Squatter settlements have, in many cases, provided the only form of shelter. Their development has been by organized invasion, by gradual accretion, and even encouraged by government initiative. Also referred to as *spontaneous settlements* because of the speed with which they appear.

The quality of shanty dwellings is rudimentary, initial building using any materials available – wood, cardboard, zinc sheets, etc. There is a severe absence of public services – roads are unpaved, sanitation systems are crude, water supplies, educational and medical services inadequate. The occupants of squatter settlements are usually the urban poor, since they act as reception areas for migrants, whom they assist in adapting to urban life. In Latin America they also attract families from inner-city tenements. They are *transitional settlements* in which a process of economic and social change is taking place. Where a strong sense of community exists, along with a spirit of self-help and protection, plus some organized co-operative effort, squatter settlements which have the capacity to improve may be regarded as ◊ *slums of hope*.

Squatter settlements are known by various local names, e.g. barracas (Guatemala, Venezuela), barriadas (Peru), barrios (Venezuela), barrios piratas (Colombia), bidonvilles (Algeria, Morocco), bustees (India), callampa (Chile), campamientos (Guatemala), cantegrill (Uruguay), champas (Guatemala), colonias proletarias (Mexico), courts (Haiti), favelas (Brazil), gecekoudu (Turkey), gourbivilles (Tunisia), kampongs (South-East Asia), ranchos (Venezuela), solares (Chile), villas miserias (Argentina).

squatting The illegal appropriation of land or property. The term was first used in respect of the illegal settlement of land which is a feature of periods of ◊ *population pressure*, e.g. in England the 16th and 17th centuries witnessed extensive encroachment of the manorial ◊ *waste* by appropriation of small plots on which cottages or smallholdings were established. It was a common belief that a cottage erected on the waste overnight entitled its builder to undisputed possession and rights to land as far as an axe could be thrown.

The term is now more commonly applied to the taking-over of vacant dwellings in the ◊ *inner city* by the homeless. Such squatting is the result of the failure of housing allocation mechanisms in advanced capitalist societies, since the squatters do not qualify for mortgage finance or public housing and cannot compete in the dwindling private rented sector.

S–R theory ◊ *stimulus–response theory.*

stabilization A policy of intervention in an economic ◊ *market* to reduce fluctuations of prices (or other indicators of concern, such as employment).

stable population A ◊ *closed population* subjected to constant age-specific ◊ *fertility* and ◊ *death rates*. Such a population tends towards a constant rate of increase and a constant proportion of persons in the different age groups. A ◊ *stationary population* is a special case of a stable population.

stage model of industrial location A descriptive model of changes in industrial location patterns in manufacturing industry suggested by G. Bloomfield on the basis of a study of motor vehicle manufacturing. Four stages are proposed:
(i) *Experimental.* There is widespread entry of many small firms at scattered locations. Since entrepreneurs are preoccupied with technical success, choice of location is not considered important – but few of the firms are successful.
(ii) *Small-scale engineering production.* New firms continue to enter the industry and successful firms grow in size, developing factory production and becoming increasingly reliant on skilled labour. A degree of localization is apparent, reflecting the emergence of ◊ *agglomeration* and ◊ *external economy* advantages.
(iii) ◊ *Mass production.* A limited number of firms survive because of the high capital cost of plant necessary for large-scale production. Thus the industry becomes more concentrated in both structure and organization. Increased mechanization provides opportunities to use semi-skilled and unskilled labour. In general mass producers expand at their existing sites.
(iv) *Industrial maturity and dispersion.* With standardization of product design and production methods, along with continued (but slower) growth of the market, dispersion of assembly facilities occurs. Most site selection is deliberately located by large corporations, but with increased government involvement in the location process. ◊ *filter-down theory of industrial location.*

stage theory of growth ◊ *development stages theory of growth.*

stages of growth ◊ *Rostow model.*

staith, staithe A wharf equipped with rails from which waggons may discharge coal directly into cargo ships. They were common along the lower Tyne.

standard deviation In statistics, an absolute measure of the spread of values in a ◊ *frequency distribution*, i.e. a descriptive measure of ◊ *dispersion* based on ◊ *interval* or ◊ *ratio data*. It is the square root of the ◊ *variance*, i.e. the root mean square deviation from the ◊ *arithmetic mean* and is normally calculated as

$$\text{Standard deviation} = \sigma = \sqrt{\frac{\Sigma|x - \bar{x}|^2}{n}}$$

where $x - \bar{x}$ = the difference of each value from the arithmetic mean

n = the number of values

Standard deviation, the second ◊ *moment measure*, is the most commonly used of all statistical yardsticks since it is a measure of dispersion in which values of all observations are taken into account.

standard distance Or *standard distance deviation*. A simple and concise measure of spatial ◊ *dispersion*, providing a measure of the areal spread of points around the ◊ *mean centre*. It is analogous to the ◊ *standard deviation* in conventional statistics, and is normally calculated in respect to two orthogonal axes by finding the deviations of the x co-ordinates from $\bar{x}$ and of the y co-ordinates from $\bar{y}$, squaring them and taking the square root of the sum, i.e.

Standard distance =

$$S_D = \sqrt{\frac{\sum_{i=1}^{N}|x_i - \bar{x}|^2 + \sum_{i=1}^{N}|y_i - \bar{y}|^2}{N}}$$

where N = number of points

x_i = x co-ordinate (longitude or northing) of the ith point

y_i = y co-ordinate (latitude or easting) of the ith point

The resultant value of S_D may be plotted on a map by describing a circle of that radius about the mean centre and can be used in the same way as standard deviation. Just as in a ◊ *normal distribution* in conventional statistics, approximately two-thirds of the occurrences will be within one standard deviation of the arithmetic mean, so in a 'normal' area distribution two-thirds of all points should be within the circle of radius S_D. Where points represent occurrences of varying magni-

tude, a *weighted standard distance* can be calculated using the value at each point as the weight. ◊◊ *index of dispersion*.

standard ellipse Or *standard deviational ellipse*. A method of summarizing ◊ *dispersion* in a point pattern in terms of an ellipse centred on the ◊ *mean centre*, with its long axis in the direction of maximum dispersion and its short axis in the direction of minimum dispersion. Where a spatial distribution departs from a circular pattern the standard ellipse is to be preferred to ◊ *standard distance* because it takes account of the fact that the spread about the mean centre is different in different directions.

standard error A ◊ *probability* statement used in assessing the reliability of an estimate based on a sample result, i.e. used to define the ◊ *confidence interval* within which the true population value lies. Standard errors are a special form of ◊ *standard deviation*, and can be calculated for various sample statistics – arithmetic mean, standard deviation, regression coefficient, etc. For example, the *standard error of the mean* (*SE$\bar{x}$*) is the standard deviation of a set of arithmetic means from ◊ *samples* of n observations, i.e. the standard deviation of a sampling distribution. It is a measure of the average dispersion of the sample means about the population mean. If an infinite number of equal-sized samples are drawn from a given population the mean of each sample will be an estimate of the true population mean, but not all of the sample means will be identical. The pattern of these sample means will constitute a ◊ *normal distribution* and its standard deviation will be the standard error. It is calculated by dividing the sample standard deviation by the square root of the number of observations in the sample. *SE$\bar{x}$* provides an estimate of the range of error that could arise from using a sample rather than the entire population under investigation: the smaller *SE$\bar{x}$* the greater the likelihood that the sample mean is close to the population mean.

Calculations can also be undertaken to establish the *standard error of the standard deviation*, the *standard error of proportions*, the *standard error of the regression estimate* of the dependent variable, etc.

standard industrial classification A government classification of economic activities for statistical purposes aimed at securing uniformity and comparability in official statistics. Details of classifications vary from one country to another and, over time, individual countries modify and up-grade their scheme, but the general principle of classifying industries first of all into very broad groups, e.g. primary metals industries, and then subdividing more finely, e.g. steel tubing (within primary metals), appears to be universal. In the United Kingdom such a classification was first introduced in 1948.

Standard Metropolitan Labour Area (SMLA) ◊ *Labourshed* areas of major urban centres which have been defined in Great Britain. Although having no official status they may be regarded as the British equivalent of the American ◊ *Standard Metropolitan Statistical Area*. Each SMLA consists of two parts: a labour centre or core and a metropolitan ring of surrounding areas strongly related to that core. SMLAs are amalgamations of local authority areas, with the core defined on three basic criteria: (a) the density of jobs in a local authority area must exceed 13·75/hectare (5/acre), (b) the total number of jobs in the area constituting the core must exceed 20,000 and (c) local authority areas which are part of the same core must be geographically contiguous. For inclusion in the metropolitan ring, in addition to the contiguity constraint, over 15% of a local authority area's resident and economically ◊ *active population* must work in the urban core. The combined population of the core and the ring must

exceed 70,000. SMLAs are spatially more restricted than ◊ *Metropolitan Labour Market Areas*.

Standard Metropolitan Statistical Area (SMSA) An area adopted in the USA for the official measurement of the extent of urbanization. The US Bureau of Census had pioneered the concept of the extended urban area since 1910 and introduced the SMSA in 1960. SMSAs are currently defined as:
(1) Either one ◊ *central city* with a population of at least 50,000, or two contiguous cities constituting a single community with a combined population of over 50,000 and a minimum population of 15,000 for the smaller of the two.
(2) The remainder of the county to which the central city belongs.
(3) Adjacent counties, if (i) 75% or more of the labour force is non-agricultural, (ii) at least 15% of workers resident in the county work in the central city or at least 25% of employment in the county is filled by workers resident in the central city, (iii) at least 50% of the population resident in the county lives at densities of 150 persons/ml^2 (58/km^2) or more, or the non-agricultural employment in the county totals at least 10,000 or is at least 10% of non-agricultural employment in the central city.

standard normal deviate ◊ *z-scores*.

standard nutrition unit The number of calories per year needed by each human being. ◊ *nutritional requirements*.

standard of living The level of material comfort enjoyed by a person, community or nation. The term *level of living* has been used in respect of given spatial areas and is a similar, if somewhat extended, concept. The level of living of a person resident in an area reflects the overall composition of housing, health, education, employment, wealth, leisure and social stability exhibited aggregatively in the area, together with those aspects of demographic structure, general physical environment and social institutions which have a bearing on the extent to which the needs and desires of residents are met. ◇ *quality of life*.

standard scores ◇ *z-scores*.

standard time The mean time at a meridian located centrally over a country or zone. It is used for timekeeping throughout the country or zone because of the difficulties which result if each place keeps its own ◇ *local time*. In general, the world is divided into a number of ◇ *International Time Zones*. These *standard time zones* differ from the time at the Greenwich meridian (◇ *Greenwich Mean Time*) by multiples of $7\frac{1}{2}°$ or $15°$, i.e. an exact number of hours or half-hours. Time zones normally extend $7\frac{1}{2}°$ on either side of the central or standard meridian, and countries with a large east–west extent, e.g. the USSR, adopt several standard time zones.

In the summer months many countries in mid-latitudes adopt what is called *summer time* or *daylight saving time*, normally one hour in advance of the zone standard time (◇ *British Summer Time*).

standardized birth rate ◇ *birth rates*.

standardized death rate ◇ *death rates*.

staple The main ◇ *commodity* produced by an area. While customarily thought of as describing products of extractive industry, the concept has been extended to include products of secondary or tertiary industry where these form the principal items of trade or consumption of an area. The range of staples may be closely related to an area's level of ◇ *development* (◇ *staple theory of economic development*).

staple theory of economic development Also referred to as the *staple export model*. A theory of national or regional economic growth which emphasizes the leading role of the exports of ◇ *staples* (of natural resource origin). External demands for these staples triggers both the initial and continued growth. In this context it is a special case of ◇ *economic base theory*.

Staple theory appears particularly applicable to the ◇ *development* of 'new' countries which have a favourable ◇ *population–resource* ratio. It was developed by the Canadian economic historian H. A. Innis, on the basis of his work on the fur, lumber and mining industries of Canada.

state (1) An area of land, or land and sea, with clearly defined and internationally recognized ◇ *boundaries* and which has de jure (legal) independence, i.e. the government exercises ◇ *sovereignty* over the territory. ◇ *nation-state*. ◇ *country*, *divided state*, *pristine state*, *protected state*, *secondary state*.
(2) A component part of a ◇ *federal state*. ◇ *unitary state*.

state capitalism An ◇ *economic system* in which the government owns and directs substantial sectors of the economy in competition with private capitalist sectors. ◇ *capitalism*.

state socialism An ◇ *economic system* in which the economy is managed or planned by the government through the ownership and control of virtually all of the economic sectors and in which principles of competition and profit are minimal. ◇ *collectivism*.

stationarity, spatial An assumption, in certain statistical techniques, that the relationship between values of the processes generating data is the same for every pair of points whose relative locations are the same. This implies that ◇ *moment measures* (and joint moments such as autocorrelation) of the series do not vary with time or distance. Thus, in a spatial context, if direction was unimportant, the degree to which the variables related would depend only on distance between the points. Such an assumption is unrealistic for socio-economic variables.

stationary population A special case of a ◊ *stable population* in which fertility equals mortality (births = deaths) and the rate of population increase is zero. The age distribution is also the ◊ *life table* distribution. ◊ *zero-growth population*.

statistics (1) In colloquial use, collections of numerical information, e.g. population statistics. Statistics in this sense are important to government and industry. ◊ *economic statistics, social statistics*.
(2) More strictly, the scientific approach to drawing conclusions from numerical information, i.e. the methods used to collect, process and interpret quantitative data. Such methods are highly dependent on the mathematical theory of ◊ *probability*. Two branches are normally recognized: (i) ◊ *Descriptive statistics*, which summarize data, and (ii) *Inferential statistics*, which seek to identify relationships between sets of observations. An alternative breakdown, used in social science, is between ◊ *exploratory statistics*, which seek hypotheses, and ◊ *confirmatory statistics*, which test hypotheses. ◊ *non-parametric tests, parametric tests*.

status variable A ◊ *variable* in a ◊ *model* which specifies the conditions of the model that are held constant throughout its operation, e.g. in the case of a model economic system, the specific form of economic organization.

statute acre ◊ *acre*.

statute mile A unit of linear measurement in English-speaking countries, equal to 1,760 yards, possibly derived from the Roman marching unit of 1,000 paces. ◊ *nautical mile*.

statutory undertaker A body, usually a nationalized industry or a ◊ *public utility*, which, by statute, is charged with the duty of providing a certain service for the public at large.

steady-state equilibrium ◊ *equilibrium*.

stepwise migration A ◊ *migration* flow in which movement takes place through a series of places, e.g. from village to town and then on up the ◊ *urban hierarchy*. ◊ *chain migration*.

sterilization A method of ◊ *birth control* in which a man or a woman is made incapable of having children.

stimulus–response theory (S–R theory) A psychological theory which links a particular stimulus in the external environment (i.e. an object or event, such as the ringing of a telephone) to a response (i.e. a decision or activated reply, such as the hearer getting up and answering the telephone) in the manner of a reflex action. Such links are reinforced through repetition, i.e. ◊ *learning* influences ◊ *perception*.

S–R theory is a very simplistic interpretation and is of limited value in understanding environmental behaviour because it does not establish what goes on between the stimulus and the response, i.e. the mediating events in a person's mind while a decision is actually being made.

stint A unit of allocation for rights of common grazing, i.e. the number of animals a holder of common right is entitled to graze on ◊ *common land*. ◊ *souming, stocking rates, surcharging*.

stochastic process A mathematical–statistical ◊ *model* incorporating a truly random element (◊ *randomness*) and describing the sequence of outcomes in passing from one observation or state to the next in ◊ *probability* terms. Since the process is one that develops in time or over space according to probability rules, future behaviour cannot be predicted with any certainty: indeed the same process can theoretically produce an infinite number of different outcomes. Stochastic processes are therefore quite different from deterministic models, in which a fixed rule or relation governs passing from one state to the next and only one outcome is possible. Geographical applications have included the modelling of both temporal and spatial sequences, e.g. in the latter case by treating industrial locations and settlements as point patterns that could have resulted from a random process. Most of the models assume ◊ *stationarity*. ◊◊ *Monte Carlo method, Markov chain.*

stock resource ◊ *resource.*

stockbroker belt A term applied to areas of residence of high-income office workers on the fringes of metropolitan areas. Such belts normally seek out areas with the most pleasant site characteristics.

stocking rate A measure of stock ◊ *carrying capacity*, expressed in terms of the number of livestock units per unit area per unit time.

Stone Age The first of the major phases of prehistoric culture (◊◊ *Bronze Age, Iron Age*) recognized by archaeologists – the period of time when people used implements and weapons made of stone. This was during the later part of the Pleistocene and part of the Post-Glacial (prior to the Bronze Age), extending, in Britain, from about 23,000 BC to around 18,000 BC. The period is subdivided into the ◊ *Palaeolithic* (Old Stone Age), ◊ *Mesolithic* (Middle Stone Age) and ◊ *Neolithic* (New Stone Age).

Stop Notice A device introduced under the 1968 Town and Country Planning Act to help provide an effective means of enforcing planning control. The stop notice is an attempt to prevent delays in other enforcement procedures by prohibiting the continuation (i.e. requiring an immediate stop) of the ◊ *development* which is alleged in an ◊ *enforcement notice* to be in breach of planning control. ◊◊ *development control, planning permission.*

store cattle Cattle bred or bought in for fattening, to be sold as fat cattle to the butcher.

stow (1) An areal unit of the smallest order in J. F. Unstead's hierarchy of regional divisions.
(2) An areal unit of the second order in D. L. Linton's system of morphological regions. ◊ *synthetic regionalization.*

stranded area A ◊ *region* that was once economically equal with contiguous areas but which has suffered a loss of ◊ *comparative advantage* and a curtailment of opportunity. Consequently the region has been by-passed in terms of economic development as surrounding areas have continued to grow, i.e. it appears stranded, with relatively lower levels of production and income per capita. ◊◊ *depressed region.*

Strassendorf A term of German origin for the type of nucleated settlement commonly associated with the colonization of forested lands in Europe. The ◊ *village* plan was usually one in which the houses were ranged on either side of a main street – hence the Anglicized term *street village*. ◊◊ *Gewanndorf, Haufendorf, Marschhufendorf, Waldhufendorf.*

strategic decision A decision which is required when some ◊ *stress tolerance threshold* is exceeded. Strategic decisions are of a non-programmed nature, occurring infrequently for any given person or organization. They look to a different future, and the decision-maker has limited or no previous experience of the situation, i.e. the problem is novel and unfamiliar. Hence the decision will be genuine and must involve a search process (◊ *search behaviour*). All location decisions are strategic ones, since they involve the redeployment of a firm's or household's assets, changing the relationship between the firm or household and its environment in order to achieve new objectives or goals. ◊ *decision-making.* ◊◊ *routine decisions.*

stratified sample ◊ *sampling*.

stratified society A ◊ *society* whose members fall into obvious strata, ◊ *classes*, ◊ *castes* or estates, and in which there is a marked difference in material well-being, attitudes, beliefs, etc. between the different strata. ◊ *social stratification*.

street An urban ◊ *road*, designed primarily to give access to the buildings fronting it.

street furniture A collective term for all the varied, minor but essential items of equipment to be found in streets or public places, e.g. traffic signs, lamp standards, electricity and telegraph poles, post boxes and telephone boxes, street names, litter bins, guard rails, bollards, seats, etc. In existing towns many of these elements are the responsibility of different authorities and there has been a lack of co-ordination in their siting or positioning, frequently resulting in visual intrusion or disfigurement. Disfigurement is especially prominent in the case of ◊ *wirescape*.

street village ◊ *Strassendorf*.

stress tolerance threshold A critical level of stress, perceived by an individual or firm, in terms of an undesirable imbalance between the household or firm and its ◊ *environment*. *Stress* is defined as any influence, arising from the internal or external environment of the household or firm, which disturbs or threatens to disturb the existing balance or equilibrium. Certain stresses are only minor and occur frequently: the problems created can be solved by ◊ *routine decisions*, which involve no change in basic behaviour patterns. If the stress tolerance level is reached or exceeded, the problem can be solved only by a ◊ *strategic decision*, bringing a significant change in behaviour. For any individual or firm the stress tolerance level depends on experience and expectations (◊ *aspiration level*). The concept has been applied in human geography, especially in industrial location, to relocation decisions.

strip The unit of tenure in the ◊ *open field* system. Each strip contained about an ◊ *acre* of land, supposedly equivalent to a day's ploughing, and was made up of a number of ridges. Strips were separated by a double furrow or ◊ *balk*. A tenant could hold several strips of differing sizes and running in different directions in different parts of the open field. ◊ *ridge and furrow*.

strip cropping A conservational practice to reduce soil erosion in which ploughing follows the contour and strips of close-growing crops alternate with rows of clean-tilled crops. ◊ *contour ploughing*.

strip field ◊ *Open field* cultivated in long narrow ◊ *strips*, each in separate ownership or occupation.

strip mining A method of mining (also called *opencast*, *open-cut* or *open-pit mining*) in which mineral deposits are stripped from the surface without recourse to mine shafts or tunnels. It is an extensive form of excavation which is only practicable where mineral deposits are near the surface, since any overlying material – the *overburden* – is removed and the exposed deposit worked by large-scale equipment such as excavators and draglines. It is widely used in coal-mining, particularly in the extraction of lignite. The environmental consequences can be highly detrimental, e.g. ◊ *hill and dale*.

Two types are distinguished. (i) *Area strip mining*, which is carried out on level or gently sloping terrain: parallel trenches are cut to expose the deposit, each trench being used for dumping the overburden removed from the next in the succession. (ii) *Contour mining*, which is practised in mountainous areas: a bench is created along the outcrop of the deposit, bounded on the up-slope side by a sheer face of solid rock, and on the down-slope side by a steep spoil-covered slope which may be unstable.

structural assimilation ◊ *assimilation*.

structural region ◊ *uniform region.*

structural time Time related to the social system and to the passage of people through that system. It therefore involves longer cycles than ◊ *oecological* and ◊ *socio-ecological time.*

structural unemployment ◊ *unemployment.*

structuralism An approach to the study of underlying patterns of social life, as represented in social behaviour and in the beliefs and ideas held by members of society. Observable phenomena are viewed as particular outputs of a given set of mechanisms (or structures). Explanations of these observed patterns must be sought in these general structures which underpin all phenomena but are not identifiable within those phenomena. Structuralism represents a holistic method of inquiry into the underlying meanings of these structures, based on concepts of totality, self-regulation and transformation. The leading exponent of structuralism is the French social anthropologist C. Lévi-Strauss.

The major impact of structuralist approaches in human geography has been as part of the critique of ◊ *positivism* in the 1970s. Structuralism does not, however, provide a single coherent set of concepts, and a distinction is drawn between approaches which regard 'structure as construct' and those viewing 'structure as process'. The former emphasize a few basic structures as universally imprinted on the human mind, whereas the latter argue that structures are based in the material conditions of society. In geography particular attention has been paid to structure as a process by geographers seeking an understanding of how scarce resources are allocated, ◊ *Marxist geography* being a prominent example.

structure plan The basic statutory planning document required under the 1968 Town and Country Planning Act which, along with ◊ *local plan(s)*, constitutes the new-style ◊ *development plan.* Structure plans are prepared by county councils and are intended to outline the general lines along which ◊ *development* should proceed in an area. 'Structure' refers to the social, economic and physical systems of an area (in so far as they are subject to planning control or influence), i.e. the structure is the planning framework for an area and includes such matters as distribution of population, activities and the inter-relationships between them, the pattern of land use and development that the activities give rise to, along with the transport networks and public utility systems.

Structure plans are intended to translate national and regional economic and social policies into a local context and, in doing so, provide a framework within which local plans can be formulated and implemented; to contain a statement of overall ◊ *development control* policy; and to provide a basis for co-ordinating decisions between various local authority departments. In practice, structure plans take the form of a written statement accompanied by any necessary supporting diagrammatic illustrations. They must indicate ◊ *action areas* and at various stages in their preparation provision is made for ◊ *public participation*, as well as requiring the approval of the Secretary of State for the Environment.

student's *t*-test ◊ *t-test.*

subject plan ◊ *local plan.*

subjective probability A concept – also known as *imputed risk* or *personal probability* – central to much behavioural theory. It represents the extent to which an individual thinks a given event is likely to occur. The importance of subjective probability derives from a basic behavioural hypothesis that human decisions reflect a tendency to maximize expected ◊ *utility* (which is the product of the utility of a pay-off occurring). In situations where individuals are forced to make decisions, i.e. there are no known probabilities, the outcomes suggest that people attempt to maximize expected utility based on subjective probability rather than on objective or real probability. Subjective probability depends on personal characteristics, such as degree of optimism, and on the previous experience of the decision-maker.

subjective sampling ◊ *sampling.*

submerged economy ◊ *informal economy.*

subsequent boundary ◊ *boundary.*

subsidence The vertical displacement of the ground surface resulting from the removal of mineral deposits by underground mining. The settlement is usually gradual and involves an accompanying horizontal displacement (◊ Fig. 155). The form and extent of vertical displacement depends on factors such as the thickness of the seam, the depth and width of the deposit extracted, variations in geological structure and the method of underground working. Horizontal displacement is generally proportional to the extent of vertical subsi-

dence and inversely proportional to the depth of mining. Subsidence caused by coal-mining is the most widespread form of dereliction caused by underground mining. It is referred to as *ground movement* by the National Coal Board in Britain.

subsidy Grant from the government to particular industries or organizations. The purposes are extremely varied, e.g. to promote exports, to keep prices of goods (especially food) down, to increase production, to support uneconomic activity or protect it from competition, to assist local government to provide services, etc.

subsistence agriculture An ◊ *agricultural system* in which the final products are not primarily for sale, but are consumed by the farmer's household. The essential feature is the lack of any surplus. Subsistence farming is usually dependent on the growing of crops, although small numbers of livestock may be kept as well. ◊ *primitive agriculture, sedentary agriculture, shifting cultivation.*

subsistence economy An ◊ *economic system,* involving relatively simple technology, in

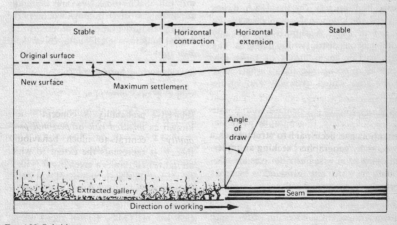

Fig. 155 Subsidence

which the people produce the bulk of what they need directly, by their own efforts. There is virtually no exchange of goods outside the family or extended family – which is both producer and consumer – and the base of the economy is frequently agricultural (◊ *subsistence agriculture*).

subsistence migration ◊ *migration*.

substitution In productive activity, the process of substituting one ◊ *factor of production* for another. This process continues until a margin or threshold is reached at which either factor will be indifferently applied and where the net efficiency of either factor will be proportional to the cost of applying it. Such factor substitution is especially common between labour and capital. ◊ *elasticity of substitution*.

subtopia Ian Nairn's term 'idealizing' the universal low-density mass of ◊ *suburbia*. It was intentionally satirical, drawing attention to the chaos and blight caused by urban expansion into the countryside in spite of the existence of a comprehensive planning system.

suburb, suburbia Suburbia generally refers to the outer residential parts of a continuously built-up city (in the USA it lies beyond the municipal boundaries of the ◊ *central city*). A suburb is a socially homogeneous district within that area. The term carries connotations of fairly low densities of occupance and of a particular ◊ *life style* suited to family and leisure needs.

succession ◊ *invasion-succession concept*.

suitcase farmer In the USA, a farmer who lives more than 48 km (30 ml) away from his holding(s), i.e. usually outside the county in which the farmland is located. Commonly associated with cereal farming. ◊ *sidewalk farmer*.

sulung An ancient subdivision of the land in South-East England, probably equi-

valent to the ◊ *hide*, used as a fiscal unit of assessment for the payment of tribute to the king in Anglo-Saxon times. It was divided into four ◊ *yokes*.

summer fallow ◊ *fallow*.

summer time ◊ *British Summer Time*.

sunk costs Resources which have been committed by past decisions and which cannot be diverted to present alternative use, e.g. capital invested in a road, a railway, a factory or office. Without costly conversion, such capital is sunk forever in its existing use.

sunlight indicators Sunlight is required not only inside buildings but also in gardens, sitting-out places (e.g. patios), play spaces, shopping precincts, etc. Sunlight indicators are standards, not mandatory, in the form of angle controls to assist planning authorities and developers in ensuring good sunlight conditions in local environments. They allow an estimation, for any point in a layout plan, of the length of time the sun will be visible (on a clear day) round the side or over the top of buildings and other obstacles and of where shadows of buildings and other obstacles will fall. Such indicators are especially important in determining whether the spacing and orientation of proposed residential buildings is adequate. ◊ *daylight indicators*.

super-absorbing barrier ◊ *diffusion barrier*.

superimposed boundary ◊ *boundary*.

super powers The two continental powers of the USA and the USSR which emerged as super powers in the 20th century. They have in common huge continental interiors, large populations, extensive reserves of mineral wealth and a large measure of self-sufficiency in foodstuffs.

supermarket A self-service store with at least 185 m² (2,000 ft²) of retail selling space. It is characterized by fast turnover and low profit margins on individual lines stocked. Customers benefit from low prices and the convenience of buying many basic goods under one roof. The retailer's profits depend on ◊ *economies of scale* arising from bulk buying, own brands and centralized management services. ◊ *hypermarket, superstore.*

superstore The term has been used interchangeably with ◊ *hypermarket*, but when defined on grounds of floorspace a superstore is a freestanding, single-storey retail outlet with 2,325–4,650 m² (25,000–50,000 ft²) of selling space. A superstore retails a wide range of clothing, household and electrical goods as well as foodstuffs, using self-service methods to keep prices low, and located on the edge of town where extensive parking can be provided for customers. The ratio of sales to storage area is of the order of 2/3:1/3, but more than 50% of the sales floorspace is given over to foodstuffs.

supplementary costs ◊ *overhead costs.*

supplementary labour costs ◊ *fringe benefits.*

supplementary product A product which is produced as a sideline in order to promote the fuller use of indivisible factor inputs (◊ *indivisibility*) employed to produce another product, the latter being the main rationale of the enterprise. The demand for inputs to produce the main product exceeds some minimum threshold necessary to justify their employment in the first place, but leaves some spare capacity which can be employed, at no extra marginal cost, on producing the supplementary product.

supply The quantity of a particular good or service which sellers will offer for sale at various prices, on the assumption that sellers seek to maximize profit at the given price. A *supply curve* is a graphical representation of a supply function showing how much of a good will be supplied per unit of time at any given price, assuming that the other influences governing supply, e.g. level of technology, number of producers, factor prices, remain unchanged. With quantity supplied on the horizontal axis and price on the vertical axis, the supply curve typically rises towards the right, indicating that the higher the price the more producers will supply.

The terms 'expansion' and 'contraction' of supply describe changes in supply attributable to changes in the price of the good only. The slope of the supply curve at any point reflects the ◊ *elasticity of supply*. The terms 'increase' and 'decrease' in supply are reserved for changes in supply attributable to changes in other factors, i.e. number of producers, factor prices, since they mean more or fewer goods are supplied at any given price than formerly, i.e. a point on a new supply curve.

The market ◊ *price* of a good is determined by the interaction of ◊ *demand* and supply.

support lending scheme A scheme introduced in Britain in 1975 after public expenditure cuts reduced the extent of local authority mortgage lending. Under the scheme, building societies agreed to relax their priority system, but not their lending criteria, for applicants referred to them by local authorities. ◊ *housing policy.*

surcharging (the common) Overstocking the ◊ *common land*. This could occur either because more animals were turned on to the common than it could feed (◊ *stocking rates*) or because holders of pasture rights kept more animals than they were entitled to (◊ *stint*). Sometimes referred to as *overpressing.*

surface A mathematical concept referring to the generalized representation of an infinite set of points describing a three-dimensional reality in two-dimensional space (i.e. on flat paper). This can be achieved by conventional means, e.g. the fitting of ◊ *isolines*, or by techniques applying curve fitting, filtering or smoothing operations, e.g. ⟡ *potential surface*, ⟡ *trend surface*. ⟢ *cost surface, profit surface, revenue surface*.

surname geography The study of personal names for their intrinsic geographical interest. Because of the hereditary nature of surnames, surname studies are of geographical value in demonstrating the district of origin of a name, in providing supporting information regarding name derivation and in providing evidence of ethnic origins, ⟡ *migration* patterns and place-loyalty.

surplus value Marx's term for that portion of the value of the results of human labour which accrues to persons other than the worker (in the form of profits, rents, etc.), i.e. the difference between the *use value of labour* (the revenue gained by an employer from the sale of goods a worker has produced) and the *exchange value of labour* (the wage paid to the worker). ⟡ *Marxian economics*.

survey analysis A general term for the variety of research methods used in the collection of data from people and their subsequent analysis (hence also *social survey*). The methods range from 'journalistic' interviews to systematic methods (especially questionnaires), from ⟡ *sample* surveys to full ⟡ *censuses*. The aim is to supply information of a descriptive, explanatory, predictive or evaluative nature which is not available from other sources, especially as a basis for drawing up policies and plans but also for wider educational reasons, e.g. reporting survey results is one way of educating the public regarding social or environmental questions.

survey population The ⟡ *population* actually covered in a survey, whether in total or by ⟡ *sampling*.

survival ratio In the analysis of manufacturing plants in a region the survival ratio is the ratio between the number of

new plant entries surviving at the end of the period under consideration and the number of all plant entries during that time period. ⟢ *entry ratio, exit ratio*.

survival table ⟡ *life table*.

survivorship curve A plot of the number of people who are still alive against the years since their birth.

sustained port dominance The ability of certain ⟡ *ports* to maintain their relative importance over a long period of time. Also termed *process of dominance ranking*. ⟢ *anyport*.

sustained yield A ⟡ *resource management* policy designed to produce a constant volume of output, in perpetuity, from a renewable ⟡ *resource*, such as ocean fisheries or forest. ⟢ *maximum sustainable yield*.

sustained yield capacity standard The optimum number of user-units per unit area that a recreation site can be designed or managed to accommodate at any one time so that normal patterns of usage will result in total annual use being just below or equal to the annual ⟡ *recreation carrying capacity*.

swidden ⟡ *shifting cultivation*.

switch trading ⟡ *countertrade*.

symbiosis A term derived from biology, where it refers to two different organisms living together to their mutual advantage, which has been used in human geography to describe the coexistence in the same group or society of a number of dissimilar institutions and activities, but which are functionally complementary or interdependent.

symbolic model ⟡ *model*.

sympolis A series of urban centres which have merged together at different scalar levels, e.g. the Bay Area in California. ⟢ *megalopolis*.

synchronic analysis The study, at a given point in time, of a ◊ *system*'s structure of internal linkages, e.g. in classical ◊ *historical geography* the taking of ◊ *cross-sections*.

synthetic regionalization J. F. Unstead's term to describe regional hierarchical classification. It involves a grouping procedure to obtain ◊ *regions* and progresses from the feature (the smallest unit area of the earth's surface), to ◊ *stows* (first-order regions comprising features grouped on the basis of resemblance), to higher-order groupings called tracts, sub-regions, minor regions and major regions.

system A set of interrelated components or objects which are connected together to form a working unit or unified whole. A consequence of the links is that any change in one part of the system will react on, and be reflected in changes in, all the other parts. A system is therefore not just a totality of parts but rather a totality of relations among and including those parts. Every system consists of (i) a set of fixed components with variable characteristics, (ii) a set of connections between those components and (iii), since every system exists in relation to an environment, a set of connections between the components and its environment. The structure of the internal connections can be described either through ◊ *graph theory* measures of ◊ *connectivity* or through ◊ *information theory* indices of ◊ *entropy*.

Depending on whether the system exchanges materials or energy with its environment it may be classed as an ◊ *open system* or a ◊ *closed system*. A further distinction is between *simple action systems* (in which the chain of cause and effect runs in one direction) and *feedback systems* (which involve not only action but reaction). Feedback systems are divided into *uncontrolled* and *controlled* (*cybernetic*) *systems*, the latter having at least one component or variable kept at a constant

level. Most systems studied by geographers are of the open and feedback varieties. Geographers analyse systems on four levels of abstraction:

(i) The *morphological system*, which consists of the physical properties of its components, expressed through a web of statistical correlations, e.g. a spatial association.

(ii) The *cascading system*, in which relationships between components involve the transfer or throughput of mass or energy, whereby the output of one component becomes the input of another, e.g. vertical linkage in manufacturing.

(iii) The *process-response system* – a hybrid of (i) and (ii), with a capacity for self-regulation, e.g. determination of price by demand and supply.

(iv) The *control system* – a process-response system modified by human intervention (i.e. decision-making agencies) at certain points to alter the disposition of throughputs in the cascading sub-system and hence change the equilibrium relationships in the morphological sub-system, e.g. land use planning.

The relationships between the four types of system are shown in ◊ Fig. 156.

system load factor The ◊ *load factor* of an electricity supply system, being the average demand for power divided by the simultaneous maximum demand on that system, expressed as a percentage, i.e.

$$\text{System load factor} = \frac{\text{Total electricity supplied}}{\text{No. of hours in one year}} \times \frac{100}{\text{Sim. max. demand}}$$

◊ *load duration curve*.

systematic geography The study of the ◊ *areal differentiation* of one particular or a few related aspects of the human environment or human population. The branches of systematic geography are labelled according either to the phen-

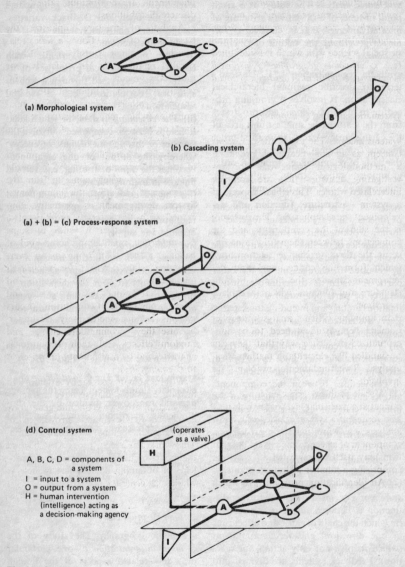

(a) Morphological system

(b) Cascading system

(a) + (b) = (c) Process-response system

(d) Control system

A, B, C, D = components of
a system
I = input to a system
O = output from a system
H = human intervention
(intelligence) acting as
a decision-making agency

(operates
as a valve)

H

Fig. 156 Systems

omenon studied (e.g. ◊ *agricultural geography*, ◊ *electoral geography*, ◊ *medical geography*, ◊ *transport geography*, ◊ *urban geography*) or to the sub-field of natural or social science with which it is identified (e.g. ◊ *economic geography*, ◊ *historical geography*, ◊ *political geography*, ◊ *social geography*).

systematic sampling ◊ *sampling*.

systems analysis The use of the ◊ *systems* concept as an analytical tool, providing a methodological framework for investigating activities that are complex interrelated wholes. Three basic aspects of a system – structure, function and development – are emphasized. The structure is the sum of the components and the connections between them; function concerns the flows (exchange relationships) which form the connections; and development considers the changes in both structure and function which take place over time.

In applying systems analysis the phenomena being studied need to be conceptualized in such a way that they can be handled like elements in mathematical analysis. Two fundamental problems are involved:

(1) A scale problem – an element or component at a particular level of analysis may also represent a system at a lower level of analysis, e.g. a firm may be regarded as a component of an economic system but that firm may itself be regarded as a system comprising a number of branch plants.

(2) An identification problem – in which phenomena are continuous rather than discrete distributions.

Analysis of structure emphasizes the basic forms of connection – a series relationship (a single causal relationship), parallel relationships (in which two or more components affect a third or, inversely, where one component affects two or more others), and feedback relationships (which may be negative or positive), or any combination of these three basic forms. Analyses of function are concerned with internal flows in a system and of the development of systems primarily with influences which come in from the environment and affect the components. System development is especially concerned with the internal stability of a system, i.e. whether it tends to some ◊ *equilibrium*, maintaining some kind of balance, rather than being in an ever-changing state. Where *morphogenesis* (changes in a system's form, structure and state so that it comes to exist at a new and more complex level of equilibrium) occurs systems become increasingly dissimilar, because they accommodate change and random effects and their structure is characterized by multifinality (as opposed to ◊ *equifinality*).

Within human geography attempts to introduce systems analysis have characterized certain areas of economic geography concerned with economic growth in an international, regional or urban context. This work has rarely progressed beyond the model-building stage because of problems of obtaining data to test models as wholes. ◊◊ *general systems theory*.

T

t–test A robust ◊ *parametric test* of the significance of the difference between two samples measured on an ◊ *interval scale*. It is based on the ◊ *arithmetic means* of the samples: the greater the difference between the means the more likely the sample difference is to be a real difference, but the greater the variability in the scores the less likely this is to be so. These two factors are taken into account in the *t*-test, which provides an index of the relationship between the difference between the means and the standard error of this difference, i.e.

$$t = \frac{\text{difference between the means}}{\text{standard error of the difference in means}}$$

namely, how many times greater than the standard error the observed difference really is. The *t*-test is particularly useful when comparing small samples.

tail A statistical term for the tapering end of a ◊ *frequency distribution*, i.e. that furthest away from the ◊ *arithmetic mean*. In tests of ◊ *significance* a *one-tailed test* considers only one end of the distribution, a *two-tailed test* both ends (◊ Fig. 35). The phrasing of the alternative ◊ *hypothesis* determines whether a test is one- or two-tailed. In the case of a one-tailed test a 'directional' hypothesis is being tested, e.g. *A* is greater than *B*, *X* is positively correlated with *Y*. A two-tailed test is appropriate where the hypothesis is merely stating a difference, e.g. *X* is significantly different from *Y*. ◊ *critical region*.

take-off A crucial stage in the economic ◊ *development* of a nation when its econ-omy and society are transformed by ◊ *industrialization* in such a way that a steady state of growth can thereafter be sustained. Take-off is characterized by a rise in the rate of productive investment, the emergence of one or more substantial manufacturing sectors with rapid growth rates, and the development of a political, social and institutional framework which encourages growth. ◊ *Rostow model*.

take-over The acquisition of one firm by another (◊ *acquisition behaviour*). The motive is usually to increase profits but may also reflect a desire to reduce competition, or secure supplies of components or materials. ◊◊ *merger*.

TAP (technique for area planning) A hybrid technique, somewhere between an ◊ *input–output* model and an ◊ *economic base* study, used to analyse the major economic activities in an area. TAP divides an area's industries into major and minor sectors on the basis of ◊ *location quotients*, size, and rapid growth or decline. The full inter-industry input–output linkages are then established for the major sectors only (the minor industries being grouped with the household sector). TAP works best for small, specialized areas, when it is reckoned to be almost as effective as a full input–output study, but needing far less data.

tapering The observed pattern by which the benefits from a ◊ *public good* diminish, or taper off, with distance from the point at which the good is supplied. This ◊ *distance-decay* effect is sometimes seen as an example of a ◊ *neighbourhood effect*.

target population (1) ◊ *population* (*statistical*).

(2) In planning, the size and composition of the ◊ *population* which is expected to result from the implementation of a proposed physical plan for an area, taking into account current demographic trends. It is used as a basis for estimating future service needs, from roads to schools and hospitals.

target price ◊ *intervention price*.

tariff A tax or *customs duty* charged by a country on its ◊ *imports* from other countries. The tax may be imposed on an *ad valorem* basis, i.e. a proportion of the value of the goods, or on a *specific basis*, i.e. a fixed amount per unit of weight or volume, and may be *preferential*, i.e. favouring some importers over others, or *non-discriminatory*, i.e. where all importers are treated alike. Tariffs are normally imposed to reduce imports for a variety of reasons, e.g. to reduce the total imports bill because of ◊ *balance of payments* problems, or to protect ◊ *infant industries*, strategic industries or home industry suffering from foreign competition.

task environment ◊ *behavioural environment*.

tau ◊ *Kendall's tau*.

tau effect A perceptual response to a journey made in two parts. The tau effect describes the situation where the two parts of the journey cover the same distance but the one taking longer seems to cover more distance than the other. ◊ *Kappa effect*.

tax, taxation A tax represents a transfer of funds by sanction of law from individuals, firms and organizations to the government. *Direct taxes* are levied on incomes and wealth, *indirect taxes* are price surcharges on expenditures.

From the viewpoint of ability to pay, taxation may be (a) *proportional*, i.e. the rate of taxation with respect to ability to pay is constant over all groups in a society; (b) *progressive*, in which case the rate of tax increases with ability to pay; or (c) *regressive*, where rate of taxation decreases as level of ability increases.

Taxation provides government with its main source of revenue to meet ◊ *public expenditure* but also gives effect to the government's economic and social policy, the objects of which may include:

(i) Increasing the economic welfare of society as a whole by reducing inequalities of income and wealth.

(ii) Reducing/increasing purchasing power through raising/lowering indirect taxes.

(iii) Checking ◊ *imports* in order to help correct an adverse ◊ *balance of payments* (◊ *tariff*).

(iv) Influencing the rate of economic growth.

technological index A combinatorial measure, representing transport, trade, energy consumption and production, and national product, developed by B. J. L. Berry in his factor analysis of ◊ *development* variables. ◊ *demographic index*.

technological unemployment ◊ *unemployment*.

technology park ◊ *science park*.

teleology A form of explanation in which phenomena and observations are understood as outcomes, i.e. it focuses on the ends as a means to understanding the cause, e.g. the 'reason' for an acorn is that it will become an oak tree. It is often regarded as the opposite of ◊ *causal analysis*.

temporal analysis Or *historical analysis*. A form of ◊ *causal analysis* which explains phenomena in relation to their development over time. ◊ *genetic approach*.

temporal autocorrelation Or *serial autocorrelation*. A systematic variation in data through time (note that the dependence in time can only extend backwards). The values display interdependence because events at one time influence outcomes in subsequent time periods. ◇ *correlogram analysis*. ◇◇ *space–time autocorrelation, spatial autocorrelation*.

temporary necessitarian A person who lives, of necessity, in a ◇ *slum* but whose residence there is likely to be temporary. Such persons are 'respectable poor' and their values differ from those of normal slum-dwellers (◇ *permanent necessitarian*).

temporary opportunist A person who uses their stay in a ◇ *slum* to pursue those values, e.g. independence, savings, property ownership, that society has taught them are worth pursuing, but who expects to move on to better things. Temporary opportunists have been subdivided into (i) *beginners* – unattached migrants to the city with no helpful contacts who need time to get oriented; (ii) *climbers* – who are similar to beginners but whose plans are longer-term and more ambitious; and (iii) *entrepreneurs* – a special type of climber dependent upon small (slum) business activity to generate savings. ◇◇ *permanent opportunist*.

tenancy A system of rights and duties associated with the occupation and use of ◇ *land* (◇ *landlord capital and tenant capital*). The landlord retains ownership rights while granting use and possession rights to the tenants, in return for which the tenant agrees to a schedule of periodic payments (in the form of a cash rent, a share of the crop or even a pledge of labour services to the landlord).

Cash tenancy is the commonest form of ◇ *land tenure* in those countries whose socio-economic development lies between that of ◇ *shifting cultivation* and owner-occupation farming. Under this system the tenant's outgoings in the form of the ◇ *farm rent* are fixed, whereas the income from farming may vary widely. The tenant takes the lease for the land for a period of years,

but generally without any assurance that the lease will be renewed at the end of the period. ◇◇ *share-cropping, tied tenancy*.

tenant capital ◇ *landlord capital and tenant capital*.

tenant right A tenant's right to occupy a holding so long as the rent is paid, and to his/her interest if the land is transferred to another owner.

tenement A term deriving from the narrow plots of land held under burgage tenure (◇ *burgess*) in Scottish towns but, from the 17th century, used to describe the particular form of building erected on such plots to cater for the rapid growth of urban population. Thus, in Scotland, the tenement became a four- or five-storeyed urban building, served by a common staircase from which passages ran, each containing two or four or more dwellings, i.e. it was equivalent to a block of flats. As the original inhabitants moved out, tenements were often further subdivided and allowed to deteriorate, so becoming ◇ *slums*.

terminal costs An element in ◇ *transport costs*, being the costs incurred in loading and unloading freight at the points of origin and destination. They are levied for each use of the terminal, i.e. each shipment, and are independent of the distance the shipment is to be moved (◇ *line-haul costs*). ◇◇ *freight rates, transfer costs*.

terminal port ◇ *port*.

terms of trade The relationship between prices of ◇ *exports* and prices of ◇ *imports*, i.e. a measure of a country's ability to exchange its own products for those of other countries. The terms of trade deteriorate for a country if the price of imports rises relative to the price of exports.

ternary diagram A triangular graph, also referred to as a *facies diagram* or *nomo-*

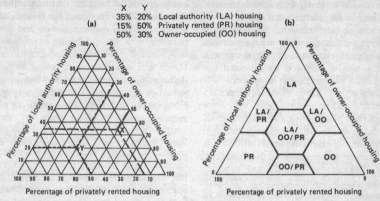

Fig. 157 Ternary diagram

graph, used for showing the influence of three variables. It can be used whenever data can be converted into percentage form, with each of the three sides of an equilateral triangle forming scales graduated from 0–100% (so that each apex represents zero on two scales and 100 on the other). From each scale lines at an angle of 60° are drawn to carry values on that scale across the graph. Provided that the values for the three variables for any observation total 100% they may be represented by a single point on the diagram (✷ Fig. 157a). The position of the point within the triangle reflects the relative importance of each variable and provides an objective method of grouping data according to the relative dominance of each (✷ Fig. 157b).

terrace cultivation A method by which mountain and hill slopes are cultivated. Terraces or benches are cut into slopes to create areas of flat land, which are surrounded (and divided) by walls to retain soil and (irrigation) water. The practice is common in mountainous areas where land is scarce and rainfall uncertain, e.g. India, Java, certain Mediterranean countries.

territorial justice The spatial application of the principles of ✷ *social justice*. The needs of the population of different areas is a primary variable in determining territorial justice.

territorial planning ✷ *physical planning*.

territorial production complex A Soviet development of the ✷ *industrial complex* concept which is used as a tool for planning the distribution of industry on a macro-spatial scale. As used in spatial economic planning, the formation of territorial production complexes, reflecting ✷ *production cycles*, is seen as a means of optimizing the spatial distribution of industry within the hierarchical structure of a centrally planned economy.

territorial sea A ✷ *maritime zone*, immediately offshore of a coastal state, being the belt of sea (also called *marine belt* or *marginal sea*) adjoining the coast over which the coastal ✷ *state* exercises ✷ *sovereignty* (✷ Fig. 29). It is measured seaward from a ✷ *baseline*, the conventional one being the mean low-water mark, although, since 1951, states with indented coastlines use baselines drawn by connecting promontories. Enclosed within the baselines of a coastal state are its ◊ *internal waters*.

There is no international consensus on the width of the territorial sea. For some 300 years a distance of three nautical miles was generally accepted (based on the area that could be defended by cannon from the coast), but in the last forty years various countries have made attempts to extend this, and every coastal state now has a right to establish a territorial sea of up to twelve nautical miles in breadth. However, the extent of the territorial sea is still subject to considerable disagreement, and international law has not yet succeeded in determining a uniform standard. Because of the importance of fisheries in coastal waters and of the mineral resources of the ◊ *continental shelf* claims of up to 200 nautical miles have been made by some countries and special rights are recognized in ◊ *contiguous zones* and ◊ *exclusive economic zones*.

The territorial sea is treated as part of the national state, hence all national laws apply (i.e. to the control of airspace, waters and seabed). The only exception is that ships of other states have the right of innocent passage in peacetime (although such vessels may be challenged at any time by the sovereign state). ◊◊ *archipelagic waters, boundary waters, Hedberg zone, high seas, historic bay, zone of diffusion, zone of exclusive fisheries*.

territorial social indicator A ◊ *social indicator* applied to the areal differentiation of ◊ *social well-being*.

territorial waters Waters under the territorial jurisdiction of a ◊ *state*, comprising the ◊ *territorial sea* and inland or ◊ *internal waters*.

territoriality A behavioural phenomenon associated with people's evaluation and organization of ◊ *space* into spheres of influence or clearly demarcated ◊ *territories* which are made distinctive and considered at least partially exclusive by their occupants. It reflects the need that individuals and groups have for space for reasons of security, identity and stimulation and has parallels with the behaviour of animals which identify with and defend territories. Hence it is commonly interpreted as the defence of the area over which an individual or group wishes to assert control. For humans such territorial realms are of variable extent, ranging from, at the smallest scale, ◊ *personal space*, through home territory, to ◊ *social space*, before phasing into public territory.

territory (1) A general term for a legally ◊ *bounded space* belonging to a sovereign ◊ *state*.
(2) In a behavioural context, ◊ *spaces* related to individuals, groups and their activities. Such perceived territories are ◊ *place*-based and may be classified as:
(i) *Primary territories*, which are owned and used exclusively by an individual or group and controlled on a relatively permanent basis. Such territories are clearly recognized by other people and are related to the day-to-day lives of their occupants, e.g. an individual's house as *home territory*.
(ii) *Secondary territories*, comprising a wide range of environmental settings from areas around people's homes to institutional settings, such as clubs. Such territories are less closely identified with particular individuals and therefore less exclusive.
(iii) *Public territories*, which may be used by almost anyone providing they conform to basic social norms or standards, e.g. public parks, libraries. ◊◊ *personal space, social space, tribal territory*.

tertiary activity, tertiary sector Economic activity concerned with the exchange and consumption of goods and services (hence also *service industry*). It includes all those activities associated with commerce and ◊ *distribution* (i.e. ◊ *wholesaling* and ◊ *retailing*), the provision of business, ◊ *per-*

sonal and ◇ *professional services*, as well as transport and entertainment services. Such activities can give ◇ *time* and ◇ *place utility* to products that have already passed through the ◇ *primary* and ◇ *secondary* sectors. ◇◇ *quaternary activities*.

Theil's entropy index A measure of spatial inequality, derived from ◇ *information theory*, used, in particular, to distinguish the contributions of 'between-region' and 'within-region' inequality to areal differentiation. The index may be calculated as:

$$I(y) = N_{i=1} \ y_i \log \frac{y_i}{1/N} =$$

$$R_{r=1} \ Yr \log \frac{Yr}{NrN} + R_{r=1} \ Yr \ i \ r \frac{y_i}{Yr} \log \frac{y_i/y_r}{1/Nr}$$

where $I(y)$ = overall entropy index of spatial inequality

y_i = percentage share of i sub-region of the overall or national position

y_r = sum of the percentages of all sub-regions in region r

N_r = number of sub-regions in region r

N = total number of sub-regions in the overall or national area

R = total number of regions in the national area

thematic map A map illustrating a particular topic or feature, usually, in the case of human geography, demonstrating statistical variation of abstract objects such as population density or unemployment.

theorem A theoretical proposition, logically deduced from a set of ◇ *axioms*, embodying something to be proved.

theory A high-order intellectual structure comprising a deductively connected set of ◇ *laws* and representing a more or less established or verified explanation, i.e. a structure composed of laws and the rules by which those laws are put together.

Theory may be constructed from relationships established by observation and measurement (◇ *positive theory*), or derived wholly deductively (◇ *normative theory*).

theory of administrative behaviour A theory, suggested by H. A. Simon, to explain ◇ *decision-making*. Its central theorem is that decision-makers will examine alternative courses of action sequentially and will select the first satisfactory one evaluated (◇ *satisficer concept*). No matter how adaptive the behaviour of an individual or group is in choice situations this adaptiveness will fall short of the 'maximization' ideal postulated in classical economics. *Administrative man*, behaving rationally only with respect to his limited knowledge of alternatives and consequences, provides an alternative to ◇ *economic man*. ◇◇ *bounded rationality*.

theory of riskless choice A ◇ *normative theory* of rational ◇ *decision-making* based on ◇ *economic man*. It requires that the decision-maker can rank in a preference set all the possible courses of action available, and that choice will be made so as to make the maximum possible personal or collective profit. It underlies the classical approach in economics and in location theory.

theory of risky choice An explanation of ◇ *decision-making* which recognizes that certain elements of ◇ *risk* can be identified and probabilities assigned to their occurrence. The theory distinguishes between risk and ◇ *uncertainty* and has received attention in its modern form as ◇ *game theory*.

Thiessen polygon ◇ *Dirichlet polygon*.

thinning The removal of a proportion of immature trees from a ◇ *forest* in order to improve the growth and form of those remaining. The object is to remove as much timber volume as possible in the form of thinnings without any appreciable reduction in overall volume production – between 50 and 60% by volume and 80 and 90% by number of trees can be removed by thinning during a rotation. *Thinning intensities* and *cycles* are determined by species and ◊ *yield classes*.

Selective thinning may be either low, in which case trees are removed from the lower canopy, i.e. the sub-dominants and suppressed trees, or *crown*, where trees are removed from the upper canopy, i.e. the dominants and co-dominants. Such thinning is expensive, and *systematic thinning*, in *line* or *chevron* patterns, is more usual today in commercial forests.

third-party effects ◊ *externalities*.

Third World One of the three major worlds of ◊ *development* recognized in a global generalization of economic patterns. The term *tiers monde* was coined during the Cold War period of the 1950s to refer to those countries uncommitted to the major power blocs of the Western, capitalist ◊ *First World* and the Eastern, communist ◊ *Second World*. However, the term Third World is now used to denote the less developed (or developing) countries in general, the United Nations singling out the twenty-five least developed countries as a group increasingly referred to as the ◊ *Fourth World* (or even the ◊ *Fifth World* if OPEC is considered as a separate group). Third World countries are therefore non-aligned, non-satellite nations with mixed economic systems (although tending to socialism) having an important ◊ *peasant farming* sector, heavily reliant on foreign aid and with a rapidly urbanizing ◊ *primate city*.

According to K. Buchanan the existence of the Third World is a malfunction of the world economic system consequent upon ◊ *imperialism*.

Thompson-Notestein theory ◊ *demographic transition*.

three-age system The division of prehistory into three successive technological stages characterized by use of stone, bronze and iron. ◊ *Bronze Age, Iron Age, Stone Age*.

three-field system A ◊ *field system*, widespread in medieval Europe and probably introduced into Britain by the Anglo-Saxons, in which the ◊ *arable* land was

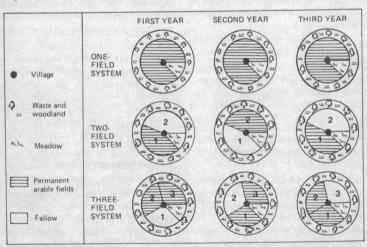

Fig. 158 Three-field system

divided into three ◊ *open fields*. Each of the three fields was rested in turn for a year. One-, two- and three-field systems are compared in ◊ Fig. 158. The system disappeared with ◊ *enclosure*.

threshold The minimum level of demand needed to support an economic activity. In ◊ *central place theory* it is the marketing equivalent of the inner ◊ *range*.

threshold analysis A technique, developed in Poland in the 1960s, which provides physical and economic planners with a common approach to ◊ *development*, particularly alternative ways of catering for urban expansion. Its conceptual basis is the idea of thresholds of urban growth. In any process of expansion, towns encounter certain limitations to their spatial growth (thresholds). There are three types:
(a) *Physical*, i.e. topographic features such as steep slopes or marshland.
(b) *Quantitative*, reflecting the maximum capacity of public utilities, such as sewage plant.
(c) *Structural*, created by the internal pattern of land use.

Such thresholds can be overcome, but only at disproportionately high capital investment costs – the *threshold costs*.

The aim of threshold analysis is to identify for any particular town these thresholds and to evaluate them in cost terms. It has been used in four main situations: for evaluating the relative effectiveness of particular alternative schemes for the expansion of a single town, for comparing the development possibilities of towns within a region (or nation), for providing guidelines for programming public investment, and for rationalizing the planning process.

Threshold analysis has been criticized on a number of grounds. Since thresholds arise from many different types of constraint it is unlikely that any two will coincide in time or space and the cost fluctuations will be evened out over the long term, especially where thresholds can be postponed by increasing existing densities. The most serious criticism is that it is a cost-minimizing technique, concentrating on the capital costs of urban expansion and ignoring the benefit side of the equation.

threshold price ◊ *intervention price*.

tidal energy ◊ *water power*.

tied accommodation Or *tied tenancy*. Residential accommodation whose occupancy by the tenant depends on his or her continued employment by the landlord, e.g. tied cottages of agricultural workers, married quarters of military personnel. Loss of job means loss of housing.

tile-hanging A method of weather-proofing external walls, introduced into England in the 17th century from the Low Countries. Clay tiles are hung on wooden laths so that each tile overlaps two others.

tillage Land annually cultivated for any other crop than grass. ◊ *arable*.

time budget A tabulation of the proportion of a person's time spent on different kinds of activity during a given period of time.

time distance A measure of the ◊ *distance* two locations are apart in terms of the time taken to travel between them. ◊ *cost distance, geodesic distance*.

time geography, time–space geography An approach to geographical study, developed by the Lund school of geography led by T. Hägerstrand in the 1960s, which seeks to add a temporal dimension to the spatial analysis of activities and to demonstrate the temporal structuring of ◊ *space*. Time and space are regarded as resources which constrain human activity and it is the allocation of those scarce resources which forms the basis of the social realities – patterns and processes – studied by human geographers.

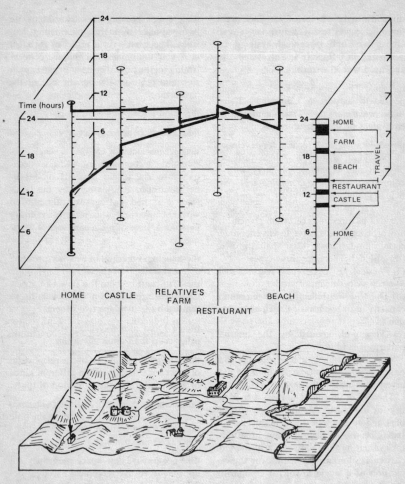

Fig. 159 Time geography

Analysis begins at the individual scale with ◇ *time–space routines*. Individuals have different possibilities of movement in space, but time imposes limitations on everyone. Once regularities in behaviour are understood at the micro-level (◇ Fig. 159), the competition between individuals for available time–space paths can be generalized, with the collective outcome

dependent on three sets of interrelated constraints: ◇ *authority constraints, capability constraints, coupling constraints*.

Time geography therefore provides a method of mapping spatial behaviour subject to temporal constraints. Such 'timing of space' involves processes that are routinized systems of exchange and interaction. Invariances or regularities in time use at the level of the day, week, month, season and year produce invariances in space use, e.g. rush-hour journey to work, peak holiday season, etc.

The alternative term *chronogeography* has not gained wide acceptance. ⟨⟩ *time–space prism*.

time preference rate The relative weight one gives to the consumption of a given quantity of goods or receipt of a given income at some future date compared with the consumption of that same quantity of goods or income at the present time, i.e. the marginal rates of substitution between present and deferred consumption. *Private time preference rates* differ widely between individuals. The *social time preference rate* is usually lower than individual ones as government places more value on longer-term consequences than individuals.

time signal A world-wide radio signal transmitted at frequent intervals to indicate an exact moment of time for the regulation of chronometers (and therefore the calculation of longitude).

time–space convergence A concept developed to examine the changing nature of spatial relations. As a result of improvements in transport and communications technologies, the travel time required between places decreases and the relative importance of distance declines. More distant places converge on each other at a greater rate than closer places. Such locational change in relative ◊ *space* can be measured for two places as

$$\text{Convergence (mins/yr)} = \frac{TT_1 - TT_2}{Y_2 - Y_1}$$

where TT_1 and TT_2 = travel times between the two places in year 1 and some later year 2, respectively

Y_1 and Y_2 = the two years in question

time–space prism Human behaviour is limited by ◊ *capability constraints* because of an individual's biological construction or the tools commanded. Some constraints

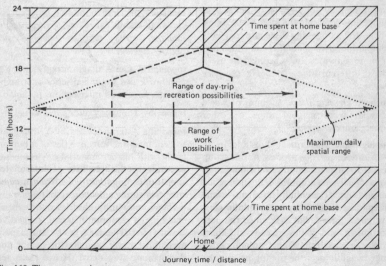

Fig. 160 Time–space prism

are temporal, e.g. the need to rest or eat, others are spatial. These constraints can be represented in a time–space prism, e.g. ◊ Fig. 160 for daily activities of an individual based at home.

time–space routine A routinized or rhythmic pattern of behaviour followed by an individual, i.e. habitual behaviour. Large parts of a day can proceed with a minimum of planning and decision if an individual has established a series of time–space routines in their daily or weekly schedule. Time–space routines mix with ◊ *body ballets* in a supportive physical environment to create ◊ *place ballet*.

time utility The ◊ *utility* which derives from making a good or service available at a different time than normally available, e.g. by storage. ◊◊ *form utility, place utility*.

time zone A longitudinal division, usually comprising 15°, devised for convenience and within which the ◊ *standard time* adopted is the mean time of a meridian near the centre of the zone. ◊ *International Time Zones*.

time zoning A solution to disputes over competing demands for land or facilities, where the competing uses are partially compatible (◊ *compatibility*), in which two or more activities are scheduled to use a site at different times. ◊ *zoning*. ◊◊ *space zoning*.

tip heap Or *slag heap*. A dump of waste material from a coal mine or other underground working.

tipping-point The critical threshold in an ◊ *invasion-succession* process. As one group begins to displace another in a particular ◊ *neighbourhood* a tipping-point is reached beyond which the initially dominant ethnic group begins to leave in large numbers, e.g. in an inter-racial case, once the proportion of non-whites exceeds the limits of the original inhabitants' tolerance for inter-racial living – the tipping-point – the whites move out.

tithes A form of taxation, introduced in England towards the end of the 4th century, for the support of the church and clergy. Originally the payment was a tenth part of the produce of the soil, and for centuries tithes constituted the only form of regular taxation in medieval England. The 1836 Tithes Commutation Act commuted tithes into money rents and in 1936 *tithe rent* charges were extinguished and sixty-year redemption annuities substituted. The last vestige of the system will therefore disappear in 1996 (except for any *tithe barns* – originally built to store the produce – which still exist). There were three types of tithe: (i) *predial*, payable on crops, (ii) *agistment*, payable on animal products, and (iii) *personal*, payable on gains from labour and industry such as milling and fishing.

toft, toft-head, toftstead Originally a homestead, the site of a house and its outbuildings, having full common rights.

toll The tax or duty paid for the use of a public road or bridge.

tonnage A measure of the amount of cargo, etc. that a ship can carry. ◊ *deadweight tonnage, gross register tonnage, net register tonnage*.

topological map A diagram representing a ◊ *network* as a simplified series of straight lines (◊ *edge*) and intersections (◊ *node*).

toponymy The study of ◊ *place names*.

topophilia A term devised by Yi-Fu Tuan to denote all the affective ties of a human being with his/her material environment, particularly the positive emotional response or feeling for ◊ *place*. The nature of such ties varies enormously but generally involves pleasurable landscape experiences, i.e. a response of warm, suggestive emotion to particular types of landscape – even those never seen by the person (or that cannot even exist). Hence there are powerful links with the human dream of

◊ *utopia* and heaven. ◊ *geosophy*, *topophobia*.

topophobia Dislike of a landscape which presents images of a very much less pleasing nature than in ◊ *topophilia*, i.e. experiences of places which are distasteful or induce anxiety, depression, fear and even suffering.

total fertility rate The average number of children born per woman in a population, assuming all experience the age-specific ◊ *fertility rates* of a specified fertility schedule.

total height index ◊ *central business height index*.

tourism The temporary movement of people to destinations outside their normal places of work and residence, the activities undertaken during their stay in those destinations and the facilities created to cater for their needs. Such travel is normally undertaken during ◊ *leisure* time and is primarily for recreational or holiday purposes, the distinction between tourism and ◊ *recreation* being that the former is defined to include a stay away from home of at least one night, whereas the latter involves activities of less than twenty-four hours away from home.

tourist function A measure used for comparing the relative importance of ◊ *tourism* in the economic life of regions. It is the ratio between the capacity of a region for receiving visitors and the number of hosts to receive them, i.e.

$$\text{Tourist function} = \frac{N \times 100}{P}$$

where N = number of tourist beds available in the area

P = resident population of the area

It has been applied at scales from the individual town to entire countries.

tourist irritation ◊ *index of tourist irritation*.

town Originally a nucleated farming settlement with a clear identity, but now generally an ◊ *urban* settlement which is larger and more regularly built up than a ◊ *village* and which has a more independent form of local government. This implies a minimum population threshold and a range of retail and business functions. Within ◊ *central place theory*, a town is distinguished from a city on the basis of size: towns have a population range of 2,500 to 20,000 (mean size 10,000) and serve a total population of between 25,000 and 100,000.

town and country planning ◊ *physical planning*.

town density ◊ *residential density*.

town plan The cartographic representation of the spatial structure of an urban (built-up) area. It is made up of three elements – the street system, the plot pattern and the building pattern. ◊ *grid plan, radial-concentric plan*.

townscape The urban equivalent of ◊ *landscape*, being the visual patterning of the town or city. It is a physical entity integrating street plan or layout, architectural style or building fabric, and land use and function and can be related to the urban dweller's 'image of the city'.

township An Old English unit of settlement involving a community of proprietors having separate ownership of the arable land but common use of the pasture (or the estate of an owner whose tenants occupy the lands of a village under a similar system). The word is in current use in Scotland to describe a ◊ *crofting* community, which operates on the same principle. ◊ *vill*.

tract (1) An areal unit of the second smallest order in J. F. Unstead's hierarchy of regional divisions.
(2) An areal unit of the third order in

D. L. Linton's system of morphological regions.

(3) In Canada and the USA, a census area unit. ◊ *synthetic regionalization*.

trade The flow of ◊ *commodities* and ◊ *goods* from producers to consumers. Flows take place within and between urban areas, regions and nations, hence the recognition of intra- and inter-urban trade, intra- and interregional trade, intra- and international trade. Two general explanations are given for the existence of trade: the classical one explains it in terms of ◊ *comparative advantage* and the more modern view in terms of exchange relationships within and between ◊ *modes of production*. ◊ *bilateral trade, countertrade, free trade, multilateral trade, reach of trade, terms of trade*.

trade acreage ◊ *ghost acreage*.

trade area ◊ *market area*.

trade creditor nation A nation or state with an excess of ◊ *exports* over ◊ *imports*. ◊ *trade debtor nation*.

trade cycle ◊ *business cycle*.

trade debtor nation A nation or state with an excess of ◊ *imports* over ◊ *exports*. ◊ *trade creditor nation*.

trade-off When a conflict of choice arises, a move towards one objective can be attained only at the expense of moving away from another objective, i.e. a trade-off exists between the two objectives − more/better of one must be played off against less/worse of the other. This implies knowledge on the part of the decision-maker of the benefits involved in pursuing one objective and the costs of not being able to achieve the other. Thus a storekeeper choosing a location in a city may wish to be both close to the city centre and to buy a cheap site; since land prices usually increase with nearness to the central business district the shopkeeper will have to trade-off cheap land against accessibility.

traffic The movement, resulting from ◊ *transport*, of people and vehicles along ◊ *roads*, railways, sea lanes, navigable inland waterways and air routes. A distinction is made between *essential traffic* (business, commercial and industrial traffic necessary to maintain and service the activities and life of an area) and *optional traffic* (arising from the exercise of choice to use a vehicle for a journey when the option existed either not to make the journey at all or to make it by some other means). ◊ *extraneous traffic*.

traffic capacity The design specification of a routeway in terms of the maximum number of vehicles which can pass over a given section of routeway in a given time period. ◊ *traffic density, traffic volume*.

traffic density A measure of the average number of vehicles per unit length of roadway over a given period of time. The *critical density* occurs when the volume of traffic is at the possible capacity (◊ *traffic capacity*) on a given roadway. ◊ *traffic volume*.

traffic intensity index A simple measure of the average waiting time in a flow, based on the relationship between time-dependent inputs and outputs. Average waiting time (e) is a function of the arrival rate of 'inputs' and the time taken to 'service' each arrival, i.e.

$$e = \frac{\text{average service time}}{\text{average inter-arrival time}}$$

If e is greater than 1.0, average waiting time and the length of the queue increases. ◊ *queuing theory*.

traffic lane The basic unit of carriageway width on a ◊ *road*. It is wide enough to accommodate safely a single line of traffic. Width varies with the design speed of the road, increasing progressively from local roads to motorways.

traffic management The organization of a more efficient movement of traffic within a given road network, e.g. a town centre, by rearranging the flows, controlling the intersections and regulating the times and places for parking.

traffic noise index Road traffic ◊ *noise* is disturbing as a result of its general level and variability with time. There are both short-term fluctuations, due to the passage of particular vehicles, and longer-term variations, which reflect changing volumes and composition of the traffic at different times of day. The annoyance or nuisance experienced by residents is seen as a function, not only of the steady background noise level, but also of the peak noise levels. This can be measured by an index known as L_{10}, or the 10% level: L_{10} is the sound level in dB(A) (◊ *decibel A-scale*) which is exceeded for just 10% of a given period of time. In the United Kingdom L_{10}(18 hrs) – the average of L_{10} values for each hour between 6 a.m. and 12 midnight on a normal weekday – gives a satisfactory correlation with nuisance and has been recommended for design use since 1973, e.g. the recommended minimum acceptable standard for new housing is 70 dB(A) external L_{10} measured 1 m from the building façade and 50 db(A) internal L_{10} indoors with the windows closed. ◊ *noise indices*.

traffic principle ◊ *transport principle*.

traffic segregation The separation of different types of traffic, most common in the case of pedestrians and vehicles. ◊ *grade separation*.

traffic shadow A concept, developed in air transport, to describe the inhibiting effect the existence of a major ◊ *airport* has on the development of rival airports in the surrounding area. This most frequently occurs where several cities are located close together and the largest city in the cluster acts as both the receiving and generating point of air traffic for the entire cluster, its airport offering the most frequent and faster flights.

traffic volume The number of vehicles moving in a specified direction (or directions) on a given lane or ◊ *road* that pass a given point during a specified period of time (hour, day, etc.). ◊ *traffic capacity*, *traffic density*.

trailer-on-flat-car (TOFC) ◊ *piggy-back principle*.

transfer costs The total costs of moving goods from one place to another, including not only the direct or ◊ *transport costs* but also the indirect costs, such as insurance and inventory costs. ◊ *freight rates*.

transfer economies ◊ *linkage*.

transfer orientation A situation in which the location of an economic activity is dominated by the differential advantages of sites with respect to the supply of transferable inputs, the demand for transferable outputs, or both. Industries most likely to be transfer- or transport-oriented are those for which the total freight bill will show the largest difference between costs at alternative sites. Their chief location problem is to find the point where ◊ *transfer costs* are lowest. ◊ *market orientation*, *material orientation*.

transfer payment Payment made by government which is not in return for goods and services currently produced. A prime objective is a redistribution of income; hence the most common are *income transfer payments*, especially in the form of social security benefits, e.g. unemployment benefits, sickness benefits, disability pensions, old-age pensions, family allowances, etc., but capital transfer payments may be made to alleviate disasters.

transfer pricing A term used to describe price-setting for transactions within the same company (i.e. as distinct from market prices). ◊ *Multinational firms* use transfer pricing to adjust the prices of their inter-plant transactions so that profits are declared in countries where taxes are lowest.

transferability The degree to which a good or service may be transported. It is one of ◊ *Ullman's bases for interaction* and considers the ◊ *transport cost* characteristics of the different goods and services, emphasizing their ability to bear those costs relative to their value.

transformation Or *scale transformation*. Any rule which enables one set of raw data to be converted into another set which is more useful than the original in a particular context, e.g. to facilitate the comparison or combination of data on variables measured in different ways. In a statistical context there is often a need to alter the 'shape' of a ◊ *frequency distribution* in order to apply certain parametric tests, and such transformation is usually referred to as ◊ *normalization*.

transformation function A function which expresses all possible ◊ *substitution* relations for two variables, usually presented in graphical form; hence *transformation curve*. Its prime application has been to depict the various combinations of outputs of two products that can be produced with fixed inputs (◊ *production possibilities curve*).

transhumance The seasonal practice, among settled pastoral farmers, of moving domesticated animals between two areas of different climatic conditions. It implies the movement of some members of the farming community with the flocks or herds to stay for a period of weeks during the grazing season. The grazings may be some distance away from the permanent settlement in either a horizontal or vertical direction. It is common in Alpine or mountainous areas, where movement is from the valley floors to high summer pastures (◊ *alp*, *saeter*), and also in the Mediterranean area, where it represents a movement from the drought and heat of the lowlands in summer into the mountains. In Britain the ◊ *shieling* system was extensive in the Scottish Highlands until the end of the 18th century. Its equivalent in Ireland was *booleying*.

transient workers ◊ *guest workers*.

transition theory ◊ *demographic transition*.

transition zone ◊ *zone in transition*.

transitional settlement ◊ *squatter settlement*.

transmitted deprivation The idea that certain families are more likely than others to suffer from a combination of social problems and that these tend to persist from one generation to another. ◊◊ *cycle of poverty*.

transport (transportation) The action of carrying or conveying goods and people from one place to another.

transport (traffic) bottleneck A pinch-point or point of constriction on a line of communications or transport where inadequate ◊ *traffic capacity* can lead to delay.

transport costs The direct costs of moving goods from one place to another, comprising ◊ *line-haul costs* and ◊ *terminal costs*. ◊ *transfer costs*. ◊◊ *back haul*, distribution costs, freight rate, in-transit privilege, procurement costs, rate-group principle.

transport geography Transport geography is concerned with patterns of ◊ *transport* as they exist at any particular point in time (present, past or future), not only the characteristics and patterns of the ◊ *transport network* but also the patterns created by the flow of traffic (people and goods) through the network, the factors influencing the development of these patterns and the consequences of transport upon other human activities. Early studies in transport geography adopted a modally based approach in which the characteristics, technology and spatial patterns of the different forms of transport (road, rail, etc.) were examined in turn. Increasingly a systems-based approach is being adopted, reflecting, in part, the tendency for transport systems to become intermodal.

transport gradient The increasing cost of shipping a unit of a commodity with increasing distance of the place of production from the market. The concept is used in location theory (◊ *von Thünen model*).

transport infrastructure (1) The transport facilities needed for all forms of economic and social activities.
(2) Fixed transport installations, such as networks of roads, railways and canals, as well as terminals, including airports and docks, and associated sites, buildings and equipment.

transport mode Type of transport, e.g. road, rail, air, inland water, etc. ◊◊ *modal split.*

transport mode development stages A ◊ *transport mode* goes through a three-stage development sequence involving:
(1) *Symbiosis* – a new mode of transport develops and is introduced to provide feeder routes to established modes, i.e. it is complementary, with nodes at ◊ *transshipment* or ◊ *break-of-bulk* connections between the old and the new. At this stage the new mode is characterized by a pattern of short, unconnected routes.
(2) The *predominant* stage, during which the new mode is adopted almost universally to compete with and even replace older modes. This stage witnesses considerable network extension, both in terms of integration into a complete or connected system and in terms of intensification to shorten routes between certain nodes.
(3) The *auxiliary* stage, in which the mode becomes subsidiary to a new mode and is effectively used only for a limited number

of commodities travelling over part of the former network, i.e. there has been a certain amount of pruning of the network in which unprofitable routes are closed or allowed to decay.

transport network An inter-connected system of lines of movement or communication by road, rail, water or air. Sometimes referred to as a *communications network*.

transport network development model Or *route development model.* A stage model of transport network evolution which recognizes broad regularities in the growth of internal transport routes. It was proposed by E. J. Taaffe, R. L. Morrill and P. R. Gould on the basis of a comparative analysis of the experiences of underdeveloped countries. There are four main stages:
(1) A scatter of small ◊ *ports* and trading posts along the coast, each with a limited internal trading area and little or no interconnection (◊ Fig. 161a).
(2) The emergence of a few major *penetration lines* (◊ Fig. 161b) connecting the most vigorous ports to inland trading centres. Such ports extend their ◊ *hinterlands* and differential growth of the coastal ports is initiated.
(3) The development of *feeder routes* and the beginnings of lateral interconnection (◊ Fig. 161c and d) as one port tries to capture the hinterland of another. At this stage some intermediate trading centres grow up between the coastal and inland terminals.
(4) Finally, complete linkage and concentration (◊ Fig. 161e and f), followed by the emergence of high-priority routes to connect the most important centres. ◊◊ *port development model.*

transport (transportation) plan A programme of action to provide for present and future demands for movement of people and goods. Such a programme is preceded by a ◊ *transport study* and

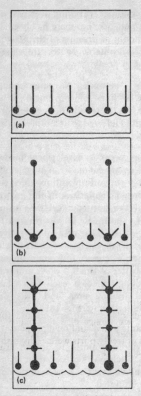

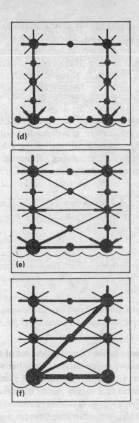

Fig. 161 Transport network development model

necessarily includes consideration of the various modes of transport. ⟡ *transport policy and programme*.

transport policy and programme (TPP) Comprehensive statements of the objectives and policies which a local transport authority intends to pursue. Prepared annually at the county level each TPP includes an estimate of transport expenditure for the coming financial year, a statement of transport objectives (covering roads, public transport, parking, traffic management and freight movement), an outline strategy for the next five years, a statement of short-term investment proposals and a summary of past expenditure. TPPs form the basis of the allocation of the *transport supplementary grant* (which was effective from 1975/6).

transport principle Or *traffic principle*. ⟡ *central place theory*.

transport (transportation) problem A special case of the ⟡ *linear programming* problem concerned with a general supply and demand situation operating in a spatial setting. It involves finding the optimum or least-cost flow of goods between a set of origins and a set of destinations given data on the volumes of supply and demand and on transport costs.

transport (transportation) study Sometimes called *land use–transportation study*, because it is based on the close relationship between land use patterns and patterns of traffic movement in a particular area at a particular point in time. The basic objective is to record existing traffic movements within the study area and to collect data on the factors affecting these movements (in particular, the distribution and characteristics of households and places of employment). The interaction of all the dependent variables is then simulated in a mathematical model which can be used, by modifying the variables to take account of estimated future population, etc., to predict the future pattern of traffic movements which would result from alternative transport strategies. These results are compared from operational, economic and environmental viewpoints in order to recommend an appropriate course of action (◊ *transport plan*).

transport system The complete set of transport facilities and modes available within an area (including all terminal facilities, offices and fuel supply points). The system is fully integrated where there is considerable linkage or interchange between the transport modes.

transshipment The shifting of cargoes from one ◊ *transport mode* to another. *Transshipment points* are therefore junctions between two transport modes. ◊◊ *gateway city*.

travel resistance A term describing the characteristics of a route which reflect the ease of travel *vis-à-vis* speed, distance, travel time and level of service.

travelling salesman problem The problem of how to use a particular ◊ *transport network* in the most efficient way. The classic problem is how to determine the optimum or shortest route for visiting a

series of places, i.e. the dilemma of a travelling salesman who wants to set out from home, visit customers at different locations, and return home. The solution is the shortest ◊ *Hamiltonian circuit* that can be designed.

trawl fishing A method of catching demersal fish in which a net – the trawl – is pulled along through the water behind the fishing boat or trawler. At first a *beam trawl* was used, but this had a heavy crosspiece designed to keep the mouth open and proved a cumbersome affair. It was replaced in the 19th century by the *otter trawl*, which uses otter boards (kite-like structures) on either side of the trawl, to keep the mouth open. More recently the technique has been adapted for mid-water fishing. ◊ *fisheries*.

treaty port A sea or river ◊ *port*, especially in China, Japan and Korea, which was opened to foreign trade by treaty during the 19th century. Foreign ships were allowed to load and unload and foreign merchants to live and own property there. Rights of treaty ports were extinguished in the 1940s.

tree ◊ *spanning tree*.

tree preservation order A power exercisable by the local planning authority in the interests of amenity to prohibit the felling, lopping or wilful destruction of protected trees and woodland, and to secure replanting where the planning authority consents to felling. Such orders have been used to protect individual trees and small groups of trees as well as areas of woodland.

trend surface analysis A mathematical technique for transforming a set of discrete spatial data into a continuous surface. It is a special case of multiple ◊ *regression* analysis. For a map pattern of the dependent variable, which is measured at a number of discrete locations, the analysis involves regressing this dependent variable on two

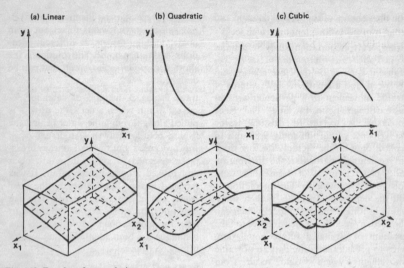

(a) Linear (b) Quadratic (c) Cubic

Fig. 162 Trend surface analysis

independent variables which are the latitudinal and longitudinal co-ordinates of those locations. The objective is to find the 'best-fit' polynomial surface. The spatial form of the surface generated depends upon the order of the fitted model. Thus trend surfaces may range from simple linear surfaces to higher-order ones, e.g. quadratic, which has a ridge or trough tilted as in a plane, or cubic, with a dome or basin. (◊ Fig. 162.)

tribal territory ◊ *Territory* associated with sedentary ◊ *tribes*.

tribe A primitive social unit formed by the alliance of a number of smaller, mainly family groups to further a common purpose. A tribe therefore consists of a number of ◊ *kinship* groups bound together by common language and common rules of social organization.

trickle-down effects ◊ *spread effects*.

triennial fallow An early pattern of ◊ *arable* farming in which two years of growing cereals on a piece of land was followed by one of ◊ *fallow*. It is thought to have been introduced into Britain by the Romans and it persisted until the introduction of modern ◊ *crop rotation*. ◊ *three-field system*.

trip A one-way movement between a point of origin and a point of destination. *Vehicle-trips* are distinguished from *person-trips*; home-based trips from non-home-based trips; and *choice trips* from *captive trips*. In choice trips there is freedom of choice between one ◊ *transport mode* and another, whereas with a captive trip there is no such freedom, either because only one method of public transport is available or because non-car owners are forced to use public transport (if they do not wish to cycle or walk). ◊ *multipurpose trip*.

trip attraction The capacity of a particular land use for attracting ◊ *trips* to it for specific activities (and trips away from it after completion of those activities). It represents the active end of a trip. ◊ *trip generation*.

trip distribution model An approach in urban transportation planning which seeks to establish the links between urban zones (not the specific routes, nor the transport modes used) in respect of trip destinations. Taking the land use pattern in, and the number of trips originating from, any urban zone as given, the trip distribution model is calibrated, for the base-year data, to reproduce the existing pattern of travel behaviour to destinations in other urban zones. Two main types of trip distribution techniques are used. *Growth factor methods* involve simple extrapolation, assuming present travel patterns can be projected into the future, using expected differential zonal growth rates. Such methods are adequate for short-term prediction or updating recent surveys. More widely used for longer-term projection are *synthetic methods*, which rely on the causal relationships behind patterns of movement, assuming them to be similar to laws of physical behaviour. The most common of these is some form of ◊ *gravity model.* ◊ *trip generation.*

trip generation The capacity of a particular location for generating ◊ *trips* away from it for varied or specific activities (and trips back to it after completion of those activities). It represents the passive end of trips. In urban transport planning, trip generation models are concerned with identifying the urban traffic zones of origin and destination of trips. Trip generation modelling is based on the premise that land use generates journeys and the number of trips originating from any zone will depend upon household socio-economic characteristics or firms' business economic characteristics and locational variables. The models are fitted to existing travel behaviour and then used to predict future situations. Two basic approaches are used in estimating trip generation. The most common is multiple ◊ *regression*, while a more recent development, *category analysis*, does not use any direct mathematical relationship between trip generation and the independent variables but identifies trip generation rates for different categories of household and business. ◊ *trip distribution model.*

tropical peasant farming A system of agriculture, common throughout the intertropical world, in which ◊ *peasants* cultivate, largely by hand, small holdings, varying in size from 1 to 12 hectares (2·5 to 30 acres). It is a type of ◊ *sedentary agriculture.* The main crops, such as millet, sorghum, rice, ground-nuts, cassava and yams, are for consumption by the peasant's family, although small amounts of ground-nuts, cacao and palm oil may be produced for sale. There is much scope for improving methods of cultivation and for increasing the marketable surplus.

truck farming The intensive, specialized production of fresh vegetables at considerable distances from the metropolitan markets in which the produce is sold. ◊ *Market gardening* is less specialized and nearer to the market. ◊ *horticulture.*

truncated firm A subsidiary firm or ◊ *branch plant* which relies on its foreign-based parent company for various services and functions and whose autonomy is circumscribed by head-office dictates. ◊ *truncation.*

truncation A term of Canadian origin describing the negative impact of foreign investment on a host economy. Truncation implies that foreign investment replaces or suppresses economically viable indigenous development that would have taken place, given the scale and complexity of the host economy. For the host economy as a whole, high levels of foreign ownership mean less internal decision-making, fewer jobs for scientists and professionals, fewer export opportunities in high value-added manufacturing, less discretion over investment policies, and increased dependence upon imported goods, services and technology. The concept underpins current geographical investigations into the local impacts of foreign-owned ◊ branch plants (◊◊ truncated firm).

trusteeship, trust territory A territory which is not yet self-governing and whose inhabitants' interests are safeguarded under the international trusteeship system provided for in the Charter of the United Nations. Trusteeships include any former League of Nations ◊ mandates yet to achieve independence.

tumulus ◊ barrow.

turbary A site where peat has been dug (◊ common rights).

turnpike Originally the gate across a road to prevent passage until a toll was paid. However, the term came to refer to the toll roads themselves, which were developed in Britain in the 17th century to meet the demand for better roads emanating from the increased industrialization. Local landowners and businessmen put up the capital, usually to improve existing roads. The turnpike system in Britain went bankrupt with the coming of the Railway Age. The term is still used in the United States to refer to certain toll roads.

turnround Time spent in ◊ port by a ship entering either to load or unload, or for both operations.

twilight economy ◊ informal economy.

twilight fringe The wilderness margin of ◊ farmscape, where farming competes with forestry, where agricultural land is marginal and where, because of the peripheral location, out-migration has left a preponderance of elderly people.

twilight zone A term used (before ◊ inner city became popular) to describe the ring of aged and obsolescent property, occupied by lower-income groups, which surrounds the central core of any large town or city. Much of the property is in multiple occupancy and some is now subject to light industrial or similar use. ◊◊ zone of transition.

two-field system A principal method of cultivating farmland in the Middle Ages in which a two-course rotation was adopted as the basis for maintaining the fertility of the ◊ arable land. The arable was divided into two sections, which were alternately cropped and fallowed (◊ Fig. 158). ◊◊ three-field system.

two-tailed test ◊ tail.

type 1 error ◊ error.

type 2 error ◊ error.

type of farming ◊ land use regions.

U

ubiquitous industry An industry whose locational pattern is in direct proportion to the distribution of population. ◊ *Market-oriented* industries, e.g. soft drink bottling, are commonly ubiquitous. ◊◊ *sporadic activities.*

ubiquity An input to a production process which is available at the same price at all the locations under consideration.

ULCC ◊ *bulk carriers.*

Ullman's bases for interaction A theory of movement or spatial interaction, developed by E. L. Ullmann on the basis of commodity flows in the USA, which combines the concepts of ◊ *complementarity*, ◊ *intervening opportunity* and ◊ *transferability.*

Umland A term used earlier in the 20th century to describe an urban area's sphere of influence. ◊ *Urban field* is a more common term now.

uncertainty The unpredictability of the outcome(s) of a particular decision or course of action. While the form of possible outcomes may be known, the ◊ *probability* of a particular outcome is not known. Uncertainty therefore differs from ◊ *risk*, where the probability of a particular outcome is known and can be insured against. Uncertainty is always present in the real-world environment in which ◊ *decision-making* operates and, in private enterprise, ◊ *profit* is the reward to the entrepreneur for bearing uncertainties.

underbounded city In the spatial delimitation of towns and cities for admin-

istrative and statistical purposes, a city where the local government or administrative unit covering it is smaller than the physical urban aggregate or built-up area. ◊◊ *overbounded city.*

underclass hypothesis The idea that municipal governments discriminate against poor and minority groups in the provision of public services.

underdeveloped region A ◊ *region* that has yet to be fully developed and in which natural ◊ *resources* are under-used. Industrial activity is limited or non-existent, and the region's inhabitants have low incomes and standards of living.

underdevelopment A condition imposed on a country or region by the international economic order, implying not just that it is underdeveloped but also that there is a barrier to ◊ *development*. Consequently, a limited, distorted and frequently dependent set of economic activities come into being. Certain opportunities are foreclosed, e.g. to export finished products, and only restricted ones are available, e.g. specialization in primary products.

underemployment (1) Generally, a situation in which an individual seeking full-time work is employed on a part-time basis or for part of the year only.
(2) In agriculture, a situation in which a full-time occupation uses time and labour inefficiently.

underground economy ◊ *informal economy.*

undernutrition Inadequacy of calorie intake. If allowed to continue for a long enough time there is either loss of normal body weight for the same physical activity, or reduction in physical activity for the same body weight, or both. ⟡ *malnutrition*, *nutritional requirements*.

underpopulation The condition of a country whose population is too small to develop its resources effectively enough to improve its standard of living. The resources could support a larger population without lowering living standards or increasing unemployment.

unemployment The condition of being out of work involuntarily. The *unemployment rate* is the number of persons able and willing to work but unable to find suitable employment, expressed as a percentage of the total number of persons available for employment at any given time. *Basic unemployment* is subdivided into:

(A) *Non-deficient demand unemployment*, comprising:

(i) *Frictional unemployment*, where some workers are temporarily unemployed because they are in the process of changing jobs, i.e. they are qualified to fill an existing vacancy in the area where they live but there is a delay or lag in finding a new job.

(ii) *Structural unemployment* (sometimes referred to as *capital-shortage unemployment*), where there is either a geographical mis-match between the demand for and supply of workers or an occupational mis-matching, or, more usually, a combination of both, i.e. unemployed persons are not qualified to fill existing vacancies in the area in which they live. Thus structural unemployment occurs not because of inadequate demand at the national level but because of inadequate demand for specific types of labour in specific labour markets. It arises because of long-term shifts in demand, changes in production methods (the term *technical* or *technological unemployment* is used where capital displaces labour from the production process), the merging of firms or the exhaustion of an old source of a raw material. Structural unemployment is a sign that new products are making old ones obsolete and causes major problems if declining industry is highly localized.

Since frictional and structural unemployment can exist at high levels of national demand for labour they may, together, be thought of as a *natural rate of unemployment* (at any level below this wage rates are ever increasing).

(B) *Demand-deficient unemployment*, which is the unemployment that would disappear if the economy were to be run so that the aggregate demand for labour at least equalled the aggregate supply of labour. It is also referred to as *cyclical unemployment*, because it corresponds to the recurring slumps in the ⟡ *business cycle*. Certain other fluctuations in unemployment show a generally consistent variation within each year, usually directly or indirectly the result of climatic variation on the demand for labour, and are referred to as *seasonal unemployment* (especially prevalent in agriculture and the tourist industry).

Official unemployment figures may underestimate the number of people out of work because of (a) *concealed* or *hidden unemployment* – that group of workers which, knowing that no jobs are available, do not actively seek work and so are not officially classified as unemployed, e.g. housewives; and (b) *disguised unemployment* – in which a fall in demand is not fully reflected in a rise in registered unemployed, workers being put on short-time (⟡ *underemployment*) because employers retain more workers than necessary, believing any recession to be temporary. ⟡ *discouraged worker hypothesis*, *employment (full)*, *labour displacement*.

unified field theory Or *idea-area chain*. A link-chain analogy in ⟡ *political geography* which views the growth of a ⟡ *state* as the product of a series of interconnected stages. It connects political ideas to political areas and provides a framework within which historical, political and geographical data can be related. Initial political *ideas* or attitudes are developed through discussion to produce a political *decision*, which in turn promotes *movement* (of people, goods and ideas) within an area or circulation *field*, and within which a defined political *area* ultimately materializes. The theory was postulated by S. B. Jones, who demonstrated its application in the case of Liberia. The idea was to abolish slavery, which prompted a decision by humanitarian societies to seek a home for repatriated slaves. Movement involved the transportation of freed slaves to West Africa, where the field represented the territory purchased for settlement, from which the area – the state of Liberia – was created.

uniform pricing Also *uniform delivered pricing, postage-stamp pricing,* and ◊ *c.i.f. pricing*. An equalized ◊ *delivered price* system in which the same price is charged to consumers buying a good regardless of their location in relation to the source of production. It is a form of discriminatory pricing, since the producers pay all the ◊ *transfer costs* involved in shipping their product and average this cost over all customers: nearby customers are thus charged more than the cost of serving them, the 'excess' being used to subsidize sales to more distant consumers. The system is common among national firms where national price advertising is important.

uniform region Or *formal region, homogeneous region* or *structural region*. A ◊ *region* in which the internal variation of specified criteria (economic, cultural, physical features, etc.) is appreciably less than the variation between the region and other areas, i.e.

$$\frac{\text{External (between region)}}{\text{Internal (within region)}}\ \frac{\text{variation}}{\text{variation}} = \text{maximum}$$

Uniform regions are non-overlapping and completely exhaust the space available.

unit value ◊ *specific value*.

unitary state A ◊ *state* in which the central (national) government is the authority which determines the degree of local self-government, i.e. local government exists at the discretion of the central authority. The latter determines the number and nature of self-governing political subdivisions and possesses the right to allocate governmental powers and responsibilities to these subdivisions. No sphere of local powers is guaranteed against expansion of central control. ◊ *federal state*.

unitization A term for *unit train operations* in which all wagons comprising a freight train carry the same item and go to the same destination. The origin and destination have specialized equipment that minimizes the time spent loading and unloading. The system needs regular, high-volume traffic flows between specific points to be economic, e.g. *merry-go-round* coal trains which travel only between coal mine and power station. ◊ *hook and haul operations*.

universal bulk ship (UBS) ◊ *'obo' vessel*.

universalism A ◊ *pattern variable* used by T. Parsons in describing ◊ *development*. It denotes an almost world-wide range of knowledge, interests or activities. Contrast ◊ *particularism*.

upward-transition region A peripheral ◊ *region* whose location relative to core areas, together with its natural resource endowment, promotes a greatly intensified use of resources through ◊ *spread effects*. ◊ *development corridor*.

urban, urban area The term 'urban' means characteristic of or situated in a ◊ *city* or ◊ *town*. It is customary to define 'urban area' in terms of physical characteristics, namely, (i) its size and the density of the continuous built-up area (the overall density is normally at least 386 persons/km² or 1,000/ml²), and (ii) functional criteria reflecting the concentration of employment in ◊ *secondary* and ◊ *tertiary activity*.

urban absorptive capacity A concept describing the ability of any city to receive ◊ *migrants*. A city's absorptive capacity is limited by any of three constraints – the number of jobs, the availability of housing and the provision of public services.

urban and regional planning ◊ *physical planning*.

urban blight ◊ *blight*.

urban centres, functional index of ◊ *functional index of urban centres*.

urban core The heart of any large ◊ *city* – the inner core area, which is generally smaller than the ◊ *central business district* and contains the highest land values, the most intensive building development and the highest concentration of pedestrian and vehicular traffic. ◊ *core–frame concept*.

urban density function (gradient) Residential population declines with increasing distance from the city centre and can be described in terms of a negative exponential function, i.e. population decreases at an increasing rate with distance:

$$Zd = Z_0 e^{-bd}$$

where Zd = population density at distance d from the centre
Z_0 = population density at the city centre
b = constant, indicating rate of decrease
d = distance from centre
e = base of natural logarithms

◊ *density gradient*.

urban ecology The conceptual work of the Chicago school of social ecology which provides a derivative source of ideas for ◊ *urban geography*. A general framework is adopted, based on a biological analogy: the city is viewed as a total environment, as a life-supporting system for the large number of people concentrated there, and within this people organize themselves and adapt to a constantly changing environment. Biology also provided the source of other concepts, e.g. ◊ *symbiosis* (interpreted as the mutual interdependence of the elements comprising the city), competition (which was translated into economic terms), ◊ *community* and ◊ *invasion-succession*. Regarded as the same as ◊ *human ecology* by some.

urban fallow Temporarily waste urban land.

urban fence A line drawn around any urban settlement to include all land where urban influences are dominant. ◊ *built-up area*.

urban field A ◊ *spatial field*, being that area surrounding a ◊ *city* which depends on it for a wide range of needs, including employment, retail goods and services, information, marketing facilities, education and banking services. It represents the latest in a series of continually expanding concepts of the city, being an enlargement of the space for urban living that represents a fusion of metropolitan and non-metropolitan spaces, extending outwards from the central city for a distance equivalent to two hours' driving time. Earlier terms used were ◊ *Umland* and urban ◊ *sphere of influence*.

urban fringe An area of land use conflict where a process of change from rural to urban use is taking place. ◊ *rural–urban fringe*. ◊◊ *land conversion process*.

urban geography The geographical study of ◊ *urbanization* and ◊ *urban areas*. It is a relatively recent branch of geography, which has experienced considerable change since the early 1960s. Since its focus is on 'area' it occupies a position between specialized ◊ *systematic* branches of geography on the one hand and ◊ *regional geography* on the other. Spatial aspects of urban development are dealt with from two points of view – the inter-urban and the intra-urban. In the former case urban areas are viewed as discrete phenomena in the general framework of settlement and concepts or generalizations are formed regarding the distribution of urban areas, their size, function and rates of growth (◊ *central place theory*). In the latter case urban areas are studied in terms of their morphology, producing concepts and generalizations related to the character and intensity of land use within the urban area and to the spatial interactions of one part of the urban area with another, i.e. internal structure and processes.

urban growth stages Five stages, suggested by W. R. Thompson, representing the economic characteristics of growth of any urban area:

(i) The recognition of *export specialism*, i.e. production for a market spatially distributed beyond the confines of the urban area.

(ii) The development of an *export complex*, involving a widening of the economic base by the attraction of linked firms and industries.

(iii) *Economic maturation* or *import replacement*, in which excessive dependence on exports and, hence, on imports of all other requirements is reduced as the increasing size of the local market allows local production to replace imports.

(iv) Where growth is achieved relatively faster than neighbouring centres, the urban area becomes a *regional metropolis* having moved up the functional ◊ *hierarchy* and exports a growing range of services to the surrounding smaller centres.

(v) Further development of ◊ *tertiary activity* means *technical-professional virtuosity* and national eminence in some special activity.

urban hierarchy ◊ *hierarchy.*

urban impact analysis (UIA) An approach, introduced in the USA with effect from the 1980 fiscal budget, designed to provide a continuing mechanism for the analysis of the urban and regional impact of new federal programmes. Originally termed *urban and community impact analysis*, later shortened to UIA. As an integral part of policy development machinery UIA is concerned with the unintended consequences for urban areas of non-urban federal initiatives. UIAs are prepared by the federal agencies responsible for each initiative and are submitted to the Office of Manpower and Budget (OMB) as part of the annual budgetary cycle. All major new federal actions – expenditure, tax policy and regulations – are to be covered, with the analysis highlighting the impact of new initiatives on employment, especially minority employment; population size and distribution; income, particularly that of low-income households; and the fiscal condition of state and local government. Five types of area for which the impacts of new initiatives should be analysed were identified – central cities, suburban communities, non-metropolitan communities, communities with above-average unemployment and communities with below-average per capita incomes. Qualitative as well as quantitative impacts have to be considered, but the contents of UIAs are confidential to the OMB, thus preventing external scrutiny. ◊ *environmental impact assessment.*

urban limit line A form of land use control in North America designed to prevent ◊ *development* of land outside areas adequately provided with services.

urban managerialism An approach in ◊ *urban geography* which focuses on the role of *urban managers* and *urban/social gatekeepers* in allocating scarce urban resources and facilities. Such managers and gatekeepers are professionals and bureaucrats who, directly or indirectly, distribute and control resources, especially housing, among competing individuals and groups in the urban area. They function as individuals within the frameworks of the larger organizations which they serve: in many instances they conform to policies or rules laid down within the organization but there is also evidence that they interpret those rules in an individualistic way and that their judgements are conditioned by local issues. They are also concerned individually to advance as professionals and collectively to maintain the boundaries between themselves and other professional interest groups. Examples of urban managers are housing officers, local government councillors, local authority planners; of gatekeepers – solicitors, estate agents, financiers. Managers operate mainly in the public sector.

urban mesh The geometrical pattern of the relations of ◊ *urban areas*. ◊ *urban system*.

urban morphology The systematic study of the form, shape and plan of an urban area, in terms of its origin, growth and function.

urban origins The traditional theory of urban origins, associated with V. A. Childe, argues that the emergence of urban areas was consequential to a process of agricultural change. It is essentially an environmental theory involving the concept of surplus food production enabling people to be relieved of the necessity of devoting all their energies to mere survival, i.e. a freedom to develop other specializations. Other explanations have been proposed, including economic ones (which view the city as a market place for the exchange of both local products and long-distance trade), military ones (which see the city as a strong point where people could gather for protection) and religious ones (where the city acts as temple).

urban programme A central government approach to the improvement of urban conditions. In Britain an *urban aid programme* was established in 1968 as one component in a more general examination of levels of social provision; it involved ◊ *positive discrimination* projects designed to provide for localized areas which suffer ◊ *multiple deprivation*.

urban realm M. Webber's term for ◊ *non-place community*.

urban renewal A continuing process of remodelling ◊ *urban areas* by means of ◊ *rehabilitation* and conservation as well as ◊ *redevelopment*. Urban renewal programmes are generally undertaken by public authorities (or local government/private ◊ *partnerships*) because of the need to amalgamate many small property ownerships in order to redefine plot boundaries and realign streets and public utility services. The emphasis is on those parts of the city which have fallen below current standards of public acceptability. These are commonly to be found in the residential parts of the ◊ *inner city*, as well as in the ◊ *central business district* itself. The former face problems of inadequate housing, environmental ◊ *deprivation*, social malaise and the presence of non-conforming uses; the latter problems of traffic ◊ *congestion* and ◊ *obsolescence* of buildings and sites. ◊◊ *conservation area, general improvement area, housing action area, improvement grant, slum clearance*.

urban rent theory A theory, based on ◊ *bid-rents*, which provides an explanation of the land use pattern within urban areas. It reflects the highly competitive bidding for sites among the various urban activities and the differential ability of those activities to bid for sites at increasing distances from the urban centre.

urban road hierarchy A network of ◊ *roads* in an urban area which seeks to segregate the different types of ◊ *traffic* in order to improve traffic flows and road safety. A *primary network* of principal traffic roads carries the main flow of traffic from one part of the town to another, as well as through traffic which cannot use a by-pass. It gives access at a limited number of intersections to a *secondary network* of district distributor roads, which carry the main traffic flow within each district. These roads in turn connect to local development or access roads, from which buildings are accessible.

urban settlement area A little-used term for the zone beyond the urban built-up area or ◊ *urban tract* which has very close economic and social ties with that urban area. It is basically the area of regular deliveries of consumer goods from the urban area, and of daily movements of people to the urban centre for business and shopping and to the industrial districts for their daily work. Beyond lies the ◊ *city region.* Also known as *zone du voisinage.* ◊◊ *daily urban system.*

urban shadow A term used in North America, especially Canada, to describe the area beyond the ◊ *rural–urban fringe* (◊ Fig. 145), in which the physical evidence of urban influences on the landscape is minimal. The urban or metropolitan presence is, however, felt in terms of some non-farm ownership of land, a scattering of non-farm residences and country estates, as well as the ◊ *commuting* patterns that develop from these and outlying villages.

urban size ratchet A threshold idea, advanced by W. R. Thompson, that there is some critical size of urban area (250,000 population?). Short of this size continued growth is not inevitable, but beyond this size absolute decline is highly unlikely, even though the rate of growth may slacken at times. The critical size is a function of the urban area's industrial diversification, political power, infrastructure, rich local market and steady supply of industrial leadership. ◊◊ *threshold analysis.*

urban sprawl A term describing the physical pattern of low-density expansion of large urban areas under market conditions into the surrounding agricultural areas. Sprawl lies in advance of the principal lines of urban growth and implies little planning control of land subdivision. Development is patchy, scattered and strung out, with a tendency to discontinuity because it leapfrogs over some areas, leaving agricultural enclaves. Its three major forms are low-density continuous development, ◊ *ribbon development* and leap-frog sprawl. ◊◊ *decentralization, dispersed city.*

urban system A set of interdependent urban areas comprising a region or nation, normally characterized by a step-like ◊ *hierarchy.*

urban tract An alternative term for the continuous ◊ *built-up area.*

urban village H. J. Gans' term for one of the two major types of low-rent neighbourhoods in the ◊ *inner city* (◊◊ *skid row*) which acts as an area of first or second settlement for urban migrants. The term implies the nature of social life in the area, as the migrants try to adapt their non-urban institutions and cultures to the urban milieu. As enduring concentrations of relatively impoverished people with similar cultural and ethnic characteristics, they are often referred to in ethnic terms, e.g. 'Little Italy', 'Black Belt'. ◊◊ *ghetto, slum.*

urbanism L. Wirth argued that an ◊ *urban area* could be distinguished by the ◊ *life style* (urbanism) of its inhabitants. The size, density and heterogeneity of the population in an urban area affects relations between persons, increasing differentiation and leading ultimately to ◊ *segregation.* Urban dwellers meet in segmented roles and their face-to-face relations are impersonal and superficial.

urbanization The spatial concomitant of the processes of ◊ *social change,* ◊ *mod-*

ernization and population concentration. Three concepts of urbanization therefore emerge in geography:

(i) A *demographic interpretation*, which views urbanization as a process in which an increasing proportion of a country's population is concentrated in ◊ *urban areas*, as well as an increasing proportion in the country's largest urban centres.

(ii) A *structural* or *economic interpretation*, which is related to the activities of the whole population but primarily to changes in economic structure accompanying ◊ *industrialization* under ◊ *capitalism*. The degree of urbanization is correlated with the level of economic ◊ *development*.

(iii) A *behavioural interpretation* based on the experience of people over time and their patterns of behaviour, i.e. ◊ *urbanism* as a way of life. ◊◊ *industrial specialization model*, *primary urbanization*, *secondary urbanization*.

urbanization economies A form of ◊ *agglomeration economies* which arise from the location in a given urban area of many firms engaged in many different industries. They are associated with the increase in total size (in terms of population, industrial output, income and wealth) of the urban area for all activities taken together and reflect the size of the market, the supply of labour, and the developed commercial and transport facilities. ◊◊ *localization economies*.

Urlandschaft Natural ◊ *landscape*, i.e. the original landscape of an area before the entry of people. ◊◊ *wilderness*.

use capacity The relative ability of a given

unit of ◊ *land* to produce a surplus of returns and/or satisfactions above its cost of utilization. ◊◊ *carrying capacity*.

Use Classes Order A categorization of the uses of buildings into classes, e.g. light industry, shops, within which change of use is permissible without constituting ◊ *development*, but between which change is regarded as 'material' and therefore requiring ◊ *planning permission*.

use-height index ◊ *central business height index*.

use period A term used in ◊ *recreation* to describe the participation of one ◊ *user unit* in an activity for one day or part of a day.

use value ◊ *utility*.

useful energy ◊ *energy*.

user unit The spatially significant unit by which ◊ *recreation* use is measured. It may be one person, one motor vehicle, one boat, etc.

utility The capacity of a good or service to give satisfaction of wants to the consumer; hence also *use value* because it is realized in the process of consumption. ◊◊ *form utility*, *place utility*, *time utility*.

utopia A term first used by Sir Thomas More for the imaginary and ideal island, described in his book *Utopia* (1516), which represented a just, tolerant and sensibly run society. Hence, a place or state where everything is perfect, especially in laws, government and social conditions – an earthly conception of paradise. ◊◊ *eftopia*, *topophilia*.

V

vacancy chain A sequence of moves by households generated in a housing stock by an initial vacancy. Such vacancies may be introduced into the housing stock of an area by the addition of new dwellings or by the release of existing housing through the migration of households outside the area. Households moving into the initial vacancies leave behind units available for a second group of households to occupy. This group in turn leaves behind units for a third group, and so on – hence vacancy chain. ⟡ *filtering.*

vacancy rate The proportion of sound properties in an area standing empty or unoccupied.

vacation house ⟡ *second home.*

vacationist A tourist (⟡ *tourism*) who is concerned with seeing as many places as possible in a given time and for whom the journey involved may be as significant as, or more significant than, any activity *en route.* A *recreational vacationist* will spend the time, e.g. a main holiday, at one place (often a considerable distance from their home) and engage in a particular activity. ⟡⟡ *recreationist.*

valuation roll, valuation list A property roll compiled annually by local authorities for rating purposes (⟡ *rates*).

value There are two interpretations: (i) *use value*, or the ⟡ *utility* given by a particular good to its possessor, and (ii) *exchange value*, or the power a good possesses of acquiring other goods and services by means of ⟡ *exchange.* ⟡⟡ *option value*, *place value*, *surplus value.*

value added The difference between the selling price of a unit of output and the cost of the material inputs needed to produce it, i.e. it represents the value added in the production process to those material inputs which is attributable to the efforts of other ⟡ *factors of production* – ⟡ *labour* (earning wages), ⟡ *capital* (dividends) and ⟡ *land* (rent).

value judgement A decision involving basic issues of fairness, justice and morality, i.e. a moral or ethical judgement about what is good or bad.

value system The system of shared cultural and social standards of a group against which actions and desires, attitudes and needs, can be judged and compared by members of that group.

variability, index of ⟡ *coefficient of variation.*

variable A measurable property of any person, place or phenomenon of interest, i.e. a characteristic that enables one member of a statistical population to be distinguished from another. A basic distinction (⟡ Fig. 163) is between *qualitative*

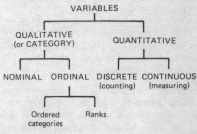

Fig. 163 Variables

493

variables (where the level of measurement is on a ◊ *nominal* or ◊ *ordinal scale*) and *quantitative variables* (where a fixed unit of measurement is defined on ◊ *interval* or ◊ *ratio scales*). The latter can be subdivided into ◊ *discrete* and ◊ *continuous variables*.

In an experiment or statistical test an *independent variable* is recognized which can be directly manipulated and whose value determines or constrains the value assumed by the *dependent variable*. In modelling a distinction is made between an *endogenous variable* (whose value is determined by forces operating within a model) and an *exogenous variable* (whose value is determined by forces outside the model and is therefore unexplained by the model).

variable cost analysis An approach in locational analysis which emphasizes the spatial variation in production costs. It provides the theoretical base for ◊ *comparative cost analysis* and, along with ◊ *variable revenue analysis*, was a classical approach to ◊ *industrial location theory*.

variable costs ◊ *Costs* that are zero at zero output and which vary directly with variations in the volume of output. The major variable costs are those of labour and raw materials. ◊◊ *fixed costs*.

variable proportions, law of ◊ *diminishing returns*.

variable revenue analysis One of the two classical approaches (◊◊ *variable cost analysis*) to ◊ *industrial location theory* which emphasizes spatial variations in revenue. Revenue is a function of quantity demanded and of price (◊◊ *pricing policies*). Variable revenue analysis forms a basis for ◊ *market area analysis*.

variance A measure of ◊ *dispersion* about the ◊ *arithmetic mean* of an ◊ *interval* or ◊ *ratio scale* data set. It is the mean of the sum of the squares of all the deviations from the arithmetic mean, and hence is

also termed *mean square deviation*, i.e.

$$V = \sigma^2 = \frac{\sum |x - \bar{x}|^2}{n}$$

where n = number of values in data set
$\sum |x - \bar{x}|^2$ = sum of squares of all deviations from the mean

Variance emphasizes the larger deviations from the mean at the expense of the smaller ones. The square root of the variance is the ◊ *standard deviation*. ◊◊ *analysis of variance*.

variance-ratio test ◊ *analysis of variance*.

Varignon frame A mechanical model of weights used for demonstrating certain principles of industrial location, in particular the point of minimum transport cost (◊ Fig. 164).

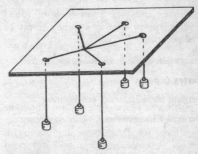

Fig. 164 Varignon frame

vega Irrigated land in Spain, usually restricted to an area which produces only one crop per year. Contrast ◊ *huerta*.

vegeculture The ◊ *cultivation* of plants reproduced by vegetative propagation, mainly tropical roots such as arrowroot, manioc, sweet potatoes, taro, yams.

vegetation mark ◊ *crop mark*.

Verdoorn's law An assertion that the rate of growth of labour productivity is determined by the rate of growth of output, i.e. the faster the rate of growth of output the faster the rate of growth of labour productivity. It is generally thought to reflect the influence of ◊ *economies of scale*, but also takes into account the induced effects on output of technical progress and ◊ *capital deepening*.

vernacular region A ◊ *region* perceived to exist by its inhabitants and other members of the population at large – hence also *popular region* or *perceptual region*. Such regions exist as part of the popular or folk culture and represent composites of the ◊ *mental maps* of ordinary people, i.e. the shared, spontaneous image of territorial reality present in their minds.

Verstehen The understanding (rather than explanation) of phenomena in a direct way through experience of the phenomena being studied, i.e. the imaginative or interpretative understanding of what really happened. It is an experiential form of common-sense knowledge of human affairs available to academic and non-academic alike. Verstehen lies at the root of the ◊ *hermeneutic* tradition. ◊ *idealism*.

vertex ◊ *node*.

vertical combination ◊ *combination*.

vertical disintegration ◊ *disintegration*.

vertical expansion The growth of a firm by involvement in further stages of a production sequence via backward and/or forward ◊ *integration*.

vertical integration ◊ *integration*.

vertical linkage ◊ *linkage*.

vertical mobility ◊ *labour mobility*.

vertical theme A theme or process operating within a society and influencing its landscape over time. The identification and tracing through of such themes was characteristic of classical ◊ *historical geography*, e.g. H. C. Darby's description of the evolving English landscape in terms of six themes – woodland clearance, marsh drainage, heath reclamation, changing arable, landscape garden and industrial-urban growth. ◊ *diachronic analysis*.

vicarious benefit The satisfaction derived by an individual from the knowledge of the existence of a particular natural phenomenon (e.g. rare or endangered species, 'natural wonders'), even though they may never see or visit it. ◊ *option value*.

vill A basic unit of settlement or territorial division under the feudal system (as described in the Domesday Book). It was of variable size, from two to three households to several hundred people, and was equivalent to the Old English ◊ *township* and the modern ◊ *parish*.

village A characteristic form of nucleated rural settlement, usually containing a church and other local functions for which there is a constant demand. Villages have been classified according to (i) physical controls on location, e.g. at the head of a valley, spring line, etc.; (ii) function, e.g. a fishing village, an agricultural village, etc.; and (iii) morphology, e.g. ◊ *Gewanndorf*, ◊ *green village*, ◊ *Haufendorf*, ◊ *Marschhufendorf*, ◊ *planned village*, ◊ *Runddorf*, ◊ *Strassendorf* (street village), ◊ *Waldhufendorf*. Within ◊ *central place theory*, village is distinguished from ◊ *town* and ◊ *hamlet* on the basis of size and range of functions: villages have a population range of 500 to 2,500 (mean 1,000) and serve an area of up to 10,000 people. ◊ *deserted village, lost village, metropolitan village*.

villeneuve ◊ *bastide town*.

virgate An early measure of the amount of land required to support a farming unit, namely, the ploughland for one yoke of oxen. It is the Low Latin equivalent of the English ◊ *yardland*. Virgates varied in size between ◊ *townships*.

virtual space A subjective ◊ *space* containing only those objects perceived by an individual. ◊ *awareness space, preference space*.

visit The unit of measurement of recreation facility use, defined as the attendance of one individual at a recreation site during all or any part of a twenty-four-hour period from midnight to midnight.

visual intrusion index An attempt to measure loss of visual amenity as a consequence of development. A new development in an existing visual environment brings a change of view; it may or may not affect the quality of that visual environment. Change of view occurs where a development is visible from an observation point and can be assessed quantitatively, whereas change of visual amenity occurs when the change in view is judged to be more or less pleasing, i.e. a subjective aesthetic judgement. The visual intrusion index seeks to assess the latter as a direct function of the perceived size of the intruding development. The index

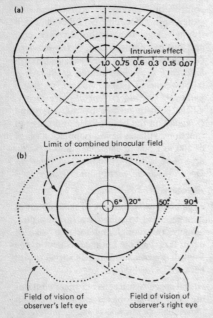

(a)

(b)

Fig. 165 Visual intrusion index

takes into account the relative sensitivity of a person's field of vision to intrusion, the central part of the visual field being most sensitive to the intrusive effects of a static object compared to the peripheral field. The field is not, however, symmetrical, intrusiveness falling off more rapidly in the upward vertical direction ($\Diamond$ Fig. 165a) than either downwards or horizontally left to right. The visual field is divided into three position zones ($\Diamond$ Fig. 165b): (i) from the centre to $20°$ radius, (ii) from $20°$ to $50°$ radius (the latter representing the usual limit of combined binocular field where both eyes function equally), and (iii) from $50°$ to the extreme periphery (approximately $90°$ radius). The subjective magnitude of the intrusion of a development in the visual field is then expressed as an index based on the solid angle subtended by the development at the observing point and a position factor (reflecting the zone of visual field occupied by the image of the artefact), i.e.

$$VI \text{ index} = k\Sigma(W_1P_1 + W_2P_2 + \ldots W_nP_n)$$

where W and P respectively are the solid angular subtenses and position factors for each individual element of the development causing intrusion. The index has been used especially to compare the relative visual intrusion caused by the siting of urban motorways.

vital events Those events – births, marriages, divorces, deaths, etc. – which are part of the record of continuous processes of change affecting a $\Diamond$ *population*. $\Diamond$ *vital rates, vital registration*.

vital index A term sometimes used for the ratio of the $\Diamond$ *birth rate* to the $\Diamond$ *death rate*. $\Diamond\Diamond$ *natural increase*.

vital rates $\Diamond$ *Vital events* expressed per thousand population. $\Diamond$ *birth rates, death rates, fertility rates*.

vital registration, vital statistics The continuous and compulsory (legal) recording of ◊ *vital events*, usually immediately after their occurrence. Registration is distinguished from enumeration (a periodic count of a population and its characteristics as in a ◊ *census*). Vital statistics are the numerical record of the number of vital events in a specified time period.

viticulture The growing of grapes (vines) for wine.

VLCC ◊ *bulk carriers*.

Volksgüter An East German state farm. ◊ *collective farming*. ◊◊ *sovkhoz*.

von Thünen model The classical model of ◊ *agricultural location theory* based on the work of J. H. von Thünen. It is a partial equilibrium approach designed to explain the type of agricultural production that would be best carried out at a given location, i.e. it is deterministic and ◊ *normative*. The model assumes a single market centre, which sets the price for all agricultural commodities, surrounded by farmland of

equal fertility. Transport costs are assumed to increase with distance at the same rate in all directions. Locations are therefore given, and the problem is to calculate the optimum crop and cropping system in response to market price and cost of transport to market.

Within the assumptive framework von Thünen developed a concept of ◊ *economic rent* or land rent. A farmer will produce the crop which has the highest land rent. Land rent (R) is a function of production costs per unit of crop (a), market price per unit of crop (p), transport cost per unit of distance per unit of crop (f), the crop yield per unit of land (E), and distance from the farm to the market centre (k), i.e.

$$R = E(p - a) - Efk$$

Under the assumed conditions E, p, a and f are constants and, with increasing distance from the market, transport costs are greater and net revenue lower, until a point is reached where net revenue equals trans-

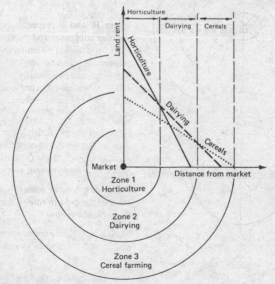

Fig. 166 Von Thünen model

497

port cost, the land rent is zero and the extensive margin of cultivation has been reached.

If only one crop was being cultivated the intensity of production would decrease with increasing distance from the market, since intensity of production depends on the net return the farmers get for their crop (which can be cultivated using different factor combinations). This aspect of the von Thünen model is referred to as the *intensity theory*.

More common is the *crop theory*, in which several crops are considered, with the importance of transport costs varying according to the bulk and perishability of the crops. In this case the crop on which the greatest savings in transport costs can be made will be grown nearest to the market, i.e. be prepared to bid the highest land rent. Crops with relatively lower transport costs will be grown at greater distances away from the market. A zonal pattern of land use – the *von Thünen rings* – is the result ($\diamondsuit$ Fig. 166). The model has been modified by relaxing certain of the assumptions, e.g. to account for differences in soil fertility, and for restricted access to lines of rapid transport to market. The idea has been applied at spatial scales ranging from the global to that of the individual farm, but it has been criticized for its neglect of behavioural factors and of farm size, and because it is a static model.

Voronoi polygons $\diamondsuit$ *Dirichlet polygons*.

W

wages A comprehensive term covering all the different forms of earnings of ◊ *labour*.

wage spread Or *skill margin*. The range of wage levels among the different occupations within a single labour market. Wage spread is generally widest in less-developed and slowly growing regions. It is explained in terms of the lower educational standards and the smaller proportion of semi-skilled manufacturing jobs in such areas.

waiting costs In ◊ *development*, those costs which arise because of the waiting period that elapses between the time of the developer's first outlay of capital and labour and the time when the developer can liquidate the investment or put the completed development into use. The two principal types of waiting costs include allowances for interest on the investment and any taxes that must be paid during the development and normal sales period. A closely related and sometimes overlapping concept is ◊ *ripening costs*.

Waldhufendorf A forest ◊ *village*. The term relates to villages, especially in central Europe, which originated during the period of forest clearances from the 9th to the 14th centuries. The village form usually comprised a double or single row of farmhouses, e.g. along a stream in a valley bottom, with the farmland in a consolidated unit stretching back upslope from each farmhouse. ◊ *Gewanndorf, Haufendorf, Runddorf, Strassendorf*.

wapentake An ancient subdivision of a ◊ *shire*, equivalent to the ◊ *hundred*, in those shires where the Danish influence was strong. It was subdivided into ◊ *carucates*.

ward An administrative division of a ◊ *borough* or ◊ *city*. Its present function is usually as a district which elects its own councillors to represent it on the borough or town council.

warehousing Temporary storage, especially associated with the ◊ *wholesale trade* and the local marketing of produce. It provides a 'time cushion' between producer and consumer.

warren In medieval times a legal term for land over which the king had granted rights to take certain game, usually the lesser forms such as hares, rabbits and many birds. Such areas were generally extensive and unenclosed. Later the term had the more limited meaning of an enclosure for keeping rabbits (hence *rabbit warren*). Such enclosures were in use until the 19th century, and the term is preserved in place names. Today the term is applied to any piece of ground where rabbits breed.

Warsaw Pact A political–military ◊ *alliance*, established by the Eastern European Mutual Assistance Treaty signed in Warsaw in 1955, which ties the Soviet Union to its satellites in Eastern Europe. The alliance is for mutual defence (to counterbalance the ◊ *North Atlantic Treaty Organization*) and combines the armed forces of the Russian satellites under Soviet hegemony.

waste, waste land A term which covers a

wide variety of types of land, all of which are either uncultivated or uncultivable or uninhabited. In medieval Britain it referred to the little used ◊ *common land*, which served as rough grazing for livestock, as a source of fuel and of materials for the repair of houses, and which later allowed the expansion of the arable area by enclosure and improvement. The use of the term waste for any remaining such land has disappeared because of the value of such commons as recreational open space. More recently the term has been applied to *industrial waste*, meaning ◊ *derelict land* resulting largely from 19th-century industrial activity.

waste factor The amount of domestic and municipal waste (solid and liquid) released into the environment (directly, or indirectly, through municipal sewers or through the municipal waste collection and treatment network) per head per year in a given area. ◊◊ *pollution factor, waste load.*

waste load The total amount of domestic and municipal waste (refuse) released into the environment (directly, or indirectly, through municipal sewers or through the municipal waste collection and treatment network) by a given area (parish, town, state, etc.) during a given period of time. ◊◊ *pollution load, waste factor.*

water power ◊ *Energy* obtained from moving or falling water. Such power is derived from two main sources: river flow and tidal movement. Whereas the water power of rivers was formerly used directly to drive water-wheels in mills, etc., it is now commonly used to generate electricity (◊ *hydroelectric power*). Similarly with *tidal energy*, which was used in the Middle Ages to operate tidal mills but today relies on tidal barrages for the generation of electricity. ◊◊ *wave energy.*

water use Three types of water use are distinguished:

(i) *Withdrawal*, where water is taken from a river, or surface or underground reservoir, and after use returned to a natural water body, e.g. water used for cooling in industrial processes. Such return flows are particularly important for downstream users in the case of water taken from rivers.

(ii) *Consumptive*, which starts with withdrawal, but in this case without any return, e.g. irrigation, steam escaping into the atmosphere, water contained in final products, i.e. it is no longer available directly for subsequent uses.

(iii) *Non-withdrawal*, i.e. the *in situ* use of a water body for navigation (including the floating of logs by the lumber industry), fishing, recreation (e.g. swimming, boating), effluent disposal and ◊ *hydroelectric power* generation.

watering place An obsolete term, previously used for:
(1) A place on a river or lake where animals are brought to drink.
(2) A place where a ship could obtain fresh water.
(3) A fashionable ◊ *resort* for sea bathing, or for drinking or bathing in the waters of a mineral spring (◊◊ *spa*).

waterway A line of water, especially a river, used for transport.

wave energy ◊ *Energy* derived from the motion of waves. As a form of ◊ *renewable energy*, with few environmental disadvantages, wave energy is now being considered as a potential source of electricity, but current proposals are all at a pilot stage.

wayleave The right of passage across another's land. ◊◊ *easement.*

wealth A stock of physical assets (goods, etc.), financial assets and non-tangible assets which can be exchanged for money.

Weaver's crop combination index ◊ *crop combinations.*

Weber's theory of industrial location The

classical model of ◊ *industrial location theory*, based on the work of Alfred Weber, in which the optimum location of a manufacturing firm is explained in terms of cost minimization, hence also termed the *least cost theory of industrial location*. Entrepreneurs locate their firms at the points of minimum cost in response to three basic locational factors – relative transport costs, labour costs and agglomeration costs. Holding two of these factors constant, Weber deduced how a firm would locate with respect to the third factor.

The approach is deterministic and ◊ *normative*, assuming that an area is physically, culturally, politically and technologically uniform; sources of raw materials and centres of consumption are given; transport costs are a function of weight and distance; there is perfectly competitive pricing.

Within this assumptive framework transport costs are viewed as the primary determinant of a firm's location. Weber demonstrates the derivation of the least transport cost location by means of the ◊ *locational triangle*, taking a simplified case of a firm with two material sources and a single market, the optimum location being the point at which the total transport costs of assembling raw materials at the place of production and of distributing the finished products to the market are minimized. The resultant location may be either ◊ *material-oriented* or ◊ *market-oriented* depending on the relationship between the weight of materials and the weight of products (◊ *material index*). Material orientation occurs when there is a sizable weight loss during the production process, market orientation when there is a weight gain.

The labour factor is then considered, in terms of the extent to which a cheap labour location might divert a firm from the least transport cost point. This will happen if the savings in labour costs exceed the additional transport costs incurred at the low labour cost location – ◊ *isodapane* analysis is used to demonstrate this point. To measure the importance of labour for any industry Weber used an ◊ *index of labour cost* and a ◊ *labour coefficient*. Agglomeration economies are treated in a similar way: the firm is diverted to an alternative location where the savings due to agglomeration economies more than offset the additional transport costs involved.

The theory has been criticized for its assumptions, especially those relating to transport costs and the spatial uniformity of demand or revenue conditions, and its high degree of abstraction from the real world. As a partial equilibrium theory it is most applicable to the single-product, single-plant firm controlled by a single, highly rational entrepreneur. Weber's basic model has been easily modified to provide a more general ◊ *variable cost theory*.

weekend cottage ◊ *second home*.

weekend farmer ◊ *hobby farmer*.

weight-loss ratio The loss in weight of a material used in a finished product as a result of the production process. Normally expressed as the ratio of the raw material(s) weight to the finished product weight. ◊◊ *locational weight, material index*.

welfare geography An approach to human geography whose fundamental objective is to map and understand social and spatial variations in the ◊ *quality of life*, i.e. 'who gets what, where and how'. 'Who' considers the population of an area (subdivided by class, race, etc. as appropriate); 'what' embraces all things from which human satisfaction, positive or negative, is derived (i.e. goods, services, social relations, environmental quality, etc.); 'where' recognizes that place of residence underlies differences in quality of life; and 'how' looks at the processes which distribute resources within society and so generate patterns of inequality. Welfare geography was part of the radical reaction (◊ *radical geography*) to the 1960s emphasis on quantification and model-building, which emphasized ◊ *logical positivism* as an approach. The latter was not seen as relevant to contemporary problems. Thus, from the early 1970s much work in human geography took up welfare issues, such as homelessness, poverty, crime, lack of access to educational opportunity and other social services, and recognized explicitly the part played by discrimination in creating the patterns of inequality. This reorientation of effort in human geography complemented trends in society at large, where a shift from narrow economic criteria to a broader concern for quality of life was discernible. Much early work in welfare geography was descriptive, the identification of spatial variations involving the development of a wide range of multivariate indexes, e.g. ◊ *physical quality of life index*, ◊ *social indicator*. There followed a search for theoretical understanding which often emphasized conflict over access to sources of power and focused on the role of the state in capitalist society; the objective of welfare geography, in a policy context, being to make recommendations which will bring about a more equitable distribution of resources and opportunities. ◊◊ *economic welfare, social welfare*.

welfare state A nation organized to provide minimum standards of living, health, housing and education for its least prosperous citizens (i.e. those members of the population whose means are inadequate to provide these standards for themselves).

wet-point settlement A settlement owing its site selection to the availability of a water supply. ◊◊ *dry-point settlement*.

wet-rice cultivation Or *paddy farming*. A distinctive type of ◊ *agricultural system*, which supports the majority of the rural population in the Far East. It is a ◊ *labour-intensive* form of ◊ *subsistence* farming and requires very large amounts of water. Wet rice has to be submerged beneath slowly moving water to an average depth of 100–150 mm (0·4–0·6 in) for three-quarters of its growing period. This restricts its cultivation to flat lands near rivers, where the rice is grown in small levelled fields (i.e. *paddies*) surrounded by low earthen bunds which keep the water in, and which can be easily breached to drain the field.

wheat belt A term sometimes used to describe that part of the North American prairies on which wheat is extensively cultivated.

wheat crescent The crescent-shaped zone extending along the drier, western margin of the South American Pampas on which wheat is widely cultivated.

wheel of retailing hypothesis A hypothesis concerning retail development in which new retailers enter the market as low-status, low-margin, low-price operators and gradually acquire more elaborate outlets, which require higher investment and incur higher operating costs. These retailers eventually reach a position of high-cost and high-price outlets, vulnerable to new low-price competitors. This circular process is called the wheel of retailing. As the retailer progresses around the 'wheel' so the location of shops changes from less convenient low-rent sites to more accessible and consequently more expensive sites.

white land Land which is given no particular allocation on a ◊ *development plan*, the presumption being that the existing land use will be retained.

white man's grave An obsolete term for the hot, humid coastlands of West Africa, especially Sierra Leone. The concept is derived from the lethal tropical diseases, such as yellow fever, which afflicted the area, but the reputation of the area for unhealthiness has long been revised in view of the control of such diseases by modern medicine, etc.

wholesale trade, wholesaling That part of the ◊ *tertiary sector* which facilitates the movement of products from the manufacturing sector to the ◊ *retailing* sector. It reflects the geographical separation of the point of production from the point of final sale. Wholesalers therefore act as intermediaries between the manufacturer (or farmer) and the retailer: they buy in large quantities from the producer and sell in small quantities to individual retailers, i.e. wholesalers have customers who are ◊ *entrepreneurs* rather than simple consumers. The manufacturer, who specializes in one or a few products for wide distribution, is relieved of the task of having to find a market and is saved from having to handle countless small orders from retailers. The retailer, who stocks a very wide variety of items, is saved from having to order small amounts from countless producers and may also find favourable credit terms offered by the wholesaler.

Wholesaling moves goods from areas of surplus to areas of need, anticipating times of possible oversupply and undersupply (i.e. it performs also a storage or ◊ *warehousing* function), and avoids costly long-haul shipments of small lots because transport scale economies can be enjoyed on the large volume movement from producers to wholesalers. At the same time it allows the benefit of much quicker delivery.

The wholesale trade is concentrated in the larger ◊ *central places* and various wholesaling districts have been identified. The *traditional wholesaling district* was sited near the city centre, at the focal point of inter-city transport facilities, in order to receive goods and supply the surrounding market. With time more specialized districts have emerged: ◊ *produce district, product comparison district, will-call*

delivery district, manufacturing stocks district, and office wholesaling district (specializing in office equipment and supplies).

Various types of wholesaler have also been recognized: (i) *merchant wholesalers,* the standard entrepreneurial traders on a large scale, (ii) *manufacturer's agents,* owned by the manufacturer(s), (iii) *brokers,* dealing in orders rather than goods, (iv) *factors* or *commission merchants,* agents who serve producers by selling their products in particular markets, (v) *export–import agents,* specializing in foreign trade.

As the retail trade has been absorbed by large firms, wholesalers have become less important, their role, in certain sectors, being taken over by retailers such as supermarket chains, which deal direct with manufacturers.

Wilcoxon test A ◊ *non-parametric* test for paired samples on an ◊ *interval scale* in which the differences between the pairs of data from the two samples are ranked irrespective of sign, i.e. put on an ◊ *ordinal scale.* The significance levels depend upon the allocation of ranks between those cases where the first sample value is greater than the second sample value and those where the second sample exceeds the first. The test is intermediate between the ◊ *sign test* and the correlation ◊ *t-test* and has a rationale similar to the ◊ *Mann–Whitney U test.*

wildcat well An exploratory or test well drilled, on the basis of seismic and similar surveys, in the hope of discovering a new oilfield. If it produces neither oil nor gas it is called a *dry hole* or *duster* and is plugged and abandoned. If it yields oil or gas it becomes a *completed well,* but will not become productive until further ◊ *appraisal wells* have been drilled to assess the extent of the field. ◊◊ *development well.*

wilderness Today, the ultimate in natural environments – an area which retains its primeval character and influence, without permanent improvements or human habitation and where people are infrequent visitors. For much of history the word held a negative connotation as a place of evil and danger, of dark and hostile forces and as a desolate waste: a wilderness was to be avoided if at all possible or else it was to be tamed, controlled and exploited. It is now thought of positively, by people and governments, as something to be valued and managed with care and respect, to be conserved for future generations (◊ *conservation*). It is perceived by people as a large natural area where plants and animals live undisturbed, and where the natural ecosystem can be experienced as it is, providing outstanding opportunities for solitude or a primitive and unconfined type of recreation.

For the individual one of the main benefits of a wilderness experience is the spiritual satisfaction obtained. Other advantages are the physical and mental stimulation, the aesthetic appreciation of beautiful scenery, and the experience of conditions similar to those encountered by the first settlers of an area. Wilderness therefore serves as a sanctuary as well as having a role to play in nature conservation and scientific research. ◊ *wildscape*, *zapovedniki*.

wildscape An area dominated by natural features – vegetation, rock outcrops, glaciers, water, etc.

will-call delivery district An area of centrally located ◊ *wholesaling* units which exist to supply undercapitalized retailers of products such as auto parts and plumbing supplies, and retailers of products liable to rapid changes in taste, e.g. hit records. The retailer calls at the wholesaler's base in order to secure immediate delivery.

wind energy The kinetic ◊ *energy* associated with the movement of large air masses over the earth's surface. Such movement is the result of the uneven heating effect of solar radiation on the seas and land masses and varies with season and location.

Wind energy was one of the earliest forms of energy to be exploited – the Chinese operated windmills some 2,000 years ago – for power for grinding, pumping, forging and milling. From the late 19th century it has been harnessed to provide electricity on a small scale, but the change towards a few large power sources diverted attention away from diffuse energy sources (such as wind) towards ◊ *fossil fuels* and, later, nuclear sources. Interest is again being shown in wind-generated power because it exploits a clean ◊ *renewable energy resource*, which does not cause problems of thermal ◊ *pollution*. However, the present-day economics of wind-generated electricity are marginal.

windbreak A screen of hardy trees deliberately planted to check the force of the wind.

wirescape The webs of cables, aerials and their supports which disfigure skylines.

wood A collection of trees growing together naturally (as distinguished from a ◊ *plantation*). More extensive than a copse (◊ *coppice*) but smaller than a ◊ *forest*. ◊ *woodland*.

woodland Land covered with trees. In Britain the term is used in an official context to cover all types of wooded land (e.g. in the Census of Woodlands), whereas international practice is to use the term *forested land*. In the British context the total woodland area can be subdivided in one of two ways: into (i) private and Forestry Commission woodland, and (ii) productive woodland (including ◊ *high forest*, ◊ *coppice*, ◊ *coppice-with-standards* and utilizable scrub), unutilizable scrub and felled woodland.

worker-peasant A member of a farming family who commutes to a job in the city but still lives in the family farmhouse, working its holdings on a part-time basis. This practice is common in many parts of continental Europe, where it is known by various names, e.g. *Arbeiterbauern*, *ouvriers-paysan*.

working capital ⟡ *capital*.

working population One interpretation of the term ⟡ *active population*.

world city ⟡ *ecumenopolis*.

world geographic reference system ⟡ *georef system*.

world-island A term used by H. J. Mac-kinder in his world power theory for the combined continents of Europe, Asia and Africa, which comprise the world's largest land mass. Being surrounded by water this land mass is, by the usual definition, an island. ⟡ *heartland*.

worsenment A decrease in the value of land (including the buildings thereon) held by a person due to the actions of central and local government, e.g. the deleterious impact of a new urban motorway on adjacent residential property. On the limited occasions when payment is made to mitigate the hardship of this loss, it is described as *compensation*.

X

x-efficiency Those intangibles that motivate people to co-operate and participate in the social process of production. Such intangibles are usually more important the smaller the group or unit.

Y

yardland An old English measure of the amount of land that would keep a pair of oxen (i.e. a two-ox plough) busy throughout the year. It was not an exact unit of land measurement but varied according to soil, generally averaging 12 hectares (30 acres), i.e. it was equivalent to the Low Latin ◊ *virgate*. It was a quarter of a ◊ *hide* and was itself subdivided into two ◊ *oxgangs* of four ◊ *ferlings*.

year The period of time taken for the earth to complete one revolution in its orbit about the sun, i.e. the measure of time to complete the cycle of the ◊ *seasons*. This is the *solar year* (of 365·2422 mean ◊ *solar days*), also known as the *astronomical year*, *equinoctial year*, *nature year* and *tropical year*. It is distinguished from the ◊ *calendar year* and the *sidereal year* (comprising 365·2564 mean solar days, the time interval for the earth to complete one revolution around the sun with reference to the stars) and the *anomalistic year* (365·25764 mean solar days, the time between two successive perihelions – the point when the earth is nearest to the sun).

yeoman farming A system of small-scale farming for profit by freehold farmers who, although subject to manorial exactions, were able to respond to market opportunities by their individual effort. This form of farming developed with ◊ *enclosure* and individual farms were created, i.e. from Tudor times onwards. In the 17th, 18th and 19th centuries the term yeoman was used to indicate the status of owner-occupiers who were not members of the nobility or 'landed gentry'.

yield Output or production expressed in relation to units of input (land, labour, capital, etc.). Actual yields are contrasted against potential or theoretical yields.

yield class A measure of plantation growth potential in a forest, expressed in terms of m^3 per hectare per year and calculated as the total volume of wood produced divided by the age when the maximum mean annual increment is achieved.

yoke A quarter of a ◊ *sulung*.

youth A term applied to the first stage of economic ◊ *development* of a country or region.

Z

z-scores The most common method for standardizing ◊ *variables* measured on the ◊ *interval* or ◊ *ratio scales*. In order to compare two variables measured in different units the original values or scores are transformed into *z*-scores or *standard scores* by expressing the values in terms of ◊ *standard deviation* units, i.e.

$$z\text{-score} = \frac{\text{deviation score}}{\text{standard deviation}}$$

where the deviation score is the difference between an individual value and the ◊ *arithmetic mean*.

Each value in the distribution becomes a value equivalent to the number of standard deviation units (hence also *standard normal deviate*) that it is above or below the mean. Where all the values in a distribution are transformed into *z*-scores the distribution is said to be *standardized*: the *z*-score transformation generates a new variable with a mean of zero and a standard deviation of 1·0.

zambo The offspring of Negro and Indian parents.

zapovedniki Natural biosphere reserves in the USSR, equivalent to ◊ *wilderness* areas.

zero-growth population A fully ◊ *stationary*, stable *population* in which births equal deaths and the rate of increase is zero.

zonal model ◊ *concentric zone theory*.

zone (1) Generally, any ◊ *region* of the world defined by specific limits.
(2) One of the various 'belts' encircling the earth, which are distinguished by climatic differences. Division is by the tropics and polar circles to give a *torrid zone*, two *temperate zones* and two *frigid zones*.
(3) In ◊ *physical planning*, an area designated for a particular land use. ◊ *zoning*.

zone du voisinage ◊ *urban settlement area*.

zone in transition A term used for the area around the ◊ *central business district*, the second ring of the ◊ *concentric zone theory*. It is an area of mixed industrial, commercial and residential land use, tending towards deterioration and ◊ *blight*. The zone was built up during the 19th century primarily for residential purposes when transport lines were inflexible and there were few restrictions on the type and density of building. Many residential structures have been taken over by business and light manufacturing, thus reducing residential desirability and leading to an influx of ethnic minorities and the poor. The overcrowded, dilapidated residences be-

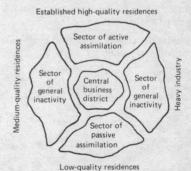

Fig. 167 Zone in transition

come ◊ *slums*. The zone, which is particularly a North American phenomenon, has been subdivided by R. E. Preston and D. W. Griffin into several sectors (◊ Fig. 167): a *sector of active assimilation*, where new uses are being developed; a *sector of passive assimilation*, involving slower change; and a *sector of general inactivity*, which is discontinuous, contains the principal slums, and where little change is in progress. ◊◊ *inner city, twilight zone*.

zone of assimilation The expansion front of the ◊ *central business district*. Although absolute areal growth of the central business district may have come to an end with the invention of the skyscraper, it is changing and shifts in its boundaries have been recognized. The area into which the central business district is migrating is the zone of assimilation and lies in the direction of the high-quality residential areas. It contains speciality shops, car showrooms, headquarter offices, professional offices and the newer hotels. ◊◊ *zone of discard*.

zone of baite Thin Alpine ◊ *pastures*, at an altitude of 2,000–2,400 m (6,550–7,850 ft).

zone of diffusion An ill-defined area beyond the ◊ *contiguous zone* in which the coastal ◊ *state* claimed certain unilateral rights, such as weapon testing, fisheries and pollution control. Now formalized as the ◊ *exclusive economic zone*. ◊◊ *zone of exclusive fisheries*.

zone of discard The area from which a ◊ *central business district* is migrating, involving a shift away from slums, railways and rivers. The zone of discard is characterized by pawn shops, family clothing stores, second-hand furniture stores, bars and low-grade restaurants, and bus stations. The process may be exacerbated where central business district retail sales are declining in the face of competition from outlying shopping centres. ◊◊ *zone of assimilation*.

zone of exclusive fisheries The desire of coastal ◊ *states* to protect their coastal ◊ *fisheries* as much as possible against foreign exploitation first led to attempts to extend their ◊ *sovereignty* beyond the state's ◊ *territorial sea*. Zones of exclusive fisheries were defined, but these have been subsumed into the now generally accepted ◊ *contiguous zone* and ◊ *exclusive economic zone*. ◊◊ *continental shelf*.

zoning A method by which ◊ *physical planning* regulates land use in the public interest, involving the allocation of land for primary purposes, such as residential, industrial, etc., in a plan for future ◊ *development*. It results in the segregation of land uses. ◊◊ *space zoning*.

Zuhube ◊ *second farm*.

FOR THE BEST IN PAPERBACKS, LOOK FOR THE

In every corner of the world, on every subject under the sun, Penguin represents quality and variety – the very best in publishing today.

For complete information about books available from Penguin – including Puffins, Penguin Classics and Arkana – and how to order them, write to us at the appropriate address below. Please note that for copyright reasons the selection of books varies from country to country.

In the United Kingdom: Please write to *Dept JC, Penguin Books Ltd, FREEPOST, West Drayton, Middlesex, UB7 0BR.*

If you have any difficulty in obtaining a title, please send your order with the correct money, plus ten per cent for postage and packaging, to *PO Box No 11, West Drayton, Middlesex*

In the United States: Please write to *Dept BA, Penguin, 299 Murray Hill Parkway, East Rutherford, New Jersey 07073*

In Canada: Please write to *Penguin Books Canada Ltd, 2801 John Street, Markham, Ontario L3R 1B4*

In Australia: Please write to the *Marketing Department, Penguin Books Australia Ltd, P.O. Box 257, Ringwood, Victoria 3134*

In New Zealand: Please write to the *Marketing Department, Penguin Books (NZ) Ltd, Private Bag, Takapuna, Auckland 9*

In India: Please write to *Penguin Overseas Ltd, 706 Eros Apartments, 56 Nehru Place, New Delhi, 110019*

In the Netherlands: Please write to *Penguin Books Netherlands B.V., Postbus 3507, NL–1001 AH, Amsterdam*

In West Germany: Please write to *Penguin Books Ltd, Friedrichstrasse 10–12, D–6000 Frankfurt/Main 1*

In Spain: Please write to *Alhambra Longman S.A., Fernandez de la Hoz 9, E–28010 Madrid*

In Italy: Please write to *Penguin Italia s.r.l., Via Como 4, I-20096 Pioltello (Milano)*

In France: Please write to *Penguin France S.A., 17 rue Lejeune, F-31000 Toulouse*

In Japan: Please write to *Longman Penguin Japan Co Ltd, Yamaguchi Building, 2–12–9 Kanda Jimbocho, Chiyoda-Ku, Tokyo 101*

FOR THE BEST IN PAPERBACKS, LOOK FOR THE 🐧

PENGUIN DICTIONARIES

Abbreviations
Archaeology
Architecture
Art and Artists
Biology
Botany
Building
Business
Chemistry
Civil Engineering
Computers
Curious and Interesting
  Words
Curious and Interesting
  Numbers
Design and Designers
Economics
Electronics
English and European
  History
English Idioms
French
Geography
German

Historical Slang
Human Geography
Literary Terms
Mathematics
Modern History 1789–1945
Modern Quotations
Music
Physical Geography
Physics
Politics
Proverbs
Psychology
Quotations
Religions
Rhyming Dictionary
Saints
Science
Sociology
Spanish
Surnames
Telecommunications
Troublesome Words
Twentieth-Century History

PENGUIN REFERENCE BOOKS

THE PENGUIN DICTIONARY OF
HUMAN GEOGRAPHY

Brian Goodall was born in 1937 and educated at Windsor Grammar School and at the London School of Economics and Political Science. After graduating in 1958 he spent one year as Fulbright Scholar at Indiana University and another as Rees Jeffreys Research Fellow, DSIR Road Research Laboratory. From 1960 to 1966 he lectured in Economics at the College of Estate Management, University of London. In 1967 he joined the Department of Geography at the University of Reading, becoming Head of Department in 1980 and Professor in 1988. He relinquished his post as Head of Department on becoming Dean of the Faculty of Urban and Regional Studies in 1990. Professor Goodall has been a member of the Institute of British Geographers since 1967 and was elected as a Fellow of The Tourism Society in 1987. His research interests include urban and land economics, environmental and resource management, recreation and tourism. He has written numerous reports and articles and is the author, with W. Lean, of *Aspects of Land Economics* (1966), and *The Economics of Urban Areas* (1972), and co-editor, with A. Kirby, of *Resources and Planning* (1979), and, with G. J. Ashworth, of *The Impact of Tourist Development on Disadvantaged Regions* (1985), *Marketing in the Tourism Industry* (1988), and *Marketing Tourism Places* (1990).